RESEARCH METHODS IN PSYCHOLOGY:

Evaluating a World of Information

Second Edition

SECOND EDITION

RESEARCH METHODS IN PSYCHOLOGY:

Evaluating a World of Information

Beth Morling

University of Delaware

W. W. Norton & Company, Inc.

New York • London

W. W. Norton & Company has been independent since its founding in 1923, when William Warder Norton and Mary D. Herter Norton first published lectures delivered at the People's Institute, the adult education division of New York City's Cooper Union. The firm soon expanded its program beyond the Institute, publishing books by celebrated academics from America and abroad. By midcentury, the two major pillars of Norton's publishing program—trade books and college texts—were firmly established. In the 1950s, the Norton family transferred control of the company to its employees, and today—with a staff of four hundred and a comparable number of trade, college, and professional titles published each year—W. W. Norton & Company stands as the largest and oldest publishing house owned wholly by its employees.

Editor: Sheri L. Snavely

Project Editor: Sujin Hong

Production Manager: Eric Pier-Hocking

Developmental Editor/Copyeditor: Betsy Dilernia

Photo Editor: Stephanie Romeo

Photo Researcher: Ted Szczepanski

Permissions Manager: Megan Jackson

Art Director: Hope Miller Goodell

Text Design: Lisa Buckley

Media Associate Editor: Callinda Taylor

Media Editor: Patrick Shriner

Editorial Assistant: Scott Sugarman

Media Assistant: George Phipps

Marketing Manager, Psychology: Lauren Winkler

Composition: CodeMantra

Manufacturing: Transcontinental Interglobe, Inc.

Library of Congress Cataloging-in-Publication Data
Morling, Beth.
 Research methods in psychology: evaluating a world of information/Beth Morling, University of Delaware.—Second Edition.
     pages cm
 Includes bibliographical references and index.
 ISBN: 978-0-393-93693-3 (pbk.: alk. paper)
 1. Psychology—Research—Methodology—Textbooks. 2. Psychology, Experimental—Textbooks. I. Title.
 BF76.5.M667 2014
 150.72'1—dc23   2014016570

W. W. Norton & Company, Inc., 500 Fifth Avenue, New York, NY 10110-0017
wwnorton.com

W. W. Norton & Company Ltd., Castle House, 75/76 Wells Street, London W1T 3QT
4 5 6 7 8 9 0

In memory of Larry H. Cohen,
a great mentor and colleague

About the Author

Beth Morling is Professor of Psychology at the University of Delaware. She attended Carleton College in Northfield, Minnesota, and received her Ph.D. from the University of Massachusetts at Amherst. Before teaching at Delaware, she held positions at Union College (New York) and Muhlenberg College (Pennsylvania). She has taught research methods at Delaware almost every semester for 10 years. In addition, she teaches undergraduate cultural psychology and a seminar on the self-concept, as well as a graduate course in the teaching of psychology. Her research in the area of cultural psychology explores how cultural practices shape people's motivations. Dr. Morling has been a Fulbright scholar in Kyoto, Japan.

Brief Contents

PART I: Introduction to Scientific Reasoning

CHAPTER 1: **Psychology Is a Way of Thinking**   3

CHAPTER 2: **Sources of Information: Why Research Is Best and How to Find It**   23

CHAPTER 3: **Three Claims, Four Validities: Interrogation Tools for Consumers of Research**   55

PART II: Research Foundations for Any Claim

CHAPTER 4: **Ethical Guidelines for Psychology Research**   89

CHAPTER 5: **Identifying Good Measurement**   121

PART III: Tools for Evaluating Frequency Claims

CHAPTER 6: **Surveys and Observations: Describing What People Do**   157

CHAPTER 7: **Sampling: Estimating the Frequency of Behaviors and Beliefs**   181

PART IV: Tools for Evaluating Association Claims

CHAPTER 8: **Bivariate Correlational Research**   203

CHAPTER 9: **Multivariate Correlational Research**   235

PART V: Tools for Evaluating Causal Claims

CHAPTER 10: **Introduction to Simple Experiments**   271

CHAPTER 11: **More on Experiments: Confounding and Obscuring Variables**   307

CHAPTER 12: **Experiments with More Than One Independent Variable**   343

PART VI: Balancing Research Priorities

CHAPTER 13: **Quasi-Experiments and Small-*N* Designs**   381

CHAPTER 14: **Replicability, Generalization, and the Real World**   413

STATISTICS REVIEW: **Descriptive Statistics**   441

STATISTICS REVIEW: **Inferential Statistics**   463

PRESENTING RESULTS: **APA-Style Reports and Conference Posters**   487

APPENDIX A: **Random Numbers and How to Use Them**   527

APPENDIX B: **Statistical Tables**   533

Glossary   547

Answers to End-of-Chapter Questions   557

References   571

Credits   583

Name Index   587

Subject Index   591

Preface

Students in the psychology major plan to pursue a tremendous variety of careers—not only to become psychology researchers. Why do psychology majors need to study research methods when they want to be therapists, social workers, teachers, lawyers, or physicians? Indeed, many students anticipate that research methods will not only be "dry" and "boring," but also irrelevant to their future goals. This book was written with these very students in mind—students who are taking their first course in research methods (usually sophomores) and who plan to pursue a wide variety of careers. Most of the students who take the course will never become researchers themselves, but they can learn to systematically navigate the research information they will encounter, in the empirical journal articles they will read in their psychology courses, and in online magazines, print magazines, newspapers, blogs, and wikis as well.

I used to tell students that by learning to plan and conduct their own research, they would be able to read and apply research later, in their chosen careers. But then I reviewed the literature on learning transfer, which reminds us that the skills involved in designing one's own studies won't easily transfer to understanding and critically assessing others' studies. If we want students to explain whether a study supports its claims, we also have to teach them how to do so. That is the approach this book attempts to teach.

Students Can Develop Research Consumer Skills

To be a systematic consumer of research, students need to know what to prioritize when assessing a study. Sometimes large or random samples matter, and sometimes they do not. Sometimes we ask about random assignment and confounds, and sometimes we do not. Students benefit from having a set of systematic steps to help them prioritize their questioning when they interrogate quantitative information. To provide that, this book presents a framework of **three claims and four validities**, introduced in Chapter 3. One axis of the framework is the three kinds of claims that researchers (as well as journalists, bloggers, and commentators) might make: frequency claims (some percentage of people do X), association claims (X is associated with Y), and causal claims (X changes Y). The second axis of the framework is the four validities that are generally agreed upon by methodologists: internal, external, construct, and statistical.

The three claims and four validities framework provides a scaffold that is reinforced throughout the book. Instead of presenting different vocabulary in every chapter, this book fits every term, technique, and piece of information into the basic framework.

The framework also helps students set priorities when evaluating a study. Good quantitative reasoners prioritize different validity questions depending on the claim. For example, for a frequency claim, we should ask about measurement (construct validity) and sampling techniques (external validity), but not about random assignment or confounds, because the claim is not a causal one. For a causal claim, we prioritize internal validity and construct validity, but external validity is generally less important.

Through engagement with a consumer-focused research methods course, students become systematic interrogators. They start to ask more appropriate and more refined questions about a study. By the end of the course, students can clearly explain why a causal claim needs an experiment to support it. They know how to evaluate whether a variable has been measured well. They know when it's appropriate to call for more participants in a study (and when it is not). And they can explain when a study must have a representative sample, and when it doesn't matter.

What About Future Researchers?

This book can also be used to teach the flip side of the question: How can producers of research design better studies? The producer angle is presented so that students will be prepared to design studies, collect data, and write papers in courses that prioritize these skills.

Future researchers will find sophisticated content in this book, presented in an accessible, consistent manner. They will learn the difference between mediation (Chapter 9) and moderation (Chapters 8 and 9), an important skill in theory building and theory testing. They will learn how to design and interpret factorial designs, even up to three-way interactions (Chapter 12). And in the all-too-common event that a student-run study fails to work, one chapter helps them explore the possible reasons for a null effect (Chapter 11). This book provides the basic statistical background, ethics coverage, and APA-style notes that are needed to guide students through study design.

Organization

The fourteen chapters in this book are arranged in six parts. Part I (Chapters 1–3) includes introductory chapters on the scientific method and the three claims, four validities framework. Part II (Chapters 4–5) covers issues that matter for any study: research ethics and good measurement. Parts III–V (Chapters 6–12) correspond to each of the three claims (frequency, association, and causal). Part VI (Chapters 13–14) focuses on balancing research priorities.

Most of the chapters will be familiar to veteran instructors, including chapters on measurement, experimentation, and factorial designs. However, unlike some methods books, this one devotes two full chapters to correlational research (one on bivariate and one on multivariate studies), which help students learn how to interpret, apply, and interrogate different types of association claims, one of the common types of claims they will encounter.

There are three supplementary chapters: Statistics Review: Descriptive Statistics, Statistics Review: Inferential Statistics, and Presenting Results: APA-Style Reports and Conference Posters. These chapters provide a review for students who've already had statistics, and provide the tools students need to create research reports and conference posters.

Two appendices are provided for reference: Random Numbers and How to Use Them, and Statistical Tables. Both of these provide important reference tools for students who are conducting their own research.

Support for Students and Instructors

The book's pedagogical features emphasize active learning and repetition of the most important points. Each chapter begins with high-level learning objectives—major skills students should expect to remember even "a year from now." Important terms in a chapter are introduced in boldface. The Check Your Understanding questions at the end of each major section provide basic review questions that allow students to revisit key concepts as they read. Each chapter ends with multiple-choice review questions and a set of Learning Actively exercises that encourage students to apply what they learned. (Answers are provided at the end of the book.) A master table of the three claims and four validities appears inside the book's front cover to remind students of the scaffold for the course.

I believe the book works pedagogically because it continually reinforces the three claims, four validities framework, building in repetition and depth. Although each chapter addresses the usual core content of research methods, students are always reminded of how a particular topic helps them interrogate the key validities. The increasingly detailed iterations of a simple message will help students remember and apply this questioning strategy in the future.

In addition to the book itself, Norton offers a carefully designed support package for instructors and students. The Instructor's Manual contains detailed teaching notes based on my own experience with the course, extra active learning activities and homework assignments, and a full Test Bank. The book comes with a number of other ancillaries to assist both new and experienced research methods instructors; a full list is available on p. xxi.

Teachable Examples on the Everyday Research Methods Blog

Students and instructors can find additional examples of psychological science in the news on my blog, Everyday Research Methods (www.everydayresearch methods.com; no password or registration required). Instructors can use the blog as a repository of teachable moments with homework style questions; they can find fresh, new examples to use in class. Students can use the entries as extra practice in reading about psychological science in the popular press.

Changes in the Second Edition

First edition users will be happy to learn that the basic organization, material, and descriptions in the text remain the same. The second edition contains several fresh examples, providing new studies and recent headlines. These new examples free instructors to assign the second edition, but teach with their favorite examples from the first.

We've added short multiple-choice quizzes to the end of each chapter to provide the self-testing opportunities that have been shown to help students learn (according to research on the testing effect). To train students to interpret tables and graphs in real contexts, certain figures are labeled as "Straight from the Source" when they have been reproduced exactly from their original journal articles. To help students get a sense of the overall structure of the chapter, the end-of-chapter summaries are presented as bulleted lists, organized under the same primary headings from the chapter, to remind students of the organization of the material. Key terms are now listed in the order of their appearance in the chapter, rather than alphabetically.

In response to consistent reviewer requests, I've split former Chapter 6 into two chapters, one on surveys and observational methods, and one on sampling techniques. Here is a detailed list of the changes made to each chapter.

Chapter	Major changes in the second edition
1. Psychology Is a Way of Thinking	The language of "cycles" is no longer used here. The same content is presented, under the theory-data cycle, the peer review process, and journal-to-journalism. A new section focuses on how researchers dig deeper—they don't stop with a single study.
2. Sources of Information: Why Research Is Best and How to Find it	Chapter 2 retains the same recurring example of the catharsis hypothesis as a frame for "sources of information." In the section on intuitive reasoning, I omitted the subsection on overconfidence, and replaced it with the bias blind spot—the sneaky tendency for us to think only other people are biased, not ourselves.
3. Three Claims, Four Validities: Interrogation Tools for Consumers of Research	The three claims, four validities framework is presented much the same, but with all new examples taken from the popular press during the past year. The long section and figure on using correlation for prediction was moved to Chapter 8 (Bivariate Correlational Research).
4. Ethical Guidelines for Psychology Research	No major changes here, except to include the recent example of social psychologist Diederik Stapel in the section on research fraud.
5. Identifying Good Measurement	While still focusing on measuring happiness, the discussion is amplified to clarify that each variable in a study can be evaluated for construct validity. The chapter now shows what happens when we investigate a claim such as "Religious people are more happy." In such research, we can evaluate the reliability and validity of two operationalizations: religiosity and happiness. Often we establish the quality of each of our operationalizations in separate data collection, before testing the relationship between them. Students struggle with this idea, and I hope the revision helps them understand it better. Because my own students tended to get unnecessarily confused by the difference between predictive and concurrent validity, I replaced both terms with the single term, criterion validity, which means that the measure correlates with a behavioral outcome of interest (either now or in the future).

Chapter	Major changes in the second edition
6. Surveys and Observations: Describing What People Do	New material attempts to convince students that self-report actually can be valid. Many of my students question the validity of any self-report, even of gender.
	I removed the term nay-saying response bias; according to research on polling, nay-saying is not that common and yea-saying is common. Fence sitting is still in the chapter.
	I use a new example of observational research, again with families, focusing on dinner conversations and emotional tone. This led to two new "Straight from the Source" figures.
7. Sampling: Estimating the Frequency of Behaviors and Beliefs	This material, on sampling, was previously combined with information on surveys and observations. Now it stands alone as its own chapter, with no other major changes.
8. Bivariate Correlational Research	There are two new examples and one modified example. The first new one is about how people who meet their spouses online are happier (providing a new example of a correlation between a categorical and quantitative variable, as well as a discussion of a study with a very small effect size). The second new example is a negative correlation, in which people who multitask the most are the worst at it. The third example is modified; it used to be "Small talk is associated with lower well-being." Now I present the complementary positive association in which "Deep talk is associated with higher well-being."
	A second major change is removal of the section on subgroups; this confused students and fits better under the sections on moderators and regression.
	I added a section on restriction of range. This section sets students up for the idea of floor and ceiling effects later on.
	The material on using correlations for prediction was moved from Chapter 3 to this chapter.
9. Multivariate Correlational Research	The examples for cross-lag panel designs and multiple-regression analyses are the same.
	The only important change is in the section on mediation, in which I emphasize more strongly that to establish mediation between variable A and B, temporal precedence is very important—the mediator must be measured after variable A, and before variable B.
	A helpful new figure distinguishes mediation, moderation, and third variables (Figure 9.13).
10. Introduction to Simple Experiments	The red/green ink example is retained, because it provides a nice example of experimental design. However, one author noted to me that he has failed to replicate a similar effect (Steele, 2014). I mention this in Chapter 14 (on replication), but instructors might wish to discuss replicability with students as they teach this chapter.
	The example on rejection and feeling cold has been replaced with a new example on the effect of serving bowl size on how much people eat.
11. More on Experiments: Confounding and Obscuring Variables	No new examples.
	I added a new metaphor for obscuring variables: two bowls of salsa that differ in how hot they are. The metaphor is intended to represent the two general causes of a null effect: not enough variance between bowls (between-groups variability) and too much variability within bowls (within-groups variability).

(continued)

Chapter	Major changes in the second edition
12. Experiments with More Than One Independent Variable	I kept the cell phone example of a 2 × 2 factorial design. A set of new examples on alcohol and aggression replaces the example on serving container size, which is now featured in Chapter 10.
13. Quasi-Experiments and Small-*N* Designs	The example of burnout and vacation is replaced with an example on how judicial decision making is affected by food breaks for judges. I replaced the example of the StayWell program with a study on the effects of cosmetic surgery.
14. Replicability, Generalization, and the Real World	I removed the section stating that statistically significant results are replicable, in response to a reviewer who pointed out the error of this reasoning. (For details, see Sohn, 1998, Replicability and statistical significance.) The example of direct replication from the Bargh et al. walking study is replaced with a study on the name-letter/birthday-number effect. I replaced the psychotherapy meta-analysis example with a meta-analysis on video games. Note that both meta-analysis examples in this chapter use *r* as the average effect size; instructors might wish to provide an example of meta-analyses in class where *d* or *g* are used as the average effect size. I added an example of the file-drawer problem, in which antidepressant trials that showed no effect were less likely to be published.

Acknowledgments

Working on this textbook has been rewarding and enriching, thanks to the many people who have smoothed the way. To start, I feel fortunate to have worked with an author-focused company and an all-around great editor, Sheri Snavely. She is both optimistic and realistic, savvy, and smart. She also made sure I got the most rigorous reviews possible and that I was supported with great Norton staff: Sujin Hong, Callinda Taylor, Eric Pier-Hocking, Hope Miller Goodell, and Scott Sugarman. My developmental editor for the second edition, Betsy Dilernia, refined each term, figure, and reference, making the book more consistent, tight, and accurate. I also remain grateful to Beth Ammerman, who helped make every aspect of the first edition well-organized and clear.

I am also thankful for the support and continued enthusiasm I have received from the Norton sales management team: Michael Wright, Allen Clawson, Annie Stewart, Dennis Fernandes, Dennis Adams, Katie Incorvia, Jordan Mendez, Lauren Greene, Shane Brisson, and Dan Horton. I also wish to thank my marketing manager Lauren Winkler for her creativity and drive to ensure my book reaches a wide audience.

I deeply appreciate the support of many colleagues. My friend Carrie Smith shares my vision for assessment and helps make this book's Test Bank an authentic measure of quantitative reasoning (as well as sending me great links to blog about). Lauren Usher carefully checked and helped revise the Test Bank for the second edition. Many thanks to Linda Juang for carefully and patiently fact-checking every chapter in this edition. Thanks, as well, to Christine Lofgren, Stefanie LoSavio, and Emily Stanley for writing and revising the questions that appear in the Coursepack created for the course management systems. The book was reviewed by a cadre of talented research method professors, and I am grateful to each of them. Some were asked to review; others cared enough to send me comments by email. Their students are lucky to have them in the classroom, and my readers will benefit from the time they spent in improving this book:

Eileen Josiah Achorn, *University of Texas, San Antonio*

Kristen Weede Alexander, *California State University, Sacramento*

Leola Alfonso-Reese, *San Diego State University*

Jennifer Asmuth, *Susquehanna University*

Gordon Bear, *Ramapo College*

Margaret Elizabeth Beier, *Rice University*

Brett Beston, *McMaster University*

Julie Boland, *University of Michigan*

Lisa Cravens-Brown, *The Ohio State University*

Victoria Cross, *University of California, Davis*

Matthew Deegan, *University of Delaware*

Kenneth DeMarree, *University at Buffalo, The State University of New York*

Jessica Dennis, *California State University, Los Angeles*

Rachel Dinero, *Cazenovia College*

Dana S. Dunn, *Moravian College*

C. Emily Durbin, *Michigan State University*

Russell K. Espinoza, *California State University, Fullerton*

Iris Firstenberg, *University of California, Los Angeles*

Christina Frederick, *Sierra Nevada College*

Christopher J. Gade, *University of California, Berkeley*

Timothy E. Goldsmith, *University of New Mexico*

Jennifer Gosselin, *Sacred Heart University*

AnaMarie Connolly Guichard, *California State University, Stanislaus*

Andreana Haley, *University of Texas, Austin*

Cheryl Harasymchuk, *Carleton University*

Deborah L. Hume, *University of Missouri*

Kurt R. Illig, *University of Virginia*

W. Jake Jacobs, *University of Arizona*

Matthew D. Johnson, *Binghamton University*

Christian Jordan, *Wilfrid Laurier University*

Linda Juang, *University of California, Santa Barbara*

Victoria A. Kazmerski, *Penn State Erie, The Behrend College*

Heejung Kim, *University of California, Santa Barbara*

Greg M. Kim-Ju, *California State University, Sacramento*

Penny L. Koontz, *Marshall University*

Ellen W. Leen-Feldner, *University of Arkansas*

Carl Lejuez, *University of Maryland*

Stella G. Lopez, *University of Texas, San Antonio*

Greg Edward Loviscky, *Pennsylvania State University*

Christopher Mazurek, *Columbia College*

Daniel C. Molden, *Northwestern University*

J. Toby Mordkoff, *University of Iowa*

Katie Mosack, *University of Wisconsin, Milwaukee*

Stephanie C. Payne, *Texas A&M University*

Anita Pedersen, *Arizona State University*

Elizabeth D. Peloso, *University of Pennsylvania*

M. Christine Porter, *College of William and Mary*

Joshua Rabinowitz, *University of Michigan*

James R. Roney, *University of California, Santa Barbara*

Carin Rubenstein, *Pima Community College*

Silvia J. Santos, *California State University, Dominguez Hills*

Mark J. Sciutto, *Muhlenberg College*

Elizabeth A. Sheehan, *Georgia State University*

Victoria A. Shivy, *Virginia Commonwealth University*

Leo Standing, *Bishop's University*

Harold W. K. Stanislaw, *California State University, Stanislaus*

Kenneth M. Steele, *Appalachian State University*

Mark A. Stellmack, *University of Minnesota, Twin Cities*

Eva Szeli, *Arizona State University*

Lauren A. Taglialatela, *Kennesaw State University*

Alison Thomas-Cottingham, *Rider University*

Allison A. Vaughn, *San Diego State University*

Jan Visser, *University of Groningen*

Christopher Warren, *California State University, Long Beach*

Jelte M. Wicherts, *Tilburg University*

Charles E. (Ted) Wright, *University of California, Irvine*

Nancy Yanchus, *Georgia Southern University*

David Zehr, *Plymouth State University*

Peggy Mycek Zoccola, *Ohio University*

I have tried to make the best possible improvements from all of these able reviewers.

My life as a teaching professor has been enriched during the last few years because of the friendship and support of many colleagues at the University of Delaware, including, but not limited to, Brian Ackerman, Ryan Beveridge, Chad Forbes, Sam Gaertner, James Jones, Mike Kuhlman, Agnes Ly, Kristen Begosh, Bob Simons, and Hal White. Colleagues old and new, far and near provide me with friendship and support, including, but not limited to, Susan Fiske, Shinobu Kitayama, Keiko Ishii, Yukiko Uchida, Steve Heine, Dana Dunn, Vinai Norassakkunkit, and all the NITOP regulars.

My boys Max, Alek, and Hugo, as usual, ensured that I never had to work on the book for too long at a stretch (thanks, guys . . .). I remain grateful to my mother-in-law, Janet Pochan, for cheerfully helping us with so many tasks on the home front. Finally, I want to thank my husband Darrin for encouraging me and for always having the right wine to celebrate the latest deadline.

Media and Print Resources for Instructors and Students

Interactive Instructor's Guide

Beth Morling, *University of Delaware*

The text's Interactive Instructor's Guide contains teaching guides to the textbook's key pedagogical features, a discussion of how to design a course that utilizes the textbook, sample syllabus and assignments, and chapter-by-chapter teaching notes and suggested activities.

Test Bank

C. Veronica Smith, *University of Mississippi,* **and**
Lauren Usher, *University of Miami*

The Test Bank provides over 750 questions using an evidence-centered approach designed in collaboration with Valerie Shute of Florida State University and Diego Zapata-Rivera of the Educational Testing Service. The Test Bank contains multiple-choice and short-answer questions that are classified by section, Bloom's taxonomy, and difficulty, making it easy for instructors to construct tests and quizzes that are meaningful and diagnostic. The Test Bank is available in Word RTF, PDF, and *ExamView®* Assessment Suite format.

Lecture PowerPoints

This edition of the book features two sets of lecture PowerPoints. One set is straight from Beth Morling's class, offering one approach to using the book. The other set offers starter slides for every section, follows the order of the text, features images and instructor notes, and is designed to be adapted to fit the needs of each individual classroom. In addition, all of the art and tables from the textbook are available in JPG and PPT formats.

The *Research Methods in Psychology* Blog: Everyday Research Methods, Interrogating the Popular Press

www.everydayresearchmethods.com

The *Research Methods in Psychology* blog offers an often-updated bank of teachable moments from the web—blogs, newspapers, research studies, online videos, speeches, and more—curated by Beth Morling and occasional guest contributors. Each blog post connects with material students encounter in the textbook and includes critical-thinking/discussion questions that an instructor may discuss in lecture or assign as homework. The blog is easily searchable, and each entry is tagged with a learning objective from the textbook and appropriate keywords.

Coursepack

Christine Lofgren, *University of California, Irvine,* **Stephanie LoSavio,**
University of Delaware, **and Emily Stanley,** *University of Delaware*

The Coursepack presents students with review opportunities that employ the text's analytical framework. Each chapter includes quizzes based on the Norton Assessment Guidelines, Chapter Outlines created by the textbook author and based on the Learning Objectives in the text, and review flashcards. The APA-style guidelines from the textbook will also be available in the Coursepack for easy access.

Contents

Preface   xi
Media and Print Resources for Instructors and Students   xxi

PART I: Introduction to Scientific Reasoning

CHAPTER 1: Psychology Is a Way of Thinking   3

Research Producers, Research Consumers   4
Why the Producer Role Is Important   4
Why the Consumer Role Is Important   5
The Benefits of Being a Good Consumer   6

How Scientists Approach Their Work   8
Scientists Are Empiricists   8
Scientists Test Theories: The Theory-Data Cycle   9
Scientists Tackle Applied and Basic Problems   13
Scientists Dig Deeper   15
Scientists Make It Public: The Publication Process   15
Scientists Talk to the World: From Journal to Journalism   16
Summary   20
Key Terms   20
Review Questions   21
Learning Actively   21

CHAPTER 2: Sources of Information: Why Research Is Best and How to Find It   23

The Research vs. Your Experience   24
Experience Has No Comparison Group   25
Experience Is Confounded   27
Research Is Better Than Experience   28
Research Is Probabilistic   29

The Research vs. Your Intuition   30
Intuition Is Biased by Faulty Thinking   30
Intuition Is Biased by Motivation   33
The Intuitive Thinker vs. the Scientific Reasoner   36

Mozart Effect— Shmozart Effect

(Intelligence, 2010)

Trusting Authorities on the Subject   36

Finding and Reading the Research   39
Consulting Scientific Sources   39
Finding Scientific Sources   42
Reading the Research   44
Finding Research in Less Scholarly Places   46
Summary   50
Key Terms   51
Review Questions   51
Learning Actively   52

CHAPTER 3: Three Claims, Four Validities: Interrogation Tools
for Consumers of Research   55

Variables   56
Measured and Manipulated Variables   56
From Conceptual Variable to Operational Definition   57

Three Claims   60
Frequency Claims   60
Association Claims   61
Causal Claims   64
Not All Claims Are Based on Research   65

Interrogating the Three Claims Using the Four Big Validities   66
Interrogating Frequency Claims   67
Interrogating Association Claims   68
Interrogating Causal Claims   72

Prioritizing Validities   77
Review: Four Validities, Four Aspects of Quality   78
Summary   82
Key Terms   83
Review Questions   83
Learning Actively   84

PART II: Research Foundations for Any Claim

CHAPTER 4: Ethical Guidelines for Psychology Research   89

Historical Examples   90
The Tuskegee Syphilis Study Illustrates Three Major Ethics Violations   90
The Milgram Obedience Studies Illustrate an Ethical Balance   92

**Whiff of
Rosemary
Gives Your
Brain a Boost**

(Body Odd,
nbcnews.com, 2012)

Core Ethical Principles   95

The Belmont Report: Principles and Applications   95

Guidelines for Psychologists: The APA Ethical Principles   98

Five General Ethical Principles   98

Ten Specific Ethical Standards   99

Ethical Decision Making: A Thoughtful Balance   112

Summary   113

Key Terms   114

Review Questions   114

Learning Actively   115

Ethical Standard 8 of the American Psychological Association   116

CHAPTER 5: Identifying Good Measurement   121

Ways to Measure Variables   122

More About Conceptual and Operational Variables   122

Three Common Types of Measures   124

Scales of Measurement   126

Reliability of Measurement: Are the Scores Consistent?   129

Introducing Three Types of Reliability   129

Using a Scatterplot to Evaluate Reliability   130

Using the Correlation Coefficient r to Evaluate Reliability   132

Reading About Reliability in Journal Articles   135

Validity of Measurement: Does It Measure What It Is Supposed to Measure?   136

Measurement Validity of Abstract Constructs   136

Face Validity and Content Validity: Does It Look Like a Good Measure?   137

Criterion Validity: Does It Correlate with Key Behaviors?   139

Convergent Validity and Discriminant Validity: Does the Pattern Make Sense?   143

The Relationship Between Reliability and Validity   146

Review: Interpreting Construct Validity Evidence   147

Interrogating a Measure of Religiosity   147

Interrogating Gallup's Headline   150

Summary   151

Key Terms   152

Review Questions   152

Learning Actively   153

Happiness Facts and Fiction

(webmd.com)

PART III: Tools for Evaluating Frequency Claims

CHAPTER 6: Surveys and Observations: Describing What People Do 157

Construct Validity of Surveys and Polls 158

Choosing Question Formats 158

Writing Well-Worded Questions 160

Encouraging Accurate Responses 163

Construct Validity of Behavioral Observations 168

Examples of Claims Based on Observational Data 169

Observations Can Be Better Than Self-Reports 172

Summary 178

Key Terms 178

Review Questions 178

Learning Actively 179

CHAPTER 7: Sampling: Estimating the Frequency of Behaviors and Beliefs 181

Generalizability: Does the Sample Represent the Population? 182

Populations and Samples 182

When Is a Sample Biased? 184

Obtaining a Representative Sample: Probability Sampling Techniques 188

Settling for an Unrepresentative Sample: Biased Sampling Techniques 192

Interrogating External Validity: What Matters Most? 194

When a Representative Sample Is Not the Top Priority 194

Larger Samples Are Not More Representative 196

Summary 198

Key Terms 198

Review Questions 199

Learning Actively 199

PART IV: Tools for Evaluating Association Claims

CHAPTER 8: Bivariate Correlational Research 203

Introducing Bivariate Correlations 204

Review: Describing Associations Between Two Quantitative Variables 206

Describing Associations with Categorical Data 208

"Should I buy these boots? They got four and a half stars on Zappos."

Interrogating Association Claims   210

Construct Validity: How Well Was Each Variable Measured?   210

Statistical Validity: How Well Do the Data Support
the Conclusion?   210

Internal Validity: Can We Make a Causal Inference from
an Association?   221

External Validity: To Whom Can the Association Be Generalized?   226

Summary   231

Key Terms   231

Review Questions   232

Learning Actively   232

CHAPTER 9: Multivariate Correlational Research   235

Reviewing the Three Causal Criteria   236

Establishing Temporal Precedence with Longitudinal Designs   237

Interpreting Results from Longitudinal Designs   238

Longitudinal Studies and the Three Criteria for Causation   240

Why Not Just Do an Experiment?   241

Ruling Out Third Variables with Multiple-Regression Analyses   242

Measuring More Than Two Variables   242

Regression Results Indicate If a Third Variable Affects
the Relationship   245

Adding More Predictors to a Regression   249

Regression in Popular Press Articles   250

Regression Does Not Establish Causation   252

Getting at Causality with Pattern and Parsimony   254

The Power of Pattern and Parsimony   254

Pattern, Parsimony, and the Popular Press   256

Mediation   257

Mediators vs. Third Variables   258

Mediators vs. Moderators   259

Multivariate Designs and the Four Validities   261

Summary   263

Key Terms   264

Review Questions   264

Learning Actively   265

*The Threee
R's? A Fourth
is crucial, Too:
Recess*

(*New York Times*, 2009)

PART V: Tools for Evaluating Causal Claims

CHAPTER 10 Introduction to Simple Experiments   271

Two Examples of Simple Experiments   272
Example 1: Seeing Red   272
Example 2: Eating Pasta   274

Experimental Variables   275
Independent and Dependent Variables   275
Control Variables   276

Why Experiments Support Causal Claims   277
Experiments Establish Covariance   277
Experiments Establish Temporal Precedence   278
Well-Designed Experiments Establish Internal Validity   279

Independent-Groups Designs   284
Independent-Groups vs. Within-Groups Designs   284
Posttest-Only Design   285
Pretest/Posttest Design   286
Which Design Is Better?   287

Within-Groups Designs   288
Concurrent-Measures Design   288
Repeated-Measures Design   289
Advantages of Within-Groups Designs   289
Covariance, Temporal Precedence, and Internal Validity in
    Within-Groups Designs   291
Disadvantages of Within-Groups Designs   293
Is Pretest/Posttest a Within-Groups Design?   294

Interrogating Causal Claims with the Four Validities   295
Construct Validity: How Well Were the Variables Measured
    and Manipulated?   295
External Validity: To Whom or What Can the Causal Claim
    Generalize?   298
Statistical Validity: How Well Do the Data Support the Causal Claim?   300
Internal Validity: Are There Alternative Explanations for
    the Outcome?   302
Summary   303
Key Terms   304
Review Questions   304
Learning Actively   305

Your Plate Is
Bigger Than
Your Stomach

(New York Times, 2007)

CHAPTER 11: More on Experiments: Confounding and Obscuring Variables   307

Threats to Internal Validity: Did the Independent Variable Really Cause the Difference?   308

The Really Bad Experiment (A Cautionary Tale)   308

Six Potential Internal Validity Threats in One-Group, Pretest/Posttest Designs   310

Three Potential Internal Validity Threats in Any Experiment   318

With So Many Threats, Are Experiments Still Useful?   321

Interrogating Null Effects: What If the Independent Variable Does Not Make a Difference?   323

Perhaps There Is Not Enough Between-Groups Difference   326

Perhaps Within-Groups Variability Obscured the Group Differences   329

Perhaps There Really Is No Difference   336

Null Effects Can Be Hard to Find   336

Summary   339

Key Terms   339

Review Questions   340

Learning Actively   341

CHAPTER 12: Experiments with More Than One Independent Variable   343

Review: Experiments with One Independent Variable   343

Experiments with Two Independent Variables Can Show Interactions   345

Intuitive Interactions   346

Factorial Designs Study Two Independent Variables   347

Factorial Designs Can Test Limits   348

Factorial Designs Can Test Theories   351

Interpreting Factorial Results: Main Effects and Interactions   353

Factorial Variations   362

Independent-Groups Factorial Designs   362

Within-Groups Factorial Designs   362

Mixed Factorial Designs   363

Increasing the Number of Levels of an Independent Variable   363

Increasing the Number of Independent Variables   365

Identifying Factorial Designs in Your Reading   370

Identifying Factorial Designs in Empirical Journal Articles   370

The Reason Why You're an Angry Drunk

(*Men's Health*, 2012)

Identifying Factorial Designs in Popular Press Articles   371
Summary   374
Key Terms   374
Review Questions   375
Learning Actively   376

PART VI: Balancing Research Priorities

CHAPTER 13: Quasi-Experiments and Small-*N* Designs   381

Quasi-Experiments   382
Two Examples of Independent-Groups Quasi-Experiments   382
Two Examples of Repeated-Measures Quasi-Experiments   385
Internal Validity in Quasi-Experiments   388
Balancing Priorities in Quasi-Experiments   396
Are Quasi-Experiments the Same as Correlational Studies?   397

Small-*N* Designs: Studying Only a Few Individuals   398
Research on Split Brains   399
Behavior-Change Studies in Clinical Settings:
    Three Small-*N* Designs   402
Other Examples of Small-*N* Studies   406
Evaluating the Four Validities in Small-*N* Designs   407
Summary   409
Key Terms   409
Review Questions   410
Learning Actively   411

CHAPTER 14: Replicability, Generalization,
                    and the Real World   413

To Be Important, a Study Must Be Replicable   414
Replication Studies   414
Replication, Importance, and the Weight of the Evidence   419
Meta-Analysis: What Does the Literature Say?   419
Replicability in the Popular Press   423

To Be Important, Must a Study Have External Validity?   424
Generalizing to Other Participants   424
Generalizing to Other Settings   425
Does a Study Have to Be Generalizable to Many People?   426
Does a Study Have to Take Place in a Real-World Setting?   433

"What is the value of an experiment with just one participant?"

Summary   438
Key Terms   439
Review Questions   439
Learning Actively   440

STATISTICS REVIEW: Descriptive Statistics   441

STATISTICS REVIEW: Inferential Statistics   463

PRESENTING RESULTS: APA-Style Reports and
                     Conference Posters   487

APPENDIX A: Random Numbers and How to Use Them   527

APPENDIX B: Statistical Tables   533
Areas Under the Normal Curve (Distribution of *z*)   533
Critical Values of *t*   539
Critical Values of *F*   541
r to *z′* Conversion   545

Glossary   547

Answers to End-of-Chapter Questions   557
Review Question   557
Guidelines for Selected Learning Actively Exercises   558

References   571

Credits   583

Name Index   587

Subject Index   591

"Would we find these same results in other cultural contexts?"

PART I

Introduction to Scientific Reasoning

Mozart Effect—Shmozart Effect

(Intelligence, 2010)

The Color Red Makes You Stronger, but More Distractable

(The Wire, 2011)

1

Psychology Is a Way of Thinking

A year from now, you should still be able to:

1. Explain what it means to reason empirically.

2. Appreciate how an understanding of psychological research methods is crucial not only for producers of information but also for consumers of information.

3. Describe five processes that shape psychological science.

Thinking back to your introductory psychology course, what do you remember learning? You probably remember studies about dogs salivating at the sound of a bell or people failing to call for help when the room they were in filled up with smoke. Or perhaps you recall studies in which people administered increasingly stronger electric shocks to an innocent man although he seemed to be in distress. There were studies about how we learn best, why we sleep, and why we can't always trust our memories. As you continue your exploration of psychology, you can anticipate learning about other landmark studies—research about the brain, cognition, social behavior, child development, and clinical disorders.

Psychological science is based on studies—on research—by psychologists. Like other scientists, psychologists are empiricists. To be an empiricist means to base one's conclusions on systematic observations. Psychologists do not simply think intuitively about behavior, cognition, and emotion; they know what they know because they have conducted studies on people and animals acting in their natural environments or in specially designed situations. If you are to think like a psychologist, then you must think like a researcher, and taking a course in research methods is crucial to your understanding of psychology. This book explains the types of studies psychologists conduct, as well as some of the potential strengths and limitations of each type of study. You will learn not only how to plan your own studies but also how to find research, read about it, and ask questions of it. While gaining a greater appreciation for the rigorous standards psychologists maintain in their research, you'll find out how to be a systematic and critical consumer of psychological science.

Research Producers, Research Consumers

Some psychology students are fascinated by the research process and intend to become *producers* of research information. Perhaps they hope to get a job studying brain anatomy, observing the behavior of pigeons or monkeys, administering personality questionnaires, observing children in a school setting, or analyzing data. They may want to write up their results and present them at research meetings. These students may dream about working as research scientists or professors.

Other psychology students may not want to work in a lab, but they do enjoy reading about the structure of the brain, the behavior of pigeons or monkeys, the personalities of their fellow students, or the behavior of children in a school setting. They are interested in being *consumers* of research information—in reading about research so they can later apply it to their work, hobbies, relationships, or personal growth. These students might pursue careers as family therapists, teachers, entrepreneurs, guidance counselors, or police officers, and they expect a psychology education to help them in these roles.

In practice, many psychologists engage in both roles. When they are planning their research and creating new knowledge, they study the work of others who have gone before them. Furthermore, psychologists in both roles require a curiosity about behavior, emotion, and cognition. Research producers and consumers share a desire to ask, answer, and communicate interesting questions. Both of them share a commitment to the practice of empiricism—to answer psychological questions with direct, formal observations, and to communicate with others about what they have learned.

Why the Producer Role Is Important

For your future coursework in psychology, it is important to know how to be a producer of research. Of course, students who decide to go to graduate school for psychology will need to know all about research methods. But even if you do not plan to do graduate work in psychology, you will probably have to write a paper following the style guidelines of the American Psychological Association (APA) before you graduate, and you may be required to do research as part of a course lab section. To succeed, you will need to know how to randomly assign people to groups, how to measure attitudes accurately, or how to interpret results from a graph. Perhaps more importantly, the skills you acquire by conducting research can teach you how psychological scientists ask questions and how they think about their discipline.

As part of your psychology studies, you might even work in a research lab as an undergraduate (**Figure 1.1**). Many psychology professors are active researchers, and you might have the opportunity to get involved in their laboratories. Your faculty supervisor may ask you to code behaviors, assign participants to different groups, graph an outcome, or write a report. If such an opportunity arises, take it! Doing so will give you your first taste of being a research producer. Although you will be supervised closely, you will be expected to know the basics of conducting research. This book will help you understand why you have to protect the anonymity of your participants, use a coding book, or flip a coin to decide who goes in which group. By participating as a research producer, you can expect to deepen your understanding of psychological inquiry.

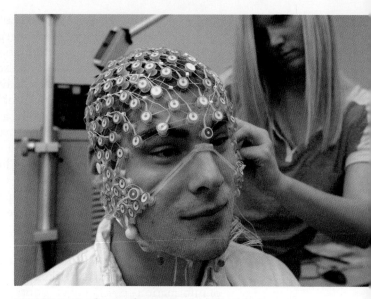

FIGURE 1.1 Producers of research. As undergraduates, some psychology majors work alongside faculty members as producers of information.

Why the Consumer Role Is Important

Although it is important to understand the psychologist's role as a producer of research, most psychology majors do not eventually become researchers. Regardless of the career you choose, however, becoming a savvy consumer of information is essential. In your psychology courses, you will read studies published by psychologists in scientific journals. You will need to develop the ability to read about research with curiosity—to understand it, learn from it, and ask appropriate questions about it.

Think about how often you encounter news stories or look up information on the Internet. Much of the time, the stories you read and the websites you visit will present information based on research. For example, during an election year, Americans may come across polling information in the media almost every day. Many online newspapers have special sections that include stories on the latest research. Entire websites are dedicated to psychology-related topics, such as treatments for autism, subliminal learning tapes, or advice for married couples. Outside the Internet, lifestyle magazines such as *Self*, *Men's Health*, and *Parents* summarize research for their readers. However, only some of the research—whether online or printed—is accurate and useful; some of it is dubious, and some is just plain wrong. How can you tell the good research information from the bad? Understanding research methods enables you to ask the appropriate questions, so you can assess information correctly. Research methods skills apply not only to research studies but also to much of the other types of information you are likely to encounter in daily life.

Finally, being a smart consumer of research could be crucial to your future career. Even if you do not plan to be a researcher—if your goal is to be a social worker, a teacher, a sales representative, a family therapist, a human resources professional, or an entrepreneur—you will need to know how to interpret published research with a critical eye. Clinical psychologists, social workers, and family therapists must read research to know which therapies are the most effective. In fact, licensure in these helping professions requires knowing the research behind **evidence-based treatments**—that is, therapies that are supported by research. Teachers also use research to find out which teaching methods work best. And the business world runs on quantitative information: Research is used to predict what sales will be like in the future, what consumers will buy, and whether investors will take risks or lie low. Once you learn how to be a consumer of information—psychological or otherwise—you will use these skills constantly, no matter what job you are in.

In this book, you will often see the phrase "interrogating information." A consumer of research needs to know how to ask the right questions, determine the answers, and evaluate a study on the basis of those answers. This book will teach you systematic rules for interrogating research information.

The Benefits of Being a Good Consumer

What do you gain by being a critical consumer of information? Imagine, for example, that you are an occupational therapist, a person who helps people with physical and mental disabilities find solutions to daily living challenges, and you're working in a private practice. You are considering taking an expensive training course in a treatment called facilitated communication (FC), in which therapists help clients communicate by guiding their hands as they type sentences on a computer. This treatment is advertised as a breakthrough for people who have autism, a disorder that appears early in childhood and is characterized, in many cases, by reduced language abilities and impoverished social interactions. The technique is also used for patients with cerebral palsy and other developmental disorders that limit the ability to speak. Before you invest your money in a weekend-long course, you decide it is your professional responsibility to look into the effectiveness of FC. Is this an evidence-based treatment?

The organizers of the training course claim that people with disabilities—even if they cannot or will not speak—are able to type coherent messages on a keyboard if their hands and arms are supported by a sympathetic adult "facilitator" as they use the keyboard. Proponents of FC believe the facilitator develops a relationship of trust and helpfulness with the client. The intent is for the clients to independently create written messages in which they express thoughts that they ordinarily cannot, because of the disability.

If you do further research, however, you would learn that some psychologists suspect that the alleged successes of FC could be cases of "unconscious cuing": While supporting the client's hands, the facilitator has many opportunities to influence what the client types (Twachtman-Cullen, 1997). Psychologists have used controlled research to test the claims about the technique. In one study, a patient and a facilitator were both presented with a drawing of a common object, and the client was asked to type its name with the help of the facilitator (Klewe, 1993). Neither the client nor the facilitator could see the other's drawing, so neither person knew that they had been shown two different objects. (For example, in one trial the client was shown a picture of a key, while the facilitator saw a picture of a sandwich.) Sure enough, the client typed out a name that fit one of the drawings—

FIGURE 1.2 Facilitated communication. One behavior that led some researchers to doubt FC was that clients were observed to type with one finger while looking away from the keyboard. (If you try it yourself, you'll notice it's virtually impossible to type coherently with one finger without looking.) Such observations meant that the facilitators, not the clients, were probably creating the typed words. Current users of FC claim to ensure that clients are always looking at the keys.

but always the drawing that the *facilitator* saw (i.e., the sandwich). The facilitators must have been cuing the clients in some way, even if they were not aware they were doing so—and even if they were trying *not* to do so (**Figure 1.2**). (For a summary of this research and an explanation of why FC may still be practiced today, see Jacobson, Mulick, & Schwartz, 1995; Janzen-Wilde, Duchan, & Higginbotham, 1995; Twachtman-Cullen, 1997). Indeed, the APA resolved that FC has "no scientifically demonstrated support for its efficacy"; it is not an evidence-based treatment (American Psychological Association, 1994).

To return to our scenario, because you are a careful consumer of information, you would probably decide to save your time and money to learn therapies that are backed up by empirical evidence. But without some ability to find, read, and understand the research on this topic, you might not have learned that FC is an unsupported technique. Training in research methods should motivate you to ask questions about this and other therapeutic techniques that you encounter.

Even if you choose a career that is not part of the field of psychology, you can benefit from reading psychological research. Consider a study on the impact of the color red, conducted by Andrew Elliot and his colleagues (2007). These researchers observed that the color red could become associated, over time, with messages of danger, caution, and avoidance. Red is the color of stop signs, stoplights, and warning signs, and teachers often use red ink or pencil to correct homework and tests. Do these associations matter for student achievement? When Elliot and his team gave college students a cognitive skills test, they scored lower if their test booklets had a red paper cover rather than a green or white one. In a second study, the students solved fewer anagrams when their participant ID number was written on each page in red ink rather than green or black ink. Elliot and his colleagues thus demonstrated that using red ink or a red cover as part of a cognitive test can inhibit performance. In a third study, students with a red-covered test (compared with students given a green or gray one) decided to work on more of the easy problems instead of the more challenging ones. The color red apparently primes people with an "avoidance" mindset—they avoid challenges and play it safe.

Just think of the real-world applications of this study. If you were a teacher preparing a test or an employer preparing a questionnaire for job candidates, you would now suspect that the color of paper and ink you use could make a difference. (Chapter 10 returns to this example and examines whether the Elliot study stands up to interrogation.)

CHECK YOUR UNDERSTANDING

1. Explain what the consumer of research and producer of research roles have in common, and describe how they differ.

2. What kinds of jobs would use consumer-of-research skills? What kinds of jobs would use producer-of-research skills?

---

1. See pp. 4–6. 2. See p. 4.

How Scientists Approach Their Work

Psychological scientists are identified not by advanced degrees or white lab coats; they are defined by what they *do*. The rest of this chapter will explain the fundamental ways that psychological scientists approach their work. First, scientists act as empiricists in their investigations, meaning that they systematically observe the world. Second, scientists test theories through research and, in turn, adapt their theories based on the resulting data. Third, scientists take an empirical approach to both applied research, which directly targets real-world problems, and basic research, which is intended to contribute to the general body of knowledge. Fourth, scientists go further: Once they have discovered an effect, they plan further research to test why, when, or for whom an effect works. Fifth, psychologists make their work public: They submit their results to journals for review and respond to the opinions of other scientists. Finally, another aspect of making work public involves sharing findings of psychological research with the popular media. Do journalists get the story right?

Scientists Are Empiricists

Empiricists do not base conclusions on intuition, on casual observations of their own experience, or on what other people say. **Empiricism**, also called the *empirical method* or *empirical research*, involves using evidence from the senses (sight, hearing, touch) or from instruments that assist the senses (such as thermometers, timers, photographs, weight scales, and questionnaires) as the basis for conclusions. Empiricists aim to be systematic, rigorous, and to make their work independently verifiable by other observers or scientists. In Chapter 2, you will learn more about why empiricism is considered the most reliable basis for conclusions when compared with other forms of reasoning, such as experience or intuition. For now, we'll focus on some of the practices in which empiricists engage.

For more on the contrast between empiricism and intuition, experience, and authority, see Chapter 2, pp. 24–38.

Scientists Test Theories: The Theory-Data Cycle

In the theory-data cycle, scientists collect data to test, change, or update their theories. Even if you have never been in a formal research situation, you have probably tested ideas and hunches of your own by asking specific questions that are grounded in theory, making predictions, and reflecting on data.

For example, imagine picking up your smart phone to check your e-mail (**Figure 1.3**). You tap on your inbox, but nothing happens. What could be wrong? Maybe your entire device is on the blink: Do the other applications work? When you test them, you find that your calculator is working, but not your online map application. In fact, it looks as if only the apps that need wireless are not working. You check your wireless indicator, and it looks low. You ask your roommate, sitting nearby, "Are you having wifi problems?" If she says no, you might restart your device, hoping to reset the wireless connection.

Notice the series of steps in this process. First, you asked a particular series of questions, all of which were guided by your theory about how such devices work. The questions you asked (Is it the phone as a whole? Is it only the wifi?) reflected your theory that e-mail applications require a working electronic device as well as a wireless connection. Because you were operating under this theory, you chose not to ask other kinds of questions. (Has a gremlin possessed my phone? Does my device have a bacterial infection?) Your theory set you up for certain questions and not others. Next, your questions led you to specific predictions, which you tested by collecting data. You tested your first idea about the problem (My device can't run any applications) by posing a specific prediction (If I test any application, it won't work). Then you set up a situation to test your prediction (Does the calculator work?). The data (The calculator does work) told you your initial prediction was wrong. You used that outcome to change your idea about the problem (It's only the wireless-based apps that aren't working). And so on. When you take systematic steps to solve a problem, you are participating in something similar to what scientists do in the theory-data cycle.

The Cupboard Theory vs. the Contact Comfort Theory

A classic example from the psychological study of attachment can illustrate the way researchers similarly use data to test their theories. You have probably observed that animals form strong attachments to their caregivers. If you have a dog, it probably is extremely happy to see you when you come home, wagging its tail and jumping all over you. Human babies, once they are able to crawl, may follow their parents or caregivers

FIGURE 1.3

Troubleshooting a smart phone. Troubleshooting an electronic device is a form of engaging in the theory-data cycle.

around, keeping close to them. Baby monkeys exhibit similar behavior, spending hours clinging tightly to the mother's fur. Why do animals form such strong attachments to their caregivers?

One theory, referred to as the cupboard theory of mother-infant attachment, is that a mother is valuable to a baby mammal because she is a source of food. The baby animal gets hungry, gets food from the mother by nursing, and experiences a pleasant feeling (reduced hunger). Over time, the sight of the mother is associated with pleasure. In other words, the mother acquires positive value for the baby because she is the "cupboard" from which food comes. If you've ever assumed your dog loves you only because you feed it, your beliefs are consistent with the cupboard theory.

An alternative theory, proposed by psychologist Harry Harlow (1958), is that hunger has little to do with why a baby monkey likes to cling to the warm, fuzzy fur of its mother. Instead, babies are attached to their mothers because of the comfort of cozy touch. This is the contact comfort theory. (In addition, it provides a less cynical view of why your dog is so happy to see you!)

In the natural world, a mother offers both food and contact comfort at once, so when the baby clings to her, it is impossible to tell why. To test the alternative theories, Harlow had to separate the two influences—food and contact comfort. The only way he could do so was to create "mothers" of his own. He built two monkey foster "mothers"—the only mothers his lab-reared baby monkeys ever had. One of the mothers was made of bare wire mesh with a bottle of milk built in. This wire mother offered food but not comfort. The other mother was covered with fuzzy terrycloth and was warmed by a lightbulb suspended inside, but she had no milk. This cloth mother offered comfort but not food.

Note that this experiment offers three possible outcomes. The contact comfort theory would be supported if the babies spent most of their time clinging to the cloth mother. The cupboard theory would be supported if the babies spent most of their time clinging to the wire mother. Neither theory would be supported if monkeys divided their time equally between the two mothers.

When Harlow put the baby monkeys in the cages with the two mothers, the evidence in favor of the contact comfort theory was overwhelming. Harlow's data showed that the little monkeys would cling to the cloth mother for 12–18 hours a day (**Figure 1.4**). When they were hungry, they would climb down, nurse from the wire mother, and then at

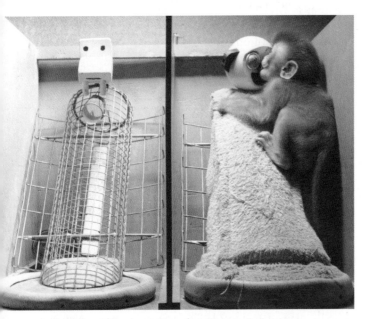

FIGURE 1.4 The contact comfort theory. As the theory hypothesized, Harlow's baby monkeys spent most of their time on the warm, cozy cloth mother, even though she did not provide any food.

once go back to the warm, cozy cloth mother. In short, Harlow used the two theories to make two specific predictions about how the monkeys would interact with each mother. Then he used the data he recorded (how much time the monkeys spent on each mother) to support only one of the theories. The theory-data cycle in action!

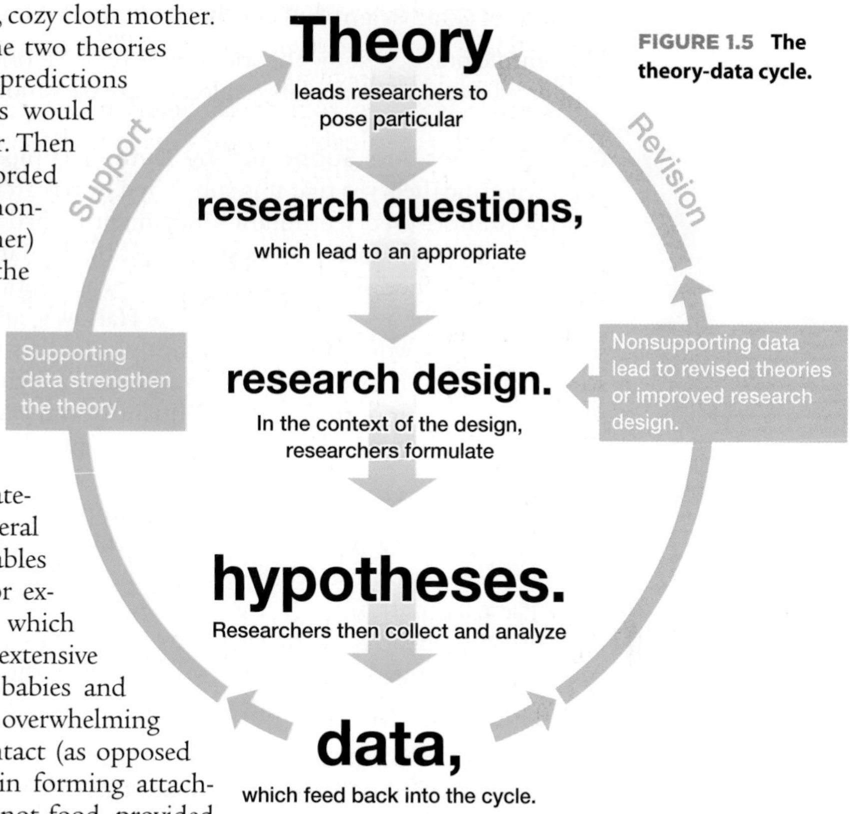

Theory, Hypothesis, and Data

A **theory** is a set of statements that describes general principles about how variables relate to one another. For example, Harlow's theory, which he developed in light of extensive observations of primate babies and mothers, was about the overwhelming importance of bodily contact (as opposed to simple nourishment) in forming attachments. Contact comfort, not food, provided the primary basis for a baby's attachment to its mother. This theory led Harlow to investigate particular kinds of questions—he chose to pit contact comfort against food in his research. The theory meant that Harlow also chose *not* to study unrelated questions, such as the babies' food preferences or sleeping habits.

The theory not only led to the questions; it also led to specific hypotheses about the answers. A **hypothesis**, or *prediction*, is a way of stating the specific outcome the researcher expects to observe if the theory is accurate. Harlow's hypothesis related to the way the baby monkeys would interact with two kinds of mothers. He predicted that the babies would spend more time on the cozy mother than the wire mother. Notably, a single theory can lead to a large number of predictions, because a single hypothesis is usually not sufficient to test the entire theory—it is intended to test only part of it. Most researchers test their theories with a series of empirical studies, each designed to test an individual hypothesis.

Data are a set of observations. (Harlow's data were the amount of time the baby monkeys stayed with each mother.) Depending on whether or not the data are consistent with hypotheses based on a theory, the data may either support or challenge the theory. Data that match the theory's hypotheses strengthen the researcher's confidence in the theory. When the data do not match the theory's hypotheses, however, those results indicate that the theory needs to be revised. **Figure 1.5** shows how these steps work as a cycle.

FIGURE 1.5 **The theory-data cycle.**

Theory leads researchers to pose particular

research questions, which lead to an appropriate

research design. In the context of the design, researchers formulate

hypotheses. Researchers then collect and analyze

data, which feed back into the cycle.

Support

Revision

Supporting data strengthen the theory.

Nonsupporting data lead to revised theories or improved research design.

Features of Good Scientific Theories

In scientific practice, some theories are better than others. The best theories are supported by the data, are falsifiable, and are parsimonious.

Good Theories Are Supported by Data. The most important feature of a good scientific theory is that it is supported by research data. In this respect, the contact comfort theory of infant attachment turned out to be better than the cupboard theory, because it was supported by the data. Clearly, primate babies need food, but food is not the source of their emotional attachments to their mothers. In this way, good theories, like Harlow's, are consistent with our observations of the world. More importantly, scientists need to conduct multiple studies, using a variety of methods, to address different aspects of their theories. A theory that is supported by a large quantity and variety of evidence is a good theory.

Good Theories Are Falsifiable. A second important feature of a good scientific theory is **falsifiability**. A theory must lead to hypotheses that, when tested, could actually fail to support the theory. Remember that theories have to be supported by the data, but data are only useful if they can convince us that the theory is either correct or incorrect. When you were troubleshooting your e-mail problems, you used falsifiable theories (If my wifi is broken, then no wireless applications will work). The following unique theory may help illustrate this concept:

> I have discovered the underlying brain mechanism that controls behavior. You will soon be reading about this discovery (in the *National Enquirer*, available at your local supermarket). In the left hemisphere of the brain near the language area reside two tiny green men. . . . [T]o make a long story short, they basically control everything. There is one difficulty, however. The green men have the ability to detect any intrusion into the brain (surgery, X-rays, etc.) and when they do sense such an intrusion, they tend to disappear (I forgot to mention that they have the power to become invisible). (Stanovich, 2010, p. 25)

Can we falsify this theory? If so, how? If we could see the little green men, that would support the theory. But if we look and we do not see the little green men, that would support the theory, too. The theory would seem to be supported either way.

Of course, Stanovich himself does not believe this theory; he invented it to make a point about falsifiability. Would anybody actually reason this way? Unfortunately, yes. In fact, some of the proponents of facilitated communication (discussed earlier) have argued that the technique cannot be empirically tested because empirical tests introduce skepticism, which breaks down the necessary trust between the facilitator and client. Furthermore, some FC proponents assert that expressing doubt (e.g., doubting that previously illiterate clients can write surprisingly complex sentences) shows a lack of faith in people with disabilities (Twachtman-Cullen, 1997). This trust and faith, they claim, are key ingredients to FC and make FC much more difficult to test scientifically. If these claims are true, the theory behind facilitated communication is not falsifiable. In contrast, in developing a truly scientific theory, researchers must take risks. With every prediction they make, they must take the risk that their theory might not be supported.

Good Theories Have Parsimony. A third important feature of a good scientific theory is that it exhibits **parsimony**: *All other things being equal, the simplest solution is the best.* (This notion is sometimes referred to as Occam's razor.) If two theories explain the data equally well but one is simpler, most scientists will opt for the simpler, more parsimonious theory. Stanovich's disappearing green men theory is not parsimonious, because its creatures require us to make several complex assumptions that contradict most principles of physics and biology.

Parsimony sets a standard for the theory-data cycle. As long as a simple theory predicts the data well, there should be no need to make the theory more complex. Harlow's theory was parsimonious because it posed a simple explanation for infant attachment: Contact comfort drives attachment more than food does. As long as the data continue to support the simple theory, the simple theory stands. However, when the data contradict the theory, the theory has to change in order to accommodate the data. For example, over the years, psychologists have collected data showing that baby monkeys do not always form an attachment to a soft, cozy mother. If monkeys are reared in complete social isolation during their first, critical months, they seem to have problems forming attachments to anyone or anything. Thus, the contact comfort theory had to change a bit, so it would emphasize the importance of contact comfort for attachment *especially in the early months of life.* The theory is slightly less parsimonious now, but it does a better job of accommodating the data.

Theories Don't Prove Anything

The word *prove* is rarely used in science. Researchers never say they have proved their theories. At most, they will say that some data *support* or *are consistent with* a theory, or they might say that some data *are inconsistent with* or *complicate* a theory. But no single confirming finding can prove a theory. New information might require researchers, tomorrow or the next day, to change and improve current ideas. Similarly, a single, disconfirming finding does not lead researchers to scrap a theory entirely. The disconfirming study may itself have been designed poorly. Or perhaps the theory needs to be modified, not discarded. Rather than thinking of a theory as proved or disproved by a single study, scientists evaluate their theories based on the **weight of the evidence**, for and against.

For more on weight of the evidence, see Chapter 14, p. 419.

Scientists Tackle Applied and Basic Problems

The scientist's empirical approach can be used for both applied and basic research questions. **Applied research** is done with a practical problem in mind; the researchers hope their findings will be directly *applied* to the solution of that problem in a particular real-world context. An applied research study might ask, for example, if a school district's new method of teaching mathematics is working better than the former one. It might test the efficacy of a treatment for depression in a sample of trauma survivors. Applied researchers might be looking for better ways to identify those who are likely to do well at a particular job. And applied researchers can use empirical evidence to answer a nonprofit organization's questions.

Basic research, in contrast, is not intended to address a specific, practical problem; the goal is to enhance the general body of knowledge. Basic researchers might want to understand the structure of the visual system, the capacity of the human memory, the motivations of a depressed person, or the limitations of the infant attachment system. Basic researchers do not just gather facts at random; in fact, the knowledge they generate may be applied to real-world issues later on. In most cases, solid basic research is an important basis for later, applied studies.

Translational research is the use of lessons from basic research to develop and test applications to health care, psychotherapy, or other forms of treatment and intervention. Translational research represents a dynamic bridge from basic to applied research. For example, basic research on approach and avoidance goals has also shown that these orientations can lead to different kinds of moods. Translational researchers applied this knowledge to depression, developing a therapy that teaches depressed people to reframe their avoidance goals into approach goals (Strauman et al., 2006), which seems to work well for some depressed people. Basic research on the biochemistry of cell membranes might be translated into a new drug for schizophrenia. **Figure 1.6** shows the interrelationship of the three types of research.

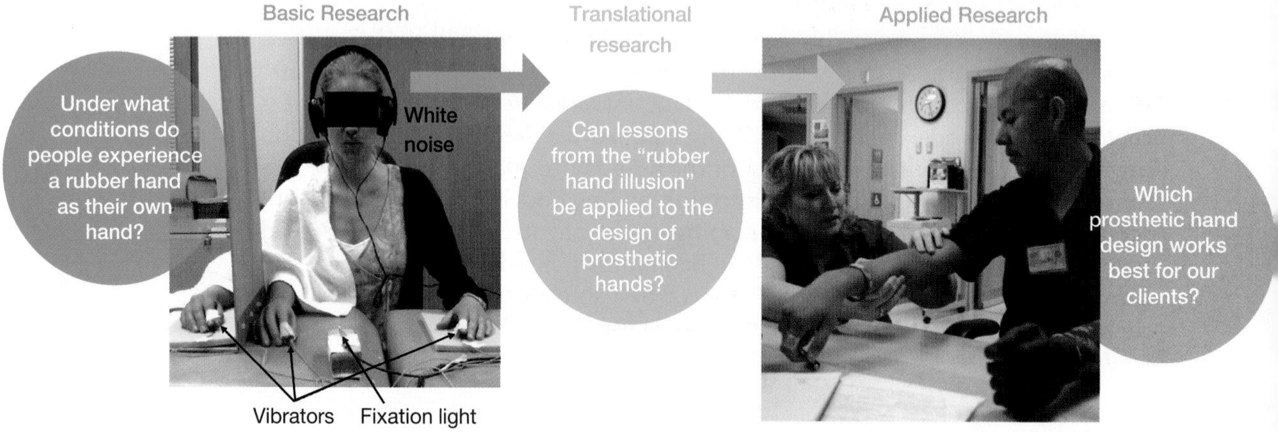

Basic Research   Translational research   Applied Research

Under what conditions do people experience a rubber hand as their own hand?

White noise

Vibrators   Fixation light

Can lessons from the "rubber hand illusion" be applied to the design of prosthetic hands?

Which prosthetic hand design works best for our clients?

FIGURE 1.6 **Basic, applied, and translational research.** Basic researchers may not have an applied context in mind, and applied researchers may be less familiar with basic theories and principles. Translational researchers attempt to translate findings of basic science into applied arenas.

FIGURE 1.7 The effect of color on behavior. Did participants walk fast to meet a person in a red shirt or a blue shirt? It depended on whether they were expecting a date or a job interview. Thus, the way color affects a person's behavior depends on the context.

Scientists Dig Deeper

Psychological scientists rarely conduct a single investigation and then stop. Instead, each study leads them to ask a new question. Scientists might start with a simple effect, such as the effect of comfort on attachment, and then ask, "Why does this occur?" "When does this happen the most?" "For whom does this apply?" "What are the limits?"

Elliot and his colleagues, for example, did not stop after their own first study, in which red paper test covers made people do worse on a cognitive task. They dug deeper. In their second study, they used red and green pens to write ID numbers, rather than paper covers. They also pushed themselves to test a variety of cognitive tasks, such as anagrams, analogies, and mathematics problems.

Their curiosity did not stop there. In later research, Elliot and his team tested the effects of color in other domains, such as physical strength and romantic contexts. They found that the color red made students squeeze a handle more forcefully and quickly than the colors blue or gray (Elliot & Aarts, 2011). They also found that when people thought they are going to a job interview, the color red made them walk to the interview room more slowly, as past work might have predicted (**Figure 1.7**). But when people thought they were going to an interview with a dating partner, the color red actually made them walk to the interview room more quickly (Meier, D'Agostino, Elliot, Maier, & Wilkowski, 2012). In romantic contexts, red incites passionate approach motives, not avoidance motives. This work illustrates that the effect of color on behavior depends upon context (Elliot & Maier, 2012).

Scientists Make It Public: The Publication Process

When scientists want to tell the scientific world about the results of their research, whether basic or applied, they write a paper and submit it to a scientific **journal**. Like magazines, journals usually come out every month and contain articles written by various qualified contributors. But unlike popular newsstand magazines, the articles in a scientific journal are *peer-reviewed*. When an editor receives a manuscript, the editor sends it to three or four experts on the subject. The experts tell the editor about the manuscript's virtues and flaws, and the editor decides whether the paper deserves to be published in the journal.

The peer-review process in the field of psychology is rigorous. Peer reviewers are kept anonymous, so even if they know the author of the article professionally or personally, they can feel free to give an honest assessment of the research. They comment on how interesting the work is, how novel it is, how well the research was done, and how clear the results are. Ultimately, peer reviewers are supposed to ensure that the articles published in scientific journals contain innovative, well-done studies. When the peer-review process works, research with major flaws does not get published. However, the process continues even after a study is published. Other scientists can cite an article and do further work on the same subject. Moreover, scientists who find flaws in the research (perhaps overlooked by the peer reviewers) can publish letters, commentaries, or competing studies. Through publishing their work, scientists make the process of their research transparent, and the scientific community evaluates it.

Scientists Talk to the World: From Journal to Journalism

One goal of this textbook is to teach you how to interrogate information about psychological science that you find not only in journals but also in more mainstream sources that you encounter in daily life. Psychology's scientific journals are read primarily by other scientists and by psychology students; the general public almost never reads them. **Journalism**, in contrast, includes the kinds of news and commentary that most of us read or hear on television, in magazines and newspapers, and on Internet sites—articles in *Psychology Today* and *Men's Health*, topical blogs, relationship advice columns, and so on. These sources are usually written by journalists or laypeople, not scientists, and they are meant to reach the general public; they are easy to access, and understanding their content does not require specialized education.

How does the news media find out about the latest scientific findings? A journalist might become interested in a particular study by reading the current issue of a scientific journal, or by hearing scientists talk about their work at a conference. The journalist turns the research into a news story by summarizing it for a popular audience, giving it an interesting headline, and writing about it using nontechnical terms.

Benefits and Risks of Journalism Coverage

Psychologists can benefit when journalists publicize their research. By reading about psychological research in the newspaper, the general public can learn what psychologists really do. Those who read or hear the story might also pick up important tips for living: They might understand their children or themselves better; they might set different goals or change their habits. These important benefits of science writing depend on two things, however. First, journalists need to report on the most important scientific stories, and second, they must describe the research accurately.

Is the Story Important? When journalists report on a study, have they chosen research that has been conducted rigorously, that tests an important question, and that has been peer-reviewed? Or have they chosen a study simply because it is cute or eye-catching? Sometimes journalists do follow important stories, especially when covering research that has already been published in a selective, peer-reviewed journal. But sometimes journalists choose the sensational story over the important one. For example, some years ago, a story about whether parents buckled their children into shopping carts hit the science headlines (Bakalar, 2005). The study found that "cute" children were more likely to be buckled into shopping carts than "ugly" children. Of course, this story was ripe for public consumption—it was shocking, easy to understand, and even a little funny. However, the original study had been presented only at a local conference and had not been peer-reviewed. Its importance, methods, and conclusions had not yet been assessed by scientists in the field. Indeed, years later, this study has yet to be published in a scientific journal.

Is the Story Accurate? Even when journalists report on reliable, important research, they don't always get the story right. Some science writers do an excellent, accurate job of summarizing the research, but not all of them do (**Figure 1.8**). Perhaps the journalist does not have the scientific training, the motivation, or the time before deadline to understand the original science very well. Maybe the journalist dumbs down the details of a study to make it more accessible to a general audience.

Media coverage of a phenomenon called the "Mozart effect" provides an example of how journalists might misrepresent science when they write for a popular audience (Spiegel, 2010). In 1993, researcher Frances Rauscher found that when students heard Mozart music played for 10 minutes, they performed better on a subsequent spatial intelligence test when compared with students who had listened to silence or to a monotone speaking voice (Rauscher, Shaw, & Ky, 1993). Rauscher said in a radio interview, "What we found was that the students who had listened to the Mozart sonata scored significantly higher on the spatial temporal task." However, Rauscher added, "It's very important to note that we did not find effects for general intelligence . . . just for this one aspect of intelligence. It's a small gain and it doesn't last very long" (Spiegel, 2010). But despite the careful way the scientist described the results, the media that reported on the story exaggerated its importance:

> The headlines in the papers were less subtle than her findings: "Mozart makes you smart" was the general idea. . . . But worse, says Rauscher, was that her very modest finding started to be wildly distorted. "Generalizing these results to children is one of the first things that went wrong.

FIGURE 1.8 Getting it right. Cartoonist Jorge Cham parodies what can happen when journalists report on scientific research. Here, an original study reported a relationship between two variables. Although the University Public Relations Office relates the story accurately, the strength of the relationship and its implications become distorted with subsequent retellings, much like a game of "telephone."

Somehow or another the myth started exploding that children that listen to classical music from a young age will do better on the SAT, they'll score better on intelligence tests in general, and so forth." (Spiegel, 2010)

Perhaps because the media distorted the effects of that first study, a small industry sprang up, recording child-friendly sonatas for parents and teachers (**Figure 1.9**). However, according to research conducted since the first study was published, the effect of listening to Mozart on people's intelligence test scores is not very strong, and it applies to most music, not just Mozart (Pietschnig, Voracek, & Formann, 2010).

The journalist Ben Goldacre (2011) catalogs many examples of how journalists and the general public misinterpret scientific data when they write about it for a popular audience. Some journalists create dramatic stories about employment statistics that show, for example, a 0.9% increase in unemployment claims. Journalists may conclude that these small increases show an upward trend—when in fact, they may simply reflect a sampling error. Another example comes from a happiness survey of 5,000 people in the United Kingdom. Local journalists picked up on tiny city-to-city differences, creating headlines about, for instance, how

FIGURE 1.9 The Mozart effect. Journalists sometimes misrepresent research findings. Exaggerated reports of the Mozart effect even inspired a line of consumer products for children.

the city of Edinburgh is the "most miserable place in the country." But the differences the survey found between the various places were not statistically significant (Goldacre, 2008). Even though there were slight differences in happiness from Edinburgh to London, the differences were small enough to be caused by random variation. The researcher who conducted the study said, "I tried to explain issues of [statistical] significance to the journalists who interviewed me. Most did not want to know" (Goldacre, 2008).

How can you prevent being misled by a journalist's coverage of science? One idea is to find the original source, which you'll learn to do in Chapter 2. Reading the original scientific journal article is the best way to get the full story. Another approach is to maintain a skeptical mindset when it comes to popular sources. Chapter 3 explains how to ask the right questions before you allow yourself to accept the journalist's claim. To see some recent examples of how journalists cover science in the news, visit www.everydayresearchmethods.com and click the box for Chapter 1.

To learn about sampling error, see Chapter 7, pp. 196–197.

CHECK YOUR UNDERSTANDING

1. What happens to a theory when the data do not support the theory's hypotheses? What happens to a theory when the data do support the theory's hypotheses?

2. Explain the difference between basic research and applied research, and describe how the two interact.

3. After an initial study, what are some of the further questions scientists might ask in their research?

4. What are the benefits when scientists publish their data?

5. What are two ways that journalists might distort the science they attempt to publicize?

1. See the discussion of Harlow's monkey experiment on pp. 9–11. 2. See pp. 13–14. 3. See p. 15. 4. See pp. 15–16. 5. See pp. 16–19.

Summary

- Thinking like a psychologist means thinking like a scientist, and thinking like a scientist involves thinking about empirical data.

Research Producers, Research Consumers

- Some students need skills as producers of research; they develop research methods skills to work in research laboratories and discover new knowledge.
- Some students need skills as consumers of research; they need to be able to find, read, and evaluate the research behind important policies, therapies, and workplace decisions.
- Having good consumer of research skills means being able to evaluate the evidence behind the claims of a salesperson, journalist, or researcher, and making better, more informed decisions by asking the right questions.

How Scientists Approach Their Work

- As scientists, psychologists are empiricists; they base their conclusions on systematic, unbiased observations of the world.
- Using the theory-data cycle, researchers propose theories, make hypotheses (predictions), and collect data. A good scientific theory is supported by data, is falsifiable, and is parsi-

monious. A researcher might say that a theory is well supported or well established, rather than proved, meaning that most of the data have confirmed the theory and very little have disconfirmed it.

- Applied researchers address real-world problems, and basic researchers work for general understanding. Basic research can become translational research, which applies solutions for specific issues.
- Scientists usually follow up an initial study with more questions about why, when, and for whom a phenomenon occurs.
- The publication process is part of worldwide scientific communication. Scientists publish their research in journals, following a peer-review process that leads to sharper thinking and improved communication. Even after publication, published work can be approved or criticized by the scientific community.
- Journalists are writers for the popular media who are skilled at transforming scientific studies for the general public, but they don't always get it right. Think critically about what you read in the papers, and when in doubt, go directly to the original source—peer-reviewed research.

Key Terms

evidence-based treatments, p. 6
empiricism, p. 8
theory, p. 11
hypothesis, p. 11
data, p. 11

falsifiability, p. 12
parsimony, p. 13
weight of the evidence, p. 13
applied research, p. 13
basic research, p. 14

translational research, p. 14
journal, p. 15
journalism, p. 16

 To see samples of chapter concepts in the popular press, visit www.everydayresearchmethods.com and click the box for Chapter 1.

Review Questions

1. Which of the following jobs most likely involves producer-of-research skills rather than consumer-of-research skills?
   a. Police officer
   b. University professor
   c. Physician
   d. Journalist

2. To be an empiricist, one should:
   a. Base one's conclusions on direct observations.
   b. Strive for parsimony.
   c. Be sure that one's research can be applied in a real-world setting.
   d. Discuss one's ideas in a public setting, such as an online chat room.

3. A statement, or set of statements, that describes general principles about how variables relate to one another is a(n) _____.
   a. prediction
   b. hypothesis
   c. empirical observation
   d. theory

4. Why is publication an important part of the empirical process?
   a. Because publication enables practitioners to read the research and use it in applied settings.
   b. Because publication contributes to making empirical observations independently verifiable.
   c. Because journalists can make the knowledge available to the general public.
   d. Because publication is the first step of the theory-data cycle.

5. Which of the following research questions best illustrates an example of basic research?
   a. Has our company's new marketing campaign led to an increase in sales?
   b. How satisfied are our patients with their wait-time in the waiting room? How satisfied are our patients with the sensitivity of the nursing staff?
   c. Do neuro-boosting soft drinks really work?
   d. Can 2-month-old human infants discern the difference between four objects and six objects?

Learning Actively

1. To learn more about the theory-data cycle, look in the textbooks from your other psychology courses for examples of theories. In your introductory psychology book, you might look up the James Lange theory or the Cannon-Bard theory of emotion. You could look up Piaget's theory of cognitive development, the Young-Helmholz theory of color vision, or the stage theory of memory. How do the data presented in your textbook show support for the theory? Does the textbook present any data that does not support the theory?

2. Go to the website www.msnbc.com and visit the Health section. Find a headline that is reporting the results of a recently published study. Read the story, and ask: Has the research in the story been published yet? Does the journalist mention the name of a journal in which the results appeared? Or has the study only been presented at a research conference? Then, use the Internet to find examples of how other journalists have covered the same story. What variation do you notice in their stories?

Does Venting Anger Feed or Extinguish the Flame?

(Personality and Social Psychology Bulletin, 2002)

Venting Frustration Will Only Make Your Anger Worse

(Lifehacker.com, 2010)

2

Sources of Information: Why Research Is Best and How to Find It

Have you ever tried one of the "stress-relief games" from the Internet? One on-line source includes *Whack Your Boss, Justin Bieber Bash*, and *Spank the Banker*. The descriptions explain that you can "take out your anger on your boss" and that the games help you "vent your aggression." But does venting aggression really make people feel better? Does expressing aggression make aggression go away?

Many sources of information promote the idea that venting anger works. You might try a game yourself and feel good while playing it. Or you may hear from guidance counselors, friends, or online sources that venting negative feelings is a healthy way to manage anger. But is it accurate to base your conclusions on what authorities—even well-meaning ones—say? Should you believe what everyone else believes? Does it make sense to base your convictions on your own personal experience?

This chapter discusses three sources of evidence for people's beliefs—experience, intuition, and authority—and compares them to a superior source of evidence: *empirical research*. We will focus on a particular type of response to the

FIGURE 2.1 Anger management. Some people believe that venting physically or playing violent video games is the best way to work through anger, but what does the research suggest?

question about handling anger: the idea of cathartically releasing pent-up anger and tension by hitting a punching bag, screaming, or playing a violent video game (**Figure 2.1**). Is catharsis a healthy way to deal with feelings of anger and frustration? Does hitting a punching bag make your anger go away? How could you find credible research on this subject if you wanted to read about it? And why should you trust the conclusions of researchers instead of those based on your own experience or intuition?

The Research vs. Your Experience

When we need to decide what to believe, our own experiences are powerful sources of information. "I've used tanning beds for 10 years. No skin cancer yet!" "I think this NeuroBliss drink really works! I feel more calm and serene after I drink one" "When I'm mad, I feel so much better after I hit the punching bag at my gym." Often, too, we base our opinions on the experiences of friends and family. For instance, suppose you're considering buying a new car. You want a car that will have the fewest possible repairs, so after consulting *Consumer Reports*, you decide on a Honda Accord, because the reports of 1,000 Accord owners indicate that the repair history for that car is excellent. But then your father reminds you that the worst car he ever owned was a Honda Accord. Why shouldn't you trust your own experience—or that of someone you know and trust—as a source of information?

Experience Has No Comparison Group

There are many reasons not to base beliefs solely on personal experience, but perhaps the most important is that when we do so, we usually do not take a comparison group into account. Research, by contrast, asks the critical question: "Compared to what?" A **comparison group** enables us to compare what would happen both with and without the thing we are interested in—both with and without tanning beds, online games, or neuro drinks (**Figure 2.2**).

Here's a disturbing example of why a comparison group is so important: Centuries ago, Dr. Benjamin Rush drained blood from people's wrists or ankles as part of a "bleeding," or bloodletting, cure for illness (Eisenberg, 1977). The practice emerged from the belief that too much blood was the cause of illness, particularly yellow fever. To restore an "appropriate" balance, a doctor might remove up to 100 ounces of blood from a patient over the course of a week. Of course, we now know that draining blood is one of the last things a doctor would want to do to a sick patient. Why did Dr. Rush keep on using such a practice? Why did he believe that bloodletting was a cure?

FIGURE 2.2 **Your own experience.** You may feel better after drinking a so-called "neuro drink." Should your experience convince you that such drinks really work?

In those days, a doctor who used the bleeding cure would have noticed that some of his patients recovered and some died. That was the doctor's personal experience. Indeed, every time a patient recovered from yellow fever after bloodletting, it *seemed* to support Rush's theory that the treatment worked. What if a patient died after being bled? Although regrettable, the death of the patient posed no problem for Rush's theory: The patient was too sick to recover and would have died anyway. Part of the problem here is that the doctor's theory was not *falsifiable*. (He was right if the patient recovered and still right if the patient died.) Another problem was that Dr. Rush never set up a systematic comparison.

To test the bleeding cure, doctors would have had to systematically count death rates among patients who were bled versus those who received some comparison treatment (or no treatment). How many people were bled and how many were not? Of each group, how many died and how many recovered? Putting all the records together, the doctors could have come to an empirically derived conclusion about the effectiveness of bloodletting.

Suppose, for example, Dr. Rush had kept records and found that 20 patients who were bled recovered, and 10 patients who refused the bleeding treatment recovered. At first, it might look like the bleeding cure worked; after all, twice as many bled patients as untreated patients improved. But you need to know all the numbers—the number of bled patients who died and the number of untreated patients who died, in addition to the number of patients in each group

TABLE 2.1 Baseline Comparisons

	Bled	Not bled
Number of patients who recovered	20	10
Number of patients who died	80	40
(Number recovered divided by total number of patients)	20/100	10/50
Percentage recovered	**20%**	**20%**

TABLE 2.2 One Value Decreased

	Bled	Not bled
Number of patients who recovered	20	10
Number of patients who died	80	1
(Number recovered divided by total number of patients)	20/100	10/11
Percentage recovered	**20%**	**91%**

TABLE 2.3 One Value Increased

	Bled	Not bled
Number of patients who recovered	20	10
Number of patients who died	80	490
(Number recovered divided by total number of patients)	20/100	10/500
Percentage recovered	**20%**	**2%**

who recovered. In order to compare all of these numbers, you might find it helpful to create a table, or matrix, that looks something like **Table 2.1**. If you consider all four cells (boxes) in the table, you'll see that there is no relationship at all between treatment and improvement. Although twice as many bled patients as untreated patients recovered, twice as many bled patients as untreated patients died, too. If you calculate the percentages, the recovery rate among people who were bled was 20%, and the recovery rate among people who were not treated was also 20%: The proportions are identical. (Keep in mind that all of these data are invented for the purposes of illustration; doctors did not make systematic comparisons like this back in the 1700s.)

To make this comparison, we needed to know the values in all four cells of the table, including the number of untreated patients who died. **Table 2.2** shows an example of what might happen if the value in only that cell changes. In this case, the number of untreated patients who died is much lower, so the treatment is shown to have a *negative* effect. Only 20% of the treated patients recovered, compared with 91% of the untreated patients. In contrast, if the number in the fourth cell were increased drastically, as in **Table 2.3**, the treatment would be shown to have a *positive* effect. The recovery rate among bled patients is still 20%, but the recovery rate among untreated patients is a mere 2%.

Notice that in all three tables, changing only one value led to dramatically different results. Drawing conclusions about a treatment—whether the bleeding treatment, ways of venting anger, or a blissful neuro drink—requires comparing data systematically from all four cells: the treated/improved cell, the treated/unimproved cell, the untreated/improved cell, and the untreated/unimproved cell. These comparison cells show the relative rate of improvement of using the treatment, compared with no treatment.

Because Dr. Rush bled every yellow fever patient, he never had the chance to see how many patients would recover without the bleeding treatment (**Figure 2.3**). Similarly, when you rely on personal experience to decide what is true, you usually do not have a systematic comparison group because you're observing only one "patient": yourself. The neuro drink you have been using may seem to be working, but what would have happened to your mood *without* the drink? Perhaps your mood would have improved anyway, as the day progressed. Or you might think playing the *Whack Your Boss* game makes you feel better when you're angry, but would you have felt better anyway, even if you had played a nonviolent game? What if you had done nothing and just let a little time pass?

Basing conclusions on personal experience is problematic because life often does not offer a comparison experience. In contrast, basing conclusions on systematic data collection has the simple but tremendous advantage of providing a comparison group. Only a systematic comparison can show you whether your mood improves when you have a neuro drink (compared with when you do not), or whether your anger goes away when you play violent games (compared with doing nothing).

FIGURE 2.3 Bloodletting in the eighteenth century. Describe how Dr. Rush's faulty attention to information led him to believe that bloodletting therapy was effective.

Experience Is Confounded

Another problem with basing conclusions on personal experience is that in everyday life, too much is going on at once. Even if a change has occurred, we often cannot be sure what caused it. When a patient bled by Dr. Rush got better, that patient might also have been trying other treatments—eating special foods, drinking more fluids. Which one caused the improvement? When you notice a difference in your mood after having a neuro drink, maybe you also had an easy day or a good night's sleep. Which one caused your mood to improve? If you play *Whack Your Boss*, it certainly provides violent content, but you might also be distracting yourself from your anger or increasing your heart rate. Is it these factors or the game's violence that causes you to feel better after playing it?

In real-world situations, there are several possible explanations for an outcome. In research, these alternative explanations are called **confounds**. Confounded can also mean confused. Essentially, a confound occurs when you think one thing caused an outcome but in fact other things changed, too, so you are confused about what the cause really was. You might think the neuro drink improved your mood, but since you were also taking a study break, tasting something sweet, or simply expecting to feel better, you can't determine which of these factors (or which combination of factors) caused the improvement.

For more on confounds and how to avoid them in research design, see Chapter 10, pp. 279-284.

What can we do about confounds like these? For a personal experience, it is hard to isolate variables. Think about the last time you were sick to your stomach—which of the many things you ate that day made you sick? Or your allergies—which of the blossoming spring plants are you allergic to? In a research setting, though, scientists can use careful controls to be sure they are changing only one factor at a time.

Research Is Better Than Experience

What happens when scientists do set up a systematic comparison that controls for potential confounds? For example, by using controlled, systematic comparisons, several groups of researchers have tested the hypothesis that venting anger is beneficial (e.g., Berkowitz, 1973; Bushman, Baumeister, & Phillips, 2001; Feshbach, 1956; Lohr, Olatunji, Baumeister, & Bushman, 2007). One such study was conducted by researcher Brad Bushman (2002). To examine the effect of venting, or catharsis, Bushman systematically compared what happened if angry people were allowed to vent their anger with what happened if angry people did not vent their anger.

First, Bushman needed to make people angry. He invited 600 undergraduate students to arrive, one by one, to a laboratory setting, where each student wrote a political essay. Next, each essay was shown to another person, called Steve, who was actually a **confederate**, an actor playing a specific role for the experimenter. Steve insulted the student by criticizing the essay, calling it "the worst essay I've ever read" and delivering other unflattering comments. (Bushman knew that this technique made students angry because he had used it in previous studies, in which students whose essays were criticized had reported feeling angrier than students whose essays were not criticized.)

Bushman then randomly divided the angry students into three groups, to systematically compare the effects of venting and not venting anger. Group 1 was instructed to sit quietly in the room for 2 minutes. Group 2 was instructed to punch a punching bag for 2 minutes, having been told it was a form of exercise. Group 3 was instructed to punch a punching bag for 2 minutes while imagining Steve's face on it. (This was the important catharsis group.) Finally, all three groups of students were given a chance to get back at Steve. In the course of playing a quiz game with him, students had the chance to blast Steve's ears with a loud noise. (However, they only thought they were blasting Steve's ears; since Steve was a confederate, he did not actually experience these noise blasts.)

Which group gave Steve the loudest, longest blasts of noise? The catharsis hypothesis predicts that Group 3 should have calmed down the most, and as a result, this group should not have blasted Steve with very much noise. This group, however, gave Steve the loudest noise blasts of all! Compared with the other two groups, those who expressed their anger at Steve through the punching bag continued to punish him when they had the chance. (**Figure 2.4** shows the results in the form of a graph.) In contrast, Group 2, those who hit the punching bag for exercise, subjected him to less noise (it was not as loud and did not last as long). Those who sat quietly for 2 minutes punished Steve the least of all. So much for the catharsis hypothesis. When the scientists set up the comparison groups, they found that the opposite was true: People's anger will subside more quickly if they just sit in a room quietly than if they try to vent it.

Notice the power of systematic comparison here. In a controlled study, scientists can set up the conditions such that they include at least one comparison group, thereby avoiding confounds. Compare the researcher's larger view with more subjective views, in which each person consults only his or her own experience. If you had asked some of the students in Group 3, for example, whether using the punching bag helped their anger subside, these participants could only consider their own experiences. When Bushman looked at the pattern overall—taking into account all three groups—the results indicated that Group 3 still felt the angriest. The researcher thus has a privileged view—the view from the outside, including all possible comparison groups. In contrast, when you are the one acting in the situation, yours is a view from the inside, and you only see one possible condition.

Researchers can also control for potential confounds. In Bushman's study, all three groups felt equally angry at first. Bushman even separated the effects of aggression only (using the punching bag for exercise) from the effects of aggression toward the person who made the participant mad (using the punching bag as a stand-in for Steve). In real life, these two effects—exercise and the venting of anger—would usually occur at the same time.

Bushman's study is, of course, only one study on catharsis. In other studies, researchers have made people angry, presented them with an opportunity to vent their anger (or not), and then watched their behavior. Over and over again, researchers have found that people who physically express their anger at a target actually become *more* angry than when they started. Thus, practicing aggression just seems to teach people how to be aggressive (Berkowitz, 1973; Bushman et al., 2001; Feshbach, 1956; Geen & Quanty, 1977; Lohr et al., 2007; Tavris, 1989). The important point is that the results of a single study, such as Bushman's, are certainly better evidence than experience. In addition, consistent results from several similar studies mean that scientists will feel confident in the findings. As more and more studies amass evidence on the subject, theories about how people can effectively regulate their anger gain increasing support.

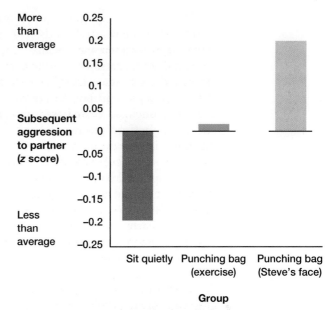

FIGURE 2.4 Results from controlled research on the catharsis hypothesis. In this study, after Steve (the confederate) insulted all the students in three groups by criticizing their essays, those in Group 1 sat quietly for 2 minutes, Group 2 hit a punching bag while thinking about exercise, and Group 3 hit a punching bag while imagining Steve's face on it. Later, students in all three groups had the chance to blast Steve with loud noise. (Source: Adapted from Bushman, 2002, Table 1.)

For more on the value of conducting multiple studies, see Chapter 14, pp. 414–419.

Research Is Probabilistic

Although research is usually more accurate than individual experience, sometimes our personal stories contradict the research results. Personal experience is powerful, and we often let a single experience distract us from the lessons of more rigorous research. Should you disagree with the results of a study when your own experience is different? Should you continue to play online games when you're angry because you believe they work for you? Should you disregard *Consumer Reports* because your father had a terrible experience with a Honda Accord?

At times, your experience (or your aunt's, or your father's) may be an exception to what the research finds. The question is: Should that exception undermine the general research results? Not at all. Behavioral research is **probabilistic**, which means that its findings are not expected to explain all cases all of the time. Instead, the conclusions of research are meant to explain a certain proportion (preferably a high proportion) of the possible cases. In practice, this means that scientific conclusions are based on patterns that emerge only when researchers set up comparison groups and test many people. Your own experience is only one point in that overall pattern. Thus, for instance, even though bleeding does not cure yellow fever, some sick patients did recover after being bled. However, those exceptional patients who recovered do not change the conclusion derived from all of the data. And even though your father's Honda did not run well, his case is only one out of 1,001 Honda owners, so it does not invalidate the general trend. Similarly, just because there is a strong general trend (that Hondas are reliable), it does not mean that your Honda will be reliable too. The research may suggest that there is a *strong probability* that your Honda will be reliable, but the prediction is not perfect.

CHECK YOUR UNDERSTANDING

1. What are two general problems with basing beliefs on experience? How does empirical research work to correct these problems?
2. What does it mean to say that research is probabilistic?

1. See pp. 25–29. 2. See pp. 29–30.

The Research vs. Your Intuition

Personal experience is one way that we often reach conclusions. Another is intuition. While we certainly think our intuition is a good source of information, it can lead us to make less effective decisions. Why? Because most people are not scientific thinkers. We are biased. When we don't pay attention, certain biases of intuition can sneak up on us, and we don't even notice. Other times, we might be aware that we have the potential to be biased, but we are too busy or not motivated enough to correct and control for these biases.

Biases of intuition fall into two overlapping categories: cognitive biases and motivational biases. The more you practice applying scientific principles, the more you can guard against the pull of these biases and the better decisions you will make.

Intuition Is Biased by Faulty Thinking

At times, intuition is biased simply because the human mind works imperfectly. We can be too easily swayed by a story that "makes sense," even when it is wrong. In addition, some kinds of information come to mind more readily than others.

Being Swayed by a Good Story

One example of cognitive biases in our thinking is when we accept a conclusion just because it "makes sense." We tend to believe good stories—even ones that are false. For example, to many people, bottling up negative emotions seems unhealthy, and expressing anger is sensible. As with a pimple or a boiling kettle of water, it might seem better to release the pressure. One of the early proponents of catharsis was the neurologist Sigmund Freud, whose models of mental distress focused on the harmful effects of suppressing one's feelings and the benefits of releasing them. Some biographers have speculated that Freud's ideas were influenced by the industrial technology of his day (Gay, 1989). Back then, engines used the power of steam to create vast amounts of energy. If the steam was too compressed, it could have devastating effects on a machine. Freud seems to have reasoned that the human psyche functions the same way. Catharsis makes a good story, because it draws on a metaphor (steam) that was, and still is, familiar to most people.

Here's another commonsense story that turned out to be wrong. Stomach ulcers were once thought to be caused by stress and excess stomach acid. Doctors treated ulcers with antacid medications and advised patients with ulcers to avoid acidic foods, such as hot sauce and carbonated drinks. Their intuition makes sense, doesn't it? Ulcers feel "hot" and they look like burns; they seem to get worse when people are under stress. Therefore, it seems sensible to treat them with calming, antiacidic methods. However, the intuition about "hot" ulcers was wrong, and this approach to treatment probably delayed the discovery of the true cause of many ulcers: a bacterium called *H. pylori* (Marshall & Warren, 1983, 1984). As it turns out, common antibiotics can cure stomach ulcers. So much for that hot story. (The real story was so important that the doctors who discovered it were awarded the Nobel Prize in Physiology or Medicine in 2005.)

Sometimes a "good story" will turn out to be accurate, of course, but it's important to be aware of the limitations of common sense. When empirical evidence contradicts what your common sense tells you, be ready to adjust your beliefs on the basis of the research. Believing in a "commonsense" story can lead you astray.

Being Persuaded by What Comes Easily to Mind

Another example of cognitive biases in thinking is the **availability heuristic**, which states that things that pop up easily in our mind tend to guide our thinking (Tversky & Kahneman, 1974). When events or memories are vivid, recent, or memorable, they come to mind more easily—and that can bias our thinking.

Here's an example. Give a quick, intuitive answer to this question before reading on: Which is more frequent—death by fire or death by falling? Most people think death by fire is more common, but death by falling is far more frequent (1.5 per 100,000 deaths by fire versus 6 per 100,000 deaths by falling; Ropeik & Gray, 2002). Why do people make this mistake? Deaths by fire may be more memorable and more easily imagined, so they come to mind easily and we inflate the risk associated with them. In contrast, deaths by falling seldom get much press. By thinking specifically about the difference between falls and fires, we realize that a large number of falling deaths probably occur among older adults. Often we are too busy (or too lazy) to think beyond the easy answer. We decide the answer that comes to mind easily must be the correct one.

The availability heuristic might lead us to wrongly estimate the number of something or how often something happens. For example, if you were to visit my campus, you would see some women wearing a headcovering (hijab), and conclude that there are lots of Muslim women on my campus. The availability heuristic could lead you to overestimate, simply because Muslim women stand out visually. People from many other religions do not stand out, so you may underestimate their frequency.

The availability heuristic can lead us to overestimate any frequency. A professor may complain that everybody uses a cell phone during his class, when in fact only one or two students do so; it's just that their annoying behavior stands out. You might overestimate how frequently cars cut you off in traffic because the frustration of this experience is so memorable. You may complain that the wait is always too long at your favorite coffee shop, but only because you hardly notice the times when you breeze right through the line. What comes to mind easily can bias our thinking.

Failing to Think About What We Cannot See

The availability heuristic heightens our reliance on facts or events that we notice easily. A related problem is that we also forget to seek out negative information. In the story "Silver Blaze," the fictional detective Sherlock Holmes investigates the theft of a prize racehorse. The horse was stolen at night while two stable hands and their dog slept, undisturbed, nearby. Holmes reflects on the dog's "curious" behavior that night. When the other inspectors protest that "the dog did nothing in the night-time," Holmes replies, "That was the curious incident." Because the dog did *not* bark, Holmes deduces that the horse was stolen by someone familiar to the dog at the stable (Doyle, 1892/2002, p. 149; see Gilbert, 2005). Holmes solves the crime because he notices the *absence* of something.

The rest of us often fail to look for absences; in contrast, it is easy to notice what is present. This tendency, referred to as the **present/present bias**, is related to the need for comparison groups (discussed earlier). Dr. Rush may have fallen prey to the present/present bias when he was observing the effects of the bloodletting practice on his patients. He focused on patients who *did* receive the treatment and *did* recover (the first cell in Table 2.1 where bleeding treatment was "present" and the recovery was also "present"). He did not fully account for the untreated patients or those who did *not* recover (the other three cells back in Table 2.1 where treatment was "absent" or recovery was "absent").

The present/present bias might even lead you to think the book you are holding must be really great: "Look at these famous people who said this book is terrific! They say so right there on the back cover!" Be careful. Think about how many famous people may have read the book and did not endorse it.

Similarly, regarding the best way to handle anger, the present/present bias means that we will easily notice the times we *did* express frustration at the gym, at the dog, or in traffic and subsequently felt better. In other words, we notice

TABLE 2.4 The Present/Present Bias

	Expressed frustration (treatment present)	Did nothing (treatment absent)
Felt better (outcome present)	5 Present/present	10 Absent/present
Felt worse (outcome absent)	10 Present/absent	5 Absent/absent

Note: The number in each cell represents the number of times the two events coincided. We are more likely to focus on the times when two factors were both present or two events occurred at the same time (the shaded present/present cell), rather than on the full pattern of our experiences.

the times when both the treatment (catharsis) and the desired outcome (feeling better) are present, but are less likely to notice the times when we didn't express our anger and still felt better—when the treatment was absent but the outcome was still present (**Table 2.4**). If our cognitive biases are active, we would focus only on experiences that fall in the present/present cell, and we would notice the five instances in which catharsis seemed to work. But if we think harder and look at the whole picture, we would conclude that catharsis does not work well at all.

In short, most people are not automatically scientific reasoners. We are overly swayed by good stories and by information that comes the most easily to mind.

Intuition Is Biased By Motivation

Sometimes we draw the wrong conclusions simply because human cognition is imperfect. At other times, we do not *want* to challenge our preconceived ideas: We are motivated to think what we want to think.

Focusing on the Evidence We Like Best

When we look at evidence, we may only seek out the information we like. Because we don't want to let go of our beliefs, we "cherry-pick" the information we take in—seeking and accepting only the evidence that supports what we already think and what we want to think.

One study specifically showed how people select only their preferred evidence. The participants took an IQ test and then were told their IQ was either high or low. Shortly afterward, they all had a chance to look at some magazine articles about IQ tests. Those who were told their IQ was low spent more time looking at articles that *criticized* the validity of IQ tests, whereas those who were told their IQ was high spent more time looking at articles that *supported* IQ tests as valid measures of intelligence (Frey & Stahlberg, 1986). They all wanted to think they were smart, so they analyzed the available information in biased ways that supported this belief. People keep their beliefs intact (in this case, the motivated belief that they are smart) by selecting only the kinds of evidence they want to see.

Another way we enable ourselves to think what we want is by asking questions that are likely to give the desired or expected answers. Take, for example, a study in which the researchers asked students to interview fellow undergraduates (Snyder & Swann, 1978). Half the students were given the goal of deciding whether their target person was extraverted, and the other half were given the goal of deciding whether their target person was introverted.

Before the interview, the students selected their interview questions from a prepared list. As it turned out, when the students were trying to find out whether their target was extraverted, they chose to ask questions such as "What would you do if you wanted to liven things up at a party?" and "What kind of situations do you seek out if you want to meet new people?" You can see the problem here: Even introverts will look like extraverts when they answer questions like these. The students were asking questions that would tend to confirm that their targets were extraverted. The same thing happened with the group of students who were trying to find out if their target was introverted: They chose to ask questions such as "In what situations do you wish you could be more outgoing?" and "What factors make it hard for you to really open up to people?" Again, in responding to these questions, wouldn't just about anybody seem introverted? Later, when the students asked these questions, targets gave answers that supported the interviewers' expectations. The researchers asked some judges to listen in on what the targets said during the interviews. Regardless of their personality, the targets who were being tested for extraversion acted extraverted, and the targets who were being tested for introversion acted introverted.

Overall, then, the students selected questions that would lead them to a particular, expected answer. This phenomenon is formally called **confirmatory hypothesis testing**. However, unlike the hypothesis testing process in the theory-data cycle (see Chapter 1), this process is conducted in a way that is decidedly not scientific. If interviewers were testing the hypothesis that their target was an extravert, they asked the questions that would confirm that hypothesis and did not ask questions that might disconfirm that hypothesis. Indeed, even though the students could have chosen neutral questions (such as "What do you think the good and bad points of acting friendly and open are?"), they hardly ever did. In follow-up studies, Snyder and Swann found that student interviewers chose hypothesis-confirming questions even if they were offered a big cash prize for being the most objective interviewer, suggesting that even when people are motivated to be accurate, they cannot always be.

FIGURE 2.5 Confirmatory hypothesis testing. This therapist suspects her client has an anxiety disorder. What kinds of questions should she be asking that would both potentially confirm and potentially disconfirm her hypothesis?

Confirmatory hypothesis testing is another example of how scientific thinking simply does not come naturally to people. Without scientific training, we are not very rigorous in gathering evidence to test our ideas. Over and over again, psychological research has found that when people are asked to test a hypothesis, they tend to ask only the questions that support their expectations (Copeland & Snyder, 1995; Klayman & Ha, 1987; Snyder & Campbell, 1980; Snyder & White, 1981). As a result, people tend to gather only a certain kind of information, and then they conclude that their hypotheses are supported. This bias is one reason clinical psychologists and other therapists are required to get a research methods education (**Figure 2.5**).

Biased About Being Biased

As if all these cognitive and motivational biases are not enough, there's an even bigger one: We are biased about being biased. Even though we read about the biased ways people think (such as in a research methods textbook like this one), we nevertheless conclude that those biases do not apply to *us*. Most of us have what's called a bias blind spot (Pronin, Gilovich, & Ross, 2004; Pronin, Lin, & Ross, 2002). The **bias blind spot** is the belief that we are unlikely to fall prey to the cognitive biases previously described. Most of us think we are less biased than others. Furthermore, when we notice that our own views of a situation are different from somebody else's view, the bias blind spot leads us to conclude that "I'm the objective one here" and "you are the biased one."

In one study, researchers interviewed U.S. airport travelers, most of whom said that the average American is much more biased than themselves (Pronin et al., 2002). For example, the travelers said that others were much more likely to take personal credit for successes than they themselves would. They believed other Americans were much more likely to believe that people who are nice are also smart and competent, but that they themselves do not have this bias. They believed other Americans would tend to "blame the victim" of random violence for being in the wrong place at the wrong time, but that they themselves would do no such thing. As another example, people who like the president may think anybody who disagrees with him must be unintelligent, failing to recognize their own bias in the president's favor (**Figure 2.6**).

The bias blind spot might be the sneakiest of all of the biases in human thinking. It makes us trust our faulty reasoning all the more. In addition, it can make it difficult for us to initiate the scientific theory-data cycle. We might say, "I don't need to test this conclusion; I already know it is correct." Part of learning to be a scientist is learning not to use feelings of confidence as evidence for the truth of our beliefs. Rather than thinking what they want to, careful scientists use data.

FIGURE 2.6 The bias blind spot. Do other people's politics bias the way they view the U.S. president? Do your own politics bias the way you view him? The bias blind spot means you notice other people's political biases, more than your own.

The Intuitive Thinker vs. the Scientific Reasoner

When we think intuitively rather than scientifically, we make mistakes. Because of our cognitive and motivational biases, we tend to notice and actively seek information that confirms our ideas. To counteract your own biases, try to adopt the empirical mindset of a researcher. Recall from Chapter 1 that empiricism involves basing beliefs on systematic information from the senses. Now we have added an additional nuance to what it means to reason empirically: To be a good empiricist, you must also strive to interpret the data that you collect in an objective way—by guarding against common biases.

Researchers—scientific reasoners—create comparison groups and look at all the data. Rather than accept the first evidence that pops into mind, researchers need to dig deeper and generate data through rigorous studies. Knowing they should not just go along with the story that everybody believes, they train themselves to test their hunches with systematic, empirical observations. They strive to ask questions objectively and collect potentially disconfirming evidence, not just evidence that confirms their hypotheses. Keenly aware they have biases, scientific reasoners allow the data to speak more loudly than their own confidently held—but possibly biased—ideas. In short, while researchers are not perfect reasoners themselves, they have trained themselves to guard against the many pitfalls of intuition—and they make smarter decisions as a result.

CHECK YOUR UNDERSTANDING

1. This section described three ways that faulty thinking biases intuition and three ways that motivation biases intuition. Can you name all six?
2. Do you think you might improve your own reasoning by simply learning about these biases? How so?

---

1. See pp. 30–35. 2. Answers will vary.

Trusting Authorities on the Subject

You should be cautious about basing your beliefs and conclusions on your own personal experiences and on those of people you know. What about advice that is given by someone who is (or claims to be) an authority? How reliable was your guidance counselor's advice on anger management? How reliable is the advice of Dr. Phil—a former clinical psychologist who has a successful talk show? How reliable is the advice of a psychology professor who is a specialist in emotion regulation? All these people have some authority—as cultural messengers, as professionals with advanced degrees, as people with significant life experience. Should you trust them?

How about this example of anger management advice from John Lee, a person with a master's degree in psychology, several published books on anger management, a thriving workshop business, and his own website. He's certainly an authority on the subject, right? Here is his advice:

Punch a pillow or a punching bag. Yell and curse and moan and holler. . . . If you are angry at a particular person, imagine his or her face on the pillow or punching bag, and vent your rage. . . . You are not hitting a person, you are hitting the ghost of that person . . . a ghost alive in you that must be exorcised in a concrete, physical way. (Lee, 1993, p. 96)

Knowing what you know now, you probably do not trust John Lee's advice. In fact, this is a clear example of how a self-proclaimed "expert" might be wrong.

Before taking the advice of authorities, ask yourself about the source of their ideas. Did the authority systematically and objectively compare different conditions, as a researcher would do? Maybe they have read the research and are interpreting it for you; they might be practitioners who are basing their conclusions on empirical evidence. In this respect, an authority with scientific degree may be better able to accurately understand and interpret scientific evidence (**Figure 2.7**). If you know that this is the case—in other words, if an authority refers to research evidence—their advice might be worth attending to. However, authorities can also base their advice on their own experience or intuition, just like the rest of us. And they, too, might present only the studies that support their own side.

Keep in mind, too, that not all research is equally reliable. The research that an expert uses to support his or her argument might have been conducted poorly. In the rest of this book, you will learn how to interrogate others' research and form conclusions about its quality. Also, the research someone cites to support

FIGURE 2.7 Which authority to believe? Jenny McCarthy (left), an actress and celebrity, claims that giving childhood vaccines later in life would prevent autism disorders. Dr. Paul Offit (right), a physician-scientist who has both reviewed and conducted scientific research on childhood vaccines, says that early vaccines save lives and that there is no link between vaccination and autism diagnosis.

an argument may not accurately and appropriately support that particular argument. In Chapter 3, you will learn more about what kinds of research support which kinds of claims. **Figure 2.8** shows a concept map illustrating the sources of information reviewed in this chapter. Conclusions based on research, highlighted in the concept map, are the most likely to be correct.

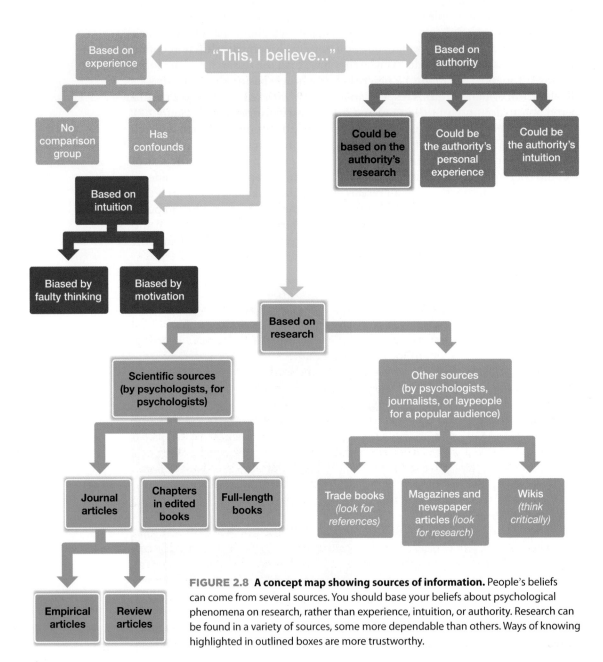

FIGURE 2.8 A concept map showing sources of information. People's beliefs can come from several sources. You should base your beliefs about psychological phenomena on research, rather than experience, intuition, or authority. Research can be found in a variety of sources, some more dependable than others. Ways of knowing highlighted in outlined boxes are more trustworthy.

1. When would it be sensible to accept the conclusions of authority figures? When might it not?

1. See pp. 36–38.

Finding and Reading the Research

In order to base your beliefs on empirical evidence rather than on experience, intuition, or authority, you will, of course, need to read about that research. But where do you find it? What if you wanted to read Bushman's studies on venting anger? How would you locate those studies? And how would you locate research by other psychologists on the same topic?

Consulting Scientific Sources

Psychological scientists usually publish their research in three kinds of sources. Most often, research results are published as articles in scholarly journals. In addition, psychologists may describe their research in stand-alone chapters in edited books. Some researchers are also authors of full-length scholarly books.

Journal Articles: Psychology's Most Important Source

Scientific journals come out monthly or quarterly, as magazines do. Unlike popular magazines, however, scientific journals usually do not have glossy, colorful covers or advertisements. You are most likely to find scientific journals in college or university libraries or in online academic databases, which are generally available through university libraries. For example, the study by Bushman (2002) described earlier was published in the journal *Personality and Social Psychology Bulletin*.

Journal articles are written for an audience of other psychological scientists and psychology students. There are hundreds of journals in psychology, and **Table 2.5** presents a partial list of some of the most prominent ones in selected categories.

Journal articles can be either empirical articles or review articles. **Empirical journal articles** report, for the first time, the results of an (empirical) research study. Empirical articles contain details about the study's method, the statistical tests used, and the numerical results of the study. **Figure 2.9** is an example of an empirical journal article.

Review journal articles provide a summary of all the published studies that have been done in one research area. A review article by Anderson and his colleagues (2010), for example, summarizes 130 studies on the effects of playing violent video games on the aggressive behavior of children. Sometimes a review article uses a quantitative technique called **meta-analysis**, which combines the results of many studies and gives a number that summarizes the magnitude, or the **effect size**, of a relationship. In the Anderson review (2010), the authors computed the average effect size across all the studies. This technique is valued by

For a full discussion of meta-analysis, see Chapter 14, pp. 419–423.

TABLE 2.5 Selected Journals in Psychology

Clinical Psychology Journals

Behavior Therapy

Cognitive Therapy and Research

Counseling Psychologist

Journal of Abnormal Psychology

Journal of Consulting and Clinical Psychology

Psychological Assessment

Applied Psychology Journals

Applied Developmental Psychology

Consulting Psychology Journal: Practice and Research

Journal of Applied Psychology

Journal of Educational Psychology

Journal of Experimental Psychology: Applied

School Psychology Quarterly

Cognitive Psychology Journals

Acta Psychologica

Cognition

Journal of Experimental Psychology: Human Perception and Performance

Journal of Experimental Psychology: Learning, Memory, and Cognition

Social and Personality Psychology Journals

Journal of Experimental Social Psychology

Journal of Personality and Social Psychology

Journal of Research in Personality

Personality and Social Psychology Bulletin

Personality and Social Psychology Review

Social Cognition

Developmental Psychology Journals

Adolescence

Child Development

Developmental Psychology

Psychology and Aging

Neuroscience Journals

Behavioral Neuroscience

Brain and Cognition

Developmental Psychobiology

Nature: Neuroscience

Physiological Psychology

Psychophysiology

Journals Containing Review Articles

American Psychologist

Behavioral and Brain Sciences

Psychological Bulletin

Psychological Review

Review of General Psychology

Psychology Journals Spanning Several Topics

Current Directions in Psychological Science

Emotion

Journal of Social Issues

Psychological Methods

Psychological Science

Note: Some subfields of psychology—language, cultural psychology, child clinical psychology, and others—are not included here.

Does Venting Anger Feed or Extinguish the Flame? Catharsis, Rumination, Distraction, Anger, and Aggressive Responding

STRAIGHT *from the* SOURCE

Brad J. Bushman
Iowa State University

Does distraction or rumination work better to diffuse anger? Catharsis theory predicts that rumination works best, but empirical evidence is lacking. In this study, angered participants hit a punching bag and thought about the person who had angered them (rumination group) or thought about becoming physically fit (distraction group). After hitting the punching bag, they reported how angry they felt. Next, they were given the chance to administer loud blasts of noise to the person who had angered them. There also was a no punching bag control group. People in the rumination group felt angrier than did people in the distraction or control groups. People in the rumination group were also most aggressive, followed respectively by people in the distraction and control groups. Rumination increased rather than decreased anger and aggression. Doing nothing at all was more effective than venting anger. These results directly contradict catharsis theory.

The belief in the value of venting anger has become widespread in our culture. In movies, magazine articles, and even on billboards, people are encouraged to vent their anger and "blow off steam." For example, in the movie *Analyze This*, a psychiatrist (played by Billy Crystal) tells his New York gangster client (played by Robert De Niro), "You know what I do when I'm angry? I hit a pillow. Try that." The client promptly pulls out his gun, points it at the couch, and fires several bullets into the pillow. "Feel better?" asks the psychiatrist. "Yeah, I do," says the gunman. In a *Vogue* magazine article, female model Shalom concludes that boxing helps her release pent-up anger. She said,

> I found myself looking forward to the chance to pound out the frustrations of the week against Carlos's (her trainer) mitts. Let's face it: A personal boxing trainer has advantages over a husband or lover. He won't look at you accusingly and say, "I don't know where this irritation is

coming from." . . . Your boxing trainer knows it's in there. And he wants you to give it to him. ("Fighting Fit," 1993, p. 179)

In a *New York Times Magazine* article about hate crimes, Andrew Sullivan writes, "Some expression of prejudice serves a useful purpose. It lets off steam; it allows natural tensions to express themselves incrementally; it can siphon off conflict through words, rather than actions" (Sullivan, 1999, p. 113). A large billboard in Missouri states, "Hit a Pillow, Hit a Wall, But Don't Hit Your Kids!"

Catharsis Theory

The theory of catharsis is one popular and authoritative statement that venting one's anger will produce a positive improvement in one's psychological state. The word *catharsis* comes from the Greek word *katharsis*, which literally translated means a cleansing or purging. According to catharsis theory, acting aggressively or even viewing aggression is an effective way to purge angry and aggressive feelings.

Sigmund Freud believed that repressed negative emotions could build up inside an individual and cause psychological symptoms, such as hysteria (nervous outbursts). Breuer and Freud (1893-1895/1955) proposed that the treatment of hysteria required the discharge of the emotional state previously associated with trauma. They claimed that for interpersonal traumas, such as

Author's Note: I would like to thank Remy Reinier for her help scanning photo IDs of students and photographs from health magazines. I
also wou[...]
an early [...]
should b[...]
Iowa Sta[...]
iastate.e[...]

PSPB, V[...]
© 2002 b[...]

724

FIGURE 2.9 Bushman's empirical article on catharsis. The first page is shown here, as it appeared in *Personality and Social Psychology Bulletin*. The inset shows how the article appears in an online search in that journal. Clicking "Full Text pdf" takes you to the article shown. (Source: Bushman, 2002.)

FIGURE 2.10 The variety of scientific sources. You can read about research in empirical journal articles, review journal articles, edited books, and full-length books.

psychologists because it weighs each study proportionately (and does not allow cherry-picking particular studies).

Before being published in a journal, both empirical articles and review articles must be peer-reviewed (see Chapter 1). Both types of articles are prestigious forms of publication by psychological scientists.

Chapters in Edited Books

An edited book is a collection of chapters on a common topic, in which each chapter is written by a different contributor. For example, Kristin Scott and Stefan Thau published a chapter entitled "Social Exclusion in Work Groups" in an edited book, *The Handbook of Social Exclusion* (2013). There are 27 other chapters, all written by different authors. The editor, Nathan DeWall, invited all the other authors to contribute. Generally, a book chapter is not the first place a study is reported; instead, the scientist is summarizing a body of research and explaining the theory behind it. Edited book chapters can therefore be a good place to find a summary of a set of research a particular psychologist has done. (In this sense, book chapters are similar to review articles in journals.) Chapters are not peer-reviewed as rigorously as empirical journal articles or review articles. However, the editor of the book is careful to invite only experts—researchers who are intimately familiar with the empirical evidence on a topic—to write the chapters. The audience for these chapters is usually other psychologists and psychology students (**Figure 2.10**).

Full-Length Books

Psychologists might describe their research in full-length books. In some other disciplines (e.g., anthropology, art history, or English), full-length books are a common way for scholars to publish their work. Psychologists do not write many full-length scientific books for other psychologists, but those books that have been published are most likely to be found in a university library. (Psychologists may also write full-length books for a general audience, as discussed below.)

Finding Scientific Sources

You can find trustworthy, scientific sources on psychological topics by starting with the tools in your college or university's library. The library's reference staff can be extremely helpful in teaching you how to find appropriate articles or chapters. Working on your own, you can use databases such as PsycINFO to conduct searches.

PsycINFO

The best, most comprehensive tool for sorting through the vast number of psychological research articles is a search engine and database called PsycINFO; it is maintained and updated weekly by the APA. Doing a search in PsycINFO is like using Google, but instead of searching the Internet, it searches only sources in psychology, plus a few sources from related disciplines, such as communication, marketing, and education. PsycINFO's database includes more than 2.5 million records, mostly peer-reviewed articles. You cannot use PsycINFO from just any computer—you must have access to a college or university library that subscribes to it.

Using PsycINFO has many advantages. It can show you all the articles written by a single author (e.g., "Brad-Bushman") or under a single keyword (e.g., "autism"). It tells you whether each source was peer-reviewed or not. It also shows you which other articles have cited each target article (listed under "Cited by") and which articles this target article has cited (listed under "References").

The best way to learn to use PsycINFO is to simply try it yourself. A reference librarian can show you or your class the basic steps in a few minutes, and an online tutorial can also be helpful. (Online tutorials sponsored by the APA can be accessed at http://www.apa.org/pubs/databases/training/tutorials.aspx.)

A challenge to using any database is translating your curiosity into the right keywords. Sometimes the search you run will give you too many results to sort through easily. Other times your search words won't yield the kinds of articles you were expecting to see. **Table 2.6** presents some strategies for turning your questions into successful searches.

TABLE 2.6 Tips for Turning Your Question into a Successful Database Search

1. Focus on the nouns in your question. **Use the "Thesaurus" tool** in PsycINFO search window to find the proper search term.

Example question: *Do eating disorders happen more frequently in families that eat dinner together?*

Search terms to try: "binge-eating disorder," "binge eating," "risk factor," "family environment," "home environment"

Example question: *What motivates people to study?*

Search terms to try: "achievement motivation," "academic achievement motivation," "academic self concept," "study habits," "homework," "learning strategies"

Example question: *Is the Mozart effect real?*

Search terms to try: "Mozart-effect," "music," "performance," "cognitive processes," "reasoning"

2. If you get too few hits, expand with "or" (*or* gives you *more*):

Example: "anorexia" or "bulimia" or "eating disorder"

Example: "false memory" or "early memory"

3. Use an asterisk to make sure you get all related terms:

Example: "adolescen*" searches for "adolescence" and "adolescents" and "adolescent"

4. If you get too many hits, restrict using "and" or use "not":

Example: "anorexia" and "adolescen*"

Example: "repressed memory" and "physical abuse"

Example: "repressed memory" not "physical abuse"

Alternatives to PsycINFO

What if you want to find empirical research but you don't have access to PsycINFO? First, if you happen to know the author of the research you are looking for, and if that author is a college or university professor, you can try visiting his or her home page. Many psychology researchers maintain a home page that includes a summary of their research interests, a list of their publications, and even PDFs of the original articles for personal use.

Second, you can use the tool Google Scholar (scholar.google.com). This site works just like the regular Google search engine, but it indexes only empirical journal articles and scholarly books. Google Scholar is easy to use: You just type a name or subject heading in the search box. The hits sometimes send you directly to a PDF version of the article. Google Scholar is an acceptable alternative if you do not have access to PsycINFO through a university library. However, it does not allow you to search as easily in specific fields (such as restricting your search to key words in an abstract). In addition, it doesn't categorize the articles it finds, for example, as peer-reviewed or not, whereas PsycINFO does. And whereas PsycINFO indexes only psychology articles, Google Scholar contains articles from all scholarly disciplines. It may take more time for you to sort through the articles it returns, because the output of a Google Scholar search is less well organized.

Although you can easily find citation information in Google Scholar, you might not be able to read the articles for free. If this is the case, see whether your library subscribes to the print version of the journal you want, or offers online access to that journal. If not, you can request a copy of the article through your college's interlibrary loan office, or possibly by visiting the author's home page.

Reading the Research

Once you have found an empirical journal article or chapter, then what? You might wonder how to go about reading the material. At first glance, some journal articles contain an array of statistical symbols and unfamiliar terminology. Even the titles of journal articles and chapters can be intimidating. Take this one, for example: "Object Substitution Masking Interferes with Semantic Processing: Evidence from Event-Related Potentials" (Reiss & Hoffman, 2006). How is a student supposed to read this sort of thing? It helps to know what you will find in an article, and to read with a purpose.

Components of an Empirical Journal Article

Most empirical journal articles (those that report the results of a study for the first time) are written in a standard format, as recommended by the *Publication Manual of the American Psychological Association* (APA, 2010). Most empirical journal articles include certain sections in the same order: abstract, introduction, method, results, discussion, and references. Each section contains a specific kind of information.

Abstract. The abstract is a concise summary of the article, about 120 words long. It briefly describes the study's hypotheses, method, and major results. When you are collecting articles for a project, the abstracts can help you quickly decide whether each article describes the kind of research you are looking for, or whether you should move on to the next article.

Introduction. The introduction is the first section of regular text, and the first paragraphs typically explain the topic of the study. The middle paragraphs lay out the theoretical and empirical background for the research. What theory is being tested? What have past studies tested? What makes the present study important? Pay attention to the final paragraph, which states the specific research questions, goals, or hypotheses for the current study.

Method. The Method section explains in detail how the researchers conducted their study. It usually contains subsections such as Participants, Materials, Procedure, and Apparatus. An ideal Method section gives enough detail that if you wanted to repeat the study, you could do so without having to ask the authors any questions.

Results. The Results section describes the quantitative and, as relevant, qualitative results of the study, including the statistical tests the authors used to analyze the data. It usually provides tables and figures to summarize key results. Although you may not understand all the statistics used in the article (especially early in your psychology education), you might still be able to understand the basic findings by looking at the tables and figures.

Discussion. The opening paragraph of the Discussion section generally summarizes the study's research question and methods and indicates how well the data supported the hypotheses. Next, the authors usually promote their study's contributions. They discuss the study's significance: Perhaps their hypothesis was new, or the method they used was a creative and unusual way to test a familiar hypothesis, or the participants were unlike others who had been studied before. In addition, the authors may discuss alternative explanations for their data and pose interesting questions raised by the research.

References. The reference list contains a full bibliographic listing of all the sources the authors cited in writing their article, enabling interested readers to locate these studies. When you are conducting a literature search, reference lists are excellent places to look for additional articles on a given topic. Once you find one relevant article, the reference list of that article will contain a treasure trove of related work.

Reading with a Purpose: Empirical Journal Articles

Here's some revolutionary advice: Don't read every word of every article, from beginning to end. Instead, *read with a purpose*. In most cases, this means asking two questions as you read: (1) What is the argument? (2) What is the evidence to support the argument? The obvious first step toward answering these questions is to read the abstract, which provides an overview of the study. What should you read next?

Empirical articles are stories from the trenches of the theory-data cycle (see Figure 1.5 in Chapter 1). Therefore, an empirical article reports on data that are generated to test a hypothesis, and the hypothesis is framed as a test of a particular theory. After reading the abstract, you can skip to the end of the introduction to find the primary goals and hypotheses of the study. After reading the goals and hypotheses, you can read the rest of the introduction to learn more about the theory that the hypotheses are testing. Another place to find information about the argument of the paper is the first paragraph of the Discussion section, where most authors summarize the key results of their study and state whether the results supported their hypotheses.

Once you have a sense of what the argument is, you can look for the evidence. In an empirical article, the evidence is contained in the Method and Results sections. What did the researchers do, and what results did they find? How well do these results support their argument (i.e., their hypotheses)?

Reading with a Purpose: Chapters and Review Articles

Chapters and review articles often do not have specific sections, such as Method, Results, and Discussion. Instead of using the predetermined headings of empirical journal articles, these authors usually create headings that make sense for their particular topics.

You can still read these sources with a purpose, asking: What is the argument? What is the evidence? The argument will be the purpose of the chapter or review article—the author's stance on the issue. In a review article or chapter, the argument often presents an entire theory (whereas an empirical journal article usually tests only one part of a theory). Here are some examples of arguments you might find in chapters or review articles:

- Playing violent video games causes children to be more aggressive. (Anderson et al., 2010)
- Memory impairments in people with autism depend on their function states (high-functioning or moderate- to low-functioning). (Boucher, Mayes, & Bigham, 2012)
- Having low self-esteem increases people's vulnerability to depression. (Sowislo & Orth, 2013)

In a chapter or review article, the evidence is the research that the author reviews. How much previous research has been done? What have the results been? How strong are the results? For example, to support the third argument above, "Having low self-esteem increases people's vulnerability to depression," Sowislo and Orth (2013) summarized the results of 77 studies. With practice, you will get better at reading efficiently. You'll learn to categorize what you read as argument or evidence, and you will be able to evaluate how well the evidence supports the argument.

Finding Research in Less Scholarly Places

Reading about research in its original form is the best way to get a thorough, accurate, and peer-reviewed report of scientific evidence. There are other sources for reading about psychological research, too, such as nonacademic books written for the general public, websites, and popular newspapers and magazines. These can be good places to read about psychological research, as long as you choose and read your sources carefully.

The Retail Bookshelf

If you browse through the psychology section in a bookstore, you will mostly find what are known as trade books about psychology, written for a general audience (**Figure 2.11**). Unlike the scientific sources we've covered, these books are written for people who do not have a psychology degree. They are written to help people, to inform, to entertain, and to make money for their authors.

FIGURE 2.11 Finding research in a popular bookstore. You can find some great descriptions of psychology at your local bookstore. Be sure to choose books that contain a long list of scientific sources in their reference section.

The language in trade books is much more readable than the language in most journal articles. Trade books can also show how psychology applies to your everyday life, and in this way they can be useful. But how well do trade books reflect current research in psychology? Do they help you apply the best research to your real-life problems? Or do they simply present an uncritical summary of common sense, intuition, or the author's own experience?

The best way to tell is to look at the end of the book, where you may find footnotes or references documenting the research studies on which the arguments are based. For example, *The Secret Life of Pronouns*, by psychologist James Pennebaker (2011), contains 54 pages of notes—mostly citations to research discussed in the rest of the book. David McRaney's book *You Are Not So Smart* (2011) contains 24 pages of citations and notes. Barbara Fredrickson's *Love 2.0: How Our Supreme Emotion Affects Everything We Feel, Think, Do, and Become* (2013) contains 31 pages of references. A book related to this chapter's theme, *Anger: The Misunderstood Emotion* (Tavris, 1989), contains 25 pages of references. These are excellent examples of trade books based on research that are written by psychologists for a general audience.

In contrast, if you flip to the end of some other trade books, you may not find any references or notes. For example, *The Everything Guide to Narcissistic Personality Disorder*, by Cynthia Lechan and Barbara Leff (2011), suggests a handful of books, but includes no reference section. *Healing ADD: The Breakthrough Program that Allows You to See and Heal the 6 Types of ADD,* by Daniel Amen (2002), cites no research, nor does *The Hoarder in You*, by Robin Zasio (2012). Perhaps not surprisingly, *The Psychology of Twilight*, by Klonsky et al. (2011), contains no references either. The book *Why Mars and Venus Collide: Improving Relationships by Understanding How Men and Women Cope Differently with Stress*, by John Gray (2008), has four pages of references. Four pages is better than nothing but seems a little light, given that literally thousands of journal articles have been devoted to the scientific study of gender differences.

If you find a book that claims to be about psychology but does not have any references, consider it to be light entertainment (at best) or irresponsible (at worst). Vast, well-conducted bodies of literature exist on such topics as self-esteem, ADHD, gender differences, mental illnesses, and coping with stress, but some authors ignore this scientific literature and instead rely on hand-selected anecdotes from their own clinical practice. By now, you know that you can do better. If a psychology trade book does not contain references to research, keep looking until you find one that does.

Wikis as a Research Source

Wikis can provide quick, easy-to-read facts about almost any topic. What kind of animal is a narwhal? What years were the *Hunger Games* movies released? How many albums has Beyoncé released? Wikis are democratic encyclopedias. Anybody can create a new entry, anybody can contribute to the content of a page, and anybody can log in and add details to an entry. Theoretically, wikis are self-correcting: If one user posts an incorrect fact, another user would come along and correct it.

Can you rely on wikis for psychology research? Yes and no. Sometimes you will find a full review of a psychological phenomenon; sometimes you won't. When you search Wikipedia for psychological terms, you might find something very different from what you wanted. Searching for the term *catharsis* is a good example. If you look up that term on Wikipedia, the first article you will find is not related to psychology at all; instead, it is about the role of catharsis in classical drama.

You probably know about the other downsides to using a wiki. First, wikis are not comprehensive in their coverage: You cannot read about a topic if no one has created a page for it. Second, although wiki pages might include references, these references are not a comprehensive list; they are only what the contributors have chosen. Third, the details on the pages might be incorrect, and they will stay incorrect until somebody else fixes them. Although vandalism is a potential problem (sometimes people intentionally insert errors into pages), Wikipedia has developed digital robots to detect and delete the most obvious errors—often within seconds (Nasaw, 2012).

If more scientists make a point of contributing to them, wikis might become more comprehensive, more accurate, and more likely to include references to relevant journal articles. But be careful. Wikis may be written only by a small, enthusiastic, and not necessarily expert group of contributors. Although Wikipedia may be your first hit from many Google searches, you should always double-check the information found there. And be aware that many psychology professors do not accept wikis as sources in academic assignments.

The Popular Press

Overall, popular press coverage is good for psychology. Journalists play an important role in telling the public about exciting findings in psychological science.

TABLE 2.7 Examples of Sources for Reading About Psychological Science, Directed at a Popular Audience

American Psychological Association and Association for Psychological Science websites (www.apa.org and www.psychologicalscience.org)

Current Directions in Psychological Science (journal)

Psychology Today (magazine and website)

Science News Daily (website; mind and brain section)

Science sections of major newspapers (print and web)

Scientific American Mind (magazine)

Psychological research is covered in magazines (such as *Time* and *Newsweek*), in daily newspapers, on TV news programs, on radio news shows, in web-based magazines (such as msnbc.com), and in blogs. Some magazines, such as *Psychology Today* and *Scientific American Mind*, are devoted exclusively to covering psychology research for a popular audience (**Table 2.7**).

Chapter 1 explained that journalists who specialize in science writing are trained to faithfully represent journal articles for a popular audience, but journalists who are not trained in science writing might not correctly summarize a journal article. Therefore, keep in mind that popular press stories are meant to tell you about a new research area or an interesting study. They can pique your interest and keep you somewhat informed. However, plan to use your developing skills as a consumer of information to read the journalism critically. If you really want to delve into the topic the journalist is covering, use PsycINFO to locate the original article and read the research at its source.

CHECK YOUR UNDERSTANDING

1. How are empirical journal articles different from review journal articles? How is each type of article different from a chapter in an edited book?
2. What two guiding questions can help you read any academic research source?
3. What are the differences between PsycINFO and Google Scholar?
4. If you encounter a psychological trade book, what signals that the information it contains is research-based?

1. See pp. 39–42. 2. See pp. 45–46. 3. See pp. 42–44. 4. See pp. 47–48.

Summary

- People's beliefs can be based on their own experience, their intuition, on authorities, or on controlled research. Of these, research information is the most accurate source of knowledge.

The Research vs. Your Experience

- Beliefs based on personal experience may not be accurate. One reason is that personal experience usually does not involve a comparison group. In contrast, research explicitly asks, "Compared to what?"
- In addition, personal experience is often confounded. In daily life, many things are going on at once, and it is impossible to know which factor is responsible for a particular outcome. In contrast, researchers can closely control for confounding factors.
- Research has an advantage over experience, because researchers design studies that include appropriate comparison groups.
- Conclusions based on research are probabilistic. Research findings are not able to predict or explain all cases all of the time; instead, they can predict or explain a high proportion of cases. Individual exceptions to research findings will not nullify the results.

The Research vs. Your Intuition

- Intuition can be affected by cognitive biases. For instance, people are likely to accept the explanation of a story that makes sense intuitively, even if it is not true.
- People can be lulled into faulty thinking if they consider only readily available thoughts, those that come to mind most easily.
- People find it easier to notice what is present than what is absent. Present/present reasoning occurs when people forget to look at the information that would falsify their original belief.
- Intuition is also subject to motivational biases. Because we do not like to challenge our ideas,

we tend to focus on the data that support our ideas and criticize or discount data that disagree.
- We may also be motivated to ask leading questions, whose answers are bound to confirm our initial ideas.
- We all seem to have a bias blind spot and believe we are less biased than everyone else.
- Scientific researchers are aware of their potential for biased reasoning, so they create special situations in which they can systematically observe behavior. They create comparison groups, consider all the data, and allow the data to change their beliefs.

Trusting Authorities on the Subject

- Authorities may attempt to convince us to accept their claims. If their claims are based on their own experience or intuition, we should probably not accept them. If they use empirical evidence to support their claims, we can be more confident about taking their advice.

Finding and Reading the Research

- Tools for finding research in psychology include the online database PsycINFO, available through college and university libraries. You can also use Google Scholar or the websites of researchers.
- Journal articles, chapters in edited books, and full-length books should be read with a purpose, by asking: What is the theoretical argument? What is the evidence—what do the data say?
- Trade books, wikis, and popular press articles can be good sources of information about psychology research, but they can also be misleading. Such sources should be evaluated by asking whether they are based on research and whether the coverage is comprehensive, accurate, and responsible.

Key Terms

comparison group, p. 25
confound, p. 27
confederate, p. 28
probabilistic, p. 30
availability heuristic, p. 31

present/present bias, p. 32
confirmatory hypothesis
   testing, p. 34
bias blind spot, p. 35
empirical journal article, p. 39

review journal article, p. 39
meta-analysis, p. 39
effect size, p. 39

 To see examples of chapter concepts in the popular press, see www.everydayresearchmethods.com and click the box for Chapter 2.

Review Questions

1. Basing our conclusions on personal experience is faulty because experience has confounds. In this context, a confound means:
   a. In real-world experiences, more than one thing changes at the same time.
   b. The conclusion we draw from the experience has left us puzzled, or confused.
   c. There has been no comparison group.
   d. We will have trouble thinking of counterexamples.

2. What does it mean to say that research is probabilistic?
   a. Researchers refer to the probability that their theories are correct.
   b. Research predicts all possible results.
   c. Research conclusions are meant to explain a certain proportion of possible cases, but not all possible cases.
   d. If there are exceptions to a research result, it means that the theory is probably incorrect.

3. After two students from his school commit suicide, Marcelino concludes that the most likely cause of death in teenagers is suicide. In fact, suicide is *not* the most likely cause of death in teens. What happened?
   a. Marcelino was probably a victim of the bias blind spot.

   b. Marcelino was probably influenced by the availability heuristic; he was too influenced by cases that came easily to mind.
   c. Marcelino thought about too many examples of teens who died from other causes besides suicide.
   d. Marcelino did not consider possible confounds.

4. When is it a good idea to base conclusions on the advice of authorities?
   a. When authorities have an advanced degree, such as a Ph.D. or a master's degree.
   b. When authorities have conducted the research on which their advice is based, by systematically and objectively comparing different conditions.
   c. It is never a good idea to base conclusions on the advice of authorities.
   d. When authorities have several years of experience in their specialty area.

5. Which of the following is not a place where psychological scientists publish their research?
   a. Scientific journals
   b. Popular magazines
   c. Chapters in edited books
   d. Full-length books

6. In reading an empirical journal article, what are the two questions you should be asking as you read?
   a. What is the argument? What is the evidence to support the argument?
   b. Why was this research done? Were there any significant findings?
   c. How reputable is (are) the author(s)? Did the findings include support for the hypotheses?
   d. How does this research relate to other research? What are ways to extend this research further?

Learning Actively

1. Each of the examples below is a statement, based on experience, that does not take a comparison group into account:
   a. Reading e-books hurts my eyes.
   b. Yoga has made me feel more peaceful.
   c. Younger teachers are better with kids.

For each statement: (a) Ask one or more comparison group questions that would help you evaluate the conclusion. (b) Draw a 2x2 matrix for systematically comparing outcomes. (c) Name as many confounds as you can.

Example: "Since I cut sugar from their diets, I've noticed that the campers in my cabin are much more cooperative!"

   (a) Comparison group question: Would the campers have improved anyway, without the change in diet?
   (b) A systematic comparison should be set up as follows:

	Reduce sugar in diet (treatment)	No change in diet (no treatment)
Kids are cooperative (outcome present)		
Kids are not cooperative (outcome absent)		

   (c) Possible confounds: What else might have changed at the same time as the low-sugar diet? Could the campers simply have gotten used to camp and settled down? Is it possible that the new swimming teacher made a difference? Might the weather have improved during the same time?

2. Using what you have learned in this chapter, write a sentence or two explaining why the reasoning reflected in each of the following statements is sound or unsound. (a) What are you being asked to believe in each case? (b) What further information might you need to determine the accuracy of the speaker's conclusions? (c) On what is the speaker basing her claim—experience, intuition, or authority?
   a. "I'm positive my cousin has an eating disorder! I hardly ever see her eat anything other than diet bars."
   b. A friend tells you, "I read something cool in the paper this morning: They said that violent video games don't cause aggression when they are played cooperatively as team games. They were talking about some research somebody did."
   c. "It's so clear that our candidate won that debate! Did you hear all the zingers he delivered?"
   d. "I read online that doing these special puzzles every day helps grow your brain. It's been proven by neuropsychology."

e. "There are way more dogs than cats in this city. That's all you see in the parks—dogs dogs dogs!"

f. "Binge drinking is totally normal on my campus. Everybody does it almost every weekend."

g. "I'm afraid of flying—planes are so dangerous!"

h. "Decluttering your closets makes a huge difference in your happiness. Just ask me: it worked!"

i. "Wow—look at how many happy couples got married after meeting on Match.com! I think I'm going to try it, too."

3. Finding sources on PsycINFO means figuring out the right search terms. Use the PsycINFO Thesaurus tool to find keywords that will help you do searches on these research questions. Table 2.6 has some suggestions for turning research questions into helpful searches.

a. Are adults with autism more violent?

b. Does having PTSD put you at risk for alcoholism?

c. Can your diet make you smarter?

d. What is it like to date a narcissist?

e. What kinds of managers do employees like the best?

4. Choose one of the search terms you worked on in Question 3. Try doing the same search on three platforms: Google (or another general search engine such as Yahoo or Ask), Google Scholar, and PsycINFO.

a. What kind of information did you get from the Google (or Yahoo or Ask) searches? Are any of them based on research, or do you see more commercial websites or blogs? How might you refine your Google search to get more research-based hits?

b. Which of the three search platforms is the easiest to use when you want a general overview of a topic? Which of the three search platforms will give you the most up-to-date research? Which of the three makes it easiest to find peer-reviewed information?

Shy People Are Better at Reading Facial Expressions

(*LiveScience*, 2012)

CDC: Nearly 60% of Teens Text While Driving

(MSNBC.com, 2012)

Whiff of Rosemary Gives Your Brain a Boost

(*Body Odd*, nbcnews.com, 2012)

3

Three Claims, Four Validities: Interrogation Tools for Consumers of Research

LEARNING OBJECTIVES

A year from now, you should still be able to:

1. Differentiate the three types of claims: frequency, association, and causal.
2. Ask appropriate questions to help you interrogate each of the four big validities: construct validity, statistical validity, external validity, and internal validity.
3. Explain which validities are most relevant for each of the three types of claims.

Articles about psychology research written for a general audience regularly appear in the popular press. Headlines about psychology can attract readers, because many people are interested in topics such as shyness, ADHD (attention-deficit/hyperactivity disorder), and intelligence. As a psychology student, you are probably interested in these subjects as well, but to what extent should you believe the information you read online? Journalists who write about psychological science should simply report what the researchers did and why the study was important, but sometimes they end up misrepresenting or overstating the research findings. They may do so unintentionally, because they do not have the appropriate training to properly critique the findings, or intentionally, to draw readers' attention.

What about the research reported directly, in an empirical journal article? How well does the study support the claims a researcher might make? Your research methods course will help you understand both popular and research-based articles at a more sophisticated level. It will teach you how to raise the appropriate questions for interrogating the information behind a writer's claims about human behavior. By extension, the skills you use to evaluate information behind the research you read will also help you plan your own studies if you intend to become a producer of information.

Think of this chapter as a scaffold. All the information in later chapters will have a place in the framework of three claims and four validities presented here. The three types of claims—frequency claims, association claims, and causal claims—make statements about variables or about relationships between variables. Therefore, learning some basics about variables comes first.

Variables

Variables are the core unit of psychological research. A **variable**, as the word implies, is something that varies, so it must have at least two **levels**, or *values*.

Take this headline: "Nearly 60% of teens text while driving." Here, texting while driving is the variable, and its levels are "whether a person does text while driving or does not text while driving." Similarly, the study that inspired the headline "Shy people are better at reading facial expressions" has two variables: shyness (whose levels might be "less shy" and "more shy") and the ability to read facial expressions (whose levels are "more skilled" and "less skilled"). In contrast, in research on fathers, gender would not be a variable, because it has only one level: Every father in the study would presumably be male. Gender, therefore, would be a constant in this study, not a variable. A **constant** is something that could potentially vary but that has only one level in the study in question.

Variables can have more than two levels. Shyness might have just two levels, less shy and more shy. Depending on how shyness is being measured in a specific context, though, it might have three levels (low, medium, and high) or even 10 levels, based on a 10-point scale from low shyness to high shyness.

Measured and Manipulated Variables

The researchers in any study either measure or manipulate each variable. The distinction is important because some claims are tested with measured variables, while other claims must be tested with both measured and manipulated variables. A **measured variable** is one whose levels are simply observed and recorded. Some variables, such as height, IQ, and blood pressure, are typically measured in the familiar sense of the word (using scales, rulers, or devices). Other variables, such as gender and hair color, are also said to be "measured." To measure abstract variables, such as depression and stress, researchers might devise a set of questions to represent the various levels. In each case, measuring a variable is a matter of recording an observation, a statement, or a value as it occurs naturally.

In contrast, a **manipulated variable** is a variable a researcher controls, usually by assigning participants to the different levels of that variable. For example, a researcher might give some participants 10 milligrams of a medication, other participants 20 mg, and still others 30 mg. Or a researcher might assign some people to take a test in a room with many other people, and assign other people to take the test alone. In both examples, the participants could end up at any of the levels, because the researchers do the manipulating, assigning participants to be at one level of the variable or another.

Some variables cannot be manipulated—they can only be measured. Gender cannot be manipulated because researchers cannot assign people to be male or female; they can only measure what gender they already are. IQ cannot be manipulated, because researchers cannot assign some people to have a high IQ and others to have a low IQ; they can only measure each person's IQ. Even if the researchers choose the 10% of people with the highest IQ and the 10% with the lowest IQ, it is still a measured variable because people cannot be assigned to the highest or lowest 10%. A trait such as suicidality is difficult or impossible to change for the purposes of a study. Other variables cannot be manipulated because it would be unethical to do so. For example, in a study on the long-term effects of elementary education, you could not ethically assign children to "high-quality school" and "low-quality school" conditions. Nor could you ethically assign people to conditions that put their physical or emotional well-being at risk.

For a complete discussion of ethical guidelines in research, see Chapter 4.

Some variables, however, can be either manipulated or measured, depending on the goals of a study. If childhood extracurricular activities were the variable of interest, you could *measure* whether children already do take music lessons or drama lessons, or you could *manipulate* this variable if you assigned some children to take music lessons and others to take drama lessons. If you wanted to study hair color, you could *measure* hair color by recording whether people are blond or brunette. You could also *manipulate* this variable if you assigned some willing people to dye their hair blond and others to dye their hair brown.

From Conceptual Variable to Operational Definition

Each variable in a study can be described in two ways (**Table 3.1**). When researchers are discussing their theories and when journalists write about research, they use concept-level language. These are **conceptual variables**: abstract concepts such as "shyness" or "intelligence." A conceptual variable is sometimes called a **construct**. Conceptual variables must be carefully defined at the theoretical level, and these definitions are called **conceptual definitions**.

To test hypotheses, researchers have to do something specific in order to gather data. When testing their hypotheses with empirical research, they create **operational definitions** of variables, also known as **operational variables**, or *operationalizations*. To **operationalize** means to turn a concept of interest into a measured or manipulated variable.

TABLE 3.1 Describing Variables

Variable name (conceptual variable)	Operational definition (one possibility)	Levels of this variable	Is the variable measured or manipulated in this context?
Vocal fry	Researchers audiorecorded women talking and coded the degree to which the speaker uses a low, gutteral vibration at the end of a sentence	3 levels: low, medium, and high amounts of vocal fry, as determined by coders	Measured
Whiff of rosemary	Researchers exposed participants to rosemary essential oil, compared to a neutral fragrance	2 levels: presentation of the rosemary oil or a neutral fragrance	Manipulated
Gender	Researchers asked people to circle "male" or "female" on their questionnaire form	2 levels: male and female	Measured
Sleep quality	In a sleep clinic, researchers used sleep monitors and timed the number of minutes participants engaged in Stage IV sleep	This variable has multiple possible levels, because it is measured in minutes	Measured

For example, a researcher's interest in the conceptual variable "shyness" might be operationalized as a structured set of questions used by a trained therapist to diagnose each person as "not shy" or "mildly shy" or "severely shy." Alternatively, the same concept might be operationalized by asking people to answer a single Internet survey question, rating their own level of shyness from 1 ("low") to 10 ("high").

Sometimes this operationalization step is simple and straightforward. For example, a researcher interested in a conceptual variable such as "weight gain" in laboratory rats would probably just weigh them. Or a researcher who was interested in the conceptual variable "having a TV in the bedroom" might operationalize this variable by asking each child's parents about their bedroom contents. In these two cases, the researcher is able to operationalize the conceptual variable of interest quite easily.

Often, however, concepts researchers wish to study are difficult to see, touch, or feel, so they are also harder to operationalize. Examples are personality traits, states such as "argumentativeness," and behavior judgments such as "attempted suicide." The more abstract nature of these conceptual variables does not stop psychologists from operationalizing them; it just makes studying them a little more difficult. In such cases, researchers spend extra time clarifying and defining the conceptual variables they plan to study. They

Conceptual variable

How often do you text and drive?

- almost always
- frequently
- occasionally
- never

Operational variables

Self-report questionnaire   Direct observation   Friends' observations

FIGURE 3.1 Operationalizing "texting while driving." A single conceptual variable can be operationalized in a number of ways.

might develop creative or elegant operational definitions to capture the variable of interest.

Most often, variables are stated at the conceptual level. To discover how the variable "texting while driving" was operationalized, you need to ask: How did the researchers measure "texting while driving" in this study? To determine how the variable "intellectual abilities" was operationalized, ask: What do they mean by "intellectual abilities" in this research? **Figure 3.1** shows how texting while driving might be operationalized.

CHECK YOUR UNDERSTANDING

1. What is the difference between a variable and its levels?

2. Explain why some variables can only be measured, not manipulated.

3. What is the difference between the conceptual variable and the operational definition of a variable? How might the conceptual variables "affection," "intelligence," and "stress" be operationalized by a researcher?

---

1. See p. 56. 2. See pp. 56–57. 3. See pp. 57–59.

Three Claims

TABLE 3.2 Examples of Each Type of Claim

Claim type	Sample headlines
Frequency claims	**1 in 25 U.S. teens attempts suicide**
	79% think regifting is acceptable
	More than 2/3 of college women use "vocal fry" sounds
Association claims	**Mixed-weight couples argue more**
	Smart jocks: Fit kids do better at math, reading
	Bedroom TVs may boost kids' risk of fat, disease
Causal claims	**Music lessons enhance IQ**
	Texting blamed for rising teen pedestrian injuries
	Study: Creepy people literally give us the chills
	Shape of glass may influence how fast you drink

A **claim** is the argument someone is trying to make. Internet bloggers might make claims based on personal experience or observation ("The media coverage of congressional candidates has been sexist"). Politicians might make claims based on rhetoric ("I am the candidate of change!"). Literature scholars make claims based on textual evidence ("Based on my reading of the text, I argue that *Frankenstein* is an antifeminist novel"). In this textbook, we focus on claims made by journalists, researchers, or scientists—claims that are based on empirical research. Recall from Chapters 1 and 2 that psychological scientists use systematic observations, or data, to test and refine theories and claims. A psychologist might claim, based on data he or she has collected, that a certain percentage of teens attempted suicide last year, or that mixed-weight couples argue more, or that music lessons can improve a child's IQ.

Notice the different wording in the boldfaced headlines in **Table 3.2**. In particular, the first highlighted claim merely gives a percentage of people who attempted suicide; this is a *frequency claim*. The highlighted claim in the middle about mixed weight and arguing, is an *association claim*: It suggests that the two variables go together, but does not claim that mixed-weight status causes arguing or that arguing causes mixed-weight status. The last highlighted claim, however, is a *causal claim*: The strong verb *enhance* indicates that the music lessons actually cause the improvement in IQ. The kind of claim a psychological scientist is able to make must be backed up by the right kind of study. How can you identify the types of claims researchers make, and how can you evaluate whether their studies are able to support each type of claim? If you conduct research yourself, how will you know what kinds of study will support the type of claim you wish to make?

Frequency Claims

1 in 25 U. S. Teens Attempts Suicide

44% of Americans Struggle to Stay Happy

58% of Boulder Residents Exercise Frequently

Frequency claims describe a particular rate or degree of a single variable. In the first example above, "1 in 25" is the frequency of suicide attempts among teens in the United States. In the second example, "44%" is the rate (the proportion) of adults who are not always happy. These headlines claim how frequent or common something is. Claims that mention the percentage of a variable, the number of people who engage in some activity, or a certain group's level on a variable can all be called frequency claims.

The best way to distinguish frequency claims from the other two types of claims (association and causal claims) is that they focus on only one variable—such as depression, happiness, or rate of exercise. Another distinguishing feature is that in frequency claims, the variables are always measured, not manipulated. In the examples above, the researchers have measured levels of suicide using some kind of measure, such as a questionnaire or an interview, and have reported the results.

Some reports give a list of single-variable results, all of which count as frequency claims. Take, for example, a 2012 report by the U.S. Centers for Disease Control and Prevention (CDC) on the health behaviors of U.S. residents. This report noted that 32% of adults were physically inactive. It also reported that 28% of adults were obese. These are two separate frequency claims—they measure single variables one at a time. The researchers were not trying to show associations between these single variables; that is, the report did not claim that the adults who are inactive were more likely to be obese. Instead, these scientists simply reported that a certain percentage of U.S. adults are inactive and a certain percentage of adults are obese.

Association Claims

Shy People Are Better at Reading Facial Expressions
People Who Multitask the Most Are the Worst at It
Screen Time Not Linked to Physical Activity in Kids

These headlines are all examples of association claims. An **association claim** argues that one level of a variable is likely to be associated with a particular level of another variable. Variables that are associated are sometimes said to **correlate**, or *covary*, meaning that when one variable changes, the other variable tends to change, too. More simply, they may be said to be *related*.

Notice that there are two variables in each example above. In the first, the variables are the amount of shyness and the ability to read facial expressions: Being more shy is associated with a greater ability to read facial expressions (and therefore being less shy goes with a lower ability to read facial expressions). In the second example, the variables are the frequency of multitasking and the ability to successfully multitask: More frequent multitasking goes with a worse ability to multitask.

An association claim must involve at least two variables, and the variables are measured, not manipulated. (This is one feature that distinguishes an association claim from a causal claim.) To make an association claim, the researcher measures the variables and then uses descriptive statistics to see whether the two variables are related. There are at least three basic types of associations among variables: positive association, negative association, and zero association.

For more on correlation patterns, see Chapter 8.

Three Claims   **61**

Positive Association

The headline "Shy people are better at reading facial expressions" suggests that, on average, the more shy people are, the better they can read facial expressions. The type of association in this example, in which high goes with high and low goes with low, is called a **positive association**, or a *positive correlation*. Stated another way, high scores on shyness go with a high ability to read facial expressions, and low scores on shyness go with a lower ability to read facial expressions.

One way to represent an association is to use a **scatterplot**, a graph in which one variable is plotted on the y-axis and the other variable is plotted on the x-axis; each dot represents one participant in the study, measured on the two variables. **Figure 3.2** shows what scatterplots of the associations in the three headlines would look like. (The data are fabricated for illustration purposes, and the numbers are arbitrary units.) Notice that the dots in **Figure 3.2A** form a cloud of points, as opposed to a straight line. If you were to draw a straight line that best fit through that cloud of points, however, the line would incline upward; in other words, the mathematical slope of the line would be positive.

Negative Association

The study behind the second headline example, "People who multitask the most are the worst at it," is a negative association. In a **negative association** (or *negative correlation*), high goes with low and low goes with high. In other words, high rates of multitasking go with a low ability to multitask, and low rates of multitasking go with a high ability to multitask.

A scatterplot representing this association would look something like the one in **Figure 3.2B.** Each dot represents a person who has been measured on two variables. However, in this example, a line drawn through the cloud of points would slope downward; it would have a negative slope.

Keep in mind that the word *negative* refers only to the slope; it does not mean the association is somehow bad. In this example, the reverse of the association—that people who multitask the least are the best at it—is another way to phrase this negative association. In other words, a negative association does not necessarily indicate negative news. To avoid this kind of confusion, some people prefer the term *inverse association*.

Zero Association

The study behind the headline "Screen time not linked to physical activity in kids" is an example of a **zero association**, or no association between the variables (*zero correlation*). In a scatterplot of this association, both low and high levels of screen time are associated with all levels of physical activity (**Figure 3.2C**). This cloud of points has no slope—or more specifically, a line drawn through it would be nearly horizontal, and a horizontal line has a slope of zero.

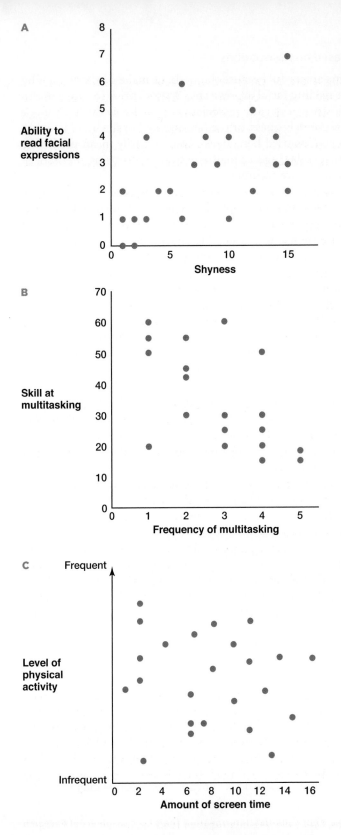

FIGURE 3.2 Scatterplots showing three types of associations. (A) Positive association: "Shy people are better at reading facial expressions." (B) Negative association: "People who multitask the most are the worst at it." (C) Zero association: "Screen time not linked to physical activity in kids." Data are fabricated for illustration purposes.

Some association claims are useful because they help us make predictions. Who is going to be better at reading facial expressions? Who's at risk for poor multitasking skill? With a positive or negative association, if we know the level of one variable, we can more accurately guess, or predict, the level of the other variable. Note that the word *predict*, as used here, does not necessarily mean predicting into the future. It means predicting in a mathematical sense—using the association to make our estimates more accurate.

To return to the headlines, according to the positive association described in the first example, if we know how shy somebody is, we can predict how well she did on a facial expression task. Therefore, if we know a person is very shy, we might predict she will be very good at reading facial expressions. According to the negative association in the second example, if you know someone spends a lot of time multitasking, we can predict that he will be less good at it. Are these predictions going to be perfect? No—they will usually be off by a certain margin. The stronger the relationship between the two variables, the more accurate our prediction will be; the weaker the relationship between the two variables, the less accurate our prediction will be. But if two variables are even somewhat correlated, it helps us make much better predictions than if we didn't know about this association.

Both positive and negative associations can help us make predictions. In contrast, zero associations cannot. If we wanted to predict how much physical activity a kid gets, we could not do so just by knowing his hours of screen time, because these two variables are not correlated. With a zero correlation, we cannot predict the level of one variable from the level of the other. In sum, positive and negative associations let us predict one variable from another, but zero associations do not.

For more on predictions from correlations, see Chapter 8, pp. 212–213.

Causal Claims

Music Lessons Enhance IQ
Whiff of Rosemary Gives Your Brain a Boost
Family Meals Curb Teen Eating Disorders

Whereas an association claim merely notes a relationship between two variables, a **causal claim** goes even further, arguing that one of the variables is responsible for changing the other. Note that each of the causal claims above has two variables, just like association claims: music lessons and IQ, a whiff of rosemary and brain activity, family meals and eating disorders. In addition, like association claims, the causal claims above suggest that the two variables in question covary—children who take music lessons have higher IQs. People who get a whiff of rosemary have more brain activity than those who do not.

Causal claims start with positive, negative, or zero associations. Music lessons are positively associated with IQ, and family meals are negatively associated with eating disorders (the more family meals, the fewer eating disorders). Occasionally you might also see a causal claim based on a zero association; it would report lack of cause. For example, you might read that a particular vaccine does not cause autism or that daycare does not cause behavior problems.

Causal claims, however, go beyond a simple association between the two variables. They use language to suggest that one variable causes the other—verbs such as *cause, enhance,* and *curb.* In contrast, association claims use verbs such as *link, associate, correlate, predict, tie to,* and *being at risk for.* In **Table 3.3,** notice the difference between these types of verbs and verb phrases. The causal verbs tend to be more exciting; they are active and forceful, suggesting that one variable acts on the other. It is not surprising, then, that journalists may be tempted to describe family meals as *curbing* eating disorders, for example, because it makes a better story than family meals just *being associated with* eating disorders.

TABLE 3.3 Verb Phrases That Distinguish Association and Causal Claims

Association claim verbs	Causal claim verbs	
is linked to	causes	promotes
is at higher risk for	affects	reduces
is associated with	may curb	prevents
is correlated with	exacerbates	distracts
prefers	changes	fights
are more/less likely to	may lead to	worsens
may predict	makes	increases
is tied to	sometimes makes	trims
goes with	hurts	adds

Here's another important point: A causal claim that contains tentative language—*could, may, seem, suggest, sometimes, potentially*—is still a causal claim. If the first headline read "Music lessons *may* enhance IQ," it would be more tentative, but it still would be a causal claim. The causal verb *enhance* makes it a causal claim, regardless of any softening or qualifying language.

Advice is also a causal claim; it implies that if you do X, then Y will get better. For example: "Best way to deal with jerks? Give them the cold shoulder." "Want to live longer? Get happy."

Causal claims are a step above association claims, and because they make a stronger statement, we hold them to higher standards. To move from the simple language of association to the language of causality, a study has to satisfy three criteria. First, it must establish that the two variables (the cause variable and the outcome variable) are correlated; the relationship cannot be zero. Second, it must show that the causal variable came first and the outcome variable came later. Third, it must establish that no other explanations exist for the relationship. (Later in this chapter, you will learn how to evaluate these three criteria and how special types of studies, called experiments, enable researchers to support causal claims.)

Not All Claims Are Based on Research

Besides the types of claims mentioned above, you may also encounter stories in the popular press that are not based on research, even if they are related to psychology, such as:

I Feel I've Overcome ADHD

Stress Ball Factory Worker Attacks Boss

91-Year-Old Yoga Teacher: Why Should I Quit?

Such headlines do not report the results of research. They may report a person's solution to a problem, an ironic story, or an expert's advice, but they do not say anything about the frequency of a problem or what research has shown to work. The ADHD story is about a single person's experience with this condition, but it is not arguing that his treatment would work for others. The factory worker's behavior is unexpected, but the story does not report systematic research about stress balls and work violence.

These kinds of headlines may be interesting, and they might be related to psychology, but they are not frequency, association, or causal claims, in which a writer summarizes the results of a poll, survey, or other research study. Such anecdotal stories are about isolated experiences, not about empirical studies. And as you read in Chapter 2, experience is not as good a source of information as empirical research.

CHECK YOUR UNDERSTANDING

1. How many variables are there in a frequency claim? An association claim? A causal claim?
2. How can the language used in a claim help you differentiate between association and causal claims?
3. How are causal claims special, compared with the other two claims?
4. What are the three criteria that causal claims must satisfy?

---

1. one; at least two. See pp. 60–61, p. 61, and p. 64. 2. See p. 64 and p. 65 and Table 3.3. 3. See p. 65. 4. See pp. 64–65.

Interrogating the Three Claims Using the Four Big Validities

You now have the tools to differentiate among the three major claims you will encounter in research journals and in the popular media—but your job is just getting started. Once you identify the kind of claim a writer is making, you need to ask targeted questions as a critically minded consumer of information. The rest of this chapter will sharpen your ability to evaluate the claims you come across, using what will be called the four big validities: construct validity, external validity, statistical validity, and internal validity. **Validity** refers to the appropriateness of a conclusion or decision, and in general, a *valid* claim is reasonable, accurate, and justifiable. In psychological research, however, we do not say that a claim is simply "valid." Instead, psychologists specify which of the validities they are applying. As a psychology student, you will learn to pause before you declare a study to be "valid" or "not valid," and to specify which of the four big validities the study has achieved.

Although the focus for now is on how you can evaluate other people's claims based on the four big validities, you will also use this same framework if you plan to conduct your own research. Depending on whether you plan to test a frequency claim, an association claim, or a causal claim, you will need to plan your research carefully, emphasizing the validities that are most important for your goals.

Interrogating Frequency Claims

To evaluate how well a study supports a frequency claim, you will focus on two of the big validities: construct validity and external validity. You may wish to ask about statistical validity, too.

Construct Validity of Frequency Claims

Construct validity refers to how well a conceptual variable operationalized. When asking about the construct validity of a frequency claim, the question to consider is how well the researchers measured their variables. Consider this claim: "60% of teens text while driving." There are several ways to evaluate whether a person texts while driving. You could ask teenagers to tell you on an Internet survey how often they text while driving. You could stand near an intersection and record the behaviors of teenage drivers. You could possibly even use cell phone records to see if a text was sent at the same time a person was known to be driving. In other words, there are a number of ways to operationalize such a variable, some of which are better than others.

When you ask how well a study measured or manipulated a variable, you are interrogating the construct validity: how accurately a researcher has operationalized each variable—be it depression, happiness, texting, gender, body mass index, or self-esteem. For example, you would expect a study on obesity rates to use an accurate scale to weigh participants. Similarly, you should expect a study about texting among teenagers to use an accurate measure, and perhaps observing behavior is a better measure than casually asking, "Have you ever texted while driving?" To ensure construct validity, researchers must establish that each variable has been measured reliably (i.e., be sure the measure gives similar scores on repeated testings), and that different levels of a variable accurately correspond to true differences in, say, depression or happiness. (For more detail on construct validity, see Chapter 5.)

External Validity of Frequency Claims

The second important question to ask about frequency claims concerns **generalizability**: How did the researchers choose the study's participants, and how well do those participants represent the intended population? Consider this example: "44% of Americans struggle to stay happy." Did the researchers survey every American to come up with this number? Of course not. They surveyed only a small proportion of Americans, so the next question is, which Americans did they ask? That is, how did they choose their participants? Did they ask a few friends? Did they ask 100 college students? Did they dial random numbers on the telephone? Did they stop shoppers in the mall?

Such questions address the study's **external validity**: how well the results of a study generalize to, or represent, people or contexts besides those in the study itself.

For more on the procedures that researchers use to ensure external validity, see Chapter 7, pp. 188–192.

If a researcher asked 100 of his Facebook friends how happy they were and 44 of them said they struggled to stay happy, the researcher cannot claim that 44% of Americans struggle to stay happy. The researcher cannot even argue that 44% of his own friends struggle to stay happy, because the 100 people who responded to his Facebook question may not be a representative selection of his friends. To claim that 44% of Americans struggle to stay happy, the researchers in this study needed to ensure that the participants in the sample adequately represented all Americans.

Statistical Validity of Frequency Claims

Researchers use statistics to describe their data. **Statistical validity**, also called *statistical conclusion validity*, is the extent to which a study's statistical conclusions are accurate and reasonable. How well do the numbers support the claim?

Statistical validity questions will vary depending on the claim. In the case of frequency claims, percentages are usually accompanied by a **margin of error estimate**, a statistical figure, based on sample size for a poll, that indicates where the true value in the population probably lies. For example, in the report about Americans struggling to stay happy, the 44% value was accompanied by this note: "The margin of error is +/−3 percentage points." This means that the true percentage of "struggling" Americans probably lies between 41–47%. In other words, the 44% value is an estimate, and the true value is probably between 41% and 47%. Asking about the statistical validity of a frequency claim means reminding yourself that the number associated with the claim is an estimate, and it has a specific amount of error associated with it.

Interrogating Association Claims

As we've seen, the studies that lead to association claims measure two variables instead of just one. Such studies describe how these variables are related to each other. A study that measures two or more variables is a **correlational study**. To interrogate an association claim, you ask how well the correlational study behind the claim supports construct, external, and statistical validities.

Construct Validity of Association Claims

To support an association claim, a researcher has to measure two variables, so you need to assess the construct validity of *each* variable. For the headline "People who multitask the most are the worst at it," you should ask how well the researchers measured the frequency of multitasking and how well they measured the ability to multitask (**Figure 3.3**). For example, the ability to multitask could be measured quite accurately using a computer-scored task that involves doing two things at once; a much less accurate measure would be obtained by asking people to answer the question, "How good are you at multitasking?" Similarly, frequency of

FIGURE 3.3 Interrogating an association claim. To interrogate the claim that "people who multitask are the worst at it," you'd ask about construct, external, and statistical validities.

multitasking might be measured accurately through asking people to document their day, or by following people around and observing when they are multitasking.

In any study, measuring variables is a fundamental strength or weakness—and construct validity questions assess how well such measurements were conducted. If you conclude that one of the variables was measured poorly, you would not be able to trust the conclusions related to that variable. However, if you conclude that the construct validity in the study was excellent, you can have more confidence in the association claim being reported.

External Validity of Association Claims

You might also interrogate the external validity of association claims, asking whether the association claim in question can generalize to other populations, as well as to other contexts, times, or places. For the association between shyness and an ability to read facial expressions, you would ask whether the results from this study's participants (perhaps a group of volunteers aged 20-30 from a university in Montana) would generalize to other people and settings. Would these same results be obtained if all of the participants were women in Dallas aged 35–40? You can ask about generalization to other contexts by asking, for example, if shyness might also be linked to other social skills besides reading facial expressions, such as interpreting gestures or vocal tones. (**Table 3.4** summarizes the four big validities used in this text.)

TABLE 3.4 The Four Big Validities

Type of validity	Description
Construct validity	How well the variables in a study are measured or manipulated.
	The extent to which the operational variables used in a study are a good approximation of the conceptual variables.
External validity	The extent to which the results of a study generalize to some larger population (e.g., whether the results from this sample of children apply to all U.S. schoolchildren), as well as to other times or situations (e.g., whether the results based on this type of music apply to other types of music).
Statistical validity	Addresses the strength of an effect and its statistical significance (the probability that the results could have been obtained by chance if there really is no effect). Also addresses the extent to which a study minimizes the probabilities of two errors: concluding that there is an effect when in fact there is none (a "false positive," or Type I error), or concluding that there is no effect when in fact there is one (a "miss," or Type II error).
Internal validity	In a relationship between one variable (A) and another (B), the extent to which A, rather than some other variable (C), is responsible for the effect on B.

Statistical Validity of Association Claims: Strength and Significance

When applied to an association claim, statistical validity is the extent to which the statistical conclusions are accurate and reasonable. One aspect of statistical validity is strength: How strong is the association? Some associations—such as the association between height and shoe size—are quite strong. People who are tall almost always have larger feet than people who are short, so if you predict shoe size from height, you will predict fairly accurately. Other associations—such as the association between height and income—might be very weak. For example, it turns out that because of a stereotype that favors tall people (tall people are more admired in North America), taller people do earn more money than short people. However, the relationship is not very strong. Though you can predict income from height, your prediction will be less accurate than when you predict height from shoe size.

For more about association strength and statistical significance, see Chapter 8, pp. 206–207 and pp. 214–217.

Another question worth interrogating is the statistical significance of a particular association. Some associations that are reported by researchers might simply be due to chance connections in that particular sample. However, if an association is statistically significant, it is probably *not* due to chance connections in that one sample. For example, if the association between multitasking ability and multitasking frequency is statistically significant, it would mean that the association is probably not a chance result from that sample alone.

Statistical Validity of Association Claims: Avoiding Two Mistaken Conclusions

Another aspect of statistical validity has to do with two kinds of mistakes. First, a study might mistakenly conclude, based on the results from a sample of people, that there is an association between two variables (e.g., shyness and reading facial expressions) when there really is *no* association in the real population. Careful researchers try to minimize the chance that they will make this kind of mistake, known as a "false positive," or **Type I error**. They want to increase the chances that they will find associations only when they are really there.

For more on Type I and Type II errors, see Statistics Review: Inferential Statistics, pp. 468–474.

Second, a study might mistakenly conclude from a sample that there is no association between two variables (e.g., screen time and physical activity) when there really *is* an association in the full population. Careful researchers try to minimize the chances of making this kind of mistake, too; it is known as a "miss," or **Type II error**. Obviously, they want to reduce the chances that they will miss associations that are really there.

As you might imagine, evaluating statistical validity can be complicated. Full training in how to assess statistical validity requires a separate, semester-long statistics class. This book introduces you to the basics. We will focus mainly on asking about statistical significance and the strength of an effect.

In sum, when you come across an association claim, you should ask about three validities: construct, external, and statistical. You can ask how well the two variables were measured (construct validity). You can ask whether you can generalize the result to a population (external validity). And you can ask about whether the researchers might have made any statistical conclusion errors, as well as evaluating the strength and significance of the association (statistical validity).

Table 3.5 gives an overview of the three claims, four validities framework. Before reading about how to interrogate causal claims, use the table to review what we've covered so far.

TABLE 3.5 Interrogating the Three Types of Claims Using the Four Big Validities

Type of Validity	Frequency claims ("Nearly 60% of teens text while driving")	Association claims ("Shy people are better at reading facial expressions")	Causal claims ("Music lessons enhance IQ")
Construct validity	How well has the researcher measured the variable in question?	How well has the researcher measured each of the two variables in the association?	How well has the researcher measured or manipulated the variables in the study?
Statistical validity	What is the margin of error of the estimate?	What is the effect size? How strong is the association? Is the association statistically significant? If the study finds a relationship, what is the probability the researcher's conclusion is a false positive? If the study finds no relationship, what is the probability the researcher is missing a true relationship?	What is the effect size? Is there a difference between groups, and how large is it? Is the difference statistically significant?
Internal validity	Frequency claims are usually not asserting causality, so internal validity is not relevant.	People who make association claims are not asserting causality, so internal validity is not relevant to interrogate. A researcher should avoid making a causal claim from a simple association, however (see Chapter 8).	Was the study an experiment? Does the study achieve temporal precedence? Does the study control for alternative explanations by randomly assigning participants to groups? Does the study avoid several internal validity threats (see Chapters 10 and 11)?
External validity	To what populations, settings, and times can we generalize this estimate? How representative is the sample—was it a random sample?	To what populations, settings, and times can we generalize this association claim? How representative is the sample? To what other problems might the association be generalized?	To what populations, settings, and times can we generalize this causal claim? How representative is the sample? How representative are the manipulations and measures?

Interrogating Causal Claims

An association claim says that two variables are related, but a causal claim goes beyond, saying that one variable causes the other. Instead of using such verb phrases as *is associated with*, *is related to*, and *is linked to*, causal claims use directional verbs such as *affects*, *leads to*, or *reduces*. When you interrogate such a claim, your first step will be to ensure that it is backed up by research that fulfills the three criteria for causation: covariance, temporal precedence, and internal validity.

Three Criteria for Causation

Of course, one variable usually cannot be said to cause another variable unless the two are related. **Covariance** is the first criterion a study must satisfy in order to establish a causal claim. But to justify using a causal verb, the data must do more than just show that two variables are associated. A study must satisfy two additional criteria to justify the use of causal language: temporal precedence and internal validity (**Table 3.6**).

To say that one variable has **temporal precedence** means that it comes first in time, before the other variable. To make the claim "Music lessons enhance IQ," a study must show that the music lessons came first and the gains in IQ came later. Although this statement might seem obvious, it is not always so. In a simple association, it might be the case that music lessons made the children smart, but it is also possible that children who start out smart are more likely to want to take music lessons. It is not always clear which one came first. Similarly, to make the claim "Family meals curb teen eating disorders," the study needs to show that family meals came first and the drop in eating disorders came later.

Another criterion, called **internal validity**, or the *third-variable criterion*, means that a study should be able to eliminate alternative explanations for the association. For example, to claim that "Music lessons enhance IQ" is to claim that the music lessons *cause* the increase in IQ. But an alternative explanation could be that certain kinds of parents might both encourage academic achievement (leading to higher IQ scores) *and* encourage their kids to take music lessons. In other words, there could be an internal validity problem: It is a certain type of parent, not the music lessons, that causes these children to score higher on IQ

TABLE 3.6 Three Criteria for Establishing Causation Between Variable A and Variable B

Criterion	Definition
Covariance	As A changes, B changes; e.g., high levels of A go with high levels of B, and low levels of A go with low levels of B.
Temporal precedence	A comes first in time, before B.
Internal validity	There are no possible alternative explanations for the change in B; A is the only thing that changed.

tests. In Chapter 2 you read about confounds in personal experience. Such confounds are also examples of internal validity problems.

Experiments Can Support Causal Claims

What kind of study can satisfy all three criteria for causal claims? Usually, to support a causal claim, researchers must conduct a well-designed **experiment**, in which one variable is manipulated and the other is measured.

Experiments are considered the gold standard of psychological research because of their potential to support causal claims. In daily life, people tend to use the word *experiment* rather loosely, to refer to any trial of something to see what happens ("Let's experiment and try making the popcorn with olive oil instead"). In psychology, an experiment is more than just "a study." When psychologists conduct an experiment, they *manipulate* the variable they think is the cause and *measure* the variable they think is the effect. In the context of an experiment, the manipulated variable is called the **independent variable**, and the measured variable is called the **dependent variable**. For example, to see whether music lessons enhance IQ, the researchers in that study had to manipulate the music lessons variable and measure the IQ variable.

Remember: To *manipulate* a variable means to assign participants to be at one level or the other. In the music example, the researchers might assign some children to take music lessons, some children to take another kind of lesson, and a third group to take no lessons. In an actual study that tested this claim in Toronto, Canada, researcher Glen Schellenberg (2004) manipulated the music lesson variable by assigning some children to take music lessons (either keyboard lessons or voice lessons), other children to take drama lessons, and still others to take no lessons. After several months of lessons, he measured the IQs of all the children. At the conclusion of his study, Schellenberg found that the children who took keyboard and voice lessons gained an average of 3.7 IQ points more than the children who took drama lessons or no lessons (**Figure 3.4**). This was a statistically significant gain. Thus, he established the first part of a causal claim: covariance.

Temporal Precedence and Internal Validity. Why does the process of manipulating one variable and measuring the other help scientists make causal claims? For one thing, manipulating the causal variable ensures that it comes first. By showing that the music lessons came before the increase in IQ, Schellenberg ensured temporal precedence in his study.

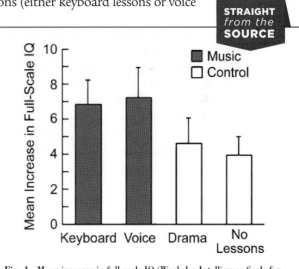

STRAIGHT *from the* SOURCE

Fig. 1. Mean increase in full-scale IQ (Wechsler Intelligence Scale for Children–Third Edition) for each group of 6-year-olds who completed the study. Error bars show standard errors.

FIGURE 3.4 Interrogating a causal claim. What key features of Schellenberg's study of music lessons and IQ made it possible for him to claim that music lessons increase children's IQ? (Source: Schellenberg, 2004.)

In addition, when researchers manipulate a variable, they have the potential to control for alternative explanations; that is, they can ensure internal validity. For example, when Schellenberg was investigating whether music lessons could enhance IQ, he did not want the children in the music lessons groups to have more involved parents than those in the drama lessons group or the no lessons group, because then the involvement of parents would have been a plausible alternative explanation for why the music lessons enhanced IQ. He did not want the children in the music lessons groups to come from a different school district than those in the drama lessons group or the no lessons group, because then the schools' curricula or teacher quality might have been alternative explanations. Instead, Schellenberg used a technique called **random assignment** to ensure that the children in the four groups were as similar as possible. He used a method such as rolling a die to decide whether each child in his study would take keyboard lessons, voice lessons, drama lessons, or no lessons. Only by randomly assigning children to one of the groups could Schellenberg ensure that the children who took music lessons were as similar as possible, in every other way, to those who took drama lessons or no lessons. Random assignment increased internal validity by allowing Schellenberg to control for potential alternative explanations.

Because Schellenberg's experiment met all three criteria of causation—covariance, temporal precedence, and internal validity—he was justified in making a causal claim from his data. His study found that music lessons really do enhance—that is, *cause* an increase in—IQ.

For more on how random assignment helps ensure that experimental groups are similar, see Chapter 10, pp. 282–283.

When Causal Claims Are a Mistake

Let's use two other causal claims to illustrate how to interrogate causal claims by writers and journalists.

Do Family Meals Really Curb Eating Disorders? To interrogate the causal claim "Family meals curb teen eating disorders," we start by asking about covariance in the study behind this claim. Is there an association between family meals and eating disorders? Yes: The news report says that 26% of girls who ate with their families fewer than five times a week had eating-disordered behavior (e.g., the use of laxatives or diuretics, or self-induced vomiting), whereas only 17% of girls who ate with their families five or more times a week engaged in eating-disordered behavior. The two variables are associated. What about temporal precedence? Did the researchers make sure that family meals had increased before the eating disorders decreased? The best way to ensure temporal precedence is to assign some families to have more meals together than others. Sure, families who eat more meals together may have fewer daughters with disordered eating behavior, but the temporal precedence simply is not clear from this association. Indeed, one of the symptoms of an eating disorder is embarrassment about eating in front of others, so perhaps the eating disorder came first and the reduction in family meals came second. Daughters with eating disorders may simply find excuses to avoid eating with their families.

Internal validity is a problem here, too. Without an experiment, we cannot rule out a wide variety of alternative, third-variable explanations. Perhaps girls from single-parent families are both less likely to eat with their families and to be vulnerable to eating disorders, whereas girls who live with both parents are not. Perhaps high-achieving girls are too busy to eat with their families and are also more susceptible to disordered dieting behavior. These are only two of many possible alternative explanations. Only a well-run experiment could have controlled for these internal validity problems (the alternative explanations), using random assignment to ensure that the girls who had frequent family dinners and those who had less-frequent family dinners were identical in all other ways: high versus low scholastic achievement, single-parent versus two-parent households, and so on. However, it would be impractical and probably unethical to do an experiment like this. Although the study's authors reported the findings appropriately, the journalist jumped to a causal conclusion by saying that family dinners *curb* eating disorders. The journalist should probably just have said, "Family dinners *are linked to* eating disorders."

Do Early Language Skills Reduce Preschool Tantrums? Another example of a dubious causal claim is this headline, which uses the strong causal verb "reduce": "Early language skills reduce preschool tantrums, study finds." In the story, the journalist reported on a study that measured two variables in a set of children—one variable was language skills and the other was ability to cope with frustration. In a study that followed the kids for a few years, the researchers measured their language skills as toddlers, and measured frustration in the same kids later, when they were 4 years old. The researchers tested the 4-year-old children's ability to cope with frustration by having them wait for 8 minutes before they could open an exciting gift. The researchers found that the kids who had had more advanced language skills as toddlers were better able to wait patiently at age 4.

Let's see if this study's design is adequate to support the journalist's conclusion—that language skills cause fewer tantrums. The study certainly does have covariance; good language skills go with reduced anger during the waiting task. It also has temporal precedence. The language skills were measured when they were only 18 months old, and the waiting task was conducted later, when the same kids were 4. So we know that the language variable came first in time. However, this study did not rule out possible alternative explanations (internal validity), because it was not an experiment. Several possible outside variables could potentially correlate with both language skill and the ability to wait for a gift. One might be that children who have better social skills (perhaps they are high on social intelligence) can develop language skills early and also are able to wait longer. Another might be that the children who have been to preschool develop both language skill and the ability to be patient.

An experiment would have had the potential to rule out such alternative explanations. In this particular example, though, it may be difficult to conduct an experiment. A researcher cannot randomly assign children to have good or poor language skills as toddlers (though they may attempt to improve the skills of

one group of toddlers through a training program). Because the research he was reporting on was not enough to support a causal claim, the journalist should have simply written an association headline: "Early language skills *predict* better ability to control anger" (**Figure 3.5**).

Other Validities to Interrogate in Causal Claims

A study can support a causal claim only if the research behind it shows covariance, and only if the variables were studied in a way that ensures both temporal precedence and internal validity. Therefore, internal validity is only important for interrogating a causal claim. In addition, it is one of the most important validities to evaluate for causal claims. Besides internal validity, the other three validities discussed in this chapter—construct validity, statistical validity, and, to a lesser extent, external validity—should be interrogated, too.

FIGURE 3.5 Support for a causal claim? Without conducting an experiment, we cannot support the causal claim that early language skills reduce tantrums.

For more on how researchers use data to check the construct validity of their manipulations, see Chapter 10, pp. 295–298.

Construct Validity of Causal Claims. Take the headline, "Music lessons enhance IQ." First, we could ask about the construct validity of the measured variable in this study. How well was IQ measured? Was an established IQ test administered by trained testers? Then we would need to interrogate the construct validity of the manipulated variable, too. In operationalizing manipulated variables, researchers need to create a specific task or situation that will represent each level of the variable. In the current example, how well did the researchers manipulate music lessons? Did students take private lessons for several weeks or have a single group lesson, for example?

External Validity of Causal Claims. We could ask, as well, about external validity. If the study used children in Toronto, Canada, as participants, do the results generalize to Japanese children? Do the results generalize to rural Canadian children? If Japanese students or rural students take music lessons, will their IQs go up, too? What about generalization to other settings? Could the results generalize to other music lessons? Would flute lessons and violin lessons also work? In Chapters 10 and 14, you will learn more about how to evaluate the external validity of experiments and other studies.

Statistical Validity of Causal Claims. We can also interrogate statistical validity. To start, we would want to ask: How strong is the relationship between music lessons and IQ? In the study in question, the students who were assigned to take music lessons gained 7 points in IQ, whereas students who did not gained an average of 4.3 points in IQ—a net gain of about 3.7 IQ points. Is this a large gain? (In this case, the difference between these two groups is about 0.35 of a standard deviation, which is considered a moderate difference between the two groups.) Next, asking whether the difference between the lessons groups was statistically significant helps ensure that the covariance criterion was met; it helps us be more sure that the difference is not just due to a chance difference in this sample alone. Finally, as we did with association claims, we could ask how well the design of the study allowed the researchers to minimize the probability of making the relevant conclusion mistake—a false positive (concluding that music raises IQ when it really does not). You will learn more about interrogating the statistical validity of causal claims in Chapter 10.

For more on determining the strength of a relationship between variables, see Statistics Review: Descriptive Statistics, pp. 452–456.

Prioritizing Validities

Which of the four validities is the most important? It depends. Although the validities are all important, no study can be perfect. In fact, when researchers plan studies to test hypotheses and support claims, they usually find it impossible to conduct a study that satisfies all four validities at once. Indeed, depending on their goals, sometimes researchers do not even try to satisfy some of them. Why is that okay? Researchers decide what their priorities are—and so will you, when you participate in producing your own research.

External validity, for instance, is not always possible to achieve—and sometimes it may not even be relevant. As you will learn in Chapter 7, to be able to generalize results from a sample to a wide population requires a representative sample from that population. Consider the study by Schellenberg (2004) on music lessons and IQ. Because he was planning to test a causal claim, he wanted to emphasize internal validity, so he focused on making his different groups—music lessons, drama lessons, or no lessons—absolutely equivalent. His focus was on internal validity, so he was not prioritizing external validity. He did not try to sample children from all over Canada. However, Schellenberg's study is still important and interesting because it used an internally valid experimental method—even though it did not have perfect external validity. Furthermore, even though he used a sample of children from Toronto, Canada, there may be no theoretical reason to assume that music lessons would not improve the IQ's of rural children, too. Future research could confirm that music works in other kinds of children too, but there is no obvious reason to expect otherwise.

In contrast, if some researchers were conducting a telephone survey and did want to generalize its results to the entire Canadian population—to maximize external validity—they would have to randomly select Canadians from all ten provinces. One way the researchers might do so would be to use a random-digit telephone dialing system to call people in their homes, but this technology is expensive. When researchers do use formal, randomly sampled polls, they often have to pay the polling company a fee to administer each question. Therefore, a researcher who wants to evaluate, say, the depression levels in a large population may be forced by economics to use a simple one- or two-question measure of depression. Often, a 2-item measure of depression is not as good as a 15-item measure, but the longer measure would cost more money. In this example, the researcher might sacrifice some construct validity in order to achieve external validity.

You will learn more about these priorities in Chapter 14. The point, for now, is simply that in the course of planning and conducting a study, scientists weigh the pros and cons of research choices and decide which validities are most important. When you read about a study, you should not necessarily conclude that the study is faulty just because it did not meet one of the validities.

CHECK YOUR UNDERSTANDING

1. Which of the four big validities should you apply to a frequency claim? An association claim? A causal claim?
2. What question(s) would you ask to interrogate a study's construct validity?
3. In your own words, describe at least three things that statistical validity addresses.
4. Define external validity, using the term *generalize* in your definition.
5. What is internal validity? Why is it mostly relevant for causal claims?
6. Why don't researchers usually aim to achieve all four of the big validities at once?

1. See pp. 67–68, pp. 68–71, and pp. 76–77. *2.* See p. 67. *3.* See pp. 70–71. *4.* See p. 67 and Table 3.4. *5.* See p. 72. *6.* See pp. 77–78.

Review: Four Validities, Four Aspects of Quality

As a review, let's apply the four validities discussed in this chapter to another headline from a popular news source: "Whiff of rosemary gives your brain a boost." The journalist's story appeared in NBCNEWS.com, and the original research was published in the scientific journal, *Therapeutic Advances in Psychopharmacology*. Should we consider this a well-designed study? How well does it hold up on each of the four validities? At this stage in the course, your focus should be on asking the right questions for each validity (e.g., **Figure 3.6**). In later chapters, you will also learn how to evaluate the answers to those questions.

A
B

FIGURE 3.6 Evaluating the external validity of a study. Can the results of the study, which used manufactured rosemary oil, be generalized to other settings, such as smelling a (A) real rosemary plant or (B) rosemary bread?

Table 3.7 shows how you might work through this example, asking questions about each validity. The table also includes what kinds of answers are provided by the journalist's story. If you read the original article in the scientific journal, you would get even more detailed answers to your four validity questions. These answers are provided in Table 3.7, too. Don't worry if you are confused by certain passages or unfamiliar terms. You can always look up definitions of new terms, and as you progress in this course, you'll get better at reading journal articles in general.

What might you conclude from the "whiff of rosemary" study? As the table explains, the study appears to have strong construct validity. And, as needed to support a causal claim, the study really was an experiment with apparently strong internal validity. Although the study did not appear to use a generalizable sample of participants, researchers usually do not prioritize that in an experiment. Indeed, when it comes to external validity, there seems to be no strong reason to suspect that the cognitive skills of these 20 volunteers would respond in some special way to the rosemary odor, compared to a more representative sample of people.

Indeed, each validity addresses a different aspect of a study: The evidence it provides for a causal statement, the measurements used, the study's generalizability, and the statistical accuracy of its conclusions. Asking questions about each validity in turn is a good way to make sure you have considered all the important aspects of the study's quality.

For more on external validity, see Chapter 8, pp. 226–230; Chapter 10, pp. 298–300; and Chapter 14, pp. 424–437.

TABLE 3.7 **Applying the Four Validities to a Journalist's or Researcher's Claim**

Journalist's headline: Whiff of Rosemary Gives Your Brain a Boost

Type of claim: Causal claim (to "give a boost" is a causal verb phrase)

Validities to interrogate: All four, with less priority to external validity

Type of Validity	Information from the journalist (NBC News)	Information from the journal article in *Therapeutic Advances in Psychopharmacology*
Construct validity	**How well did the researchers manipulate "whiff of rosemary"?**	
	The journalist reports that "a cohort of 20 subjects were exposed to varying levels of the aroma."	The empirical journal article reports that participants were exposed to the Tisserand brand of rosemary essential oil by sitting in a cubicle with it for 4, 6, 8, or 10 minutes. This appears to be a straightforward manipulation of exposure to rosemary.
	How well did they measure "brain boost"?	
	The journalist reports that the participants were given a "battery of cognitive tests and mood" assessments.	The journal article describes three tasks, all of which seem to be tests of cognitive attention. For example, participants were shown a computerized stream of digits and were asked to press the space bar when they detected sequences of three consecutive odd or even numbers. This appears to be a reasonable measure of cognitive attention.
Statistical validity	**How large was the difference in cognitive performance between the different rosemary groups?**	
	Was the difference in cognitive performance between the different rosemary groups statistically significant?	
	The journalist does not mention how far apart the cognitive scores were. The journalist does not mention whether the difference was statistically significant.	The journal article reports that the more of the chemical 1.8 cineole was in each participant's blood (1.8 cineole is increased by rosemary oil), the better they did at the three cognitive tasks. The effect was large and statistically significant.
Internal validity	**Was it an experiment?**	
	Since the journalist reports that the participants were exposed to different amounts of the aroma and then given a battery of cognitive tests, you can assume that aroma was manipulated, so this was an experiment.	The journal article reports that participants were randomly assigned to the different lengths of exposure to essential oil, making this an experiment.

Type of Validity	Information from the journalist (NBC News)	Information from the journal article in *Therapeutic Advances in Psychopharmacology*
	Can they support temporal precedence and internal validity?	
	Temporal precedence: Since the rosemary aroma came first, and then the cognitive tests, the study did have temporal precedence.	
	Internal validity: Because this was an experiment, you can be reasonably sure that the groups differed only on the amount of rosemary aroma they were exposed to.	The journal article asserts that the groups were exactly the same on all variables except the amount of the aroma; there were no confounds (e.g., the different amounts of aroma were not confounded with time of day). Therefore, internal validity appears acceptable.
External validity	**Can you generalize from the 20 people in this sample to other kinds of people?**	
	The journalist does not indicate if the 20 people in this study were a representative sample or not. They probably were not randomly selected; however, when researchers conduct experiments to support causal claims, their priority is usually internal validity, not external validity.	The journal article reports that the 20 participants were healthy volunteers. They were not a random sample of a population; however, when researchers conduct experiments to support causal claims, their priority is usually internal validity, not external validity.
	Can you generalize from the aromas used in this study to other settings?	
	The subjects in this study smelled rosemary from essential oil. Does this exposure to rosemary generalize to smelling it from an actual rosemary plant? Would it generalize to smelling other sources of rosemary, such as rosemary baked into bread or into a pizza?	

Summary

- The three claims, four validities framework, providing the structure for the content of this textbook, enables you to systematically evaluate any study you read, in a journal article or a popular press story. It can also guide you in making choices for research you might conduct yourself.

Variables

- Variables, concepts of interest that vary, form the core of psychological research. A variable has at least two levels.
- Variables can be measured or manipulated.
- Variables in a study can be described in two ways: as conceptual variables (as elements of a theory) and as operational definitions (as specific measures or manipulations in order to study them).

Three Claims

- As a consumer of information, you will need to identify three types of claims that researchers, journalists, and other writers make: frequency, association, and causal claims.
- Frequency claims make arguments about the level of a single, measured variable in a group of people.
- Association claims argue that two measured variables are related to each other. An association can be positive, negative, or zero. When you know how two variables are associated, you can use one to predict the other.
- Causal claims state that one variable is responsible for changes in the other variable. To support a causal claim, a study must meet three criteria—covariance, temporal precedence, and internal validity—which is accomplished by experimentation.

Interrogating the Three Claims Using the Four Big Validities

- To interrogate a frequency claim, ask questions about the study's construct validity (the quality of the measurements), external validity (its generalizability to a larger population), and statistical validity (the degree of error in the percentage estimate).
- To interrogate an association claim, ask about its construct and external validity and also its statistical validity. Statistical validity addresses the strength of a research finding, and whether or not a finding is statistically significant. It also is the degree to which a study can minimize the probability of making a false positive conclusion or of missing a true effect.
- To interrogate a causal claim, ask whether the study conducted was an experiment, which is the only way to establish internal validity and temporal precedence. If it was an experiment, further assess internal validity by asking whether the study was designed with any confounds, and whether the researchers used random assignment for making participant groups. You can also ask about the study's construct, external, and conclusion validity.
- Because researchers cannot usually achieve all four validities at once in an experiment, they prioritize the validities. This situation is most common when researchers who want to make a causal claim emphasize internal validity: Their interest in making a causal statement means that they may sacrifice internal validity for some loss of external validity.

Key Terms

variable, p. 56
level, p. 56
constant, p. 56
measured variable, p. 56
manipulated variable, p. 57
conceptual variable, p. 57
construct, p. 57
conceptual definition, p. 57
operational definition, p. 57
operational variable, p. 57
operationalize, p. 57
claim, p. 60

frequency claim, p. 60
association claim, p. 61
correlate, p. 61
positive association, p. 62
scatterplot, p. 62
negative association, p. 62
zero association, p. 62
causal claim, p. 64
validity, p. 66
construct validity, p. 67
generalizability, p. 67
external validity, p. 67

statistical validity, p. 68
margin of error estimate, p. 68
correlational study, p. 68
Type I error, p. 70
Type II error, p. 70
covariance, p. 72
temporal precedence, p. 72
internal validity, p. 72
experiment, p. 73
independent variable, p. 73
dependent variable, p. 73
random assignment, p. 74

To see samples of chapter concepts in the popular press, visit
www.everydayresearchmethods.com and click the box for Chapter 3.

Review Questions

1. Which of the following variables is manipulated, rather than measured?
   a. Number of pairs of shoes owned, in pairs.
   b. A person's height, in cm.
   c. Amount of aspirin a researcher gives a person to take, either 325 mg or 500 mg.
   d. Degree of happiness, rated on a scale from 1 to 10.

2. Which of the following headlines is an association claim?
   a. Chewing gum can improve your mood and focus.
   b. Want to cheer up? Cheer harder. Hard-core sports fans show less depression.
   c. Swine flu shot tied to narcolepsy, study finds.
   d. Eating kiwis may help you fall asleep.

3. Which of the following headlines is a frequency claim?
   a. Obese kids less sensitive to tastes.
   b. Exercise: 45% of you shake your booty in Zumba.

   c. Feeling fat? Maybe Facebook is to blame.
   d. Daycare and behavior problems are not linked.

4. Which of the following headlines is a causal claim?
   a. Holding a gun may make you think others are, too.
   b. Younger people can't read emotions on wrinkled faces.
   c. Strange but true: Babies born in the autumn are more likely to live to 100.
   d. Check the baby! Many new moms show signs of OCD.

5. Which validity would you be interrogating by asking: How well did the researchers measure sensitivity to tastes in this study?
   a. Construct validity
   b. Statistical validity
   c. External validity
   d. Internal validity

6. Which validity would you be interrogating by asking: How did the researchers get their sample of people for this survey?
   a. Construct validity
   b. Statistical validity
   c. External validity
   d. Internal validity

7. In most experiments, trade-offs are made between validities because it is not possible to achieve all four at once. What is the most common trade-off?
   a. Internal and external validity
   b. Construct and statistical validity
   c. Statistical and internal validity
   d. External and statistical validity

Learning Actively

1. For each boldfaced variable below, indicate the variable's levels, whether the variable is measured or manipulated, and how you might describe the variable conceptually and operationally.

Variable in context	Conceptual variable	Levels of this variable	Measured or manipulated	Operational definition
A questionnaire study asks for various demographic information, including participants' **gender**.	Participant's gender	Male Female	Measured	Asking participants to circle "male" or "female" on a form
A questionnaire study asks about **self-esteem**, measured on a 10-item Rosenberg self-esteem scale.				
A study of readability gives people a passage of text. The passage to be read is printed in one of three **colors** (black, red, or blue).				
A study of **school achievement** requests each participant to report his or her SAT score, as a measure of college readiness.				
A researcher studying self-control and **blood glucose levels** asks participants to come to an experiment at 1:00 P.M. Some of them are told not to eat anything before the experiment; others are told to eat lunch before arriving.				
A professor who wants to know more about **study habits** among his students asks students to report the number of minutes they studied for the midterm exam.				
In a study on **self-esteem**'s association with self-control, the researchers give a group of students a self-esteem inventory. Then they invite participants who score in the top 10% and the bottom 10% of the self-esteem scale to participate in the next step.				

2. Imagine you encounter each of the following headlines. First, classify each headline as a frequency, association, or causal claim. Second, what questions would you ask if you wanted to understand more about the quality of the study behind the headline? For each of your questions, indicate which of the four validities your question is addressing. Follow the model in Table 3.7.
   a. Chewing gum can improve your mood and focus.
   b. Obese kids less sensitive to tastes.
   c. 45% of you shake your booty to Zumba.

3. Imagine you wanted to test the causal claim that "chewing gum can improve your mood and focus." How could you design an experiment to test this claim? What would the variables be? Would each be manipulated or measured? What results would you expect? Sketch a graph of the outcomes you would predict. Would your experiment fulfill the three criteria for supporting a causal statement?

PART II

Research Foundations
for Any Claim

**Respect
for Persons**

Beneficence

Justice

IF YOU'RE
HERE FOR
A PSYCH
STUDY GO
RIGHT TO
LOBBY...

4

Ethical Guidelines for Psychology Research

A year from now, you should still be able to:

1. Define the three ethical principles of the Belmont Report and describe how each one is applied. Recognize the similarities between the Belmont Report's principles and the five APA Ethical Principles.

2. Describe the procedures that are in place to protect human participants and animal subjects in research.

3. Articulate some of the ways that ethical decision making requires balancing priorities, such as research risks versus benefits, individual participants versus society, participation versus coercion.

No matter what type of claim researchers are investigating, they are obligated—by law, by morality, and by today's social norms—to treat the participants in their research with kindness, respect, and fairness. In the 21st century, researchers are bound to follow basic ethical principles in the treatment of humans and other animals. Researchers are also bound to produce research that is meaningful and helpful to society. How can we know when a study is conducted ethically? This chapter introduces the criteria for evaluating whether a set of research was conducted appropriately.

Historical Examples

In the past, researchers may have held different ideas about the ethical treatment of study participants. Two examples of research, one from medicine and one from psychology, follow. The first one clearly illustrates several ethics violations. The second illustrates the difficult balance of priorities researchers might face when evaluating a study's ethicality.

The Tuskegee Syphilis Study Illustrates Three Major Ethics Violations

In the late 1920s and early 1930s, people working with poor men in the southern United States were concerned that up to 35% of Black men living in the South were infected with syphilis. The disease was largely untreatable at the time, and it interfered with men's ability to work, contribute to society, and climb their way out of poverty. The available treatment involved infusions of toxic metals; when it worked at all, this method had serious—even fatal—side effects. In 1932, the U.S. Public Health Service (PHS), cooperating with the Tuskegee (Alabama) Institute, began a study of 600 Black men. About 400 of them were already infected with syphilis, and about 200 were not. The researchers wanted to study the effects of untreated syphilis on the men's health over the long term. At the time, not treating the men was a reasonable choice, because the risky treatments that were available in 1932 were unlikely to work (Jones, 1993). The men were recruited in their community churches and schools, and many of them were enthusiastic about participating in a project that would allow them access to medical care for the first time in their lives (Reverby, 2009). However, there is little evidence that the men were told the study was actually about syphilis.

Early in the project, the researchers decided to follow the men infected with syphilis until each one had died, to obtain valuable data on how the disease progresses when untreated. The study lasted 40 years, during which the researchers made a long series of ethically questionable choices (**Figure 4.1**). The men were not informed they had syphilis; they were told they had "bad blood." The researchers told them they were being treated, and all of them were required to come to the Tuskegee clinic for evaluation and testing. But they were never given any beneficial treatment. At one point, in fact, the researchers had to conduct a painful, potentially dangerous spinal tap procedure on every participant in order

FIGURE 4.1 The Tuskegee Syphilis Study. A doctor takes a blood sample from a participant. What ethically questionable decisions were made by the researchers who conducted the Tuskegee Syphilis Study?

to follow the progression of the disease. To ensure that they would come in for the procedure, the researchers lied, telling the men that the procedure was a "special free treatment" for their illness (Jones, 1993).

As the project continued, 250 of the men registered for the U.S. Armed Forces, which were then engaged in World War II. As part of the draft process, the men were diagnosed (again) with syphilis and told to reenlist after they had been treated. Instead of following these instructions, however, the researchers interfered by preventing the men from being treated. As a result, they could not serve in the armed forces or receive subsequent G.I. benefits (Final Report of the Tuskegee Study Ad Hoc Advisory Panel, 1973).

In 1943, the PHS approved the use of penicillin for treating syphilis, yet the Tuskegee Institute did not provide information about this new cure to the participants in their study. In 1969, PHS employee Peter Buxtun raised concerns with officials at the CDC. However, the researchers decided to proceed as before. The study continued until 1972, when Buxtun told the story to the Associated Press (Gray, 1998; Heller, 1972). Over the years, many men got sicker, and dozens died. Several men inadvertently infected their wives, in some cases causing congenital syphilis in their children (Jones, 1993; Reverby, 2009).

FIGURE 4.2 **An official apology in 1997.** The U.S. government issued an apology to survivors of the Tuskegee Syphilis Study.

In 1974, the families of the participants reached a settlement in a lawsuit against the U.S. government. In 1997, President Bill Clinton formally apologized to the survivors on behalf of the nation (**Figure 4.2**). Nonetheless, the Tuskegee Syphilis Study has contributed to an unfortunate legacy. As a result of this study, some African Americans are suspicious of government health services and research participation (McCallum, Arekere, Green, Katz, & Rivers, 2007).

Three Kinds of Ethics Violations

The researchers conducting this infamous study made a number of choices that are ethically questionable from today's perspective. Later writers have identified these choices as falling into three distinct categories (Childress, Meslin, & Shapiro, 2005; Gray, 1998). First, the men were *not treated respectfully*. The researchers lied to them about the nature of their participation, and withheld information (such as penicillin as a cure for the disease); in so doing, they did not give the men a chance to provide full, informed consent for participating in the study. If they had known in advance the true nature of the study, some might still have consented to participate, but others might not. After the men died, the doctors offered a generous burial fee to the families, but mainly so they could be sure of studying the men via autopsy. These low-income families may have felt coerced into agreeing to an autopsy only because of the large payment.

Second, the men in the study were *harmed*. They were not told about a treatment for a disease that, in the later years of the study, could be easily cured. (Many of the men were illiterate and thus unable to learn about the penicillin cure on their own.) They were also subjected to painful and dangerous tests. Third, the researchers *targeted a disadvantaged social group* in this study. Syphilis affects people from all ethnicities and social backgrounds, yet all the men in this study were poor and African American (Gray, 1998; Jones, 1993).

The Milgram Obedience Studies Illustrate an Ethical Balance

The Tuskegee Syphilis Study provides several clear examples of ethics violations, but decisions about ethical matters are not always so clear. Social psychologist Stanley Milgram's series of studies on obedience to authority, conducted in the early 1960s, illustrates some of the difficulties of ethical decision making.

Imagine yourself as a participant in one of Milgram's studies. You are told that there will be two participants: you, the "teacher," and another participant, the "learner." As teacher, your job is to punish the learner when he makes mistakes in a learning task. The learner slips into a cubicle where you cannot see him, and the session begins (Milgram, 1963, 1974).

As the study goes on, you are told to punish the learner for errors by administering electric shocks at increasingly higher intensities, as indicated on an imposing piece of equipment in front of you: the "shock generator." At first, while receiving the low-voltage shocks, the learner does not complain. But he keeps making mistakes on a word association test he is supposed to be learning, and you are required by the rules of the study to deliver shocks that are 15 volts higher after each mistake (**Figure 4.3**). As the voltage is increased, the learner begins to grunt with pain. At about 120 volts, the learner shouts that the shocks are very painful and says he wants to quit the experiment. At 300 volts, the learner screams that he will no longer respond to the memory task; he stops responding. The experimenter, sitting behind you in a white lab coat, tells you to keep delivering shocks to the man—15 volts more each time, until the machine indicates you're delivering 450-volt shocks. Whereas before the learner screamed in pain with each new shock,

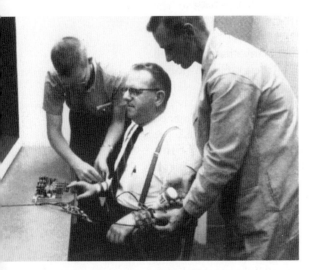

FIGURE 4.3 **The Milgram obedience studies.** In one version, the "experimenter" (right) and the true participant (left) help connect the "learner" to the electrodes that would supposedly shock him. Was it ethical for the researchers to invent this elaborate situation, which ultimately caused participants so much stress?

after 300 volts you now hear nothing from him. You cannot tell whether he is even conscious in his cubicle.

If you protest (and you probably do), the experimenter behind you says calmly, "Continue." If you protest again, the experimenter says, again calmly, "The experiment requires that you continue," or even, "You have no choice, you must go on." What would you do now?

You may believe you would have refused to obey the demands of this inhumane experimenter. However, in the original study, about 65% of the participants followed the experimenter's demands and delivered the 450-volt shock to the learner. Only two or three participants (out of hundreds) refused to give even the first, 15-volt shock. Virtually all participants subjected another person to one or more electric shocks—or at least they thought they did. Fortunately, the learner was actually a confederate of the experimenter; he was a paid actor playing a role, and he did not in fact receive any shocks. The participants did not know this; they thought the learner was an innocent, friendly man.

Milgram conducted 18 or more variations of this study. In each variation, 40 new participants were asked to deliver painful shocks to the learner. In one variation, the learner mentioned that he had a heart condition; this made no difference, and the level of obedience remained at about 65%. In another variation, Milgram changed laboratory locations, from his original Yale University lab to a seedy storefront in Bridgeport, Connecticut. This change also made no difference; the level of obedience for the full study stayed at about 65%. In one other variation, the learner sat right in the room with the teacher-participant; in this condition, obedience dropped to 40%. Another time, the experimenter supervised the situation from down the hall, giving his instructions ("Continue," "The experiment requires that you continue") over the phone. In this condition, the obedience level also dropped, and only 20% of participants delivered all the shocks.

Ethical Questions

Was Milgram acting ethically when he conducted this series of studies? Writers have pointed to two sources of ethical concern. First, the study itself was extremely stressful to the teacher-participants (Baumrind, 1964). Milgram relayed an observation by one of his research assistants:

> I observed a mature and initially poised businessman enter the laboratory smiling and confident. Within 20 minutes he was reduced to a twitching, nervous wreck, who was rapidly approaching a point of nervous collapse. He constantly pulled on his earlobe, and twisted his hands. At one point he pushed his fist into his forehead and muttered, "Oh, God, let's stop it." And yet he continued to respond to every word of the experimenter, and obeyed to the very end. (Milgram, 1963, p. 377)

Was it ethical of Milgram to put unsuspecting volunteers through such a stressful experience?

FIGURE 4.4 Balancing ethical concerns. In one version, participants were required to force the learner's arm onto a (fake) electric plate. How do you balance potential harm to participants with the benefits of knowledge in the Milgram obedience studies?

The second ethical question concerns the lasting effects of the study (Baumrind, 1964). In an interview after the study, the participants were **debriefed**; they were carefully informed about the study's hypotheses, and they were introduced to the (unharmed) learner. However, despite the careful debriefing process, some participants were dramatically affected by learning that they were willing to harm another human being, simply because someone in authority told them to do it (Perry, 2013). Even though the debriefing probably lessened their initial feelings of stress, the sense that they may have harmed someone stuck with some for a long time (**Figure 4.4**).

According to Milgram, most of his participants reported that they felt they had learned something important and valuable about themselves. Milgram hired a psychiatrist to interview participants months later about their current state of well-being. Most of them said they were not suffering from the experience, and some still felt they had learned something important. For example, one participant reported: "What appalled me was that I could possess this capacity for obedience and compliance. . . . I hope I can deal more effectively with future conflicts of values I encounter" (Milgram, 1974, p. 54).

Balancing Risk to Participants with Benefit to Society

At first, the results of the Milgram studies—65% obedience—surprised even Milgram himself, he claimed (Milgram, 1974). Experts at the time predicted that only 1–2% of people would obey the experimenter up to 450 volts. After the first variation of the study, however, Milgram knew what kind of behavior to expect, and he had already seen firsthand the stress the participants were going through. Once he knew that many of the people in the study would have anxiety and stress, Milgram might have taken steps to stop, or modify, the procedure, and yet he did not.

Some writers, both at the time and more recently, have found Milgram's choices unethical (e.g., Baumrind, 1964; Perry, 2013). Other psychologists, in contrast, have pointed out that Milgram's studies contributed crucial lessons about obedience to authority and the "power of the situation"—lessons we would not have learned without his research (Blass, 2002). Thus, we are faced with a fundamental conundrum in deciding whether this research is ethical. We try to balance the potential *risks to participants* and *the value of the knowledge* we can gain. In cases like the Milgram studies, it is not an easy decision.

1. What three categories of ethics violations are illustrated by the Tuskegee Syphilis Study?

2. What are two primary concerns that have been raised against the Milgram obedience studies? How did Milgram and his supporters counter these concerns?

1. See pp. 91–92. 2. See pp. 93–94.

Core Ethical Principles

Organizations around the world have developed formal statements of ethics. Following World War II, the Nuremberg Trials revealed the horror of medical experiments conducted on concentration camp victims in Nazi-occupied Europe, and resulted in the Nuremberg Code. Although it is not a formal law in any nation, the ten-point Nuremberg Code influences the ethical research laws of many countries (Shuster, 1997). In addition, many national leaders have signed the Declaration of Helsinki, which guides ethics in medical research and practice. Within the United States, ethical systems are also based on the Belmont Report, which defines the ethical guidelines researchers should follow. All of these ethical statements are grounded in the same core principles.

The Belmont Report: Principles and Applications

In 1976, a commission of physicians, ethicists, philosophers, scientists, and other citizens gathered at the Belmont Conference Center in Eldridge, Maryland, at the request of the U.S. Congress. They had been called together for an intensive discussion of basic ethical principles researchers should follow when conducting research with human participants. The commission was called partly in response to the egregious ethics violations of the Tuskegee Syphilis Study (Jonsen, 2005). The contributors produced a short document called the Belmont Report, which outlines three main principles for guiding ethical decision making: respect for persons, beneficence, and justice. The guidelines are intended for use in many disciplines, including medicine, sociology, anthropology, and basic biological research, as well as psychology.

The Principle of Respect for Persons

In the Belmont Report, the **principle of respect for persons** includes two provisions. First, individuals participating in research should be treated as autonomous agents: They should be free to make up their own minds about whether they wish to participate in a research study. Applying this principle means that every participant is entitled to the precaution of **informed consent**: each person learns about the research project, knows the risks and benefits, and decides whether to participate. In obtaining informed consent, researchers are not allowed to mislead people about the study's risks and benefits. Nor may they coerce or unduly influence a person into participating in research; doing so would violate the principle of respect for persons. Coercion occurs when researchers explicitly or implicitly suggest that those who do not participate will suffer a negative consequence (e.g., a professor implying that students' grades will be lower if they do not participate in a particular study). Undue influence occurs when researchers offer an incentive too attractive to refuse (e.g., an irresistible amount of money in exchange for participating). The report notes that financially poor individuals may be more easily swayed into participating if a research study provides a large payment.

The second provision of respect for persons states that some people have less autonomy, so they are entitled to special protection when it comes to informed consent. For example, children, people with intellectual or developmental disabilities, and prisoners should be protected, according to the Belmont Report. Children and certain other individuals may not be able to give informed consent because they might not understand the procedures involved well enough to make informed choices (**Figure 4.5**). Prisoners are especially susceptible to coercion, according to the Belmont Report, because they may perceive requests to participate in research as demands, rather than as invitations. All these populations should be treated with special consideration.

FIGURE 4.5 Vulnerable populations in research. Why might children be considered a vulnerable population that requires special ethical consideration?

The Principle of Beneficence

To comply with the **principle of beneficence**, researchers must take precautions to protect research participants from harm and to ensure their well-being. Researchers need to carefully assess the risks and benefits of the research they plan to conduct. In addition to considering the potential benefits and risks to the study participants, they must also consider others who might benefit or be harmed. Will a community gain something of value from the knowledge this research is producing? Will there be costs to a community if this research is not conducted?

The Tuskegee Syphilis Study failed to treat the participants in accordance with the principle of beneficence. The researchers harmed participants through risky and invasive medical tests, and they harmed the participants' families by exposing them to untreated syphilis. The researchers also withheld benefits from the men in the study. Today, researchers may not withhold treatments that are known to be helpful to study participants. For example, if a researcher discovers halfway through a study that a treatment is proving to be advantageous for an experimental group, the researcher must give the participants in the control group the opportunity to receive that treatment, too.

Harm and benefit are generally easy to assess when it comes to physical health, the type measured in medical research. Is a person's health getting worse or better? Is the community going to be healthier because of this research, or not? In contrast, some psychological studies can expose participants to emotional or psychological harm, such as anxiety, stress, depression, or cognitive strain, and these may be harder to assess.

Consider the participants in the Milgram studies, who were clearly experiencing stress. How might you quantify the harm done in this situation? Would you measure the way participants felt at that time? Would you ask how they felt about it a year later? Would you measure what they say about their own stress, or what an observer would say? Just as it's hard to quantify emotional or psychological harm, it is difficult to evaluate how damaging a study like Milgram's might be. However, the principle of beneficence demands that researchers consider such risks (and benefits) before beginning each study. As a point of reference, some institutions ask researchers to estimate how stressful a study's situation is compared with the normal stresses of everyday life.

The other side of the balance—the benefits of psychological research to the community—may not be easy to assess, either. One could argue that Milgram's results are valuable, but their value is impossible to quantify in terms of lives or dollars saved. Nevertheless, to apply the principle of beneficence, researchers must attempt to predict the risks and benefits of their research—both to participants and to the larger community.

The Principle of Justice

The **principle of justice** calls for a fair balance between the kinds of people who participate in research and the kinds of people who benefit from it. For example, if a research study discovers that a procedure is risky or harmful, the participants, unfortunately, "bear the burden" of that risk, while other people—those not in the study—are able to benefit from the research results (Kimmel, 2007). The Tuskegee Syphilis Study illustrates a violation of this principle of justice: Anybody, regardless of race or income, can contract syphilis, but the participants in the study—who bore the burden of untreated syphilis—were all poor, African American men. Therefore, even though the researchers originally intended to help this population, the participants bore an undue burden of risk.

When the principle of justice is applied, it means that researchers might first ensure that the participants involved in a study are representative of the kinds of people who would also benefit from its results. If researchers decide to study a sample from only one ethnic group, or only a sample of institutionalized individuals, they must demonstrate that the problem they are studying is especially prevalent in that ethnic group or in that type of institution. For example, it might violate the justice principle if researchers studied a group of prisoners mainly because they were convenient. However, it might be perfectly acceptable to study only institutionalized people for a study on tuberculosis, for example, because tuberculosis is particularly prevalent in institutions, where people live together in a somewhat confined area.

Ethical Principles in Practice

The ethical principles of the Belmont Report must be interpreted in order to be used. Just as panels of judges interpret a country's laws, panels of people interpret the guidelines in the Belmont Report (Jonsen, 2005). Most universities and research hospitals have committees who decide whether research and practice are complying with ethical guidelines. In the United States, federally funded agencies must follow the common rule, which describes detailed ways the Belmont Report should be applied in research (U.S. Department of Health and Human Services, 2009). For example, it explains informed consent procedures and ways to approve research before it is conducted.

CHECK YOUR UNDERSTANDING

1. Name and describe the three main principles of the Belmont Report.
2. Each principle in the Belmont Report has a particular application. For example, the principle of respect for persons has its application in the informed consent process. What are the applications of the other two principles?

---

1. See p. 95 for principles and pp. 95–98 for definitions. 2. See pp. 96–97.

Guidelines for Psychologists: The APA Ethical Principles

In addition to the Belmont Report, local policies, and federal laws, American psychologists can consult another layer of ethical principles and standards written by the American Psychological Association (2002), the Ethical Principles of Psychologists and Code of Conduct (**Figure 4.6**). This set of guidelines governs the three most common roles of psychologists: research scientists, educators, and practitioners (usually as therapists). Psychological associations in other countries have similar codes of ethics, and other professions have codes of ethics as well (Kimmel, 2007).

Five General Ethical Principles

The APA outlines five general principles for guiding individual aspects of ethical behavior. These principles are intended to protect not only research participants,

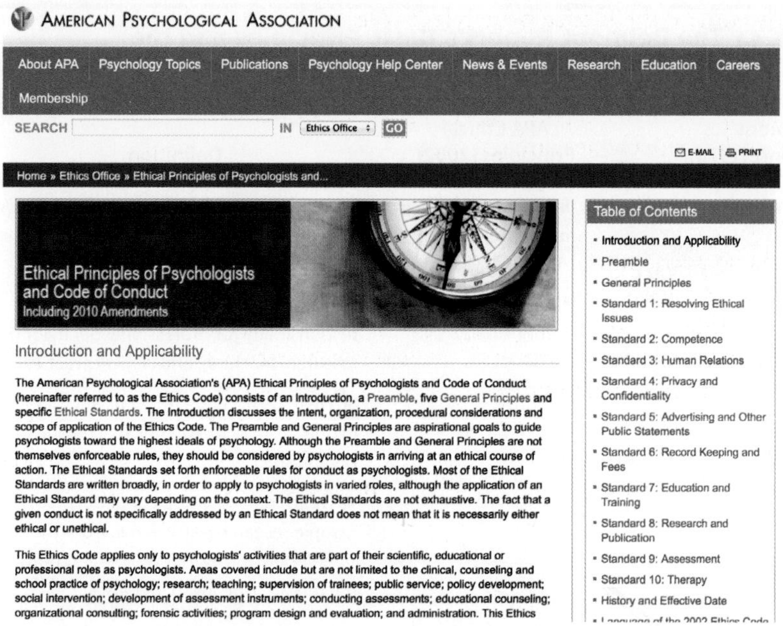

FIGURE 4.6 **The APA website.** The full text of the APA's ethical principles can be found on the website.

but also students in psychology classes and clients of professional psychologists. As you can see in **Table 4.1**, three of the APA principles are identical to the three main principles of the Belmont Report (beneficence, justice, and respect for persons). The other two are integrity (e.g., professors are obligated to teach you accurately, and therapists are required to stay up-to-date on the empirical evidence for therapeutic techniques) and fidelity and responsibility (e.g., a clinical psychologist who teaches in a university may not serve as a therapist to one of his or her classroom students, and psychologists must avoid sexual relationships with their students or clients).

Ten Specific Ethical Standards

In addition to the five general principles, the APA lists ten specific ethical standards. These standards are similar to enforceable rules or laws. Psychologist members of the APA who violate any of these standards can lose their professional license or may be disciplined in some other way by the association.

Of the ten ethical standards, Ethical Standard 8 is the one most relevant in a research methods book; it is written specifically for psychologists in their role as researchers. (The other standards are more relevant to their roles as therapists, consultants, and teachers.) Ethical Standard 8 is reprinted on pp. 116–119. You will notice that some of them are familiar (e.g., informed consent, Standard 8.02, and protection of vulnerable groups, Standard 8.04), but some deserve more explanation. The next sections outline the details of the APA's Ethical Standard 8, noting how they work together with other layers of guidance a researcher must follow.

TABLE 4.1 The Belmont Report's Basic Principles and the APA's Five General Principles Compared

Belmont Report (1979)	APA Ethical Principles (2002)	Definition
Beneficence	**A. Beneficence and nonmaleficence**	Treat people in ways that benefit them. Do not cause suffering. Conduct research that will benefit society.
	B. Fidelity and responsibility	Establish relationships of trust; accept responsibility for professional behavior (in research, teaching, and clinical practice).
	C. Integrity	Strive to be accurate, truthful, and honest in one's role as researcher, teacher, or practitioner.
Justice	**D. Justice**	Strive to treat all groups of people fairly. Sample research participants from the same populations that will benefit from the research. Be aware of biases.
Respect for persons	**E. Respect for people's rights and dignity**	Recognize that people are autonomous agents. Protect people's rights, including the right to privacy, the right to give consent for treatment or research, and the right to have participation treated confidentially. Understand that some populations may be less able to give autonomous consent, and take precautions against coercing such people.

Note: The principles in boldface are shared by both documents and specifically involve the treatment of human participants in research. The APA guidelines are broader; they apply not only to how psychologists conduct research, but also to how they teach and conduct clinical practice.

The website of the APA Ethics Office provides the full text of the APA's ethics documents. If you are considering becoming a therapist or counselor someday, you may find it interesting to read the other ethical standards that are written specifically for practitioners.

Institutional Review Boards (Standard 8.01)

An **institutional review board (IRB)** is a committee responsible for interpreting ethical principles and ensuring that research using human participants is conducted ethically. Most colleges and universities, as well as hospitals and other institutions that conduct research, have an IRB. In the United States, IRBs are mandated by federal laws. If an institution conducts research using federal money (such as research grants from the government), then a designated IRB is required.

An IRB panel in the U.S. includes at least five people, some of whom must come from specified backgrounds. At least one member must be a scientist, one has to have academic interests outside the sciences, and one (or more) should be a community member who has no ties to the institution (such as a local pastor, a community leader, or an interested citizen). In addition, when the IRB discusses a proposal to use prison participants, one member must be recruited as a designated prisoner advocate. The IRB must consider particular questions for any research involving children. IRBs in most other countries follow similar mandates for their composition.

At regular meetings, the IRB reviews proposals from individual scientists. Before conducting a study, researchers must fill out a detailed application describing their study, its risks and benefits (both to participants and to society), its procedures for informed consent, and its provisions for protecting people's privacy—even describing how and for how long the data will be stored. Researchers must demonstrate to the IRB that they have taken all appropriate safeguards for their participants' welfare. The IRB then reviews each application. Different IRBs have different procedures. In some universities, when a study is judged to be of little or no risk (such as a completely anonymous questionnaire), the IRB might not meet to discuss it in person. In most institutions, though, any study that poses risks to humans or that involves vulnerable populations must be reviewed by an in-person IRB meeting.

In many cases, IRB oversight provides a neutral, multiperspective judgment on any study's ethicality. An effective IRB should not permit research that violates people's rights, research that poses unreasonable risk, or research that lacks a sound rationale. However, an effective IRB should not obstruct valuable research, either. It should not prevent controversial—but still ethical—research questions from being investigated. In the ideal case, the IRB attempts to balance the welfare of research participants against the researcher's goal of contributing important knowledge to the field.

Informed Consent (Standard 8.02)

As mentioned earlier, informed consent is the researcher's obligation to explain the study to potential participants in everyday language, and give them a chance to decide whether to participate. In most studies, informed consent is obtained by providing a written document that outlines the procedures, risks, and benefits of the research, including a statement about any treatments that are experimental (**Figure 4.7**). Everyone who wishes to participate signs two copies of the document—one for the researcher to store, and one for the participant to take home.

In certain circumstances, the APA standards (and other federal laws that govern research) indicate that informed consent procedures are not necessary (see Standard 8.05, Dispensing with Informed Consent for Research). Specifically, researchers may not need to have participants sign informed consent forms if the study is not likely to cause harm and if it takes place in an educational setting.

Certificate of Informed Consent

Title of study: Group Decision Making Processes
Investigators: Matthew Deegan, Dr. Sam Gaertner

In this study you will be asked to work on a group task so that we can investigate group decision making processes. In addition to working on these group tasks you will be asked to complete questionnaires regarding your perceptions of these group interactions and to complete a learning task involving categorizing words on a computer screen. You may also be asked to complete additional attitudes questionnaires unrelated to this study.

Risks and Benefits: Your responses will be kept confidential, and all experiment data will be linked to your identity only via a unique 4-digit ID number. The link between participant names and ID numbers will be stored on an encrypted, password-protected, hard drive and a hard copy will be stored in a locked filing cabinet, as such there is a risk of a possible breach in confidentiality. Your data will be kept for a minimum of five years. One benefit that you may gain by participating is an increased knowledge of the way research is conducted in psychology.

Contacts: If you have any questions about the procedures used in this experiment, please contact Samuel Gaertner, Professor, Department of Psychology (831-2268). If you have questions about your rights as a subject or about any issues concerning the use of human subjects in research, please contact the Chair, Human Subjects Review Board at 302-831-2137.

Participation: Participation in this research is voluntary. You are free to withdraw from the experiment at any time without penalty. If you elect not to participate or withdraw your participation before the completion of the study, you will be required to write a paper summarizing one of the articles available from the subject pool website in the place of participation. Links to these articles are available at: http://fleen.psych.udel.edu/studenthomepage.php

For completing the experiment you will receive one hour of research credit.

Please keep your copy of this document of informed consent, so that you have proof you participated in the study today, should there be any questions in the future regarding your participation.

Age Requirement: You must be at least 18 years of age to participate in this study. By signing below you are indicating that you meet this age requirement. By signing below, you are also indicating that the project for which you have appeared has been explained to you and that you agree to participate.

Date: ______/______/______

Name- (print): ______________________________
Signature:______________________________
Age: _____

Please check the appropriate line:

_____ I choose to participate in this study _____ I choose not to participate in the study

FIGURE 4.7 Informed consent. This is an informed consent form for a study conducted by the author's colleagues at the University of Delaware.

Written informed consent might not be needed when participants answer a completely anonymous questionnaire, in which their answers are not linked to their names in any way. Written consent forms may not be required when the study involves naturalistic observation of participants in low-risk public settings, such as a museum, classroom, or mall—where people can reasonably expect to be observed by others anyway. The individual institution's regulations determine whether written informed consent is necessary in such situations. Such studies still must be approved by an IRB; however, the IRB will allow the researcher to proceed without obtaining formal, written consent forms from every participant. Nevertheless, researchers are always ethically obligated to inform participants of their rights.

According to Ethical Standard 8 (and most other ethical guidelines), obtaining informed consent also involves informing people whether the data they provide in a research study will be treated as private and confidential. Nonconfidential data might put participants at some risk. For example, in the course of research people might report on their health status, political attitudes, test scores, or study habits—information they might not want others to know. Therefore, informed consent procedures ordinarily outline which parts of the data are confidential and which, if any, are not. If data are to be treated as confidential, researchers agree to remove names and other identifiers. Such things as handwriting, birthdays, or photographs might reveal personal data, and researchers must be careful to protect that information if they have promised to do so. At many institutions, confidentiality procedures are not optional. Many institutions require researchers to store any identifiable data in a locked area or on secure computers.

Deception (Standard 8.07)

You may have read about psychological research in which the researchers lied to participants. Consider some of the studies you've learned about in your psychology courses. In the Milgram studies described earlier, the participants did not know the learner was not really being shocked. In another study, an experimental confederate posed as a thief, stealing money from a person's bag while an unsuspecting bystander sat reading at a table (**Figure 4.8**). In some versions of this study, the "thief," the "victim," and a third person who sat calmly nearby, pretending to read, were all experimental confederates. That makes three confederates and a fake crime—all in one study (Shaffer, Rogel, & Hendrick, 1975).

FIGURE 4.8 Deception in research. A study on bystander action staged a theft at a library table.

Even in the most straightforward study, participants may not be told about all the comparison conditions. For example, participants might have been aware they are writing in a booklet with a red cover, but they did not know the covers of other participants' booklets were green or gray (Elliot et al., 2007). All these studies contained an element of **deception**: Researchers withheld some details of the study from participants—deception through *omission*; in some cases, they actively lied to them—deception through *commission*.

Consider how these studies might have turned out if there had been no such deception. Suppose the researchers had said, "We're going to see whether you're willing to help prevent a theft. Wait here. In a few moments, we will stage a theft and see what you do." Or "We want to know whether you make more mistakes because your test booklet has a scary red cover. Go!" Obviously, the data would be useless. Deceiving research participants by lying to them or by withholding information is, in many cases, necessary in order to obtain meaningful data.

Is deception ethical? Of course, lying to people seems to violate the principle of respect for persons. The principle of beneficence also applies: What are the ethical costs and benefits of doing the study with deception, compared with the ethical costs of not doing it this way? It is important to find out what kinds of situational factors influence people's willingness to report a theft. In achievement contexts, it is important to understand incidental factors that might affect performance. Because most people consider these questions important, some researchers argue that the gain in knowledge seems worth the cost of lying (temporarily) to the participants (Kimmel, 1998). Even then, the APA principles and federal guidelines require researchers to avoid using deceptive research designs except as a last resort, and to debrief participants after the study.

Despite such arguments, some psychologists believe that deception undermines people's trust in the research process and should never be used in a study design (Ortmann & Hertwig, 1997). Still others suggest that deception is acceptable under constrained circumstances (Bröder, 1998; Kimmel, 1998; Pittenger, 2002). Some researchers have studied how undergraduate students respond to participating in a study that uses deception. Such studies have concluded that students usually tolerate minor deception and even some discomfort or stress, considering them necessary parts of research. When students do find deception to be stressful, these negative effects are diminished when the researchers fully explain the deception in a debriefing session (Bröder, 1998; Sharpe, Adair, & Roese, 1992; Smith & Richardson, 1983).

Debriefing (Standard 8.08)

When researchers have used deception, they must spend time after the study debriefing each participant in a structured conversation. In a debriefing session, the researchers describe the nature of the deception and explain why it was necessary. Emphasizing the importance of their research, they attempt to restore an honest relationship with the participant. As part of the debriefing process, the researcher describes the design of the study, thereby giving the participant some insight about the nature of psychological science.

Although debriefing is considered essential for studies in which deception is used, nondeceptive studies normally include a debriefing session, too. At many universities, all student participants in research receive a written description of the study's goals and hypotheses, along with references for further reading. The intention is to make participation in research a worthwhile educational experience, so students can learn more about the research process in general, understand how their participation fits into the larger context of theory testing, and learn how their participation might benefit others. In debriefing sessions, researchers might also offer to share results with the participants. Even months after their participation, people can request a summary of the study's results.

Research Misconduct

Most discussions of ethical research focus on protection and respect for research participants, and rightly so. However, the publication process also involves ethical decision making. As an example, it is considered ethical to publish one's results. After participants have spent their time in a study, it is only fair to make the results known publicly for the benefit of society. Psychologists must also treat their data and their sources accurately.

Data Fabrication (Standard 8.10) and Data Falsification. Two forms of research misconduct are data fabrication and data falsification. **Data fabrication** occurs when, instead of recording what really happened in a study (or sometimes instead of running a study at all), researchers invent data that fit their hypotheses. **Data falsification** occurs when researchers influence the study's results, perhaps by selectively deleting observations from a data set or by influencing their research subjects to act in the hypothesized way.

A recent case exemplifies both of these breaches. In 2012, social psychologist Diederik Stapel was fired from his job as a professor at Tilburg University, in the Netherlands, because he fabricated data in dozens of his studies (Stapel Investigation, 2012). Three graduate students became suspicious of his actions and bravely informed their department head. Soon thereafter, committees at the three universities where he had worked began documenting years of fraudulent data collection by Stapel. In written statements, he admitted that at first, he changed occasional data points (data falsification), but that later he found himself typing in entire datasets to fit his and his students' hypotheses (data fabrication). The scientific journals that published his fraudulent data have retracted over 50 articles to date (**Figure 4.9**).

Creating fabricated or falsified data is not just unethical; it also has far-reaching consequences. Scientists use data to test their theories, and they can do so only if they know that previously reported data are true and accurate. When they fabricate data, they mislead others about the actual state of support for a theory. Fabricated data might inspire other researchers to spend time following a promising (but false) lead. They might lead researchers to be more confident in theories than they should be. If journalists unknowingly write about fabricated data, it might cause people to waste time on unsupported techniques or therapies.

For more on the theory-data cycle, see Chapter 1, pp. 9–13.

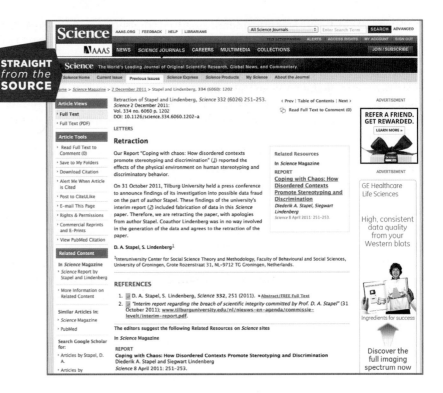

FIGURE 4.9 Fabricated and falsified data.
After admitting that he fabricated the data in over 50 published papers, each of Stapel's published articles is now presented with a formal statement of retraction, like this one in the journal *Science*.

In the case of Stapel, the fraud also cast a shadow over the careers of the graduate students and coauthors he worked with. Even though investigators declared that the collaborators did not know about or participate in the fabrication, Stapel's collaborators subsequently found many of their own published papers on the retraction list. The fraud even prompted some scientists to warn that Stapel's entire field, social psychology, has come under suspicion (Kahneman, 2012).

Why might a researcher fabricate or falsify data? In many universities, the reputations, income, and promotions of professors are based on their publications and their influence on the field. In such high-pressure circumstances, the temptation might be great to delete contradictory data or create supporting data. In addition, some researchers may simply be convinced of their own hypotheses and believe that any data that do not support their predictions must be inaccurate. Writing about his first experience, Stapel said: "I changed an unexpected 2 into a 4 . . . I looked at the [office] door. It was closed. When I saw the new results, the world had returned to being logical" (quoted in Borsboom & Wagenmakers, 2013). Unethical scientists may manipulate their data to coincide with their intuition rather than with formal observations, as a true empiricist would.

For a review of the quality of different sources of information, see Chapter 2, pp. 39–49 and Figure 2.8.

When the colleagues or students of a researcher in the U.S. suspect such misconduct, they may report it to the scientist's institution. If the research project is federally funded, suspected misconduct can be reported to the Office of Research Integrity, a branch of the Department of Health and Human Services, which then has the obligation to investigate.

Plagiarism (Standard 8.11). Another form of research misconduct is **plagiarism**, usually defined as representing the ideas or words of others as one's own. A formal definition, provided by the U.S. Office of Science and Technology Policy, states that plagiarism is "the appropriation of another person's ideas, processes, results, or words without giving appropriate credit" (Federal Register, 2000). Academics and researchers consider plagiarism a violation of ethics because it is unfair for a researcher to take credit for another person's intellectual property: It is a form of stealing.

To avoid plagiarism, a writer must cite the sources of all ideas that are not his or her own, to give appropriate credit to the original authors. There are many acceptable formats. Psychologists usually follow the style guidelines for citations in the *Publication Manual of the American Psychological Association* (APA, 2010). Specifically, when a writer describes or paraphrases another person's ideas, the writer must cite the original author's last name and the year of publication. When quoting (or very closely paraphrasing) another person's ideas, the writer puts quotation marks around the quoted text and indicates the page number where the quotation appeared in the original source. Complete source citations are included in the References section of the publication for all quoted or paraphrased works (**Figure 4.10**). (For an abbreviated version of the APA guidelines, see Presenting Results at the end of this book.)

---

palled me was that I could possess this capacity for obedience and compliance. . . . I hope I can deal more effectively with future conflicts of values I encounter" (Milgram, 1974, p. 54).

Balancing Risk to Participants with Benefit to Society

At first, the results of the Milgram studies—65% obedience—surprised even Milgram himself, he claimed (Milgram, 1974). Experts at the time predicted that only 1–2% of people would obey the experimenter up to 450 volts. After the first variation of the study, however, Milgram knew what kind of behavior to expect, and he had already seen firsthand the stress the participants were going through. Once he knew that many of the people in the study would have anxiety and stress, Milgram might have taken steps to stop, or modify, the procedure, and yet he did not.

References

Milgram, S. (1974). *Obedience to authority*. New York: Harper & Row.

FIGURE 4.10 Acknowledging sources. This textbook cites sources in APA style. Within the text, the source of ideas is acknowledged with the author's last name and year of publication. Direct quotes require quotation marks and a page number as well. Full bibliographic information is presented in the references.

Plagiarism is a serious offense—not only in published work by professional researchers, but also in papers students submit for college courses. Every university and college has plagiarism policies that prohibit students from copying the words or ideas of others without proper credit. Students who plagiarize in their academic work are subject to disciplinary action—including expulsion, in some cases.

Animal Research (Standard 8.09)

Psychologists do not study only human participants. Indeed, in some branches of psychology, research is conducted almost entirely on animal subjects: rats, mice, cockroaches, sea snails, dogs, rabbits, cats, chimpanzees, and others. The ethical debates surrounding animal research can be just as complex as those for human participants. Many people have a profound respect for animals and compassion for their well-being. Most people—psychologists and nonpsychologists alike—want to protect animals from undue suffering.

Legal Protection for Laboratory Animals. In Standard 8.09, the APA lists ethical points for the care of animals in research laboratories. Psychologists who use animals in research must care for them humanely, must use as few animals as possible, and must be sure their research is valuable enough to justify the use of animals.

In addition to these APA standards, psychologists must follow federal and local laws for animals care and protection. In the United States, for example, animals in research are also protected by government oversight. The Animal Welfare Act (AWA) outlines standards and guidelines for the treatment of animals (Animal Welfare Act, 1966 and later). The AWA applies not only to many species of animals in research laboratories, but also to animals in pet stores, agriculture, and even zoos and circuses.

The AWA mandates that each institution at which animal research takes place must have a local board called the Institutional Animal Care and Use Committee (IACUC, pronounced "EYE-a-kuk"). Similar to an IRB, the IACUC must approve any animal research project before it can begin (Animal Welfare Act, 1966 and later). Also like an IRB, the IACUC must comply with federal guidelines. It must contain at least three members: a veterinarian, a practicing scientist who is familiar with the goals and procedures of animal research, and a member of the community at large who is unconnected with the institution. The IACUC requires researchers to submit an extensive protocol that specifies how animals will be used, what will happen to each one, what precautions researchers plan to take to minimize animal distress (such as anesthetics or analgesics), and if and how the animals will be euthanized at the end of the study. The IACUC application also includes the scientific justification for the research: Applicants must demonstrate that the proposed study has not already been done, and explain why the research is important. Curiosity is not enough.

After approving a research project, the IACUC monitors the care and treatment of animals throughout the research process. It inspects the labs every 6 months. If a laboratory violates a procedure outlined in the proposal, the IACUC or a government agency can stop the experiment, shut the lab down, or discontinue government funding for the laboratory. If violations are severe enough, the government can choose to withdraw all federal funds from the entire university or institution. In short, in the U.S., animal care and treatment are enforced quite rigorously by clear guidelines and by federal and local oversight. In European countries and Canada, similar laws apply.

Animal Care Guidelines and the Three R's. Animal researchers in the United States, along with IACUC committees, use the resources of the *Guide for the Care and Use of Laboratory Animals*, which focuses on the "three R's": replacement, refinement, and reduction (National Research Council, 2011).

- *Replacement* means researchers should find alternatives to animals in research when necessary. For example, some studies can use computer simulations instead of animal subjects.
- *Refinement* means researchers must modify experimental procedures and other aspects of animal care to minimize or eliminate animal distress.
- *Reduction* means researchers should adopt experimental designs and procedures that require the fewest animal subjects possible.

In addition, the manual provides guidelines for housing facilities, diet, and other specifics of animal care in research. For example, it specifies that nonhuman primates be housed in enclosures that are wide and tall enough to accommodate these species' normal activities, and requires that primates be housed in social groups; members of this species do not thrive when isolated. The guide also specifies cage sizes, temperature and humidity ranges, air quality, lighting and noise conditions, and sanitation procedures, and makes suggestions for toys, bedding, and other enrichments.

Attitudes of Scientists and Students Toward Animal Research. In surveys, the majority of students and psychologists support the use of animals in research (Plous, 1996a). However, many students report being unsure about whether laboratory animals are treated humanely. For the most part, student and psychologist samples say they support monitoring the pain of animals in research and support the federal regulations that protect the well-being of primates used in studies (Plous, 1996b).

In addition, having conducted a survey of 494 active animal researchers, Plous and Herzog (2000) reported that the vast majority of them supported extending the AWA's protections to laboratory mice, rats, and birds. (Current versions of the AWA protect primates, dogs, cats, hamsters, guinea pigs, and rabbits.) Although somewhat dated, these surveys suggest that animal researchers are in favor of protecting their animals from pain. They support the promotion of animal *welfare*.

Attitudes of Animal Rights Groups. Since the mid-1970s in the United States, some groups have increased their visibility and have assumed a more extreme po-

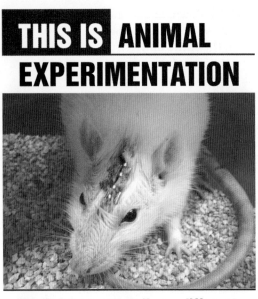

THIS IS ANIMAL EXPERIMENTATION

Don't let anyone tell you different.

P*e*TA

FIGURE 4.11 A poster opposing animal research.

sition—arguing for animal rights, rather than animal welfare (**Figure 4.11**). Groups such as People for the Ethical Treatment of Animals (PETA), as well as other groups, both mainstream and marginal, violent and nonviolent, have tried to discover and expose cruelty to animals in research laboratories.

Animal rights groups generally base their activities on one of two arguments (Kimmel, 2007). First, they may believe animals are just as likely as humans to experience suffering. They feel humans should not be elevated above other animals: Because all kinds of animals can suffer, all of them should be protected from painful research procedures. In this view, a certain type of research with animals could be allowed, but only if it might also be permitted with human participants. Second, some groups also believe animals have inherent rights, equal to those of humans. These activists argue that most researchers do not treat animals as creatures with rights; instead, animals are treated as resources to be used and discarded (Kimmel, 2007). In a way, this argument draws on the principle of justice, as outlined in the Belmont Report and the APA Ethical Principles: Animal rights activists do not believe animals should unduly bear the burden of research that benefits a different species (humans). Both arguments lead animal rights groups to conclude that many research practices using animals are morally wrong. Some activists accuse researchers who study animals of conducting cruel and unethical experiments (Kimmel, 2007).

The members of these groups may be politically active, vociferous, and sincerely devoted to the protection of animals. In a survey, Herzog (1993) concluded that the members of these organizations are "intelligent, articulate, and sincere." He added that they were "eager to discuss their views about the treatment of animals" with a scientist (quoted in Kimmel, 2007, p. 118). Consistent with this view, Plous (1998) polled animal rights activists and found most in his sample to be open to compromise—to a respectful dialogue with animal researchers.

Ethically Balancing Animal Welfare, Animal Rights, and Animal Research. Given the careful laws governing animal welfare, and given the broad awareness (if not universal endorsement) of animal rights arguments, you can be sure that today's research with animals in psychological science is not conducted lightly or irresponsibly. On the contrary, though research with animals is widespread, animal researchers are generally careful, thoughtful, and respectful of animal welfare.

Animal researchers defend their use of animal subjects with three primary arguments. The first and central argument is that animal research has resulted in numerous benefits to humans and animals alike (**Figure 4.12**). Animal research has contributed countless valuable lessons about psychology, biology, and neuroscience; discoveries about basic processes of vision, the organization of the brain, the course of infection, disease prevention, and therapeutic drugs. Animal research has made fundamental contributions to both basic and applied science, for both humans and animals. Therefore, as outlined in the Belmont Report and APA Ethical Principles, ethical thinking means that research scientists and the public must evaluate the costs and benefits of research projects—in terms of both the subjects used and the potential outcomes.

Best Supporting Role in a Medical Drama.
FOUNDATION FOR BIOMEDICAL RESEARCH

FIGURE 4.12 **A poster in support of animal research.** How do researchers achieve an ethical balance between concern for animal welfare and the benefits to society from research using animals?

Second, supporters of animal research argue that researchers are sensitive to animal welfare. They think about the pain and suffering of animals in their studies and take steps to avoid or reduce it. The IACUC oversight process and the *Guide for the Care and Use of Laboratory Animals* help ensure that animals are treated with care. Third, researchers have successfully reduced the number of animals they need to use, because they have developed new procedures that do not require animal testing (Kimmel, 2007). Indeed, some animal researchers believe animal rights groups have exaggerated (or even fabricated, in some cases) the cruelty of animal research (Coile & Miller, 1984), and that some activists have largely ignored the valuable scientific and medical discoveries that have resulted from animal research.

CHECK YOUR UNDERSTANDING

1. What are the five ethical principles outlined by the APA? Which two are not included in the three principles of the Belmont Report?

2. The APA has ten ethical standards. Ethical Standard 8 outlines ethical practices in research for psychologists. Name and define each of the separate points included in Ethical Standard 8.

1. See pp. 98–99 and Table 4.1. **2.** See Ethical Standard 8 on pp. 116–119 and the discussion on pp. 100–111.

Ethical Decision Making:
A Thoughtful Balance

Ethical decision making, as you have learned, does not involve simple yes-or-no decisions; it requires a balance of priorities. When faced with a study that could possibly harm human participants or animals, researchers (and their IRBs) consider the potential benefits of the research: Will it contribute something important to society? Many people believe that research with some degree of risk is justified, if the benefit from the knowledge gained from the results is great. In contrast, if the risk to participants becomes too high, the new knowledge may not be valuable enough to justify the harm.

Another example of this careful balance comes from the way researchers implement the informed consent process. On the one hand, researchers may want to demonstrate their gratitude and respect for their participants by compensating them with money or some other form of reward or credit. Paying participants might help ensure that the samples represent a variety of populations, as the principle of justice requires, because some people might not participate in a study without a financial incentive. On the other hand, if the rewards researchers offer are too great, they could tip the balance. If monetary rewards become too influential, potential participants may no longer be able to give free consent.

Although in some cases it is easy to conduct important research that has a low degree of risk to participants, other ethical decisions are extremely difficult. Researchers try to balance respect for animal subjects and human participants, protections from harm, benefits to society, and awareness of justice. As this chapter has emphasized, they do not weigh the factors in this balance alone. Influenced by IRBs, IACUCs, peers, and sociocultural norms, they strive to conduct research that is valuable to society, and to do it in an ethical manner.

Ethical research practice is not performed according to a set of permanent rules. It is an evolving and dynamic process that takes place in historical and cultural contexts. Researchers refine their ethical decision making in response to good and bad experiences, changing social norms, and scientific discoveries. By following ethical principles, researchers make it more likely that their work will benefit, and be appreciated by, the general public.

CHECK YOUR UNDERSTANDING

1. Give some examples, from the preceding discussion, of how the ethical practice of research is conducted as a thoughtful balance of priorities.

1. Answers will vary.

Summary

- No matter whether psychologists are testing a frequency, association, or causal claim, they strive to conduct their research ethically. Psychologists are guided by standard ethical principles as they plan and conduct their research.

Historical Examples

- The Tuskegee Syphilis Study, which took place in the U.S. during the 1930s through the 1970s, illustrates the ethics violations of harming people, not asking for consent, and targeting a particular group in research.
- The Milgram obedience studies illustrate the gray areas in ethical research, including how researchers define harm to participants, and how they balance the importance of a study with the harm it might do.

Core Ethical Principles

- Achieving an ethical balance in research is guided by standards and laws. Many countries' ethical policies are governed by the Nuremberg Code and the Declaration of Helsinki. In the U.S., federal ethical policies are based on the common rule, which is grounded in the Belmont Report.
- The Belmont Report outlines three main principles for research: respect for persons, beneficence, and justice. Each principle has specific applications in the research setting.
- Respect for persons involves the process of informed consent and the protection of special groups in research, such as children and prisoners.

- Beneficence involves the evaluation of risks and benefits, both to participants in the study and to society as a whole.
- Justice involves the way participants are selected for the research. One group of people should not bear an undue burden for research participation, and participants should be representative of the groups that will also benefit from the research.

Guidelines for Psychologists: The APA Ethical Principles

- The APA guides psychologists by providing a set of principles and standards for research, teaching, and other professional roles.
- The APA's five general principles include the three Belmont Report principles, plus two more: the principle of integrity and the principle of fidelity and responsibility.
- The APA's Ethical Standard 8 provides enforceable guidelines for researchers to follow. It includes specific information for informed consent, institutional review boards, deception, debriefing, research misconduct, and animal research.

Ethical Decision Making: A Thoughtful Balance

- No matter what type of claim psychologists are investigating, ethical decision making requires balancing a variety of priorities.
- Psychologists must balance benefits to society with risks to research participants, and balance compensation for participants with undue coercion for their participation.

Key Terms

debriefed, p. 94
principle of respect for persons, p. 95
informed consent, p. 95

principle of beneficence, p. 96
principle of justice, p. 97
institutional review board (IRB), p. 100

deception, p. 104
data fabrication, p. 105
data falsification, p. 105
plagiarism, p. 107

 To see samples of chapter concepts in the popular press, visit www.everydayresearchmethods.com and click the box for Chapter 4.

Review Questions

1. Which of the following is not one of the three principles of the Belmont Report?
   a. Respect for persons
   b. Justice
   c. Beneficence
   d. Fidelity

2. In a study of a new drug for asthma, a researcher finds that the group receiving the drug is doing much better than the control group, whose members are receiving a placebo. Which principle of the Belmont Report requires the researcher to also give the control group the opportunity to receive the new drug?
   a. Informed consent
   b. Justice
   c. Beneficence
   d. Respect for persons

3. In order to study a sample of participants from only one ethnic group, researchers must first demonstrate that the problem being studied is especially prevalent in that ethnic group. This is an application of which principle from the Belmont Report?
   a. Respect for persons
   b. Beneficence
   c. Special protection
   d. Justice

4. Which two principles are included in the APA Ethical Principles and not in the Belmont Report?
   a. Integrity; fidelity and responsibility
   b. Justice; beneficence and nonmaleficence
   c. Justice; respect for people's rights and dignity
   d. Respect for people's rights and dignity; beneficence and nonmaleficence

5. Following a study using deception, how does the researcher attempt to restore an honest relationship with the participant?
   a. By apologizing to the participant and offering monetary compensation for any discomfort or stress.
   b. By debriefing each participant in a structured conversation.
   c. By reassuring the participant that all names and identifiers will be removed from the data.
   d. By giving each participant a written description of the study's goals and hypotheses, along with references for further reading.

6. What type of research misconduct involves representing the ideas or words of others as one's own?
   a. Plagiarism
   b. Obfuscation
   c. Suppression
   d. Data falsification

7. Which of the following is not one of the three R's provided by the Guide for the Care and Use of Laboratory Animals?
   a. Reduction
   b. Replacement
   c. Restoration
   d. Refinement

Learning Actively

1. A developmental researcher applies to an institutional review board (IRB), proposing to observe children ages 2–10 playing in the local McDonald's play area. Because the area is public, the researcher does not plan to ask for informed consent from the children's parents. What ethical concerns exist for this study? What questions might an IRB ask?

2. A social psychologist plans to hand out surveys in her 300-level undergraduate class. The survey asks about student study habits. The psychologist does not ask the students to put their names on the survey; instead, students will put completed surveys into a large box at the back of the room. Because of the low risk involved in participation and the anonymous nature of the survey, the researcher requests to be exempted from formal informed consent procedures. What ethical concerns exist for this study? What questions might an IRB ask?

3. Consider the use of deception in psychological research. Does participation in a study involving deception (such as the Milgram studies described in this chapter) necessarily cause harm? Recall that when evaluating the risks and benefits of a study, the researcher considers both the participants in the study and society as a whole—anyone who might be affected by the research. What might be some of the costs and benefits to participants who are deceived? What might be some of the costs and benefits to society of studies involving deception?

4. Use the Internet to look up your college's definition of plagiarism. Does it match the one given in APA Ethical Standard 8.11? If not, what does it exclude or add? What behaviors count as plagiarism at your college? What are the consequences for plagiarism at your college?

5. Use the Internet to find out the procedures of the IRB at your college. According to your college's policies, do undergraduate students like you need special ethics training before they can conduct research? Does research conducted in a research methods class need formal IRB approval? Does your college categorize studies that are "exempt" from IRB review versus "expedited" versus "full board" review? If so, what kinds of studies are considered exempt?

Ethical Standard 8 of the American Psychological

8.01 Institutional Approval

When institutional approval is required, psychologists provide accurate information about their research proposals and obtain approval prior to conducting the research. They conduct the research in accordance with the approved research protocol.

8.02 Informed Consent to Research

(a) When obtaining informed consent as required in Standard 3.10, Informed Consent, psychologists inform participants about (1) the purpose of the research, expected duration, and procedures; (2) their right to decline to participate and to withdraw from the research once participation has begun; (3) the foreseeable consequences of declining or withdrawing; (4) reasonably foreseeable factors that may be expected to influence their willingness to participate such as potential risks, discomfort, or adverse effects; (5) any prospective research benefits; (6) limits of confidentiality; (7) incentives for participation; and (8) whom to contact for questions about the research and research participants' rights. They provide opportunity for the prospective participants to ask questions and receive answers. (See also Standards 8.03, Informed Consent for Recording Voices and Images in Research; 8.05, Dispensing with Informed Consent for Research; and 8.07, Deception in Research.)

(b) Psychologists conducting intervention research involving the use of experimental treatments clarify to participants at the outset of the research (1) the experimental nature of the treatment; (2) the services that will or will not be available to the control group(s) if appropriate; (3) the means by which assignment to treatment and control groups will be made; (4) available treatment alternatives if an individual does not wish to participate in the research or wishes to withdraw once a study has begun; and (5) compensation for or monetary costs of participating including, if appropriate, whether reimbursement from the participant or a third-party payor will be sought. (See also Standard 8.02a, Informed Consent to Research.)

8.03 Informed Consent for Recording Voices and Images in Research

Psychologists obtain informed consent from research participants prior to recording their voices or images for data collection unless (1) the research consists solely of naturalistic observations in public places, and it is not anticipated that the recording will be used in a manner that could cause personal identification or harm, or (2) the research design includes deception, and consent for the use of the recording is obtained during debriefing. (See also Standard 8.07, Deception in Research.)

8.04 Client/Patient, Student, and Subordinate Research Participants

(a) When psychologists conduct research with clients/patients, students, or subordinates as participants, psychologists take steps to protect the prospective participants from adverse consequences of declining or withdrawing from participation.

Association

(b) When research participation is a course requirement or an opportunity for extra credit, the prospective participant is given the choice of equitable alternative activities.

8.05 Dispensing with Informed Consent for Research

Psychologists may dispense with informed consent only (1) where research would not reasonably be assumed to create distress or harm and involves (a) the study of normal educational practices, curricula, or classroom management methods conducted in educational settings; (b) only anonymous questionnaires, naturalistic observations, or archival research for which disclosure of responses would not place participants at risk of criminal or civil liability or damage their financial standing, employability, or reputation, and confidentiality is protected; or (c) the study of factors related to job or organization effectiveness conducted in organizational settings for which there is no risk to participants' employability, and confidentiality is protected or (2) where otherwise permitted by law or federal or institutional regulations.

8.06 Offering Inducements for Research Participation

(a) Psychologists make reasonable efforts to avoid offering excessive or inappropriate financial or other inducements for research participation when such inducements are likely to coerce participation.

(b) When offering professional services as an inducement for research participation, psychologists clarify the nature of the services, as well as the risks, obligations, and limitations. (See also Standard 6.05, Barter with Clients/Patients.)

8.07 Deception in Research

(a) Psychologists do not conduct a study involving deception unless they have determined that the use of deceptive techniques is justified by the study's significant prospective scientific, educational, or applied value and that effective nondeceptive alternative procedures are not feasible.

(b) Psychologists do not deceive prospective participants about research that is reasonably expected to cause physical pain or severe emotional distress.

(c) Psychologists explain any deception that is an integral feature of the design and conduct of an experiment to participants as early as is feasible, preferably at the conclusion of their participation, but no later than at the conclusion of the data collection, and permit participants to withdraw their data. (See also Standard 8.08, Debriefing.)

8.08 Debriefing

(a) Psychologists provide a prompt opportunity for participants to obtain appropriate information about the nature, results, and conclusions of the research, and they take reasonable steps to correct any misconceptions that participants may have of which the psychologists are aware.

(b) If scientific or humane values justify delaying or withholding this information, psychologists take reasonable measures to reduce the risk of harm.

(c) When psychologists become aware that research procedures have harmed a participant, they take reasonable steps to minimize the harm.

8.09 Humane Care and Use of Animals in Research

(a) Psychologists acquire, care for, use, and dispose of animals in compliance with current federal, state, and local laws and regulations, and with professional standards.

(b) Psychologists trained in research methods and experienced in the care of laboratory animals supervise all procedures involving animals and are responsible for ensuring appropriate consideration of their comfort, health, and humane treatment.

(c) Psychologists ensure that all individuals under their supervision who are using animals have received instruction in research methods and in the care, maintenance, and handling of the species being used, to the extent appropriate to their role. (See also Standard 2.05, Delegation of Work to Others.)

(d) Psychologists make reasonable efforts to minimize the discomfort, infection, illness, and pain of animal subjects.

(e) Psychologists use a procedure subjecting animals to pain, stress, or privation only when an alternative procedure is unavailable and the goal is justified by its prospective scientific, educational, or applied value.

(f) Psychologists perform surgical procedures under appropriate anesthesia and follow techniques to avoid infection and minimize pain during and after surgery.

(g) When it is appropriate that an animal's life be terminated, psychologists proceed rapidly, with an effort to minimize pain and in accordance with accepted procedures.

8.10 Reporting Research Results

(a) Psychologists do not fabricate data. (See also Standard 5.01a, Avoidance of False or Deceptive Statements.)

(b) If psychologists discover significant errors in their published data, they take reasonable steps to correct such errors in a correction, retraction, erratum, or other appropriate publication means.

8.11 Plagiarism

Psychologists do not present portions of another's work or data as their own, even if the other work or data source is cited occasionally.

8.12 Publication Credit

(a) Psychologists take responsibility and credit, including authorship credit, only for work they have actually performed or to which they have substantially contributed. (See also Standard 8.12b, Publication Credit.)

(b) Principal authorship and other publication credits accurately reflect the relative scientific or professional contributions of the individuals involved, regardless of their relative status. Mere possession of an institutional position, such as department chair, does not justify authorship credit. Minor contributions to the research or to the writing for publications are acknowledged appropriately, such as in footnotes or in an introductory statement.

(c) Except under exceptional circumstances, a student is listed as principal author on any multiple-authored article that is substantially based on the student's doctoral dissertation. Faculty advisors discuss publication credit with students as early as feasible and throughout the research and publication process as appropriate. (See also Standard 8.12b, Publication Credit.)

8.13 Duplicate Publication of Data

Psychologists do not publish, as original data, data that have been previously published. This does not preclude republishing data when they are accompanied by proper acknowledgment.

8.14 Sharing Research Data for Verification

(a) After research results are published, psychologists do not withhold the data on which their conclusions are based from other competent professionals who seek to verify the substantive claims through reanalysis and who intend to use such data only for that purpose, provided that the confidentiality of the participants can be protected and unless legal rights concerning proprietary data preclude their release. This does not preclude psychologists from requiring that such individuals or groups be responsible for costs associated with the provision of such information.

(b) Psychologists who request data from other psychologists to verify the substantive claims through reanalysis may use shared data only for the declared purpose. Requesting psychologists obtain prior written agreement for all other uses of the data.

8.15 Reviewers

Psychologists who review material submitted for presentation, publication, grant, or research proposal review respect the confidentiality of and the proprietary rights in such information of those who submitted it.

Happiness Facts and Fiction

(webmd.com)

Religious Americans Enjoy Higher Well-Being

(Gallup, 2012)

Three Things You Might Not Know About the Relationship Between Income and Happiness

(*PsychologyToday.com*, 2011)

5

Identifying Good Measurement

LEARNING OBJECTIVES

A year from now, you should still be able to:

1. Interrogate the construct validity of a study's variables.
2. Describe the kinds of evidence that support the construct validity of a measured variable.

Whether studying the speed of a chemical reaction, the number of polar bears left in the Arctic Circle, the strength of a bar of steel, or the level of human happiness, every scientist faces the challenge of measurement. When researchers test theories or pursue empirical questions, they have to systematically observe the phenomena by collecting data. Such systematic observations require measurements, and these measurements must be good ones—or else they are useless.

Measurement in psychological research can be particularly challenging. Many of the phenomena psychologists are interested in—motivation, emotion, thinking, reasoning—are difficult to measure directly. Happiness, the topic of much research, is a good example of a construct that could be difficult to measure. Is it really possible to quantify how happy people are? Are the measures accurate? Before testing the idea that religious people are more happy, we might ask whether we can really measure happiness. Maybe people misrepresent their level of well-being, or maybe people aren't aware of how happy they are. How do we measure who is really happy and who isn't? This chapter explains how to ask questions about the quality of a study's measures—the construct validity of measures of happiness, religiosity, or wealth. Construct validity, remember, refers to how well a study's variables are measured or manipulated.

For a review of measured and manipulated variables, see Chapter 3, pp. 56–57.

Construct validity is a crucial piece of any psychological research study—for frequency, association, or causal claims. This chapter focuses on the construct validity of *measured variables*. You will learn, first, about different ways researchers measure variables. Then you'll learn how you can assess the reliability and validity of those measurements. The construct validity of *manipulated variables* is covered in Chapter 10.

Ways to Measure Variables

The process of measuring variables involves some key decisions. As researchers decide how they should operationalize each variable in a study, they choose among three common types of measures: self-report, observational, and physiological. They also decide on the most appropriate scale of measurement for each variable they plan to investigate.

More About Conceptual and Operational Variables

In Chapter 3, you learned about operationalization, the process of turning a concept of interest into a measured or manipulated variable (see Figure 3.1). Any variable can be expressed in two ways: as a *conceptual variable* (also called a conceptual definition or construct) and as an *operational definition* (an operational variable). The conceptual definition, or construct, is the researcher's definition of the variable in question at a theoretical level. The operational definition of a variable represents a researcher's specific decision about how to measure or manipulate the conceptual variable.

Operationalizing "Happiness"

Let's take the variable "happiness," for example. One researcher, Ed Diener, began his study of happiness by developing a precise conceptual definition. Specifically, Diener reasoned that the word *happiness* might have a variety of meanings, so he explicitly limited his interest to "subjective well-being" (i.e., well-being from a person's own perspective).

After defining happiness at the conceptual level, Diener and his colleagues developed an operational definition. Because they were interested in people's perspectives on their own well-being, they chose to operationalize subjective well-being, in part, by asking people to report on their own satisfaction with life in a questionnaire format. Furthermore, Diener and his team decided that people should use their own criteria to define what a "good life" is (Pavot & Diener, 1993). They worded their questions such that people could think about the definition of life satisfaction that was appropriate for them. Ultimately, these researchers operationally defined (i.e., measured) subjective well-being by asking people to respond to five items about their life satisfaction, using a 7-point scale. On the scale, 1 corresponded to "strongly disagree" and 7 corresponded to "strongly agree":

_____ 1. In most ways my life is close to my ideal.

_____ 2. The conditions of my life are excellent.

_____ 3. I am satisfied with my life.

_____ 4. So far I have gotten the important things I want in life.

_____ 5. If I could live my life over, I would change almost nothing.

The unhappiest people would get a total score of 5 on this self-report scale, because they would answer "strongly disagree," or 1, to all five items ($1 + 1 + 1 + 1 + 1 = 5$). The happiest people would get a total score of 35 on this scale, because they would answer "strongly agree," or 7, to all five items ($7 + 7 + 7 + 7 + 7 = 35$). Those at the neutral point would score 20—right in between satisfied and dissatisfied ($4 + 4 + 4 + 4 + 4 = 20$). Diener and Diener (1996) reported some data on this scale, concluding that most people are happy, meaning most people scored above 20. For example, 63% of high school and college students scored above 20 in one study, and 72% of disabled adults scored above 20 in another study.

In choosing this operational definition of subjective well-being, Diener started with only one possible measure, even though there are many other ways to study this concept. Another way to measure happiness is to use a single question called the Ladder of Life (Cantril, 1965). The question goes like this:

Imagine a ladder with steps numbered from 0 at the bottom to 10 at the top. The top of the ladder represents the best possible life for you and the bottom of the ladder represents the worst possible life for you. On which step of the ladder would you say you personally stand at this time?

On this measure, participants respond by giving a value between 0 and 10. The Gallup polling organization uses the Ladder of Life item to measure well-being in its daily Healthways Index.

You might be thinking that one of these operational definitions seems like a better measure of happiness than the other. Which one do you think is best? Or maybe they both do a good job of measuring the construct? Researcher Diener and the Gallup organization have both decided that their measures of happiness are accurate, based on the data they have collected on them.

Operationalizing Other Conceptual Variables

To study conceptual variables other than happiness, researchers follow a similar process: They start by stating a definition of their construct (the conceptual variable) and then create an operational definition. For example, to measure the association between wealth and happiness, researchers need to measure not only happiness, but also wealth. They might operationally define wealth by asking about salary in dollars, by asking for bank account balances, or even by observing the kind of car people drive.

TABLE 5.1 Variables and Operational Definitions

Variable	One possible operational definition (operationalization)	Another possible operational definition
Religiosity	Asking people if they agree with the statement: "My religious faith is the most important influence in my life."	Asking people how frequently they attend religious services (never, several times per year, monthly, nearly weekly, or weekly).
Gender	Asking people to report on a survey if they are male or female.	In phone interviews, a researcher guesses gender through the sound of the voice.
Wealth	Asking people to report their income on a variety of ranges (less than $20,000, between $20,000 and $50,000, and more than $50,000).	Coding the value of a car from 1 (older, lower-status vehicle) to 5 (new, high-status vehicle in good condition).
Working memory span	Administering a digit-span test, in which people are asked to repeat longer and longer strings of letters.	Asking people to recall as many words as possible from a verbal list of 30 words.
Well-being (happiness)	10-point Ladder of Life scale.	Diener's 5-item subjective well-being scale.

Consider another variable: religiosity. Researchers who measure religiosity might operationalize it by asking people how often they attend religious services or by asking people about their spiritual commitment. Even a simple variable, such as gender, must be operationalized. As **Table 5.1** shows, any conceptual variable can be operationalized in a number of ways. In fact, operationalizations are one place where creativity comes into the research process, as researchers work to develop new and better measures of their constructs.

Three Common Types of Measures

The types of measures psychological scientists typically use to operationalize variables generally fall into three categories: self-report, observational, and physiological.

Self-Report Measures

A **self-report measure** operationalizes a variable by recording people's answers to questions about themselves in a questionnaire or interview. Diener's five-item scale and the Ladder of Life question are both examples of self-report measures about life satisfaction. Similarly, asking people how frequently they attend religious services, or asking people their gender, are both self-report measures. If stress was the variable being studied, researchers might ask people to report on the frequency of specific events they might have experienced in the past year, such as marriage, divorce, or moving (e.g., Holmes & Rahe, 1967).

In research on children, self-reports may be replaced with parent reports or teacher reports. Similar to self-reports, these reports ask parents or teachers to respond to a series of questions about the child. For example, the parent or teacher might be asked to describe the child's recent life events, the words a child knows, or the child's typical classroom behaviors. (Chapter 6 discusses situations when self-report measures are likely to be accurate and when they might be biased.)

Observational Measures

An **observational measure**, sometimes called a *behavioral measure*, operationalizes a variable by recording observable behaviors or physical traces of behaviors. For example, a researcher could operationalize happiness by observing how many times a person smiles. Intelligence tests can be considered observational measures, because the people who administer such tests in person are observing people's intelligent behaviors (such as being able to correctly solve a puzzle or quickly detect a pattern). Coding how much a person's car cost would be an observational measure of wealth (Piff, Stancato, Côté, Mendoza-Denton, & Keltner, 2012).

Observational measures may record physical traces of behavior. Stress behaviors could be measured by counting the number of tooth marks left on a person's pencil, or a researcher could measure stressful events by using public legal records to record whether people have recently married, divorced, or moved. (Chapter 6 addresses how an observer's ratings of behavior might be accurate and how they might be biased.)

Physiological Measures

A **physiological measure** operationalizes a variable by recording biological data such as brain activity, hormone levels, or heart rate. Physiological measures usually require the use of equipment to amplify, record, and analyze biological data. For example, moment-to-moment happiness has been measured using facial electromyography (EMG)—a way of electronically recording tiny movements in the muscles in the face. Facial EMG can detect a happy facial expression, because people who are smiling show particular patterns of muscle movement around the eyes and cheeks.

Other constructs might be measured using a brain scanning technique called functional magnetic resonance imaging, or fMRI. In a typical fMRI study, people engage in a carefully designed series of psychological tasks (such as looking at three types of photos or playing a series of rock-paper-scissors games) while they are lying in an MRI machine. The MRI apparatus (and computers associated with it) record and code the relative change in blood flow in particular regions of the brain, as shown in **Figure 5.1**. When more blood flows to a brain region during certain tasks, researchers conclude that that area of the brain is working harder during that task. Some research points to a way fMRI might be used to measure intelligence in the future. Specifically, the brains of people with higher intelligence are more efficient at solving complex problems; their fMRI scans show relatively less brain activity for complex problems (Deary, Penke, & Johnson, 2010). Therefore, future researchers may be able to use efficiency of brain activity as a physiological measure

FIGURE 5.1 **Images from fMRI scans.**
In this study of how people respond to rewards and losses, the researchers tracked blood flow patterns in the brain when people had either won, lost, or tied a rock-paper-scissors game played with a computer. They found virtually every area of the brain was influenced by the type of outcome. (Source: Vickery, Chun, & Lee, 2011.)

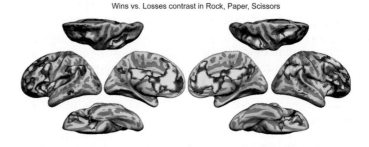

Wins vs. Losses contrast in Rock, Paper, Scissors

of intelligence. Another physiological measure, one that turned out to be flawed, comes from a century ago, when people used head circumference to measure intelligence, under the mistaken impression that smarter brains would be stored inside larger skulls (Gould, 1996).

A physiological way to operationalize people's level of stress might be to measure the degree of the hormone cortisol that is released in their saliva, because people under stress show higher levels of cortisol (Carlson, 2009). Skin conductance, an electronic recording of the activity in the sweat glands of the hands or feet, is another way to measure stress physiologically. People under more stress have more activity in these glands.

Other physiological measures used in psychology research include the detection of hormones, such as testosterone, oxytocin, or catecholamine; and the detection of electrical patterns in the brain using electroencephalography (EEG).

Which Operationalization Is Best?

A single construct can be operationalized in several ways, from self-report to behavioral observation to physiological measures. Many people erroneously believe that physiological measures are bound to be the most accurate, but even they have to be validated by using other measures. For instance, as mentioned above, researchers used fMRI to learn that the brain works more efficiently relative to level of intelligence. But how is intelligence measured? Before doing the fMRI scans, the researchers gave the participants an IQ test—an observational measure (Deary et al., 2010). Similarly, researchers might trust an fMRI pattern to indicate when a person is genuinely happy. However, the only way a researcher could know that some pattern of brain activity was associated with happiness is by asking each person about his or her happiness at the same time the brain scan was being done. As you'll learn later in this chapter, it is best if self-report, observational, and physiological measures show similar patterns of results.

Scales of Measurement

All variables must have at least two levels (see Chapter 3). The levels of operational variables, however, can be coded using different scales of measurement.

Categorical vs. Quantitative Variables

Operational variables are primarily classified as categorical or quantitative. The levels of **categorical variables**, as the term suggests, are categories. (Categorical variables are also called *nominal variables*.) Examples are sex, whose levels are male and female; and species, whose levels in a study might be rhesus macaque, chimpanzee, and bonobo. A researcher might decide to assign numbers to the levels of a categorical variable (e.g., using a 1 to represent rhesus macaques, 2 for chimps, and 3 for bonobos) during the data-entry process. However, the numbers do not have numerical meaning—a bonobo is different from a chimpanzee, but being a bonobo (a 3) is not quantitatively "higher" than being a chimpanzee (a 2).

In contrast, the levels of **quantitative variables** are coded with *meaningful* numbers. Height and weight are quantitative because they are measured in numbers, such as 150 centimeters or 45 kilograms. Diener's scale of subjective well-being is quantitative too, because a score of 35 represents more happiness than a score of 7. IQ score, level of brain efficiency, and amount of salivary cortisol are also quantitative variables.

Three Types of Quantitative Variables

For certain kinds of statistical purposes, researchers may need to further classify a quantitative variable in terms of ordinal, interval, or ratio scale.

An **ordinal scale** of measurement applies when the numerals of a quantitative variable represent a ranked order. For example, a bookstore's website might display the top 10 best-selling books. We know that the #1 book sold more than the #2 book, and that #2 sold more than #3, but we don't know whether the number of books that separates #1 and #2 is equal to the number of books that separates #2 and #3. In other words, the intervals may be unequal. Maybe the first two rankings are only 10 books apart, and the second two rankings are 150,000 books apart. Similarly, a professor might use the order in which exams were turned in to operationalize how fast students completed the exam. This represents ordinal data because the fastest exams are on the bottom of the pile—ranked 1. However, this variable has not quantified *how much* faster each exam was turned in, compared with the others.

An **interval scale** of measurement applies to the numerals of a quantitative variable that meet two conditions: First, the numerals represent equal intervals (distances) between levels, and second, there is no "true zero" (a person can get a score of 0, but the 0 does not really mean "nothing"). An IQ test is an interval scale—the distance between IQ scores of 100 and 105 represents the same as the distance between IQ scores of 110 and 115. However, a score of 0 on an IQ test does not mean a person has "no intelligence." Body temperature in degrees Celsius is another example of an interval scale—the intervals between levels are equal; however, a temperature of 0 degrees does not mean that a person has "no temperature." Most researchers assume that questionnaire scales like Diener's (scored from 1 = *strongly disagree* to 7 = *strongly agree*) are interval scales. They do not have a true zero but assume that the distances between numerals, from 1 to 7, are equivalent. Because they do not have a true zero, interval scales cannot allow a researcher to say things like "twice as hot" or "three times happier."

TABLE 5.2 Measurement Scales for Operational Variables

Type of variable	Characteristics	Examples
Categorical	Levels are categories.	Gender. Nationality. Favorite song.
Quantitative	Levels are coded with meaningful numbers.	
Ordinal	A quantitative variable in which numerals represent a rank order. Distance between subsequent numerals may not be equal.	Order of finishers in a swimming race. Ranking of 10 movies from most to least favorite.
Interval	A quantitative variable in which subsequent numerals represent equal distances, but there is no true zero.	IQ score. Shoe size. Degree of agreement on a 1–7 scale.
Ratio	A quantitative variable in which numerals represent equal distances and there is a true zero.	Number of exam questions answered correctly. Number of seconds to respond to a computer task. Height in cm.

Finally, a **ratio scale** of measurement applies when the numerals of a quantitative variable have equal intervals and when the value of 0 truly means "nothing." On a test a researcher might measure how many items people answer correctly. Some people might answer 0 items correctly, and their score of 0 represents truly "nothing correct" (0 answers correct). A researcher might measure how frequently people blink their eyes in a stressful situation; number of eyeblinks is a ratio scale because people could blink their eyes 0 times. Because ratio scales do have a true zero, one can meaningfully say something like "Miguel answered twice as many problems as Diogo."

Table 5.2 summarizes all the above variations.

CHECK YOUR UNDERSTANDING

1. Explain why a variable will usually have only one conceptual definition but can have multiple operational definitions.
2. Name the three common ways in which researchers operationalize their variables.
3. In your own words, describe the difference between categorical and quantitative variables. Describe the differences between ordinal, interval, and ratio scales.

1. See pp. 123–124. 2. See pp. 124–126. 3. See pp. 127–128.

Reliability of Measurement: Are the Scores Consistent?

Now that we've established different types of operationalizations, we can ask the important question: How do you know if a study's operationalizations are good ones? How can you tell whether the study's measures have construct validity? The construct validity of a measure has two aspects. **Reliability** refers to how consistent the results of a measure are, and **validity** concerns whether the operationalization is measuring what it is supposed to measure. Both are important, and the first step is reliability.

Introducing Three Types of Reliability

Before using their measures in a study, researchers collect data to be sure the measures are reliable. They collect data because establishing the reliability of a measure is an empirical question. A measure's reliability is just what the word suggests: whether or not you can rely on a particular score. If your measurement is reliable, you get a consistent pattern of scores every time. Reliability can be assessed in three ways, depending on how a variable was operationalized, and all three involve consistency in measurement. With **test-retest reliability**, the researcher gets consistent scores every time he or she uses the measure. With **interrater reliability**, consistent scores are obtained no matter who measures or observes. With **internal reliability** (also called *internal consistency*), a study participant gives a consistent pattern of answers, no matter how the researcher has phrased the question.

Test-Retest Reliability

To illustrate test-retest reliability, suppose a sample of people took an IQ test today. When they take it again 1 month later, the scores should be consistent. The pattern should be the same: People who scored the highest at Time 1 should also score the highest at Time 2. Even if all the scores from Time 2 are higher than all the scores from Time 1 (perhaps because of practice), the pattern should be consistent: The highest Time 1 person should still be the highest (or one of the highest) at Time 2. Test-retest reliability can apply whether the operationalization is self-report, observational, or physiological. However, it is primarily relevant when researchers are measuring constructs (such as intelligence, personality, religiosity) that they expect to be relatively stable in most people. Subjective well-being, for example, may reasonably fluctuate from month to month or from year to year for a particular person, so less consistency would be expected in this variable.

Interrater Reliability

With interrater reliability, two or more independent observers will come up with consistent (or very similar) findings. Interrater reliability is most relevant for observational measures. For example, say you are assigned to observe the number of times each child smiles in 1 hour on a daycare playground. Your lab partner is assigned to sit on the other side of the playground and make his own count of the same children's smiles. If, for one child, you record 12 smiles during the first hour, and your lab partner also records 12 smiles in that hour for the same child, there is interrater reliability. Any two observers watching the same children at the same time should agree about which child has smiled the most and which child has smiled the least.

Internal Reliability

As an example of the third kind of reliability, internal reliability, suppose a sample of people take Diener's five-item subjective well-being scale. The questions on his scale are worded differently, but each item is intended to be a measure of the same construct. Therefore, people who agree with the first item on the scale should also agree with the second item (as well as with Items 3, 4, and 5). Similarly, people who disagree with the first item should also disagree with Items 2, 3, 4, and 5. If the pattern is consistent across items in this way, the scale has internal reliability.

Using a Scatterplot to Evaluate Reliability

Before using a particular measure to test a hypothesis, researchers often collect data to see if it is reliable. Researchers may use two statistical devices for data analysis: scatterplots (see Chapter 3) and the correlation coefficient r (discussed below). In fact, evidence for reliability is a special example of an association claim—the association between one version of the measure and another, between one coder and another, or between an earlier time and a later time.

How are correlations used for establishing reliability? Years ago, when people thought smarter people had larger heads, they may have tried to use head circumference as an operationalization of intelligence. Would this measure be reliable? Probably. Suppose you record the head circumference, in centimeters, for everyone in a classroom, using an ordinary tape measure. To see if the measurements were reliable, you could measure all of the heads twice (test-retest reliability) or you could measure them first, and then have someone else measure them (interrater reliability).

Figure 5.2 shows what the results of such a measurement might look like, in the form of a data table and a scatterplot. In the scatterplot, the first measurements of head circumference for four students are plotted on the y-axis. The circumferences as measured the second time—whether by you again (test-retest) or by a second observer (interrater)—are plotted on the x-axis. In this scatterplot, each dot represents a person measured twice.

We would expect the two measures of head circumference to be about the same for each person. They are, so the dots on the scatterplot all fall almost exactly on the sloping line that would indicate perfect agreement. The two measures will not always be exactly the same because there is likely to be some measurement error that will lead to slightly different scores even for the same person (such as variations in exactly where the tape measure was placed in each trial).

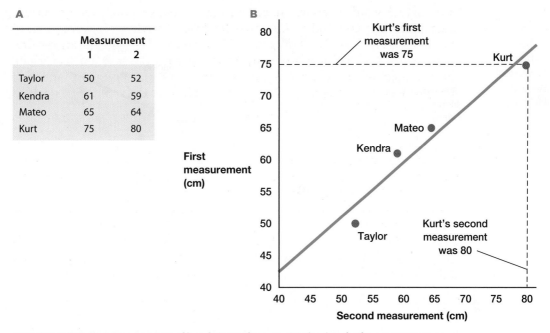

FIGURE 5.2 Two measurements of head circumference. (A) The data for four participants in table form. (B) The same data presented in a scatterplot.

Scatterplots Can Show Interrater Agreement or Disagreement

In a different scenario, suppose ten young children are being observed on a playground. Two independent observers, Mark and Matt, rate how happy each child appears to be, on a scale of 1 to 10. They later compare notes to see how well their ratings agree. From these notes, they create a scatterplot, plotting Observer Mark's ratings on the x-axis and Observer Matt's ratings on the y-axis.

If the data looked like those in **Figure 5.3A**, the ratings would have high interrater reliability. Both Observer Mark and Observer Matt rate Jay's happiness as 9. Observer Mark rates Jackie a 2; Observer Matt rates her 3, and so on. The two observers do not show perfect agreement, but there are no great disagreements either. Again, the points are scattered around the plot a bit, but they hover close to the sloping line that would indicate perfect agreement.

In contrast, suppose the data looked like **Figure 5.3B**, which shows much less agreement. Here, the two observers are Mark and Peter, and they are watching the same children at the same time, but Mark gives Jay a rating of 9 and Peter thinks he rates only a 6. Mark considers Jackie's behavior to be shy and withdrawn and rates her a 2, but Peter thinks she seems calm and content and rates her a 7. Here the interrater reliability is low—in fact, for most purposes, it would be considered unacceptably low. One reason it is low could be that the observers did not have a clear enough operational definition of "happiness" to work with. Another reason could be that one or both of the coders has not been trained well enough yet.

A scatterplot can thus be a helpful tool for assessing the agreement between two administrations of the same measurement (test-retest reliability) or between two coders (interrater reliability). Using a scatterplot, you can see whether

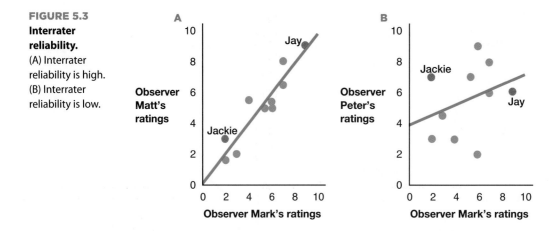

FIGURE 5.3
Interrater reliability.
(A) Interrater reliability is high.
(B) Interrater reliability is low.

the two ratings agree (if the individual dots are close to a straight line drawn through them) or whether they disagree (if the individual dots scatter widely from a straight line drawn through them).

Using the Correlation Coefficient *r* to Evaluate Reliability

Scatterplots are an important first step in evaluating reliability. However, a more common and efficient way to evaluate reliability relationships is to use the correlation coefficient. Researchers can use a single number, called a **correlation coefficient**, or *r*, to indicate how close the dots on a scatterplot are to a line drawn through them.

Notice that the scatterplots in **Figure 5.4** differ in two important ways. One difference is that the scattered clouds of points slope in different directions. In Figure 5.4A and Figure 5.4B the points slope upward from left to right, in Figure 5.4C they slope downward, and in Figure 5.4D they do not slope up or down at all. This slope is referred to as the direction of the relationship, and the **slope direction** can be positive, negative, or zero—that is, sloping up, sloping down, or not sloping at all.

The other way the scatterplots differ is that in some, the dots are close to a straight, sloping line; in others, the dots are more spread out. This spread corresponds to the **strength** of the relationship. In general, the relationship is strong when dots are close to the line; it is weak when dots are spread out.

The numbers below the scatterplots are the correlation coefficients, or *r*. The *r* indicates the same two things as the scatterplot: the direction of the relationship and the strength of the relationship, both of which psychologists use in evaluating reliability evidence. Notice that when the slope is positive, *r* is positive; when the slope is negative, *r* is negative. The value of *r* can fall only between 1.0 and −1.0. When the relationship is strong, *r* is close to either 1.0 or −1.0; when the relationship is weak, *r* is closer to zero. An *r* of 1.0 represents the strongest possible positive relationship, and an *r* of −1.0 represents the strongest possible negative relationship. If there is no relationship between two variables, *r* will be .00 or close to .00 (i.e., .02 or −.04).

Those are the basics. How do psychologists use the strength and direction of *r* to evaluate reliability evidence?

For more on the slope of a scatterplot, see Chapter 3, pp. 61–64.

For more on how to compute *r*, see Statistics Review: Descriptive Statistics, pp. 454–456.

CHAPTER 5 Identifying Good Measurement

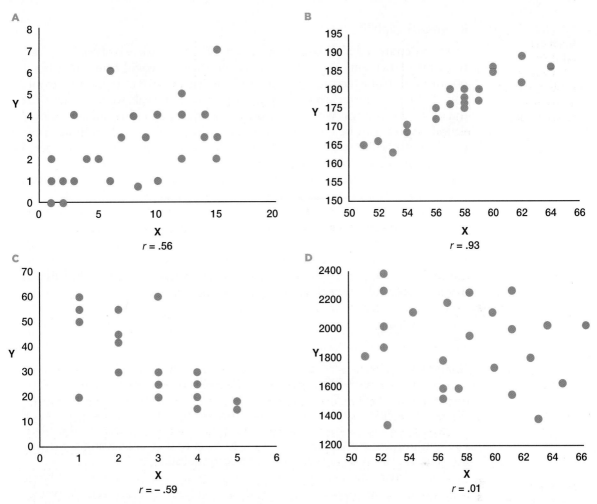

FIGURE 5.4 Correlation coefficients. Notice the differences in the correlation coefficients (*r*) in these scatterplots. The correlation coefficient describes the direction and strength of the association between the two variables, regardless of the scale on which the variables are measured.

Test-Retest Reliability

To assess the test-retest reliability of some measure, we would measure the same set of participants on that measure at least twice—at Time 1 and Time 2. Then we could compute *r*. If *r* is positive and strong (for test-retest, we might expect .50 or above), we would have very good test-retest reliability. If *r* is positive but weak, we would know that participants' scores on the test changed from Time 1 to Time 2. This result would be a sign of poor measurement reliability if we are measuring something that should stay the same over time. For example, a trait like intelligence is not usually expected to change over a few months, so if we assess the test-retest reliability of an IQ test and obtain a low *r*, we would be doubtful about the reliability of this test. However, if we were measuring flu symptoms or work stress, we would expect test-retest reliabilities to be low, simply because these constructs do not stay the same over time.

Interrater Reliability

To test interrater reliability of some measure, we might ask two observers to rate the same participants at the same time, and then we would compute r. If r is positive and strong (according to many researchers, $r = .70$ or higher), we would have very good interrater reliability. If r is positive but weak, we could not trust the observers' ratings. We would retrain the coders or refine our operational definition so it can be more reliably coded. A negative r would indicate a big problem. In the daycare example, that would mean Observer Mark considered Jay very happy but Observer Peter considered Jay very unhappy, Observer Mark considered Jackie unhappy but Peter considered Jackie happy, and so on. When you are assessing reliability, a negative correlation is rare and undesirable.

Although r can be used to evaluate interrater reliability when the observers are rating a quantitative variable, a more appropriate statistic, called *kappa*, is used when the observers are rating a sample on a categorical variable. Although the computations are beyond the scope of this book, kappa measures the extent to which two raters place participants into the same categories. As with r, a kappa close to 1.0 means that the two raters agreed.

Internal Reliability

Internal reliability is relevant for measures that use more than one item to get at the same construct. Researchers who use self-report scales, such as the questions on Diener's five-item subjective well-being scale, often ask the same question in multiple phrasings, because each wording of the question might leave room for some measurement error. When researchers assess the internal reliability of a multi-item scale, they are evaluating whether people's responses to the different wordings are consistent. They want to be sure they are getting consistent answers every time, no matter how they ask the question.

A set of items has internal reliability if its items correlate strongly with one another. If they correlate strongly, the researcher can reasonably take an average to create a single overall score for each person.

Let's consider the following version of Diener's well-being scale. Would a group of people give consistent answers to all of these items?

_____ 1. In most ways my life is close to my ideal.
_____ 2. The conditions of my life are excellent.
_____ 3. I am fond of polka dots.
_____ 4. I am a good swimmer.
_____ 5. If I could live my life over, I would change almost nothing.

Obviously, these items would probably not be correlated in a sample, so we could not average them together for a meaningful well-being score. Items 1 and 2 are probably correlated, since they are similar to each other, but Items 1 and 3 are probably not correlated, since people can like polka dots whether or not they are living their ideal lives. Item 4 is probably not correlated with any other item, either. But how could we quantify these intuitions? How do we know that this subjective well-being scale, or any other measure, has internal reliability?

Most commonly, researchers will run a correlation-based statistic called **Cronbach's alpha** (or *coefficient alpha*) to see if their measurement scales have internal reliability. First, they collect data on the scale from a large sample of participants, and then they compute all possible correlations among the items. (Does Item 1 correlate with Item 2? Does Item 1 correlate with Item 3? Does Item 2 correlate with Item 3? And so on.) The formula for Cronbach's alpha returns one number, computed from the average of the inter-item correlations and the number of items in the scale. The closer the Cronbach's alpha is to 1, the better the scale's reliability. (For self-report measures, researchers are looking for Cronbach's alpha of .70 or higher.) If the internal reliability is good, the researchers can average all the items together. If the internal reliability is low, the researchers are not justified in combining all the items into one scale. They have to go back and revise the items—or average together only those items that correlate strongly with one another.

Reading About Reliability in Journal Articles

Authors of empirical journal articles often present reliability information for the measures they are using. One example of such evidence is in **Figure 5.5**, which comes from an actual journal article. According to the table, the subjective well-being scale was used in six studies. The table shows the internal reliability (labeled as coefficient alpha) from each of these studies, as well as test-retest reliability for each one. The table did not present interrater reliability because their scale is a self-report measure, and interrater reliability is relevant only when two or more observers are doing the ratings. Based on the evidence in this table, we can conclude that the subjective well-being scale has excellent internal reliability and excellent test-retest reliability.

Table 2

Estimates of Internal Consistency and Temporal Reliability for the Satisfaction with Life Scale

STRAIGHT *from the* SOURCE

Sample	Coefficient alpha	Test–retest	Temporal interval
Alfonso & Allison (1992a)	.89	.83	2 weeks
Pavot et al. (1991)	.85	.84	1 month
Blais et al. (1989)	.79–.84	.64	2 months
Diener et al. (1985)	.87	.82	2 months
Yardley & Rice (1991)	.80, .86	.50	10 weeks
Magnus, Diener, Fujita, & Pavot (1992)	.87	.54	4 years

FIGURE 5.5 Reliability of the well-being scale. The researchers created this table to show how six studies supported the internal and test-retest reliability of their scale. (Source: Pavot & Diener, 1993, Table 2.)

1. Reliability is about consistency. Define the three kinds of reliability, noting what kind of consistency each is designed to show.

2. For each of the three common types of operationalizations—self-report, observational, and physiological—indicate which type(s) of reliability would be relevant.

3. Which of the following correlations is the strongest: $r = .25$, $r = -.65$, $r = -.01$, or $r = .43$?

1. See pp. 129–130. 2. Self-report: test-retest and internal may be relevant; observational: interrater would be relevant; physiological: interrater may be relevant. 3. $r = -.65$.

Validity of Measurement: Does It Measure What It Is Supposed to Measure?

Before using particular measures in a study, researchers not only check to be sure the measures are reliable; they also want to be sure that they measure the conceptual variables they were intended to measure. That's validity. You might ask whether the five-item well-being scale Diener uses really reflects how subjectively happy people are. You might ask if a self-report measure of religiosity really reflects how religious people are. You might ask if recording the value of the car a person drives really reflects that person's wealth.

Measurement reliability and measurement validity are separate steps in establishing construct validity. To demonstrate the difference between them, consider the example of head circumference as an operationalization of intelligence. Although head circumference measurements may be very reliable, almost all studies have shown that head circumference is not related to intelligence (Gould, 1996). Therefore, like an inaccurate bathroom scale (**Figure 5.6**), the head circumference test may be reliable, but it is not valid as an intelligence test: It does not measure what it is supposed to measure.

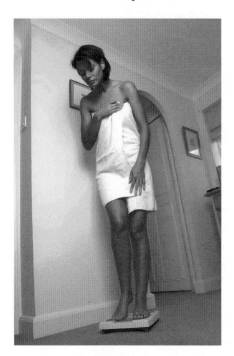

FIGURE 5.6 Reliability is not the same as validity. This person's bathroom scale may report that she weighs 300 pounds (136 kg) every time she steps on it. The scale is certainly reliable, but it is not valid.

Measurement Validity of Abstract Constructs

Did you know that the U.S. National Institute of Standards and Technology (NIST) has a platinum-iridium bar, kept in a special case at a constant temperature, that represents the international standard for measuring a meter? (Several governments around the world have identical meter sticks in their measurement collections.) Suppose I have a plain wooden meter stick, received as a promotional gift from my local garden store, that I've been using to measure the height of my tomato plant. I always take the daily measurement twice and always get the same result both times, so I know it is a reliable meter stick. I don't know, though, whether it is an accurate meter. Maybe it warped over the years, or maybe it was made from a bad batch of wood, or the ends have worn down. If I took my meter stick to NIST and compared it to theirs, would mine match the platinum-iridium standard? If so, then my wooden meter stick is a valid measure of a meter: It measures what it is supposed to measure.

Physical scientists are fortunate to have such standards for measurement so they can make sure they are measuring things reliably and precisely. But psychological scientists often want to measure abstract constructs, such as happiness, intelligence, stress, or self-esteem, for which there is no standard "meter stick" (Cronbach & Meehl, 1955; Smith, 2005a, 2005b).

Construct validity is therefore important in psychological research, especially when a construct is not directly observable. Take happiness: We have no means of directly measuring how happy a person is. We could estimate it in a number of ways, such as scores on a well-being inventory, daily smile rate, blood pressure, stress hormone levels, or even the activity levels of certain brain regions. Yet each of these measures of happiness is indirect. For some abstract constructs, there really is no single, direct measure. And that is the challenge: How can we know if indirect operational measures of a construct are really measuring happiness and not something else?

We know by collecting data. Before using a measure in a study, researchers either collect their own data on the measure, or they consider data collected by others, to evaluate validity. Furthermore, the evidence for construct validity is always a matter of degree. Psychologists do not say that a particular measure is or is not valid. Instead, they ask: What is the weight of evidence in favor of this measure's validity? There are a number of kinds of evidence that can convince a researcher of a measure's validity.

Figure 5.7 summarizes the reliability and validity concepts covered in this chapter.

Face Validity and Content Validity: Does It Look Like a Good Measure?

A measure has **face validity** to the extent that it appears to experts to be a plausible measure of the variable in question. Face validity is a subjective judgment: If it looks as if it should be a good measure, it has face validity. A measure of head circumference has high face validity as a measure of people's hat size, but it has low face validity as a measure of intelligence. In contrast, rapidity of problem solving, vocabulary size, or creativity would have higher face validity than head circumference as measures of intelligence. Researchers generally check face validity by consulting experts. For example, we might assess the face validity of Diener's well-being scale by asking a panel of judges (e.g., personality psychologists) how reasonable they think the scale is as a way of estimating happiness.

Content validity also involves subjective judgment about a measure. To ensure **content validity**, a measure must capture all parts of a defined construct. For example, consider this conceptual definition of intelligence, containing

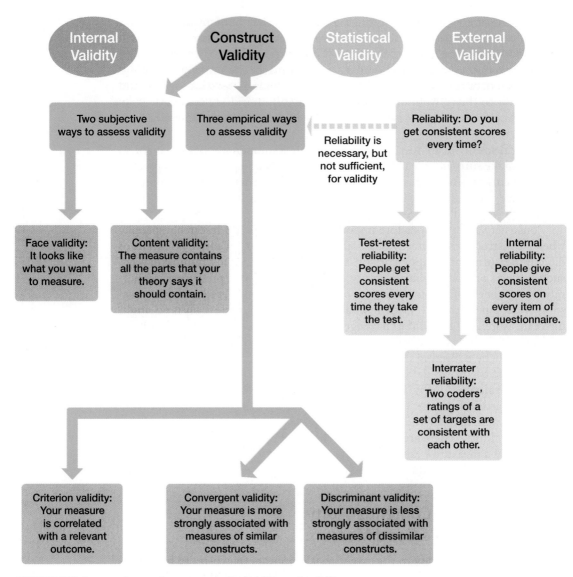

FIGURE 5.7 A concept map of measurement reliability and validity.

distinct elements such as the ability to "reason, plan, solve problems, think abstractly, comprehend complex ideas, learn quickly, and learn from experience" (Gottfredson, 1997, p. 13). To have adequate content validity, any operationalization of intelligence should include questions or items to assess each of these components. Indeed, most IQ tests have multiple categories of items, such as memory span, vocabulary, and problem-solving sections.

Criterion Validity: Does It Correlate with Key Behaviors?

To evaluate the validity of a measure, face and content validity are a good place to start, but most psychologists prefer to rely on more than a subjective judgment: They prefer to see empirical evidence of a measure's validity. There are several ways to collect data on a measure, but in all cases, the point is to make sure the measurement is associated with something it *should* be associated with. In some cases, such relationships can be illustrated by using scatterplots and correlation coefficients. They can be illustrated with other kinds of evidence too, such as comparisons of groups with known properties.

Correlational Evidence for Criterion Validity

Criterion validity evaluates whether the measure under consideration is related to a concrete outcome, such as a behavior, that it should be related to, according to the theory being tested. Suppose you work for a company that wants to predict how well job applicants would do as salespeople. For a few years the company has been using IQ to predict sales aptitude, and they want to establish a better measure, so they hire a consultant to develop a paper-and-pencil scale to measure sales aptitude. How valid is the consultant's measure? The items might look good on a face validity level, but do the test scores correlate with a key behavior: success in selling? This is an empirical question; you would collect unbiased observations about whether the new sales aptitude test is correlated with success in selling.

You could give the sales test to each current sales representative and then measure their sales figures (a measure of their selling behavior) sometime later—say, 3 months. You would then compute the correlation between the new sales aptitude measure and the relevant behavioral outcome. We can use scatterplots or *r* to assess the validity of the sales measure. **Figure 5.8A** shows results for one possible test of criterion validity. The score on the sales ability test is plotted on the x-axis, and actual sales performance is plotted on the y-axis. (Alex scored 39 on the test and brought in $38,000 in sales, whereas Irina scored 98 and brought in $100,000.) **Figure 5.8B**, in contrast, shows the association of sales performance with IQ, the measure the company formerly used.

Looking at these two scatterplots, we can see that the relationship in the first one is much stronger than in the second one. In other words, future sales performance is correlated more highly with scores on the sales ability test than with scores on the IQ test. If the data looked like this, the company would conclude that the sales ability test has good criterion validity as a measure of sales aptitude. In contrast, the other results show that scores on an IQ test are a poorer indicator of future sales performance. The IQ test has poor criterion validity as a measure of sales aptitude.

The behavioral criteria provided by criterion validity provide excellent evidence for construct validity. No matter what type of operationalization is used, if it is a good measure of its construct, it should correlate with a criterion behavior or outcome that is related to that construct.

Here's another example. Most colleges in the United States use standardized tests, such as the SAT and ACT, to measure the construct "aptitude for college-level work." To demonstrate that these tests have criterion validity, an

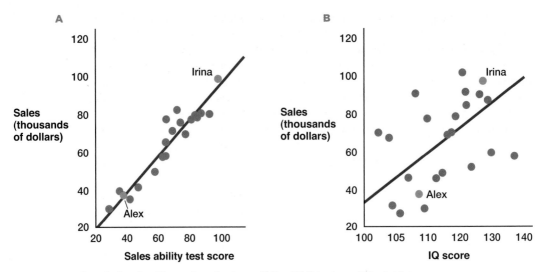

FIGURE 5.8 Correlational evidence for criterion validity. (A) Criterion validity is high. (B) Criterion validity is lower.

educational psychologist might want to show that scores on these measures are correlated with college grades (an outcome that represents "college-level work").

The Gallup organization presents criterion validity correlations for the ten-point Ladder of Life scale they use to measure happiness. They report, for instance, that across different regions of the U.S., regions with higher levels of happiness also have a higher life expectancy and lower rates of poverty. Such correlational evidence provides criterion validity for the Ladder of Life measure—the measure correlates with key outcomes in ways that make sense (Gallup Healthways, n.d.).

If an IQ test has criterion validity, it should be correlated with behaviors that capture the construct of intelligence, such as how fast people can learn a complex set of symbols (an outcome that represents the conceptual definition of intelligence). Of course, the ability to learn quickly is only one component of that definition. Further criterion validity evidence could show that IQ scores are correlated with other outcomes and behaviors that are theoretically related to intelligence, such as ability to solve problems and indicators of life success (e.g., graduating from college, being employed in a high-level job, or earning a large income).

Known-Groups Evidence for Criterion Validity

Although evidence for criterion validity is commonly represented with correlation coefficients, it does not have to be. Another way to gather evidence for criterion validity is to use a **known-groups paradigm**, in which researchers see whether scores on the measure can discriminate among a set of groups whose behavior is already well understood.

For example, to validate the use of salivary cortisol as a measure of stress, a researcher could compare the salivary cortisol levels in two groups of people: those who are about to give a speech in front of a classroom, and those who are in the audience. Public speaking is recognized as being a stressful situation for many. Therefore, if salivary cortisol is a valid measure of stress, people in the speech group should have higher levels of cortisol than those in the audience group.

Lie detectors are another good example. These instruments record a set of physiological measures (such as skin conductance and heart rate) whose levels are supposed to indicate which of a person's statements are truthful and which are lies. If skin conductance and heart rate are valid measures of lying, we could conduct a known-groups test in which we know in advance which of a person's statements are true and which are false. The physiological measures should be elevated only for the lies, not for the true statements. (For a review of the mixed evidence on lie detection, see Saxe, 1991.)

Known groups can also be used to validate self-report measures. Psychiatrist Aaron Beck and his colleagues developed the Beck Depression Inventory (BDI), a 21-item self-report scale with items that ask about major symptoms of depression (Beck, Ward, Mendelson, Mock, & Erbaugh, 1961). People are asked to circle one of four choices, such as the following:

0 I do not feel sad.
1 I feel sad.
2 I am sad all the time and I can't snap out of it.
3 I am so sad or unhappy that I can't stand it.

0 I have not lost interest in other people.
1 I am less interested in other people than I used to be.
2 I have lost most of my interest in other people.
3 I have lost all of my interest in other people.

A clinical scientist adds up the scores on each of the 21 groups of items for a total BDI score, which can range from a low of 0 (not at all depressed) to a high of 63 .

To test the criterion validity of the BDI, Beck and his colleagues gave this self-report scale to two known groups of people. Some were suffering from clinical depression and some were not, as determined by four psychiatrists who conducted clinical interviews and diagnosed the individuals. The researchers computed the mean BDI scores of the two groups and created a bar graph, shown in **Figure 5.9**. The evidence supports the criterion validity of the BDI: As you can see from the graph, the average BDI score of the known group of depressed people was higher than the average score of the known group of people who were not depressed. The BDI is still widely used today when researchers need a quick and valid way to identify people who are vulnerable to depression.

Beck also used the known-groups paradigm to calibrate scores on the BDI. After the psychiatrists interviewed the people in the sample, they indicated the level of depression in each person: none, mild, moderate, or severe. As expected,

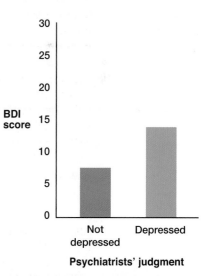

FIGURE 5.9 Known-groups evidence for criterion validity. Patients judged to be more depressed by psychiatrists also scored higher on the BDI. (Source: Adapted from Beck et al., 1961.)

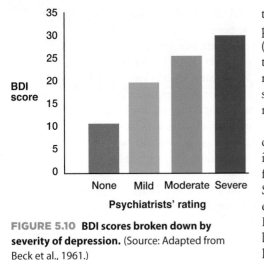

FIGURE 5.10 **BDI scores broken down by severity of depression.** (Source: Adapted from Beck et al., 1961.)

the BDI scores of the groups rose as their level of depression (assessed by psychiatrists) was more severe (**Figure 5.10**). This result was even clearer evidence that the BDI was a valid measure of depression. It also means that researchers can use specific ranges of BDI scores to categorize how severe a person's depression might be.

Diener's subjective well-being (SWB) scale is another example of using known-groups criterion validity. In one article, he presented the SWB scale averages from several different studies. Each study had given the SWB scale to different groups of people who could be expected to vary in happiness (Pavot & Diener, 1993). For example, male prison inmates, a group that would be expected to have low subjective well-being, showed lower scores on the scale, compared with Canadian college students, who averaged much higher (**Table 5.3**). Such known-groups patterns provide strong evidence for the criterion validity of the SWB scale. Researchers can use this scale in their studies with confidence.

What about the Ladder of Life scale, the measure of happiness used by the Gallup organization? This measure also has some known-groups evidence to support its criterion validity. For one, Gallup reported that Americans' well-being was especially low in 2008 and 2009, a period corresponding to a significant downturn in the U.S. economy. Well-being is a little bit higher in American summer months, as well. These results fit what we would expect if the Ladder of Life is a valid measure of well-being (**Figure 5.11**).

TABLE 5.3 Subjective Well-Being (SWB) Scores for Different Known Groups, as Studied by Various Researchers

Sample characteristics	N	M	SD	Study reference
American college students	244	23.7	6.4	Pavot & Diener (1993)
French Canadian college students (male)	355	23.8	6.1	Blais et al. (1989)
Moscow State University students	61	18.9	4.5	Balatsky & Diener (1993)
Korean university students	413	19.8	5.8	Suh (1993)
Older American adults	39	24.2	6.9	Pavot et al. (1991)
Printing trade workers	304	24.2	6.0	George (1991)
Veterans Affairs hospital inpatients	52	11.8	5.6	Frisch (1991)
Abused women	70	20.7	7.4	Fisher (1991)
Male prison inmates	75	12.3	7.0	Joy (1990)

Note: N = Number of people in group. M = Group mean on SWB. SD = Group standard deviation.
Source: Adapted from Pavot & Diener, 1993, Table 1.

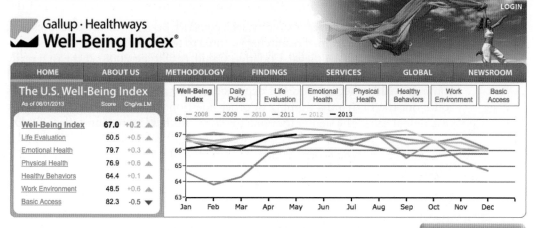

Gallup · Healthways
Well-Being Index®

| HOME | ABOUT US | METHODOLOGY | FINDINGS | SERVICES | GLOBAL | NEWSROOM |

The U.S. Well-Being Index
As of 06/01/2013

	Score	Chg/vs.LM
Well-Being Index	67.0	+0.2 ▲
Life Evaluation	50.5	+0.5 ▲
Emotional Health	79.7	+0.3 ▲
Physical Health	76.9	+0.6 ▲
Healthy Behaviors	64.4	+0.1 ▲
Work Environment	48.5	+0.6 ▲
Basic Access	82.3	-0.5 ▼

The Gallup-Healthways Well-Being Index® is the first-ever daily assessment of U.S. residents' health and well-being. By interviewing at least 500 U.S. adults every day, the Well-Being Index provides real-time measurement and insights needed to improve health, increase productivity, and lower healthcare costs. Public and private sector leaders use data on life evaluation, physical health, emotional health, healthy behavior, work environment, and basic access to develop and prioritize strategies to help their communities thrive and grow. Journalists, academics, and medical experts benefit from this unprecedented resource of health statistics and behavioral economic data to inform their research and reporting.

2012 Well-Being Index Findings

Gallup and Healthways have released in-depth 2012 state reports, which include city and congressional district level findings for each state. To download these reports, click here.

To download the 2012 Composite City, State and Congressional District Ranking Report, click here.

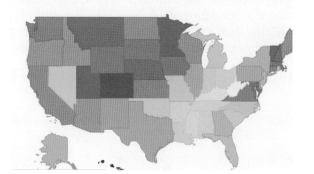

FIGURE 5.11 The Gallup Healthways Well-Being Index. Yearly and seasonal patterns in the Well-Being Index provide some criterion validity evidence for this measure.

Convergent Validity and Discriminant Validity: Does the Pattern Make Sense?

Criterion validity examines whether a measure correlates with key outcomes and behaviors. Another form of validity evidence is whether there is a meaningful pattern of similarities and differences. The measure should correlate more strongly with other measures of the same constructs—showing **convergent validity**; and it should correlate less strongly with measures of different constructs—demonstrating **discriminant validity** (or *divergent validity*).

Convergent Validity

As an example of convergent validity, let's consider Beck's measure of depression, the BDI, again. One team of researchers wanted to test the convergent and discriminant validity of the BDI (Segal, Coolidge, Cahill, & O'Riley, 2008). If the BDI really measures depression, the researchers reasoned, it should be correlated with (should converge with) other measures of depression. They asked a sample of 376 adults to fill out the BDI and a number of other questionnaires, including a self-report instrument called the Center for Epidemiologic Studies Depression scale (CES-D).

As expected, the BDI was positively, strongly correlated with the CES-D ($r = .68$). People who scored as depressed on the BDI measure of depression also scored as depressed on the CES-D measure of depression; likewise, those who scored as not depressed on the BDI also scored as not depressed on the CES-D. **Figure 5.12** shows a scatterplot of the results. (Notice that most of the points fall in the lower left-hand portion of the scatterplot, because most people in the sample are not depressed: They score low on both the BDI and the CES-D.) This correlation between similar measures of the same construct (depression) provided good evidence for the convergent validity of the BDI.

For more on the strength of correlations, see Chapter 8, Table 8.4, and Statistics Review: Descriptive Statistics, pp. 452–456.

Testing for convergent validity can feel circular. Even if researchers validate the BDI with the CES-D, for instance, there is no assurance that the CES-D measure is the gold standard. Indeed, its validity would need to be established, too! The researchers might next try to validate the CES-D with a third measure, but that measure's validity would also need to be supported with evidence. Eventually, however, they might be satisfied that a measure is valid after evaluating the *weight* and *pattern* of the evidence. Many researchers are most convinced when measures have been associated with a variety of behaviors (using criterion validity). However, no single definitive test will establish validity (Smith, 2005a).

FIGURE 5.12 Evidence supporting the convergent validity of the BDI. The BDI is strongly correlated with another measure of depression, the CES-D ($r = .68$), providing evidence for convergent validity. (Source: Segal et al., 2008.)

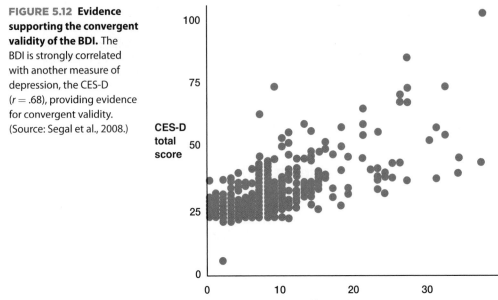

Discriminant Validity

Whereas the BDI should correlate with another measure of depression, it should not correlate strongly with measures of constructs other than depression. In other words, it should show discriminant validity with those measures. For example, depression is not the same as a person's perception of his or her overall physical health. Although mental health and physical health probably do overlap somewhat, we would not expect the BDI to be strongly correlated with a measure of perceived physical health. More importantly, we would expect the BDI to be more strongly correlated with the CES-D than it is with physical health. In fact, Segal and his colleagues found, as expected, a correlation of only $r = -.17$ between the BDI and a measure of perceived physical health. This weak correlation shows that the BDI is different from people's perceptions of their physical health, so we can say that the BDI has discriminant validity (divergent validity) with physical health. **Figure 5.13** shows a scatterplot of the results.

Notice something important: What matters is that this correlation is weak, not that it is negative. To provide evidence for discriminant validity, we care about the pattern: We expect that the (discriminant) correlation of the BDI with physical health is not as strong as its (convergent) correlation with CES-D. (Notice also that most of the points fall in the upper left-hand portion of the scatterplot, because most people in the sample are both physically healthy and not depressed: They score low on the BDI and high on the physical health scale.)

As another example, consider that many developmental disorders have similar symptoms, but diagnoses might be different. It might be important to specify, for instance, whether a child has autism or whether she has a language delay only. Therefore, a screening instrument that is supposed to determine if a child has autism should have discriminant validity; it should not accidentally

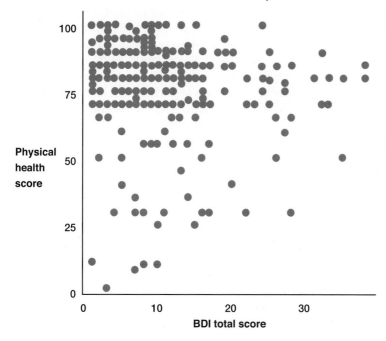

FIGURE 5.13 Evidence supporting the discriminant validity of the BDI. As expected, the BDI is only weakly, negatively correlated with physical health ($r = -.17$), providing evidence for discriminant validity. (Source: Segal et al., 2008.)

diagnose those same children as having language delay. Similarly, a scale that is supposed to diagnose learning disabilities should not be correlated with IQ, because learning disabilities are not related to general intelligence.

It is usually not necessary to establish discriminant validity between a measure and something that is completely unrelated. Because depression is not likely to be associated with how many movies you watch or the number of siblings you have, we would not need to examine its discriminant validity with these variables. Instead, researchers worry about discriminant validity when they want to be sure that their measure is not accidentally capturing a similar but different construct. Does the BDI measure depression or perceived health? Does Diener's SWB measure capture enduring happiness or just temporary mood? Does a measure capture autism, or language delay? Before researchers use a measurement tool, they need to be sure of what it really measures.

Convergent validity and discriminant validity are usually evaluated together, as a pattern. A measurement should correlate more strongly with similar traits (convergent validity) and less strongly with dissimilar traits (discriminant validity). There are no hard-and-fast rules for what the correlations should be. Instead, the overall pattern of convergent and discriminant validity helps researchers decide whether their operationalization really measures the construct they want it to measure—as opposed to other constructs.

The Relationship Between Reliability and Validity

One essential point is worth reiterating: The validity of a measure is not the same as its reliability. A journalist might claim that some measure of behavior is "a very reliable test," but to say that a measure is "reliable" is only half the story. A measure (such as a measure of head circumference) can be extremely reliable but still may not be valid for an intended use (as a measure of intelligence).

Although a measure may be less valid than it is reliable, it cannot be more valid than it is reliable. Intuitively, this statement makes sense. Reliability has to do with how well a measure correlates with itself. For example, an IQ test is reliable if it is correlated with itself over time. Validity, however, has to do with how well a measure is associated with something else, such as a key behavior or another indicator of intelligence. An IQ test is valid if it is associated with another variable, such as school grades or life success. If a measure does not even correlate with itself, then how can it be more strongly associated with some other variable? Therefore, reliability is necessary (but not sufficient) for validity.

CHECK YOUR UNDERSTANDING

1. What do face validity and content validity have in common?
2. To establish criterion validity, researchers make sure the scale or measure is correlated with _____.
3. Which requires stronger correlations for its evidence: convergent validity or discriminant validity?

---

1. See pp. 137–138. **2.** Some relevant behavior or outcome; see pp. 139–142. **3.** Convergent validity.

146   **CHAPTER 5**   Identifying Good Measurement

Review: Interpreting Construct Validity Evidence

Before using a stopwatch in a track meet, coaches probably want to be sure the stopwatch is working well. Before testing a patient's blood pressure, a nurse may want to be sure the cuff she is using is reliable and accurate. Similarly, before conducting a study, researchers want to be sure the measures they plan to use are reliable and valid ones. When you read a research study, you should be asking: Do the authors provide evidence that the measures they are using have construct validity?

How will you identify good measurement when you read about a study? Authors often include reliability and validity evidence in their Method section, where they describe their measures. How might they present this evidence, and how can you evaluate it?

Interrogating a Measure of Religiosity

Sasaki and Kim (2011) examined the variable of religiosity in a series of studies published in an empirical journal article. They explored how religiosity is related to coping in different cultures. The measure of religiosity they used is introduced in the Method section of the article:

> The background questionnaire included a 10-item reliable, validated scale to assess level of general religiosity (Worthington et al., 2003; $\alpha = .95$). Example items include "My religious beliefs lie behind my whole approach to life," and "I enjoy working in the activities of my religious organization." (p. 409)

This statement tells you four things about the measure of religiosity these researchers used. First, they used a 10-item self-report measure. Second, the authors report the internal reliability of the 10-item scale. The value $\alpha = .95$ indicates that people in Sasaki and Kim's study answered the 10 items in a consistent manner. A Cronbach's alpha level of .95 is considered very good internal reliability because it is close to 1.0. Third, it says that the 10-item measure of religiosity was developed by a researcher named Worthington and his colleagues. Fourth, the statement informs you that the 10-item scale by Worthington is "reliable" and "validated."

Sasaki and Kim do not say anything else about the specific evidence for the validity of the religiosity measure. To learn more about how it was validated, you can look up the Worthington et al. (2003) journal article. Using the information in Sasaki and Kim's references section, you can locate the Worthington article in the *Journal of Counseling Psychology* and read about the evidence it presents.

The Worthington article documents the reliability and validity evidence for that team's 10-item religiosity scale, which they call the Religious Commitment

Item

1. I often read books and magazines about my faith.
2. I make financial contributions to my religious organization.
3. I spend time trying to grow in understanding of my faith.
4. Religion is especially important to me because it answers many questions about the meaning of life.
5. My religious beliefs lie behind my whole approach to life.
6. I enjoy spending time with others of my religious affiliation.
7. Religious beliefs influence all my dealings in life.
8. It is important to me to spend periods of time in private religious thought and reflection.
9. I enjoy working in the activities of my religious organization.
10. I keep well informed about my local religious group and have some influence in its decisions.

FIGURE 5.14 The Religious Commitment Inventory. Each item is answered on a scale from 1 ("not at all true of me") to 5 ("totally true of me"). Does this scale have criterion validity? Are people who agree with these items more likely to attend religious services? (Source: Worthington et al., 2003.)

Inventory, or RCI (**Figure 5.14**). Over several years, the researchers administered the RCI to several samples of people, including undergraduates at state schools, undergraduates at Christian schools, religiously diverse undergraduates, and clients who were attending counseling sessions. They presented all the RCI data in their journal article.

In the text of the article, you can read about the reliability of the scale. The authors write:

> The coefficient alpha for the new RCI-10 . . . was .93 for the full scale. (Worthington, et al., 2003, p. 87)

They also include test-retest reliability information:

> The 5-month test-retest reliability was also high, $r(121) = .84, p < .001$. (Worthington et al., 2003, p. 91)

The first statement, about a Cronbach's alpha of .93, means that the 10 items in the RCI were all answered in a consistent manner by their participants. A value of .93 for Cronbach's alpha is very high. (Cronbach's alpha will vary slightly from sample to sample, which explains why this value is different in the Sasaki and Kim study.) The second statement means the scores were very stable over time. A correlation of .84 is a very high test-retest correlation. Thus, the scale is reliable, because the scores are consistent.

In terms of validity, the researchers present a variety of correlational evidence that supports the validity of the RCI. **Figure 5.15** shows one example of this evidence, taken from a study of 213 clients who had come in for counseling. In the first column of the table, the yellow-highlighted values show the mean score on the RCI for subgroups of the full sample. Protestants and Roman Catholics reported higher mean scores than those who reported a religious denomination

Table 4
Means and Standard Deviations of Religious Commitment for Clients, With Correlations (Study 6)

	Full scale RCI–10		Intrapersonal RCI		Interpersonal RCI		RCI–10 correlation with		
	M	*SD*	*M*	*SD*	*M*	*SD*	Attendance	Single-item religious commitment	Intensity of spiritual life
Counselors									
Full sample (*N* = 51)	38.7	12.4	24.1	7.4	14.5	5.2			
Agency									
Christian (*n* = 33)	45.9	4.4	28.5	1.8	17.4	3.0			
Secular (*n* = 18)	25.5	11.3	16.2	7.2	9.3	4.4			
Clients									
Full sample (*N* = 213)	33.7	12.5	21.2	7.6	12.5	5.4	.76	.82	.66
Gender									
Female (*n* = 151)	33.3	12.9	21.2	7.8	12.2	5.5			
Male (*n* = 59)	34.2	11.4	21.2	7.0	13.1	5.0			
Ethnicity									
European American (*n* = 170)	33.6	12.7	21.2	7.8	12.5	5.4			
African American (*n* = 24)	37.3	9.8	23.4	5.7	14.0	4.7			
Asian American (*n* = 6)	22.7	10.9	14.2	5.6	8.5	6.0			
Denomination									
Protestant (*n* = 140)	37.9	10.3	23.6	6.3	14.3	4.6	.60	.72	.70
None (*n* = 36)	22.3	10.6	14.9	7.0	7.8	4.4	.77	.80	.58
Roman Catholic (*n* = 19)	30.1	13.9	19.0	8.6	11.1	5.5	.83	.86	.76
Other (*n* = 11)	27.6	12.4	17.5	7.2	10.2	5.8	.94	.92	.61

Note. RCI–10 = Religious Commitment Inventory—10. For all correlations, *p* < .001.

FIGURE 5.15 Validity evidence for the RCI. The values highlighted in yellow provide known-groups criterion validity, and the values highlighted in blue provide criterion validity and convergent validity. (Source: Adapted from Worthington et al., 2003, Table 4.)

of "none" or "other." These data provide evidence for known-groups criterion validity: People who report affiliating with a religious denomination are more religious than those who do not.

The blue-highlighted correlations on the right side of the table provide evidence for the scale's criterion validity and convergent validity. The RCI-10 is correlated .76 with reported church attendance; this is criterion validity evidence because religious attendance is a key behavior that should correlate with the RCI. In addition, the RCI-10 correlates with two other similar measures of religiosity: it correlates .82 with a one-item measure of religious commitment and .66 with a measure of the intensity of spiritual life. These values are evidence of convergent validity.

Finally, the article presents some evidence for the RCI's discriminant validity. Worthington and his colleagues explain that the RCI-10 is not correlated with another self-report scale that asked about morality: "Morality was not significantly related to religious commitment as measured by the full-scale RCI–10, *r* (154) = .09" (Worthington et al., 2003, p. 88). Because religiosity is a different construct than morality (people can act morally without being religious), the two should not be correlated, and indeed they are not. The low correlation of .09 provides discriminant validity evidence; the RCI is measuring religiosity—not morality.

In their published journal article, the Worthington research team present a variety of empirical evidence on the RCI's internal reliability, test-retest reliability, criterion validity, and convergent and discriminant validity. You should be very convinced of this measure's overall construct validity. Now you are better informed about why Sasaki and Kim called the RCI a "reliable, validated scale" (2011, p. 409). They chose a good scale of religiosity to use in their research.

Interrogating Gallup's Headline

Religious Americans Enjoy Higher Well-Being

The American polling organization Gallup also asks Americans about religiosity. In fact, their data are behind one of this chapter's opening headlines. As a final example, you can interrogate the construct validity behind the Gallup headline.

You would look for validity evidence behind each of the two variables—religiosity and well-being. You already know about one of these; Gallup measures well-being with the Ladder of Life scale, which does seem to have good validity evidence. What about their measure of religiosity? Gallup does not use the Worthington RCI scale. Instead, Gallup polls typically ask only one item per topic, and they use the following question:

> How important would you say religion is in your own life—very important, fairly important, or not very important?

Is this single-item measure of religiosity a reliable and valid one? What kind of evidence would support its construct validity? You might ask if people give consistent scores over time: What is the test-retest reliability of this item? You might also ask if people's answer to this question is associated with religious behaviors (that would be criterion validity) or with other measures of religiosity—even Worthington's (that would be convergent validity). Unfortunately, although the Gallup organization includes some details about how it conducts its research, it does not include any reliability and validity evidence for this item about religion. If Gallup has conducted a pilot test on the item, the results of that work are not publicly available on its website.

It is possible that Gallup does not expect general readers to be appropriately trained or motivated to ask for data on the construct validity of their polling questions. (If this is the case, Gallup may be willing to share additional reliability and validity details on request.) If you were interrogating Gallup's measure of religiosity, you'd have to conclude that you do not have enough information. In this case, "I don't know" is the answer: You don't have a lot of evidence that this item has construct validity.

Although Gallup has not published any data that specifically addresses the item's construct validity, it is worth noting that results fit what you would expect. For example, Gallup reports that Utah and some Southern states, such as Mississippi, have higher percentages of people who claim to be "very religious," and some New England states, such as Vermont, have much lower percentages of religious people. The regional pattern counts as known-groups criterion validity evidence. Other observers have concluded that Utah and the U.S. South are very religious regions, so the fact that Gallup's item shows this pattern means the item has some criterion validity.

Summary

- The construct validity of a study's measured variables is something you will interrogate for any type of claim.

Ways to Measure Variables

- Psychological scientists measure variables in every study they conduct. Three common types of measures are self-report, in which a person reports on his or her own behaviors, beliefs, or attitudes; observational measures, in which raters record the visible behaviors of people or animals; and physiological measures, in which researchers measure biological data, such as heart rate, brain activity, and hormone levels.
- Depending on how they are operationalized, variables may be categorical or quantitative. The levels of categorical variables are categories. The levels of quantitative variables are meaningful numbers, in which higher numbers represent more of some variable.
- Quantitative variables can be further classified in terms of ordinal, interval, or ratio scales.

Reliability of Measurement: Are the Scores Consistent?

- Both measurement reliability and measurement validity are important for establishing a measure's construct validity.
- Researchers use scatterplots and correlation coefficients (among other methods) to evaluate evidence for a measure's reliability and validity.
- To establish a measure's reliability, researchers collect data to see whether the measure works consistently. There are three types of measurement reliability.
- Test-retest reliability establishes whether a sample gives a consistent pattern of scores at more than one testing.

- Interrater reliability establishes whether two observers give consistent ratings of a sample of targets.
- Internal reliability is established when a sample of people answer a set of similarly worded items in a consistent way.
- Measurement reliability is necessary but not sufficient for measurement validity.

Validity of Measurement: Does It Measure What It Is Supposed to Measure?

- Measurement validity can be established with subjective judgments (face validity and content validity) or with empirical data.
- Empirically derived validity tests include criterion validity as well as convergent and discriminant validity.
- Criterion validity requires showing that an operationalization is correlated with outcomes that it should correlate with, according to the understanding of the construct.
- Convergent and discriminant validity require showing that a measure is correlated in a pattern—more strongly with measures of similar constructs than with measures of dissimilar constructs.

Review: Interpreting Construct Validity Evidence

- You can read about a measure's reliability and validity by looking at the details reported in the Method section of empirical journal articles. Such evidence may be reported in the text, as a table of results, or through reference to a longer article that presents full reliability and validity evidence.
- Polling organizations might present data on the construct validity of their questions on their websites.

Key Terms

self-report measure, p. 124
observational measure, p. 125
physiological measure, p. 125
categorical variable, p. 127
quantitative variable, p. 127
ordinal scale, p. 127
interval scale, p. 127
ratio scale, p. 128

reliability, p. 129
validity, p. 129
test-retest reliability, p. 129
interrater reliability, p. 129
internal reliability, p. 129
correlation coefficient r, p. 132
slope direction, p. 132
strength, p. 132

Cronbach's alpha, p. 135
face validity, p. 137
content validity, p. 137
criterion validity, p. 139
known-groups paradigm,
   p. 140
convergent validity, p. 143
discriminant validity, p. 143

 To see samples of chapter concepts in the popular press, visit
www.everydayresearchmethods.com and click the box for Chapter 5.

Review Questions

1. Classify each operational variable below as categorical or quantitative. If the variable is quantitative, further classify it as ordinal, interval, or ratio.
   a. Degree of pupil dilation in a person's eyes in a study of romantic couples (measured in millimeters).
   b. Number of books a person owns.
   c. A book's sales rank on Amazon.com.
   d. Location of a person's hometown (urban, rural, or suburban).
   e. Nationality of the participants in a cross-cultural study of Canadian, Ghanaian, and French students.
   f. A student's grade in school.

2. Which of the following correlation coefficients best describes the pictured scatterplot?
   a. $r = .78$ c. $r = .03$
   b. $r = -.95$ d. $r = .45$

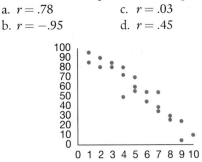

3. Classify each of the following results as an example of internal reliability, interrater reliability, or test-retest reliability.
   a. A researcher finds that people's scores on a measure of extroversion stay stable over 2 months.
   b. An infancy researcher wants to measure how long a 3-month-old baby looks at a stimulus on the right and left sides of a screen. Two undergraduates watch a tape of the eye movements of ten infants and time how long each baby looks to the right and to the left. The two sets of timings are correlated $r = .95$.
   c. A researcher asks a sample of 40 people a set of five items that are all capturing how extroverted they are. The Cronbach's alpha for the five items is found to be .65.

4. Classify each result below as an example of face validity, content validity, convergent and discriminant validity, or criterion validity.
   a. A professor gives a class of 40 people his five-item measure of conscientiousness (e.g., "I get chores done right away," "I follow a schedule," "I do not make a mess of things"). Average scores are correlated ($r = -.20$) with how many times each student has been late to class during the semester.

b. A professor gives a class of 40 people his five-item measure of conscientiousness (e.g., "I get chores done right away," "I follow a schedule," "I do not make a mess of things"). Average scores are more highly correlated with a self-report measure of tidiness ($r = .50$) than with a measure of general knowledge ($r = .09$).

c. The researcher e-mails his five-item measure of conscientiousness (e.g., "I get chores done right away," "I follow a schedule,"

"I do not make a mess of things") to 20 experts in personality psychology, and asks them if they think his items are a good measure of conscientiousness.

d. The researcher e-mails his five-item measure of conscientiousness (e.g., "I get chores done right away," "I follow a schedule," "I do not make a mess of things") to 20 experts in personality psychology, and asks them if they think he has included all the important aspects of conscientiousness.

Learning Actively

1. For each measure below, indicate which kinds of reliability would need to be evaluated. Then, draw a scatterplot indicating that the measure has good reliability and another one indicating that the measure has poor reliability. (Pay special attention to how you label the axes of your scatterplots.)

   a. Researchers place unobtrusive video recording devices in the living rooms of 20 children. Later, coders view tapes and code how many minutes each child spends playing video games.

   b. Clinical psychologists have developed a seven-item self-report measure to quickly identify people who are at risk for panic disorder.

   c. Psychologists measure how long it takes a mouse to learn an eyeblink response. For 60 trials, they present a mouse with a distinctive blue light followed immediately by a puff of air. The 5th, 10th, and 15th trials are test trials, in which they present the blue light alone (without the air puff). The mouse is said to have learned the eyeblink response if observers record that it blinked its eyes in response to a blue light test trial. The earlier in the 60 trials the mouse shows the eyeblink response, the faster it has learned the response.

   d. A restaurant owner uses a response card with four items in order to evaluate how satisfied customers are with the food, service, ambience, and overall experience. Each item is scaled from one to four stars.

   e. Educational psychologists use teacher ratings of classroom shyness (on a nine-point scale, where 1 = "not at all shy in class" and 9 = "very shy in class") to measure children's temperament.

2. Consider how you might validate the nine-point classroom shyness rating example in question 1e. First, what behaviors might be relevant to use to test this rating's criterion validity? Draw a scatterplot showing the results of a study in which the classroom shyness rating has good criterion validity (be careful how you label the axes). Second, come up with ways to evaluate the convergent and discriminant validity of this rating system. What traits should correlate strongly with shyness? What traits should correlate only weakly or not at all? Explain why you chose those traits. Draw a scatterplot showing the results of a study in which the shyness rating has good convergent or discriminant validity (be careful how you label the axes).

PART III

Tools for Evaluating Frequency Claims

"Should I buy these boots? They got four and a half stars on Zappos."

"I'm not taking that class. The professor has a frowny face on ratemyprofessors .com."

"What's the difference between a pit bull and a hockey dad? There is no difference."

(*Star Tribune*, 2008)

6

Surveys and Observations: Describing What People Do

A year from now, you should still be able to:

1. Explain how carefully prepared questions improve the construct validity of a poll or survey.
2. Describe how researchers can make observations with good construct validity.

You should be able to identify the three statements that open this chapter as single-variable frequency claims. Each claim is based on data from one variable: the rated quality of a pair of boots, opinions about a professor, or beliefs about the aggression of hockey fans. Where do the data for such claims come from? This chapter focuses on the construct validity of surveys and polls, in which researchers ask people questions, as well as observational studies, in which researchers watch the behavior of people or other animals, often without asking any questions at all. Researchers use surveys, polls, and observations to measure variables for any type of claim. However, in this chapter and the next, we primarily focus on how surveys and observations are used to measure one variable at a time—for frequency claims.

Construct Validity of Surveys and Polls

Researchers use surveys and polls to ask people questions over the telephone, in door-to-door interviews, through the mail, or over the Internet. You may have been asked to take surveys in various situations. Perhaps after you purchased a new pair of shoes, you got an e-mail asking you to post an online review. While you were reading an online newspaper, maybe a survey popped up. A polling organization, such as Gallup or Pew Research Center, may have called you at home.

The word *survey* is often used when people are asked about a consumer product, whereas the word *poll* is used when people are asked about their social or political opinions. However, these two terms can be interchangeable, and in this book, **survey** and **poll** both mean the same thing: a method of posing questions to people on the phone, in personal interviews, on written questionnaires, or online. Psychologists might conduct national polls as part of their research, or they may use the polling information they read (as consumers of information) to inspire further research.

How much can you learn about a phenomenon just by asking people questions? It depends on how you ask. As you will learn, researchers who develop their questions carefully can support frequency claims that have excellent construct validity.

Choosing Question Formats

Survey questions can follow many formats. Researchers may ask **open-ended questions** that allow respondents to answer any way they like. For example, they might ask people to name the public figure they admire the most. They might ask a sample of people to describe their views on immigration. They might ask students, "What are your comments about this professor?" The various responses to open-ended questions provide researchers with spontaneous, rich information. The drawback is that the responses must be coded and categorized, a process that can often be difficult and time-consuming. In the interest of efficiency, therefore, researchers in psychology often restrict the answers people can give. There are several approaches.

One specific way to ask survey questions is in a **forced-choice format**, in which people give their opinion by picking the best of two or more options. This type of question is frequently used in political polls, such as asking which of two or three candidates respondents are most likely to vote for, or asking for opinions on current issues or preference between two choices.

An example of a psychology measure that uses the forced-choice format is the Narcissistic Personality Inventory (NPI; Raskin & Terry, 1988). This instrument asks people to choose one statement from each of 40 pairs of items, such as the following:

1. _____ I really like to be the center of attention.
   _____ It makes me uncomfortable to be the center of attention.
2. _____ I am going to be a great person.
   _____ I hope I am going to be successful.

To score a survey like this, the researcher adds up the number of times people choose the "narcissistic" response over the "non-narcissistic" one (in the example items above, the narcissistic response is the first option).

In another question format, people are presented with a statement and are asked to use a rating scale to indicate their degree of agreement. When such a scale contains more than one item and is anchored by the terms *strongly agree, agree, neither agree nor disagree, disagree,* and *strongly disagree*, it is often called a **Likert scale** (Likert, 1932). If it does not follow this format exactly, it may be called a *Likert-type scale*. A commonly used measure of self-esteem, the Rosenberg self-esteem inventory, uses a Likert-type scale (Rosenberg, 1965). Here is one of its ten items:

I am able to do things as well as most other people.

1	2	3	4	5
Strongly disagree				Strongly agree

Instead of degree of agreement, respondents might be asked to rate a target object using a numeric scale that is anchored with adjectives; this is called a **semantic differential format**. For example, on the Internet site ratemyprofessors.com, students give their opinions about a professor using the following adjectives:

Easiness:
Easy   1   2   3   4   5   Hard

Helpfulness:
Useless   1   2   3   4   5   Very helpful

Clarity:
Confusing   1   2   3   4   5   Crystal clear

The five-star rating format that many Internet shopping sites use is another example of this technique (**Figure 6.1**). Generally one star means "poor" or "I don't like it," and five stars means "outstanding" or "I love it."

There are other question types, of course, and researchers might even combine formats on a single survey. The point is that the format of a question (open-ended, forced-choice, or Likert scale) does not make or break its construct validity.

Customer Reviews

★★★★☆ (6)
4.2 out of 5 stars

5 star		3
4 star		2
3 star		0
2 star		1
1 star		0

Share your thoughts with other customers

Write a customer review

See all 6 customer reviews

FIGURE 6.1 A five-star product rating on the Internet. The ratings of products people might buy online are examples of frequency claims. Are such five-star ratings valid indicators of a product's quality?

The way the questions are worded, and the order in which they appear, are much more important.

Writing Well-Worded Questions

As with other research findings, when you interrogate a survey result, your first question is about construct validity: How well was that variable measured? The way a question is worded and presented in a survey can make a tremendous difference in how people answer. It is crucial that each question be clear and straightforward to answer. The creators of the survey work to ensure that the wording and order of the questions do not influence respondents' answers.

Leading Questions

An example of the way question wording can affect survey responses comes from a study in which the researcher asked people about their views on U.S. race relations in a Gallup poll (Wilson, 2006). Half the participants heard this (forced-choice) version of the question:

> Do you think that relations between Blacks and Whites
> —Will always be a problem?
> —Or that a solution will eventually be worked out?

The other half heard this version:

> Do you think that relations between Blacks and Whites
> —Are as good as they're going to get?
> —Or will they eventually get better?

On the surface, these two questions seem to measure the same thing—how optimistic respondents felt about race relations. However, the results of the study showed that they elicited very different responses. Only 45% of respondents who heard the first version of the question reported being optimistic about race relations; only 45% said that relations "will eventually work out." Of those who heard the second version, 73% reported being optimistic, saying that race relations "will eventually get better." Why would the responses be so different when the questions seem to be asking the same thing? Clearly, they are **leading questions**; there is a difference in meaning because of the wording of the two versions. Framing race relations as a "problem" that needs to be "worked out" is more negative than framing race relations as "good" and possibly getting "better." From this study, you can't tell if the negative version primed people to be negative or if the positive version primed people to be positive—or whether both happened. You have learned, however, that the wording of the question definitely matters.

In general, if the intention of a survey is to capture respondents' true opinions, the survey writers might attempt to word every question as neutrally as possible. When researchers want to measure the extent to which question wording matters for their topic, the best way is to word the questions more than one way. If the results are the same regardless of the wording, they can conclude that question wording does not affect people's responses to that particular topic. If the results are different, then they may need to report the results separately for each version of the question.

Double-Barreled Questions

The wording of a question can become so complicated that respondents have trouble answering in a way that accurately reflects their opinions. In a survey, it is always best to ask a simple question. When people can understand the question, they can give a clear, direct, and meaningful answer, but sometimes survey writers forget this rule. For example, an online survey from the National Rifle Association asked this question:

> Do you agree that the Second Amendment to our United States Constitution guarantees your individual right to own a gun and that the Second Amendment is just as important as your other Constitutional rights?
> ❑ Support
> ❑ Oppose
> ❑ No opinion

This is called a **double-barreled question**; it asks two questions in one. Double-barreled questions have poor construct validity, because people might be responding to the first half of the question, the second half, or both. Therefore, the item could be measuring the first construct, the second construct, or both. Careful researchers would have asked each question separately:

> Do you agree that the second amendment guarantees your individual right to own a gun?
> ❑ Support
> ❑ Oppose
> ❑ No opinion

> Do you agree that the second amendment is just as important as your other constitutional rights?
> ❑ Support
> ❑ Oppose
> ❑ No opinion

Negative Wording

Negatively worded questions can also make survey items unnecessarily complicated. Whenever a question is cognitively difficult for people, it can cause confusion and thus reduce the construct validity of a survey.

An example comes from a survey on Holocaust denial, which found that 20% of Americans denied that the Nazi Holocaust ever happened. In the months that followed the publication of this survey's results, writers and journalists decried and analyzed the "intensely disturbing" news (Kagay, 1994).

Upon further investigation, the Roper polling organization reported that the people in the original telephone poll were asked, "Does it seem possible or does it seem impossible to you that the Nazi extermination of the Jews never happened?" Think for a minute about how you would answer that question. If you wanted to convey the opinion that the Holocaust did happen, you would have to say, "It's impossible that it never happened." In order to give your opinion about the Holocaust accurately, you must also be able to unpack the double negative of *impossible* and *never*. So instead of measuring people's beliefs, the question may be measuring people's working memory or their motivation to pay attention.

We know that the awkward question wording may have affected people's responses because the same polling organization repeated the survey less than a year later, asking the question more clearly: "Does it seem possible to you that the Nazi extermination of the Jews never happened, or do you feel certain that it happened?" This time, only 1% responded that the Holocaust might not have happened; 8% did not know, and 91% said they were certain that it happened (Kagay, 1994). This new result, as well as other polls reflecting similarly low levels of Holocaust denial, indicate that because of the original wording, the question had poor construct validity: It probably did not measure people's true beliefs.

Sometimes even one negative word can make a question difficult to answer. For example, consider the following question:

Abortion should never be restricted.

1	2	3	4	5
Disagree				Agree

To answer this question, those who oppose abortion must think in the double negative ("I *disagree* that abortion should *never* be restricted"), while those who support abortion rights would be able to answer more easily ("I agree—abortion should never be restricted"). When possible, negative wording should be avoided, but researchers sometimes ask questions both ways, like this:

Abortion should never be restricted.

1	2	3	4	5
Disagree				Agree

I favor strict restrictions on abortion.

1	2	3	4	5
Disagree				Agree

After asking the question both ways, the researchers can study the items' internal consistency (using Cronbach's alpha) to see whether people respond similarly to both questions (in this case, agreement with the first item should covary with disagreement with the second item). Like double-barreled questions, negatively worded questions can reduce construct validity because they might capture people's ability or motivation to do the cognitive work, rather than their true opinions.

Question Order

The order in which questions are asked can also affect the responses to a survey. The earlier questions can change the way respondents understand and answer the later questions. For example, a question on a parenting survey such as "How often do your children play?" would have different meanings if the previous questions had been about sports versus music versus daily activities.

Consider this example: Political opinion researcher David Wilson and his colleagues asked people whether they supported affirmative action for different groups (Wilson, Moore, McKay, & Avery, 2008). Half of the participants were asked two forced-choice questions in this order:

1. Do you generally favor or oppose affirmative action programs for women?
2. Do you generally favor or oppose affirmative action for racial minorities?

The other half were asked the same two questions, but in the opposite order:

1. Do you generally favor or oppose affirmative action for racial minorities?
2. Do you generally favor or oppose affirmative action programs for women?

Wilson found that Whites reported more support for affirmative action for minorities when they had first been asked about affirmative action for women. Presumably, most Whites support affirmative action for women more than they do for minorities. To be consistent, they might feel obligated to express support for affirmative action for racial minorities if they have just indicated their support for affirmative action for women.

The most direct way to control for order effects is to prepare different versions of a survey, with the questions in different sequences. That way, researchers can look for order effects. If the results for the first order differ from the results for the second order, researchers can report both sets of results separately. In addition, they might be safe in assuming that people's endorsement of the first question on any survey is unaffected by previous questions.

Encouraging Accurate Responses

Careful researchers pay attention to how they word and order their survey questions. But what about the people who answer them? People can give meaningful responses to many kinds of questions. In certain situations, however, people are less likely to respond accurately. It's not because they are intentionally being dishonest; they might give inaccurate answers because they don't make an effort to think about each question, because they want to look good, or because they are simply unable to report accurately about their own motivations and memories.

Giving Meaningful Responses Efficiently

Some students are skeptical that people can *ever* report accurately on surveys. Despite what you might think, though, self-reports can sometimes be ideal. People are able to report their own gender, socioeconomic status, ethnicity, and so on; there is no need to use more expensive or difficult measures to collect such information.

More importantly, self-reports often provide the most meaningful information you can get. Diener and his colleagues, in their studies of well-being (see Chapter 5), were specifically interested in subjective perspectives on happiness, so it made sense to ask participants to self-report on aspects of their life satisfaction.

In some cases, self-reports might be the only option. For example, researchers who study dreaming can monitor brain activity to identify *when* someone is dreaming, but they need to use self-reports to find out the *content* of the person's dreams, because only the dreamer experiences the dream. Other traits are not very observable, such as how anxious somebody is feeling. Therefore, it is meaningful and effective to ask people to self-report on their own subjective experiences (Vazire & Carlson, 2011).

Using Shortcuts

Response sets, also known as *nondifferentiation*, are a type of shortcut respondents can take when answering survey questions. Although response sets do not cause many problems for answering a single, stand-alone item, people might adopt a consistent way of answering all the questions—especially toward the end of a long questionnaire (Lelkes, Krosnick, Marx, Judd, & Park, 2012). Rather than thinking carefully about each question, people might answer all of them positively, negatively, or neutrally. Response sets weaken construct validity because these survey respondents are not saying what they really think.

One common response set is **acquiescence**, or *yea-saying*; this occurs when people say "yes" or "strongly agree" to every item instead of thinking carefully about each one. For example, a respondent might answer "5" to every item on Diener's scale of subjective well-being—not because she is a happy person, but because she is using a yea-saying shortcut (**Figure 6.2**). People apparently have a bias to agree with (say "yes" to) any item—no matter what it states (Krosnick, 1999). Acquiescence can

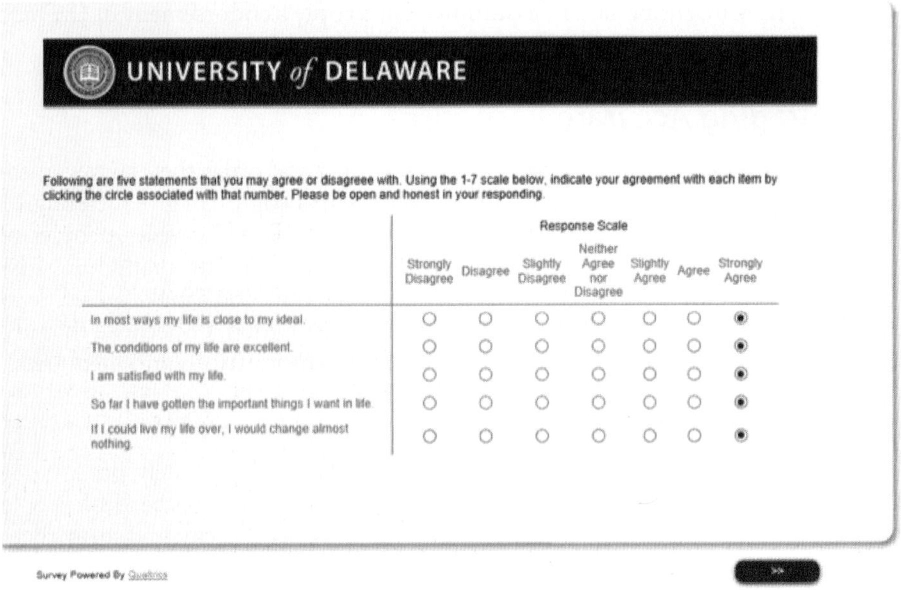
UNIVERSITY *of* DELAWARE

Following are five statements that you may agree or disagreee with. Using the 1-7 scale below, indicate your agreement with each item by clicking the circle associated with that number. Please be open and honest in your responding.

	Response Scale						
	Strongly Disagree	Disagree	Slightly Disagree	Neither Agree nor Disagree	Slightly Agree	Agree	Strongly Agree
In most ways my life is close to my ideal.	○	○	○	○	○	○	◉
The conditions of my life are excellent.	○	○	○	○	○	○	◉
I am satisfied with my life.	○	○	○	○	○	○	◉
So far I have gotten the important things I want in life.	○	○	○	○	○	○	◉
If I could live my life over, I would change almost nothing.	○	○	○	○	○	○	◉

Survey Powered By Qualtrics

>>

FIGURE 6.2
Response sets.
When people use an acquiescent response set, they agree with almost every question or statement. It can be hard to know whether they really mean it, or whether they're being a little bit lazy. (Source: Diener, Emmons, Larsen, & Griffin, 1985.)

threaten construct validity, because instead of measuring the construct of true feelings of well-being, the survey could be measuring the tendency to agree, or the lack of motivation to think and rate carefully.

How can researchers tell the difference between a respondent who is yea-saying and one who really does agree with all the items? The most common way is by including reverse-worded items. (Diener might have asked, for instance, "If I had my life to live over, I'd change almost *everything*.") One benefit is that reverse-worded items might slow people down so they answer more carefully. (Before computing a scale average for each person, the researchers rescore only the reverse-worded items such that, for example, "strongly disagree" becomes a 5 and "strongly agree" becomes a 1.) The scale with reverse-worded items would have more construct validity because high or low averages would be measuring true happiness or unhappiness, instead of acquiescence. A drawback of reverse-wording is that sometimes the result is negatively worded items, which are more difficult to answer.

Another specific response set is **fence sitting**—playing it safe by answering in the middle of the scale, especially when survey items are controversial. People might also answer in the middle (or say "I don't know") when a question is confusing or unclear. Fence sitters can weaken a survey's construct validity when middle-of-the-road scores suggest that some responders do not have an opinion, when they actually do. Of course, some people honestly may have no opinion on the questions; in that case, they choose the middle option for a valid reason. It can be difficult to distinguish those who are unwilling to take a side from those who are truly ambivalent.

Researchers may try to jostle people out of this tendency. One approach is to take away the neutral option. Compare these two formats:

Race relations are going well in this country.

    ○   ○   ○   ○   ○

Strongly disagree   Strongly agree

Race relations are going well in this country.

    ○   ○   ○   ○

Strongly disagree   Strongly agree

When a scale contains an even number of response options, the person has to choose one side or the other, because there is no neutral choice. The drawback of this approach is that sometimes people really do not have an opinion or an answer, so for them, having to choose a side is an invalid representation of their truly neutral stance. Therefore, researchers must carefully consider which format is best.

Another common way to get people off the fence is to use a forced-choice format, in which people must pick one of two answers. Although this reduces fence sitting, again it can frustrate people who feel their own opinion is somewhere in the middle of the two options. In some telephone surveys, interviewers will write down a response of "I don't know" or "No opinion" if a person volunteers that response. Thus, more people get off the fence, but truly ambivalent people can also validly report their neutral opinions.

Trying to Look Good

Most of us want to look good in the eyes of others, but when survey respondents give answers that make them look better than they really are, these responses decrease the survey's construct validity. This phenomenon is known as **socially desirable responding**, or **faking good**. The idea is that because respondents are embarrassed, shy, or worried about giving an unpopular opinion, they will not tell the truth on a survey or other self-report measure. A similar, but less common, phenomenon is called **faking bad**.

To avoid socially desirable responding, a researcher might ensure that the participants know their responses are anonymous—perhaps by conducting the survey online, or by having people put their unsigned responses into a large, closed box. However, anonymity may not be a perfect solution. Anonymous respondents may treat surveys less seriously: In one study, anonymous respondents were more likely to start using response sets in long surveys. In addition, anonymous people were less likely to accurately report a simple behavior, such as how many candies they had just eaten, which suggests they were paying less attention to things (Lelkes et al., 2012).

One way to minimize this problem is to include special survey items that identify socially desirable responders with target items like these:

> My table manners at home are as good as when I eat out in a restaurant.
> I never hesitate to go out of my way to help someone in trouble.

If people agree with many such items, researchers may discard that data from the final set, under suspicion that they are exaggerating on the other survey items, or not paying close attention in general.

Researchers can also ask people's friends to rate them. When it comes to domains where we want to look good (e.g., on how rude or how smart we are), others know us better than we know ourselves (Vazire & Carlson, 2011). Thus, researchers might be better off asking people's friends to rate them on traits that are observable but desirable.

Finally, researchers increasingly use special, computerized measures to evaluate people's implicit opinions about sensitive topics. One widely used test, the Implicit Association Test, asks people to respond quickly to positive and negative words on the right and left of a computer screen (Greenwald, Nosek, & Banaji, 2003). Intermixed with the positive and negative words may be faces from different social groups, such as Black and White faces. People respond to all possible combinations, including positive words with Black faces, negative words with White faces, negative words with Black faces, and positive words with White faces. When people respond more efficiently to the White-positive/Black-negative combination than to the White-negative/Black-positive combination, researchers infer that the person may hold negative attitudes on an implicit, or unconscious, level.

Self-Reporting "More Than They Can Know"

As researchers strive to encourage accurate responses, they also ask whether people are *capable* of reporting accurately on their own feelings, thoughts, and actions. Everyone knows his or her opinions better than anyone else does, right? Only *I* know my level of support for a political candidate. Only *you* know how much you liked a professor. Only *the shopper* knows how much she liked those boots. In some cases, however, self-reports can be inaccurate, especially when people are asked to describe *why* they are thinking, behaving, or feeling the way they do. When asked, most people willingly provide an explanation or an opinion to a researcher, but sometimes they unintentionally give inaccurate responses.

Psychologists Richard Nisbett and Timothy Wilson (1977) conducted a set of studies to demonstrate this phenomenon. In one study, they put six pairs of nylon stockings on a table and asked female shoppers in a store to tell them which of the stockings they preferred. As it turned out, almost everyone selected the last pair on the right. The reason for this preference was something of a mystery—especially

FIGURE 6.3 The accuracy of self-reports. If you ask this shopper why she chooses one of these items, she will probably give you a reasonable answer. But does her answer represent the true reason for making her choice?

since all the stockings were exactly the same! Next, Nisbett and Wilson asked each woman why she selected the pair she did. Every participant reported that she selected the pair on the right for its excellent quality. Even when the researchers suggested that they might have chosen the pair because it was on the far right side of the table, the women insisted they made their choices based on the quality of the stockings. In other words, the women easily formulated answers for the researchers, but their answers had nothing to do with the real reason they selected the one pair of stockings (**Figure 6.3**). Moreover, the women did not seem to be aware that they were inventing a justification for their preference. They gave a sincere, reasonable response—one that just happened to be wrong. Therefore, researchers cannot assume the reasons people give for their own behavior are their actual reasons. People may not be able to accurately explain why they acted.

Self-Reporting Memories of Events

Even if people cannot always self-report reasons behind their behaviors, surely they know what those behaviors were, right? In fact, psychological research has shown that people's memories for the events they have participated in are not very accurate. For example, many Americans can say exactly where they were when they heard the news that two planes had crashed into New York's World Trade Center on September 11, 2001, and their memories are often startlingly vivid. Cognitive psychologists have checked the accuracy of such "flashbulb memories." To conduct such a study, researchers have administered a short questionnaire to their students on the day after a dramatic event, asking them to recall where they were, whom they were with, and so forth. A few years later, the researchers ask the same students the same questions as before, and also ask them to rate their confidence in their memories. Such studies have shown that overall accuracy is very low: For example, about 73% of students recalling their memories of the 9/11 attacks recalled seeing the first plane hit the World Trade Center on TV, when in fact no such footage was shown at that time (Pezdek, 2004).

The other important finding from these studies is that people's confidence in the accuracy of their memories is virtually unrelated to how accurate the memories actually are. Three years later, people who are extremely confident in their memories are about as likely to be wrong as people who report their memories with little or no confidence. In one study, when researchers showed participants what they wrote years ago, on the day after significant events, they were genuinely stumped, saying, "I still think of it as the other way around" or "I mean, like I told you, I have no recollection of [that version] at all" (Neisser & Harsch, 1992, p. 21). Studies like these remind us to question the construct validity of even the most vivid and confidently held "memories" of the past. In other words, asking people what they remember is probably not the best operationalization for studying what really happened to them.

In sum, self-reports are not appropriate for evaluating all research questions. Surveys and polls can be excellent measures of people's subjective states, of what they *think* they are doing, and of what they *think* is influencing their behavior. But if you want to know what people are *really* doing or what *really* influences behavior, you should probably watch them. If you want to know how hot a person subjectively feels, you can ask him or her to tell you, but if you want to know how hot it actually is, you should check a thermometer. Indeed, many researchers prefer to observe behavior directly, rather than rely on self-reports.

CHECK YOUR UNDERSTANDING

1. What are three potential problems related to the wording of survey questions? Can they be avoided?
2. For which topics, and in what situations, are people most likely to answer accurately to survey questions?
3. What are some ways to ensure that survey questions are answered accurately?

1. See pp. 160–163. 2. See p. 163. 3. See pp. 164–168.

Construct Validity of Behavioral Observations

Survey and poll results are one of the most common types of data used to support a frequency claim—the kind you read most often in newspapers or on websites. Researchers also study people simply by watching them in action. When a researcher watches people or animals and systematically records how they behave or what they are doing, it is called **observational research**. Many scientists believe that observing behavior is better than self-reports collected through surveys, because people cannot always report on their behavior or past events accurately. Given the potential for question order effects, response sets, socially desirable responding, and other problems, many psychologists trust behavioral data more than survey data.

Observational research can be the basis for frequency claims. Researchers might record how much people eat in fast-food restaurants. They might observe drivers, counting how many will stop for a pedestrian in a crosswalk. They might listen in on the comments of parents watching a hockey game. Observational research, however, is not just for frequency claims: Observations can also be used to operationalize variables in association claims and causal claims. Regardless of the type of claim, it is important that observational measures have good construct validity.

Examples of Claims Based on Observational Data

Many researchers use data from direct observations to make frequency claims about what people do. In certain cases, these observations provide much richer, more accurate information than survey and poll data.

Observing How Much People Talk

One example of how observational methods have been used in psychology comes from researcher Matthias Mehl, who has observed what people say in everyday contexts. He recruited several samples of students and asked them to wear an electronically activated recorder (EAR) for 2–10 days (depending on the sample). This device contains a small, clip-on microphone and a digital sound recorder similar to an iPod (**Figure 6.4A**). At 12.5-minute intervals throughout the day, the EAR records 30 seconds of ambient sound. Later, research assistants transcribe everything the person says during the recorded time periods. The published data demonstrate that on average, women speak 16,215 words per day, while men speak 15,669 words per day (**Figure 6.4B**). This difference is not statistically significant. Therefore, despite stereotypes of women being the chattier sex, women and men showed the same level of speaking (Mehl, Vazire, Ramirez-Esparza, Slatcher, & Pennebaker, 2007).

For more detail on statistical significance, see Chapter 3, p. 70, and Statistics Review: Inferential Statistics, pp. 482–483.

Observing Hockey Moms and Dads

Another example of observational research comes from Canadian researchers who investigated popular press stories about parents who had acted violently at youth ice hockey games (Bowker et al., 2009). To see how widespread this "problem" was, the researchers decided to observe a sample of hockey games and record the frequency of violent, negative behavior (as well as positive, supportive behavior) by parents. Although the press had reported dramatic stories about fights among parents at youth hockey games, these few instances seem to have been an exception. After sitting in the stands at 69 boys' and girls' hockey games in one Canadian city, the researchers found that 64% of the parents' comments were positive, and only 4% were negative. The authors

Table 1. Estimated number of words spoken per day for female and male study participants across six samples. *N* = 396. Year refers to the year when the data collection started; duration refers to the approximate number of days participants wore the EAR; the weighted average weighs the respective sample group mean by the sample size of the group.

Sample	Year	Location	Duration	Age range (years)	Sample size (*N*)		Estimated average number (SD) of words spoken per day	
					Women	Men	Women	Men
1	2004	USA	7 days	18–29	56	56	18,443 (7460)	16,576 (7871)
2	2003	USA	4 days	17–23	42	37	14,297 (6441)	14,060 (9065)
3	2003	Mexico	4 days	17–25	31	20	14,704 (6215)	15,022 (7864)
4	2001	USA	2 days	17–22	47	49	16,177 (7520)	16,569 (9108)
5	2001	USA	10 days	18–26	7	4	15,761 (8985)	24,051 (10,211)
6	1998	USA	4 days	17–23	27	20	16,496 (7914)	12,867 (8343)
				Weighted average			16,215 (7301)	15,669 (8633)

FIGURE 6.4 Observational research on daily spoken words. This table shows the study's results, as they were reported in the original empirical journal article. (Source: Mehl et al., 2007, Table 1.)

concluded that their results were "in stark contrast to media reports, which paint a grim picture of aggressive spectators and out-of-control parents" (Bowker et al., 2009, p. 311).

Observing Families in the Evening

A final example comes from a study of families in which both parents work (Campos, Wang, Plaksina, Repetti, Schoebi, Ochs, & Beck, 2013). The researchers trained camera crews to follow both parents from a sample of 30 dual-earner families, from the time they left work, around 5:00 P.M., until 8:00 P.M. Later, teams of trained coders coded a variety of behaviors from the resulting tapes. The researchers studied two aspects of family life: the emotional tone of the parents, and the topics of conversation during dinner.

To code emotional tone, they rated each parent on a 7-point scale as they watched the tapes. The rating scale went from 1 (cold/hostile) to 4 (neutral) to 7 (warm/happy) (**Figure 6.5**). The results from the Campos study showed that emotional tone in the families was slightly positive in the evening hours (around 4.2 on the 7-point scale). In addition, they found that kids and parents differed in what they discussed at dinnertime. The kids were more likely to express distaste at the food, while the parents talked about how healthy it was (**Figure 6.6**).

Emotional tone. To measure emotional tone, coders rated the extent to which the behavior of each parent was marked by verbal and nonverbal markers of coldness/hostility or warmth/happiness on a Likert scale (1 = *cold/hostile*; 4 = *neutral*; 7 = *warm/happy*). Cold/hostile emotional tone was defined as short communication, flat or angry affect, and no evidence of positive affect. Neutral tone was defined as a task oriented, practical tone that was neither cold/hostile nor warm/happy. Warm/happy emotional tone was defined as warm voice tones, smiles, laughter, and head nods with no evidence of negative affect. Coders independently rated a parent's emotional tone when they appeared in the video (a) alone, (b) with their partner (if present), or (c) with their 7- to 12-year-old child (if present). The latter rating was restricted to the 7- to 12-year-old child that all families were required to have to standardize interaction that might otherwise vary with stage of child development. Thus, up to three emotional tone variables could be rated for each parent in each 30-s video slice. Interrater reliabilities for emotional tone alone (ICC = .92), with partner (ICC = .91), and with child (ICC = .95) were high.

STRAIGHT *from the* SOURCE

A

Dinnertime talk. Coders documented whether each family member present engaged in each of the following six types of food-related talk: (a) expressions of appreciation, (b) expressions of distaste, (c) reference to health, (d) reference to pleasure, (e) reference to food as a reward, and (f) negotiation over the terms of food rewards or penalties.

STRAIGHT *from the* SOURCE

B

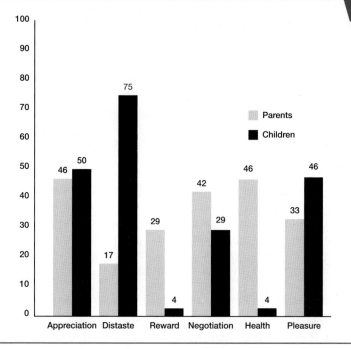

Observations Can Be Better Than Self-Reports

The previous examples illustrate a variety of ways researchers have conducted observational studies, either through direct means, such as sitting in the stands during a hockey game, or by using technology, such as an EAR or a video camera. Let's reflect on the benefits of behavioral observation in these cases. What might have happened if the researchers had asked the participants to self-report? The college students certainly would not have been able to state how many words they spoke each day. The hockey parents might have reported that their own comments at the rink were mostly positive, but they might have exaggerated their reports of other parents' degree of negativity. And while parents could report on how they were feeling, they might not have been able to describe how emotionally warm their expressions appeared to others—the part that matters to their partners and children. Observations can sometimes tell a more accurate story than self-reporting.

Making Reliable and Valid Observations

Observational research is a way to operationalize a conceptual variable, so when interrogating a study we need to ask about the construct validity of any observation. What is the variable of interest, and did the observations accurately measure that variable? Although observational research may seem straightforward, researchers actually work quite diligently to be sure their observations are reliable and valid.

The construct validity of observations can be threatened by three problems: Observer bias, observer effects, and reactivity. Observations have good construct validity to the extent that they can avoid these three problems.

Observer Bias: When Observers See What They Expect to See

Observer bias occurs when observers' expectations influence their interpretation of the participants' behaviors or the outcome of the study. Instead of rating behaviors objectively, observers rate behaviors according to their own expectations or hypotheses. In one study, psychoanalytic therapists were shown a videotape of a 26-year-old man talking to a professor about his feelings and work experiences (Langer & Abelson, 1974). Some of the therapists were told the young man was a patient, while others were told he was a job applicant. After seeing the videotape, the clinicians were asked for their observations. What kind of person was this young man?

Although all the therapists saw the same videotape, their reactions were not the same. Those who thought the man was a job applicant described him with such terms such as "attractive," "candid," and "innovative." Those who saw the videotape thinking the young man was a patient described him as a "tight, defensive person," "frightened of his own aggressive impulses" (Langer & Abelson, 1974, p. 8). Since everyone saw the same tape, these striking differences can only have reflected the biases of the observers in interpreting what they saw.

Observer Effects: When Participants Confirm Observer Expectations

It is problematic when observer biases affect their own interpretation of what they see. It is even worse when the observers actually change the behavior of those they are observing, such that participants' behavior changes to match observer expectations. Known as **observer effects**, or *expectancy effects*, this phenomenon can occur even in seemingly objective observations.

Bright and Dull Rats. In a classic study of observer effects, researchers Rosenthal and Fode (1963) gave each student in an advanced psychology course five rats to test as part of a final lab experience in the course. Each student timed how long it took for their rats to learn a simple maze, every day for several days. Although each student actually received a randomly selected group of rats, the researchers told half of them that their rats were bred to be "maze-bright" and the other half that their rats were bred to be "maze-dull."

Even though all the rats were genetically the same, those that were believed to be maze-bright completed the maze a little faster each day and with fewer mistakes. In contrast, the rats that were believed to be maze-dull did not improve their performances over the testing days. This study showed that observers not only see what they expect to see; sometimes they even cause the behavior of those they are observing to conform to their expectations.

Clever Hans. A horse nicknamed Clever Hans provides another classic example of how observers' subtle behavior changed a subject's behavior, and how scientifically minded observers corrected the problem. More than 100 years ago, a schoolteacher named William von Osten tutored his horse, Hans, in simple mathematics. If he asked Hans to add 3 and 2, for example, the horse would tap his hoof five times and then stop. After 4 years of daily training, Clever Hans could perform subtraction, multiplication, and division at least as well as an average fifth-grader (**Figure 6.7**). Von Osten allowed many scientists to test his horse's abilities, and they were satisfied that von Osten was not giving Hans cues on the sly, because he apparently could do arithmetic even when his owner was not in the room (Pfungst, 1911).

Just when other scientists had concluded that Hans was truly capable of simple math, an experimental psychologist, Oskar Pfungst, came up with a more rigorous set of checks. Suspecting that Hans was sensing subtle cues from his human questioners, Pfungst set up situations in which the questioners did not know what question the horse heard. For example, one of the onlookers would whisper into Hans' ear, "Seven." Then another observer would whisper into the horse's ear, "Plus four." The horse got the question, but neither questioner knew the correct answer.

Under these conditions, Hans was helpless. He would go on tapping his hoof indefinitely. As it turned out, the

FIGURE 6.7 William von Osten and Clever Hans. The horse Clever Hans could detect nonverbal gestures from anybody—not just his owner—so his behavior even convinced a special commission of experts in 1904.

horse *was* extremely clever—but not at math. He was very good at detecting the subtle changes in breathing and posture his questioners would make as his taps approached the right answer. A slight lean at the waist, a furrowed eyebrow—Hans had learned that signs like these were cues to stop tapping.

Preventing Observer Bias and Observer Effects

Researchers must ensure the construct validity of observational measures by taking steps to avoid observer bias and observer effects. First and foremost, careful researchers train their observers well. They create clear rating scales, often called *codebooks*, so the observers can make reliable judgments with less bias. **Figure 6.8** shows an example of how the parents' comments were coded in the hockey games study.

Researchers can assess the construct validity of a coded measure by using multiple observers. Doing so allows the researchers to assess the interrater reliability of their measures. Refer back to Figure 6.5, the excerpt from the Campos et al. (2013) article, in which the researchers discuss the interrater reliability of the emotional tone ratings. The abbreviation ICC is a correlation that quantifies degree of agreement. The closer the correlation is to 1.0, the more the observers agreed with one another. The coders in this case showed acceptable interrater reliability.

Using multiple observers does not eliminate anyone's biases, of course, but if two observers of the same event agree on what happened, the researchers can be

Positive, General (Pg). These comments were defined as positive in tone and as directed at the team in general, with no instructional content (e.g., "Go Crusaders"; "Nice try"; "Good work").

Positive, Specific (Ps). These comments were defined as being positive, but directed at a specific player (e.g., "Nice play JD"; "Way to go LJ").

Corrective/Instructional (Cor). These comments were defined as including a specific action or play that the player was instructed to do. They included comments which were positive in nature (e.g., "Go after it"), and those with a more negative tone (e.g., "Get back"; "You've got to cover him").

Negative (Neg). These comments were defined as those meant to criticize the target in some way (usually directed toward the referee). Much of the time, the negativity of the comment was due to a sarcastic tone (e.g., "What kind of call is that?"; "Come on ref, you call that a penalty?").

Neutral (Neu). These comments were defined as those not fitting into any of the other categories, and/or were unrelated to the game (e.g., "Did you book your hotel room for the tournament?").

Each remark was coded for intensity, based on a three-point scale: 1 = spoken relatively quietly, with little to no emotion; 2 = louder, more intense speech, stronger emotion, but controlled; 3 = loud, intense speech, extreme emotional content.

FIGURE 6.8 Codebooks can improve the construct validity of observations. This information was included in the empirical journal article's Method section. (Source: Adapted from Bowker et al., 2009.)

more sure it really happened that way. If there is disagreement, the researchers may need to train their observers better, develop a clearer coding system for rating the behaviors, or both.

For more on interrater reliability, see Chapter 5, pp. 129–135.

Even when an operationalization has good interrater reliability, it still might not be valid. Even if two observers agree with each other, they might share the same biases, so their common observations are not necessarily valid. Think about the therapists in the Langer and Abelson (1974) study. Those who were told the man in the videotape was a patient might have showed interrater reliability in their descriptions of how defensive or frightened he appeared. But because they shared similar biases, their reliable ratings were not valid descriptions of the man's behavior. Therefore, interrater reliability is only half of the story; researchers should employ methods that minimize observer bias and observer effects.

Masked Research Design. The Rosenthal and Fode (1963) study and the "Clever Hans effect" both demonstrate that observers can give unintentional cues that affect how their subjects act. A common way to prevent observer bias and observer effects is to use a **masked design**, or *blind design*, in which the observers are unaware of the conditions to which participants have been assigned and are unaware of what the study is about.

If Rosenthal and Fode's students had not known which rats were expected to be bright and dull, they would not have evoked different behavior in their charges. Similarly, when Clever Hans' observers did not know the right answer to the questions they were asking, the horse acted differently; he looked much less intelligent. These examples make it clear that coders and observers should not be aware of a study's hypotheses, or should take steps to mask the conditions they are observing.

Reactivity: When Participants React to Being Watched

Sometimes the mere presence of an outsider is enough to change the behavior of those being observed. Imagine you visit a first-grade classroom to observe the children's behavior. You walk quietly to the back of the room and sit down to observe what the children do. What will you see? A roomful of little heads swiveled around looking at you! Do first graders usually spend most of their time staring at the back of the room? Of course not. What you are witnessing is an example of reactivity.

Reactivity occurs when people change their behavior (react) in some way when they know another person is watching. They might be on their best behavior—or in some cases, their worst behavior—rather than display their typical behavior. Reactivity occurs not only with human participants but also with animal subjects. Psychologist Robert Zajonc once demonstrated that even cockroaches behave differently in front of an audience of other cockroaches (Zajonc, Heingartner, & Herman, 1969). If people and animals can change their behavior just because they are being watched, what should a careful researcher do?

FIGURE 6.9 Unobtrusive observations. This one-way mirror lets researchers unobtrusively record the behaviors of children in a preschool classroom.

Solution 1: Blend In. One way to avoid observer effects is to make **unobtrusive observations**—that is, make yourself less noticeable. Developmental researchers might sit behind a one-way mirror, like the one shown in **Figure 6.9**, so they can observe how children interact in a classroom without letting them know. In a public setting, a researcher might act like a casual onlooker—another face in the crowd—to observe the behavior of other people. In the Bowker hockey games study, observers collected data in plain sight by posing as fans in the stands. Across the 69 hockey games they observed, only two parents ever asked the observer what he or she was doing, suggesting that the observer's presence was unobtrusive.

Solution 2: Wait It Out. Another solution is to wait it out. A researcher who plans to observe at a school might let the children get used to his or her presence until they forget about being observed. Jane Goodall, in her studies of chimpanzees in the wild, used a similar tactic. When she began introducing herself to the chimps in the Gombe National Park in Africa, they fled, or dropped whatever else they were doing to focus on her. After several months, the chimps got used to having her around and were no longer afraid to go about their usual activities in her presence. Similarly, participants in the Mehl EAR study reported that after a couple of days of wearing the device, they did not find it to be invasive (Mehl & Pennebaker, 2003).

Solution 3: Measure the Behavior's Results. Another way to avoid reactivity is to use unobtrusive data. Instead of measuring behavior, researchers measure the traces that a behavior leaves behind. For example, in a museum, wear-and-tear on the flooring can signal which areas of the museum are the most popular, and the height of smudges on the windows can indicate the age of visitors; the number of empty liquor bottles in residential garbage cans can indicate how much alcohol is being consumed in a community (Webb, Campbell, Schwartz, & Sechrest, 1966).

Observing People Ethically

Is it ethical for researchers to observe the behaviors of others? It depends. Most psychologists believe it is ethical to observe people behaving in museums, classrooms, hockey games, or even at the sinks of public bathrooms, because in those settings people can reasonably expect their behavior to be public, not private. Of course, when psychologists report the results of such observational studies, they do not specifically identify any of the people who were observed. More secretive methods, such as one-way mirrors or covert video recording, are also considered ethical in some conditions. In most cases, psychological scientists doing research must obtain permission in advance to watch or to record people's private behavior. If hidden video recording is used, the researcher must explain the recording at the conclusion of the study. If people object to having been recorded, the researcher must erase the file without watching it. However, ethical decisions may also be influenced by the policies of a university where a study is conducted. As discussed in Chapter 4, institutional review boards (IRBs) assess each study to decide whether it can be conducted ethically.

CHECK YOUR UNDERSTANDING

1. What is the difference between observer bias and observer effects? How can such biases be prevented?
2. What is reactivity? What three approaches can researchers take to be sure people do not react to being observed?

1. See pp. 172–175. 2. See pp. 175–176.

Summary

- Surveys, polls, and observational methods are used to support frequency claims; they also measure variables for association and causal claims. When interrogating a claim based on data from survey or an observational study, we ask about the construct validity of the measurement.

Construct Validity of Surveys and Polls

- Survey question formats include open-ended, forced-choice, Likert scale, and semantic differential.
- Leading questions might not capture true opinions, and double-barreled and negatively worded questions are difficult to answer in a valid way.
- People sometimes answer survey questions with an acquiescent or fence-sitting response tendency, or in a way that makes them look good. Researchers can add items to a survey, or change the way questions are written, in order to avoid some of these problems.
- Surveys are efficient and accurate ways to assess people's subjective feelings and opinions; they may be less appropriate for assessing people's motivations or memories.

Construct Validity of Behavioral Observations

- Good observations record people's true behavior, rather than what the observer wanted to see or what the observer caused to happen.
- Well-trained coders and clear codebooks help ensure that observations will be reliable and not influenced by observer expectations.
- Some observational studies are susceptible to reactivity. Masked designs and unobtrusive observations make it more likely that observers will not make biased ratings, and that participants will not change their behavior in reaction to being observed.

Key Terms

survey, p. 158
poll, p. 158
open-ended question, p. 158
forced-choice format, p. 158
Likert scale, p. 159
semantic differential format, p. 159
leading question, p. 160

double-barreled question, p. 161
negatively worded question, p. 161
response set, p. 164
acquiescence, p. 164
fence sitting, p. 165
socially desirable responding, p. 166

faking good, p. 166
faking bad, p. 166
observational research, p. 168
observer bias, p. 172
observer effect, p. 173
masked design, p. 175
reactivity, p. 175
unobtrusive observation, p. 176

To see samples of chapter concepts in the popular press, visit www.everydayresearchmethods.com and click the box for Chapter 6.

Review Questions

1. The following item appears on a survey: "Is your cell phone new and does it have all the latest features?" What is the biggest problem with this wording?
   a. It is a leading question.
   b. It involves negative wording.
   c. It is a double-barreled question.
   d. It is not on a Likert scale.

2. When people are using an acquiescent response set they are:
   a. Trying to give the researcher the responses they think he or she wants to hear.

b. Misrepresenting their views to appear more socially acceptable.

c. Giving the same, neutral answer to each question.

d. Tending to agree with every item, no matter what it says.

3. In which of the following situations do people most accurately answer survey questions?
   a. When their answers are anonymous.
   b. When they are describing the reasons for their own behavior.
   c. When they are describing what happened to them, especially after important events.
   d. When they are describing their subjective experience; how they personally feel about something.

4. Which of the following makes it more likely that behavioral observations will have good interrater reliability?
   a. A masked study design
   b. A clear codebook

c. Using naive, untrained coders
d. Open-ended responses

5. Which one of the following is a means of controlling for observer bias?
   a. Using unobtrusive observations.
   b. Waiting for the participants to become used to the observer.
   c. Making sure the observer does not know the study's hypotheses.
   d. Measuring physical traces of behavior rather than observing behavior directly.

6. Which of the following is a way of preventing reactivity?
   a. Waiting for the participants to become used to the observer.
   b. Making sure the observers do not know the study's hypotheses.
   c. Making sure the observer uses a clear codebook.
   d. Ensuring the observers have good interrater reliability.

Learning Actively

1. Consider the various survey question formats: open-ended, forced-choice, Likert scale, and semantic differential. For each of the following research topics, write a question in each format, keeping in mind some of the pitfalls in question writing. Which of the questions you wrote would have the best construct validity, and why?
   a. A study that measures attitudes about women serving in combat roles in the military.
   b. A customer service survey asking people about their satisfaction with their most recent online shopping experience.
   c. A poll that asks people which political party they have supported in the past.

2. Find an online opinion poll. Classify the item types as forced-choice, Likert scale, semantic differential, or some other format. Does each

item appear to be leading, negatively worded, or double barreled? Do you think the items would be easy to answer?

3. Plan an observational study to see which kind of drivers are more likely to stop for a pedestrian in a crosswalk: male or female drivers. Think about how to maximize your construct validity. Will observers be biased about what they record? How might they influence the people they observe, if at all? Where should observers stand to observe driver behavior? How will you evaluate the interrater reliability of your observers? Write a two- to three-sentence operational definition of what it means to "stop for a pedestrian in a crosswalk." Your operational definition should be clear enough that if you asked two friends to use it to code "stopping for pedestrian" behavior, it would have good reliability and validity.

"8 out of 10 pediatricians use Johnson & Johnson products on their own children."

70% of Canadians "Felt Well-Rested Yesterday"

(Gallup Worldview, 2014)

61% Said This Shoe "Felt True to Size"

(Zappos.com)

 *Fit Survey:* **61%** Felt true to size

7

Sampling: Estimating the Frequency of Behaviors and Beliefs

LEARNING OBJECTIVES

A year from now, you should still be able to:

1. Explain why external validity often matters for a frequency claim.
2. Describe which sampling techniques allow generalizing from a sample to a population of interest, and which ones do not.

The claims that open this chapter address a variety of topics: shopping patterns, sleep habits, and the fit of a pair of shoes. The target population in each case is different. One example is about pediatricians, one applies to Canadians (presumably all of them), and the last apparently represents online shoppers. In all three claims, we are being asked to believe something about a larger group of people (e.g., all pediatricians or all Canadians), based on data from a smaller sample that was actually studied. In this chapter, you'll learn about when we can use a sample to generalize to a population, and when we cannot. In addition, you'll learn when we really care about being able to generalize to a population, and when we care less.

Generalizability: Does the Sample Represent the Population?

When interrogating external validity, we ask whether the results of a particular study can be generalized to some larger population of interest. External validity is often extremely important for frequency claims. To interrogate the external validity of frequency claims such as those discussed in Chapter 6 and also presented here, we might ask the following types of questions:

> "Do the students who rated the professor on this website adequately represent all of the professor's former students?"

> "Does the sample of pediatricians who were asked about Johnson & Johnson products adequately represent all pediatricians?"

> "Can the 70% of Canadians in the sample who felt well-rested yesterday generalize to all Canadians?"

> "Do the people who reviewed the fit of these shoes represent the population of people who wear them?"

and even . . .

> "Can we predict the results of the presidential election from the results of this poll if the sample consisted of 1,500 people?"

Recall that external validity concerns both *samples* and *settings*. A researcher may intend the results of a study to generalize to the other members of a certain population, as in the questions above. Or a researcher may intend the results to generalize to other settings, such as other shoes from the same manufacturer, other products, or other classes taught by the same professor. However, this chapter focuses primarily on the external validity of samples.

Populations and Samples

Have you ever been offered a free sample in a grocery store? Say you tried a sample of spinach mini-quiche and you loved it. You probably assumed that all 50 in the box would taste just the same. Maybe you liked one baked pita chip and assumed all the chips in the bag would be good, too. The single bite you tried is the sample. The box or bag it came from is the population. A **population** is the entire set of people or products in which you are interested. The **sample** is a smaller set, taken from that population. You do not need to eat the whole bag (the whole population) to know whether you like the chips; you only need to test a small sample. If you did taste every chip in the population, you would be conducting a **census**.

Researchers usually don't need to study every member of the population either—that is, they do not need to do a census. Instead, they study a sample of people, assuming that if the sample behaves a certain way, the population will do the same. The external validity of a study concerns whether the sample used in the study is adequate to represent the unstudied population. If the sample can generalize to the population, there is good external validity. If the sample is biased in some way, there is not.

What Is the Population of Interest?

The world's population is around 7 billion human beings, but researchers rarely have that entire population in mind when they conduct a study. Before researchers can decide whether a sample is biased or unbiased, they have to specify a population to which they want to generalize: the *population of interest*. Instead of "the population" as a whole, a research study's intended population is more limited. The population of interest might be laboratory mice. It might be undergraduate women. It might be men with dementia. At the grocery store, the population of interest might be the 50 mini-quiches in the box, or the 200 pita chips in the bag.

Similarly, we might be interested in only the population of Canadians, not other North Americans, in a particular survey. If we used the opinions of a sample of people who rated a pair of shoes on how well they fit, we would be interested in generalizing to the population of people who have worn those shoes. If we are interrogating the results of a national election poll, we might primarily care about the population of people who will vote in the next election in the country. In order to say that a sample generalizes to a population, we have to decide which population we are interested in.

Coming from a Population vs. Representing That Population

For a sample to be representative of a population, the sample must come from the population. However, coming from the population is not sufficient by itself; that is, just because a sample *comes from* a population does not mean it *is representative of* that population. Just because a sample consists only of Canadians does not mean it represents all Canadians. Just because a sample contains 200 undergraduate women doesn't mean the sample can generalize to the population of undergraduate women.

Samples are either biased or representative. In a **biased sample** (or *unrepresentative sample*), some members of the population of interest have a much higher probability of being included in the sample compared to other members. In a **representative sample** (or *unbiased sample*), all members of the population have an equal chance of being included in the sample. Only representative samples allow us to make inferences about the population of interest. **Table 7.1** lists a few examples of biased and representative samples.

TABLE 7.1 Biased and Representative Samples of Different Populations of Interest

Population of interest	Biased sampling technique	Representative sampling technique
Democrats in Texas	Recruiting people sitting in the front row at the Texas Democratic Convention.	Obtaining a list of all registered Texas Democrats from public records, and calling a sample of them through randomized digit dialing.
Pediatricians	Asking only the pediatricians who are working on the day you visit six pediatrics clinics.	Obtaining a list of licensed pediatricians, and selecting a sample using a random number generator.
Students who have taken a class with Professor A	Including only students who have written comments about Professor A on an online website.	Obtaining a list of all of Professor A's current and former students, and selecting every fifteenth student for study.

When Is a Sample Biased?

Let's return to the food examples to explore biased and representative samples further. If you reached all the way to the bottom of the bag to select your sample pita chip, that sample would be *biased*, or *unrepresentative*. Broken chips at the bottom of the bag are not representative of the population, and choosing a broken chip would cause you to draw the wrong conclusions about the quality of that bag of chips. Similarly, suppose the box of 50 quiches was a variety pack, containing various flavors of quiche. In that case, a sample spinach quiche would be unrepresentative, too. If the other types of quiche are not as tasty as the spinach, you would draw incorrect conclusions about the varied population.

In a consumer survey or an online opinion poll, a biased sample could be like getting a handful from the bottom of the bag, where the broken pita chips are more likely to be. In other words, a researcher's sample might contain too many of the most *unusual* people. For instance, the students who rate a professor on a website might tend to be the ones who are angry or disgruntled, and they might not represent the rest of the professor's students very well. A biased study sample could also be like an unrepresentative spinach quiche. A researcher's sample might include only one kind of people, when the sample of interest is more like a variety pack. Imagine a poll that sampled only Democrats when the population of interest contains Republicans, Democrats, and people with other political views (**Figure 7.1**). Or imagine a study that sampled only men when the population of interest contains both men and women.

Of course, the population is what the researcher says it is, so if the population is only Democrats, it is appropriate to use only people who are registered Democrats in the sample. But even then, the researcher would want to be sure the Democrats in the sample are representative of the population of Democrats.

FIGURE 7.1 **Unrepresentative samples.** If the population of interest includes members of all political parties, a sample from a single party's political convention would not provide a representative sample to study.

Ways to Get a Biased Sample

A sample could be biased in at least two ways. Researchers might study only those cases they are able to contact easily or only the people who are most eager to respond. These two biases can threaten the external validity of a study, because people who are convenient or more willing might have different opinions from those who are less handy and less willing.

Sampling Only Those Who Are Most Easy to Contact. Many studies incorporate **convenience sampling**, using a sample of people who are readily available to participate. Psychology studies are often conducted by psychology professors who find it easy to study a sample of college students; the Mehl study on how much people talk is an example (see Chapter 6). However, those convenient college students may not be representative of other populations that are more educated, less educated, older, or younger (e.g., Connor Snibbe & Markus, 2005).

Here's another example. Imagine you are conducting an exit poll during a presidential election, and you've hired interviewers to ask voters, as they are leaving the polling station, whom they voted for. (Exit polls are widely used in the United States to help the media predict the results of an election before the votes are completely counted.) The sample for your exit poll might be biased in a couple of ways. For one, maybe you had only enough money to send pollsters to polling stations that were nearby and easy to reach. The resulting sample might be biased, because the neighboring polling precincts might be different from the district as a whole. Therefore, it would be better to send interviewers to a sample of precincts that represent the entire population of precincts. In addition, at a particular precinct, the pollsters might approach the population of exiting voters in a biased way. Exit poll workers may feel most comfortable approaching voters who look friendly, look similar to themselves, or look as if they are not in a hurry. For instance, younger pollsters might find it easiest to approach younger voters. Yet because younger voters tend to be more liberal, that sample's result might lead you to conclude that the voters at that location are more liberal than they really are. In this case, sampling only the people who are easy to reach would lead to a biased sample. Effective pollsters insist that their staff interview exiting voters according to a strict (usually randomized) schedule.

Researchers might also end up with a convenience sample if they are *unable* to contact an important subset of people. They might not be able to study those who live far away, who don't show up to a study appointment, or who don't answer the phone. Such circumstances may result in a biased sample when the people the researchers *can* contact might be different from the population to which they want to generalize.

During past election cycles, for instance, U.S. opinion pollsters have almost always selected their samples from landline telephone numbers. Until recently, this approach made sense, because almost all American voters had telephones in their homes. Yet a growing proportion of voters now use only cell phones. Excluding cell-phone-only users would bias a poll's results if the cell-phone-only group is different from the group of people who have landlines. In fact, a study by the Pew Research Center concluded that in the U.S., people who only have cell phones are more likely to be young, less affluent, unmarried, and more liberal on political questions. Recent statistics suggest that 25% of U.S. households had cell phones only (no landlines), but about half (51%) of U.S. adults ages 25–29 had cell phones only (Pew Research, n.d.). These differences can translate into biased polling results. In the 2010 U.S. congressional election, polls conducted using a landline-only sample showed much more support for Republican candidates, because younger voters are less likely to vote Republican, and are more likely to be excluded from landline-only samples (**Table 7.2**; Keeter, Christian, & Dimock, 2010).

TABLE 7.2 Opinions Based on Type of Telephone Use

2010 congressional vote	Landline and cell phone sample (%)	Landline only sample (%)	Difference (%)
Republican	49.6	52.1	2.5
Democrat	42.0	39.4	2.6
Other/Don't know	8.4	8.5	
Rep-Dem margin	+7.6	+12.7	5.1

Note: Pew Research Center. Based on combined data among likely voters from surveys conducted in Fall 2010. Figures may not add to 100% because of rounding.

Source: Adapted from Keeter, Christian, & Dimock, 2010.

FIGURE 7.2 Online polls. Can you trust the Internet poll's finding that 32% of children learn to read by age 3?

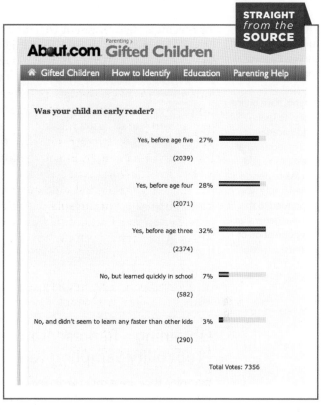

Sampling Only Those Who Invite Themselves. Another way a sample might be biased is through **self-selection**, a term used when a sample is known to contain only people who volunteer to participate. Self-selection is ubiquitous in online polls, and it can cause serious problems for external validity. One Internet poll asked parents, "Was your child an early reader?" The poll found, surprisingly, that 32% of children learn to read before age 3 (**Figure 7.2**). In truth, however, most children in the United States are taught to read in kindergarten, at about age 5 or 6. The reason the online poll had such unusual results is that the respondents were self-selected: The parents who would most likely respond to such a poll might be those who want to brag about their children.

In addition, this poll appeared in a forum for parents of "gifted" children, and gifted children are more likely to start reading early. Therefore, there are two selection biases at work: The result may apply only to the populations of parents who think their children are gifted, and to those who want to boast about when their child learned to read.

Self-selection occurs on most Internet polls. Whenever Internet users rate anything—a product on Amazon.com, a story on msnbc.com, a professor on ratemyprofessors.com—they are self-selecting when doing so. This self-selection may lead to biased samples, because the people who rate the items are not necessarily representative of the population of all people who have bought the product, read the story, or taken the class. All these ratings are made by people who care enough to take a survey. Researchers do not know much yet about how Internet "raters" differ from "nonraters," but they speculate that the people who take the time to rate things on the Internet might have stronger opinions, might be more willing to share ideas with others, and are perhaps more engaged with Internet content in general (**Figure 7.3**).

Obtaining a Representative Sample: Probability Sampling Techniques

Samples that are convenient or self-selected are not likely to represent the population of interest. In contrast, when external validity is vital and researchers need a representative sample from a population, probability sampling is the best option. There are many techniques for probability sampling, but they all involve an element of random selection. In **probability sampling**, also called *random sampling*, every member of the population of interest has an equal chance of being selected for the sample, regardless of whether they are close by, easy to contact, or motivated to respond. Therefore, probability samples have excellent external validity. They can generalize to the population of interest, because all members of the population are equally likely to be represented.

Simple Random Sampling

The most basic form of probability sampling is **simple random sampling**. To visualize this process, imagine that each member of the population of interest has his or her name written on a ticket. The tickets are tossed into a hat and stirred, and someone reaches in and selects a number of tickets equal to the size of the desired sample. The people whose names are on the selected tickets will make up the sample.

Another way to create a simple random sample is to assign a number to each population member's name, and then use a table of random numbers to select a sample from the population. Professional researchers do randomizing using computer programs that generate numbers that are random, or very nearly so (**Figure 7.4**). When pollsters need a random sample, they set up computer systems that randomly select telephone numbers from a database of eligible cell phone and landline numbers.

For a sample table of random numbers, see Appendix A, pp. 529–532.

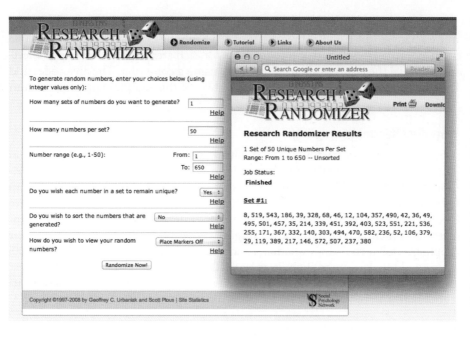

FIGURE 7.4
Computerized randomizers. This website generates lists of random numbers. In this example, the user requested a list of 50 random members of a population of 650. Each individual in the original population must first be assigned a number from 1 to 650. The randomizer tool determines which of the 50 individuals should be in the random sample. (Source: www.randomizer.org.)

Although simple random sampling works well in theory, it can be surprisingly difficult and time consuming. It can be nearly impossible to find and enumerate every member of the population of interest, and researchers usually use variants of the basic technique. The variants below are just as externally valid as simple random sampling, because they all contain an element of random selection.

Cluster Sampling and Multistage Sampling

In **cluster sampling**, clusters of participants within a population of interest are randomly selected, and then all individuals in each selected cluster are used. If a researcher wanted to randomly sample college students in the state of Pennsylvania, for example, he could start with a list of colleges (clusters) in that state, randomly select five of those colleges (clusters), and then include every student from each of those five colleges in the sample. The Bowker hockey games study (2009) used a version of cluster sampling (see Chapter 6). The researchers selected 69 games at random out of 630 possible hockey games in Ottawa, Canada, that they could have attended during the season. They then sampled every single comment at each game.

In the related technique **multistage sampling**, two random samples are selected: a random sample of clusters, then a random sample of people within those clusters. In the earlier example, the researcher starts with a list of colleges (clusters) in the state and selects a random five of those colleges. Then, instead of selecting all members of the cluster, the researcher selects a random sample of students from within each of the five selected colleges. Both cluster sampling and multistage sampling are easier than sampling from all Pennsylvania colleges, and both should still produce a representative sample.

Professional pollsters might use three-stage multistage sampling to select phone numbers for telephone polls. They first select a random sample of area codes out of all possible area codes in the country. Next, they select a random sample of the exchanges (the middle three digits of a U.S. phone number) out of all possible exchanges in each selected area code. Then, for each area code and exchange selected, they dial the last four digits at random, using a computer. The area codes and exchanges are considered clusters. At each stage of this sampling process, random selection is used.

Stratified Random Sampling

Another multistage technique is **stratified random sampling**, in which the researcher selects particular demographic categories on purpose and then randomly selects individuals within each of the categories. For example, a group of researchers might want to be sure their sample of 1,000 Canadians includes people of South Asian descent in the same proportion as in the Canadian population (which is 4%). Thus, they might have two categories (strata) in their population: South Asian Canadians and other Canadians. In a sample of 1,000, they would make sure to include at least 40 members of the category of interest (South Asian Canadians). Importantly, however, all 1,000 members of both categories are selected at random.

Oversampling

A variation of stratified random sampling is called **oversampling**, in which the researcher intentionally overrepresents one or more groups. Perhaps a researcher wants to sample 1,000 people, making sure to include South Asians in the sample. Imagine further that the researcher's population of interest has a low percentage of South Asians (say, 4%). Because 40 individuals may not be enough to accurately detect trends in the data, the researcher decides that of the 1,000 people she samples, a full 100 will be sampled at random from the Canadian South Asian community. In this example, the ethnicities of the participants are still the categories, but the researcher is oversampling the South Asian population: The South Asian group will constitute 10% of the sample, even though it represents only 4% of the population. A survey that includes an oversample adjusts the final results so that members in the oversampled group are weighted to their actual proportion in the population. However, this is still a random sample, because the 100 South Asians in the final sample were sampled randomly from the population of South Asians.

Systematic Sampling

For more on random numbers and how to use them, see Appendix A, pp. 527–528.

In **systematic sampling**, using a computer or a random number table , the researcher starts by selecting two random numbers—say, 4 and 7. If the population of interest is a roomful of students, the researcher would start with the fourth person in the room and then count off, choosing every seventh person until the sample was the desired size. Mehl and his colleagues (2007) used the EAR device to sample conversations every 12.5 minutes (see Chapter 6). Although they did not choose this value (12.5 min) at random, the effect is essentially the same as being a random sample of participants' conversations. (Note that although external validity often involves generalizing to populations of *people*, researchers may also generalize to settings—in this case, to a population of conversations.)

Combining Techniques

As you read about studies in the news or in empirical journal articles, you will probably come across methods of sampling that combine the techniques mentioned here. Researchers might do a combination of multistage sampling and oversampling, for example. But as long as clusters or individuals were selected at random, the sample will represent the population of interest. It will have good external validity.

In addition, researchers might supplement random selection with other techniques to control for bias. Consider the technique used by the Pew Research Center. This organization calls telephone numbers using a multistage technique, but then first asks to speak to the "youngest male, 18 years of age or older, who is now at home." If no eligible male is at home, they ask to speak to the "youngest female, 18 years of age or older, who is now at home" (Pew Research Center, n.d.). Why? If the interviewer talked only to the person who first picked up the phone, the resulting sample would have too many older women and not enough young people or men. (Presumably, Pew has found that in most U.S. homes, Mom is most likely to answer the phone.)

In sum, there are many acceptable ways to obtain a representative sample. Because all these techniques involve a component of randomness, they all ensure that each individual, cluster, or systematic interval has an equal chance of being selected. In other words, people are not excluded from the sample for any of the reasons that might lead to bias. **Figure 7.5** provides a visual overview of representative and biased sampling techniques.

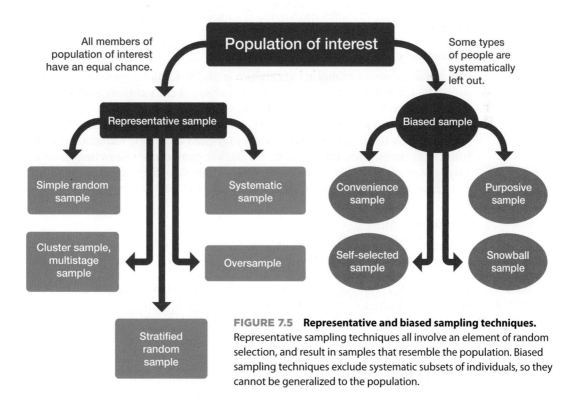

FIGURE 7.5 **Representative and biased sampling techniques.** Representative sampling techniques all involve an element of random selection, and result in samples that resemble the population. Biased sampling techniques exclude systematic subsets of individuals, so they cannot be generalized to the population.

Random Sampling vs. Random Assignment

Be careful not to confuse random sampling and random assignment. With random sampling (probability sampling), researchers create a sample using some random method, such as drawing names from a hat or using a random-digit phone dialer, so that each member of the population has an equal chance of being in the sample. Random sampling enhances *external validity*.

Random assignment is used only in experimental designs. When researchers want to place participants into different groups (often a treatment group and a comparison group), they usually assign them at random, by flipping a coin, for example. Random assignment enhances *internal validity* by helping ensure that the comparison group and the treatment group have the same kinds of people in them, thereby controlling for alternative explanations. For example, in a study of a treatment's effect on overall health, random assignment would make it likely that the people in the treatment and comparison groups are about equally healthy to start with. (For more detail on random assignment, see Chapters 3 and 10.)

Settling for an Unrepresentative Sample: Biased Sampling Techniques

In cases where external validity is not vital to a study's goals, the researchers might be content with a biased, unrepresentative kind of sampling. Depending on the type of study they are conducting, researchers can choose among a number of techniques for gathering such a sample.

Convenience Sampling

The most common sampling technique in behavioral research, convenience sampling (introduced earlier) uses samples that are chosen merely on the basis of who is easy to access. Many psychologists study students on their own campuses because they are the easiest participants to reach. The researchers may ask for volunteers in an introductory psychology class or among residents of a dormitory. In the Bowker (2009) study on hockey games, the researchers sampled games only in their own city, instead of randomly sampling games from all over the Canadian province (see Chapter 6).

Purposive Sampling

If researchers want to study only certain kinds of people, they recruit only those particular participants. When this is done in a nonrandom way, it is called **purposive sampling**. Researchers who wanted to study, for example, the effectiveness of a particular intervention for smoking would include smokers in the sample. Notice that limiting a sample to only one type of participant does not make a sample purposive. If smokers are recruited by phoning a random sample of community members, that sample would not be considered purposive because it is a random sample. However, if researchers recruit the sample of smokers by posting flyers at a local tobacco store, that action makes it a purposive sample, because only smokers will participate, and because the smokers are not randomly selected. Researchers studying a weight management program might study only people in a diabetes clinic. Such a sample would not be, and might not need to be, representative of the population of obese people in some area.

Snowball Sampling

One variation on purposive sampling that can help researchers find rare individuals is **snowball sampling**, in which participants are asked to recommend a few acquaintances for the study. For a study on coping behaviors in people who have Crohn's disease, for example, a researcher might start with one or two who have the diagnosis, and then ask them to recruit people from their support groups for that disease. Each of those participants might, in turn, recruit one or two more acquaintances, until the sample is large enough. Snowball sampling is nonrepresentative because people are recruited via social networks, which are not random. You might be familiar with this approach from online surveys that let you forward the survey link to a few more people. (Many Facebook quizzes work like this, even though they are created for entertainment, not for research.)

Quota Sampling

Similar to stratified random sampling, in **quota sampling** the researcher identifies subsets of the population of interest and then sets a target number for each category in the sample (e.g., 80 Asian Americans, 80 African Americans, and 80 Latinos). Next, the researcher samples from the population of interest nonrandomly until the quotas are filled. As you can see, both quota sampling and stratified random sampling specify subcategories and attempt to fill targeted percentages or numbers for each subcategory. However, in quota sampling the participants are selected nonrandomly (perhaps through convenience or purposive sampling), and in stratified random sampling they are selected using a random selection technique.

CHECK YOUR UNDERSTANDING

1. What are five techniques for selecting a representative sample of a population of interest? Where does randomness enter into each of these five selection processes?

2. In your own words, describe the difference between random sampling and random assignment.

3. What are four ways of selecting a biased sample of a population of interest? Which subsets are more likely to be selected in each case?

4. Why are convenience, purposive, snowball, and quota sampling *not* examples of representative sampling?

1. See pp. 188–191. 2. See p. 192 3. See pp. 192–193. 4. Answers will vary.

Interrogating External Validity: What Matters Most?

Frequency claims, as you know, are claims about how often something happens in a population. When you read headlines such as "66% of younger Americans support marriage equality" or "70% of Canadians felt well-rested yesterday" or "1% of Americans are Holocaust deniers," it might be obvious to you that external validity is important. If the opinion pollers used sampling techniques that did not include cell phones, the estimate of marriage equality opinions would be too low, since younger Americans support marriage equality the most. If the Canadian poll's sampling methods were not based on random sampling, the estimate of 70% being well-rested might be wrong. In such claims, external validity, which relies on random sampling techniques, is crucial.

In some cases, the external validity of surveys based on random samples can actually be confirmed. The best example is in political races, where the results of pre-election opinion polling can be compared with the final voting results. During major U.S. elections, polling websites and blogs compete to make the most accurate predictions, and some analysts combine polls from several sources to come up with their estimates. For instance, blogger Nate Silver analyzed multiple opinion polls before the 2012 U.S. presidential election, combining estimates based on the accuracy of their sampling techniques (as well as, incidentally, the construct validity of the questions they asked). Based on his analysis of the polls, Silver predicted that 50.8% of the popular vote would support Obama. In fact, Obama won 51.1%—pretty close to Silver's prediction. Apparently, Silver knew how to identify polls with the best external validity, and weighted those polls more in his analysis (Silver, 2012).

In most cases, however, researchers are not able to check the accuracy of their samples' estimates, because they hardly ever complete a full census of a population on the variable of interest. For example, a psychologist could never evaluate all the citizens of Canada to find out the true percentage who felt well-rested. Similarly, a researcher can't find all the owners of a particular pair of shoes to ask them whether their shoes "fit true to size." Because you usually cannot directly check accuracy when interrogating a frequency claim, the best you can do is interrogate the sampling techniques used, asking how the researchers obtained the sample. As long as they used a random sampling technique, you can be more confident in the external validity of the result.

When a Representative Sample Is Not the Top Priority

Although external validity is crucial for many frequency claims, external validity may not be a priority when researchers study association or causal claims. Many associations and causes can still be accurately detected even in a convenient or haphazard sample. However, what should you think if you encounter a frequency claim that is not based on a random (probability) sample? It might matter a lot, or it might not. You will need to carefully consider whether the reason for the sample's bias is relevant to the claim.

Nonrandom Samples in the Real World

Consider, for a moment, whether self-selection affects the results of an online shopping rating, as in one of this chapter's opening examples: "61% said this shoe felt true to size." You can be pretty sure the people who rated these shoes on their fit are self-selected and therefore do not represent all the people who own those shoes. The raters obviously have Internet access, whereas some of the shoe owners might not. They probably do more online shopping, whereas some of the shoe owners bought their pairs in bricks-and-mortar stores. More importantly, the raters cared enough to rate the shoes online; most of them probably responded because they either loved or hated the shoes. Those who are in-between may not be motivated enough to log in and rate their new shoes.

Another reason people care enough to respond might be that they are conscientious. They like to keep others informed, so they tend to rate everything they buy. In this case, the shopping rating sample is self-selected to include people who are more helpful than average.

The question is: Do the opinions of these nonrandom shoppers apply to other shoppers, and to how the shoes will fit *you*? Are the feet of opinionated or conscientious raters likely to be very different from those of the general population? Probably not, so their opinions about the fit of the shoes seem likely to generalize. The raters' fashion sense might even be the same as yours, too. (After all, they were attracted to the same image online.) If you believe that on the relevant dimensions the members of this self-selected sample are roughly the same as the general population, it might be safe to trust them.

For more on when external validity may not be a priority, see Chapter 8, p. 227; Chapter 10, pp. 298–300; and Chapter 14.

In an analogous situation, let's say a driver calls the radio station to report bad traffic near Exit 9 on Highway 35. This driver is not a randomly selected sample of drivers on that stretch of road; in fact, he is more conscientious than the other drivers there, and probably more willing to place calls to the radio station. Of course, these personality traits are not that relevant to the report of traffic. Traffic is the same for everybody, conscientious or not, so even though this driver is a nonrandom sample, the report of the traffic can probably generalize to the other drivers on that road. The feature that has biased the sample (being conscientious) is not relevant to the variable being measured (being in traffic).

In short, when you know that a sample is not representative, you should think carefully about how much it matters. Are the characteristics that make the sample biased actually relevant to what you are measuring? On some occasions, you will be perfectly fine in trusting the reports of an unrepresentative sample.

Nonrandom Samples in Research Studies

Let's use this reasoning to work through a couple of other examples. Recall from Chapter 6 the 30 dual-earner families who allowed the researchers to videotape their evening activities (Campos et al., 2013). It is probably a special kind of family that will let researchers place video cameras in their homes and permit them to walk around the house with laptops, recording the behavior of each member of the family. What does this mean for the conclusions of the study? Here, it seems possible that a family that is open to such intrusion could also exhibit a different emotional tone; perhaps the full population of dual-earning families has an emotional tone that is less warm than the self-selected sample of dual-earning families that volunteered to participate. Without more data on families who do not readily agree to be taped, we cannot know for sure. The researchers may have to live with some uncertainty about the generalizability of their data.

Let's return to the Mehl study (2007) on how many words people speak in a day (see Chapter 6). The sample of participants was not drawn randomly from a population of college students; instead, it was a convenience sample who participated because they were trying to earn class credit or a few extra dollars. Could the qualities that make these students likely to volunteer for the study also be qualities that affect how many words they would say? Probably not, but it is possible. Again, we live with some uncertainty about whether the Mehl findings would generalize—not only to other college students, but to other populations outside the college setting as well. We know that Mehl found the same results among college students in Mexico, but we do not know if the results for these college samples will apply to samples of middle-aged or older adults. However, just because we don't know whether the finding generalizes to other populations doesn't mean Mehl's results from college students are wrong or even uninteresting. Indeed, future research by Mehl and his colleagues could investigate this question in new populations.

Larger Samples Are Not More Representative

In research, is a bigger sample always a better sample? The answer may surprise you: Not necessarily. The idea that larger samples are more representative than smaller samples is perhaps one of the hardest myths to dispel in a research methods class.

When a phenomenon is rare, we do need a large sample in order to locate enough instances of that phenomenon for analysis. For example, we might need to sample 10,000 children to locate a sufficient number of them with a diagnosis of autism or ADHD, for analysis. But when researchers are striving to generalize from a sample to a population, the size of a sample is in fact much less important than how that sample was selected. When it comes to the external validity of the sample, it's *how*, not *how many*.

Suppose you want to try to predict the outcome of a national presidential election by polling 4,000 people at the Republican National Convention. You would have a grand old sample, but it would not tell you anything about the opinions of the entire country's voting population because everyone you sampled would be a member of one political party. Similarly, some Internet polls are so popular that thousands of people choose to vote in them. Even so, 100,000 self-selected people are not likely to be representative of the population. Look back at the poll about children reading early (see Figure 7.2). More than 7,000 parents voted, yet the results are completely ungeneralizable.

In fact, when researchers conduct public opinion polls, it turns out that 1,000–2,000 people are all they usually need—even for populations as large as the U.S. population of 313 million. For reasons of statistical accuracy, many polls shoot for, at most, a sample of 2,000. A researcher chooses a sample size for the poll in order to optimize the margin of error of the estimate. As introduced in Chapter 3, the margin of error estimate is a statistic that quantifies the degree of sampling

TABLE 7.3 Margins of Error Associated with Different Random Sample Sizes

If the percentage is estimated on a random sample of size	The margin of error on the percentage is
2,000	Plus or minus 2%
1,500	Plus or minus 3%
1,000	Plus or minus 3%
500	Plus or minus 4%
200	Plus or minus 7%
100	Plus or minus 10%
50	Plus or minus 14%

Note: Margin of error estimates in this table are based on a 50% polling result.

error in a study's results. For instance, you might read that 28% of Canadians in some poll support the Liberal Party, plus or minus 3%. In this example, the margin of error ("plus or minus 3%") means that if the researchers conducted the same poll many times and computed margins of error, 95% of the ranges would include the true value of support. In other words, it would mean that the true percentage of Canadians who support the Liberal Party is probably between 25% and 31%.

Table 7.3 shows the margin of error for samples of different sizes. You can see in the table that the larger the sample size, the smaller the margin of error—that is, the more accurately the sample's results reflect the views of the population. However, after a sample size of 1,000, it takes many more people to gain just a little more accuracy in the margin of error. That's why many researchers consider 1,000 to be an optimal balance between accuracy and effort. A sample of 1,000 people, *as long as it is random*, allows them to generalize to the population (even a population of 313 million) quite accurately. In effect, sample size is not an external validity issue; it is a statistical validity issue.

CHECK YOUR UNDERSTANDING

1. Why do you think researchers might decide to use an unrepresentative sample, even though a random sample would ensure external validity?
2. When will it be most important for a researcher to use a representative sample?
3. Which of these samples is more likely to be representative of a population of 100,000?
   a. A snowball sample of 10,000 people
   b. A randomly selected sample of 100 people
4. Explain why a larger sample is not necessarily more representative than a smaller one.

1. See pp. 194–196. 2. See p. 194. 3. b. 4. See pp. 196–197.

Summary

- When a claim makes a statement about a population of interest, you can ask how well the sample that was studied (such as a sample of online shoppers) represents the population in the claim (all online shoppers).

Generalizability: Does the Sample Represent the Population?

- The quality of a frequency claim usually depends on the ability to generalize from the sample to the population of interest. Researchers use samples to estimate the characteristics of a population.
- When generalization is the goal, random sampling techniques—rather than sample size—are vital, because they lead to unbiased estimates of a population.
- Nonrandom and self-selected samples do not represent the population. Such biased samples may be obtained when researchers sample only those who are easy to reach or only those who are more willing to participate.
- Probability sampling techniques can result in a representative sample; they include simplified random sampling, cluster sampling, multistage sampling, stratified random sampling, oversampling, systematic sampling, and combinations of these. All of them select people or clusters at random, so all members of the population of interest are equally likely to be included in the sample.
- Biased sampling techniques include convenience sampling, purposive sampling, snowball sampling, and quota sampling. Such sampling methods do not allow generalizing from the sample to a population.

Interrogating External Validity: What Matters Most?

- When researchers intend to generalize from the sample to the population, probability sampling (random sampling) is essential.
- Random samples are crucial when researchers are estimating the frequency of a particular opinion, condition, or behavior in a population. Nonrandom samples can occasionally be appropriate when the cause of the bias is not relevant to the survey topic. Representative samples may be less important for association and causal claims.
- For external validity, the size of a sample is not as important as whether or not the sample was selected randomly.

Key Terms

population, p. 182
sample, p. 182
census, p. 183
biased sample, p. 183
representative sample, p. 183
convenience sampling, p. 185
self-selection, p. 187

probability sampling, p. 188
simple random sampling,
    p. 188
cluster sampling, p. 189
multistage sampling, p. 189
stratified random sampling,
    p. 190

oversampling, p. 190
systematic sampling,
    p. 190
random assignment, p. 192
purposive sampling, p. 192
snowball sampling, p. 193
quota sampling, p. 193

To see samples of chapter concepts in the popular press, visit www.everydayresearchmethods.com and click the box for Chapter 7.

Review Questions

1. Which of the following four terms does not belong?
   a. Generalizable sample
   b. Externally valid sample
   c. Representative sample
   d. Biased sample

2. A researcher's population of interest is New York City dog owners. Which of the following samples is most likely to generalize to this population of interest?
   a. A sample of 25 dog owners visiting dog-friendly New York City parks.
   b. A sample of 25 dog owners who have appointments for their dogs at veterinarians in the New York City area.
   c. A sample of 25 dog owners selected at random from New York City pet registration records.
   d. A sample of 25 dog owners who regularly log into the nycdog.org website.

3. Which of the following samples is most likely to generalize to its population of interest?
   a. A convenience sample of 12,000.
   b. A quota sample of 120.
   c. A cluster sample of 120.
   d. A self-selected sample of 120,000.

4. Externally valid samples are more important for some research questions than for others. For which of the following research questions will it be most important to use an externally valid sampling technique?
   a. Estimating the proportion of U.S. teens who are depressed.
   b. Testing the association between depression and illegal drug use in U.S. teens.
   c. Testing the effectiveness of support groups for teens with depression.

Learning Actively

1. During a recent U.S. election, the news media interviewed a group of women in Florida. Although opinion polls supported the liberal candidate, these conservative women were still optimistic that their own side would win. One woman said, "I don't think those polls are very good—after all, they've never called *me*. Have they called any of you ladies?" Is this woman's critique of polling techniques appropriate? Why or why not?

2. Imagine you're planning to estimate the price of the average book at your college bookstore. The bookstore carries 13,000 titles, but you plan to sample only 200 books. You will select a sample of 200 books, record the price of each book, and use the average of the 200 books to estimate the average price of the 13,000 titles in the bookstore. Assume that the bookstore can give you access to a database that lists all 13,000 titles that it carries. Based on this information, answer the following questions:
   a. What is the sample in this study, and what is the population of interest?
   b. How might you collect a simple random sample of books?
   c. How might you collect a stratified random sample?
   d. How might you collect a convenience sample?
   e. How might you collect a systematic random sample?
   f. How might you collect a cluster sample?
   g. How might you collect a quota sample?

PART IV

Tools for Evaluating Association Claims

Talk Deeply, Be Happy?

(New York Times, 2010)

Meeting Spouse Online Linked to a Better Marriage

(PsychCentral, 2013)

8

Bivariate Correlational Research

A year from now, you should still be able to:

1. Explain what types of studies support association claims: Measured variables, not any particular statistic, make a study correlational.

2. Interrogate construct validity, statistical validity (and, less importantly, external validity) of an association claim.

3. Resist the temptation to make a causal inference from an association claim.

The two statements that open this chapter are examples of association claims that are supported by data. Each one is an association claim because it describes a relationship between two measured variables: number of substantive conversations ("talking deeply") and happiness; where people met their spouse and marital satisfaction.

Even without reading the full details of each study, we can be pretty sure the variables in these claims were measured, because it would be difficult to manipulate them. Researchers can measure people's deep conversations and their levels of happiness, but they may not be able to assign people to have deep conversations, and they cannot assign people to have certain levels of happiness. Researchers can measure where people met their spouses, but they cannot reasonably assign people to meet their spouse either online or in person. They can measure people's marital satisfaction, but they cannot assign people to be satisfied or not.

Because it's a plausible assumption that the two variables in each claim were measured, we can infer that they are association claims. Notice, too, that the verbs in each case are not strong, causal verbs. Instead, less ambitious language is used to indicate association. The first one simply notes that people who exhibit a particular behavior also exhibit a higher level of happiness. The second statement uses the neutral verb *linked* to indicate an association claim. Neither of the statements argues that X *causes* Y, or X *makes* Y *happen*, or X *increases rates of* Y. (If they did, they would be causal claims instead of association claims.)

This chapter describes the kinds of studies that lead to association claims, explains what kinds of graphs and statistics are used to describe the associations, and shows how you can systematically interrogate an association claim using the four big validities framework. What kinds of questions should you ask when you encounter an association claim? What should you keep in mind if you plan to conduct a study to test such a claim?

Introducing Bivariate Correlations

An association claim describes the relationship found between two measured variables. A **bivariate correlation**, or *bivariate association*, is an association that involves exactly two variables. Chapter 3 introduced the main types of associations: positive, negative, and zero. To investigate associations, researchers need to measure the first variable and then measure the second variable—in the same group of people. Then they use graphs and simple statistics to describe the type of relationship between the variables.

To investigate the association between deep, substantive conversations and happiness, Matthias Mehl and his colleagues (2010) measured people's happiness by combining two measures: Pavot and Diener's (1993) subjective well-being (SWB) scale (see Chapter 5) and a measure of overall happiness. Then they measured people's level of "deep talk" by having them wear an electronically activated recorder (EAR) for 4 days. (The EAR, introduced in Chapter 6, is an observational measurement device, an unobtrusive microphone worn by a participant that records 30 seconds of ambient sound every 12.5 minutes.) After people's daily conversations were recorded and transcribed, researchers coded the extent to which the recorded snippets represented "deep talk" or "substantive conversation." Each participant was assigned a value representing the percentage of time spent on substantive conversation. Those with more deep conversations had higher well-being scores.

To test the relationship between meeting one's spouse online and marital satisfaction, researcher John Cacioppo and his colleagues arranged to send an e-mail survey to thousands of people who participate in uSamp, an online market research center (Cacioppo, Cacioppo, Gozaga, Ogburn, & Vander-Weele, 2013). Respondents answered questions about where they met their spouse—online or not. Then, to measure marital satisfaction, the researchers used a 4-item measure called the Couples Satisfaction Index (CSI), which asks questions such as "Indicate the degree of happiness, all things considered, of your marriage," with a 7-point rating scale from 1 ("extremely unhappy") to 7 ("perfect"). People who met online scored a little higher on the CSI.

Another correlational study investigated this claim: "People who multitask the most are the worst at it" (introduced in Chapter 3). David Sanbonmatsu and his colleagues tested people on two variables: their frequency of media multitasking and their ability to do it (Sanbonmatsu, Strayer, Medeiros-Ward, & Watson, 2013). To measure frequency of media multitasking, the researchers asked participants to complete a Media Multitasking Inventory (MMI) in which they indicated how many hours a day they spent using each of 12 kinds of media (web surfing, text messaging, music, computer video, TV, etc.), and also how often they used each one at the same time as doing another task. To measure *ability* to multitask, they gave participants the OSPAN task. In this difficult task, people alternately read letters on the computer screen and solve basic math problems in their head. When prompted, they have to report all the letters and give the answers to all the math problems they have recently seen. In the Sanbonmatsu study, those who reported doing the most media multitasking did the worst on the OSPAN task.

Excerpts from the data sets for each of the studies described above appear in **Tables 8.1**, **8.2**, and **8.3**. In the three sets of data, notice that each row shows one person's scores on two measured variables. Notably, even though each study measured more than two variables, an analysis of bivariate correlations looks at only two variables at a time. Therefore, a correlational study might have measured multiple variables, but the authors present the bivariate correlations between different pairs of variables separately.

TABLE 8.1 Sample Data from the Mehl Study on Well-Being and Deep Talk

Person	Score on well-being scale	Percentage of conversations rated as deep talk
A	4.5	80
B	3.0	52
C	3.2	35
D	4.1	42
E	4.9	74
...	...	...
ZZ	2.8	16

Note: Values are fabricated for illustration purposes.
Source: Adapted from Mehl et al., 2010.

TABLE 8.2 Sample Data from the Cacioppo Study on Marital Satisfaction

Respondent	Where did you meet spouse?	Marital satisfaction rating
a	Online	6.2
b	Offline	5.5
c	Online	7.0
d	Offline	4.2
e	Offline	5.0
...	...	...
yy	Online	7.0

Note: Values are fabricated for illustration purposes.
Source: Adapted from Cacioppo et al., 2013.

TABLE 8.3 Representative Data from the Sanbonmatsu Study on Multitasking Frequency and Ability

Student	MMI score for multitasking frequency	Accuracy score on OSPAN task for multitasking ability
Alek	3.65	27
Jade	4.21	48
Sofia	2.91	31
Deangie	2.06	62
Max	8.44	25
...		...
Yuri	4.56	32

Source: Adapted from Sanbonmatsu et al., 2013.

Review: Describing Associations Between Two Quantitative Variables

After recording the data, the next step in testing an association claim is to describe the relationship between the two measured variables using scatterplots and the correlation coefficient r. We could create a scatterplot for the relationship between deep talk and well-being, for example, by placing scores on the well-being scale on the x-axis and percentage of conversations that include deep talk on the y-axis, then placing a mark on the graph to represent each person (**Figure 8.1**).

In addition to creating the scatterplot, Mehl and his team computed the correlation coefficient for their data and came up with an r of .28. As discussed in Chapter 3, the positive r means that the relationship is positive: High scores on one variable go with high scores on the other. In other words, high percentages of substantive conversation go with high levels of well-being, and low percentages of substantive conversation go with low levels of well-being. The magnitude of r is .28, which indicates a relationship that is moderate in strength.

FIGURE 8.1

Scatterplot of the association between deep talk and well-being.
(Source: Adapted from Mehl et al., 2010.)

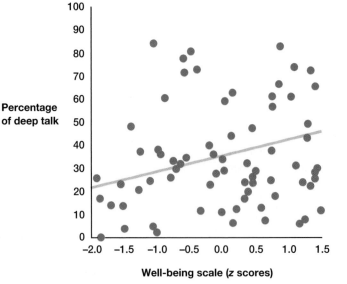

The reason we know an association of .28 is moderate is that psychological scientists typically follow a set of guidelines provided by the psychological statistician Jacob Cohen (1992). Recall that *r* has two qualities: direction and strength. Direction refers to whether the association is positive, negative, or zero; strength refers to how closely related the two variables are—how close *r* is to 1 or −1. To help researchers label the strength of their associations as small, medium, or large, Cohen provided a set of benchmarks, shown in **Table 8.4**. According to these conventions, the magnitude of the deep talk/well-being association is medium. (These conventions are discussed in more detail later in the chapter.)

TABLE 8.4 Cohen's Guidelines for Evaluating Strengths of Association (Based on *r*)

An *r* of approximately	Would be considered to have an effect size that is
.10 (or −.10)	Small, or weak
.30 (or −.30)	Medium, or moderate
.50 (or −.50)	Large, or strong

Source: Cohen, 1992.

Figure 8.2 shows a scatterplot for the study correlating frequency of multitasking with ability to multitask. When Sanbonmatsu's team computed the correlation coefficient between ability to multitask and frequency of doing it, they found an *r* of −.19. The negative *r* means that more frequent media multitasking is associated with lower scores on the OSPAN task, and less frequent media multitasking is associated with higher scores. According to Cohen's conventions, the size of the correlation, .19, means that this association is small to medium in strength.

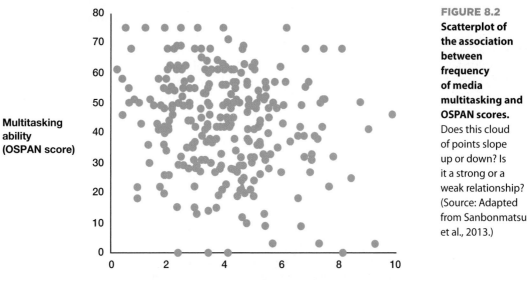

Multitasking ability (OSPAN score)

Frequency of media multitasking (MMI score)

FIGURE 8.2
Scatterplot of the association between frequency of media multitasking and OSPAN scores. Does this cloud of points slope up or down? Is it a strong or a weak relationship? (Source: Adapted from Sanbonmatsu et al., 2013.)

Describing Associations with Categorical Data

In the examples we have discussed so far, the nature of the association can be described with scatterplots and the correlation coefficient *r*. In the association between marital satisfaction and online dating, however, the dating variable is *categorical*; its values fall in either one category or another. A person meets his or her spouse either online or offline. The other variable in this association, marital satisfaction, is not categorical; it is *quantitative*; 7 means more marital satisfaction than 6, 6 means more than 5, and so on.

For more on categorical and quantitative variables, see Chapter 5, p. 127.

Graphing Associations When One Variable Is Categorical

When both variables in an association are measured on quantitative scales (as were number of substantive conversations and happiness), a scatterplot is usually the best way to represent the data. But is a scatterplot the best representation of an association in which one of the variables is measured categorically? **Figure 8.3** shows what a scatterplot for the association between online/offline meeting and marital satisfaction might look like.

As in all scatterplots, one variable is plotted on the x-axis and the other on the y-axis, and one dot represents one person. You can even look for an association in this graph: Do the scattered points slope up from right to left, do they slope down, or is the slope flat? If you answered that you see a slight downward slope, you would be right. You would conclude from this scatterplot that there is an association between where people meet their spouse and marital satisfaction, such that people who meet their spouses online are slightly higher in marital satisfaction, just as the researchers found when they conducted their study (Cacioppo et al, 2013). If you computed the correlation between these two variables, you would get a very weak, or small, correlation: $r = .06$.

Although you can make a scatterplot of such data, it is far more common for researchers to plot the results of an association with a categorical variable as a bar graph, as in **Figure 8.4**. Each person is not represented by one data point; instead, the graph shows the **mean** marital satisfaction rating (the arithmetic average) for all the people who met their spouses online and the mean marital satisfaction for all the people who met their spouses in person.

In a bar graph, you would examine the *difference* between the group averages to see whether there is an association. In the graph of meeting location

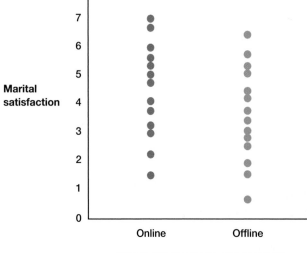

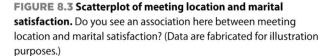

FIGURE 8.3 Scatterplot of meeting location and marital satisfaction. Do you see an association here between meeting location and marital satisfaction? (Data are fabricated for illustration purposes.)

and marital satisfaction in Figure 8.4, you can see that the average satisfaction score is slightly higher in the online than the offline group, indicating that this study found a weak association between where people met their spouse and marital satisfaction.

Analyzing Associations When One Variable Is Categorical

When at least one of the variables in an association claim is categorical, as in the online dating example, researchers may use different statistics to analyze the data. Although they occasionally use r, it is more common to test whether the difference between means (group averages) is statistically significant, usually by using a statistic called the **t test**, or other statistical tests.

Two Measured Variables Make a Study Correlational

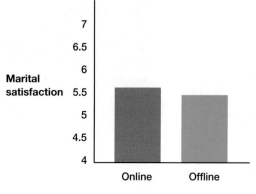

Where did you meet your spouse?

FIGURE 8.4 Bar graph of meeting location and marital satisfaction. This is the same outcome as in Figure 8.3, graphed differently. Do you see an association here between meeting location and marital satisfaction? (Source: Adapted from Cacioppo et al., 2013.)

It might seem confusing that association claims can be depicted by either scatterplots or bar graphs, or that association claims can be described using a variety of statistics, such as r or t tests. It's important to remember that no matter what kind of graph you make, no matter what kind of statistic you use, when both variables are measured, the study is correlational, and therefore it can support an association claim. (In contrast, recall from Chapter 3 that if one of the variables is *manipulated*, you have an experiment, which is more appropriate for testing a causal claim.) An association claim is not supported by a particular kind of statistic or a particular kind of graph; it is supported by a study design in which both of the variables are measured.

For more detail about the *t* test, see Statistics Review: Inferential Statistics, pp. 475–479.

CHECK YOUR UNDERSTANDING

1. At minimum, how many variables are there in an association claim?
2. What characteristic of a study's variables makes a study correlational?
3. Sketch three scatterplots: one showing a positive correlation, one showing a negative correlation, and one showing a zero correlation.
4. Sketch two bar graphs: one showing a correlation and one showing a zero correlation.
5. When do researchers typically use a bar graph, as opposed to a scatterplot, to display correlational data?

---

1. Two. 2. Both variables are measured; see p. 209. 3. Answers may vary; see Figures 8.1, 8.2, and 8.3 for models. 4. A bar graph that shows a correlation should have bars at different heights; a bar graph with a zero correlation would show two bars of the same height. 5. See p. 208.

Interrogating Association Claims

With an association claim, the two most important validities to interrogate are construct validity and statistical validity. You might also ask about the external validity of the association. Although internal validity is not usually relevant to an association claim, you need to know why it is not relevant. We'll now discuss the questions you'll use to interrogate each of the four big validities specifically in the context of association claims.

Construct Validity: How Well Was Each Variable Measured?

An association claim describes the relationship between two measured variables, so it is relevant to ask about the construct validity of *each* variable. How well was each of the two variables measured?

To interrogate the Mehl study, for example, you would ask questions about the researchers' operationalizations of—the way they measured—deep talk and well-being. Recall that deep talk in this study was observed via the EAR recordings and coded later by research assistants, while well-being was measured using the SWB scale. Once you know what kind of measure was used for each variable, you can ask questions to assess each one's construct validity: Does the measure have good reliability? Is it measuring what it is intended to measure? What is the evidence for its face validity, its concurrent validity, its discriminant and convergent validity? **Table 8.5** gives a specific example of how you might interrogate the construct validity of the claim that couples who meet online have happier marriages.

Statistical Validity: How Well Do the Data Support the Conclusion?

When you ask about the statistical validity of an association claim, you are asking about factors that might have affected the scatterplot, correlation coefficient r, bar graph, or difference score that led to your association claim. You need to consider the effect size and statistical significance of the relationship, any outliers that might have affected the overall findings, restriction of range, and whether a seemingly zero association might actually be curvilinear.

Statistical Validity Question 1: What Is the Effect Size?

All associations are not equal; some are stronger than others. As you'll recall from Chapter 2, the **effect size** describes the strength of an association. As an example, **Figure 8.5** depicts two associations: Both are positive, but the one in part B is stronger (its r is closer to 1). In other words, part B depicts a stronger effect size.

	Variable 1: Where people met their spouse	Variable 2: Marital satisfaction
Operationalization (How was the construct measured?)	Self-report answer to the question, "Did you meet your spouse online?" Yes or No.	Self-report answers to 4-item Couples Satisfaction Index (CSI), including "Indicate the degree of happiness, all things considered, of your marriage" and "In general how satisfied are you with your marriage?" Responses range from 1 (*extremely unhappy*) to 7 (*perfect*)
Reliability Questions		
Test-retest reliability	Do people give consistent answers to the question every time they take the survey?	Do people give consistent answers to the CSI every time they take it?
Internal reliability	(Not relevant, since this was a one-item measure)	Are the four CSI items correlated with each other; is there a strong Cronbach's alpha?
Interrater reliability	(Not relevant for self-report measures)	(Not relevant for self-report measures)
Measurement Validity Questions		
Face validity, content validity	Does this item look like a good measure of where people met their spouse?	Do the CSI items look like good ways to ask about marital satisfaction?
Criterion validity	Do people's answers to this item correlate with where they really met their spouse? For example, can answers be corroborated with online membership records at dating sites?	Do people's answers to the CSI items correlate with behaviors or outcomes related to marital satisfaction, such as divorce rate or number of arguments?
Convergent validity	If there is more than one measure of where people met, do they correlate with each other?	Do the CSI items correlate strongly with a second measure of marital satisfaction that was used in the same study, an 11-item measure of "chemistry"? (In fact, it was correlated, $r = 0.78$.)
Discriminant validity	Is this question about meeting online/offline really getting at where people met, or something else, such as their ability to remember accurately?	Do the CSI items correlate more weakly with dissimilar measures, such as people's agreeableness or conscientiousness?

Recall Cohen's conventions for labeling correlations as small, medium, or large in strength. In the Mehl study, the association between deep talk and well-being was $r = .28$, a relationship of medium strength. In the Sanbonmatsu study, the size of the association between multitasking frequency and ability was $r = -.19$, a negative relationship of small to medium strength. However, in the Cacioppo study, the relationship between meeting location and marital satisfaction was very small—a correlation of about $r = .06$. Therefore, of the three examples in this chapter, the strongest one is the deep talk/well-being relationship. But how strong is .28 compared with −.19? What is the logic behind these conventions?

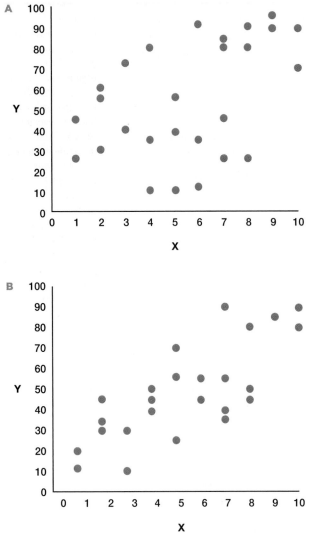

Larger Effect Sizes Give More Accurate Predictions. One meaning of the word "strong" when applied to effect size is that strong effect sizes enable predictions that are more accurate. When two variables are correlated, the correlation lets us make predictions of one variable from another. The more strongly correlated two variables are (the larger the effect size), the more accurate our predictions can be.

To understand how an association can help us make more accurate predictions, suppose we want to guess how tall a 2-year-old (we'll call him Hugo) will be as an 18-year-old. If we know absolutely nothing about Hugo, our best bet would be to predict that Hugo's adult height will be exactly average. Hugo might be taller than average or shorter than average, so we would do best to split the difference. In the United States, the average height (or 50th percentile) for an 18-year-old boy is 175 centimeters, so we should guess that Hugo will be 175 cm tall at age 18.

Now suppose we happen to know that Hugo is a relatively short 2-year-old; his height is 83 cm, within the 25th percentile for that age group. In this case, we would lower our prediction of Hugo's adult height accordingly. Specifically, since we know that there is a strong correlation between 2-year-old height and adult height, we could use a prediction line associated with this correlation (**Figure 8.6A**). Starting at Hugo's 2-year-old height of 83 cm, we'd read up to the prediction line and predict 172 cm as his 18-year-old height.

FIGURE 8.5 Two scatterplots depicting different association strengths. Both of these are positive associations. Which scatterplot shows the stronger relationship, part A or part B?

Are our predictions of Hugo's adult height likely to be perfect? Of course not. Let's say we find out that Hugo actually grew up to be 170 cm tall at age 18. We had guessed 172, so our prediction was off by 2 cm. That's the error of prediction. Our 2 cm difference is an error, but it's a smaller error than the 5 cm error we would have made before, using average adult height.

Errors of prediction get larger when associations get weaker. Suppose we want to predict Hugo's adult height but we don't know his 2-year-old height anymore; all we know is the height of his mother. The correlation between mothers' height and sons' height is positive, but weaker than the correlation between one's

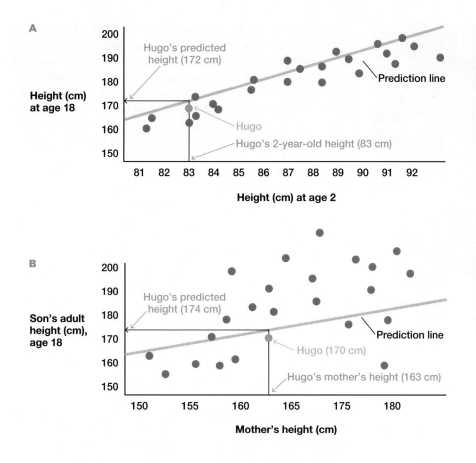

FIGURE 8.6
Stronger correlations mean more accurate predictions.
(A) If we use Hugo's 2-year-old height to predict Hugo's adult height, we would be off by 2 cm. (B) If we use Hugo's mother's height to predict Hugo's adult height, we would be off by 4 cm. Weaker correlations allow predictions, too, but their errors of prediction are larger. (Data are fabricated for illustration purposes.)

2-year-old height and one's adult height. As shown in **Figure 8.6B**, the scatterplot is more spread out. We can still use the prediction line associated with this correlation, but the fact that the correlation is weaker means that our errors of prediction will be larger. If Hugo's mother's height is 163 cm, we might use this and its associated prediction line to predict that Hugo's adult height would be 174 cm (a little taller than average). Our prediction is now off by 4 cm (recall that Hugo grew up to be 170 cm); our prediction error was larger than when we used 2-year-old height.

In sum, positive and negative associations can allow us to predict one variable from another, and the stronger the effect size, the more accurate, on average, our predictions will be.

Larger Effect Sizes Are Usually More Important. In addition to indicating the accuracy of predictions, effect sizes can also indicate the importance of a result. When all else is equal, a larger effect size is often considered more important than a small one. By this criterion, the association between deep talk and happiness is more important than the much smaller association between meeting online and having a happier marriage.

FIGURE 8.7 Effect size and importance. Larger effect sizes are usually more important than smaller ones. In some studies, however, such as those showing that an aspirin a day can reduce heart attack risk, even a very small effect size can be an important result.

However, there are exceptions to this rule. Depending on the context, even a small effect size can be important. A medical study on heart disease provides one famous example in which a small r was considered extremely important. The study (reported in McCartney & Rosenthal, 2000) found that taking an aspirin a day was associated with a lower rate of heart attacks, though the size of the association was only $r = .03$. According to the guidelines in Table 8.4, this is a very weak association, but in terms of the number of lives saved, even this small association was substantial. The full sample in the study consisted of about 22,000 people. Comparing the 11,000 in the aspirin group to the 11,000 in the placebo group, the study showed 85 fewer heart attacks in the aspirin group. An r of only .03 therefore represented 85 heart attacks avoided. This outcome was considered so dramatic that the doctors ended the study early and told everyone in the non-aspirin group to start taking aspirin (**Figure 8.7**). In such cases, even a tiny effect size, by Cohen's standards, can be considered important, especially when it has life-or-death implications.

When the outcome is not as extreme as life or death, however, a very small effect size might indeed be negligible in importance. For instance, at $r = .06$, the effect size of the association between meeting online and marital satisfaction corresponds to a difference on the 7-point satisfaction scale of .16 (5.64 versus 5.48). It's hard to picture what sixteen one-hundredths of a point difference means in practical terms, but it doesn't seem like a large effect. Similarly, the Cacioppo team also collected the divorce rates in the two groups. They found that the divorce rate for online-originated marriages was 5.96%, compared to 7.67% for marriages that met offline, which corresponds to an effect size of $r = .02$. That is also a very small effect size. In your opinion, is it important?

Statistical Validity Question 2: Is the Correlation Statistically Significant?

Whenever researchers obtain a correlation coefficient (r), they not only establish the direction and the strength (effect size) of the relationship but also determine whether the correlation is statistically significant. In the present context, **statistical significance** refers to the conclusion a researcher reaches regarding how likely it is they'd get a correlation of that size just by chance, assuming that there's no correlation in the real world.

For more on statistical significance, see Statistics Review: Inferential Statistics, pp. 482–483.

The Logic of Statistical Inference. Determining statistical significance is a process of inference. Researchers usually cannot study everybody in a population, so they study only one sample at a time and make an inference from the sample about the population. The sample's result usually mirrors what is happening in the population, but not always. If there is an association between two variables in a population, we will probably observe an association between those two variables in the sample, too. And if there is no association between two variables in a population, we will probably observe no association between those two variables in the sample.

Sometimes, however, even if there is zero association between two variables in a population, just by chance a study happens to use a sample in which an association shows up. The correlation from that particular sample would have been caused by mere chance. Because such chance results sometimes occur, when we find an association in a sample, we can never know for sure whether there really is an association in the larger population or whether there is not.

Here's an example. A researcher conducts a study on a sample of 310 college students and finds that ability to multitask correlates with frequency of multitasking at $r = -.19$. That correlation might really exist in the whole population of college students, but it could also be a fluke—a result of mere chance from that particular sample. Even if there is no real-world correlation between multitasking ability and frequency, once in a while a sample may, for reasons of chance alone, find such a correlation.

Statistical significance calculations help researchers evaluate the probability that the result (such as $r = -.19$) came from a population in which the association is really zero. Even though we can never know for sure whether our sample's result mirrors the population, we can nevertheless estimate the probability that our sample's result is a fluke. The calculations estimate the following: What kinds of r results would we typically get from a zero-correlation population if we conducted the same study many, many times with samples of the same size? How often would we get an r of $-.19$ just by chance, even if there is no association in the population?

What Does a Statistically Significant Result Mean? Statistical significance calculations provide a probability estimate (p, sometimes abbreviated as sig for significance). The p value helps researchers evaluate the probability that the sample's association came from a population in which the association is zero. If the probability (p) associated with the result is very small—that is, less than 5%—we know that the result is very *unlikely* to have come from a "zero-association" population. The correlation is considered statistically significant. The r of $-.19$ in the Sanbonmatsu study was statistically significant ($p < .05$), so we can conclude that their result is statistically significant.

What Does a Nonsignificant Result Mean? By contrast, if the probability (p) of getting some correlation just by chance is relatively *high* (i.e., higher than $p = .05$), the result is usually considered to be "nonsignificant" or "not statistically significant." It means we cannot rule out the possibility that the result came from a population in which the association is zero.

Effect Size, Sample Size, and Significance. Statistical significance is related to effect size; usually, the stronger a correlation (the larger its effect size), the more likely the correlation will be statistically significant. That's because the stronger an association is, the less likely it could have been sampled, just by chance, from a population in which the association is zero. But we can't tell whether a particular correlation is statistically significant by looking at its effect

For more detail on effect size, sample size, and statistical significance, see Statistics Review: Inferential Statistics, pp. 471–477 and pp. 482–483.

size alone. We also have to look for the significance calculations—the p values—associated with it.

Statistical significance calculations depend not only on effect size but also on sample size. A very small effect size (say, $r = .06$) will be statistically significant if it is identified in a very large sample (say, a sample of 1,000 or more). For example, in the Cacioppo study on online meeting and marriages, the researchers found a very small effect size, but it was statistically significant because the sample size was extremely large: more than 20,000. That same small effect size of $r = .06$ would not have been statistically significant if the study used a small sample (say, 30). A small sample is more easily affected by chance events than a large sample is. In other words, in a population in which the association is zero, studies with small samples might show weak correlations relatively frequently. Therefore, a weak correlation based on a small sample is more likely to be the result of chance variation and is more likely to be judged "not significant."

Reading About Significance in Journal Articles. In an empirical journal article, statistically significant associations are recognizable by their p values. Significance information may also be indicated by an asterisk (*), which usually means that an association is significant, or with the word sig, or with a notation such as $p < .05$ or $p < .01$. See, for example, **Figure 8.8**, from the Mehl

STRAIGHT *from the* **SOURCE**

Table 1. Daily Interaction Variables: Reliabilities and Correlations With Well-Being

Interaction variable	Intercoder reliability	Overall correlation with well-being			Correlation with well-being on weekdays	Correlation with well-being on weekends[b]	Correlation with well-being after accounting for personality differences
		Well-being index	Satisfaction with life	Happiness			
Alone[a]	.97	−.35**	−.36**	−.27*	−.29**	−.35**	−.40**
Talking to others[a]	.95	.31**	.31**	.26*	.30**	.30**	.39**
Small talk[a]	.76	−.07	−.03	−.10	−.01	−.09	.08
Small talk as a percentage of all conversations	—[c]	−.33**	−.25*	−.35**	−.30**	−.34**	−.17
Substantive conversations[a]	.84	.31**	.26*	.30**	.27*	.31**	.36**
Substantive conversations as a percentage of all conversations	—[c]	.28**	.20	.31**	.28**	.27*	.22*

Note: $N = 79$. Intercoder reliabilities were computed as intraclass correlations, $ICC(2, k)$, from a training set of 221 Electronically Activated Recorder (EAR) sound files that were independently coded by all coders. Satisfaction with life was assessed using participants' responses on the Satisfaction With Life Scale (Diener, Emmons, Larsen, & Griffin, 1985); happiness was assessed using self-reports and informant reports on a single item. The happiness and life-satisfaction measures were combined to create the well-being index. Personality was measured using self-reports and informant reports on the Big Five Inventory (John & Srivastava, 1999).
[a]These variables were calculated as the proportion of the total number of sampled sound files in which the indicated activity occurred. [b]The weekend was defined as beginning Friday at 6:00 p.m. and ending Sunday at midnight. [c]No reliability is reported because the variable is a quotient of two coded variables.
*$p \leq .05$ (two-tailed). **$p < .01$ (two-tailed).

FIGURE 8.8 Statistical significance in an empirical journal article. This table presents a variety of bivariate correlations. It also presents interrater reliability information for the variables that were coded from the EAR. (The last column shows a multiple-regression analysis; see Chapter 9.) (Source: Mehl et al., 2010.)

et al. (2010) journal article. Some of the correlations have asterisks next to them; the footnote explains that one asterisk indicates a p value less than .05, and two asterisks indicate a p value less than .01. Therefore, the probability is low that these starred correlations came from a population in which the correlation is zero, so they are statistically significant. In contrast, a popular press article usually will not specify whether a correlation is significant or not. The only way to know for sure is to track down the original study.

Statistical Validity Question 3: Could Outliers Be Affecting the Association?

An **outlier** is an extreme score—a single case (or sometimes a few) that stands out far away from the pack. Depending on where it sits in relation to the rest of the sample, a single outlier can have a strong effect on the correlation coefficient r. The two scatterplots in **Figure 8.9** show the potential effect of an outlier, a single person who happened to score high on both x and y. Why would a single outlier be a problem? As it turns out, adding that one data point changes the correlation depicted in the scatterplot from $r = .26$ to $r = .37$! Depending on where the outlier is, it can make a medium-sized correlation appear stronger, or a strong correlation appear weaker, than it really is.

Outliers can be problematic for an association claim, because even though they are only one or two data points, they may exert disproportionate influence. Think of an association as a seesaw. If you sit close to the center of the seesaw, you don't have much power to make it move, but if you sit way out on one end, you can have a much larger influence on whether it moves. Outliers are like people on the far ends of a seesaw: They can have a large impact on the direction or strength of the correlation.

In a bivariate correlation, outliers are mainly problematic when they involve extreme scores on *both* of the variables. In evaluating the correlation between height and weight, for example, a person who is both extremely tall and extremely heavy would make the r appear stronger; a person who is extremely short but extremely heavy would make the r appear weaker. When interrogating an association claim, it is therefore important to ask whether a sample has any outliers. The best way to find them is to look at the scatterplots and see if one or a few data points stand out.

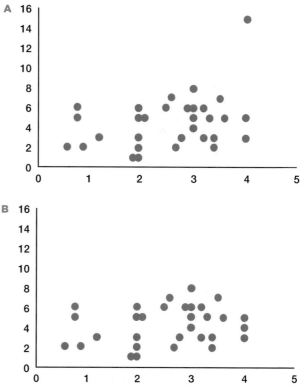

FIGURE 8.9 The effects of an outlier. These two scatterplots are identical, except for the outlier in the upper right-hand corner of part A. (A) $r = .37$. (B) $r = .26$.

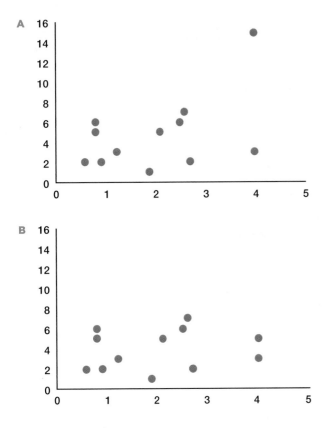

Outliers matter the most when a sample is small (**Figure 8.10**). If there are 500 points in a scatterplot (a whole bunch of people sitting in the middle of the seesaw), one outlier is not going to have as much impact. But if there are only 12 points in a scatterplot (only a few people in the middle of the seesaw), an outlier has much more influence on the pattern.

FIGURE 8.10 Outliers matter most when the sample is small. Again, these two scatterplots are identical except for the outlier. However, in this case, removing the outlier changed the correlation from $r = .49$ to $r = .15$; this is a much bigger jump than in Figure 8.9, which has more data points.

Statistical Validity Question 4: Is There Restriction of Range?

In a correlational study, if there is not a full range of scores on one of the variables in the association, it can make the correlation appear smaller than it really is. This situation is known as **restriction of range**.

To understand the problem, imagine a selective college (College S) that admits only students with high SAT scores. To support their admissions practices, the college might claim that SAT scores are good predictors of academic success. To support their claim with data, they would want to report the correlation between SAT scores and first-year college grades. (Those grades are an appropriate measure for such a study, because for many students, first-year college courses are similar in content and difficulty.)

Suppose College S plots the correlation between its own students' SAT scores and first-year college grades, getting the results shown in **Figure 8.11**. You'll see that the scatterplot shows a wide cloud of points. It has a positive slope, as you might expect, but it does not appear very strong. In fact, in real analyses of similar data, the correlation between SAT and first-year college grades is about $r = .33$ (Camara & Echternacht, 2000). As you have learned, such a correlation is considered moderate in strength. Is this the strong evidence that College S was looking for? Maybe not.

Here's where restriction of range comes in. As you may know, student scores on the SAT can range from 600 to 2400. But our selective College S admits only students who score 1800 or higher on their SATs, as shown in **Figure 8.12A**. Therefore, the true range of SAT scores is *restricted* in College S; it ranges only from 1800 to 2400 out of a possible 800 to 2400.

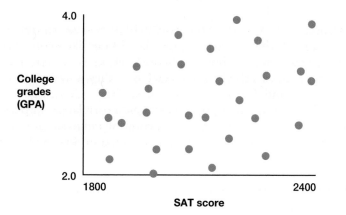

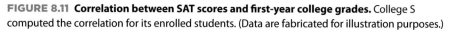

FIGURE 8.11 Correlation between SAT scores and first-year college grades. College S computed the correlation for its enrolled students. (Data are fabricated for illustration purposes.)

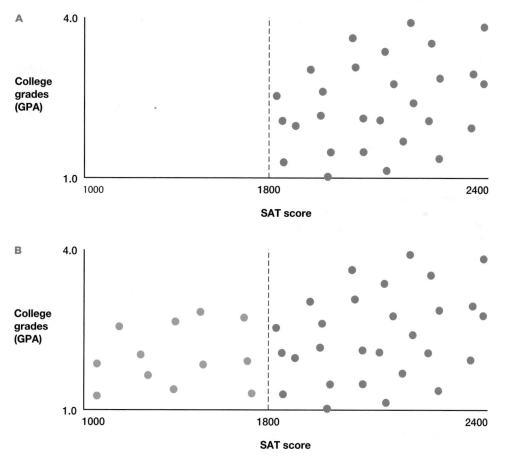

FIGURE 8.12 Restriction of range underestimates the true correlation. (A) College S admits only those students whose SAT scores are above 1800, so its observed correlation between SAT and GPA is about $r = .33$. (B) If we include estimates of the scores for students who were not admitted, the correlation between SAT and GPA would be stronger, about $r = .57$.

If we assume that the pattern observed in Figure 8.12A continues in a linear fashion, we can see what the scatterplot would look like if the range on SAT scores were not restricted, as shown in **Figure 8.12B**. The admitted students' scatterplot points are in exactly the same pattern as they were before, but now we have scatterplot points for the unadmitted students. Compared to the range-restricted correlation in part A, the full sample's correlation in part B appears much stronger. In other words, the restriction of range situation means that College S originally *underestimated* the true correlation between SAT scores and grades.

What do researchers do when they suspect restriction of range? A study could obtain the true correlation between SAT scores and college grades by admitting all students to College S, regardless of their SAT scores, see what grades they obtained, and compute the correlation. Of course, College S would not be very keen on that idea. The second option is to use a statistical technique, *correction for restriction of range*. The formula is beyond the scope of this text, but it estimates the full set of scores based on what we know about an existing, restricted set, and then recomputes the correlation. Actual studies that have corrected for restriction of range have estimated a correlation of $r = .57$ between SAT scores and college grades—a much stronger association and much more convincing evidence for the predictive validity of the SAT.

Restriction of range is similar to ceiling and floor effects; see Chapter 11, pp. 326–327.

Restriction of range can apply when, for any reason, one of the variables has very little variance. For example, if researchers were testing the correlation between parental income and child school achievement, they would want to have a sample of parents that included all levels of income. If their sample of parents was entirely upper middle class, there would be restriction of range on parental income, and researchers would underestimate any true correlation. Similarly, in the Sanbonmatsu et al. (2013) study, to get at the true correlation they would ideally want to include people who do a lot of media multitasking and very little, as well as those who perform well on the OSPAN task and those who perform poorly. In addition, the Mehl team (2010) would ideally want to have people who have both a lot of deep conversations and very few, as well as people who are very happy and who are less happy.

Because restriction of range makes correlations appear smaller, we would ask about it primarily when the correlation is weaker than expected. When restriction of range might be a problem, researchers could either use statistical techniques that let them correct for restriction of range, or, if possible, recruit more people at both ends of the spectrum.

Statistical Validity Question 5: Is the Association Curvilinear?

In rare cases, when a study reports that there is no relationship between two variables, the relationship might truly be zero. In other cases, however, there might be a **curvilinear association** (or *curvilinear correlation*), in which the relationship between two variables is not a straight line—for example, the relationship might be positive up to a point, and then become negative. In **Figure 8.13**, as people's age increases, their use of the health care system decreases up to a point. Then,

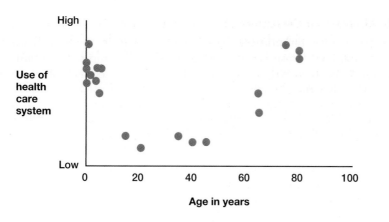

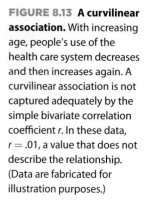

FIGURE 8.13 **A curvilinear association.** With increasing age, people's use of the health care system decreases and then increases again. A curvilinear association is not captured adequately by the simple bivariate correlation coefficient *r*. In these data, *r* = .01, a value that does not describe the relationship. (Data are fabricated for illustration purposes.)

as they approach age 60 and beyond, health care use increases again. A curvilinear association clearly exists between age and the use of health care services. However, when we compute a simple bivariate correlation coefficient *r* on these data, we get only *r* = −.01, because *r* is designed to describe the slope of the best-fitting *straight line* through the scatterplot. When the slope of the scatterplot goes up and then down (or down and then up), *r* does not describe the pattern very well. The straight line that fits best through this set of points is flat and horizontal, with a slope of zero. Therefore, if we looked only at the *r* and not at the scatterplot, we might conclude there is no relationship between age and use of health care. When researchers suspect a curvilinear association, the statistically valid way to analyze it is to compute the correlation between one variable and the square of the other.

Internal Validity: Can We Make a Causal Inference from an Association?

Even though we do not have to formally interrogate internal validity for an association claim, we still need to think about internal validity every time we read one. Why? Because we always have to guard against the *causal temptation*—the powerful automatic tendency to make a causal inference from any association claim we read. We hear that couples who meet online have happier marriages, so we advise our single friends to sign up for Match.com (thinking that online dating will *make* their future marriages more happy). We hear that deep talk goes with higher well-being, and we vow to participate in more substantive conversations. In fact, when an online newspaper reported on Mehl et al.'s finding, the journalist included this sentence: "Deep conversations made people happier than small talk, one study found." Oops; the strong verb *made* turned the association claim into a causal one (Rabin, 2010). The temptation to make a causal claim is pervasive.

Applying the Three Causal Criteria

Because the causal temptation is so strong, we have to remind ourselves repeatedly that correlation is not causation. Why is a simple association insufficient to establish causality? As discussed in Chapter 3, to establish causation, a study has to satisfy three criteria:

1. *Covariance of cause and effect.* There must be correlation, or association, between the cause variable and the effect variable.
2. *Temporal precedence.* The causal variable must precede the effect variable; it must come first in time.
3. *Internal validity.* There must be no plausible alternative explanations for the relationship between the two variables.

The temporal precedence criterion is sometimes called the **directionality problem**, because we don't know which variable came first. The internal validity criterion is often called the **third-variable problem**: When we can come up with an alternative explanation for the association between two variables, that alternative explanation is the third variable. **Figure 8.14** provides a shorthand description of these three criteria.

Let's apply these criteria to the deep talk and well-being association, to determine whether we can conclude from this association that substantive conversations *cause* an increase in well-being:

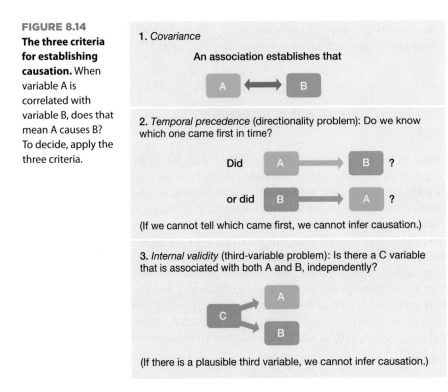

FIGURE 8.14

The three criteria for establishing causation. When variable A is correlated with variable B, does that mean A causes B? To decide, apply the three criteria.

1. *Covariance*

An association establishes that

A ⟷ B

2. *Temporal precedence* (directionality problem): Do we know which one came first in time?

Did A ⟶ B ?

or did B ⟶ A ?

(If we cannot tell which came first, we cannot infer causation.)

3. *Internal validity* (third-variable problem): Is there a C variable that is associated with both A and B, independently?

C ⟶ A
C ⟶ B

(If there is a plausible third variable, we cannot infer causation.)

1. *Covariance of cause and effect*. From the study's results, we already know deep conversations are associated positively with well-being. As the percentage of deep conversation goes up, well-being goes up, thus showing covariance of the proposed cause and the proposed effect.

2. *Temporal precedence*. The study measured deep talk and well-being during the same, short time period, so we cannot be sure whether an increase in deep talk came first, followed by an increase in well-being, or whether people were happy first and then engaged in more deep conversations.

3. *Internal validity*. The association between deep talk and well-being could be attributable to some third variable that is connected to both deep talk and well-being. For instance, a busy, stressful life might lead people to both report lower well-being and have less time for substantive conversations. Or perhaps in this college sample, having a strong college-preparatory background is associated with both deep conversations and having higher levels of well-being in college (because those students are more prepared). But be careful—not any third variable will do. The third variable, to be plausible, must correlate logically with *both* of the measured variables in the original association. (For example, we might propose that income is an alternative explanation, arguing that people with higher incomes will have higher well-being. For income to work as a plausible third variable, though, we would have to explain how higher income is related to more deep talk, too.)

As you can see, the bivariate correlation between well-being and deep conversation doesn't let us make the causal claim that high levels of substantive conversation cause high levels of well-being. It also does not allow us to make a causal claim the other way around—that high levels of well-being cause people to engage in more deep conversations. Although the two variables are associated, the study has established only one of the three causal rules: covariance. Further research using a different kind of study would be needed to establish temporal precedence and internal validity before we would accept this relationship as causal.

What about the article showing that meeting one's spouse online is associated with a happier marriage? Does this finding justify this headline from a blogger? "Meeting online leads to better marriages" (Kamenetz, 2013). Let's see how this study stands up to the three causal criteria:

1. *Covariation of cause and effect*. The study reported an association between meeting online and greater marital satisfaction. As discussed earlier, the association was very weak, but it was statistically significant.

2. *Temporal precedence*. We can be sure that the "meeting" variable came first and the marital satisfaction came later. People have to meet somebody (either online or offline) before getting married!

3. *Internal validity*. This criterion is not met by the study. It is possible that people of certain backgrounds are more likely to meet people online and be happier in their marriages. For example, people who are especially motivated to be in a relationship may be more likely to sign up for, and meet their spouses at, online dating sites. And such relationship-motivated people may be especially prepared to feel happy in their marriages.

In this case, the two variables are associated, so the study has established covariance, and the temporal precedence criterion has also been satisfied. However, the study does not establish internal validity, so we cannot make a causal inference.

More on Internal Validity: When Is That Potential Third Variable a Problem?

When we think of a reasonable third variable explanation for an association claim, how do we know if it is an internal validity problem? In the Mehl study about deep talk and happiness, level of education might be a third variable that explains this association. As mentioned earlier, it could be that better-educated people are happier and also have more substantive conversations, and that's why deep talk is correlated with happiness. Educational level makes a reasonable third variable here, because well-educated people seem likely to have more substantive conversations, and research also shows that educated people tend to be happier. But is education really responsible for the relationship the Mehl team found? We have to dig deeper.

What would it look like if education really was the third variable responsible for the correlation between deep talk and happiness? We can use a scatterplot to illustrate. Looking at **Figure 8.15** overall—blue and green dots together—we see a moderate, positive relationship between deep talk (substantive conversa-

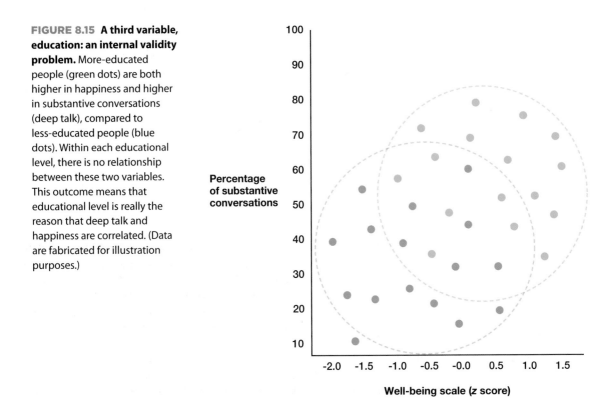

FIGURE 8.15 A third variable, education: an internal validity problem. More-educated people (green dots) are both higher in happiness and higher in substantive conversations (deep talk), compared to less-educated people (blue dots). Within each educational level, there is no relationship between these two variables. This outcome means that educational level is really the reason that deep talk and happiness are correlated. (Data are fabricated for illustration purposes.)

tions) and happiness, just as we know exists. But let's think about separating people who are more and less educated into two subgroups. In Figure 8.15, the more-educated people are represented by green dots and the less-educated by blue dots. The more-educated people (green dots) are generally higher on both happiness and substantive conversations, and the less-educated (blue dots) are generally lower on both variables.

Furthermore, if we study the scatterplot pattern within the green dots alone, we see that *within* the subgroup of well-educated people, there is no positive relationship between deep talk and happiness. The cloud of green dots is spread out and has no positive slope at all. Similarly, if we study the pattern within the blue dots alone, the same thing occurs—less educated people are lower on both happiness and deep talk, and within this subgroup, the cloud of blue dots shows no positive relationship between the two.

The outcome shown in Figure 8.15 means that the only reason deep talk and happiness are correlated is because well-educated people are higher on both of these variables. In other words, education presents a third variable problem. In such situations, the original relationship is referred to as a **spurious association**; the association is only there because of some third variable.

The results could have come out differently, however. In **Figure 8.16**, as before, the green dots (more-educated) are higher on both happiness and substantive

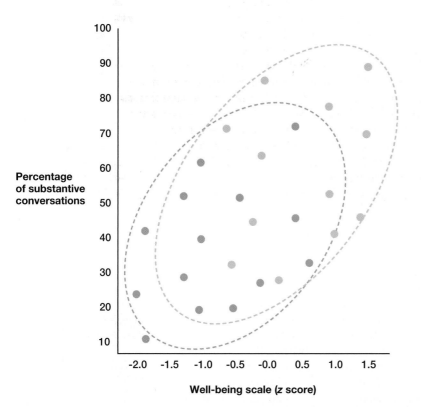

FIGURE 8.16 A third variable, education: not an internal validity problem. More-educated people (green dots) are both higher in happiness and higher in substantive conversations (deep talk), compared to less-educated people (blue dots). However, within each educational level, there is still a positive relationship between deep talk and happiness. This outcome means that educational level is not an internal validity problem; deep talk and happiness are still correlated even within the two subgroups. (Data are fabricated for illustration purposes.)

conversations and the blue dots (less-educated) are lower on both. But this time, when we study the pattern within the green dots alone, we see that within this subgroup of people, there is still a positive association between deep talk and happiness; the cloud of green dots still has a positive slope. Similarly, within the blue dots alone, there is an overall positive relationship between deep talk and happiness. Therefore, the situation in Figure 8.16 indicates that although we thought level of education might be a third variable explanation for Mehl's result, a closer look at the data puts us at ease: Deep talk and happiness are still correlated within subgroups of more and less educated people.

When we propose a third variable that could explain a bivariate correlation, it's not necessarily going to present an internal validity problem. Instead, it's a reason to dig deeper and ask more questions. We can ask the researchers if their bivariate correlation is still present within potential subgroups. Until we find out, however, we should definitely refrain from making a causal claim.

For more on subgroups and third variables, see Chapter 9, pp. 242–245.

In sum, when we're interrogating a simple association claim, it is not necessary to focus on internal validity as long as it's just that: an association claim. However, we must keep reminding ourselves that covariance satisfies only the first of the three criteria for causation. Before assuming that an *association* suggests a *cause*, we have to apply what we know about temporal precedence and internal validity.

External Validity: To Whom Can the Association Be Generalized?

When interrogating the external validity of an association claim, you ask whether the association can generalize to other people, places, and times. For example, consider again the association between media multitasking frequency and ability to multitask. To interrogate the external validity of this association, the first questions would be who the participants were and how they were selected. If you check the original article (Sanbonmatsu et al., 2013), you'll find that the sample consisted of 310 undergraduates: 176 women and 134 men.

For more on sampling techniques, see Chapter 7, pp. 185–193.

As you interrogate external validity, recall that the *size* of the sample does not matter as much as the *way* the sample was selected from the population of interest. Therefore, you would next ask whether the 310 students in the sample were selected using random sampling. If that was the case, you could then generalize from these 310 students to their population—college students at the University of Utah. If the students were not chosen by a random sample of the population of interest, you could not be sure the sample's results would generalize to that population.

As it turns out, the Sanbonmatsu team do not say in their article whether the 310 students were a random sample of University of Utah students or not. And of course, because the college students in this sample were from only Utah, the study results may not generalize to other college students in other areas of the country. Finally, because the sample consisted entirely of college students, the association may not generalize to nonstudents and older people. The Sanbonmatsu study seems to come up short when you interrogate its external validity.

How Important Is External Validity?

What should you conclude when a study does not use a random sample? Is it fair to disregard the entire study? In the case of the Sanbonmatsu study, the construct validity is excellent; the measures of multitasking frequency and ability to multitask have been used in other studies and have been shown to be valid and reliable measures of these concepts. In terms of statistical validity, the correlation is statistically significant, and the effect size is moderate. The sample was large enough to avoid the influence of outliers, and there did not seem to be a curvilinear relationship or restriction of range. The researchers did not make any causal claims that would render internal validity relevant. In most respects, this association claim stands up; it lacks only external validity.

A bivariate correlational study may not have used a random sample, but you should not automatically reject the association for that reason. Instead, you can accept the study's results and leave the question of generalization to the next study, which might test the association between these two variables in some other population.

Furthermore, many associations do generalize—even to samples that are very different from the original one. You might think the association claim for multitasking would not generalize to older adults, ages 70–80, because maybe you assume they are less likely to multitask with many forms of media, and perhaps they're less capable of multitasking, compared to a younger, college-aged population. You would probably be right about these mean (average) differences between the samples. However, *within* a sample of people in the 70–80 age range, those who *do* tend to multitask the most may still be the ones who are the worst at it. The new sample of people might score lower, on average, on both variables in the association claim, but even so, the association might still hold true within that new sample. A scatterplot that includes both these samples, such as the one in **Figure 8.17**, looks similar to the one in Figure 8.16, where the association holds true within each subgroup and when both groups are studied together.

Moderating Variables

In association research, when the relationship between two variables changes depending on the level of another variable, that other variable is called a **moderator**. Let's consider another study using the EAR recorder (Mehl, Gosling, & Pennebaker, 2006). This study also recorded people's daily events using the EAR, but this time, they measured personality traits. One of the results found that people who scored high on extroversion were also more likely to be recorded as talking during the sampling periods ($r = .30$). This result matches what you'd probably expect: Extroverted people talk more.

The researchers also considered what percentage of the participants' conversations took place specifically in a group. The results are in **Table 8.6**. The association between extroversion and group conversations depends on gender. For men, extroversion is not related to having a higher percentage of group conversations. For women, though, extroversion is positively related to having more group conversations. In this example, you'd say *that gender moderates the association between extroversion and group conversations*. In other words, the association

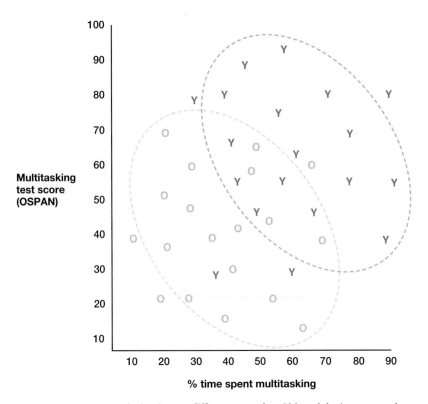

FIGURE 8.17 An association in two different samples. Older adults (represented by O) might engage in less multitasking than college students (Y), and they might perform worse on multitasking tests, such as the OSPAN task. But the same association between the two variables *within* each sample of people may exist. (Data are fabricated for illustration purposes.)

TABLE 8.6 Gender Moderates the Relationship Between Extroversion and Group Conversations

Gender group	Association (*r*) between extroversion and percentage of group conversations
Males	.07
Females	.49*

Note: Extroversion and group conversations are correlated for women, but not for men. *$p < 0.05$; result is statistically significant. Source: Adapted from Mehl et al., 2006.

TABLE 8.7 Gender Does Not Moderate the Relationship Between Extroversion and Being Alone

Gender group	Association (r) between extroversion and being alone
Males	−.33*
Females	−.42*

Note: Extroversion is associated with being alone less often, for both women and men. *$p < 0.05$; result is statistically significant.
Source: Adapted from Mehl et al., 2006.

between extroversion and group conversation depends on gender. Extroverted women spend more time talking in groups, but extroverted men do not.

In the same study, the researchers tested the association between extroversion and being alone during the sampling period (Mehl et al., 2006). This relationship did not depend on gender. As shown in **Table 8.7**, there was a negative, moderate correlation between extroversion and being alone for both subgroups, men and women. Therefore, we say *that gender does not moderate the association between extroversion and spending time alone.*

In their happiness study, Mehl et al. (2010) looked for moderators in the relationship they found between deep talk and well-being. They wondered if the relationship would differ depending on whether substantive conversations took place on a weekend or a weekday. However, the results suggested that weekend/weekday status did not moderate the relationship between deep talk and well-being: The relationship was positive and of equal strength in both time periods (**Table 8.8**).

In Chapter 12, you will learn that another way of understanding moderators is to describe them as interactions; see p. 350.

TABLE 8.8 Weekend/Weekday Status Does Not Moderate the Relationship Between Deep Talk and Well-Being

Day of week	Association (r) between percentage of substantive conversations and well-being
Weekday	.28*
Weekend	.27*

Note: Substantive conversations are associated with happiness on both weekdays and weekends. *$p < 0.05$; result is statistically significant.
Source: Adapted from Mehl et al., 2006.

In correlation research, moderators can inform external validity. When an association is moderated by day of the week, gender, or some other variable, we know that the association may not generalize from one of these situations to the others. For example, in asking whether the association between multitasking frequency and ability would generalize to 70–80-year-olds, you were asking whether that association would be moderated by age. Similarly, the Mehl team found that the association between deep talk and well-being does generalize well from the weekends to weekdays: The strength of the association is almost the same in the two contexts.

CHECK YOUR UNDERSTANDING

1. In one or two brief sentences, explain how you would interrogate the construct validity of a bivariate correlation.
2. What are five questions you can ask about the statistical validity of a bivariate correlation? Do all the statistical validity questions apply the same way when bivariate correlations are represented as bar graphs?
3. Which of the three rules of causation is almost always met by a bivariate correlation? Which two rules might not be met by a correlational study?
4. Give examples of some questions you can ask to evaluate the external validity of a correlational study.

1. See p. 210. 2. See pp. 210–221; questions about outliers and curvilinear relationships may not be relevant for correlations represented as bar graphs. 3. See pp. 221–223. 4. See pp. 226–230.

Summary

- Association claims involve two variables, both of which are measured in a set of participants. (If either of the variables is manipulated, the study is an experiment, which could potentially test a causal claim.)

Introducing Bivariate Correlations

- The variables in a bivariate correlational study can be either quantitative or categorical. If both variables are quantitative, the data are usually depicted in a scatterplot; if one variable is categorical, the data are usually depicted in a bar graph.
- For a scatterplot, the correlation coefficient r can be used to describe the relationship. For a bar graph, the difference between the two group means is used to describe the relationship.
- Regardless of whether an association is analyzed with scatterplots or bar graphs, if both variables are measured, the study is correlational.

Interrogating Association Claims

- Because an association claim involves two measured variables, the construct validity of each measure must be interrogated in a bivariate correlation study.
- Interrogating the statistical validity of an association claim involves five areas of inquiry: effect size (strength of r), statistical significance, the presence of outliers, possible restriction of range, and whether the association is curvilinear.
- Internal validity addresses the degree to which a study supports a causal claim. Although it is not necessary to interrogate internal validity for an association claim because it does not make a causal statement, it can be tempting to assume causality.
- Correlational studies do not satisfy all three criteria for a causal claim: They may show covariance, but do not usually satisify temporal precedence or internal validity.
- Interrogating the external validity of an association claim involves asking whether the sample can generalize to some population. If a correlational study does not use a random sample of people or contexts, the results cannot necessarily generalize to the population from which the sample was taken.
- A lack of external validity should not disqualify an entire study. If the study fulfills the other three validities, and its results are sound, the question of generalization can be left for a future investigation.
- A bivariate correlation is sometimes moderated; the relationship changes, depending on the levels of another variable, such as gender or age.

Key Terms

bivariate correlation, p. 204
mean, p. 208
t test, p. 209
effect size, p. 210

statistical significance, p. 214
outlier, p. 217
restriction of range, p. 218
curvilinear association, p. 220

directionality problem, p. 222
third-variable problem, p. 222
spurious association, p. 225
moderator, p. 227

 To see samples of chapter concepts in the popular press, visit www.everydayresearchmethods.com and click the box for Chapter 8.

Review Questions

1. Suppose you hear that conscientious people are more likely to get regular health checkups. Which of the following correlations between conscientiousness and getting checkups would probably support this claim?
   a. $r = .03$
   b. $r = .45$
   c. $r = -.35$
   d. $r = -1.0$

2. Which of these associations will probably be plotted as a bar graph rather than a scatterplot?
   a. The more conscientious people are, the more likely to get regular health checkups.
   b. Level of depression is linked to the amount of chocolate people eat.
   c. Students at private colleges get higher GPAs than those at public colleges.
   d. Level of chronic stomach pain in kids is linked to later anxiety as adults.

3. A study found that people who like spicy foods are generally risk takers. Which of the following questions interrogates the construct validity of this correlation?
   a. Is the result statistically significant?
   b. Did the study use a random sample?
   c. Were there any outliers in the relationship?
   d. How well did they measure risk taking and liking spicy foods?

4. Darrin reads a story reporting that students at private colleges get higher GPAs than those at public colleges. He wonders if this means going to a private college causes you to have a higher GPA; if so, he'll go to a private college! Applying the three causal criteria, Darrin knows there is covariance here. He also knows there is temporal precedence, because you choose a college first, and then you get your GPA. Which of the following questions would help Darrin ask about the third criterion, internal validity?
   a. Could there be restriction of range?
   b. Is the link between private college and high grades the same for both men and women?
   c. How did they decide what qualifies a college as "private" or "public"?
   d. Is there some other reason why these two are related? Maybe better students are more likely to go to private colleges, and they are also going to get better grades?

5. Which of the following sentences describes a moderator for the relationship between risk taking and liking spicy foods?
   a. There is a positive relationship between liking spicy foods and risk taking for men, but no relationship for women.
   b. There is a positive relationship between liking spicy foods and risk taking, and it is equally strong for both older and younger adults.
   c. The relationship between liking spicy foods and risk taking does not depend on where you grew up.

Learning Actively

1. For each of the following examples, sketch a graph of the result (either a bar graph or a scatterplot). Then, interrogate the construct validity, the statistical validity, and the external validity of each association claim. What questions would you ask? What answers would you expect?
   a. "Chronic stomach pain in kids is linked to adult anxiety disorders in later life." In this study, the researchers "followed 332

children between the ages of 8 and 17 who were diagnosed with functional abdominal pain and 147 with no pain for an average of eight years. . . . On follow-up, the researchers interviewed the volunteers—who were on average age 20 at that point—either in person or by phone. . . . Of adults who had abdominal pain as children, 51 percent had experienced an anxiety disorder during their lives, compared to 20 percent of those who didn't experience tummy aches as children" (Carroll, 2013).

b. "Kids with ADHD may be more likely to bully." In this study, the researchers "followed 577 children—the entire population of fourth graders from a municipality near Stockholm—for a year. The researchers interviewed parents, teachers and children to determine which kids were likely to have ADHD. Children showing signs of the disorder were then seen by a child neurologist for diagnosis. The researchers also asked the kids about bullying. [The study found that] children with attention deficit hyperactivity disorder are almost four times as likely as others to be bullies"(Carroll, 2008).

2. A researcher conducted a study of 34 scientists (Grim, 2008). He reported a correlation between the amount of beer each scientist drank per year and the likelihood of that scientist publishing a scientific paper. The correlation was reported as $r = -.55, p < .01$.

a. What does a negative correlation mean in this example? Is this relationship strong or weak?

b. What does $p < .01$ mean in this result?

c. Draw a scatterplot of this association. What might happen to this correlation if you added one person in the sample who drank much more beer than other scientists and also published far fewer papers than other scientists?

d. A popular press report about this article was headlined, "Suds seem to skew scientific success" (*San Diego Union-Tribune*, 2008). Is such a causal claim justified?

e. Perhaps scientific discipline is a moderator of this relationship. Create a moderator table, using Table 8.6 as a model, showing that the association between beer drinking and publications is negative for ecologists, but close to zero for physicists.

The Three R's? A Fourth Is Crucial, Too: Recess

(New York Times, 2009)

Kids' Aggressive Behavior Tied to TV Violence in Studies

(Columbus Dispatch, 2013)

9

Multivariate Correlational Research

LEARNING OBJECTIVES

A year from now, you should still be able to:

1. State why simple bivariate correlations are not sufficient for establishing causation.
2. Explain how longitudinal correlational designs help address temporal precedence.
3. Explain how multiple-regression analyses help address internal validity (the third-variable problem).
4. Articulate the value of pattern and parsimony, when researchers can infer causation from a variety of research results that all support a single, parsimonious causal theory.
5. Explain the function of a mediating variable.

Studies that support association claims can provide interesting new information in their own right. It might be intriguing, for instance, to note that children who watch violence on television also behave aggressively, or that classrooms with longer recess periods have fewer behavior problems. More often, however, an association claim is merely an early step in establishing a causal relationship between two variables. Psychological scientists—and the rest of us—often want to know about causes and effects, not just correlations. When reading that watching violence on TV *is associated with* imitating aggressive behavior, we may wonder whether viewing the violence on the screen *causes* the aggression. Similarly, when reading about recess being associated with fewer behavior problems, we might ask: Does the recess cause the drop in bad behavior? Or is it the case that a certain type of classroom (perhaps a private school classroom) both allows more recess and has better-behaved kids? Knowing about causes enables applied researchers to make interventions. If violent TV causes aggression, then pediatricians, teachers, or advocacy groups could try to persuade parents to limit their children's exposure to violent shows. If recess causes children to do better in school, schools should require recess periods. But unless these relationships are causal, such interventions would not work.

Because correlation is not causation, what are the options? Researchers have developed some techniques that enable them to test for cause. The best of these is experimentation: Instead of measuring both variables, researchers manipulate one variable and measure the other. (Experimental designs are covered in Chapters 10–12.) Even without setting up an experiment, however, researchers can use some advanced correlational techniques to get a bit closer to making a causal claim. This chapter outlines three such techniques: longitudinal designs, which allow researchers to evaluate temporal precedence in their data; multiple-regression analyses, which help researchers rule out certain third-variable explanations; and the "pattern and parsimony" approach, in which the results of a variety of correlational studies all support a single, causal theory. In all three techniques, as in all association studies, the variables are measured—that is, none are manipulated.

Reviewing the Three Causal Criteria

Unlike the bivariate examples in Chapter 8, which involved only two measured variables, longitudinal designs, multiple-regression designs, and the pattern and parsimony approach are **multivariate designs**, involving more than two measured variables. While these techniques are not perfect solutions to the causality conundrum, they are extremely useful and widely used tools, especially when experiments are impossible to run.

Remember that the three criteria for establishing causation are covariance, temporal precedence, and internal validity. We might apply these criteria to the association between violence on TV and aggressive behavior as follows:

- *Is there covariance?* Yes. Many studies have shown that the correlation between watching violent TV shows and acting aggressively is moderately strong, around $r = .35$ (e.g., Paik & Comstock, 1994). These two variables are clearly related.
- *Is there temporal precedence?* A typical correlational study cannot establish temporal precedence. In some early studies on TV viewing and aggressive behavior, researchers measured aggressive behavior at the same time as TV preferences. Such a study does not show which one comes first. It is possible that watching violent TV shows comes first and causes people to be

more aggressive. It is also possible, however, that a person's aggressiveness comes first and affects his or her TV viewing habits. (In other words, aggressive people choose to watch more violent TV shows, and less aggressive people choose to watch less violent ones.)

- *Is there internal validity?* The association between TV violence and aggressive behavior might potentially be explained by a third variable, such as a personality trait. Perhaps people who seek extreme emotional situations (known as sensation seekers) are more likely to both act aggressively *and* prefer violent TV shows. In this explanation, sensation seeking comes first and causes both aggressive behavior and a preference for violent shows. Or perhaps the third variable is gender: Men are both more likely to watch violent shows and more likely to act aggressively than women.

CHECK YOUR UNDERSTANDING

1. Why can't a simple bivariate correlational study meet all three criteria for establishing causation?

1. See pp. 235–236.

Establishing Temporal Precedence with Longitudinal Designs

A **longitudinal design** can provide evidence for temporal precedence by measuring the same variables in the same people at several points in time. Often, longitudinal research is used in developmental psychology to study changes in a trait or an ability as a person grows older. In addition, this type of design is adapted to test causal claims. For example, in a classic study that evaluated TV violence and aggression (Eron, Huesmann, Lefkowitz, & Walder, 1972), the researchers collected data on 875 children in 1960—the entire third-grade population of a small town in New York. Ten years later, the researchers were able to track down 427 of these original children, who were now teenagers. (As shorthand, they called the second study time "thirteenth grade.") At each of the two times, the researchers measured two important variables. First, they measured aggression by asking the peers of each child (and later, teen) which students in the class were most likely to hit, push, say mean things, or start fights. Second, they measured children's interest in violent TV programs by asking what their four favorite shows were. The children's parents reported the TV information when the children were in the third grade; in thirteenth grade, the teenagers self-reported the TV information.

The Eron study was longitudinal because the researchers measured the *same* variables in the *same* group of people across time—10 years apart. The study is also a multivariate correlational study because four variables were measured: preference for TV violence at Time 1, preference for TV violence at Time 2, aggression at Time 1, and aggression at Time 2.

Interpreting Results from Longitudinal Designs

Because there are more than two variables involved, a multivariate design gives several individual correlations, referred to as cross-sectional correlations, autocorrelations, and cross-lag correlations. (Note that the researchers in this study conducted their analyses on boys and girls separately, in order to investigate the causal paths for each gender separately. Only the results for the boys are presented here.)

Cross-Sectional Correlations

The first two correlations are **cross-sectional correlations**; they test to see whether two variables, measured at the same point in time, are correlated. For example, the study reports that the correlation between a preference for TV violence in third grade and aggression in third grade was $r = .21$. That correlation was not surprising, since the researchers already knew from several previous studies that TV violence was associated with aggression. There was also a correlation between preference for TV violence in thirteenth grade and aggression in thirteenth grade, but it was only $r = .05$ (not significantly different from zero). Because most studies on this topic do show a correlation, the zero result was an exception to an otherwise strong empirical pattern (Paik & Comstock, 1994). Even when the weight of the evidence shows a strong pattern (such as a relationship between TV preferences and aggression), occasional exceptions can occur, like this one. **Figure 9.1** depicts how this study was designed. These first two simple cross-sectional correlations could have been obtained from any sample that measured TV violence and aggression at the same time.

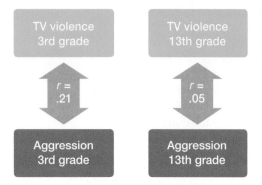

FIGURE 9.1 A longitudinal study design. First look at the correlations of the variables when measured at the same time. In third grade, a preference for TV violence is correlated with aggression; in thirteenth grade, these two variables do not appear to be correlated. Notice that the arrows point in both directions, because in these cross-sectional correlations, there is no way to know which of the variables came first in time. (Source: Adapted from Eron et al., 1972.)

Autocorrelations

The next step was to evaluate the associations of each variable with itself across time. For example, the Eron team asked whether preference for TV violence in third grade is associated with preference for TV violence in thirteenth grade, and whether aggression in third grade is associated with aggression in thirteenth grade. Such correlations are sometimes called **autocorrelations**, because they determine the correlation of one variable with itself, measured on two different occasions. The results in **Figure 9.2** suggest that TV viewing is not stable over time (the correlation is low), but that aggressive behavior is stable over time (the correlation is moderate).

Cross-Lag Correlations

So far so good. However, cross-sectional correlations and autocorrelations are generally not the researchers' primary interest. Rather, they are usually most interested in **cross-lag correlations**, which show whether the earlier measure of one variable is associated with the

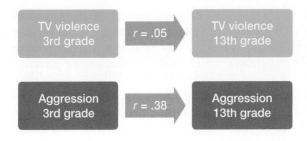

FIGURE 9.2 **Autocorrelation.** In a longitudinal study, researchers also investigate the autocorrelations. Although TV violence preferences are not stable over time, aggression levels appear to be somewhat stable. Notice that the arrows point in only one direction, because the third-grade measurements came before the thirteenth-grade measurements. (Source: Adapted from Eron et al., 1972.)

later measure of the other variable. The two cross-lag correlations thus address the directionality problem and help establish temporal precedence. In the Eron study, the cross-lag correlations would show whether preference for TV violence in third grade is correlated with aggression later on, or whether aggression in third grade is correlated with preference for TV violence later on.

By inspecting the cross-lag correlations in a longitudinal design, we can investigate how people change over time—and therefore establish temporal precedence. In this example, only one of the cross-lag correlations is statistically significant. Children who prefer more violent TV shows in third grade are more aggressive in thirteenth grade, but children who are aggressive in third grade do not prefer more violent TV shows later on. This pattern of results suggests that the preference for TV violence, not the aggression, came first.

The results of the 1972 Eron study were replicated 30 years later in another sample of 707 families (Johnson, Cohen, Smailes, Kasen, & Brook, 2002). Both studies found similar results: Watching violent TV programs at younger ages was associated with aggression at older ages, but aggression at younger ages was not as strongly related to viewing violence on TV at older ages.

Three Possible Patterns from a Cross-Lag Study. The results of the cross-lag correlations in the Eron study could have followed one of three patterns. The study did show that TV at Time 1 was strongly correlated aggression at Time 2 while aggression at Time 1 was not strongly correlated with TV at Time 2. Such a pattern indicates that TV preferences lead to aggression over time (**Figure 9.3**).

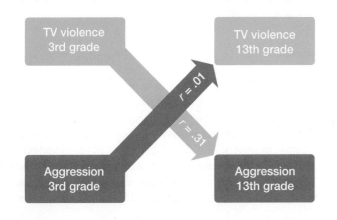

FIGURE 9.3 **Results of a cross-lag study.** The cross-lag correlations in this study suggest that viewing violent TV shows causes aggression, because a preference for TV violence in third grade predicts later aggression, but aggression in third grade does not predict later preferences for TV violence. (In this figure, the arrows point in only one direction, because in each case it is obvious which variable came first in time; third grade comes before thirteenth grade.) (Source: Adapted from Eron et al., 1972.)

However, the study could have shown the opposite results—that aggression at Time 1 was correlated with TV preferences at Time 2, but that TV preferences at Time 1 were not correlated with aggression at Time 2. Such a pattern would have indicated that the children's aggressive traits came first, leading to preferences for violent TV later.

Finally, a study might show that *both* correlations are significant—for example, if this study had shown that aggression at Time 1 predicted TV preference at Time 2 *and* that TV preference at Time 1 predicted aggression at Time 2. If that had been the result, it would mean TV preferences and aggression are mutually reinforcing; in other words, there is a cyclical, reinforcing relationship in which a preference for violent TV shows leads to aggression, and vice versa.

Longitudinal Studies and the Three Criteria for Causation

Longitudinal designs can provide some evidence for a causal relationship by means of the three criteria for causation:

1. *Covariance.* Significant relationships in longitudinal designs help establish covariance. When two variables are significantly correlated (as in the cross-sectional correlations in Figure 9.1), there is covariance.

2. *Temporal precedence.* A longitudinal design can help researchers make inferences about temporal precedence. Because each variable is measured in at least two different points in time, they know which one came first. By comparing the relative strength of the two cross-lag correlations, the researchers can see which path is stronger. If one of them is stronger (as in the TV/aggression example), the researchers move a little closer to determining which variable comes first, causing the other.

3. *Internal validity.* When conducted simply—that is, by measuring only the four key variables (Time 1 and Time 2 of the two key variables)—longitudinal studies do not help rule out third variables. For example, the Eron study cannot clearly rule out the possible third variable of sensation seeking, the desire to engage in risky or dangerous activities. Kids who are higher in sensation seeking would probably have preferred violent TV shows as third graders and might also have acted more aggressively in thirteenth grade. The study design Eron and his colleagues used does not rule out this possibility.

However, careful researchers may be able to design their studies or conduct the subsequent analyses in ways that address some third variables. For example, in the study of TV and aggression, one possible third variable is gender. Boys usually show higher levels of aggression than girls, and boys are more likely to prefer violent TV shows than girls are. Therefore, like sensation seeking, gender is undoubtedly associated with both variables. Participant gender does not threaten internal validity here, however, because, as mentioned above, Eron and his colleagues studied boys and girls separately. They found that a preference for violent TV predicts aggression for boys but not for girls. Girls showed no strong associations between the two variables (**Figure 9.4**). Thus, in the case of TV preferences and aggression, gender is a potential third variable. But by studying the longitudinal patterns of boys and girls separately, the Eron researchers were able to rule it out. (In the process, they also happened to discover that gender moderated the relationship between TV preferences and aggressive behavior.)

Why Not Just Do an Experiment?

Why would Eron and his team go to all the trouble of finding the same children after 10 years? Why didn't they just do an experiment? After all, an experiment is the best way to confirm or disconfirm causal claims. The problem is that in many cases people cannot be randomly assigned to a variable. One reason is that they cannot be assigned to preferences—people either like or dislike watching violent TV shows, and it's hard to manipulate this variable. A second reason is that it could be unethical to assign some people, especially children, to a condition in which they are forced to watch certain violent television shows for 10 years. Similarly, if researchers suspect that smoking causes lung cancer, it would be unethical (and difficult) to ask study participants to smoke cigarettes for several years. When an experiment is not practical or ethical, a longitudinal correlational design is a good option.

Nevertheless, researchers in the area of TV violence and aggressive behavior have not relied solely on correlational data. They have developed ethical experiments to study the TV/aggression relationship in both adults and children, at least over a short-term study. By randomly assigning children and adults to watch violent or nonviolent shows and then measuring their aggressive responses, researchers have produced some solid evidence that viewing violent media does, in fact, cause aggression (Bushman & Anderson, 2001). Because the ethicality of having children watch violent videos is questionable, such studies had to pass strict ethical standards before they were conducted, and the exposure time was short (1 hour or less, followed by a test of aggressive behavior). It would be much more challenging to do an ethical experimental study of the effects of long-term exposure to violent media, though, so longitudinal correlational designs become an attractive alternative.

FIGURE 9.4 Television violence and aggressive behavior. In the Eron et al. study (1972), it appeared that gender moderates the association between a preference for viewing violence on TV and aggressive behavior. Watching violent TV programs appears to lead to aggressiveness later in life, but only for boys.

CHECK YOUR UNDERSTANDING

1. Why is a longitudinal design called a multivariate design?
2. What three kinds of correlations are obtained from a longitudinal design?
3. Describe which patterns of temporal precedence are indicated by different cross-lag correlational results.

---

1. See p. 237. 2. See pp. 238–239. 3. See p. 239.

Ruling Out Third Variables with Multiple-Regression Analyses

> A study published this month in the journal *Pediatrics* studied the links between recess and classroom behavior among about 11,000 children age 8 and 9. Those who had more than 15 minutes of recess a day showed better behavior in class than those who had little or none.
> (Pope, 2009, p. D4)

The newspaper article quoted here, about a study on recess and children's behavior, reports a simple association between amount of recess time and behavior in class (Barros, Silver, & Stein, 2009). But is there a causal link? Does the recess *cause* the good behavior? Certainly there is covariance: More recess is associated with fewer behavior problems. What about temporal precedence? Did recess come before the behavior, or did the behavior come before the recess? This study is not a longitudinal design, so we don't know whether the recess policy came before the good behavior or whether the good behavior led to the recess policy. We might reason that a classroom of badly behaved children might be punished by being denied recess. In many schools, however, the recess structure was probably in place already, before any good or bad behavior was observed.

What about internal validity? Several third variables could explain the recess/behavior relationship. Perhaps recess and behavior problems are correlated because of school type—public versus private. Maybe private schools have both better-behaved students and more flexibility in their curricula to offer recess. Or perhaps grade level is a third variable: Children may be better behaved in younger grades, and younger grade levels may be more likely to have recess. Maybe income is a third variable: Children from disadvantaged groups may have more behavior problems, and they also go to schools that do not have the resources or time for a long recess.

How do we know whether one of these variables—or another one—is the true explanation for the association? The study in question used a statistical technique called **multiple regression** (or *multivariate regression*), which can help rule out some third variables. Multiple regression can help address questions of internal validity.

Measuring More Than Two Variables

To obtain the important correlation in the recess study, the researchers measured a sample of classrooms on the two key variables (Barros et al., 2009). To measure the amount of daily recess time, they asked the teacher how many minutes of recess the students got each day. To assess the level of behavior problems, they used an established measure of classroom behavior, in which each teacher rated how well-behaved his or her students were. These two variables were negatively correlated; as time for recess increased, behavior problems decreased (**Figure 9.5**).

If the researchers had stopped there and measured only these two variables, they would have conducted a bivariate correlational study. However, they also

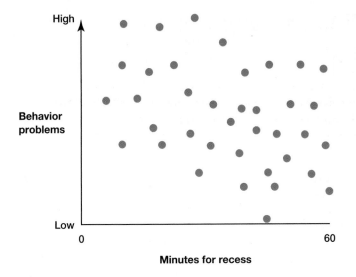

FIGURE 9.5 Correlating recess time and behavior problems. Because of the way this study was conducted, each dot represents a classroom rather than a person. The classroom is the unit of analysis; each classroom was measured on the number of behavior problems and the minutes of recess the students were allowed each day. (Data are fabricated for illustration purposes.)

measured several other variables, including the proportion of children in each classroom who were eligible for free lunch, an indicator of their family income. They also measured whether the classroom was public or private and the number of students in each classroom. By measuring all these variables instead of just two (with the goal of testing the interrelationships among them all), they conducted a multivariate correlational study.

Using Statistics to Control for Third Variables

By conducting a multivariate design, researchers can evaluate whether a relationship between two key variables still holds when they **control for** another variable. To introduce what "controlling for" means, let's focus on only one potential third variable—the measure of family income. Perhaps recess and behavior problems are correlated only because poorer children are both more likely to have behavior problems and more likely to be in schools that have less time for recess. If this is the case, all three variables are correlated with one another: Recess and behavior are correlated, as we knew, but recess and income level are also correlated with each other, and income level and behavior are correlated, too. The researchers want to know whether socioeconomic status, as a third variable correlated with both recess and behavior, can account for the relationship between recess and behavior problems. To answer the question, they will see what happens to the relationship between recess and behavior when they control for family income.

You'll learn more about multiple-regression computations in a full-semester statistics course; this book will focus on a conceptual understanding of what these analyses mean. The most statistically accurate way to describe the phrase "control for income level" is to talk about proportions of variability. Researchers are asking whether, after they take the relationship between income level and behavior into account, there is still a portion of variability in classroom behavior that is

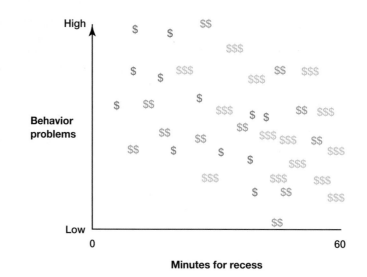

FIGURE 9.6 The association between recess time and behavior problems is still negative, even controlling for family income. The overall relationship is negative, and this negative relationship holds even after controlling for family income. (Data are fabricated for illustration purposes.)

attributable to recess. But this is extremely abstract language. The meaning is a bit like asking about the overall movement (the variance) of your wiggling, happy dog when you return home. You can ask, "What portion of the variability in my dog's overall movement is attributable to his tail moving? To his shoulders moving? To his back legs moving?" You can ask, "Will the dog still be moving when he greets me, even if I were to hold his tail constant—hold it still?"

An easier way to understand the phrase "controlling for" is to recognize that testing a third variable with multiple regression is similar to identifying subgroups. We can think of the process of controlling for income level like this: We start by looking only at the highest level of income and see whether recess and behavior are still correlated. Then we move to next highest level of income, then the next highest, and so on, until we have analyzed the relationship at the lowest level. We ask whether the bivariate relationship still holds at all levels.

There are a couple of possible outcomes from such a subgroup analysis, and one is shown in the scatterplot in **Figure 9.6**. Here, the overall relationship is negative—the more time for recess, the fewer behavior problems. In addition, the classrooms with the poorest children (the $ symbols) have, overall, more behavior problems and shorter recess. The classrooms with the richest children (the $$$ symbols) have, overall, fewer behavior problems and longer recess. If we look *only* at the poorer classrooms, or *only* at the middle-income classrooms, or *only* at the richer classrooms, however, we still find the key relationship between behavior problems and recess time: It is still negative even within these family income subgroups. Therefore, the relationship is still there, even when we control for income level.

In contrast, the second possible outcome is shown in **Figure 9.7**. Here, the *overall* relationship is still negative, just as before—the more time for recess, the fewer behavior problems. In addition, just as before, the classrooms with the poorest children (the $ symbols) have, overall, more behavior problems and shorter recess, and the classrooms with the richest children (the $$$

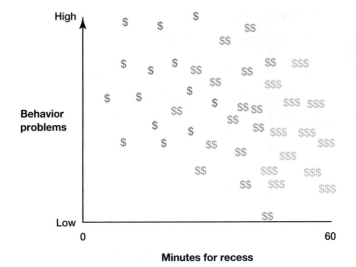

FIGURE 9.7 The association between recess time and behavior problems goes away, controlling for family income. The overall relationship is negative, but when we look *only* at subgroups of the poorest classrooms, the middle-income classrooms, or the richest classrooms, there is no relationship between the two variables. (Data are fabricated for illustration purposes.)

symbols) have, overall, fewer behavior problems and longer recess. However, this time, when we look *only* at the children from poorer classrooms or *only* at the children from the richer classrooms, the relationship between behavior problems and recess (the key relationship) is absent. The scatterplots *within* the family income subgroups do not show the relationship anymore. Therefore, the relationship between recess time and behavior problems goes away when we control for income level. In this case, family income was, indeed, the third variable that was responsible for the relationship.

Regression Results Indicate If a Third Variable Affects the Relationship

Which one of the two scatterplots, Figure 9.6 or 9.7, best describes the relationship between recess time and behavior problems? The statistical technique of multiple regression can tell us. When researchers use regression, they are testing whether some key relationship holds true even when a suspected third variable is statistically controlled for.

As a consumer of information, you are most likely to work with the end result of this process, when you encounter regression results in tables of empirical journal articles. Suppose you're reading a journal article and you come across **Table 9.1**, which shows what the regression results would look like for the recess/behavior example. What do these numbers mean? What steps did the researchers follow to come up with them?

TABLE 9.1 Multiple-Regression Results from a Study Predicting Behavior Problems from Recess Time and Family Income

Criterion (dependent) variable: Classroom behavior problems	Beta	Sig
Predictor (independent) variables:		
Minutes of recess	−0.06	*
Proportion of students eligible for free lunch	0.10	*

Note: Data are fabricated, based on results if the researchers had used only two predictor variables.
*$p < .001$.

Criterion Variables and Predictor Variables

When researchers use multiple regression, they are studying three or more variables. The first step is to choose the variable they are most interested in understanding or predicting; this is known as the **criterion variable**, or *dependent variable*. In the case of recess and behavior problems, the Barros team decided they were most interested in understanding behavior problems, so they chose that as their criterion variable. The criterion (dependent) variable is almost always specified either in the top row or in the title of a regression table.

The rest of the variables measured in a regression analysis are called **predictor variables**, or *independent variables*. In the recess/behavior study, the predictor variables are the amount of recess time each classroom had and the proportion of students eligible for free lunch. In Table 9.1, the two predictor variables are listed below the criterion variable.

Using Beta to Test for Third Variables

The point of the multiple-regression results in Table 9.1 is to see whether the relationship between recess time and behavior problems might be explained by a third variable—family income (measured by free lunch eligibility). Does the association remain, even within each level of income (as in Figure 9.6)? Or does the relationship between recess time and behavior problems go away within different levels of income (as in Figure 9.7)? The betas in Table 9.1 help answer this central question.

Beta Basics. In a regression table like Table 9.1, there is often a column labeled beta (or β, or even standardized beta). There will be one beta value for each predictor variable. Beta is similar to r, but it reveals more than r does. A positive beta, like a positive r, indicates a positive relationship between that predictor variable and the criterion variable, when the other predictor variables are statistically controlled for. A negative beta, like a negative r, indicates a negative relationship between two variables (when the other predictors are controlled for). A beta that is zero, or not significantly different from zero, means that there is no relationship (when the other predictors are controlled for). Therefore, betas are similar to correlations in that they denote the direction and strength of a relationship. The higher beta is, the stronger the relationship is between that predictor variable and the criterion variable. The smaller beta is, the weaker the relationship.

Within a single regression table, we can usually compare predictor variables that show larger betas to predictor variables with smaller betas—the larger the beta, the stronger the relationship. For example, in Table 9.1 we can say that the beta for the free lunch predictor is stronger than the beta for the recess predictor. (However, it is not appropriate to compare the strengths of betas from one regression table to the strengths of betas from another one.)

Unlike r, there are no quick guidelines for beta to indicate effect sizes that are weak, moderate, or strong. The reason is that betas change, depending on what other predictor variables are being used—being controlled for—in the regression.

Sometimes a regression table will include the symbol b instead of beta. The coefficient b is also called an unstandardized coefficient. A b is similar to beta in that the sign of *b*—positive or negative—still denotes a positive or negative association (when the other predictors are controlled for). But unlike two betas, we cannot compare two *b* values within the same table to each other. The reason is that *b* values are computed from the original measurements of the predictor variables (such as dollars, centimeters, percentages, or inches), whereas betas are computed from predictor variables that have been changed to standardized units. A predictor variable that shows a large *b* may not actually denote a stronger relationship to the criterion variable than a predictor variable with a smaller *b*.

Interpreting Beta. In Table 9.1, notice that the predictor variable "number of minutes of recess" has a beta of −0.06. This negative beta, just like a negative *r*, means that as recess minutes go up, behavior problems go down. But it also means that as recess minutes go up, behavior problems go down, even while we statistically control for the other predictor variable in this table—the free lunch. In other words, even when we hold the free lunch variable constant statistically, the relationship between recess time and behavior problems is still there. This result is consistent with the relationship depicted in Figure 9.6, not the one in Figure 9.7.

The other beta in Table 9.1, the one associated with the free lunch predictor variable, is positive. This beta means that as the proportion of students eligible for free lunch goes up, the behavior problems go up, too, *when the number of minutes of recess is controlled for.* In other words, when we hold the number of minutes of recess constant, family income levels predict behavior problems, too. In sum, the beta that is associated with a predictor variable represents the relationship between that predictor variable and the criterion variable, when the other predictor variables in the table are controlled for.

Statistical Significance of Beta. The regression tables in empirical journal articles often have a column labeled sig or *p*, or an asterisked footnote giving the *p* value for each beta. Whether in a column or a footnote, these data indicate whether each beta is statistically significantly different from zero. As discussed in Chapter 8, the *p* value gives the probability that the beta came from a population in which the relationship is zero. When *p* is less than .05, the beta (i.e., the relationship between that predictor variable and the criterion variable, when the other predictor variables are controlled for) is considered statistically significant. When *p* is greater than .05, the beta is considered not significant, meaning we cannot conclude that beta is different from zero.

In Table 9.1, both of the betas reported are statistically significant, so we can interpret them as describing replicable relationships. **Table 9.2** gives several appropriate ways to explain what these significant betas mean.

What If Beta Is Not Significant? To answer this question, we will use an example from a different line of research: family meals and child academic achievement. When these two variables are studied as a bivariate relationship, many researchers find that children who come from families that eat many meals together (dinners and breakfasts) tend to achieve more academically, compared to children who come from families that eat only a few meals together.

For more on statistical significance, see Statistics Review: Inferential Statistics, pp. 482–483.

TABLE 9.2 Describing the Significant Beta of –0.06 in Table 9.1

Each of these sentences is an appropriate description of the relationship:

- The relationship between recess time and behavior problems is negative (as recess minutes go up, behavior problems go down), even when the proportion of students eligible for free lunch is controlled for.

- The relationship between recess time and behavior problems is negative (as recess minutes go up, behavior problems go down), independent of the proportion of students eligible for free lunch.

- The relationship between recess time and behavior problems is negative (as recess minutes go up, behavior problems go down), even when the proportion of students eligible for free lunch is held constant.

- The relationship between recess time and behavior problems is negative (as recess minutes go up, behavior problems go down), and is not attributable to the third variable of family income, because it holds even when the proportion of students eligible for free lunch is held constant.

Once again, this simple bivariate relationship is not enough to show causation. There is a temporal precedence problem: Do family meals come first and reinforce key academic skills, leading to more school achievement? Or does high academic achievement come first, making it more pleasant for parents to have meals with their kids? In addition, there are third variables that present an internal validity concern. For instance, more involved parents might arrange more family meals, and more involved parents might also have higher-achieving children. A multiple-regression analysis could hold parental involvement constant and see if family meal frequency is still correlated with academic achievement. In one such study, the researchers found that when parental involvement was held constant (along with other variables), family meal frequency was no longer a significant predictor of school success (Miller, Waldfogel, & Han, 2012). This pattern of results means that the only reason family meals correlated with academic success was because of the third-variable problem of parental involvement (**Table 9.3**).

In other words, although frequency of family meals and academic success are significantly related in their bivariate relationship, that relationship goes away when potential third variables, such as parental involvement, are controlled for. When you hold parental involvement constant, there is no longer a relationship between frequency of family meals and academic success (**Table 9.4**).

TABLE 9.3 Multiple-Regression Results from a Study Predicting Academic Success from Frequency of Family Meals and Parental Involvement

Criterion (dependent) variable: Academic success	Beta	Sig
Predictor (independent) variables:		
Frequency of family meals	−0.01	Not significant
Parental involvement	0.09	*

Note: Data are fabricated, but reflect actual research. The study controlled not only for parental involvement, but also income, family structure, school quality, birth weight, school type, and a host of other possible third variables. When controlling for all these in a sample of more than 20,000 children, the researchers found that the beta for frequency of family meals was not significant.
*$p < .001$.
Source: Adapted from Miller et al., 2012.

TABLE 9.4 Describing the Nonsignificant Beta of −0.01 in Table 9.3

Each of these sentences is an appropriate description of the relationship:

- The relationship between family meal frequency and child academic achievement is not significant when controlling for parental involvement.
- The relationship between family meal frequency and child academic achievement is probably explained by the third variable of parental involvement.
- The relationship between family meal frequency and child academic achievement goes away when parental involvement is held constant.

Adding More Predictors to a Regression

Up to now, when we have considered the relationship between recess time and behavior problems, we've focused on only one potential internal validity problem—family income. But remember that there are many other potential third variables for the recess/behavior relationship. What about class size? What about private versus public schools? In fact, Barros and her colleagues measured each of those third variables and even added a few more, such as the proportion of boys in the classroom and the proportion of students in each classroom reading above grade level. **Table 9.5** shows every variable the Barros team tested, as well as the multiple-regression results for all the other variables.

TABLE 9.5 Multiple-Regression Results from a Study Predicting Behavior Problems from Recess Time and Other Variables

Criterion (dependent) variable: Behavior problems in classroom	Beta	Sig
Predictor (independent) variables:		
Availability of recess	−0.042	*
Proportion of students eligible for free lunch	0.097	*
Proportion of boys in class	0.154	*
Proportion of students above grade in math	−0.108	*
Proportion of students above grade in reading	−0.045	*
Number of students in class	0.062	*
Proportion of minorities in class	0.091	*
Parental education	−0.031	*
Private school[a]	0.041	*

*$p \leq .001$.
[a]Private school is coded so that a higher value means private school.
Source: Adapted from Barros et al., 2009.

Even when there are so many more predictor variables in the table, beta still means the same thing. The beta for the recess variable is negative: The more time for recess, the fewer behavior problems, when the researchers controlled for all the other predictors. Even after controlling for all variables listed in Table 9.5, the researchers found that longer recess time predicts fewer behavior problems.

Adding several predictors to a regression analysis can help answer two kinds of questions. First, it helps control for several third variables at once. Indeed, in the Barros study, even after all other variables were controlled for, recess still predicted fewer behavior problems. A result like that gets the researchers closer to making a causal claim, because the relationship between the suspected cause (recess) and the suspected effect (behavior problems) does not appear to be attributable to any of the other variables that were measured.

Second, by looking at the betas for all the other predictor variables, we can get a sense of which factors most strongly affect classroom behavior problems. One strong predictor is the proportion of boys in the classroom. The more boys, the more behavior problems, even when the availability of recess, free lunch, reading level, and every other variable is controlled for. In fact, we know that the effect of boys is *larger* than the effect for recess, because the beta for the "boys" predictor is larger than the beta for the "recess" predictor. Even though the authors of this study were most interested in describing the benefits of recess, they were also able to evaluate which other variables are important in predicting behavior problems. (Recall, however, that when a table presents *b* values, or unstandardized coefficients, it is not appropriate to compare their *relative* strength. We can only do so with beta, and even then, remember that betas change depending on what other predictor variables are used.)

Regression in Popular Press Articles

When you encounter association claims in the popular press, such as magazines, newspapers, and websites, the journalists will rarely discuss betas, *p* values, or predictor variables. After all, they write for a general audience, so they assume that most of their readers will not be familiar with these concepts. However, if you read carefully, you can detect that a multiple regression has been used, if a journalist uses one of these telltale phrases.

"Controlled for"

The phrase "controlled for" is the most common sign of a regression analysis. When the recess/behavior study was reported in an online newspaper, the journalist mentioned the simple relationship between recess and behavior, and then wrote:

> Although disadvantaged children were more likely to be denied recess, the association between better behavior and recess time held up *even after researchers controlled for a number of variables*, including sex, ethnicity, public or private school and class size. (Pope, 2009; emphasis added)

Similarly, when journalists covered the story about family dinners and academic achievement, they stated the findings like this:

Researchers . . . determined that there wasn't any relationship between family meals and a child's academic outcomes or behavior. To pinpoint the effect of family meal time on academic outcomes and behavior, Miller and his team also *controlled for factors* such as parental employment, television-watching, the quality of school facilities, and the years of experience the children's teachers had, among others. (Family dinner benefits, 2012; emphasis added)

The phrase "controlled for" is a clue that the study used multiple regression. (In an empirical journal article, the things that the study controlled for would be listed as the predictor variables.)

"Taking into Account"

Here is another example from a popular press story about a study of veterans. This is the headline: "Perk of a good job: aging mind is sharp."

Mentally demanding jobs come with a hidden benefit: less mental decline with age. Work that requires decision making, negotiating with others, analysis, and making judgments may not necessarily pad your bank account. But it does build up your "cognitive reserve"—a level of mental function that helps you avoid or compensate for age-related mental decline. (DeNoon, 2008)

In this story, the central association is between how mentally demanding a man's job is and his cognitive functioning as he ages. The more demanding the job, the less cognitive decline he suffers. But could there be a third variable, such as intelligence or level of education? Perhaps the veterans in the study who were better educated were more likely both to have a mentally challenging job and to experience less cognitive decline. However, the story goes on:

After taking into account both intelligence and education, Potter and colleagues found that men with more complex jobs—in terms of general intellectual demands and human interaction and communication—performed significantly better on tests of mental function. (DeNoon, 2008; emphasis added)

The phrase "taking into account" means that the researchers conducted multiple-regression analyses. Even when they controlled for education and intelligence, they still found a relationship between job complexity and cognitive decline.

"Correcting for" or "Adjusting for"

The following excerpt is from a story reporting an association between birth order and IQ. The researchers found that firstborn children are smarter than later-born siblings:

In the study, Norwegian epidemiologists analyzed data on birth order, health status and IQ scores of 241,310 18- and 19-year-old men born from 1967 to 1976, using military records. *After correcting for factors that*

The Chocolate Diet?

"Since so many complicating factors can influence results, it is difficult to pinpoint cause and effect. But the researchers adjusted their results for a number of variables, including age, gender, depression, vegetable consumption, and fat and calorie intake."

FIGURE 9.8 Multiple regression in the popular press. This journalist wrote that people who ate more chocolate had lower body mass index, and that the researchers adjusted their results for several variables. The phrase "adjusted for" signals a regression analysis, thereby ruling out those variables as internal validity problems. (Source: O'Connor, 2012.)

may affect scores, including parents' education level, maternal age at birth, and family size, the researchers found that eldest children scored an average of 103.2, about 3 percent higher than second children (100.3) and 4 percent higher than thirdborns (99.0). (Carey, 2007; emphasis added)

Again, the phrase "after correcting for" indicates that the researchers used multiple regression.

Similar terminology such as "adjusting for" also indicates multiple regression, as in this example of a study that found a relationship between chocolate consumption and weight (**Figure 9.8**).

The people who ate chocolate the most frequently, despite eating more calories and exercising no differently from those who ate the least chocolate, tended to have lower B.M.I.'s. . . . The researchers *adjusted their results for* a number of variables, including age, gender, depression, vegetable consumption, and fat and calorie intake. "It didn't matter which of those you added, the relationship remained very stably significant." (O'Connor, 2012; emphasis added)

When you encounter an association claim, one of your questions should be whether the researchers controlled for possible third variables. If you cannot tell from the news story what the researchers controlled for, it's reasonable to suspect that some third variables may be responsible for the association.

Regression Does Not Establish Causation

Multiple regression might seem to be a foolproof way to rule out all kinds of third variables. If you look at the recess and behavior problems data in Table 9.5, for example, you might think you can safely make a causal statement now, since the researchers controlled for so many internal validity problems. They seem to have thought of everything! However, there are still two problems with concluding that longer recess periods cause children to behave better. One is that even though multivariate designs analyzed with regression statistics can control for third variables, they may not be able to establish temporal precedence. Recess could cause behavior problems to decline, but it is still possible that the behavior problems in certain classrooms came first and caused teachers to restrict their classes' recess times.

The second problem is that researchers cannot control for variables they do not measure. Even though multiple regression controls for any third variables the researchers measure in the study, there could be an important third variable—one they did not consider—that accounts for the association. In the recess example, some unmeasured variable—maybe the teacher's level of experience, the quality of the food in the school, the number of windows in the classroom—is really accounting for the relationship between recess and behavior. But since those variables were not measured (or even considered), there is no way of knowing (**Figure 9.9**).

This unknown third-variable problem is one reason that a well-run experimental study is ultimately more convincing than a correlational study. An experimental study on recess, for example, would randomly assign a large sample of classrooms to a "recess condition" and a "no recess condition." The power of random assignment would make the two groups likely to be equal on any possible third variable—even the third variables the researchers did not happen to measure. The classrooms with the smartest students would be divided at random between the two experimental groups. The classrooms with the most experienced teachers and the fewest boys would also be divided at random between the two experimental groups. A randomized experiment is still the gold standard for determining causation. Multiple regression, in contrast, allows researchers to control for potential third variables, but only for the variables they choose to measure.

FIGURE 9.9 Possible third variables in the association between recess and behavior. What additional third variables, not already measured by the researchers, might explain why classrooms with more time for recess have fewer behavior problems?

1. Describe what it means to say that some variable "was controlled for" in a multivariate study.
2. How many criterion variables are there in a multiple-regression analysis? How many predictor variables?
3. What does a significant beta mean? What does a nonsignificant beta mean?
4. Give at least three phrases indicating that a study used a multiple-regression analysis.
5. What are two reasons that multiple regression analyses cannot completely establish causation?

1. See p. 243. 2. One criterion variable, and at least two predictor variables. See p. 246.
3. See pp. 247–248. 4. See pp. 250–252. 5. See pp. 252–253.

Getting at Causality with Pattern and Parsimony

So far this chapter has focused on two techniques that help researchers investigate causation, even when they are working with correlations among measured variables. Longitudinal correlational designs help satisfy the temporal precedence criterion. Multiple-regression analyses help establish internal validity by statistically controlling for some potential third variables.

In this section, we explore how researchers can investigate causality by using a variety of correlational studies that all point in a single, causal direction. This approach can be called "pattern and parsimony" because there is a pattern of results that is best explained by a parsimonious causal explanation. As discussed in Chapter 1, **parsimony** is the degree to which a good scientific theory provides the simplest explanation of some phenomenon. In the context of investigating a causal claim, parsimony means the simplest explanation of a pattern of data—the best explanation that requires making the fewest exceptions or qualifications.

The Power of Pattern and Parsimony

A great example of pattern and parsimony is the case of smoking and lung cancer. This example was first articulated by the psychological scientist Robert Abelson. Decades ago, it started becoming clear that smokers had higher rates of lung cancer than nonsmokers (the correlation has been estimated at about $r = .40$). Did the smoking *cause* the cancer? Cigarette manufacturers certainly did not want people to think so. If somebody were to argue that this correlation was causal, a critic might counter that the cigarettes were not the cause; perhaps people who smoked also had more nervous tension, which predisposed them to lung cancer. Or perhaps smokers also drank a lot of coffee, and it was the coffee, not the cigarettes, that caused cancer. The list of third-variable explanations could go on and on. Even though multiple-regression analyses could control for these third variables, critics could always argue that regression cannot control for every possible third variable.

Another problem, of course, is that even though an experiment could rule out these third-variable explanations, a smoking experiment would not be ethical or practical. A researcher could not reasonably assign a sample of volunteers to become lifetime smokers or nonsmokers. The only data that researchers had to work with were correlational.

Abelson explains that the way out of such a conundrum is to specify a mechanism for the causal path. Specifically, in the case of cigarettes, researchers proposed that cigarette smoke contains chemicals that are toxic when they come into contact with human tissue. The more contact human tissue has with these chemicals, the more toxicity people are exposed to. This simple theory leads to a set of predictions, all of which could be explained by the single, parsimonious theory that chemicals in cigarettes cause cancer (Abelson, 1995, p. 184):

1. The longer a person has smoked cigarettes, the greater his or her chances of getting cancer.
2. People who stop smoking have lower cancer rates than people who keep smoking.
3. Smokers' cancers tend to be in the lungs and of a particular type.
4. Smokers who use filtered cigarettes have a somewhat lower rate of cancer than those who use unfiltered cigarettes.
5. People who live with smokers would have higher rates of cancer, too, because of their passive exposure to the same chemicals.

This process exemplifies the theory-data cycle (see Chapter 1). A theory—cigarette toxicity—led to a particular set of research questions. The theory also led researchers to frame hypotheses about what the data should show.

Indeed, converging evidence from several individual studies, conducted by medical researchers, has supported each of these separate predictions (their evidence became part of the U.S. Surgeon General's warning in 1964), and that's where parsimony comes in. Because all five of these diverse predictions are tied back to one central principle, the toxicity of the chemicals in cigarette smoke, there is a strong case for parsimony (**Figure 9.10**).

Notice, also, that the diversity of these five empirical findings makes it much harder to raise third-variable explanations. Suppose a critic argued that coffee drinking was a third variable. Coffee drinking could certainly explain the first

FIGURE 9.10 Pattern and parsimony. Many studies, using a variety of methods, provide converging evidence to support the causal claim that cigarettes contain toxic chemicals that are harmful to humans. Although each of the individual studies has weaknesses, taken together, they all support the same, parsimonious conclusion.

result (the longer one smokes—and presumably drinks coffee, too—the higher the rates of cancer). But it cannot explain the effect of filtered cigarettes or the cancer rates among secondhand smokers. The most parsimonious explanation of this entire pattern of data—and the weight of the evidence—is the toxicity of cigarettes.

It is hard to overstate the strength of the pattern and parsimony technique. In psychology, researchers commonly use a variety of methods and many studies to explore the strength and limits of a particular research question. The TV violence and aggression connection is another good example of how a single, parsimonious causal statement (violence on TV leads to violent behavior) explains a wide body of evidence. Some of the studies on violent TV and aggressive behavior are correlational, some are experimental. Some are on children, others in adults. Some are longitudinal, others are not. But in general, the evidence all points to a single, parsimonious conclusion (Anderson et al., 2003).

Many psychological scientists build their careers by doing study after study devoted to one research question. As discussed in Chapter 1, scientists dig deeper: They use a variety of methods, combining results to develop their causal theories and to support them with converging evidence.

To review the concept of weight of the evidence, see Chapter 1, p. 13.

Pattern, Parsimony, and the Popular Press

When journalists write about science, they do not always fairly represent pattern and parsimony in research. Instead, they may report only the results of the latest study. For example, they might present a news story on the most recent nutrition research, without describing the other studies done in that area. They might report that shy people are better at reading facial expressions, but fail to cover the full pattern of studies on shyness. They might report on a single study that showed an association between eating chocolate and BMI, without mentioning the rest of the studies on that same topic, and without tying the results to the theory they are supporting.

When journalists report only one study at a time, they selectively present only a part of the scientific process. They might not describe the context of the research, such as what previous studies have revealed, or what theory the study was testing. Reporting on the latest study without giving the full context can make it seem as though scientists conduct single, unconnected studies on a whim. It might even give the impression that a single study can reverse decades of previous research. In addition, skeptics who read such science stories might find it easy to deride the results of a single, correlational study. But in fact, science accumulates incrementally. Ideally, journalists should report on the entire body of evidence, as well as the theoretical background, for a particular claim.

CHECK YOUR UNDERSTANDING

1. Why do many researchers find pattern and parsimony an effective way to support a causal claim?

2. What is a responsible way for journalists to cover single studies on a specific topic?

---

1. See pp. 254–256. 2. See p. 256.

Mediation

We have discussed the research designs and statistical tools researchers use to get closer to making causal claims. Once a relationship between two variables has been proposed, we often want to explore it further, by thinking about *why*. For example, we might ask why recess apparently leads to a drop in behavior problems. Many times, these explanations for a causal relationship involve a **mediator**, or *mediating variable*. Researchers may propose a mediating step between two of the variables. A study does not have to be correlational to include a mediator; experimental studies can also test them. However, mediation analyses often rely on multivariate tools such as multiple regression, so it makes sense to learn about mediators here.

Here's an example. We know that conscientious people are more physically healthy than less conscientious people. Why? The mediator of this relationship might be that conscientious people are more likely to adhere to medical advice and instructions, and that's why they are healthier. Following doctor's orders would be the mediator of the relationship between the trait, conscientiousness, and the outcome, better health (Hill & Roberts, 2011).

Similarly, we know there is an association between recess and behavior problems. Researchers might next propose a reason for the association—in other words, a mediator of this relationship. One likely mediator could be physical activity: Recess gives children a chance for physical activity, and the more tired they get from that activity, the fewer behavior problems they show. The researchers could draw this mediation hypothesis, as shown in **Figure 9.11**. They would propose that there is an overall relationship, *c*, between recess and behavior problems. However, this overall relationship exists only because there are two other relationships, *a* (between recess and physical activity) and *b* (between physical activity and behavior problems). In other words, physical activity mediates the relationship between recess and behavior problems. (Of course, there are other possible mediators, such as exposure to fresh air and experience in natural settings. Those mediators could be tested, too, in another study.)

The researchers could examine this mediation hypothesis by following five steps (Kenny, 2008):

1. Test for relationship *c*. Is recess associated with behavior problems? (If it is not, there is no relationship to mediate.)

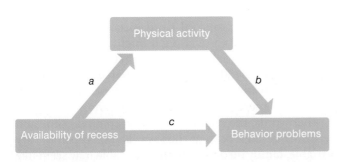

FIGURE 9.11 A proposed mediation model. More recess leads to more physical activity, which leads to fewer behavior problems. To support this model, a researcher follows five steps (see text).

2. Test for relationship *a*. Is recess associated with the proposed mediator, physical activity? Do children who have recess actually engage in more physical activity than children who do not? (If physical activity is the aspect of recess that explains why recess leads to fewer behavior problems, then logically, classes that have more recess must also show higher levels of physical activity.)
3. Test for relationship *b*. Do children who engage in more physical activity have fewer behavior problems? (Again, if physical activity explains behavior problems, then logically, classes with more physical activity must also have lower levels of behavior problems.)
4. Run a regression test, using both physical activity and recess as predictor variables to predict behavior problems, to see whether relationship *c* goes away. (If physical activity is the mediator of relationship *c*, the relationship between recess and behavior problems should drop when physical activity is controlled for. Here we would be using regression as a tool to show that recess was associated with classroom behavior in the first place because physical activity was responsible.)

A fifth important step establishes temporal precedence:

5. Mediation is definitively established only when the proposed causal variable is measured (or manipulated) first in a study, followed by the mediating variable, followed by the proposed outcome variable.

In other words, to establish mediation in this example, the researchers must conduct a study in which the amount of recess is measured first, followed shortly afterwards by a measure of physical activity. They have to measure behavior problems last of all, to rule out the possibility that the behavior problems led to having less recess.

In the example in which researchers want to examine whether following doctor's orders is the mediator of the relationship between conscientiousness and good health, the design of the study should ideally measure conscientiousness first, and then later measure medical adherence, and then later measure health. If the design establishes temporal precedence *and* the results support the steps above, there is strong evidence for mediation.

Mediators vs. Third Variables

Mediators are similar to third-variable explanations, in that both of them involve multivariate research designs, and researchers can use the same statistical tool (multiple regression) to detect them both. However, they function differently with respect to some bivariate correlations.

In a third-variable explanation, the proposed third variable is external to the two variables in the original bivariate correlation; it might even be seen as a problematic "lurking variable" that potentially distracts from the relationship of interest. For example, if family income really were a third variable that is responsible for the recess/behavior relationship, recess and behavior are correlated with each other only because each one is correlated separately with family income, as shown in **Figure 9.12**. In other words, the relationship between recess time and behavior problems is there only because both of those variables happen to vary with the external third variable, family income. The third variable may seem like

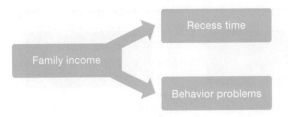

FIGURE 9.12 A third variable. In a third-variable scenario, the third variable is seen as external to the original two variables. Here, family income might be associated with both less recess and more behavior problems.

a nuisance; it might not be of central interest to the researchers. (If they are really interested in recess and behavior, they have to control for family income first.)

In contrast, when researchers propose a mediator, they are interested in isolating which aspect of the causal variable is responsible for that relationship. A mediator variable is *internal* to the causal variable and often of direct interest to the researchers, rather than a nuisance. In the recess example, the researchers believe that that physical activity is the important aspect of recess, the one responsible for reducing behavior problems.

Mediators vs. Moderators

Recall that moderators were introduced in Chapter 8. These similar-sounding names can make them confusing at first. However, testing for mediation versus moderation involves asking different questions (Baron & Kenny, 1986). When researchers test for mediating variables, they ask: Why are these two variables linked? When they test for moderating variables, they ask: Are these two variables linked the same way for everyone, or in every situation? Mediators ask: Why? Moderators ask: For whom? or When?

A mediation hypothesis could propose, for instance, that medical adherence is the reason why conscientiousness is related to better health. In contrast, a moderation hypothesis could propose that the link between conscientiousness and good health is strongest among older people (perhaps because their health problems are more severe, and most likely to benefit from medical adherence) and weakest among younger people (whose health problems are less serious).

As the name implies, the mediating variable comes in the middle of the other two variables. The word *moderate* can mean "to make less intense," and a moderating variable can make the relationship between the other two variables less intense. **Figure 9.13** diagrams the differences between mediation, moderation, and third variables.

CHECK YOUR UNDERSTANDING

1. Explain why each of the five steps in a mediation examination is important to establishing evidence for a mediator.

2. Think of a possible mediator for the relationship between having substantive conversations and being happy (from Chapter 8). Sketch a diagram of the mediator you propose, following Figure 9.11.

---

1. See pp. 257–258. 2. Diagram should resemble Figure 9.11, with proportion of substantive conversations in the left box, happiness in the right box, and your proposed mediator in the middle box.

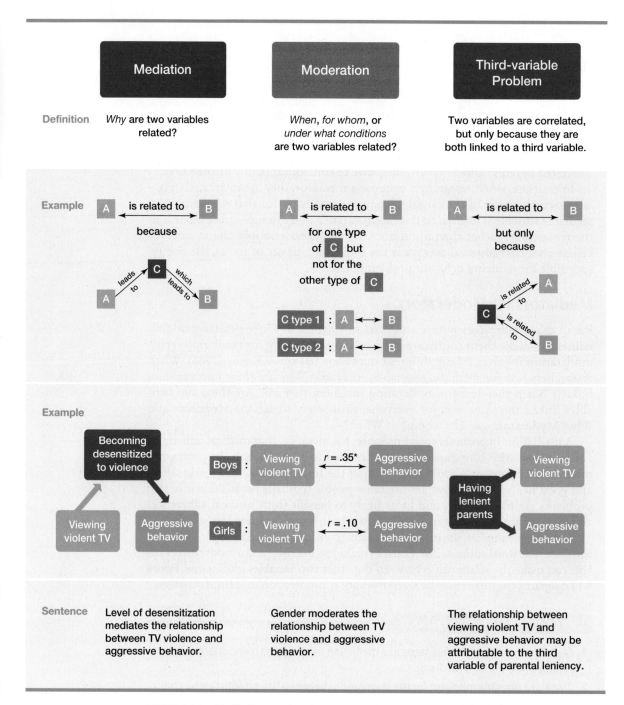

FIGURE 9.13 Mediation, moderation, and third variables. How are they different?

Multivariate Designs and the Four Validities

Researchers use multivariate correlational research, such as longitudinal designs and multiple-regression analyses, to get closer to making causal claims. Longitudinal designs help establish temporal precedence, and multiple-regression analysis helps rule out third variables, thus providing some evidence for internal validity. We must remember, however, to interrogate the other three major validities—construct, external, and statistical validity—as well.

For any multivariate design, as for any bivariate design, it is appropriate to interrogate the construct validity of the variables in the study, by asking how well each variable was measured. In the Eron study on TV violence and aggression, is asking children or their parents what TV shows they like to watch a reliable and valid way to measure their preference for media violence? What about the measure of aggression? Is asking peers a reliable and valid way to measure a child's levels of aggression? Similarly, in the Barros study, what about the measures of recess time and classroom behavior problems? Is it reliable and valid to ask teachers to rate their own students' behavior problems? Why or why not?

We can also interrogate the external validity of a multivariate design. In the TV violence and aggression study, the researchers observed every third grader in a single small town in New York. Because they used a census, not a sample, it is irrelevant to ask whether the sample was random. However, it might be appropriate to question whether the results would generalize to urban children, to children from different regions of the United States, or to children from different countries. We might also ask whether the link generalizes to other kinds of media, such as video games. Even when associations are established in a restricted sample, those associations might very well still generalize to other groups or to other media.

To interrogate the external validity of the recess and school behavior study, we can ask whether the classrooms were sampled randomly, and from what kind of population. Because the researchers measured each classroom's average family income, proportion of boys, private versus public status, and proportion of minorities, these variables may be used to evaluate how well their sample of classrooms mirrors that of the population of U.S. classrooms. We could ask: Does the percentage of private classrooms in this sample match the proportion of U.S. schoolchildren who attend private schools?

For interrogating a multivariate correlational research study's statistical validity, we can apply the issues discussed in Chapter 8. We can ask about the effect size and statistical significance. Take, for instance, the effect of recess time on classroom behavior. We know that the beta was statistically significant. However, compared with the other predictors, the effect size was smaller—beta was just -0.04 (see Table 9.5). Although there are no guidelines for what constitutes a "small" beta, we can compare it with other betas in the regression, noting, for example, that the effect of the proportion of boys on a classroom's behavior problems was larger: beta $= 0.15$. But even though the beta of -0.04 is small, the importance of a small effect size depends on the researchers' perspective. On the one hand, it is both interesting and important

TABLE 5   Bivariate Comparison of TRCB Scores According to Level of Exposure to Recess

Level of Exposure	N	TRCB Score, Mean ± SD (95% Confidence Interval)
None/minimal break	3369	3.44 ± 0.900(3.41–3.47)
Little recess[a]	595	3.62 ± 0.811(3.55–3.68)
More recess[a]	2132	3.57 ± 0.900(3.53–3.60)
A lot of recess[a]	2299	3.61 ± 0.829(3.58–3.64)
Minimal recess/lunch[a]	3027	3.60 ± 0.845(3.57–3.63)
Recess/lunch of >30 min[a]	107	3.74 ± 0.925(3.56–3.92)

[a] $P < .001$ for none/minimal break versus all other groups.

FIGURE 9.14 Statistical validity in the recess/behavior study. To illustrate the effect size of recess on behavior, the researchers indicated the behavior rating at each level of the recess variable. By comparing the behavior ratings for the highest and lowest levels of recess, you can decide if the impact of recess is strong or weak. TRCB = Teacher Rating of Classroom Behavior, ranging from 1 (misbehaves very frequently, almost always difficult to handle) to 5 (behaves exceptionally well). A confidence interval is a statistical estimate of where the population mean lies. (Source: Barros et al., 2009.)

that recess time is significantly associated with better classroom behavior, even after a large number of third variables are controlled for. On the other hand, the effect of recess time is small, so in practical terms, providing longer recess may amount to only a small decrease in classroom behavior problems. The authors of the paper presented a helpful table, presented here as **Figure 9.14**, of the true level of classroom behavior at each level of the recess variable. Do you think the effect of recess on behavior is strong? Is it important?

Other statistical validity questions apply to multivariate designs, too. When researchers use multivariate designs, they need to take precautions to look for subgroups, outliers, and curvilinear relationships, all of which can be more complicated to detect when there are more than two variables.

CHECK YOUR UNDERSTANDING

1. Give an example of a question you would ask to interrogate each of the four validities for a multivariate study.

1. See pp. 261–262.

Summary

- Research often begins with a simple bivariate correlation, but since bivariate correlations cannot establish causation, researchers use other techniques that help them get closer to making a causal claim.

Reviewing the Three Causal Criteria

- In a multivariate design, researchers measure more than two variables and look for the relationships among them.
- A simple, bivariate correlation indicates that there is covariance, but cannot always indicate temporal precedence or internal validity, so it cannot establish causation.

Establishing Temporal Precedence with Longitudinal Designs

- Longitudinal designs start with two key variables, on which the same group of people are measured at multiple points in time. Researchers can tell which variable came first in time, thus helping establish temporal precedence.
- Longitudinal designs produce cross-sectional correlations (correlations between the two key variables at any one time period) and autocorrelations (correlations between one variable and itself, over time).
- Longitudinal designs also produce cross-lag correlations. By comparing the relative strengths of the two cross-lag correlations, researchers can infer which of the variables probably came first in time (or if they are mutually reinforcing each other).

Ruling Out Third Variables with Multiple-Regression Analyses

- In a regression design, researchers start with a bivariate correlation and then measure other potential third variables that might affect it.
- Using multiple-regression analysis, researchers can see whether the basic relationship is still present, even when they statistically control for one or more third variables. If the beta is still significant for the key variable, even when the researchers control for the third variables, it means the key relationship is not explained by those third variables.
- If the beta becomes nonsignificant when the researchers control for a third variable, then the key relationship is attributable to that third variable.
- Even though regression analyses can rule out third variables, they cannot definitively establish causation, because they can only control for possible third variables that the researchers happened to measure. An experiment is the only design that definitively establishes causation.

Getting at Causality with Pattern and Parsimony

- Researchers can approach causal certainty through pattern and parsimony; they specify a mechanism for the causal relationship and combine the results from a variety of research questions. When a single causal theory explains all of the disparate results, researchers are closer to making a causal claim.

Mediation

- In a mediation hypothesis, researchers specify a variable that comes between the two variables of interest and is the reason why the two variables are associated. After collecting data on all three variables (the original two, plus the mediator), they follow specific steps to evaluate how well the data support the mediation hypothesis.

Multivariate Designs and the Four Validities

- Interrogating multivariate correlational designs involves investigating not only internal validity and temporal precedence, but also construct validity, external validity, and statistical validity. While no single study is perfect, exploring each validity in turn is a good way to systematically assess a study's strengths and weaknesses.

Key Terms

multivariate design, p. 236
longitudinal design, p. 237
cross-sectional correlation,
   p. 238

autocorrelation, p. 238
cross-lag correlation, p. 238
multiple regression, p. 242
control for, p. 243

criterion variable, p. 246
predictor variable, p. 246
parsimony, p. 254
mediator, p. 257

To see samples of chapter concepts in the popular press, visit
www.everydayresearchmethods.com and click the box for Chapter 9.

Review Questions

1. A headline in Yahoo! News made the following (bivariate) association claim: "Facebook users get worse grades in college" (Hsu, 2009). The two variables in this headline are:
   a. Level of Facebook use and college grades.
   b. High grades and low grades.
   c. High Facebook use and low Facebook use.

2. Suppose a researcher uses a longitudinal design to study the relationship between Facebook use and grades over time. She measures both of these variables in Year 1, and then measures both variables again in Year 2. Which of the following is an example of an autocorrelation in the results?
   a. The correlation between Facebook use in Year 1 with Facebook use in Year 2.
   b. The correlation between Facebook use in Year 1 with grades in Year 2.
   c. The correlation between grades in Year 1 with Facebook use in Year 2.
   d. The correlation between grades in Year 1 and Facebook use in Year 1.

3. In the longitudinal study described in question 2, which pattern of cross-lag correlations would indicate that Facebook use leads to lower grades (rather than the reverse)?
   a. Grades at Year 1 shows a strong correlation with Facebook use at Year 2 , but Facebook use at Year 1 shows a weak correlation with grades at Year 2.

   b. Grades at Year 1 shows a weak correlation with Facebook use at Year 2 , but Facebook use at Year 1 shows a strong correlation with grades at Year 2.
   c. Grades at Year 1 shows a strong correlation with Facebook use at Year 2, and Facebook use at Year 1 shows a strong correlation with grades at Year 2.

4. Consider this statement: "People who use Facebook got worse grades in college, even when the researchers controlled for the level of college preparation (operationalized by SAT scores) of the students." What does it mean?
   a. Facebook use and grades are correlated only because both of these are associated with SAT score.
   b. SAT score is a third variable that seems to explain the association between Facebook use and grades.
   c. SAT score can be ruled out as a third variable explanation for the correlation between Facebook use and college grades.

5. Which of the following statements is an example of a mediator of the relationship between Facebook use and college grades?
   a. Facebook use and college grades are more strongly correlated among nonathletes, and less strongly correlated among athletes.
   b. Facebook use and college grades are only correlated with each other because they are

both related to the difficulty of the major. Students in more difficult majors get worse grades, and those in difficult majors have less time to use Facebook.

c. Facebook use and college grades are correlated because Facebook use leads to less time studying, which leads to lower grades.

6. A news outlet reported on a study of people with dementia. The study found that among patients with dementia, bilingual people had been diagnosed 3-4 years later than those who were monolingual. What are the variables in this bivariate association?

a. Being bilingual or monolingual

b. Being bilingual or not, and age at dementia diagnosis

c. Age at dementia diagnosis

7. The journalist reported that the relationship between bilingualism and age at diagnosis did not change, even when the researchers controlled for level of education. What does this suggest?

a. That the relationship between bilingualism and dementia onset is probably attributable to the third variable: level of education.

b. That the relationship between bilingualism and dementia onset is not attributable to the third variable: level of education.

c. That being bilingual can cause people to resist dementia.

8. Researchers speculated that the reason bilingualism is associated with later onset of dementia is that bilingual people develop richer connections in the brain through their experiences in managing two languages; these connections help stave off dementia symptoms. This statement describes:

a. A mediator

b. A moderator

c. A third variable

Learning Actively

1. Studies have shown that maternal responsiveness (i.e., how quickly a mother responds to her infant's cries) is associated with the fussiness of the baby (Hubbard & van Ijzendoorn, 1991). Specifically, more responsive mothers have less fussy babies. Which variable comes first? Consider how you might design a longitudinal correlational study to test this question.

a. Using Figures 9.1, 9.2, and 9.3 for guidance, map out the different pairs of correlations you might find: cross-sectional correlations, autocorrelations, and cross-lag correlations.

b. Which pattern of cross-lag correlations would suggest that maternal responsiveness causes less fussiness? Which pattern of cross-lag correlations would suggest that infant fussiness causes less maternal responsiveness? Which pattern would suggest that these two variables are in a mutually reinforcing relationship?

2. Indicate whether each statement below is describing a mediation hypothesis, a third-variable argument, or a moderator result. First, identify the key bivariate relationship. Next, decide whether the extra variable comes between the two key variables or is causing the two key variables simultaneously. Then, draw a sketch of each explanation, following the examples in Figure 9.13.

a. Having a cognitively demanding job is associated with cognitive benefits in later years, because people who are highly educated take cognitively demanding jobs, and people who are highly educated have better cognitive skills.

b. Having a cognitively demanding job is associated with cognitive benefits in later years, but only among men, not among women.

c. Having a cognitively demanding job is associated with cognitive benefits in later years, because cognitive challenges build lasting connections in the brain.

d. Sibling aggression is associated with worse child mental health, but the link is especially strong for later-born children and is weaker in firstborn children.

e. Sibling aggression is associated with worse child mental health because child victims of sibling aggression are more likely to feel lonely at home. Sibling aggression leads to loneliness, which leads to mental health problems.

f. Sibling aggression is associated with worse child mental health only because of parental conflict. Sibling aggression is more likely among parents who argue frequently, and arguing also affects kids' mental health.

3. Do victims of sibling aggression suffer worse mental health? A recent study investigated this question (Tucker, Finkelhor, Turner, & Shattuck, 2013). The researchers wondered whether sibling aggression was linked to worse mental health in children, and whether sibling aggression was as bad for kids as peer aggression. In a large sample of children and youths,

ages 2-17, they measured several kinds of sibling aggression (e.g., physical assault, taking something away from the child, breaking the child's toys on purpose, calling names). They also measured mental health using a Trauma Symptom Checklist, on which high scores indicate the child has more symptoms of anxiety, depression, and other signs of mental disturbances. The researchers also measured parents' education, child's age, and so on. The regression table in **Table 9.6** comes from their article.

a. What is the criterion (dependent) variable in this study, and where do you find it?

b. How many predictor variables are there in this study?

c. Write a sentence that describes what the beta for the "Total types of sibling victimization" predictor means. (Use the sentences in Table 9.2 as a model.)

d. Write a sentence that describes what the beta for the "Total types of peer victimization" predictor variable means.

e. Write a sentence that describes what the beta for the "Child maltreatment" predictor variable means.

f. Write a sentence that describes what the beta for the "Internet victimization" predictor means.

g. Using the magnitude of the betas to decide, which of the predictors is most strongly associated with worse child mental health? What about the researchers' initial question: Is sibling aggression just as bad for kids as peer aggression?

TABLE 9.6 Multiple Regression Predicting Children's and Adolescents' Mental Health

Variable	Dependent var: Trauma symptom checklist score β
Parent education: some college	−0.02
College degree plus	−0.04
Ethnicity	
Black	−0.05[b]
Hispanic, any race	−0.01
Other or mixed	−0.00
Language of interview in Spanish	−0.01
Child age 10 plus	−0.13[a]
Child gender male	0.00
Child maltreatment	0.15[a]
Sexual victimization	0.06[b]
School victimization	0.05[c]
Internet victimization	0.02
Witness family violence	0.17[a]
Witness community violence	0.07[a]
Total types of sibling victimization	0.15[a]
Total types of peer victimization	0.25[a]
Total sibling × peer types of victimization	−0.02
R^2	0.27

[a] $p < .001$.
[b] $p < .01$.
[c] $p < .05$.
Source: Tucker et al., 2013.

PART V

Tools for Evaluating Causal Claims

Seeing Red Affects Achievement

(*World Science*, 2007)

Your Plate Is Bigger Than Your Stomach

(*New York Times*, 2007)

10

Introduction to Simple Experiments

LEARNING OBJECTIVES

A year from now, you should still be able to:

1. Apply the three criteria for establishing causation to experiments, and explain why experiments can support causal claims.

2. Identify an experiment's independent, dependent, and control variables.

3. Classify experiments as independent-groups and within-groups designs, and explain why researchers might conduct each type of study.

4. Evaluate three potential threats to internal validity in an experiment—design confounds, selection effects, and order effects—and explain how experimenters usually avoid them.

5. Interrogate an experimental design using the four validities.

A causal claim is the boldest kind of claim a scientist can make. A causal claim replaces verb phrases such as *related to*, *is associated with*, or *linked to* with such powerful verbs as *causes, influences, affects,* or *makes.* Causal claims are special: When researchers make a causal claim, they are also stating something about interventions and treatments. If seeing the color red affects performance or achievement, then changing a color might improve performance. If serving food in a larger bowl makes people take more food and eat more, then dieters can be advised to serve foods in smaller bowls or use smaller individual plates. Interventions are often the ultimate goal of scientific studies, and they must be based on sound, experimental research. If a treatment is difficult to implement (or if it comes at the cost of other techniques), users would want to be sure the treatment causes the intended outcome. Experiments are the only way to investigate such causal issues.

Two Examples of Simple Experiments

Let's begin with two examples of experiments that supported valid causal claims. As you read about the two studies, consider how each one differs from the bivariate correlational studies in Chapter 8. What makes each of these studies an experiment? How does the experimental design allow the researchers to make a causal claim rather than an association claim?

Example 1: Seeing Red

What do you think about when you see the color red? You might think of fire trucks, fast cars, or valentines, since red is associated with heat, speed, and passion. In many North American contexts, however, red is also associated with caution. Teachers often use a red pen to correct papers. Stop signs are red, and so are the signals for biohazards and hot stoves. Red means danger—"Be careful!"—in many contexts (**Figure 10.1**).

Andrew Elliot, a psychologist who studies academic achievement, wanted to know whether the color red could affect people's performance on academic tasks. Could a single color affect the ability to solve a math problem or finish a puzzle?

In the context of Elliot's broader theory of academic achievement, the color red was important. Through his theory and research over the years, Elliot learned something important about academic achievement: Students in school tend to do better when they have an approach orientation rather than an avoidance orientation. When students adopt an *approach orientation* toward an academic task, they try to succeed. They focus on getting questions right, learning something new, seeking challenges, and doing their best—and generally they do well. In contrast, when students adopt an *avoidance orientation* toward an academic task, they try not to fail. In the avoidance mode, students address the task of learning with anxiety and an awareness of inferiority. They may withdraw effort or choose easy problems to protect themselves from failure. As a result, students with an avoidance orientation typically do not perform as well on academic tasks.

Enter the dangerous, cautious color red. In many contexts, red signals danger and avoidance, so Elliot's theory led to a specific hypothesis: Exposing students to something red on a test booklet would cause them to withdraw effort and perform worse on an academic test.

Elliot and his colleagues conducted an experiment to test their hypothesis

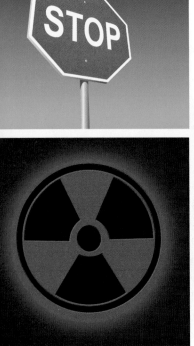

FIGURE 10.1 Red alert. The color red is often associated with caution, correction, or avoidance.

(Elliot, Maier, Moller, Friedman, & Meinhardt, 2007). They recruited 71 students into a laboratory setting, one at a time. The students took a 5-minute test in which they unscrambled anagrams (e.g., unscrambling the letters KRNID to form the word DRINK). The test booklets looked identical on the front, but inside, each student's participant number had been written in ink in the top corner of the first page. For some participants, the ID number was written in red ink; for others, the number was in green; and for still others, the number was in black. Behind the scenes, one experimenter rolled a die to decide which group each participant would be placed in (black, green, or red). Another experimenter, the one who was in the room with the participant, never saw which color the participant was assigned. Other than the color of the ID number, all other things about the test booklets were the same. The same problems were inside, students had the same amount of time to work on the problems, and the experimenter who handed the booklets to the students was always the same person.

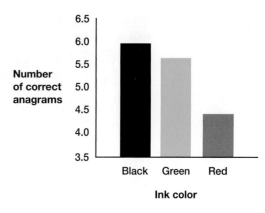

FIGURE 10.2 The effect of the color red on performance. Students whose participant numbers were written in red ink solved fewer anagrams—performed worse—than those whose numbers were written in green or black ink. (Source: Adapted from Elliot et al., 2007.)

The results Elliot and his colleagues obtained are shown in **Figure 10.2**. Students in the red ink group solved fewer anagrams than those in the two comparison groups. The color of the ID number apparently *caused* a difference in their performance on an academic test.

Because it was important to demonstrate that such a surprising result could happen again, they ran the study another time. This time, they manipulated the color in a slightly different way: by using a red, green, or gray cover page for the test booklets. The results were the same (**Figure 10.3**). In fact, Elliot and his team ran the

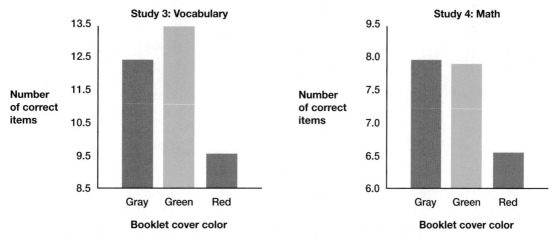

FIGURE 10.3 Replicating the effect of red on performance. In each study, the experimenters manipulated the color of test booklet covers. They measured how many vocabulary analogies (Study 3 in the original journal article) and math problems (Study 4 in the original article) the students in each group solved. (Source: Adapted from Elliot et al., 2007.)

study several more times in somewhat different ways, and each time they concluded that an ID number written in red ink or a red exam booklet cover made student scores go down. They made a causal claim: Red *caused* performance to get worse.

The results are interesting in their own right, but also because they support Elliot's longstanding theory about the ways approach and avoidance orientation work in school achievement. Think carefully about the choices Elliot and his colleagues made. Do you think their study supports the causal claim?

Example 2: Eating Pasta

The popular press piece entitled "Your plate is bigger than your stomach" summarized a line of research conducted at Cornell University's Food and Brand Lab. An example of research on how people eat was published in the *Journal of Nutrition Education and Behavior*. Researchers Ellen van Kleef, Mitsuru Shimizu, and Brian Wansink (2012) invited 68 college students to come into a kitchen laboratory during the lunch hour. The participants were divided into small groups of 16–18 students.

Behind the scenes, the researchers had assigned participants to one of two experimental sessions by flipping a coin. Half were assigned to a "large bowl" session and half were assigned to a "medium bowl" session. During the lunch, participants were invited to serve themselves pasta from a communal bowl. The bowl was continually refilled when about half the pasta was gone, so nobody felt the food was getting scarce. After they scooped pasta from the serving bowl, a research assistant weighed their individual plates to measure the amount they took. Participants were allowed to eat their pasta lunches at a comfortable pace. When they were finished, the research assistants weighed each plate again, subtracting the two weights to determine how much food each person had actually eaten.

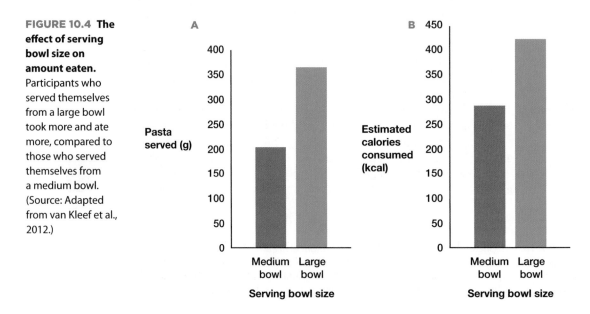

FIGURE 10.4 The effect of serving bowl size on amount eaten. Participants who served themselves from a large bowl took more and ate more, compared to those who served themselves from a medium bowl. (Source: Adapted from van Kleef et al., 2012.)

The results are shown in **Figure 10.4**. On average, the participants took more pasta from the large serving bowl than the medium one (Figure 10.4A). When the researchers converted the amount of consumed pasta into calories, it was clear that the large-bowl participants had eaten about 140 calories more than the medium-bowl ones (Figure 10.4B). The researchers used causal language in their article's conclusion: "the size of the serving bowl had a substantial influence" on what people ate (p. 70).

Experimental Variables

The word *experiment* is common in everyday use. Colloquially, "to experiment" means to try something out. A cook might say she experimented with a recipe by replacing the eggs with applesauce. A friend might say he experimented with a different driving route to the beach. In psychological science, the term **experiment** specifically means that the researchers manipulated at least one variable and measured another (as you learned in Chapter 3). Experiments can take place in a laboratory, and just about anywhere else: movie theaters, conference halls, zoos, classrooms, or daycare centers—anywhere a researcher can manipulate one variable and measure another.

A **manipulated variable** is a variable that is controlled, such as when the researchers assign participants to a particular level (value) of the variable. So, for example, Elliot and his colleagues manipulated ink color by rolling a die to determine whether each participant's number would be written in red, green, or black ink. (In other words, the participants did not choose which color was used.) Ink color was a variable because it had more than one level (red, green, or black), and it was a manipulated variable because the experimenter assigned each participant to a particular level. The van Kleef team similarly manipulated the size of the pasta serving bowl by flipping a coin ahead of time to decide which session participants were in. (Participants did not choose the bowl from which they would serve themselves.)

Measured variables take the form of records of behavior or attitudes, such as self-reports, behavioral observations, or physiological measures (see Chapter 5). After an experimental situation is set up, the researchers simply record what happens. In their first study, the Elliot team measured performance on anagram tests. After manipulating ink color, they watched and recorded—that is, they measured—how many anagrams each person solved. The van Kleef team manipulated the serving bowl size, and then measured two variables: how much pasta people took and how much they ate.

Independent and Dependent Variables

In an experiment, the manipulated variable is the **independent variable**. The name comes from the fact that the researcher has some "independence" in assigning people to different levels of this variable. A study's independent variable should not be confused with its levels, which are also referred to as **conditions**.

The independent variable in the van Kleef study was serving bowl size, which had two conditions: medium and large.

The measured variable is the **dependent variable**, or *outcome variable*. How a participant acts on the measured variable *depends* on the level of the independent variable. Researchers have less control over the dependent variable; they manipulate the independent variable and then watch what happens to people's self-reports, behaviors, or physiological responses. A dependent variable is not the same as its levels, either. The dependent variable in the van Kleef study was amount of pasta eaten (not "eating 200 calories").

Here is how to tell the two kinds of variables apart. When researchers graph their results, the independent variable is almost always on the x-axis, and the dependent variable is almost always on the y-axis (see Figures 10.3 and 10.4 for examples). A mnemonic for remembering the two types of variables is that the independent variable comes first in time (and the letter I looks like the number 1), and the dependent variable is measured afterward (or second).

Control Variables

When researchers are manipulating an independent variable, they need to make sure they are varying only one thing at a time—the potential causal force, or proposed "active ingredient" (e.g., only color, or only size of bowl). Therefore, besides the independent variable, researchers also control potential third variables (or nuisance variables) in their studies by holding all other factors constant between the levels of the independent variable. For example, Elliot and his colleagues manipulated (purposely varied) the color of the pen, but they held constant a number of other potential variables: The colored ID numbers were all the same size, the participants took the exact same anagram tests, the same experimenters ran each session, and so on. Any variable that an experimenter holds constant on purpose is called a **control variable**.

In the van Kleef study, one control variable was the quality of the food: It was always the same kind of pasta. The researchers also controlled the size of the serving spoon and the size of the plates (each participant served pasta onto a 9-inch plate).

Control variables are not really variables at all, because they do not vary; experimenters keep the levels the same for all participants. Clearly, control variables are essential in experiments. They allow researchers to separate one potential cause from another and thus eliminate alternative explanations for results. Control variables are therefore important for establishing internal validity.

CHECK YOUR UNDERSTANDING

1. What are the minimum requirements for a study to be an experiment?
2. Define independent variable, dependent variable, and control variable, using your own words.

---

1. A manipulated variable and a measured variable; see p. 275. 2. See pp. 275–276.

Why Experiments Support Causal Claims

In both of the examples above, the researchers manipulated one variable and measured another, so both studies can be considered experiments. But are these researchers really justified in making causal claims on the basis of these experiments? Yes. To understand how experiments support causal claims, you can first apply the three rules for causation to the pasta bowl study. The three rules should be familiar to you by now:

1. *Covariance.* Is the causal variable related to the effect variable? Are distinct levels of the independent variable associated with different levels of the dependent variable?
2. *Temporal precedence.* Does the causal variable come before the effect variable in time?
3. *Internal validity.* Are there alternative explanations for the results?

Experiments Establish Covariance

The experiment by van Kleef and her colleagues did show covariance between the causal (independent) variable (size of bowl) and the effect (dependent) variable (amount of pasta eaten). On average, students who were in the large-bowl condition ate 425 calories worth of pasta, and students in the medium-bowl condition ate 283 calories (see Figure 10.4). In this case, covariance is indicated by a *difference* in the group means: The large-bowl calories were different from the medium-bowl calories. The Elliot study also showed covariance: Red test covers were associated with fewer solved problems than green or gray ones.

Independent Variables Answer "Compared to What?"

The covariance criterion might seem obvious. In our everyday reasoning, though, we tend to ignore its importance, because most of our personal experiences do not have the benefit of a **comparison group**, or *comparison condition*. For instance, you might suspect that your mom's giant pasta bowl is making you eat too much, but without a comparison bowl, you cannot know for sure. An experiment, in contrast, provides the comparison group you need. Therefore, an experiment is a better source of information than your own experience, because an experiment allows you to ask and answer: Compared to what?

For a review of experience versus empiricism, see Chapter 2.

If independent variables did not vary, a study could not establish covariance. Suppose the van Kleef team had tested only one group, who had served themselves pasta from a large bowl, and found that each person consumed 425 calories worth of pasta. This study would not tell you anything: Because you would have nothing to compare the 425 to, the study would not show evidence for covariance. Instead, the real study included one other level of the variable (the medium bowl), which provided data to compare with the large bowl's data. Because experiments manipulate an independent variable, and because every independent variable has at least two levels, true experiments are always set up to look for covariance.

Covariance: It's Also About the Outcome

Manipulating the independent (causal) variable is only part of establishing co-variance, however. The outcome matters, too. Suppose the van Kleef researchers had found no difference in how much pasta people consumed in the two groups. In that case, the study would have found no covariance, and the experimenters would have had to conclude that serving bowl size does not cause people to eat more pasta. After all, if pasta consumption does not vary with serving bowl size, there is no causal impact to explain.

Control Groups, Treatment Groups, and Comparison Groups

There are a couple of ways an independent variable might be designed to show covariance. Your early science classes may have emphasized the importance of a control group in an experiment. A **control group** is a level of an independent variable that is intended to represent "no treatment" or a neutral condition. When a study has a control group, the other level or levels of the independent variable are usually called the **treatment group(s)**. For example, if an experiment is testing the effectiveness of a new medication, the researchers might assign some partici-pants to take the medication (the treatment group) and other participants to take an inert sugar pill (the control group). When the control group is exposed to an inert treatment such as a sugar pill, it is called a **placebo group**, or a *placebo control group*.

For more details on the placebo effect and how researchers control for it, see Chapter 11, pp. 319–321.

Not every experiment has—or needs—a control group, though. Often, in fact, a clear control group does not even exist. The Elliot study had two comparison groups—green and black ink color—but neither was a control group, in the sense that neither of them clearly established an "absence of red." The van Kleef study did not have a true control group either; the researchers simply used two differ-ent serving bowl sizes. Also consider the experiment by Harry Harlow (1958), discussed in Chapter 1, in which baby monkeys were put in cages with artificial "mothers" made of either cold wire or warm cloth. There was no control group, just a carefully designed comparison condition. When a study uses comparison groups, the levels of the independent variable differ in some intended and mean-ingful way. All experiments need a comparison group, so the researchers can compare one condition to another; but the comparison group does not need to be a control group.

Experiments Establish Temporal Precedence

The experiment by van Kleef's team also established temporal precedence. The experimenters manipulated the causal (independent) variable (serving bowl size) to ensure that it came first in time. Then the students picked up the spoon to serve their own pasta. The causal variable clearly did come before the effect (de-pendent) variable. This ability to establish temporal precedence, by controlling which variable comes first, is a strong advantage of experimental designs. By ma-nipulating the independent variable, the experimenter virtually ensures that the cause comes before the effect.

The ability to establish temporal precedence is a feature that makes experiments superior to correlational designs. A simple correlational study is a snapshot—all variables are measured at the same time, so when two variables covary (such as recess and school behavior, or deep conversations and well-being), it's impossible to tell which variable came first. In contrast, experiments unfold over time, and the experimenter makes sure that the independent variable comes first.

Well-Designed Experiments Establish Internal Validity

Did the van Kleef study establish internal validity? Are there any alternative explanations for why people in the large-bowl condition took more pasta than people in the medium-bowl condition?

A well-designed experiment establishes internal validity, which is one of the most important validities to interrogate when you encounter causal claims. To be internally valid, a study must ensure that the causal variable (the active ingredient), and not other factors, is responsible for the change in the effect variable. You can interrogate internal validity by exploring potential alternative explanations. For example, you might ask whether the participants in the large-bowl group were served tastier-looking pasta than those in the medium-bowl group. If so, the quality of the pasta would be an alternative explanation for why people took more. However, the researchers put the same type of pasta in both serving bowls (**Figure 10.5**). In fact, the quality of the pasta was a control variable: It was held constant for all participants, for just this reason.

For a discussion about how researchers use blind and double-blind designs to control internal validity, see Chapter 11, p. 319.

You might be wondering whether the experimenters treated the large-bowl group differently than the other group. Maybe the research assistants acted in a more generous or welcoming fashion with participants in the large-bowl group than the medium-bowl group. That would have been another threat to internal validity, so it's important to know whether the assistants knew the hypothesis of the study.

For any given research question, there can be several possible alternative explanations. Generally, these alternative explanations are called **confounds**, or potential threats to internal validity. The word *confound* can mean "confuse": When a study has a confound, you are confused about what is causing the change in the dependent variable. Is it the intended causal variable (such as bowl size)? Or is there some alternative explanation (such as the generous attitude of the research assistants)? Internal validity is subject to a number of distinct threats,

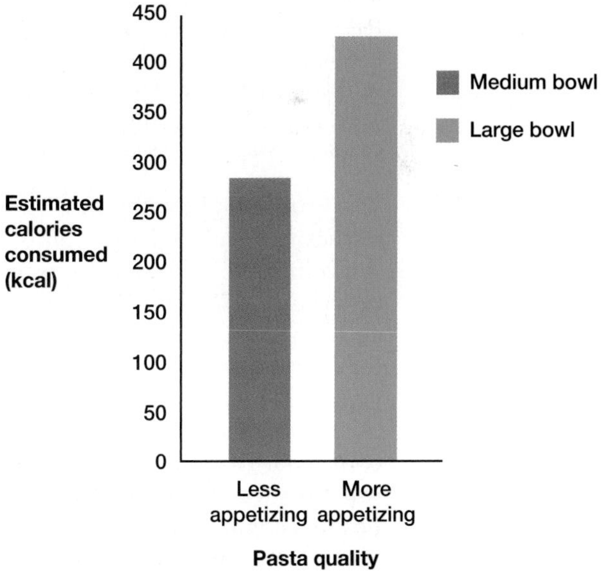

FIGURE 10.5 Internal validity. If the pasta in the large bowl had been more appetizing than the pasta in the medium bowl, that would have been a design confound in this study. (Data are fabricated for illustration purposes.)

three of which are discussed in this chapter. Design confounds and selection effects are described next, and order effects are described in a later section. The rest are covered in Chapter 11. As experimenters design and interpret studies, they keep these threats to internal validity in mind and try to avoid them.

Design Confounds

A **design confound** is an experimenter's mistake in designing the independent variable; it is a second variable that happens to vary systematically along with the intended independent variable and therefore is an alternative explanation for the results. As such, a design confound is a classic threat to internal validity. If van Kleef et al. had accidentally served a more appetizing pasta in the large bowl than the medium bowl, the study would have a design confound, because the second variable (pasta quality) would have systematically varied along with the independent variable. If the research assistants had treated the large-bowl group with a more generous attitude, the treatment of each participant would have been a design confound, too.

Consider the Elliot study on ink color. If all of the students in the red ink group had to answer more difficult anagrams, that would be a design confound. We would not know whether the difference in anagram performance was caused by the anagram difficulty or the ink color. However, the researchers did not make this error; they gave the same anagrams to all participants, no matter what color condition they were in, so there would be no systematic differences between the groups.

When an experiment has a design confound, it has poor internal validity and cannot support a causal claim. Because van Kleef et al.'s study did not have any apparent design confounds, its internal validity is sound. The researchers took care to think about confounds in advance and turned them into control variables instead. Similarly, Elliot et al. controlled for a number of potential design confounds, such as anagram difficulty, experimenter expectations, room conditions, and so on. In both cases, the steps the researchers followed helped them justify making a causal claim.

The Problem of Systematic Variability. You need to be careful before accusing a study of having a design confound. Not every potentially problematic variable is a confound. Consider the example of the pasta bowl experimenters. It might be the case that some of the research assistants were generous and welcoming, and others were reserved. The attitude of the research assistants is a problem for internal validity *only if* it shows **systematic variability** with the independent variable. Did the generous assistants work only with the large-bowl group and the reserved ones only with the medium-bowl group? Then it would be a design confound. However, if the research assistants' demeanor showed **unsystematic variability** (random or haphazard) across both groups, then their attitude would not be a confound.

Here's another example. Perhaps some of the participants in the Elliot study were really good at anagrams, and others were not. This variability in anagram ability would not be a design confound unless it varied systematically with the ink color condition students were exposed to. If the students in the red ink group all happened to be bad at anagrams and those in the green and black ink groups were really good at them, that would vary systematically with the ink color conditions—and would be a confound. But if some participants in each condition were good at anagrams and some were not, that would be unsystematic variability and would not be a confound.

Unsystematic variability can lead to other problems in an experiment. Specifically, it can obscure, or make it difficult to detect differences in, the dependent variable, as discussed fully in Chapter 11. However, unsystematic variability should not be called a design confound.

Selection Effects

A **selection effect** occurs in an experiment when the kinds of participants in one level of the independent variable are systematically different from those in the other. Selection effects can occur when the experimenters let participants choose which group they want to be in. A selection effect can also result if the experimenters assign one type of person (e.g., all the women, or all who sign up early in the semester) to one condition, and another type of person (e.g., all the men, or all those who wait until later in the semester) to another condition.

Here's a real-world example. A study was designed to test a new intensive therapy for autism, involving one-on-one sessions with a therapist for 40 hours per week (Lovaas, 1987; see Gernsbacher, 2003). To determine whether this therapy would cause a significant improvement in children's autistic symptoms, the researchers recruited 38 families that had children with autism, and arranged for some children to receive the new intensive treatment while others received their usual treatment. The researchers assigned families to either the intensive-treatment group or the treatment-as-usual group. However, some of the families lived too far away to receive the treatment; other parents protested that they would rather be placed in the intensive-treatment group. Thus, not all the families were randomly assigned to the two groups.

At the end of the study, the researchers found that the autistic symptoms of the children in the intensive-treatment group had improved more than the symptoms of those who received their usual treatment. However, this study suffered from a clear selection effect: The families in the intensive-treatment group were probably systematically different from the treatment-as-usual group, because the groups self-selected. Many parents in the intensive-treatment group were placed there because of their eagerness to try a focused, 40-hour-per-week treatment regimen. Therefore, parents in that group may have been more motivated to help their children, so there was a clear threat to internal validity. Because of the selection effect, it's impossible to tell the reason for the results (**Figure 10.6**). Did the children in that group improve because of the intensive treatment? Or did they improve because the families

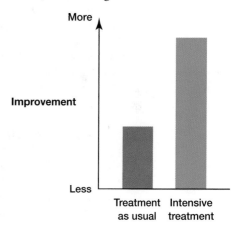

FIGURE 10.6 Selection effects. In a study by Lovaas (1987), some parents insisted that their children be in the new intensive-treatment group rather than the treatment-as-usual group. Because they had this choice, it's not possible to determine whether the improvement in the intensive group was caused by the treatment itself or by the fact that the more motivated parents chose it. (Data are fabricated for illustration purposes.)

who selected the new therapy were simply more motivated and engaged in their children's treatment? Of course, in any study that tests a therapy, some participants will be more motivated than others. This variability in motivation becomes a confound only when the more motivated folks tend to be in one group—that is, when the variability is systematic.

Avoiding Selection Effects with Random Assignment. Well-designed experiments often use **random assignment** to avoid selection effects. In the Elliot study, an experimenter rolled a die to decide which participants would be in each group, so each one had an *equal chance* of being in the red, green, or black ink group. What does this mean? Suppose that of the 71 participants who volunteered for the study, 12 were exceptionally clever people. Probabilistically speaking, the rolls of the die would have placed about 4 of them in the red group, about 4 in the green group, and about 4 in the black group. Similarly, if 15 of the participants were having a bad day on the day of the study, random assignment would place about 5 of them in each group. In other words, since the researchers used random assignment, it is very unlikely, given the random (deliberately unsystematic) way people were assigned to each group, that all the clever, lazy, or unlucky people would have been clustered in the same group.

Assigning participants at random to different levels of the independent variable—by flipping a coin, rolling a die, or using a random number generator—controls for all sorts of potential selection effects (**Figure 10.7**). In practice, random assignment does not usually create numbers that are perfectly even (e.g., the 12 exceptionally clever people may not be distributed exactly as 4, 4, and 4); however, it can often result in fairly even distributions.

Random assignment is a way of desystematizing the types of participants who end up in each level of the independent variable. Of course, some people are more motivated than others; some are more educated than others; some are

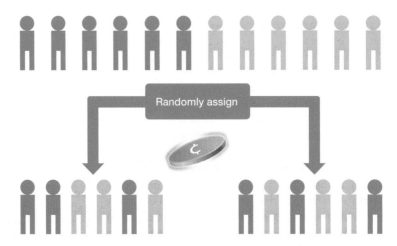

FIGURE 10.7 Random assignment. Random assignment ensures that every participant in an experiment has an equal chance to be in each group.

more extroverted. Successful random assignment spreads these differences out more evenly. It creates a situation in which the experimental groups will become virtually equal, on average, before the independent variable is applied. After random assignment (and before manipulating the independent variable), researchers should be able to test the experimental groups for intelligence, extroversion, motivation, and so on, and averages of each group should be comparable on these traits.

To review the difference between random assignment and random sampling, see Chapter 7, p. 192.

Avoiding Selection Effects with Matched Groups. In the simplest type of random assignment, researchers assign participants at random to one condition or another in the experiment. In some situations, however, random assignment does not always work exactly as planned. For example, imagine a sample of 30 people who vary on their ability to do anagrams, and who are randomly assigned to three groups. Now suppose there are 6 exceptionally clever people in the original sample. Theoretically, when assigned at random into three groups, 2 of these talented people should end up in each group.

In practice, random assignment does not always work perfectly, especially when the samples are on the small side. If the sample of 30 is randomly assigned to three groups, 4 of those clever people could end up in one group, and 1 in each of the other groups. In fact, there might be all 6 clever people in one group and none in another. Such unevenness is more likely when researchers are dealing with smaller numbers. In contrast, over a very large sample, the unevenness is less noticeable. A subset of 60 clever people might be distributed as 23, 18, and 19, but that is not as imbalanced as when a subset of 6 clever people is distributed as 4, 1, and 1.

For this reason, some researchers choose to use **matched groups**, or *matching*, especially when assigning small numbers of participants to groups. To create matched groups from a sample of 30, the researchers first would measure the participants on a particular variable that might matter to the dependent variable; IQ, for instance, might matter to anagram ability. They would next match participants up set by set; that is, they would take the three participants with the highest IQ scores and *within that matched set*, randomly assign one of them to each of the three groups. They would then take the participants with the three next-highest IQ scores and within that set again assign randomly to the three groups. They would continue this process until they reach the participants with the lowest three IQ scores and assign them at random, too (**Figure 10.8**).

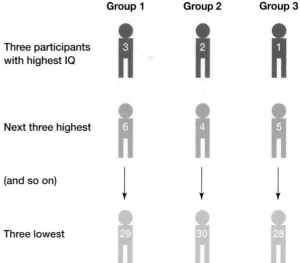

FIGURE 10.8 Matching groups to eliminate selection effects. To create three matched groups, participants are sorted from lowest to highest on some variable and grouped into sets of three. Individuals within each set are then assigned at random to the three experimental groups.

Matching has the advantage of randomness. Because each member of the matched set is randomly assigned, the technique prevents selection effects. This method also ensures that the groups are equal on some important variable, such as IQ, before the manipulation of the independent variable. The disadvantage is that the matching process requires an extra step—in this case, administering an IQ test to everyone in the sample before assigning to groups. Matching, therefore, requires many more resources than random assignment.

CHECK YOUR UNDERSTANDING

1. Why do experiments usually satisfy the three causal criteria?
2. How are design confounds and control variables related?
3. How does random assignment prevent selection effects?
4. How does using matched groups prevent selection effects?

1. See pp. 277–279. 2. See pp. 280–281; control variables are used to eliminate potential design confounds. 3. See pp. 282–283. 4. See pp. 283–284.

Independent-Groups Designs

Although the minimum requirement for an experiment is that researchers manipulate one variable and measure another, experiments can take many forms. One of the most basic distinctions is between independent-groups designs and within-groups designs.

Independent-Groups vs. Within-Groups Designs

In the Elliot and van Kleef studies, there were different participants at each level of the independent variable. In Elliot's study, some participants saw a number written in red ink, others saw a number in green ink, and still others saw black ink. In the pasta bowl study, some participants were in the large-bowl condition, and others were in the medium-bowl condition. Both of these studies used an **independent-groups design**, in which different groups of participants are placed into different levels of the independent variable. This type of design is often called a *between-subjects design* or *between-groups design*.

In a **within-groups design**, or *within-subjects design*, there is only one group of participants, and each person is presented with *all* levels of the independent variable. For example, Elliot and his colleagues might have run their study as a within-groups design if they had asked each participant to solve three sets of anagrams—one with numbers in red, one with numbers in green, and one with numbers in black.

Two basic forms of independent-groups designs are the posttest-only design and the pretest/posttest design. The two types of designs are used in different situations.

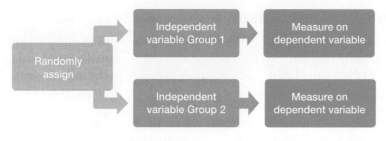

FIGURE 10.9 **A posttest-only design.**

Posttest-Only Design

The posttest-only design is one of the simplest independent-groups experimental designs. In the **posttest-only design**, also known as an *equivalent groups, posttest-only design*, participants are randomly assigned to independent variable groups and are tested on the dependent variable once (**Figure 10.9**).

The Elliot research team's study of the color red is an example of a posttest-only design (Elliot et al., 2007). Participants were randomly assigned to a red ink, black ink, or green ink group. This study was a posttest-only design, but it had three independent variable levels, as shown in **Figure 10.10**.

Posttest-only designs satisfy all three criteria for causation. They allow researchers to test for covariance by detecting differences in the dependent variable. (Having at least two groups makes it possible to do so.) They establish temporal precedence because the independent variable comes first in time. And when they are conducted well, they establish internal validity. When researchers use appropriate control variables, there should be no design confounds, and random assignment takes care of selection effects.

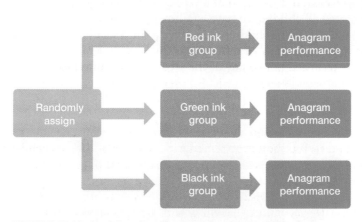

FIGURE 10.10 **Studying the effect of red: a posttest-only design.**

Pretest/Posttest Design

In a **pretest/posttest design**, or *equivalent groups, pretest/posttest design*, participants are randomly assigned to at least two groups and are tested on the key dependent variable twice—once before and once after exposure to the independent variable. If Elliot and his team had included a pretest, the experiment would have been a pretest/posttest design, as shown in **Figure 10.11**.

Researchers might use a pretest/posttest design when they want to evaluate whether random assignment made the groups equal. This type of design could be especially important when group sizes are on the small side, because chance is more likely to lead to lopsided groups when samples are small (say, less than 10 per group). In this case, a pretest/posttest design means researchers can be absolutely sure there is no selection effect in a study.

A pretest/posttest design also works well to track how participants in the experimental groups have changed over time in response to some manipulation. In one study, Mueller and Dweck (1998) asked a sample of fifth-grade children to complete a set of problems, and then randomly assigned them to hear two kinds of praise. One group of children received "process praise," such as "You must have worked hard at these problems." Another group of children received "person praise," such as "You must be smart at these problems." Because of previous research and theory, the researchers hypothesized that the process praise would be more adaptive for the children, meaning that it would be more motivating, especially after a failure.

The researchers used a pretest/posttest design. In the first stage, all the children solved fairly easy puzzles. This was the pretest, and the researchers recorded how many puzzles the children solved. As expected, the children in both groups solved about the same number of puzzles (i.e., random assignment worked by making the groups equal before the independent variable was manipulated). Right after the first stage, the independent variable was administered: The children received one kind of praise or the other.

All the children were then asked to solve a second set of problems—but these problems were intended for tenth graders, and most of the fifth-grade children did not do well. (However, no data were collected at this stage. The researchers simply wanted all children to have a failure experience, which acted as a control variable.) Finally, all the children were given a third set of puzzles; these were easy ones again, the same level of difficulty as the first set. This was the posttest. The researchers recorded how many of the second round of easy puzzles children in the two groups could solve.

FIGURE 10.11
Studying the effect of red: a pretest/posttest design. If the Elliot team had conducted their study as a pretest/posttest design, it would have looked like this.

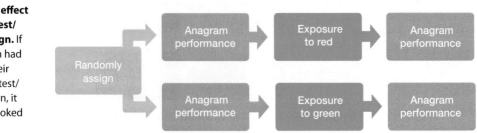

As Mueller and Dweck's theory predicted, the children who received person praise showed a decline in the number of easy puzzles they could solve after failure, while the children who received the process praise showed an improvement in the number of easy puzzles they could solve after failure (**Figure 10.12**).

In this study, because the researchers used a pretest/posttest design, they could easily track the increase and decrease in performance in the two groups. Although the two groups started out, as expected, solving about the same number of problems, after different kinds of praise followed by a failure experience, the two groups diverged dramatically.

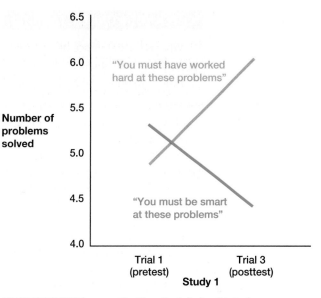

FIGURE 10.12 **Using a pretest/posttest design to study process praise and person praise.** The orange line represents process praise. The green line represents person praise. (Source: Adapted from Mueller & Dweck, 1998.)

Which Design Is Better?

Why might researchers choose to do a posttest-only experiment? Shouldn't they always make sure that groups are equal on anagram ability or pasta appetite *before* they experience a manipulation? Not necessarily.

In some situations, it is problematic to use a pretest/posttest design. Imagine how the van Kleef team might have done this. Maybe they would want to pretest participants to see how much pasta they usually eat. But if they did that, people might have felt too full to participate in the rest of the study. Instead, the researchers trusted in random assignment to create equivalent groups. Participants who were big eaters and participants who were light eaters all had an equal chance of being in either one of the serving bowl groups, and if they were distributed evenly across both groups, their effects would cancel each other out. Therefore, any observed difference in overall eating behavior between these two groups should be attributable only to the two different bowl sizes. In other words, "being a big eater" could have been a selection effect, but random assignment helped avoid it.

In contrast, a pretest/posttest design made sense for Mueller and Dweck's study. They could justify giving their sample of children multiple sets of problems, because the situation was quite similar to other classroom situations, and it was unlikely to arouse suspicion.

In short, the posttest-only design may be the most basic type of independent-groups experiment, but its combination of random assignment plus a manipulated variable can lead to powerful causal conclusions. The pretest/posttest design adds a pretesting step to the most basic independent-groups design. Researchers might use a pretest/posttest design if they want to be extra sure that two groups were equivalent at pretesting—as long as the pretest does not make the participants change their more spontaneous behavior.

1. What is the difference between independent-groups and within-groups designs?
2. Describe how posttest-only and pretest/posttest designs are both independent-groups designs. Explain how they differ.

1. See p. 284. 2. See pp. 285–287.

Within-Groups Designs

There are two basic types of within-groups design. When researchers expose participants to all levels of the independent variable, they might do so concurrently, or they might do so by repeated exposures, over time, to different levels.

Concurrent-Measures Design

In a **concurrent-measures design**, participants are exposed to all the levels of an independent variable at roughly the same time, and a single attitudinal or behavioral preference is the dependent variable. An example is a study in which infants were shown two faces at the same time, a male face and a female face; an experimenter recorded which face they looked at the longest (Quinn, Yahr, Kuhn, Slater, & Pascalis, 2002). Here, the independent variable is the gender of the face, and babies experience both levels (male and female) at the same time. The baby's looking preference would be the dependent variable (**Figure 10.13**). In fact, babies in such studies typically show a preference for looking at female faces.

Another example of a concurrent-measures design comes from Chapter 1. Harry Harlow presented baby monkeys with two "mothers": a wire mother that gave milk and a cloth mother that was warm and cozy but did not provide milk (Harlow, 1958). The monkeys indicated their preference by spending more time with one mother than the other. In Harlow's study, the type of mother was the independent variable (manipulated as within-groups), and each baby monkey's clinging behavior was the dependent variable.

FIGURE 10.13
A concurrent-measures design for an infant cognition study. Babies saw two faces simultaneously, and the experimenters recorded which face they looked at the longest.

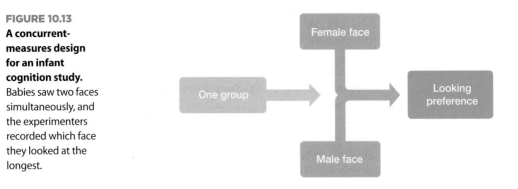

FIGURE 10.14
A repeated-measures design.

Repeated-Measures Design

A **repeated-measures design** is a type of within-groups design in which participants are measured on a dependent variable more than once—that is, after exposure to each level of the independent variable. Using a repeated-measures design, developmental researchers Bick and Dozier (2010) studied the hormone oxytocin, which is believed to be involved in social bonding. The participants were mothers whose toddlers were 2 or 3 years old. In one phase of the study, the women's oxytocin levels were monitored as they interacted closely with their own toddlers. In the other phase a couple of days later, at the same time of day, the mothers' oxytocin levels were monitored as they interacted closely with a different toddler they did not previously know. (The mothers traded toddlers with each other for this part of the study.) The researchers found that oxytocin levels were higher when women were interacting with the new child than with their own. In this experiment, the independent variable was the interaction partner and had two levels: own toddler and new toddler. The dependent variable was oxytocin levels: Oxytocin levels *depended* on the interaction partner. Because women were tested on the dependent variable (oxytocin levels) after each toddler, this was a repeated-measures design (**Figure 10.14**).

Advantages of Within-Groups Designs

The principal advantage of a within-groups design is that it ensures the participants in the two groups will be equivalent; after all, they are the same participants. For example, Bick and Dozier knew that oxytocin levels were variable across women: Some women have normally high levels of this hormone; others have low levels. If the researchers had randomly assigned women to interact with either their own toddler or a new toddler, they would have run the risk that, by chance, a few extra women with high oxytocin levels would be assigned to one group, and the groups would not be perfectly equivalent.

In Bick and Dozier's repeated-measures design, however, a woman with a naturally high or low level of oxytocin, or even a naturally high or low interest in toddlers, would bring that same baseline to her interactions with both toddlers. As a result, the only difference between the two groups should be attributable to the independent variable (which toddler a woman was with), not to individual or personal variables. Researchers say that each woman "acted as her own control," because by exposing all participants to both independent variable conditions, Bick and Dozier controlled for—kept constant—a number of individual difference variables (e.g., oxytocin levels, parenting style, personality) across conditions.

Similarly, when the Quinn team studied whether infants prefer to look at male or female faces as a within-groups design, they did not have to worry (for instance) that all the girl babies would be in one group or the other, or that babies who have older siblings were in one group or the other. Every baby saw both female and male faces, and that kept any extraneous personal variables constant across both face conditions.

In fact, the idea of "treating each participant as his or her own control" also means that matched-groups designs can be treated as within-groups designs. As discussed earlier, in a matched-groups design, researchers carefully match sets of participants on some key control variable (such as IQ) and assign each member of a set to a different group. The matched participants in the groups are assumed to be more similar to each other than in a more traditional independent-groups design, which uses random assignment.

To review matched-groups design, see pp. 283–284.

Besides providing the ability to use each participant as his or her own control, within-groups designs also give researchers more power to notice differences between conditions. Statistically speaking, when extraneous differences (unsystematic variability) in personality, living conditions, gender, ability, and so on are held constant across all conditions, researchers will be more likely to detect an effect of the independent variable manipulation if there is one. In this context, the term **power** refers to the ability of a study to show a statistically significant result when an independent variable truly has an effect in the population. For example, if seeing an ID number written in red really does affect performance or achievement, will the study show a difference? Maybe not. If extraneous differences exist

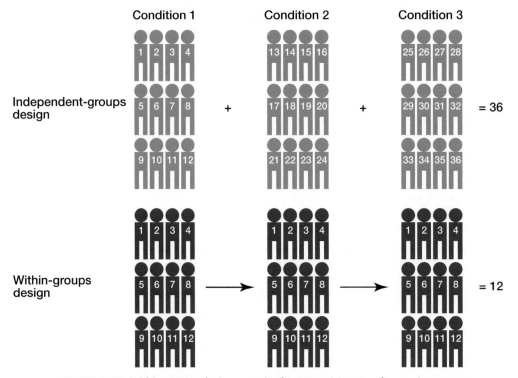

FIGURE 10.15 Within-groups designs require fewer participants. If researchers want to use 12 people in each of three experimental conditions, a within-groups design is more efficient than an independent-groups design.

CHAPTER 10 Introduction to Simple Experiments

between groups, too much unsystematic variability may be obscuring a true difference. It's like being at a noisy party—your ability to detect somebody's words is hampered when many other conversations are going on around you.

A within-groups design can also be attractive because it generally requires fewer participants overall. Suppose a team of researchers is running a study with three conditions. If they want 12 participants in each condition, they will need a total of 36 people for an independent-groups design. However, if they run the same study as a within-groups design, they will need only 12 participants, because each participant experiences all levels of the independent variable (**Figure 10.15**). In this way, a repeated-measures design can be much more efficient.

For more on power, see Chapter 11, pp. 334–335, and Statistics Review: Inferential Statistics, pp. 471–474.

Covariance, Temporal Precedence, and Internal Validity in Within-Groups Designs

Do within-groups designs allow researchers to make causal claims? In other words, do they stand up to the three causal criteria?

Because within-groups designs enable researchers to manipulate an independent variable and incorporate comparison conditions, they provide an opportunity for establishing covariance. Bick and Dozier (2010) observed, for example, that oxytocin levels covaried with the toddler with whom each woman was interacting. A repeated-measures design also establishes temporal precedence, because the experimenter controls the independent variable and can ensure that it comes first. In this study, each toddler interaction came before each oxytocin measurement.

Order Effects

Within-groups designs do have the potential for a particular threat to internal validity: Sometimes, being exposed to one condition changes how participants react to the other condition. Such responses are called **order effects**, and they happen when exposure to one level of the independent variable influences responses to the next level of the independent variable. An order effect in a within-groups design is a confound, meaning that participant performance at later levels of the independent variable might be caused not by the experimental manipulation, but rather by the sequence in which the conditions were experienced. Order effects can include **practice effects**, also known as *fatigue effects*, in which a long sequence might lead participants to get better at the task, or to get tired or bored toward the end. Order effects also include **carryover effects**, in which some form of contamination carries over from one condition to the next. For example, imagine sipping orange juice right after brushing your teeth; the first taste contaminates your experience of the second one.

Consider what might have happened if Elliot and his colleagues had conducted their 2007 study as a repeated-measures design, in which participants took the anagram quiz three times: first with an ID number written in red ink, then with the number in green ink, and finally with the number in black ink. Maybe the higher scores in the later conditions were simply due to practice—not to the color of the ink. Such a practice effect would be an internal validity threat: You wouldn't be sure whether the higher scores in the green-ink and black-ink conditions were due to color (the real independent variable) or to practice (the alternative explanation). And indeed, the practice could have also obscured the true effect of red ink: If the order had been green, black, red, the practice effect might have canceled out any avoidance effect of the red color. Similarly, Bick and Dozier might have wondered whether women who interacted with the unfamiliar toddler showed an increase in oxytocin simply as a carryover effect. Maybe the oxytocin increased only because the women were contrasting the new toddler with their own.

Avoiding Order Effects by Counterbalancing

Because order effects (e.g., practice, fatigue, aftertaste, or boredom) are potential internal validity problems in a within-groups design, experimenters want to avoid them. When researchers use **counterbalancing**, they present the levels of the independent variable to participants in different orders. With counterbalancing, any order effects should cancel each other out when all the data are collected.

Bick and Dozier used counterbalancing in their experiment (**Figure 10.16**). Half the women interacted with their own toddler first, followed by the new toddler, and the other half interacted with the new toddler first, followed by their own toddler. If oxytocin had risen over time just because of experience in the study, the increase should have occurred in the new-toddler condition for half the women and in the own-toddler condition for the other half. When all the data were combined from these two sequences, any order effect dropped out of the comparison between the own-toddler and new-toddler conditions. As a result, the researchers knew that the difference they noticed was attributable only to the different toddlers—and not to fatigue, practice, or some other order effect.

Procedures Behind Counterbalancing. When researchers counterbalance conditions (or levels) in a within-groups design, they have to split their participants into groups; each group receives one of the condition sequences. How do the experimenters decide which participants receive the first order of presentation and which ones receive the second? Through random assignment, of course! They might recruit, say, 30 participants to a study and randomly assign 15 of them to receive the order A then B, and assign the remaining 15 the order B then A.

There are two methods for counterbalancing an experiment: full and partial. When a within-groups experiment has only two or three levels of an independent variable, researchers can use **full counterbalancing**, in which all possible condition orders are represented. For example, a repeated-measures design with two conditions is easy to counterbalance; there are two orders (A → B and B → A). In

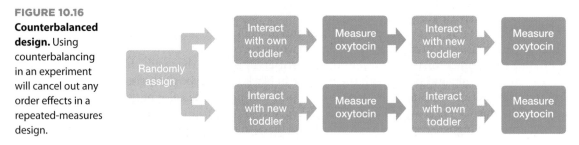

a repeated-measures design with three conditions—A, B, and C—each group of participants would be randomly assigned to one of the six following sequences:

A → B → C   B → C → A
A → C → B   C → A → B
B → A → C   C → B → A

As the number of conditions increases, however, the number of possible orders needed for full counterbalancing increases dramatically. For example, a study with four conditions requires 24 possible orders! If experimenters want to put at least a few participants in each order, the need for participants can quickly increase, counteracting the typical efficiency of a repeated-measures design. Therefore, they might use **partial counterbalancing**, in which only some of the possible condition orders are represented. One way to partially counterbalance is to present the conditions in a randomized order for each subject. (This is easy to do when an experiment is administered by a computer; the computer delivers conditions in a new random order for each participant.)

Another technique for partial counterbalancing is to use a **Latin square**, a formal system of partial counterbalancing that ensures that each condition appears in each position at least once. A Latin square for six conditions (conditions 1 through 6) might look like this:

1   2   6   3   5   4
2   3   1   4   6   5
3   4   2   5   1   6
4   5   3   6   2   1
5   6   4   1   3   2
6   1   5   2   4   3

The first row is set up according to a formula, and then the conditions simply go in numerical order down each column. Latin squares work differently for odd and even numbers of conditions. If you wish to create your own, you can find formulas for setting up the first rows of a Latin square online.

Disadvantages of Within-Groups Designs

Within-groups designs are true experiments because they involve a manipulated variable and a measured variable. They potentially establish covariance, they ensure temporal precedence, and when experimenters control for order effects, they can establish internal validity, too. So why wouldn't a researcher choose a within-groups design all the time?

Within-groups designs have three main disadvantages. First, as noted earlier, repeated-measures designs have the potential for order effects, which can threaten internal validity. But a researcher can usually control for order effects by using counterbalancing, so such effects may not be much of a concern.

A second possible disadvantage is that a within-groups design might not be possible or practical. Suppose someone has devised a new way of teaching children how to ride a bike, called Method A. She wants to compare Method A with the older method, Method B. Obviously, she cannot teach a group of children to ride a bike with Method A and then return them to baseline and teach them again with Method B. Once taught, the children are permanently changed. In such a case, a within-groups design, with or without counterbalancing, would make no sense.

A third problem occurs when people see all levels of the independent variable and then change the way they would normally act. If participants in the van Kleef study had seen both the medium and large serving bowl conditions (instead of just one or the other), participants might have begun to think, "I know I'm participating in a study at the moment; seeing these two bowls makes me wonder whether it has something to do with serving bowl size." In response to that thought, they might have changed their spontaneous behavior. When an experiment contains cues that lead participants to guess its hypotheses, the experiment is said to have **demand characteristics**, or *experimental demand*. When demand characteristics of an experiment are high, they may create an alternative explanation for a study's results. You would have to ask: Did the manipulation work? Or did the participants simply guess what the researchers expected them to do, and act accordingly?

Is Pretest/Posttest a Within-Groups Design?

You might wonder whether pretest/posttest independent-groups design should be considered a within-groups design. In one sense, it is: Participants are tested twice—at pretest and at posttest.

In a true within-groups design, however, participants are exposed to all levels of a meaningful independent variable, such as which toddler they are working with, or which kind of face they're looking at. The levels of such independent variables can also be counterbalanced. In contrast, in a pretest/posttest design, participants see only one level of the independent variable, not all levels (**Figure 10.17**).

Table 10.1 summarizes the four types of experimental designs covered in this chapter.

FIGURE 10.17
Pretest/posttest design versus within-groups design. In a pretest/posttest design, participants see only one level of the independent variable, but in a within-groups design, they see all the levels. DV = dependent variable. IV = independent variable.

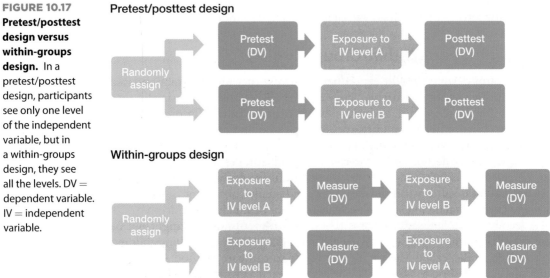

TABLE 10.1 Two Independent-Groups Designs and Two Within-Groups Designs

Independent-Groups Designs		Within-Groups Designs	
Different participants at each level of the independent variable		Same participants see all levels of the independent variable	
Posttest-only design	Pretest/posttest	Concurrent-measures design	Repeated-measures design

---

CHECK YOUR UNDERSTANDING

1. What are the two simple forms of within-groups designs?
2. Describe how counterbalancing improves the internal validity of a within-groups design.
3. Summarize the three advantages and the three potential disadvantages of within-groups designs.

1. Concurrent measures and repeated measures; see pp. 288–289. 2. See pp. 292–293. 3. See pp. 289–291 and pp. 293–294.

Interrogating Causal Claims with the Four Validities

Let's use Mueller and Dweck's (1998) study on process praise and person praise to illustrate how to interrogate an experimental design using the four big validities as a framework. What questions should you ask, and what do the answers mean?

Construct Validity: How Well Were the Variables Measured and Manipulated?

In an experiment, researchers operationalize two constructs: the independent variable and the dependent variable. When you interrogate the construct validity of an experiment, you should ask about the construct validity of each of these variables.

Dependent Variables: How Well Were They Measured?

Chapters 5 and 6 explained in detail how to interrogate the construct validity of a dependent, measured variable. To interrogate construct validity in Mueller and Dweck's study, for example, you could ask how well the researchers measured their dependent variable: student performance. In the study, the researchers measured fifth-grade children's performance by using an established test called Standard Progressive Matrices. These matrices are visual puzzles in which kids are supposed to pick the image that completes an overall pattern. Is this test a good measure of how well schoolchildren can perform—what they can achieve academically? Is it reliably scored; that is, is it easy for coders to agree on what a child's score is? Is it valid; are kids' scores on the matrices associated with their performance in an academic domain?

Mueller and Dweck do not present any empirical evidence for the reliability and validity of the Standard Progressive Matrices, but they do cite the instrument's author, Raven (1976). Many of Mueller and Dweck's readers would be familiar with this instrument, because it is a common research measure of intelligence and academic potential. By reading the reference they cite (Raven, 1976), you could learn more about the reliability and validity of this measure as a test of intelligence or academic performance.

Independent Variables: How Well Were They Manipulated?

To interrogate the construct validity of the independent variables, you would ask how well the researchers manipulated (or operationalized) them. In Mueller and Dweck's study, for example, the independent variable was process praise versus person praise. The researchers manipulated this variable by giving kids a set of matrices they could all solve easily, and then telling them either, "Wow, you did very well on these problems. You got [number of problems] right. You must have worked hard at these problems" (process praise) or "Wow, you did very well on these problems. You got [number of problems] right. You must be smart at these problems" (person praise).

To evaluate this manipulation, you can simply assess its face validity. Does the manipulation (the operationalization) fit the researchers' definition of the construct? For example, is telling a child, "You must have worked hard at these problems" a good measure of process praise? Is telling a child, "You must be smart at these problems" a good measure of person praise?

Another way to evaluate the manipulation's construct validity is to see whether and how other researchers have used this manipulation before. Have other scientists reviewed the manipulation and decided it was a meaningful one?

Manipulation Checks and Pilot Studies. In some cases, researchers use manipulation checks to collect empirical data on the construct validity of their independent variables. A **manipulation check** is an extra dependent variable that researchers can insert into an experiment to help them quantify how well an experimental manipulation worked. For example, Mueller and Dweck wanted to check to be sure the children believed the praise the experimenter gave them. Therefore, at one point in the study, they asked the kids to use two colors to fill in a circle, indicating how important both their hard work and their smartness were in explaining their performance. The results from this variable showed that those who got process praise colored in a greater proportion of the circle using the "effort" color, while kids who got person praise colored in a greater proportion of the circle using the "smartness" color.

The same procedure—exposing children to the manipulation and then asking them to indicate what kind of praise they got—might also be used in a pilot study. A **pilot study** is a simple study, using a separate group of participants, that is completed before (or sometimes after) conducting the study of primary interest. Researchers may use pilot study data to confirm the effectiveness of their manipulations.

Manipulation checks and pilot studies are not always necessary, but careful experimenters often use them. For instance, Elliot and his colleagues (2007) believed that the ink colors they used would be perceived by their participants as red, green, and black. But just to be sure, they conducted a pilot study to ask participants to describe the ink colors they used. The pilot group confirmed that, indeed, the red, green, and black pens the researchers planned to use were "conventional" and "typical" examples of these three colors. When researchers have taken such a step, you can feel more confident in the construct validity of the independent variable.

Construct Validity and Theory Testing

When evaluating the construct validity of an experiment, you assess the quality of two operationalizations: the one for the independent variable and the one for the dependent variable. The standard for evaluating these operational variables is provided by the theory the study is testing; that is, construct validity also lets researchers say that the results of the study support their theory. Recall that the Elliot team conducted the ink color study in the first place because they wanted to test a theory about avoidance orientation in academic tasks. Therefore, they should be able to show that the results came out the way they did because red ink led people to have an avoidance orientation, not some other reason.

The key independent variable condition, the color red, in the Elliot study is not just an avoidance color; it's also a warm color, compared with green and black. Therefore, a critic could argue that the results do not support Elliot's theory, since it's impossible to be sure whether the key color, red, was working because it suggested avoidance or because it was a warm color. To improve construct validity, the researchers could have added a fourth condition: a warm color, such as orange or pink ink. If the results showed that only the red ink, not the other warm colors, led to poor performance, Elliot would have stronger support for the avoidance aspect of his theory. The operationalization of his manipulation (ink color) would have been more clearly tied to the construct (avoidance) it was meant to represent.

Another way researchers can show that results support their theory is by collecting additional data. As discussed earlier, Elliot and his colleagues conducted two additional experiments. One showed that viewing a red test booklet cover (versus a green or gray one) caused participants to select easy, rather than hard, items on a test. Because people in an avoidance mode are known to prefer easy (safe) problems and avoid difficult (risky) ones, this study showed that the color red was probably working in the previous study because it prompted avoidance (and not something else). That supports the construct validity of the independent variable (**Figure 10.18**).

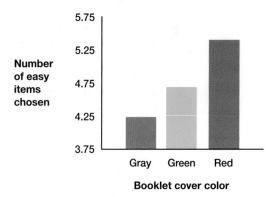

FIGURE 10.18 Construct validity and theory testing. The researchers showed that exposure to the color red made students more likely to select easy items on a test—evidence that the color red was activating the motivation to avoid challenge. This study helped support the researchers' theory about color and avoidance. (Source: Adapted from Elliot et al., 2007.)

In still another experiment, Elliot and his colleagues evaluated the brain activity of participants who received a red, green, or gray test booklet. They found that the pattern of right-brain and left-brain activity of participants with the red test booklet was consistent with an avoidance orientation, too. (Studies have shown that when people are motivated to avoid something, they have more activity in the right than in the left frontal cortex.)

Therefore, when you are interrogating the construct validity of an experiment, you can ask what evidence shows that the manipulations and measures actually represent the intended constructs in the theory.

External Validity: To Whom or What Can the Causal Claim Generalize?

Chapters 7 and 8 discussed external validity in the context of frequency claims and association claims. Interrogating external validity in the context of causal claims is similar. You ask whether the causal relationship can generalize to other people, places, and times. (Chapter 14 goes into even more detail about external validity questions.)

Generalizing to Other People

As with an association claim or a frequency claim, when interrogating a causal claim's external validity, you should ask how the experimenters recruited their participants. Remember that when you interrogate external validity, you ask about *random sampling*—randomly gathering a sample from a population. (In contrast, when you interrogate internal validity, you ask about *random assignment*—randomly assigning each participant in a sample into one experimental group or another.) Were the participants in a study sampled randomly from the population of interest? If they were, you can be relatively sure the results can be generalized, at least to the population of participants from which the sample came. In the Mueller and Dweck study (1998), the 128 fifth graders were a convenience sample (rather than a random sample) from two American schools: one in the Midwest and one in the Northeast. Because they were a convenience sample, you can't be sure if the results would generalize to other fifth graders. In addition, since the study was run on fifth graders, you can't assume the results would apply to college students or preschoolers.

Generalizing to Other Situations

External validity also applies to the types of situations to which an experiment might generalize. For example, the van Kleef study used pasta, but other researchers in the same lab found that large serving containers also cause people to consume more soup, popcorn, and snack chips (Wansink, 2006). The situation in the Mueller and Dweck study can probably generalize to other contexts where children take the Standard Progressive Matrices test. But how well does this experimental situation represent other situations in which kids get praise? Would it apply to other tasks, such as math problems or a drawing task? Mueller and Dweck reported six separate studies in their article, all of which gave person praise and process praise, and all of which showed the same pattern of results.

Schoolchildren performed worse after failure when they had been told, "You must be smart at these problems." However, all six of their studies used the same basic situation and the same matrices test. On its own, this set of studies doesn't tell you about the situations to which this effect generalizes.

Later research by Dweck and her colleagues did provide evidence that the results can generalize to other situations. For example, a team of researchers invited 4-year-old children to observe a little play with two simple puppets (Cimpian, Arce, Markman, & Dweck, 2007). The child puppet drew pictures and the teacher puppet delivered praise (**Figure 10.19**). Half the children saw the teacher puppet give person praise to the child puppet ("You are a good drawer"), and the other half saw the teacher puppet give process praise to the child puppet ("You did a good job drawing"). After four praise scenarios, the child puppet had a failure experience by making a drawing mistake, such as leaving the wheels off a bus. The researchers found that kids who had received person praise were upset by this situation, and more likely to want to "walk away" from the bad drawing; in contrast, those who'd received the process praise were more likely to say they'd "fix it" about the bad drawing.

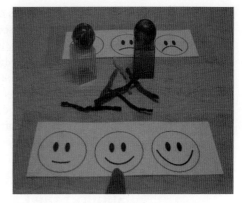

FIGURE 10.19 Generalizing to other situations. In this study, the green teacher puppet praised the red child puppet's imaginary drawings (Cimpian et al., 2007). The researchers found that even 4-year-olds react to person praise ("You are a good drawer") by withdrawing effort after failure, whereas process praise ("You did a good job drawing") led to more engagement. This study shows that the Mueller and Dweck studies can be generalized to children younger than fifth grade, and to tasks other than academic puzzles.

The Cimpian et al. (2007) study is only one example of many others that have found a similar effect of person praise versus process praise in a variety of experimental situations. As you learned in Chapter 1, researchers dig deeper. Rather than conducting a single study and calling it a day, they continue exploring why, and when, a phenomenon will work. Taken together, these studies help establish the external validity of a causal claim: Person praise makes kids withdraw effort after a failure experience.

What If External Validity Is Poor?

Should you be concerned that Mueller and Dweck did not select their participants at random from a population of fifth graders? Should you be concerned that their set of six studies all used the same kind of tasks, the Standard Progressive Matrices?

Remember from Chapter 3 that in an experiment, researchers usually prioritize experimental control—that is, internal validity. To get a clean manipulation, they may have to conduct their study in an artificial environment, such as a university laboratory. Often, such environments, and the people who participate in the studies conducted there, are not obviously representative of people in the real world. Although it is possible to achieve both internal and external validity in a single study, doing so can often be difficult. Therefore, many experimenters decide to sacrifice real-world representativeness for internal validity.

Testing their theory and teasing out the causal variable from potential confounds were the steps Mueller and Dweck, like most experimenters, took care of first. In addition, running an experiment on a relatively homogenous sample

For more discussion on prioritizing validities, see Chapter 14, pp. 424–437.

(such as fifth graders or college students) means that the unsystematic variability is less likely to obscure the effect of the independent variable (see Chapter 11). Replicating the study using several samples in a variety of contexts is a step saved for later. Although Mueller and Dweck sampled only fifth graders, we saw that other studies demonstrated that person praise and process praise also affect the motivation of 4-year-olds. Other researchers might also be interested in testing Latino children in Los Angeles or high school students in Kyoto. Such studies would help demonstrate whether person praise and process praise work the same way across different settings and at different developmental stages.

Statistical Validity: How Well Do the Data Support the Causal Claim?

In your statistics class, you will learn how to ask specific questions about experimental designs, such as whether the researchers did the right statistical tests. For the present context, interrogating the statistical validity of an experiment involves two basic concerns: statistical significance and effect size.

Is the Difference Statistically Significant?

The first question to ask is whether the difference between means obtained in the study is statistically significant. Recall from Chapter 8 that when a result is statistically significant, it is unlikely to have been obtained by chance from a population in which nothing is happening. When the difference (say, between a person-praise group and a process-praise group) in a study is statistically significant, you can be reasonably sure the difference is not a fluke result. In other words, a statistically significant result suggests that covariance exists between the variables in the population from which the sample was drawn.

When the difference between conditions is not statistically significant, you cannot conclude that there is covariance—you cannot conclude that the independent variable had a detectable effect on the dependent variable. Any observed difference between the groups found in the study is similar to the kinds of differences you would find just by chance when there is no covariance. And if there is no covariance, the study does not support a causal claim.

How Large Is the Effect?

Knowing that a result is statistically significant tells you that the result probably was not drawn by chance from a population in which there is no difference between groups. However, depending on the study, even tiny differences might be statistically significant. Therefore, asking about effect size can help you evaluate the strength of the covariance (i.e., the difference). In general, the larger the effect size, the more important, and the stronger, the causal effect. When a study's result is statistically significant, it is not necessarily the same as having a large effect size.

As discussed in Chapter 8, psychological scientists often use the correlation coefficient r to help evaluate the effect size of an association. In experiments, researchers often use a different indicator of standardized effect size, called d. This measure represents how far apart two experimental groups are on the dependent

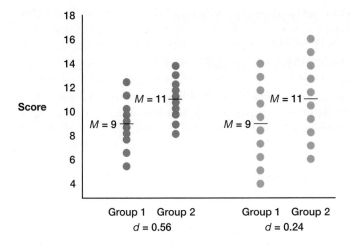

FIGURE 10.20 Effect size and overlap between groups. Effect sizes are larger when the scores in the two experimental groups overlap less. Overlap is a function of how far apart the group means are, as well as how variable the scores are within each group. On both sides of the graph, the two group means (*M*) are the same distance apart (about 2 units), but the overlap of the scores between groups is greater in the blue scores on the right. Because there is more overlap between groups, the effect size is smaller.

variable. It indicates not only the distance between the means, but also how much the scores within the groups overlap. The standardized effect size, *d*, takes into account both the difference between means and the spread of scores within each group (the standard deviation). When *d* is larger, it usually means the independent variable caused the dependent variable to change for more of the participants in the study. When *d* is smaller, it usually means the scores of participants in the two experimental groups overlap more. **Figure 10.20** shows what two *d* values might look like when a study's results are graphed showing all participants. Even though the difference between means is exactly the same in the two graphs, the effect sizes reflect the degrees of overlap between the group participants.

In Mueller and Dweck's first study (1998), the effect size for the difference in postfailure performance between the person-praise group and the process-praise group was $d = 1.37$. According to statistical conventions, a *d* that size would be considered a very large effect size indeed. Therefore, if you were interrogating the statistical validity of Mueller and Dweck's causal claim, you would conclude that the effect of type of praise on subsequent performance was very strong—and probably very important. By comparison, the effect size for the difference between the red ink and green ink groups in the Elliot et al. study (2007) was about $d = 0.64$. You previously learned, in Table 8.4 in Chapter 8, the conventions for a different measure of effect size, *r*. Here, **Table 10.2** shows how the conventions apply to *d*. According to these guidelines, a *d* of 0.64 represents a moderate effect of ink color on performance.

For more detail on standard deviation and effect size, see Statistics Review: Descriptive Statistics, pp. 446–449 and pp. 456–461.

For more questions to ask when interrogating statistical validity, such as whether the researchers used the appropriate tests or whether they made any inferential errors, see Statistics Review: Inferential Statistics, pp. 463–486.

TABLE 10.2 Cohen's Guidelines for Effect Size Strength

An effect size in which *d* =	Can be described as	And is comparable to an *r* of
0.20	Small, or weak	.10
0.50	Medium, or moderate	.30
0.80	Large, or strong	.50

Internal Validity: Are There Alternative Explanations for the Outcome?

When interrogating causal claims, internal validity is often the priority. Experimenters isolate and manipulate a key causal variable, while controlling for all possible other variables, precisely so they can achieve internal validity. If the internal validity of an experiment is sound, you know that a causal claim is almost certainly appropriate. But if the internal validity is flawed—if there is some confound—a causal claim would be inappropriate. It should instead be demoted to an association claim.

Some common threats to internal validity have already been discussed in this chapter. Recall that three fundamental internal validity questions are worth asking of any experiment:

1. Did the experimental design ensure that there were no design confounds, or did some other variable accidentally covary along with the intended independent variable? (Mueller and Dweck made sure that both groups of kids knew they'd done well at the matrices task; they just got different types of praise for their good work.)
2. If the experimenters used an independent-groups design, did they control for selection effects by using random assignment or matching? (Mueller and Dweck randomly assigned kids to receive one type of praise or the other.)
3. If the experimenters used a within-groups design, did they control for order effects by counterbalancing? (Counterbalancing is not relevant in Mueller and Dweck's design, because it was an independent-groups design.)

Chapter 11 goes into further detail on these threats to internal validity. In addition, nine more threats are covered.

CHECK YOUR UNDERSTANDING

1. How do manipulation checks provide evidence for the construct validity of an experiment? Why does theory matter in evaluating construct validity?
2. Besides generalization to other people, what other aspect of generalization does external validity address?
3. What does it mean when an effect size is large (as opposed to small) in an experiment?
4. Summarize the three threats to internal validity discussed in this chapter.

1. See pp. 295–298. 2. Generalization to other situations; see pp. 298–299. 3. See pp. 300–301. 4. See p. 302.

Summary

- Causal claims are special because they can lead to advice, treatments, and interventions. The only way to support a causal claim is to conduct a well-designed experiment.

Two Examples of Simple Experiments

- A series of experiments showed that exposure to the color red causes people to perform worse on anagrams and other problems.
- An experiment showed that providing a large serving bowl caused people to serve themselves more pasta, and to eat more of it, than a medium serving bowl.

Experimental Variables

- Experiments study the effect of an independent (manipulated) variable on a dependent (measured) variable.
- Experiments deliberately keep all extraneous variables constant as control variables.

Why Experiments Support Causal Claims

- Experiments support causal claims because they potentially allow researchers to establish covariance, temporal precedence, and internal validity.
- The three potential internal validity threats covered in this chapter that researchers work to avoid are design confounds, selection effects, and order effects.

Independent-Groups Designs

- In an independent-groups design, different participants are exposed to each level of the independent variable.
- In a posttest-only design, participants are randomly assigned to one of at least two levels of an independent variable and then measured once on the dependent variable.
- In a pretest/posttest design, participants are randomly assigned to one of at least two levels of an independent variable, and are then measured on a dependent variable twice—once

before and once after they experience the independent variable.
- Random assignment or matched groups can help establish internal validity in independent-groups designs by minimizing selection effects.

Within-Groups Designs

- In a within-groups design, the same participants are exposed to all levels of the independent variable.
- In a concurrent-measures design, participants are exposed to at least two levels of an independent variable at the same time, and then indicate a preference for one level (the dependent variable).
- In a repeated-measures design, participants are tested on the dependent variable after each exposure to an independent variable condition.
- Within-groups designs allow researchers to treat each participant as his or her own control, and require fewer participants than independent-groups designs. Within-groups designs also present the potential for order effects and demand characteristics.

Interrogating Causal Claims with the Four Validities

- Interrogating construct validity involves assessing whether the variables were manipulated and measured in ways consistent with the theory behind the experiment.
- Interrogating external validity involves asking whether the experiment's results can be generalized to other people or to other situations and settings.
- Interrogating statistical validity starts by asking how strongly the independent variable affects the dependent variable (effect size), and whether the effect is statistically significant.
- Interrogating internal validity involves looking for design confounds and seeing whether the researchers used techniques such as random assignment and counterbalancing.

Key Terms

experiment, p. 275
manipulated variable, p. 275
measured variable, p. 275
independent variable, p. 275
condition, p. 275
dependent variable, p. 276
control variable, p. 276
comparison group, p. 277
control group, p. 278
treatment group, p. 278
placebo group, p. 278
confound, p. 279
design confound, p. 280

systematic variability, p. 280
unsystematic variability, p. 280
selection effect, p. 281
random assignment, p. 282
matched groups, p. 283
independent-groups design,
   p. 284
within-groups design, p. 284
posttest-only design, p. 285
pretest/posttest design, p. 286
concurrent-measures design,
   p. 288
repeated-measures design, p. 289

power, p. 290
order effect, p. 291
practice effect, p. 291
carryover effect, p. 291
counterbalancing, p. 292
full counterbalancing, p. 292
partial counterbalancing, p. 293
Latin square, p. 293
demand characteristic, p. 294
manipulation check, p. 296
pilot study, p. 296

 To see samples of chapter concepts in the popular press, visit
www.everydayresearchmethods.com and click the box for Chapter 10.

Review Questions

Max ran an experiment in which he asked people to shake hands with an experimenter (played by a female friend) and rate the experimenter's friendliness, using a self-report measure. The experimenter was always the same person, using the same standard greeting for all participants. People were randomly assigned to either shake hands with her after she had cooled her hands under cold water, or to shake hands with her after she had warmed up her hands under warm water. Max's results found that people rated the experimenter as more friendly when her hands were warm than when they were cold.

1. Why does Max's experiment satisfy the causal criterion of temporal precedence?
   a. Because Max found a difference in rated friendliness between the two conditions, cold hands and warm hands.
   b. Because the participants shook the experimenter's hand before rating her friendliness.
   c. Because the experimenter acted the same in all conditions, except having cold or warm hands.
   d. Because Max randomly assigned people to the warm hands or cold hands condition.

2. In Max's experiment described above, what was a control variable?
   a. The participants' rating of the friendliness of the experimenter.
   b. The temperature of the experimenter's hands (warm or cold).
   c. The gender of the students in the study.
   d. The standard greeting the experimenter used while shaking hands.

3. What type of design is Max's experiment?
   a. Posttest-only design
   b. Pretest/posttest design
   c. Concurrent-measures design
   d. Repeated-measures design

4. Max randomly assigned people to shake hands either with the "warm hands" experimenter or the "cold hands" experimenter. Why did he randomly assign participants?
   a. Because he had a within-groups design.
   b. Because he wanted to avoid selection effects.
   c. Because he wanted to avoid an order effect.
   d. Because he wanted to generalize the results to the population of students at his university.

5. Which of the following questions would be interrogating the construct validity of Max's experiment?
   a. How large is the effect size comparing the rated friendliness of the warm hands and cold hands conditions?
   b. How well did Max's "experimenter friendliness" rating capture participants' actual impressions of the experimenter?
   c. Were there any confounds in the experiment?
   d. Can we generalize the results from Max's friend to other experimenters with whom people might shake hands?

Learning Actively

1. Design a posttest-only experiment that would test each of the following causal claims. For each one, identify the study's independent variable(s), identify its dependent variable(s), and suggest some important control variables. Then, sketch a bar graph of the results you would predict (remember to put the dependent variable on the y-axis). Finally, apply the three causal criteria to each study.
   a. Having a friendly (versus a stern) teacher for a brief lesson causes children to score better on a test of material for that lesson.
   b. Practicing the piano for 30 minutes a day (compared with 10 minutes a day) causes new neural connections in the temporal region of the brain.
   c. Drinking sugared lemonade (compared to sugar-free lemonade) makes people better able to perform well on a task that requires self-control.

2. For each of the following independent variables, how would you design a manipulation that used an independent-groups design? How would you design a manipulation that used a within-groups design? Explain the advantages and disadvantages of doing each independent variable as independent-groups versus within-groups.
   a. Drinking sugared versus sugar-free lemonade.
   b. Listening to a lesson from a friendly teacher versus a stern teacher.
   c. Practicing the piano for 30 minutes a day versus 10 minutes a day.

3. To study people's willingness to help others, social psychologists Bibb Latané and John Darley (1968) invited people to work on questionnaires in a lab room. After handing out the questionnaires, the female experimenter went next door and staged a loud accident: She pretended to fall off a chair and get hurt, although she actually played a tape recording of this accident. Then the experimenters observed whether each participant stopped filling out the questionnaire and went to try to help the "victim."

   Behind the scenes, the experimenters had flipped a coin to assign participants randomly to either an "alone" group, in which they were in the questionnaire room by themselves, or a "passive confederate" group, in which they were in the questionnaire room with a confederate (an actor) who sat impassively during the "accident" and did not attempt to help the "victim."

   In the end, Latané and Darley found that when participants were alone, 70% reacted, but when participants were with a passive confederate, only 7% reacted. This experiment supported the researchers' theory that during an accident, people take cues from others, looking to others to decide how to interpret the situation.
   a. What are the independent, dependent, and control variables in this study?
   b. Sketch a graph of the results of this study.
   c. Is the independent variable in this study manipulated as independent-groups or as repeated-measures? How do you know?
   d. For this study, ask at least one question for each of the four validities.

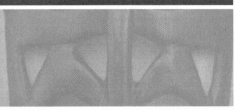
"How should
we interpret
a null result?"

"Was it really
the therapy,
or something
else, that
caused
symptoms to
improve?"

11

More on Experiments: Confounding and Obscuring Variables

A year from now, you should still be able to:

1. Interrogate an experiment to identify signs of twelve potential threats to internal validity.

2. Describe how researchers can design studies to prevent internal validity threats.

3. Interrogate an experiment with a null result, identifying possible obscuring factors.

4. Describe how researchers can design studies to minimize possible obscuring factors.

Chapter 10 covered the basic structure of an experiment, and the present chapter addresses a number of questions about experimental design. Why is it so important to use a comparison group? Why do so many experimenters create a standardized, controlled, seemingly artificial environment? Why do they use so many (or so few) participants? Why do researchers often use computers to measure their variables? Why do they insist on double-blind study designs? For the clearest possible results, responsible researchers specifically design their experiments with many factors in mind. They want to detect differences that are really there, and they want to determine conclusively when their predictions are wrong.

The first main section describes potential internal validity problems and how researchers usually avoid them. The second main section discusses some of the reasons that experiments may yield null results.

Threats to Internal Validity: Did the Independent Variable Really Cause the Difference?

When you interrogate an experiment, internal validity is the priority. As discussed in Chapter 10, three of the most common threats to internal validity are design confounds, selection effects, and order effects. All three of these threats involve an alternative explanation for the results.

With a design confound, there is an alternative explanation because the experiment was poorly designed; another variable happened to vary systematically along with the intended independent variable. Chapter 10 presented the study on pasta serving bowl size and amount of pasta eaten. If the pasta served to the large-bowl group had looked more appetizing than the pasta served to the medium-bowl group, that would have been a design confound (see Figure 10.5 in Chapter 10). It would not be clear whether the bowl size or the quality of the pasta caused the large-bowl group to take more.

With a selection effect, a confound exists because the different independent variable groups have different types of participants. In Chapter 10, the example was a study of an intensive therapy for autism, in which children who received the intensive experimental therapy did, indeed, improve over time. However, their improvement may have been caused by the therapy, or it may have been caused by greater overall involvement on the part of the parents who elected to be in the intensive therapy group. Those parents' greater motivation to treat their children could have been an alternative explanation for the improvement of children in the intensive therapy group.

With an order effect (in a within-groups design), there is an alternative explanation because the outcome might be caused by the independent variable, but it also might be caused by the order in which the levels of the variable are presented. When there is an order effect, we do not know whether the independent variable is really having an effect, or whether the participants are just getting tired, bored, or well-practiced.

These types of threats are just the beginning. There are other ways—about twelve in total—that an experiment might be at risk for a confound. Experimenters try to think about all of them, and they plan studies accordingly. Good researchers will creatively apply design strategies to prevent these threats and make strong causal statements.

The Really Bad Experiment (A Cautionary Tale)

Previous chapters have used examples of real studies to illustrate the material. In contrast, this chapter opens with three fictional experiments. They have to be fictional, because responsible scientists would never conduct studies like these.

> Nikhil, a summer camp counselor and psychology major, has noticed that his current cabin of 15 boys is an especially rambunctious bunch.

He has heard that a change in diet might help them calm down, so he eliminates the sugary snacks and desserts from the boys' meals for 2 days. As he expected, the boys are much quieter and calmer by the end of the week, after refined sugar has been eliminated from their diets.

Dr. Yuki has recruited a sample of 40 depressed women, all of whom are interested in receiving psychotherapy to treat their depression. She measures their level of depression using a standard depression inventory at the start of therapy. For 12 weeks, all the women participate in Dr. Yuki's style of cognitive therapy. At the end of the 12-week session, she measures the women again and finds that on the whole, their levels of depression have significantly decreased.

A dormitory on a university campus has started a Go Green Facebook campaign, focused on persuading students to turn out the lights in their rooms when they're not needed. Dorm residents receive e-mails and messages on Facebook that encourage energy-saving behaviors. At the start of the campaign, the head resident noted how many kilowatt hours the dorm was using by checking the electric meters on the building. At the end of the 2-month campaign, the head resident checks the kilowatt hours again and finds that the usage has dropped. He tests the two measures (pretest and posttest) and finds that they are significantly different.

Note that all three of these examples fit the same template, as shown in **Figure 11.1**. If you graphed the data of the first two studies, they would look something like the two graphs in **Figure 11.2**. Before going on, reflect on the three examples: What alternative explanations can you think of for the results of each one?

The formal name for this kind of design is the **one-group, pretest/posttest design**. A researcher recruits one group of participants, measures them on a pretest, exposes them to a treatment, intervention, or change, and then measures them on a posttest. However, a better name for this design might be "the really bad experiment." Understanding why this design is so problematic can help you learn about threats to internal validity—and appreciate how researchers can avoid them by using better research designs.

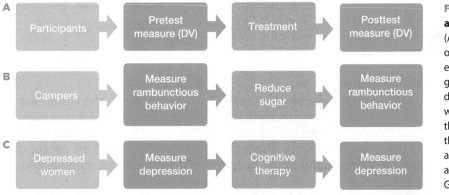

FIGURE 11.1 The really bad experiment. (A) A general diagram of the really bad experiment, or the one-group, pretest/posttest design. (B, C) Possible ways to diagram two of the examples given in the text. Using these as a model, try sketching a diagram of the Go Green example.

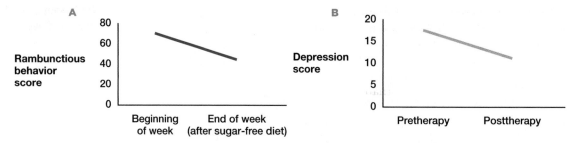

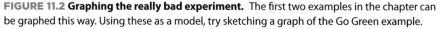

FIGURE 11.2 **Graphing the really bad experiment.** The first two examples in the chapter can be graphed this way. Using these as a model, try sketching a graph of the Go Green example.

Six Potential Internal Validity Threats in One-Group, Pretest/Posttest Designs

By the end of this chapter, you will have learned a total of twelve internal validity threats. Three of them you just reviewed: design confounds, selection effects, and order effects. Six of the internal validity threats apply especially to the really bad experiment. These include maturation threats, history threats, regression threats, attrition threats, testing threats, and instrumentation threats. And the final three threats (observer bias, demand characteristics, and placebo effects) potentially apply to any experiment.

Maturation Threats to Internal Validity

Why did the boys in Nikhil's cabin start acting better? Was it because they had eaten less sugar? Perhaps. An alternative explanation, however, is that they simply settled in, or "matured into," the camp setting after they had time to get used to the place. The boys' behavior improved on its own; the sugar-free diet may have had nothing to do with it. Such an effect is called a **maturation threat**, a change in behavior that emerges more or less spontaneously over time. People adapt to strange environments; children get better at walking and talking; plants grow taller—but not because of any outside intervention. It just happens.

Similarly, the depressed women may have improved because the cognitive therapy was effective, but an alternative explanation is that at least some of the women simply improved on their own. Sometimes the symptoms of depression or other disorders disappear, for no known reason, with time. This phenomenon, known as *spontaneous remission*, is another name for maturation.

Preventing Maturation Threats. Because the studies both Nikhil and Dr. Yuki conducted followed the model of the really bad experiment, there is no way of knowing whether the improvements they noticed were caused by maturation or by the treatments they administered. In contrast, if the two researchers had conducted true experiments, they would also have included an appropriate comparison group. Nikhil would have observed a comparison group of equally rambunctious campers who did not switch to a low-sugar diet. Dr. Yuki would have studied a comparison group of women who started out equally depressed but did not receive the cognitive therapy. If the treatment groups improved significantly more than the comparison groups did, each researcher could essentially subtract out the effect of maturation when they interpret their results. **Figure 11.3** illustrates the benefits of a comparison group in preventing a maturation threat for the depression study.

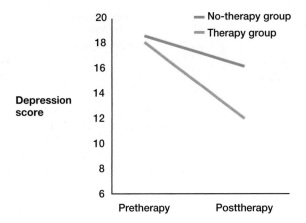

History Threats to Internal Validity

Sometimes a threat to internal validity occurs not just because time has passed, but because something specific has happened between the pretest and posttest. In the third example, why did the dorm residents use less electricity? Was it the Go Green campaign? Perhaps. But a plausible alternative explanation is that the weather got cooler and the residents did not use the air conditioning as much.

FIGURE 11.3 Maturation threats. A comparison group would help subtract out the maturation threat in Dr. Yuki's depression study. Notice that both groups improved: Even the no-therapy group showed a maturation threat. However, the therapy group showed an even larger effect, indicating that the cognitive therapy is working above and beyond the effect of maturation. The new study controls for maturation threats, since both groups experience some maturation.

Why did the campers' behavior improve? It could have been the low-sugar diet, but maybe they all started a difficult swimming course in the middle of the week, and the exercise tired them out.

These alternative explanations are examples of **history threats**, which result from a "historical" or external event that affects *most members* of the treatment group at the same time as the treatment, making it unclear whether the change in the experimental group is caused by the treatment received or by the historical factor. To be a history threat, the external factor must affect everyone or almost everyone in the group (i.e., systematically), not just a few people (i.e., unsystematically).

Preventing History Threats. As with maturation threats, a comparison group can help control for history threats. In the Go Green study, the students would need to measure the kilowatt usage in another, comparable dormitory during the same 2 months, but not give the students in the second dorm the Go Green campaign materials. (This would be a pretest/posttest design.) If both groups decreased their kilowatt usage about the same over time (**Figure 11.4A**), the decrease probably resulted from the change of seasons, not from the Go Green campaign. However, if the treatment group decreased its usage more than the comparison group did (**Figure 11.4B**), you can rule out the history threat. Both the comparison group and the treatment group should experience the same seasonal "historical" changes; therefore, including the comparison group controls for this threat.

For more on pretest/ posttest design, see Chapter 10, pp. 286–287.

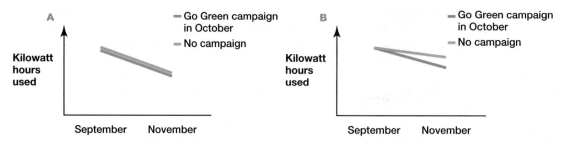

FIGURE 11.4 **History threats.** A comparison group would help subtract out the history threat of seasonal differences in electrical usage. (A) If both dorms reduced their kilowatt hours equally, the Go Green campaign did not work, because all dorms reduced their energy usage over the fall months. (B) Both dorms show a decrease in kilowatt usage in November, but the Go Green campaign dorm's usage decreased even more, indicating that the campaign worked.

Regression Threats to Internal Validity

A **regression threat** refers to a statistical concept called *regression to the mean*: When a performance is extreme at Time 1, the next time that performance is measured (Time 2), it is likely to be less extreme—that is, closer to a typical or average performance. The mean here refers to the arithmetic average of all the performances (or scores) of a particular group.

For more detail on arithmetic mean, see Statistics Review: Descriptive Statistics, p. 445.

Everyday Regression to the Mean. Everyday situations can help illustrate regression to the mean. For example, during a 2010 World Cup match in South Africa, the team from Portugal won one of their games 7–0. That's a huge score; soccer (football) scores are hardly ever that high. Without being familiar with either team, people who know about soccer would predict that in their next game, Portugal would score fewer goals. Why? Simply because most people have an intuitive understanding of regression to the mean.

Here's the statistical explanation. Portugal's score in the first game was exceptionally high partly because of the team's talent, and partly because of a unique combination of random factors that came out in Portugal's favor. The team's injury level was, just by chance, much lower than usual, and, just by chance, their opponents were a weaker team (North Korea). Just by chance, North Korea had a string of bad defense in the second half. In addition, it was raining, and Portugal's team performs well in rainy conditions. Moreover, Portugal's Tiago just happened to be having a great day and scored two goals. Therefore, despite Portugal's legitimate talent, they also benefited from randomness—a chance combination of lucky events that would probably never happen in the same combination again. Overall, the team's score in the subsequent game would almost necessarily be worse than in this game. Indeed, the team did regress; in their next game, they scored 0 goals in a tie with Brazil. In other words, Portugal finished closer to their average level of performance.

In another example, suppose you are normally cheerful and happy. On any given day, though, your usual upbeat mood can be affected by other random factors, such as the weather, your friends' moods, and even parking problems. Every once in

312   **CHAPTER 11**   More on Experiments: Confounding and Obscuring Variables

a while, just by chance, several of these random factors will affect you negatively: It will pour rain, your friends will be grumpy, and you won't be able to find a parking space. Your day is terrible! The good news is that tomorrow will almost certainly be better, because those random factors are unlikely to occur in that same, unlucky combination again. It might still be raining, but your friends won't be grumpy, and you'll quickly find a good parking space. If even one of these factors is better, your day will go better, and you will regress toward your average, happy mean.

Regression works at both extremes. An unusually good performance or outcome is likely to regress downward (toward its mean) the next time. And an unusually bad performance or outcome is likely to regress upward (toward its mean) the next time. Either extreme is explainable by an unusually lucky, or an unusually unlucky, combination of random events.

Regression and Internal Validity. Regression threats occur only in a pretest/posttest design, and only when a group has an extreme score at pretest. If the group is unusually high or low at the pretest, you can expect them to regress toward the mean somewhat when it comes time for the posttest.

The 40 depressed women Dr. Yuki studied were, on average, quite depressed. Their group average at pretest may have been partly due to their true, baseline level of depression. Because they had just volunteered for treatment, however, at least some of them were probably feeling especially bad at the time of the pretest, partly because of random events (e.g., the winter blues, a recent illness, parenting troubles, job loss, or divorce). Therefore, they were particularly interested in getting therapy just at that time. At the posttest, the random effects on the group mean probably would not be the same as they were at pretest (maybe a few saw their relationships get better, or the job situation improved for some of them), so the posttest depression average would go down. The change would not occur because of the treatment, but simply because of regression to the mean, so in this case there would be an internal validity threat.

Preventing Regression Threats. What can a researcher do to prevent regression threats? Once again, comparison groups can help, along with a careful inspection of the pattern of results. If the comparison group and the experimental group are equally extreme at pretest, the researchers can account for any regression effects in their results.

In **Figure 11.5A**, you can rule out regression and conclude that the therapy really does work: Even though both groups started out equally extreme, their depression decreases at different rates. Both groups become less depressed over time, but the levels of depression in the therapy group decrease even more. If regression played a role, it would have done so for both groups, because they were equally at risk for regression at the start. In contrast, if you saw the pattern of results shown in **Figure 11.5B**, you would suspect that regression had occurred. The therapy group did improve more than the no-therapy group, but the therapy group also started out more depressed—more extreme—than the comparison group. Regression is a particular threat in exactly this situation—when one group starts out more extreme. Even though those in the therapy group were less depressed at posttest than at pretest, the drop could be attributed to a regression

FIGURE 11.5

Regression to the mean. Regression to the mean can be analyzed by inspecting different patterns of results. (A) Regression effects can be ruled out as an internal validity threat because both groups started out equally extreme at pretest. (B) A regression threat is a possibility, because the therapy group started out more extreme than the no-therapy group; extreme pretest scores are at the most risk for regression. (C) Regression can be ruled out, because regression effects alone do not make an extreme group cross over the mean toward the other end of the scale.

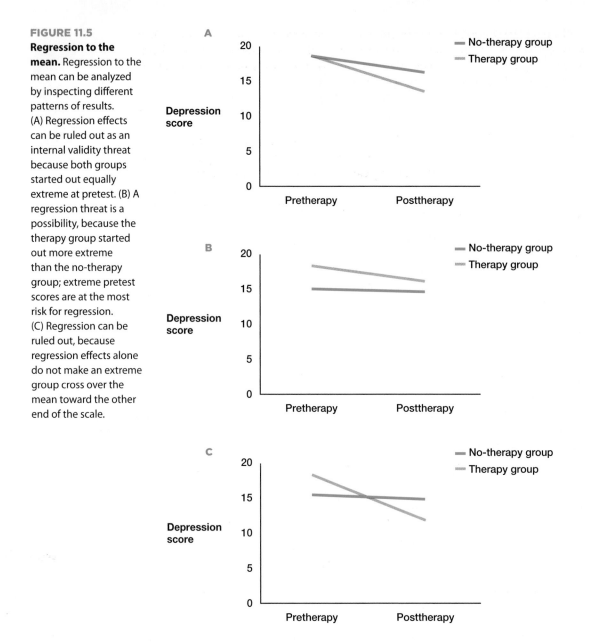

effect, rather than to the therapy. In short, the results from Figure 11.5B should not convince you that the therapy worked.

In **Figure 11.5C**, in contrast, the therapy group started out more extreme on depression, and therefore probably experienced some regression to the mean. However, this pattern shows a clear effect of therapy, too. Assuming the therapy and comparison samples are both drawn from the same population (both have the same usual Time 1 mean), it would be implausible for the therapy group to surpass the mean of the comparison group through regression alone. Regression pulls an extreme group closer to the mean, but regression alone will not cause a group to cross back over the mean to the other extreme, as depicted here. Therefore, these results suggest that the therapy probably did have an effect (in addition to a little help from regression effects).

Attrition Threats to Internal Validity

Why did the average level of rambunctiousness in Nikhil's campers decrease over the course of the week? It could have been because of the low-sugar diet, but maybe it was because the most unruly camper had to leave camp early.

Similarly, the level of depression among Dr. Yuki's patients might have decreased because of the cognitive therapy, but it might have been because three of the most depressed women in the study had symptoms so severe that they could not maintain the therapy regimen and dropped out of the study. The posttest average is lower only because these extra-high scores are not included.

In studies that have a pretest and a posttest, attrition (sometimes referred to as mortality) is a reduction in participant numbers that occurs when people drop before the end. Attrition can happen when a pretest and posttest are administered on separate days, and some participants are not available on the second day. An **attrition threat** becomes a problem for internal validity when attrition is systematic; that is, when only a certain kind of participant drops out. If just any camper leaves midweek, it might not be a problem for Nikhil's research, but it is a problem when the most rambunctious camper leaves early. His departure creates an alternative explanation for Nikhil's results: Was the posttest average lower because the low-sugar diet worked, or because one extreme score is gone?

Similarly, as shown in **Figure 11.6**, it would not be unusual if three of 40 women in the depression therapy study dropped out. However, if the three most depressed women *systematically* drop out, the mean for the posttest is going to be lower, only because it does not include these three extreme scores (not because of the therapy). Therefore, if

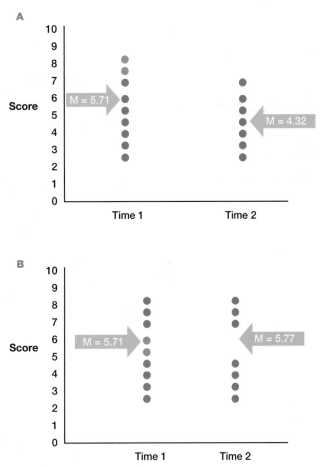

FIGURE 11.6 Attrition threats. (A) If two people drop out of a study, both of whom scored at the high end of the distribution on the pretest, the group mean changes substantially when their scores are omitted, even if all other scores stay the same. (B) If the dropouts' scores on the pretest are close to the group mean, removing their scores does not change the group mean as much.

the depression score goes down from pretest to posttest, you wouldn't know whether the decrease occurred because of the therapy or because of the alternative explanation—that the highest-scoring women had dropped out.

Preventing Attrition Threats. An attrition threat is fairly easy for researchers to identify and correct. When participants drop out of a study, most researchers will remove those participants' scores from the pretest average. That way, they look only at the scores of those who completed both parts of the study. Another approach is to check the pretest scores of the dropouts. If they have extreme scores on the pretest, their attrition is more of a threat to internal validity than if their scores are closer to the group average.

Testing Threats to Internal Validity

A **testing threat**, a specific kind of order effect, refers to a change in the participants as a result of taking a test (dependent measure) more than once. People might have become more practiced at taking the test, leading to improved scores, or they may become fatigued or bored, which could lead to worse scores over time. Therefore, testing threats include practice effects and fatigue effects (see Chapter 10).

In an educational setting, for example, students might perform better on a posttest than on a pretest, but not because of any educational intervention. Instead, perhaps they were inexperienced the first time they took the test, and they did better on the posttest simply because they had more practice the second time around. Taking a pretest might also sensitize people to particular issues; for instance, the questions on a depression pretest might have made the women in Dr. Yuki's study more sensitive to subtle symptoms of depression. They might have changed their posttest answers in response to this sensitivity, not in response to the treatment.

Preventing Testing Threats. To avoid testing threats, researchers might abandon a pretest altogether and use a posttest-only design (see Chapter 10). If they do use a pretest, they might opt to use alternative forms of the test for the two

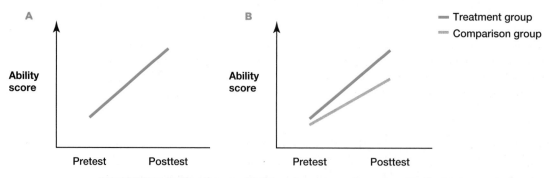

FIGURE 11.7 Testing threats. (A) If there is no comparison group, it is hard to know whether the improvement from pretest to posttest is caused by the treatment, or simply by practice. (B) The results from a comparison group can help rule out testing threats. Both groups might improve, but the treatment group improves even more, suggesting that both practice *and* a true effect of the treatment are causing the improvement.

measurements. The two forms might both measure depression, for example, but use different items to do so. A comparison group can also help. If the comparison group takes both the pretest and the posttest, too, but the treatment group shows an even larger change, testing threats can be ruled out (**Figure 11.7**).

Instrumentation Threats to Internal Validity

An **instrumentation threat**, also called *instrument decay*, occurs when a measuring instrument changes over time. In observational research, the people who are coding behaviors are the measuring instrument, and over a period of time, they might change their standards for judging behavior, by becoming more strict or more lenient. Thus, maybe Nikhil's campers did not really become less disruptive; instead, the people judging the campers' behavior became more tolerant of shoving and hitting.

Another case of an instrumentation threat would be when a researcher uses different forms for the pretest and posttest, but the two forms are not sufficiently equivalent. Dr. Yuki might have used a measure of depression at pretest on which people tend to score a little higher, and another measure of depression at posttest that tends to yield lower scores. As a result, the pattern she observed was not a sign of how good the cognitive therapy is, but merely reflected the way the alternative forms of the test are calibrated.

Preventing Instrumentation Threats. One simple way to prevent an instrumentation threat is to use a posttest-only design (in which behavior is measured only once). However, if a pretest/posttest design is required for other reasons, researchers should take steps to ensure that the pretest and posttest measures are equivalent. To do so, they might collect data from each instrument to be sure the two are calibrated the same. Or, to avoid shifting standards of behavioral coders, researchers might retrain their coders throughout the experiment, establishing their reliability and validity at both pretest and posttest. Using clear coding manuals would be an important part of this process.

Finally, to control for the problem of different forms, Dr. Yuki could also counterbalance the versions of the test, giving some participants version A at pretest and version B at posttest, and giving other participants version B, and then version A.

Instrumentation vs. Testing Threats. Because these two threats are pretty similar, here's a way to remember the difference. An instrumentation threat means the *measuring instrument* has changed from Time 1 to Time 2. A testing threat means the *participant* changes over time from having been tested before.

Combined Threats

You have learned throughout this discussion that pretest/posttest designs normally take care of many internal validity threats. However, in some cases, a study with a pretest/posttest design might combine selection threats with history or attrition threats. In a **selection-history threat**, an outside event or factor systematically affects people in the study—but only those at one level of the independent variable. For example, perhaps the dorm that was used as a comparison dorm was undergoing construction, and the construction crew used electric tools that drew on only that dorm's power supply. Therefore, the researcher won't be sure: Was it because the Go Green campaign reduced student energy usage? Or was it only because the comparison dorm used so many power tools?

Similarly, in a **selection-attrition threat**, only one of the experimental groups experiences attrition. If Dr. Yuki conducted her depression therapy experiment as a pretest/posttest design, it might be the case that the most severely depressed people dropped out—but only from the treatment group, not the control group. The treatment might have been especially arduous for the most depressed people, so they drop out of the study. Because the control group was not undergoing treatment, they are not susceptible to the same level of attrition. Therefore, selection and attrition can combine to make Dr. Yuki unsure: Did the treatment really work, compared to the control group? Or is just the case that the most severely depressed people dropped out of the treatment group?

Three Potential Internal Validity Threats in Any Experiment

Many internal validity threats are likely to occur in the really bad experiment, and these threats can often be examined simply by adding a comparison group. Doing so would result in a two-group, pretest/posttest design. The posttest-only design is another option (see Chapter 10). However, three more threats to internal validity—observer bias, demand characteristics, and placebo effects—might apply even for designs with a clear comparison group.

Observer Bias

Observer bias can be a threat to internal validity in almost any study in which there is a behavioral dependent variable. **Observer bias** occurs when researchers' expectations influence their interpretation of the results. For example, Dr. Yuki might be a biased observer of her patients' depression: She expects to see her patients improve, whether they do or do not. Nikhil may be a biased observer of his own campers: He may expect his low-sugar diet to work, so he views the campers' posttest behavior more positively.

Although comparison groups can prevent many threats to internal validity, they do not necessarily control for observer bias. Even if Dr. Yuki used a no-therapy comparison group, observer bias could still occur: If she knew which participants were in which group, her biases could lead her to see more improvement in the therapy group than in the comparison group.

Observer bias can threaten two kinds of validity in an experiment. It threatens internal validity, because an alternative explanation exists for the results. Did the therapy work, or was Dr. Yuki biased? It can also threaten the construct validity of the dependent variable, because it means the depression ratings given by Dr. Yuki do not represent the true levels of depression of her participants.

For more on observer bias, see Chapter 6, p. 172.

Demand Characteristics

Demand characteristics are a problem when participants guess what the study is supposed to be about and change their behavior in the expected direction. For example, Dr. Yuki's patients know they are getting therapy. If they think Dr. Yuki expects them to get better, they might change their self-reports of symptoms in the expected direction. Nikhil's campers, too, might realize something fishy is going on when they're not given their usual snacks. The campers' awareness of a change in their diet could certainly change the way they act.

For more on demand characteristics, see Chapter 10, p. 294.

Controlling for Observer Bias and Demand Characteristics. To avoid observer bias and demand characteristics, researchers must do more than add a comparison group to their studies. The most appropriate way to avoid such problems is to conduct a **double-blind study**, in which neither the participants nor the researchers who evaluate them know who is in the treatment group and who is in the comparison group.

Suppose Nikhil decides to test his hypothesis as a double-blind study. Nikhil could arrange to have two cabins of equally rambunctious campers and for only one group of them, replace their sugary snacks with low-sugar versions. The boys would not know which kind of snacks they were eating, and the people observing their behavior would also be blind to which boys were in which group.

When a double-blind study is not possible, a variation might be an acceptable alternative. In some studies, participants know which group they are in, but the observers do not; this is called a **masked design**, or *blind design* (see Chapter 6). The students exposed to the Go Green campaign would certainly be aware that someone was trying to influence their behavior. Ideally, however, the raters who were recording their electrical energy usage should not know which dorm was exposed to the campaign and which was not. Of course, keeping observers blind to condition is even more important when they are rating behaviors that are more difficult to code, such as symptoms of depression or behavior problems at camp.

Recall the Chapter 10 study by Elliot et al. (2007) in which the color red affected performance on tests. The research assistants in that study were blind to the ink colors each participant received, presumably so they could not subtly influence the participants' behavior. The participants themselves were not blind to the color of their materials (in fact, seeing the color was central to the researcher's manipulation). But since the test-takers participated in only one condition, they were not aware that color was an important feature of the experiment. Therefore, they were blind to the *reason* their numbers were written in a particular color.

Placebo Effects

The women who received Dr. Yuki's psychotherapy may have improved because her style of cognitive therapy really works. An alternative explanation is that there was a placebo effect: The women improved simply because they *believed* that they were receiving an effective treatment.

A **placebo effect** occurs when people receive a treatment and really improve—but only because the recipients believe they are receiving a valid treatment. In most studies on the effectiveness of medications, for example, one group receives a pill or an injection with the real drug, while another group receives a pill or an injection with no active ingredients—a sugar pill or a saline solution. People can even receive placebo psychotherapy, in which they simply talk to a friendly listener

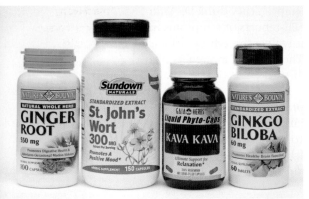

FIGURE 11.8 **Are herbal remedies placebos?** It is possible that perceived improvements in mood, joint pain, or wellness promised by herbal supplements are simply due to the belief that they will work, not because of the specific ingredients they contain.

about their problems; these placebo conversations have no therapeutic structure. The inert pill, injection, or therapy is the placebo. Often people who receive the placebo see their symptoms improve, because they believe the treatment they are receiving is supposed to be effective. In fact, the placebo effect can occur whenever any kind of treatment is used to control symptoms, such as an herbal remedy for improved wellness (**Figure 11.8**).

Placebo effects are not imaginary. Placebos have been shown to reduce real symptoms, such as depression (Kirsch & Sapirstein, 1998); post-operative pain or anxiety (Benedetti, Amanzio, Vighetti, & Asteggiano, 2006); terminal cancer pain; and epilepsy (Beecher, 1955). Placebo effects are not only psychological; they can also be physical. Nor are they always beneficial or harmless; physical side effects, including skin rashes and headaches, can be caused by placebos, too. People's symptoms appear to respond not just to the active ingredients in medications or to psychotherapy, but also to their belief in what the treatment can do to improve their situation.

A placebo can be strong medicine. Kirsch and Sapirstein (1998) reviewed studies that gave either antidepressant medication, such as Prozac, or a placebo to depressed patients, and concluded that the placebo groups improved almost as much as groups that received real medicine. In fact, up to 75% of the depression improvement in the Prozac groups was also achieved in placebo groups.

Designing Studies to Rule Out the Placebo Effect. To determine whether an effect is caused by a therapeutic treatment or by placebo effects, the standard approach is to include a special kind of comparison group. As usual, one group receives the real drug or real therapy, and the second group receives the placebo drug or placebo therapy. Crucially, however, neither the people treating the patients nor the patients themselves know whether they are in the real group or the placebo group. This experimental design is called a **double-blind placebo control study**.

The results of such a study might look like the graph in **Figure 11.9**. Notice that both groups improved, but the group receiving the real drug improved even more, showing placebo effects *plus* the effects of the real drug. If the results turn out like this, the researchers can conclude that the treatment they are testing does cause

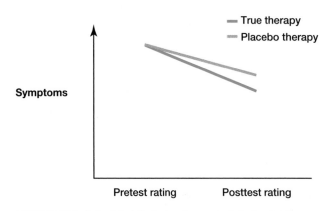

FIGURE 11.9 **A double-blind placebo control study.** Adding a placebo comparison group can help researchers subtract out a potential placebo effect from the true effect of a particular therapy.

improvement above and beyond a place-bo effect. Once again, an internal validity threat—a placebo effect—can be accounted for with a careful research design.

Is That Really a Placebo Effect? If you thought about it carefully, you probably noticed that the results in Figure 11.9 do not definitively show a placebo effect pattern. Both the group receiving the real drug and the group receiving the placebo improved over time. However, some of the improvement in both groups could have been caused by maturation, history, regression, testing, or instrumentation threats (Kienle & Kiene, 1997). If you were interested in showing a placebo effect specifically, you would have to include a no-treatment comparison group—one that receives neither drug nor placebo. Suppose your results looked something like those in **Figure 11.10**. Because the placebo group improved over time, even more than the no-therapy/no-placebo group, you can attribute the improvement to placebo and not just to maturation, history, regression, testing, or instrumentation.

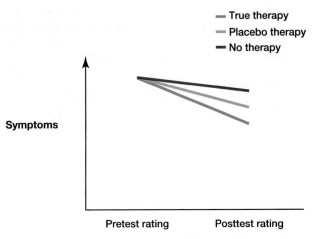

FIGURE 11.10 Identifying a placebo effect. To definitively show a placebo effect requires three groups: one receiving the true treatment, one receiving the placebo treatment, and one receiving no treatment. If there is a placebo effect, the pattern of results will show that the no-treatment group does not improve as much as the placebo group.

With So Many Threats, Are Experiments Still Useful?

After reading about a dozen ways a good experiment can go wrong, you might be tempted to assume that most experiments you read about are faulty. However, responsible researchers consciously avoid internal validity threats when they design and interpret their work. Many of the threats discussed in this chapter are a problem only in one-group pretest/posttest studies—those with no comparison group. A carefully designed comparison group will correct for many, but not all, of these threats. Researchers also use reliable coding procedures, double-blind designs, placebo conditions, and control variables to ensure the internal validity of their experiments.

Table 11.1 summarizes the internal validity threats in this chapter, and suggests ways to find out if a particular study is vulnerable.

CHECK YOUR UNDERSTANDING

1. What is a one-group, pretest/posttest design, and which threats to internal validity are especially applicable to this design?
2. Using Table 11.1 as a guide, indicate which of the internal validity threats would be relevant even to a two-group, posttest-only design.

1. See pp. 309–318. 2. See pp. 322–323.

TABLE 11.1 A Dozen Possible Internal Validity Threats in Experiments

Name	Definition	Example	Questions to ask
Design confound	A second variable that unintentionally varies systematically with the independent variable.	*From Chapter 10*: If pasta served in a large bowl appeared more appetizing than pasta served in a medium bowl.	Did the researchers turn nuisance variables into control variables, for example, keeping the pasta recipe constant?
Selection effect	In an independent-groups design, when the two independent variable groups have systematically different kinds of participants in them.	*From Chapter 10*: In the autism study, some parents insisted they wanted their children to be in the intensive treatment group rather than the control group.	Did the researchers use random assignment or matched groups to equalize groups?
Order effect	In a within-groups design, when the effect of the independent variable is confounded with carryover from one level to the other, or with practice, fatigue, or boredom.	*From Chapter 10*: All participants in a bonding study play with their own toddler, followed by a different toddler.	Did the researchers counterbalance the orders of presentation?
Maturation	An experimental group improves over time only because of natural development or spontaneous improvement.	Rambunctious boys settle down as they get used to the camp setting.	Did the researchers use a comparison group of boys who had an equal amount of time to mature but who did not receive the treatment?
History	An experimental group changes over time because of an external factor or event that affects all or most members of the group.	Dormitory residents use less air conditioning in November than September because the weather is cooler.	Did the researchers include a comparison group that had an equal exposure to the external event but did not receive the treatment?
Regression to the mean	An experimental group whose average is extremely low (or high) at pretest will get better (or worse) over time, because the random events that caused the extreme pretest scores do not recur the same way at posttest.	A group's average is extremely depressed at pretest, in part because some of the people volunteered for therapy when they were feeling much more depressed than usual.	Did the researchers include a comparison group that was equally extreme at pretest but did not receive the therapy?
Attrition	An experimental group changes over time, but only because the most extreme cases have systematically dropped out and their scores are not included in the posttest.	Because the most rambunctious boy in the cabin leaves camp early, his disruptive behavior affects the pretest mean but not the posttest mean.	Did the researchers compute the pretest and posttest scores with only the final sample included, removing any dropouts' data from the pretest group average?

Name	Definition	Example	Questions to ask
Testing	A type of order effect: An experimental group changes over time because repeated testing has affected the participants. Subtypes include fatigue effects and practice effects.	A classroom's math scores improve only because the students take the same version of the test both times and therefore are more practiced at posttest.	Did the researchers have a comparison group take the same two tests? Did they use a posttest-only design, or did they use alternative forms of the measure for the pretest and posttest?
Instrumentation	An experimental group changes over time, but only because repeated measurements have changed the quality of the measurement instrument.	Coders get more lenient over time, so the same exact behavior is coded as less rambunctious at posttest than at pretest.	Did the researchers train coders to use the same standards when coding? Are pretest and posttest measures demonstrably equivalent?
Observer bias	An experimental group's ratings differ from a comparison group's, but only because the researcher expects the groups' ratings to differ.	The researcher expects a low-sugar diet to decrease the campers' unruly behavior, so he notices only their calm behavior and ignores the wild behavior.	Were the observers of the dependent variable unaware of which condition participants were in? (A comparison group does not automatically get rid of the problem of observer bias.)
Demand characteristic	Participants guess what the study's purpose is and change their behavior in the expected direction.	Campers guess that the low-sugar diet is supposed to make them calmer, so they change their behavior accordingly.	Were the participants kept unaware of the purpose of the study? Was it an independent-groups design, which makes participants less able to guess the study's purpose?
Placebo effect	Participants in an experimental group improve only because they believe in the efficacy of the therapy or drug they receive.	Women receiving cognitive therapy improve simply because they believe the therapy will work for them.	Did a comparison group receive a placebo (inert) drug or a placebo therapy?

Interrogating Null Effects: What If the Independent Variable Does Not Make a Difference?

So far, this chapter has discussed cases in which a researcher works to ensure that any covariance found in an experiment was caused by the independent variable, not by a threat to internal validity. What happens when a study finds a **null effect** (also called a *null result*)? What if the independent variable did not make a difference in the dependent variable; there is no significant covariance between the two?

You might not read about null effects very often. Journals, newspapers, and websites are much more likely to report the results of a study in which the independent variable does have an effect. However, studies that show null effects are surprisingly common—something many students learn when they start to conduct their own studies. Often, researchers who get a null result will say their study "didn't work." Why might null effects happen?

The following three hypothetical examples illustrate null effects:

Many people believe that having more money will make them happy. But will it? One researcher, Dr. Williams, designed an experiment in which he randomly assigned people to three groups. He gave one group nothing, gave the second group a little money, and gave the third group a lot of money. The next day, he asked each group to report their happiness on a mood scale. The group who received cash (either a little or a lot) was not significantly happier, or in a better mood, than the group who received nothing.

Do GRE test preparation courses really work? An educational psychologist recruited a sample of students, all of whom wanted to raise their GRE scores. She randomly assigned the students to two groups. One group received a one-day version of a GRE test-preparation course, and one group received a "pep talk" control session, in which the same instructor gave students a pep talk and encouragement but no actual instruction on how to improve their scores. Afterward, students took a real GRE test. The GRE prep course group's scores were a little higher than those of the pep talk group, but the difference was not statistically significant.

Researchers have hypothesized that feeling anxious can cause people to reason less carefully and logically. To test this hypothesis, a group of researchers placed people in three groups: low, medium, and high anxiety. After a few minutes of being exposed to the anxiety manipulation, the researchers gave each participant reasoning problems, which required logic, rather than emotional reasoning, to solve. Although the researchers had predicted that the anxious people would do better on the problems, participants in the three groups scored roughly the same.

These three examples of null effects, shown as graphs in **Figure 11.11**, are all posttest-only designs. However, a null effect can happen in a within-groups design or a pretest/posttest design, too (indeed, even in a correlational study). In all three of these cases, the independent variable manipulated by the experimenters did not result in a change in the dependent variable. Why didn't these experiments show covariance between the independent and dependent variables?

Any time an experiment gives a null result, it might simply be the case that the independent variable really does not affect the dependent variable. In the real

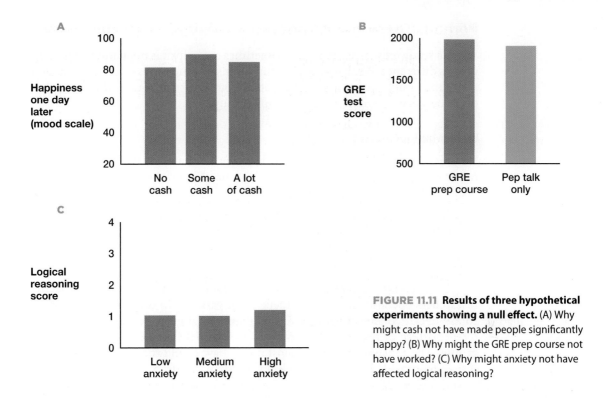

FIGURE 11.11 Results of three hypothetical experiments showing a null effect. (A) Why might cash not have made people significantly happy? (B) Why might the GRE prep course not have worked? (C) Why might anxiety not have affected logical reasoning?

world, perhaps money does not make people happier, GRE prep courses do not work, and being anxious does not affect logical reasoning. In other words, the experiment gave an accurate result, showing that the manipulation the researchers used did not cause a change in the dependent variable.

However, another possible reason for a null effect outcome is that the study was not designed or conducted carefully enough. The independent variable actually does cause a change in the dependent variable, but some obscuring factor in the study prevented the researchers from detecting the true difference. Such obscuring factors can take two general forms: There might not have been enough between-groups difference; there might have been too much within-groups variability.

To illustrate these two types of problems, suppose you prepared two bowls of salsa: one containing three shakes of hot sauce and the other containing four shakes of hot sauce. People might not taste any difference between the two bowls. One reason is that four shakes is not different enough from three; there's not enough between-groups difference. A second reason is that each bowl contains many other ingredients (tomatoes, onions, jalapenõs, cilantro, lime juice), so it's hard to detect any change in hot sauce intensity, with all those other flavors getting in the way. This is a problem of too much within-groups variability. Now let's see how this analogy plays out in psychological research.

Perhaps There Is Not Enough Between-Groups Difference

When a study returns a null result, sometimes the culprit is not enough between-groups difference. Weak manipulations, insensitive measures, and reverse design confounds might prevent an experiment from detecting a true difference that exists between two or more experimental groups.

Weak Manipulations

Why did Dr. Williams's study show that money did not affect people's mood? You might ask how much money he gave each group. What if the amounts were $0.00, $0.25, and $1.00? In that case, it would be no surprise that the manipulation didn't work; a dollar is not enough money to affect most people's mood. Like the difference between three shakes and four shakes of hot sauce, it's not enough of an increase to matter. Similarly, perhaps the one-day GRE preparation course was not sufficient to cause any change in GRE scores. Both of these would be examples of weak manipulations, which can obscure a true causal relationship.

When you interrogate a null result, it is therefore important to ask how the researchers operationalized the independent variable. In other words, you have to ask about construct validity. Dr. Williams might have obtained a very different pattern of results if he had given $0.00, $5.00, and $150.00 to the three groups. The educational psychologist might have found that GRE courses work if they are provided daily for 3 weeks rather than for just a day.

Insensitive Measures

Sometimes a study finds a null result because the researchers have not used an operationalization of the dependent variable with enough sensitivity. It would be like asking a friend who hates spicy food to taste your two bowls of salsa; he'd simply call both of them "way too spicy." If a medication reduces fever by a tenth of a degree, you wouldn't be able to detect it with a thermometer that was calibrated in one-degree increments; it wouldn't be sensitive enough. Similarly, if a GRE course improves people's test scores by about 15 points, you would not be able to detect the improvement with a simple pass/fail test (either passing the test or failing it, nothing in between). When it comes to dependent measures, it is smart to use ones that have detailed, quantitative increments—not just two or three levels.

For more on scales of measurement, see Chapter 5, pp. 126–128.

Ceiling and Floor Effects

As special cases of weak manipulations and insensitive measures, these effects cause independent variable groups to score almost the same on the dependent variable. In a **ceiling effect**, all the scores are squeezed together at the high end. In a **floor effect**, all the scores cluster at the low end.

Ceilings, Floors, and Independent Variables. Ceiling and floor effects can be the result of a problematic independent variable. For example, if Dr. Williams really did manipulate his independent variable by giving people $0.00, $0.25, or

$1.00, that would be a floor effect, because these three amounts are all low—that is, they are squeezed close to a floor of $0.00.

Consider the example of the anxiety and reasoning study. Suppose the researcher manipulated anxiety by telling the groups that they were about to receive an electric shock. The low-anxiety group was told to expect a 10-volt shock, the medium-anxiety group was told to expect a 50-volt shock, and the high-anxiety group was told to expect a 100-volt shock. This manipulation would probably result in a ceiling effect, because expecting any amount of shock would cause anxiety, regardless of the shock's intensity. As a result, the various levels of the independent variable would appear to make no difference.

Ceilings, Floors, and Dependent Variables. Poorly designed dependent variables can also lead to ceiling and floor effects. Imagine if the logical reasoning test in the anxiety study was so difficult that nobody could solve the four problems. That would cause a floor effect: The three anxiety groups would score the same, but only because the measure for the dependent variable results in low scores in all groups. Similarly, your friend has a floor effect on salsa; he rejects both versions.

> Ceiling and floor effects are examples of restriction of range; see Chapter 8, pp. 218–220.

In the money and mood study, Dr. Williams asked participants to rate their happiness on the following scale:

1 = I feel horrible.
2 = I feel awful.
3 = I feel bad.
4 = I feel fine.

Because there is only one option on this measure to indicate feeling good (and people generally tend to feel good, rather than bad), the majority would report the maximum, 4. Money would appear to have no effect on their mood, but only because the dependent measure of happiness used was subject to a ceiling effect.

Here's an even better example of a ceiling effect. Suppose you want to try to show that women and men are equally good at mathematics by asking participants in a sample to solve the problem $7 \times 5 = ?$. Almost everyone would answer this question correctly. Could you then conclude that men and women are equally good at math? Again, this measure would result in a ceiling effect, because everybody would get a perfect score; there would be no room for between-group variability on this measure (**Figure 11.12**).

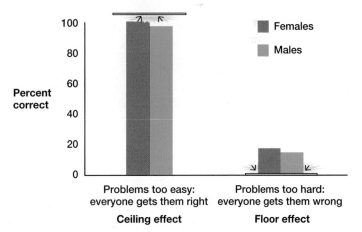

FIGURE 11.12 Ceiling and floor effects. A ceiling or floor effect on the dependent variable can obscure a true difference between groups. If problems on a test are all too easy, everyone will get a perfect score. If the problems are too difficult, everyone will score low.

When you interrogate a study with a null effect, it is important to ask how the independent and dependent variables were operationalized. Was the independent variable manipulation strong enough to cause a difference between groups? And was the dependent variable measure sensitive enough to detect that difference?

Recall from Chapter 10 that a **manipulation check** is a separate dependent variable that experimenters include in a study, just to make sure the manipulation worked. For example, in the anxiety study, after telling people they were going to receive a 10-volt, 50-volt, or 100-volt shock, the researchers might have asked: How anxious are you right now, on a scale of 1 to 10? If the manipulation check showed that participants in all three groups felt nearly the same level of anxiety (**Figure 11.13A**), you would know the researchers did not effectively manipulate what they intended to manipulate. If the manipulation check showed that the independent variable levels differed in an expected way—that the participants in the high-anxiety group really felt more anxious than those in the other two groups (**Figure 11.13B**)—then you would know the researchers did effectively manipulate anxiety, the independent variable. If the manipulation check worked, researchers would have to look for another reason for the null effect of anxiety on logical reasoning. Perhaps the dependent measure has a floor effect; that is, the logical reasoning test might be too difficult, so everyone scores low (see Figure 11.12). Or perhaps there really is no effect of anxiety on logical reasoning.

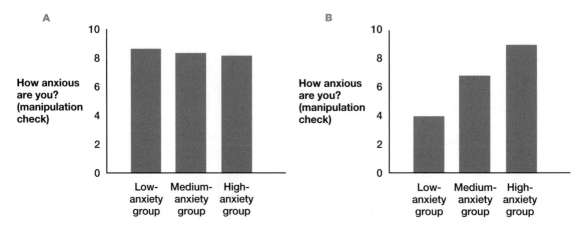

FIGURE 11.13 Possible results of a manipulation check. (A) These results suggest that the anxiety manipulation did not work, because people at all three levels of the independent variable reported being equally anxious. (B) These results suggest that the anxiety manipulation did work, because the anxiety of people in the three independent variable groups did vary in the expected way.

Design Confounds Acting in Reverse

Most of the time, confounds are considered to be internal validity threats—alternative explanations for some observed difference in a study. However, they can apply to null effects, too. A study might be designed in such a way that a design confound actually counteracts some true effect of an independent variable.

In the GRE study, for example, maybe the group assigned to take the test-preparation course was also put under extra pressure to do well, whereas the comparison group did not take a test-prep course and was not exposed to the extra pressure. In this case, the extra pressure applied to the test-prep group was a design confound that might have worked against any real effect of the course. Perhaps the students who received the most money in Dr. Williams's study happened to be given the money by a grim and grumpy experimenter, while those who received the least money were exposed to a more cheerful person; this confound would have worked against any true effect of money on mood.

Perhaps Within-Groups Variability Obscured the Group Differences

Another reason a study might return a null effect is that there is too much unsystematic variability within each group. This is referred to as **noise** (also known as *error variance* or *unsystematic variance*). In the salsa example, noise would be the great number of the other flavors in the two bowls. Noisy within-group variability can get in the way of detecting a true difference between groups.

Consider the sets of scores in **Figure 11.14**. Both sides of the figure depict the same data, but in two graphing formats. In each case, the difference *between* the two group averages is the same. However, the variability *within* each group is much larger in Figure 11.14A than in Figure 11.14B. You can see that when there is more variability within groups, it obscures the differences between the groups, because more overlap exists between the members of the two groups. It's a statistical validity problem: The greater the overlap, the smaller the effect size, and the less likely the two group means will be statistically significant; that is, the less likely the study will detect covariance.

When the data show less variability within the groups (see Figure 11.14B), the larger the effect size will be, and the more likely the mean difference will be statistically significant. The less within-group variability, the less likely it is to obscure a true group difference. If the two bowls of salsa contained only tomatoes, the difference between three and four shakes of hot sauce would be more easily detectable, because there would be fewer competing, "noisy" flavors within bowls.

In sum, the more unsystematic variability there is within each group, the more the scores in the two groups overlap with each other. The greater the overlap, the less apparent the average difference. As described next, most researchers prefer to keep within-group variability to a minimum, so they can more easily detect between-group differences. They keep in mind a few common culprits: measurement error, individual differences, and situation noise.

For more on statistical significance, see Chapter 10, p. 300; and Statistics Review: Inferential Statistics.

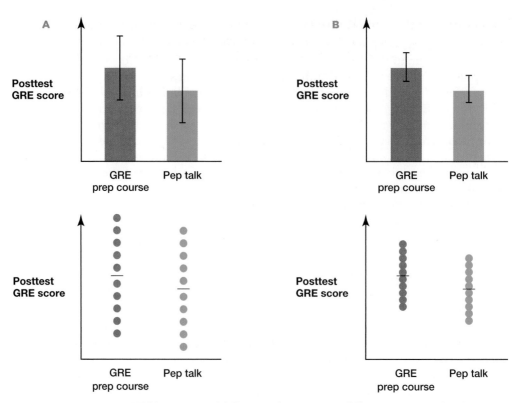

FIGURE 11.14 Within-group variability can obscure group differences. Notice that the group averages are the same in both versions, but the variability within each group is greater in part A than in part B. Part B is the situation researchers prefer, because it enables them to better detect true differences in the independent variable.

Measurement Error

One reason for high within-group variability is **measurement error**, any factor that can inflate or deflate a person's true score on a dependent measure. For example, a man who is 160 centimeters tall might be measured at 161 cm because of the angle of vision of the person reading the meter stick, or he might be measured at 159 cm because he slouched a bit during measurement.

All dependent measures involve a certain amount of measurement error, and researchers try to keep those errors as small as possible. For example, the GRE test used as a dependent variable in the educational psychologist's study is not perfect. Indeed, a group's score on the GRE represents the group's "true" GRE potential—that is, the actual level of the construct to measure in a group—plus or minus some random measurement error. Maybe one student's batch of GRE problems happened to be more difficult than average. Perhaps another student just happened to study the vocabulary words right before the test, but the rest of the students did not. Maybe one student was especially drowsy during the test, and another was especially alert. When these distortions of measurement are random, they cancel each other out across a sample of people and will not affect the group's average, or mean. Nevertheless, an operationalization with a lot of measurement error will result in a set of scores that are more spread out around the group mean (see Figure 11.14A).

A person's score on the GRE measure can be represented with the following formula:

student's GRE score =
        student's true GRE ability +/− random error of measurement

Or, more generally:

dependent variable score =
        participant's true score +/− random error of measurement

The more sources of random error there are in a dependent variable's measurement, the more variability there will be within each group in an experiment (see Figure 11.14A). In contrast, the more precisely and carefully a dependent variable is measured, the less variability there will be within each group (see Figure 11.14B). And lower within-groups variability is better, making it easier to detect a difference between independent variable groups.

Solution 1: Use Reliable, Precise Measurements. When researchers use measurement tools that have excellent reliability (internal, interrater, and test-retest), they can reduce errors in measurement (see Chapter 5). When measurement tools also have good construct validity, there will be less error in measurement as well. More precise and accurate measurements will have less measurement error.

Solution 2: Measure More Instances. A precise, reliable measurement tool is sometimes impossible to find. What then? In this case, the best alternative is to measure a larger sample (e.g., more people, more animals, more books). In other words, one solution to measuring badly is to take more measurements. When a measurement tool potentially causes a great deal of random error, the researcher can cancel out many errors simply by including more people in the sample.

Is one person's score of 10 points too high because of a random measurement error? If so, it's not a problem, as long another participant's score is 10 points too low because of a random measurement error. The more participants there are, the better the chances of having a full representation of all the possible measurement errors. The errors cancel each other out, and the result is a better estimate of the "true" average for that group. The reverse applies as well: When a measurement tool is known to have very little measurement error, the researcher can get away with having fewer participants in the study.

Individual Differences

Individual differences are another source of within-group variability. They can be a problem in independent-groups designs. In Dr. Williams's experiment on money and mood, for example, the normal mood of the participants must have varied.

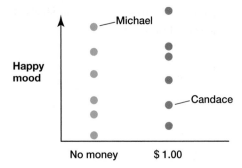
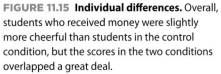

FIGURE 11.15 **Individual differences.** Overall, students who received money were slightly more cheerful than students in the control condition, but the scores in the two conditions overlapped a great deal.

Some people are more cheerful, others more churlish; such individual differences have the effect of spreading out the scores of the people within each group, as shown in **Figure 11.15**. In the $1.00 condition, you might have Candace, who is typically unhappy. The gift of $1.00 might have made her happier, but her mood would still be relatively low because of her normal level of grumpiness. Michael, a cheerful guy, was in the no-money control condition, but he still scored high on the mood measure. Looking over the data, you'll notice that, on average, the participants in the experimental condition did score a little higher than those in the control condition. But the data are mixed and far from consistent; a lot of overlap exists between the scores in the money group and the control group. Because of this overlap caused by individual differences, the effect of a gift of money might not reach statistical significance; individual differences in overall mood would obscure it. The effect of the money gift would be small in comparison to the variability within each group.

Solution 1: Change the Design. One way to accommodate individual differences is to use a within-groups design instead of an independent-groups design. In **Figure 11.16**, each pair of points, connected by a line, represents a single person whose mood was measured under both conditions. Therefore, the top pair of points represents Michael's mood both after a cash gift and after no gift. Another pair of points represents Candace's mood both after a cash gift and after no gift. Do you see what happens? The individual data points are exactly where they were in Figure 11.15, but the pairing process has turned a scrambled set of data into a clear and very consistent finding: Every participant was happier after receiving a cash gift than after no gift. This included Michael, who is always cheerful, and Candace, who is usually grumpy, as well as others in between.

A within-groups design like this, which compares each participant with himself or herself, controls for individual differences. Finally, notice that the study required only half as many participants as the original independent-groups experiment. You can see again the two strengths of within-groups designs (introduced in Chapter 10): They control for individual differences, and they require fewer participants than independent-groups comparisons.

Experimenters can achieve a similar effect with a matched-groups design. Before introducing the independent variable, Dr. Williams might measure the participants' usual daily mood. Then he might match the two most cheerful people and the two least cheerful people. The graphed results would

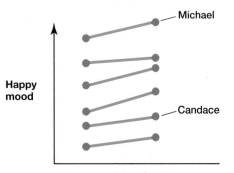

FIGURE 11.16 **Within-groups designs control for individual differences.** When each person participates in both levels of the independent variable, the individual differences are controlled for, and it is easier to see the effect of the independent variable.

look similar to Figure 11.16, but now the lines would connect matched pairs, as shown in **Figure 11.17**. Dr. Williams could then see the same reduction in individual difference variability as in the within-groups design.

Solution 2: Add More Participants. If within-groups or matched-pairs designs are inappropriate (and sometimes they are, because of order effects, demand characteristics, or practicality), another solution to individual difference variability is to measure more people. The principle is the same as it is for measurement error: When a great deal of variability exists because of individual differences, one simple thing to do is to measure a lot of people: The more people you measure, the less impact any one, extreme person will have on the group's average. Adding more participants to a study reduces the impact of individual differences *within* groups and will increase a study's ability to detect differences *between* groups.

The reason is mathematical. The number of people in a sample goes in the denominator of the statistical formula for a *t* test—used for detecting a difference between two means. As you will learn in your statistics class, the formula for the usual *t* test is:

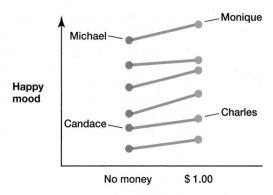

FIGURE 11.17 **Graphing the results of a matched-pairs design.** When pairs are matched on some individual difference variable (such as baseline happiness), it is easier to see the effect of the independent variable.

$$\dfrac{\text{mean difference}}{\left(\dfrac{\text{standard deviation}}{\sqrt{n}}\right)}$$

The larger *n* (the number of participants) is, the smaller the denominator of *t*. And the smaller that denominator is, the larger *t* can get, and the easier it is to find a significant *t*. A significant *t* means you do not have a null result.

For more on *t* tests, see Statistics Review: Inferential Statistics, pp. 475–479.

Situation Noise

Besides measurement error and individual differences, **situation noise**—external distractions of any kind—is a third factor that could cause variability within groups and obscure true group differences. Imagine if Dr. Williams had conducted his study on money and happiness in the middle of the student union on campus. The sheer number of distractions in this setting would make a mess of the data. The smell of the nearby coffee shop might make some participants feel peaceful, seeing friends at the next table might make some feel extra happy, and seeing the cute guy from sociology class might make some feel nervous or self-conscious. The kind and amount of distractions in the student union would vary from participant to participant and from moment to moment. The result, once again, would be variability within each group.

Situation noise, therefore, can add unsystematic variability to each group in an experiment. Unsystematic variability, like that caused by random measurement error or individual differences, will obscure true differences between groups.

Researchers often attempt to minimize situation noise by carefully controlling the surroundings of an experiment. Dr. Williams might choose to distribute money and measure people's moods in a consistently undistracting laboratory room, far from coffee shops and classmates. Similarly, the researcher studying anxiety and logical reasoning might reduce situation noise by administering the logical reasoning test on a computer in a standardized classroom environment.

Sometimes the controls for situation noise have to be extreme. Consider one study on smell (cited in Mook, 2001), in which the researchers had to control *all* extraneous odors that might reach the participants' noses. The researchers dressed the participants in steam-cleaned plastic parkas fastened tightly under the chin to trap odors from their clothes, and placed them in a steam-cleaned plastic enclosure. A layer of Vaseline over the face trapped odors from the skin. Only then did the researchers introduce the odors being studied by means of tubes placed directly in the participants' nostrils.

Obviously, researchers do not usually go to such extremes. Dr. Williams would not have to put Vaseline on people's faces, or place them in a steam-cleaned environment, to adequately study the effect of money on happiness. However, researchers typically try to control the potential distractions that might affect the dependent variable. To control the situation so it doesn't induce unsystematic variability in mood (his dependent variable), Dr. Williams would not have a TV turned on in the lab. To control the situation to avoid unsystematic variability in her dependent variable, GRE performance, the educational psychologist would limit participants' exposure to outside study guides or motivational posters. The researchers in the anxiety and reasoning study would want to control any kind of unsystematic situational factor that might add variability to people's scores on the logical reasoning test.

Another Name for These Solutions: Power

When researchers use a within-groups design, employ a strong manipulation, carefully control the experimental situation, or add more participants to a study, they are increasing the power of their study. Recall from Chapter 10 that **power**, an aspect of statistical validity, is the likelihood that a study will return a statistically significant result when the independent variable really has an effect. If GRE prep courses really do make a difference, even a small one, will the study detect it? If anxiety really affects problem solving, will the study find a significant result? A within-groups design, a strong manipulation, a larger number of participants, and less situation noise are all things that will increase the power of an experiment.

When researchers design a study with a lot of power, they are more likely to detect true patterns—even small ones. Consider the analogy of looking for an object in a dark room. If you go into the room with a big, powerful flashlight, you're more likely to find what you're looking for—even if it's something small,

Studies with low power   can find only   large effects,
                                                    not small ones

Studies with lots of power   can find   even small
                                                   effect sizes

FIGURE 11.18 Studies with more power can detect small effects. Experimenters can increase a study's power by strengthening the "light source" (through large samples or accurate measurements), or by increasing the size of the effects (through strong manipulations). Thus, a study with low power might return a null result inconclusively. If a study has high power, you can be more confident it has detected any result worth finding.

like an earring. But if you go into the room with just a candle, you're likely to miss finding smaller objects. A study with a lot of participants or low situation noise is like having a strong flashlight; it can detect even small differences in GRE scores or happiness. Similarly, a study with a strong manipulation is like increasing the size of the object you're looking for; you'll be able to find a teddy bear in the room more easily than an earring—even if you have only a candle for light (**Figure 11.18**). Good experimenters try to maximize the power of their experimental designs by strengthening their "light source" or increasing the size of their effects.

For more on power, see Statistics Review: Inferential Statistics, pp. 471–474.

Perhaps There Really Is No Difference

When an experiment reveals that the independent variable conditions are not significantly different, what should you conclude? The study might be flawed in some way, so you might first ask whether it was designed to elicit and detect between-group differences. Was the manipulation strong? Was the dependent measure sensitive enough to detect group differences? Could either variable be limited to a ceiling or floor effect? Are any design confounds working against the independent variable?

You would also ask about the study's ability to minimize within-group differences. Was the dependent variable measured as precisely as possible, to minimize measurement error? Could individual differences be obscuring the effect of the independent variable? Did the study include enough participants to counteract the effects of measurement error and individual differences? Was the study conducted with appropriate situational controls? Any of these factors, if problematic, could explain why an experiment showed a null effect. **Table 11.2** summarizes the possible reasons for a null result in an experiment.

If, after interrogating these possible obscuring factors, you find that the experiment was conducted in ways that maximized its power and yet still found a nonsignificant result, you might well conclude the independent variable truly does not affect the dependent variable. A study with a strong independent variable manipulation, a sensitive and precise dependent variable measure, careful situational controls, and a large number of participants might still return a null result. The interpretation in that case is that the independent variable in question simply does not affect the dependent variable. Perhaps money really does not buy happiness. Perhaps a GRE prep course does not help students score higher. Or perhaps anxiety really does not affect logical reasoning. In other words, if you read about a study that used a really strong flashlight, and yet still didn't find anything—that's a sign there's probably no effect to be found.

Null Effects Can Be Hard to Find

When studies are conducted with adequate power, null results can be just as interesting and just as informative as experiments that show group differences. There are many examples of true null effects in psychological science. Some therapeutic drugs and certain types of therapy apparently do not work (such as facilitated communication therapy, discussed in Chapter 1). Some commonsense hypotheses do not hold true when examined by research studies; for example, after a certain level of income, money does not appear to cause happiness (Diener, Horwitz, & Emmons, 1985; Lyubomirsky, King, & Diener, 2005; Myers, 2000). And, despite stereotypes to the contrary, women and men apparently do not differ in how much they talk (Mehl, Vazire, Ramirez-Esparza, Slatcher, & Pennebaker, 2007).

TABLE 11.2 Reasons for a Null Result

Obscuring factor	Example	Questions to ask
Not enough variability between levels		
(e.g., not enough difference between three and four shakes of hot sauce)		
Ineffective manipulation of the independent variable	A one-day GRE prep course might not improve scores (compared with a control group), but a 3-week GRE course might improve scores.	How did the researchers manipulate the independent variable? Was the manipulation strong? Do manipulation checks suggest the manipulation did what it was intended to do?
Insufficiently sensitive measurement of the dependent variable	Researchers used a pass/fail measure, when the improvement was detectable only by using a finer-grained measurement scale.	How did the researchers measure the dependent variable? Was the measure sensitive enough to detect group differences?
Ceiling or floor effects on the independent variable	Researchers manipulated three levels of anxiety by threatening people with 10-volt, 50-volt, or 100-volt shocks (all of which make people very anxious).	Are there meaningful differences between the levels of the independent variable? Do manipulation checks suggest the manipulation did what it was intended to do?
Ceiling or floor effects on the dependent variable	Researchers measured logical reasoning ability with a very hard test (a floor effect on logical reasoning ability).	How did the researchers measure the dependent variable? Do participants cluster near the top or near the bottom of the distribution?
Too much variability within levels		
(e.g., too many competing ingredients in the salsa bowls)		
Measurement error	Logical reasoning test scores are affected by multiple sources of random error, such as item selection, participant's mood, fatigue, etc.	Is the dependent variable measured precisely and reliably? Does the measure have good construct validity? If measurements are imprecise, did the experiment include enough participants to counteract this obscuring effect?
Individual differences	GRE scores are affected by individual differences in motivation and ability.	Did the researchers use a within-groups design to better control for individual differences? If an independent-groups design is used, larger sample size can reduce the impact of individual differences.
Situation noise	The money and happiness study was run in a distracting location, which introduced several external influences on the participants' mood.	Did the researchers attempt to control any situational influences on the dependent variable? Did they run the study in a standardized setting?
It's also possible that …		
The independent variable, in truth, has no effect on the dependent variable		Did the researchers take precautions to maximize between-group variability and minimize within-group variability? In other words, does the study have adequate power? If so, and they still do not find a group difference, it is reasonable to conclude that the independent variable does not affect the dependent variable.

However, if you are looking for examples of studies that found null effects in the popular press, you won't find many. There is a bias, in both what gets published in scientific journals and which stories are picked up by magazines and newspapers. Most readers are more interested in independent variables that matter than in those that do not. You might be more likely to read that a vaccine puts children at risk for autism than to read that the same vaccine has no effect on autism risk. It's more interesting to learn that dark chocolate has health benefits rather than none, and that women and men differ on a particular trait, as opposed to being the same. Differences seem more interesting than null effects, so a publication bias exists that favors differences.

CHECK YOUR UNDERSTANDING

1. How can a study maximize variability between independent variable groups? (There are four ways.)

2. How can a study minimize variability within groups? (There are three ways.)

3. In your own words, describe how within-groups designs minimize unsystematic variability.

1. See pp. 326–329 and Table 11.2. 2. See pp. 329–335 and Table 11.2. 3. See pp. 332–333.

Summary

- Responsible experimenters may conduct double-blind studies, use computers to measure variables, or put people in contrived, controlled environments to eliminate internal validity threats and to increase a study's power to avoid a null effect.

Threats to Internal Validity: Did the Independent Variable Really Cause the Difference?

- When an experiment finds that an independent variable affected a dependent variable, you can interrogate the study for twelve possible internal validity threats.
- The first three threats to internal validity (from Chapter 10) are design confounds, selection effects, and order effects.
- Six threats to internal validity are especially relevant to the one-group, pretest/posttest design: maturation, history, regression, attrition, testing, and instrumentation threats. All of them can usually be ruled out if an experimenter conducts the study using a comparison group (either a posttest-only design or a pretest/posttest design).
- Three more internal validity threats could potentially apply to any experiment: observer bias, demand characteristics, and placebo effects.
- By asking appropriate questions about a study's design and results, you can decide whether it has ruled out all twelve threats. If the study passes all your internal validity que-

ries, you can conclude with confidence that the study was a strong one: You can trust the result and make a causal claim.

Interrogating Null Effects: What If the Independent Variable Does Not Make a Difference?

- If you encounter a study in which the independent variable had no effect on the dependent variable (a null effect), you can review the possible obscuring factors.
- Obscuring factors can be sorted into two categories of problems. One is the problem of not enough between-groups difference, which results from weak manipulations, insensitive measures, ceiling or floor effects, or a design confound acting in reverse.
- The second problem is too much within-groups variability, caused by measurement error, individual differences, or situation noise. These problems can be counteracted by using multiple measurements, within-groups designs, large samples, and very controlled experimental environments.
- If you can be reasonably sure a study avoided all the obscuring factors, then it probably did have adequate power to detect a true effect. Therefore, you can trust the result and conclude that the independent variable really does not cause a change in the dependent variable.

Key Terms

one-group, pretest/posttest design, p. 309
maturation threat, p. 310
history threat, p. 311
regression threat, p. 312
attrition threat, p. 315
testing threat, p. 316
instrumentation threat, p. 317
selection-history threat, p. 317

selection-attrition threat, p. 318
observer bias, p. 318
demand characteristic, p. 318
double-blind study, p. 319
masked design, p. 319
placebo effect, p. 319
double-blind placebo control study, p. 320

null effect, p. 323
ceiling effect, p. 326
floor effect, p. 326
manipulation check, p. 328
noise, p. 329
measurement error, p. 330
situation noise, p. 333
power, p. 334

To see samples of chapter concepts in the popular press, visit www.everydayresearchmethods.com and click the box for Chapter 11.

Review Questions

1. Dr. Weber conducted a long-term study on friendship. He noticed that the most introverted people dropped out by the third session. Therefore, his study might have which of the following internal validity threats?
   a. Attrition
   b. Maturation
   c. Selection
   d. Regression

2. How is a testing threat to internal validity different from an instrumentation threat?
   a. A testing threat can be prevented with random assignment; an instrumentation threat cannot.
   b. A testing threat applies only to within-groups designs; instrumentation threats are for any design.
   c. A testing threat can be prevented with a double-blind study; instrumentation threats can be prevented with a placebo control.
   d. A testing threat refers to a change in the participants over time; instrumentation threats refer to a change in the measuring instrument over time.

3. A regression threat applies especially:
   a. When there are two groups in the study: an experimental group and a control group.
   b. When the researcher recruits a sample whose average is extremely low or high at pretest.
   c. In a posttest-only design.
   d. When there is a small sample in the study.

4. Dr. Banks tests to see how many training sessions it takes for dogs to learn to "Sit and stay." She randomly assigns 60 dogs to two reward conditions: one in which the reward is miniature hot dogs, and one in which the reward is small pieces of steak. Surprisingly, she finds that the dogs in each group learn "Sit and stay" in about an equal amount of sessions. Given the design of her study, what is the *most likely* explanation for this null effect?
   a. The dogs loved both treats (her reward manipulation has a ceiling effect).
   b. She used too many dogs.
   c. She didn't use a manipulation check.
   d. There were too many individual differences among the dogs.

5. Dr. Banks modifies her design and conducts a second study. She used the same number of dogs and the same design, except now she rewarded one group of dogs with miniature hot dogs, and another group of dogs with pieces of apple. She found a big difference, with the mini-hot-dogs group learning the command faster. Dr. Banks avoided a null result this time, because she:
   a. Increased the between-groups variability.
   b. Decreased the within-groups variability.
   c. Improved the study's internal validity.

6. When a study has a large number of participants and a small amount of unsystematic variability (low measurement error, low levels of situation noise), then it has a lot of:
   a. Internal validity
   b. Manipulation checks
   c. Dependent variables
   d. Power

Learning Actively

The scenarios described in questions 1 and 2 contain threats to internal validity. For each scenario:

    a. Identify the independent variable (IV) and dependent variable (DV).

    b. Identify the design (posttest-only, pretest/posttest, within-groups, one-group pretest/posttest).

    c. Sketch a graph of the results. (Reminder: Put the dependent variable on the y-axis.)

    d. Decide whether the study is subject to any of the internal validity threats listed in Table 11.1.

    e. Indicate whether you could redesign the study to correct or prevent any of the internal validity threats.

1. For his senior thesis, Jack was interested in whether viewing alcohol advertising would cause college students to drink more alcohol. He recruited 25 seniors for a week-long study. On Monday and Tuesday, he asked them to log in to a secure website and record how many alcoholic beverages they had consumed the day before. On Wednesday, he invited them to the laboratory, where he showed them a 30-minute TV show interspersed with entertaining advertisements for alcoholic products. Thursday and Friday were the follow-up measures: Students logged in to the secure website and recorded their alcoholic beverage consumption again. Jack found that students reported drinking more after seeing the alcohol advertising. He concluded that the advertising caused them to drink more.

2. In a cognitive psychology class, a group of student presenters wanted to demonstrate the power of retrieval cues. First, the student presenters asked the class to memorize a list of 20 words that they read in a random order. One minute later, members of the class wrote down as many words as they could remember. On average, the class recalled 6 words. Second, the student presenters told the class to try sorting the words into categories as the words were read (color words, vehicle words, and sports words). The student presenters read the words again, in a different random order. On the second test of recall, the class remembered, on average, 14 words. The student presenters told the class this experiment demonstrated that categorizing helps people remember words because they are able to develop rich connections to the words.

———

3. Dr. Dove was interested in the effects of chocolate on well-being. She randomly assigned 20 participants to two groups. Both groups ate as they normally would, but one group was instructed to eat 1-ounce square of dark chocolate after both lunch and dinner. After the participants spent 4 weeks on this diet, Dr. Dove asked each one to complete a questionnaire measuring well-being (happiness, contentment). However, Dr. Dove was surprised to find that the chocolate had no effect: Both groups, on average, scored the same on the well-being measure. Help Dr. Dove troubleshoot her study. What should she do next time to improve her chances of finding a significant effect for the chocolate-enhanced diet?

The Reason Why You're an Angry Drunk

(Men's Health, 2012)

Should Cell Phone Use by Drivers Be Illegal?

(New York Times, 2009)

12

Experiments with More Than One Independent Variable

So far, you have read two chapters about evaluating causal claims. Chapters 10 and 11 introduced experiments with one independent variable and one dependent variable. Now you are ready for experiments with more than one independent variable. Consider the headlines on the facing page. Both of them begin with one independent variable, but what happens when more independent variables are added to the mix?

Review: Experiments with One Independent Variable

Let's start with the alcohol headline: Is it true that people are angry drunks? According to research on the topic, there's almost no doubt that drunk people are more aggressive than sober people. In several studies, psychologists have brought people into comfortable laboratory settings, given them various

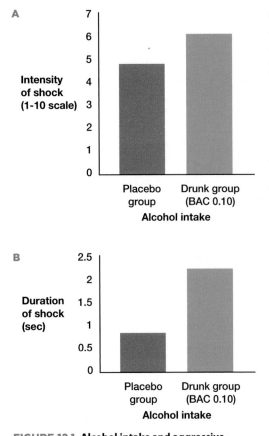

A

Intensity
of shock
(1-10 scale)

Placebo
group

Drunk group
(BAC 0.10)

Alcohol intake

B

Duration
of shock
(sec)

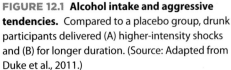

Placebo
group

Drunk group
(BAC 0.10)

Alcohol intake

FIGURE 12.1 Alcohol intake and aggressive tendencies. Compared to a placebo group, drunk participants delivered (A) higher-intensity shocks and (B) for longer duration. (Source: Adapted from Duke et al., 2011.)

To review counterbalancing, see Chapter 10, pp. 292–293.

amounts of alcohol to drink, and then placed them in a different setting to measure their aggressive tendencies. For example, a team of researchers led by Aaron Duke invited community members into their lab (Duke, Giancola, Morris, Holt, & Gunn, 2011). After screening out volunteers who had problem drinking behaviors, were pregnant, or had other risky conditions, they randomly assigned them to drink a glass of orange juice that contained different amounts of alcohol. The "active placebo" group drank orange juice with a very small amount of vodka—enough to smell and to taste, but not enough to make them drunk. Another group was assigned to drink enough vodka to reach a 0.10 blood alcohol concentration (BAC), which is legally drunk.

After confirming the two groups' intoxication levels with a breathalyzer test, the researchers had the volunteers play a computer game with an opponent who was supposedly in another room (the opponent was actually played by a computer programmed in advance). The players took turns, and when a player made a mistake, the opponent was allowed to deliver a shock as punishment. Players chose the intensity of the shock their opponents would receive for each mistake (on a scale of 1 to 10), and they could hold the shock delivery button down for different lengths of time. The researchers measured the intensity and duration of the shocks each participant delivered. The more intense the shocks and the longer their duration, the more aggressive the participants were said to be. Results showed a difference: drunk participants were more aggressive (**Figure 12.1**).

The second headline is about cell phone use while driving. The study the newspaper story cites found that using a cell phone while behind the wheel does seem to make a difference in the driver's ability to observe road safety. The evidence comes from experiments by David Strayer and his colleagues (Strayer & Drews, 2004), who asked people to talk on hands-free cell phones in a high-fidelity driving simulator (one that looked almost exactly like a real car). As the participants drove, the researchers recorded several dependent variables, including driving speed, braking time, and following distance. In a repeated-measures (within-groups) design, they had participants drive on several 10-mile segments of highway in the simulator. For two of the segments, the drivers carried on a conversation on a hands-free cell phone. For the other two segments, drivers were not on the phone (of course, their participation in the different segments was counterbalanced). The results showed that when drivers were talking on cell phones, their reactions to road hazards were 18% slower. Drivers on cell phones also took longer to regain their speed after slowing down and got into more (virtual) accidents (**Figure 12.2**).

The Strayer and Drews study, like Duke and his team's study, had one independent variable (cell phone use, manipulated as a within-groups variable) and one dependent variable (driving quality). Their study also showed a *difference*: People drove more poorly while using cell phones. Studies with one independent variable are able to show a difference between conditions. These two studies were analyzed with a simple difference score: Placebo minus drunk conditions, or cell phone minus control.

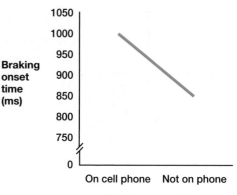

FIGURE 12.2 **Cell phone use and driver reaction time.** Drivers using hands-free cell phones were slower to hit the brakes in response to a road hazard (braking onset time in milliseconds). (Source: Adapted from Strayer & Drews, 2004.)

Experiments with Two Independent Variables Can Show Interactions

Strayer and Drews's study found that hands-free cell phones cause people to drive badly. These researchers also wondered whether that overall difference would apply in all situations and to all people. For example, might younger drivers be less distracted by using cell phones than older drivers? On the one hand, they might, because they grew up using cell phones and are more accustomed to them. On the other hand, older drivers might be less distracted, because they have more years of driving experience. If you're asking these questions, you are thinking about adding another independent variable to the original study: driver age, and the levels could be old and young. Specifically, you would be asking whether a driver's age will change the effect of driving while using a cell phone.

When you ask about the effect of an additional independent variable, you are usually wondering about the **interaction effect** (or *interaction*)—whether the effect of the original independent variable (cell phone use) *depends on* the level of another independent variable (driver age). Therefore, an interaction of two independent variables allows researchers to establish whether or not "it depends." They can now ask: Does the effect of cell phones depend on age?

The mathematical way to describe an interaction of two independent variables is to say that there is a "difference in differences." In the driving example, the *difference* between the cell phone and control conditions (cell phone minus control) might be *different* for older drivers than younger drivers.

$$\text{Interaction} = \frac{\text{a difference}}{\text{in differences}} = \begin{array}{l}\text{the effect of one independent}\\\text{variable depends on the level of}\\\text{the other independent variable}\end{array}$$

Intuitive Interactions

Behaviors, thoughts, motivations, and emotions are rarely simple; they usually involve interactions between two or more influences. Therefore, much of the most important research in psychology explores interactions among multiple independent variables. What's the best way to understand what an interaction means?

Here's one example of an interaction: Do you like hot foods or cold foods? Your preference probably depends on the food. You probably like your ice cream cold, but you like your pancakes hot. In this example, there are two independent variables: the food you are judging (ice cream or pancakes) and the temperature of the food (cold or hot). The dependent variable is how much you like the food. A graph of the interaction is shown in **Figure 12.3**. Notice that the lines cross each other; this kind of interaction is sometimes called a *crossover interaction*.

To describe this interaction, you could say that when people eat ice cream, they like their food cold more than hot; when people eat pancakes, they like their food hot more than cold. You could also apply the mathematical definition by saying that there is a *difference in differences*. You like ice cream cold more than you like it hot (cold minus hot is a positive value), but you like pancakes cold less than you like them hot (cold minus hot is a negative value).

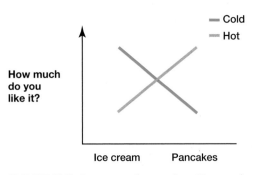

FIGURE 12.3 A crossover interaction. How much you like certain foods depends on the temperature at which they are served.

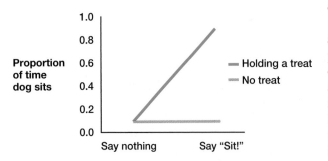

FIGURE 12.4 A spreading interaction. Whether or not my dog sits when I say "Sit" depends on whether or not I am holding a treat.

Here's another example: the behavior of my dog, Fig. Does he sit on command? It depends on whether I say "Sit," and on whether I have a treat in my hand. When I don't have a treat, Fig will not sit, even if I tell him to sit. But if I do have a treat, he will sit, but only when I say "Sit." (In other words, my stubborn dog has to be bribed.) In this example, the probability that my dog will sit is the dependent variable, and the two independent variables are what I say ("Sit" or nothing) and what I am holding (a treat or nothing). **Figure 12.4** shows a graph of this interaction. Notice that the lines are not parallel, and they do not cross over each other. This kind of interaction is sometimes called a *spreading interaction*.

This interaction could be described by saying that when I say nothing, my dog's probability of sitting is the same in both conditions: treat and no-treat. But when I say "Sit," his probability of sitting is higher in the treat than the no-treat condition. Here is the mathematical description of this interaction: When I say nothing, there is *zero* difference between the treat and no-treat conditions (treat minus no treat equals zero). When I say "Sit," there is a *large* difference between the treat and no-treat conditions (treat minus no treat equals a positive value). There is a difference in differences.

When there is an interaction, you can describe it accurately from either direction. Thus, it is equally accurate to make both of these statements: (1) When I am not holding a treat, there is zero difference between the "say Sit" and "say nothing" conditions, and (2) When I am holding a treat, there is a large difference between the "say Sit" and "say nothing" conditions.

You can also graph the interaction accurately either way—by putting the "What I say" independent variable on the x-axis, as shown in Figure 12.4, or by putting the "What I'm holding" independent variable on the x-axis, as shown in **Figure 12.5**. Although the two graphs may look a little different, each one is an accurate representation of the data.

When psychological scientists think about behavior, they might start with a simple link between an independent and a dependent variable, but often they find they need a second independent variable to tell the full story. For example, in a romantic relationship, are positive attitudes such as forgiveness healthy? (In other words, does the independent variable of positive attitudes versus negative attitudes affect the dependent variable, relationship health?) The answer depends on how severe the problems are in the relationship. When problems are minor, positive attitudes are healthy for the relationship, but when problems are severe (e.g., one partner is abusive to the other or abuses drugs), positive attitudes seem to prevent the couple from addressing the problems. Thus, the severity of the relationship's problems (minor versus severe) is the second independent variable (McNulty, 2010).

Does going to daycare hurt children's social and intellectual development? That might depend on the quality of care. When high-quality daycare is provided, children's social and intellectual development might improve (compared with that of children given only parental care); when the quality of daycare is poor, development might be impaired (Vandell, Henderson, & Wilson, 1988). Reflect for a moment: What would the dependent and independent variables be in this example?

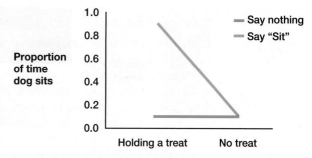

FIGURE 12.5 The same spreading interaction, graphed the other way. The data in Figure 12.4 can be graphed equally accurately with the other independent variable on the x-axis.

Factorial Designs Study Two Independent Variables

When researchers want to test for interactions, they do so with factorial designs. A **factorial design** is one in which there are two or more independent variables (also referred to as *factors*). In the most common factorial design, researchers *cross* the two independent variables; that is, they study *each possible combination* of the independent variables. Strayer and Drews, for example, created a factorial design to test whether the effect of driving while talking on a cell phone depended on the driver's age. They used two independent variables (cell phone use and driver

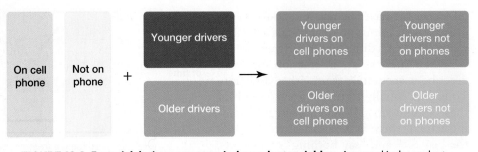

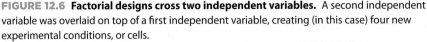

FIGURE 12.6 Factorial designs cross two independent variables. A second independent variable was overlaid on top of a first independent variable, creating (in this case) four new experimental conditions, or cells.

age), creating a condition representing each possible combination of the two. As shown in **Figure 12.6**, to cross the two independent variables, they essentially overlaid one independent variable on top of another. This overlay process created four unique conditions, or **cells**: older people driving while using cell phones, older people driving without using cell phones, younger people driving while using cell phones, and younger people driving without using cell phones.

Figure 12.6 shows the simplest possible factorial design. There are two independent variables (two factors)—cell phone use and age—and each one has two levels (driving while using a cell phone or not; older or younger driver). This particular design is called a 2 × 2 (two-by-two) factorial design, meaning that two levels of one independent variable are crossed with two levels of another independent variable. Since 2 × 2 = 4, there are four cells in this design.

Using Factorial Designs to Study Manipulated Variables or Participant Variables

You might have noticed that one of Strayer and Drews's variables, cell phone use, was truly manipulated; they had participants either talk or not talk on cell phones while driving. The other variable, age, was not manipulated; it was a measured variable. Strayer and Drews did not assign people to be older or younger; they simply selected participants who fit these levels. Age is an example of a **participant variable**—a variable whose levels are selected (i.e., measured), not manipulated. Because the levels are not manipulated, variables such as age, gender, and ethnicity are not truly "independent" variables. However, when they are studied in a factorial design, researchers often call them independent variables, for the sake of simplicity.

Factorial Designs Can Test Limits

One reason researchers conduct studies with factorial designs is to test whether an independent variable affects different kinds of people, or people in different situations, in the same way. Strayer and Drews's research on cell phone use while driving is a good example of this purpose. When they crossed age and cell phone use, they were asking whether the effect of using a cell phone was limited to one age group only, or whether it would have the same effect on people of different ages.

This research team conducted their study on a sample of 18- to 25-year-olds and a sample of 65- to 74-year-olds (Strayer & Drews, 2004). Each participant drove in the simulator for a warm-up period and then drove 10-mile stretches in simulated traffic four times. During two of the four segments, drivers carried on a conversation using a hands-free phone, chatting with a research assistant about their day (**Figure 12.7**). While the participants drove, the researchers collected data on a variety of dependent variables, including braking onset time (how long it takes, in milliseconds, for a driver to brake for an upcoming road hazard), accidents, and following distance. **Figure 12.8** shows the results for braking onset time. Notice that the same results are presented in two ways: as a table and as a graph.

The results might surprise you. In fact, the primary conclusion from this study is that the effect of talking on a cell phone did not depend on age.

FIGURE 12.7 A young driver using a hands-free cell phone while driving in a simulator.

Older drivers did tend to brake more slowly than younger ones, overall; that finding is consistent with past research on aging drivers. However, Strayer and Drews wanted to know whether the *difference* between the cell phone and control conditions would be *different* for older drivers. The answer was no. The effect of using a cell phone (i.e., the simple difference between the cell phone condition and the control condition) was about the same in both age groups. In other words, cell phone use *did not interact with* (did not *depend on*) age. At least for these two groups, the harmful effect of cell phone use was the same.

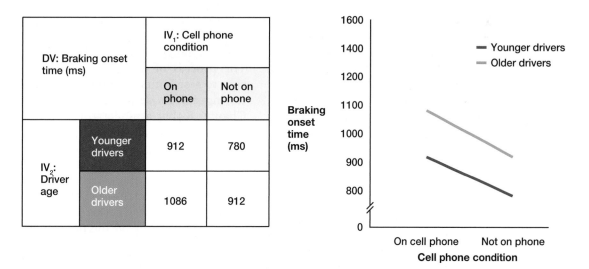

FIGURE 12.8 Factorial design results: table and graph formats. (Source: Adapted from Strayer & Drews, 2004.)

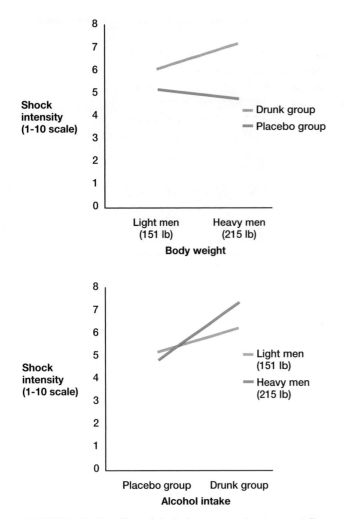

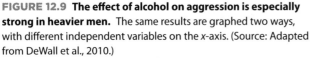

FIGURE 12.9 The effect of alcohol on aggression is especially strong in heavier men. The same results are graphed two ways, with different independent variables on the *x*-axis. (Source: Adapted from DeWall et al., 2010.)

A Form of External Validity

You might have recognized this goal of testing limits as being related to external validity. When researchers test an independent variable in more than one group at once, they are testing whether the effect generalizes. Sometimes, as in the example of age and cell phone use while driving, the independent variable affects the groups in the same way, suggesting that the effect of cell phone use generalizes to drivers of all ages.

In other cases, groups might respond differently to an independent variable. In one study, for instance, researchers tested whether the effect of alcohol on aggression depends on body weight (DeWall, Bushman, Giancola, & Webster, 2010). Using a procedure similiar to that of Duke et al. (2011), they randomly assigned men to a placebo group and a drunk group and then measured their aggression in the shock game. As shown in **Figure 12.9**, they found the effect of alcohol was especially strong for the heavier men. In other words, there may be some truth to the stereotype of the "big, drunk, aggressive guy."

Interactions Show Moderators

The process of using a factorial design to test limits is sometimes called testing for moderators. Recall from Chapter 8 that a moderator is a variable that changes the relationship between two other variables (Kenny, 2009). In factorial design language, a moderator is an independent variable that changes the relationship between another independent variable and a dependent variable. In other words, a moderator results in an interaction; the effect of one independent variable depends on (is moderated by) the level of another independent variable. When Strayer and Drews studied whether driver age would interact with cell phone use, they found that driver age did not moderate the impact of cell phone use on braking onset time. However, DeWall and his colleagues showed that body weight moderates the effect of alcohol on aggression.

To review how moderators work in correlational designs, see Chapter 8, pp. 227–230.

Factorial Designs Can Test Theories

Researchers can use factorial designs not only to test the generalizability of a causal variable but also to test theories. The goal of most experiments in psychological science is to test hypotheses derived from theories. Indeed, many theories make statements about how variables interact with one another. The best way to study how variables interact is to combine them in a factorial design and measure whether the results are consistent with the theory.

To review the theory-data cycle, see Chapter 1, pp. 9–13.

Using a Factorial Design to Test a Theory of Alcohol Cues

Once studies established that alcohol intake can lead to aggressive behavior, researchers wanted to dig deeper. They theorized about *why* alcohol causes aggression. One idea is that alcohol impairs the brain's executive functioning; it interferes with a person's ability to consider the consequences of his or her actions (Giancola, 2000). In addition to pharmacological effects, another theory suggests that through exposure to cultural messages and stereotypes about alcohol, people learn to cognitively associate alcohol with aggression. Merely *thinking* about alcohol might prime people to think about aggression. Researchers Bruce Bartholow and Adrienne Heinz (2006) sought to test the theory that alcohol can become cognitively associated with thoughts of aggression. They didn't get anybody drunk in their research; they simply exposed them to pictures of alcohol.

In the lab, participants viewed a series of images and words on a computer screen. Their task was to indicate whether a string of letters was a word or a nonword. For example, the letter string EDVIAN would be classified as a nonword, and the letter string INVADE would be classified as a word. Some of the words were aggression-related (e.g., *hit, combat,* or *fight*) and others were neutral (e.g., *sit, wonder,* or *caught*).

Before seeing each of the word strings, participants were shown a photograph on the computer screen for a brief period (300 ms). Sometimes, the photograph was related to alcohol, perhaps a beer bottle or a martini glass. Other times, the photograph was not related to alcohol; it was a photo of a plant. The researchers hypothesized that people would be faster to identify aggression-related words after seeing the photos of alcohol. They used the computer to measure how quickly people responded to the words.

As shown in **Figure 12.10**, Bartholow and Heinz were interested in the interaction of two independent variables: photo type (alcohol or plant) and word type (aggressive or neutral). The results told the story they expected: When people had just seen a photo of alcohol, they were quicker to identify an aggressive word. When people had just seen a photo of a plant, they were slower to identify an aggressive word (**Figure 12.11**).

This study is a good example of how a researcher can test a theory using a factorial design. The resulting interaction supported one reason that alcohol causes aggressive behavior: People cognitively associate alcohol cues with aggressive concepts.

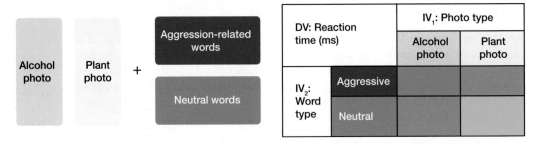

DV: Reaction time (ms)		IV₁: Photo type	
		Alcohol photo	Plant photo
IV₂: Word type	Aggressive		
	Neutral		

FIGURE 12.10 Theory testing by crossing two independent variables. This type of design creates all possible combinations of the independent variables. Here, one independent variable (photo type) is crossed with another independent variable (word type) to create all four possible combinations.

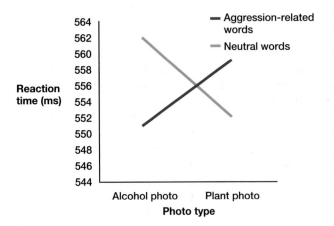

DV: Reaction time (ms)		IV₁: Photo type	
		Alcohol	Plant
IV₂: Word type	Aggressive	551	559
	Neutral	562	552

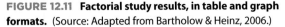

FIGURE 12.11 Factorial study results, in table and graph formats. (Source: Adapted from Bartholow & Heinz, 2006.)

Using an Interaction to Test a Memory Theory

In another example of theory testing with factorial designs, two cognitive psychologists wanted to test a theory about context-dependent memory (Godden & Baddeley, 1975). The theory predicted that when people study a list of words in order to memorize them, they associate the words with the surrounding context: the desk they're sitting at, the notebook the words are written in, even the carpet on the floor. When people try to remember the list of words later, they may be able use the desk, notebook, and carpet as reminders of what the words were—if those same objects are present when the people are trying to recall the words.

These researchers asked a group of scuba divers to memorize a list of words, and then tested them later. One group memorized the material while sitting on the edge of the water, and the other group memorized the material while underwater, 20 feet below the surface. (Both groups were tested in their full scuba gear.) That was one independent variable: learning location (on the edge or in the water). Then each group was divided in two; half the participants in each group were tested for memory while at the edge of the water, and the other half were tested underwater. That was the second

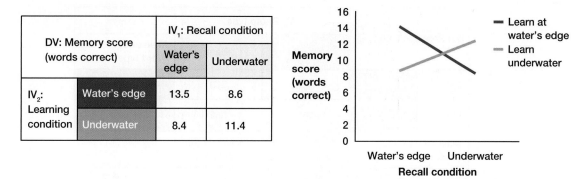

DV: Memory score (words correct)		IV₁: Recall condition	
		Water's edge	Underwater
IV₂: Learning condition	Water's edge	13.5	8.6
	Underwater	8.4	11.4

FIGURE 12.12 **A factorial study of context-dependent memory.** Do people recall material better on land or underwater? It depends on where they learned it. (Source: Adapted from Godden & Baddeley, 1975.)

independent variable: recall location (on the edge or in the water). Sure enough, participants who learned the material on the edge of the water remembered it best on the edge of the water; participants who learned it underwater remembered it best underwater. The results are shown in **Figure 12.12**.

In this example, the psychologists used a factorial design to test their theory about context-dependent memory. The study results supported the clear interaction predicted by the theory: Is memory better underwater or at the water's edge? It depends on where you learned the material: underwater or at the water's edge.

Interpreting Factorial Results: Main Effects and Interactions

After running a study with a factorial design with two independent variables, researchers, of course, want to analyze the results. In an analysis with two independent variables, there will be three results to inspect: two main effects and one interaction effect.

Main Effects: Is There an Overall Difference?

In a factorial design, researchers test each independent variable to look for a **main effect**—the overall effect of one independent variable on the dependent variable, averaging over the levels of the other independent variable. In other words, a main effect is a simple difference. In a factorial design with two independent variables, there are two main effects.

Figure 12.13 shows the data from Bartholow and Heinz's study on word association. One independent variable, type of word, is highlighted in blue; the other, type of photo, is highlighted in yellow. First, to look for a main effect of word type, you would compute the reaction time to aggressive words (averaging across the two photo conditions), and the reaction time to neutral words (averaging across the two photo conditions). The resulting two marginal means for aggressive and neutral words are shown in the far-right column of the table.

DV: Reaction time (ms)		IV₁: Photo type		
		Alcohol	**Plant**	**Main effect for IV₂:** Word type
IV₂: Word type	Aggressive	551	559	555 (average of 551 and 559)
	Neutral	562	552	557 (average of 562 and 552)
Main effect for IV₁: Photo type		556.5 (average of 551 and 562)	555.5 (average of 559 and 552)	

FIGURE 12.13 Using marginal means to look for main effects. Looking for the main effect of an independent variable involves computing the overall score for each level of that independent variable, averaging over the levels of the other independent variable. Neither main effect in this study is statistically significant. (Source: Adapted from Bartholow & Heinz, 2006.)

Marginal means are the arithmetic means for each level of an independent variable, averaging over levels of the other independent variable. If the sample size in each cell is exactly equal, marginal means are a simple average. If the sample sizes are unequal, the marginal means will be computed using the weighted average, counting the larger sample more. In Figure 12.13, notice that there is not much difference overall between reaction times to the aggressive words (555 ms) and the neutral words (557 ms). In technical terms, there appears to be no main effect of word type.

Second, to find the main effect of photo type, the other independent variable, you would compute the reaction time after seeing the alcohol photos, averaged across the two word type conditions, and the reaction time after seeing the plant photos, also averaged across the two word type conditions. These two marginal means are shown in the bottom row of the table. Here again, there is not much overall difference: On average, people are about as fast to respond after an alcohol photo (556.5 ms) as they are after a plant photo (555.5 ms). In technical terms, there appears to be no main effect of photo type.

Main Effects May or May Not Be Statistically Significant. Researchers look at the marginal means to inspect the main effects in a factorial design, and they use statistics to find out whether the difference in the marginal means is statistically significant. Recall from Chapter 10 that the Elliot team asked, in the study on the color red, whether the observed differences among the red, green, and black ink conditions were statistically significant. Similarly, Bartholow and Heinz asked whether the overall difference in reaction time to the two types of words was statistically significant. They also asked whether the overall difference in reaction time after the two types of photos was statistically significant. In their study, neither of these main effects was statistically significant. The observed difference in marginal means is about what you would expect to see by chance if there were no difference in the population.

For more on statistical significance, see Chapter 10, p. 300, and Statistics Review: Inferential Statistics, pp. 482–483.

DV: Shock intensity (1-10 scale)		IV₁: Body weight		Main effect for IV₂: Drinking condition
		Light men (151 lb)	Heavy men (215 lb)	
IV₂: Drinking condition	Placebo group	5.09	4.72	4.91 (average of 5.09 and 4.72)
	Drunk group	6.00	7.19	6.60 (average of 6.00 and 7.19)
Main effect for IV₁: Body weight		5.55 (average of 5.09 and 6.00)	5.96 (average of 4.72 and 7.19)	

FIGURE 12.14 **A study with two main effects.** The marginal means on the right show that there was a main effect of alcohol intake (such that drunk men are more aggressive than sober men). The marginal means in the bottom row show that there was also a main effect of body weight (heavy men are more aggressive than light men). (Source: Adapted from DeWall et al., 2010.)

Sometimes statistical significance tests tell you that a main effect is, in fact, statistically significant. For example, **Figure 12.14** shows results from the study that measured aggression in drunk and sober men (DeWall et al., 2010). The marginal means in this study revealed a statistically significant main effect for the drinking condition, such that drunk men were more aggressive than sober men. It also revealed a statistically significant main effect for body weight, such that heavy men were more aggressive than light men.

Main Effect = Overall Effect. The term *main effect* is usually misleading, because it seems to suggest that it is the most important effect in a study. It is not. In fact, when a study's results show an interaction, the interaction itself is the most important effect. Think of a main effect instead as an *overall effect*—the overall effect of one independent variable at a time.

Interactions: Is There a Difference in Differences?

In a factorial design with two independent variables, the first two results obtained are the main effects for each independent variable. The third result is the interaction effect. Whereas the main effects are simple differences, the interaction effect is the difference in differences.

Detecting Interactions from a Table. You can use a table to detect whether a study's results show an interaction. Because an interaction is a difference in differences, you start by computing two differences, as **Figure 12.15** shows, using the Bartholow and Heinz (2006) study. Begin with one level of the first independent variable: the alcohol photos. The difference between the aggressive and neutral words conditions for the alcohol photos is $551 - 562 = -11$. Then go to the second level of the first independent variable: the plant photos. The difference between the aggressive and neutral words for the plant photos is $559 - 552 = 7$. (Be sure to compute the difference in the same direction both

FIGURE 12.15
**Detecting
interactions
from a table
(the difference
in differences):
option 1.** This
format focuses on
row differences.
(Source: Adapted
from Bartholow &
Heinz, 2006.)

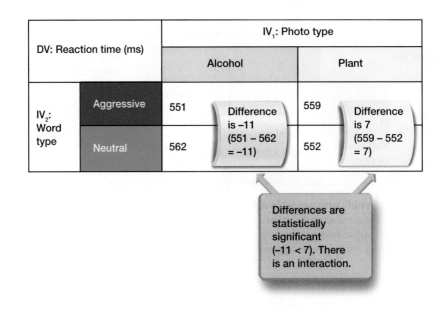

times; in this case, always subtracting the results for the neutral words from those for the aggressive words.) There are two differences: -11 and 7. These differences are different: One is negative and one is positive. Indeed, statistical tests told the researchers that the difference of 18 points is statistically significant. Therefore, you can conclude that there is an interaction in this factorial study.

You could detect the difference in differences the other way instead, by computing the difference in response time between the alcohol and plant photos, first for aggressive words ($551 - 559 = -8$) and then for neutral words ($562 - 552 = 10$). Although the values will be slightly different this time, you will reach the same conclusion: There is an interaction. The differences are different (-8 is different from 10).

Similarly, **Figure 12.16** shows how to compute the interaction for Strayer and Drews's study on using cell phones while driving. Again, if you start with one level of one independent variable, the younger drivers, the difference in braking onset time between drivers using cell phones and drivers who are not using cell phones is $912 - 780 = 132$ ms. Next, among the older drivers, the difference in braking onset time between drivers using cell phones and drivers not using cell phones is $1086 - 912 = 174$ ms. Are the two differences, 132 and 174, different? They may look a little different, but this is where statistics come in. Just as with main effects, researchers use significance tests to tell them whether a difference in differences is significantly different from zero. Strayer and Drews's statistical significance tests told them that the two differences are *not* significantly different. So, in this case, there is not a significant difference in differences. In fact, at each age level, there is a 15% drop in braking onset time.

Detecting Interactions from a Graph. While it's possible to compute interactions in a table, it is much easier to detect them from a graph. When results from a factorial design are plotted as a line graph, you simply look to see whether the

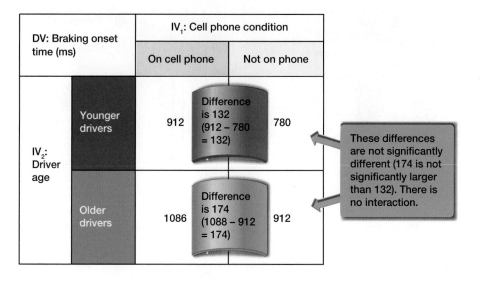

FIGURE 12.16
Detecting interactions from a table (the difference in differences): option 2. This format focuses on column differences, whereas the table format in Figure 12.15 focused on row differences. Interactions can be computed either way. (Source: Adapted from Strayer & Drews, 2004.)

The table:

DV: Braking onset time (ms)		IV₁: Cell phone condition	
		On cell phone	Not on phone
IV₂: Driver age	Younger drivers	912	Difference is 132 (912 – 780 = 132)	780
	Older drivers	1086	Difference is 174 (1088 – 912 = 174)	912

These differences are not significantly different (174 is not significantly larger than 132). There is no interaction.

lines are parallel. If the lines are not parallel, as in **Figure 12.17A**, there probably *is* an interaction. If the lines are parallel, as in **Figure 12.17B**, there probably is *no* interaction. Of course, you would also have to confirm your observations with a significance test. Notice that lines don't have to cross to show an interaction; they simply have to be nonparallel. For example, look back at the first graph in Figure 12.9, and see nonparallel lines indicating an interaction between type of drink and body weight.

You can also detect interactions from a bar graph. As you inspect the bar graphs in **Figure 12.18**, imagine connecting the tops of each matching bar (the two pink bars and the two orange bars) with straight lines. Would the resulting lines be parallel or not? Or you might look at the differences between the bars' heights on each side of the graph. Are the differences different, or are they the same?

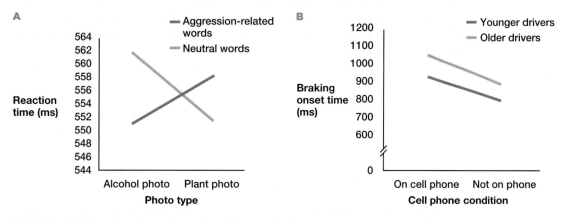

FIGURE 12.17 Detecting interactions from a line graph. (A) An interaction in the Bartholow and Heinz (2006) study—the lines are not parallel. (B) No interaction in the Strayer and Drews (2004) study—the lines are almost perfectly parallel.

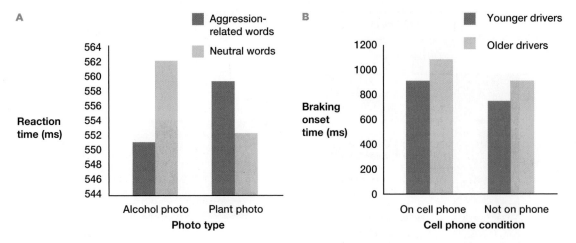

FIGURE 12.18 Detecting interactions from a bar graph. (A) Results of the Bartholow and Heinz (2006) study. (B) Results of the Strayer and Drews (2004) study. Is it easier to detect interactions in this format or in the line graphs in Figure 12.17?

Describing Interactions in Words. It's one thing to estimate that a study has an interaction effect; it's another to describe the pattern of the interaction in words. Since there are many possible patterns for interactions, there's no single best way to describe any one interaction: It depends on how the graph looks, as well as on how the researcher wants to frame the results.

One of the simpler verbal descriptions starts with one level of the first independent variable, explaining what is happening with the second independent variable at that level, then moves to the next level of the first independent variable and does the same thing. For example, for the interaction in the Bartholow and Heinz study (see Figures 12.17 and 12.18), you might describe it like this: When people saw photos of alcohol, they were quicker to recognize aggression words than neutral words, but when people saw photos of plants, they were slower to recognize aggression words than neutral words. As you move from level to level, you make it clear that the size of the effect of the other independent variable (type of word) is changing. You can also describe the pattern using phrases such as "especially for" or "depends on." **Figure 12.19** shows two examples of interactions, and how you might describe each one in words.

Interactions Are More Important Than Main Effects

When researchers analyze the results of a factorial design, they look at main effects for each independent variable, and they look for interactions. When a study shows both a main effect and an interaction, *the interaction is almost always more important.*

The study on alcohol, aggression, and body weight provides a good example of this principle (DeWall et al., 2010). This factorial design resulted in a main effect for body weight (heavy men were more aggressive than light men), a main effect for alcohol intake (alcohol made people more aggressive than the

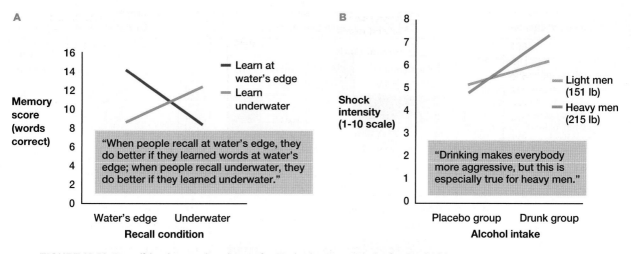

A

Memory score (words correct)

16
14
12
10
8
6
4
2
0

━ Learn at water's edge
━ Learn underwater

"When people recall at water's edge, they do better if they learned words at water's edge; when people recall underwater, they do better if they learned underwater."

Water's edge   Underwater
Recall condition

B

Shock intensity (1-10 scale)

8
7
6
5
4
3
2
1
0

━ Light men (151 lb)
━ Heavy men (215 lb)

"Drinking makes everybody more aggressive, but this is especially true for heavy men."

Placebo group   Drunk group
Alcohol intake

FIGURE 12.19 Describing interactions in words. Method 1: Start with the first level of the independent variable (IV) on the x-axis, and describe what's happening with the other IV. Then move to the second level of the IV on the y-axis, and describe what's happening with the other IV. Method 2: Describe the difference in differences, using phrases like "especially for" and "depends on."

placebo), and a significant interaction. However, the overall difference (main effect) for alcohol intake actually hides the fact that alcohol intake makes a difference *especially* for heavy men. And the overall difference (main effect) for body weight actually hides the fact that body weight affects aggression primarily when men are drunk. So there may be real differences in the marginal means, but the exciting—and most accurate—story in this study is the interaction.

Possible Main Effects and Interactions in a 2 × 2 Factorial

Figure 12.20 shows a variety of hypothetical outcomes from a single study. In all the examples, the independent variables are the same: a cell phone condition and an age condition. The dependent variable is the average number of accidents. This figure presents a variety of outcomes, all hypothetical, to show some possible combinations of main effects and interactions in a 2 × 2 factorial design. Note, too, how each main effect and interaction can be described in words.

CHECK YOUR UNDERSTANDING

1. Describe why Bartholow and Heinz's word association study on alcohol and thoughts of aggression was a factorial design.
2. What are two common reasons to use a factorial design?
3. How can you detect an interaction from a table of means? From a line graph?
4. Why might it be better to call a main effect an "overall effect"?

---

1. See p. 351. 2. See pp. 348-353. 3. See pp. 355-357. 4. See pp. 353-355.

Summary of effects	Cell means and marginal means	Line graph of the results

Row 1

Main effect for cell phone: *No*
Main effect for age: *No*
Age × cell phone interaction: *Yes* —younger drivers on a cell phone cause more accidents; older drivers on a cell phone cause fewer accidents

DV: Number of accidents	On cell phone	Not on phone	
Younger drivers	10	4	7
Older drivers	4	10	7
	7	7	

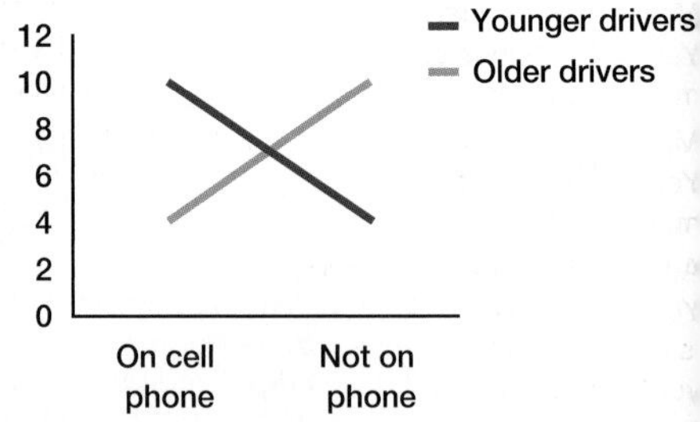

Row 2

Main effect for cell phone: *No*
Main effect for age: *Yes* —younger drivers have more accidents
Age × cell phone interaction: *No*

DV: Number of accidents	On cell phone	Not on phone	
Younger drivers	10	10	10
Older drivers	4	4	4
	7	7	

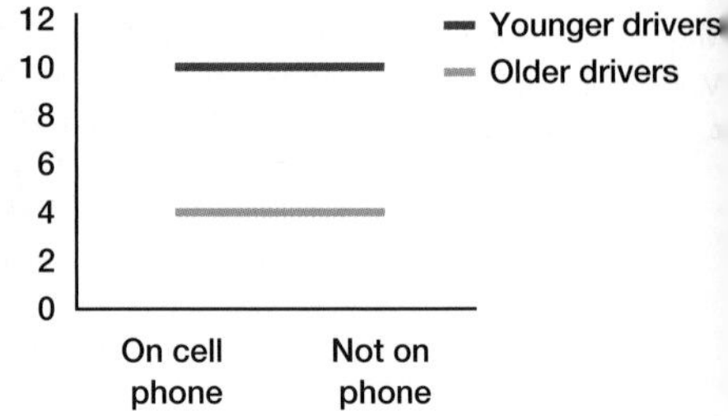

Row 3

Main effect for cell phone: *Yes* —cell phones cause more accidents
Main effect for age: *No*
Age × cell phone interaction: *No*

DV: Number of accidents	On cell phone	Not on phone	
Younger drivers	10	4	7
Older drivers	10	4	7
	10	4	

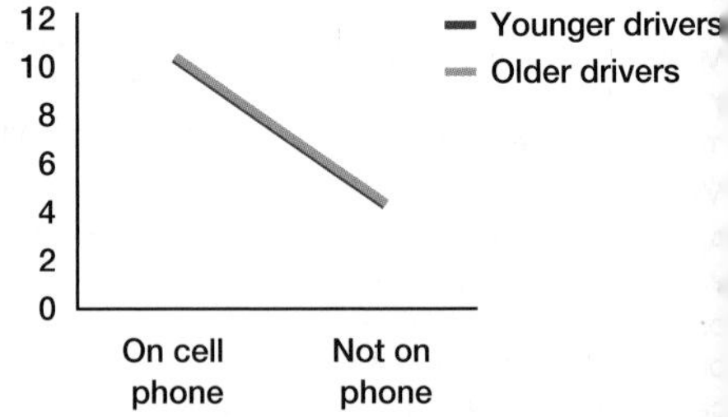

Row 4

Main effect for cell phone: *Yes* —cell phones cause more accidents
Main effect for age: *Yes* —younger drivers have more accidents
Age × cell phone interaction: *Yes* —for younger drivers, cell phones do not make a difference, but for older drivers, cell phones cause more accidents

DV: Number of accidents	On cell phone	Not on phone	
Younger drivers	10	10	10
Older drivers	10	4	7
	10	7	

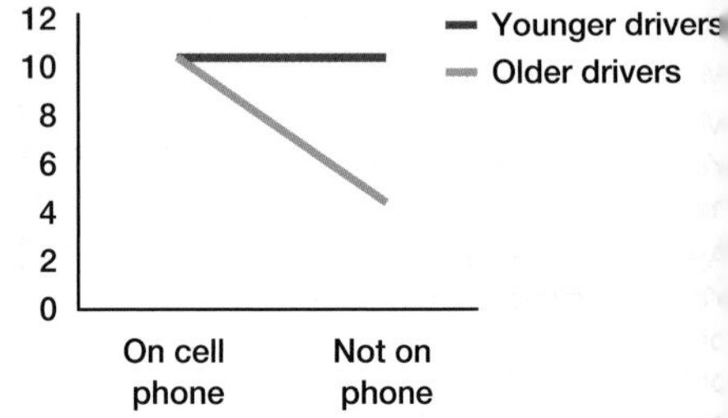

FIGURE 12.20 A range of possible outcomes from a single 2 × 2 factorial design. Use this chart to study how various outcomes result in different patterns of main effects and interactions. (Data are fabricated for illustration purposes.)

Summary of effects	Cell means and marginal means	Line graph of the results
Main effect for cell phone: *Yes*—cell phones cause more accidents. Main effect for age: *Yes*—older drivers have more accidents Age × cell phone interaction: *Yes*—impact of a cell phone is larger for older than for younger drivers	**DV: Number of accidents** — On cell phone / Not on phone Younger drivers: 8, 2, 5 Older drivers: 12, 3, 7.5 10, 2.5	
Main effect for cell phone: *No* Main effect for age: *No* Age × cell phone interaction: *No*	**DV: Number of accidents** — On cell phone / Not on phone Younger drivers: 5, 5, 5 Older drivers: 5, 5, 5 5, 5	
Main effect for cell phone: *Yes*—cell phones cause more accidents Main effect for age: *No* Age × cell phone interaction: *Yes*—for younger drivers, cell phones make no difference, but for older drivers, cell phones cause more accidents	**DV: Number of accidents** — On cell phone / Not on phone Younger drivers: 5, 5, 5 Older drivers: 8, 2, 5 6.5, 3.5	
Main effect for cell phone: *No* Main effect for age: *Yes*—younger drivers have more accidents Age × cell phone interaction: *Yes*—for younger drivers, cell phones cause more accidents, but for older drivers, cell phones cause fewer accidents	**DV: Number of accidents** — On cell phone / Not on phone Younger drivers: 8, 5, 6.5 Older drivers: 2, 5, 3.5 5, 5	

Factorial Variations

Now you're ready to explore some advanced variations on the basic 2×2 factorial design. What happens when an independent variable has more than two levels? What happens when one of the independent variables is manipulated within groups? What if we add a third independent variable?

Recall from Chapter 10 that in a simple experiment, the independent variable can be manipulated as either an independent-groups variable (different people participate at each level) or a within-groups variable (the same people participate at each level, as in a repeated-measures design). The same is true for factorial designs. Researchers can choose whether to manipulate *each* independent variable as independent-groups or within-groups.

Independent-Groups Factorial Designs

In an independent-groups factorial design (also known as a between-subjects factorial), both independent variables are studied as independent-groups. Therefore, if the design is a 2×2, there are four different groups of participants in the experiment. The DeWall team's study on alcohol, aggression, and body weight was an independent-groups factorial: Some light men drank a placebo beverage, other light men drank an alcoholic one, some heavy men drank a placebo beverage, and other heavy men drank an alcoholic one. In other words, there were different men in each cell. If the researchers decided to use 50 participants in each cell of the design, they would have needed a full 200 participants: 50 in each of the four groups.

Within-Groups Factorial Designs

In a within-groups factorial design (also called a repeated-measures factorial), both independent variables are manipulated as within-groups. Therefore, if the design is 2×2, there is only one group of participants, but they participate in all four combinations, or cells, of the design. The Bartholow and Heinz study on alcohol and thoughts of aggression was a within-groups factorial design. All participants saw both alcohol photos and plant photos, which alternated over trials. In addition, all participants responded to both aggression-related words and neutral words.

In a within-groups factorial design, all participants are involved in every possible combination. If Bartholow and Heinz had decided to use 50 people in each cell of their study, they would need a total of only 50 people; each of the 50 would participate in each of the four possible combinations of independent variables. Therefore, within-groups designs make efficient use of participants because they require fewer participants overall (**Figure 12.21**). Because it was a within-groups design, the researchers counterbalanced the order of presentation of photos and words by having the computer present the photos and their subsequent words in a different random order for each participant.

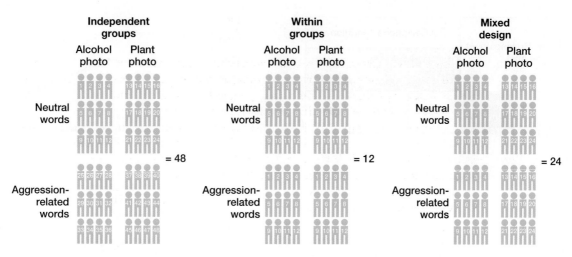

FIGURE 12.21 Within-groups designs are more efficient. To achieve a goal of 12 observations per cell, an independent-groups factorial design would need 48 participants. A within-groups factorial design would require 12 participants, and a mixed design would require 24 participants.

Mixed Factorial Designs

In a mixed factorial design, one independent variable is manipulated as independent-groups and the other is manipulated as within-groups. The Strayer and Drews study on cell phone use while driving among different age groups is an example of a mixed factorial design. Age was an independent-groups participant variable: Participants in one group were old, and those in the other group were young. But the cell phone condition independent variable was manipulated as within-groups. Each participant drove in both the cell phone and the control conditions of the study. If Strayer and Drews had wanted 50 people in each cell of their 2 × 2 mixed design, they would have needed a total of 100 people: 50 old drivers and 50 young drivers, each participating at both levels of the cell phone condition.

Increasing the Number of Levels of an Independent Variable

The discussion so far has focused on the simplest factorial design, the 2 × 2. This design has two independent variables, each with two levels, creating four conditions (2 × 2 = 4). However, researchers can add more levels to each independent variable. For example, Strayer and Drews might have manipulated their cell phone condition using three levels (handheld cell phone, hands-free cell phone, and no cell phone) and then crossed it with age (older and younger drivers). This design is represented in **Figure 12.22**. It still has two independent variables, but one has two levels and the other has three levels. This design is called a 2 × 3 factorial design, and it results in six cells (2 × 3 = 6).

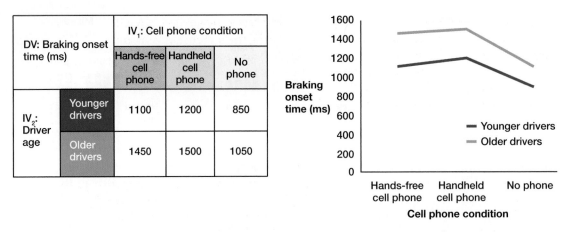

| DV: Braking onset time (ms) | IV₁: Cell phone condition | | |
	Hands-free cell phone	Handheld cell phone	No phone
IV₂: Driver age — Younger drivers	1100	1200	850
IV₂: Driver age — Older drivers	1450	1500	1050

Braking onset time (ms) — Younger drivers / Older drivers

FIGURE 12.22 A 2 × 3 factorial design. (Data are fabricated for illustration purposes.)

The notation for factorial designs follows a simple pattern. Factorials are notated in the form "__ × __." The quantity of numbers indicates the number of independent variables (a 2 × 3 design is represented with two numbers, 2 and 3). The value of each of the numbers indicates how many levels there are for each independent variable (two levels for one and three levels for the other). When you multiply the two numbers, you get the total number of cells in the design.

What would happen if Strayer and Drews also increased the number of levels of the other independent variable, age? For example, what if they used four groups of drivers: drivers in their 20s, 30s, 50s, and 70s? If the cell phone condition had three levels and age had four levels, the new design would be represented as in **Figure 12.23**. There are still two independent variables, but one of them has three levels and the other has four levels. The new design is called a 3 × 4 factorial design, and it results in 12 cells (3 × 4 = 12).

| DV: Braking onset time (ms) | IV₁: Cell phone condition | | |
	Hands-free cell phone	Handheld cell phone	No phone
IV₂: Driver age — Age 20–29	1100	1200	850
IV₂: Driver age — Age 30–49	1120	1225	820
IV₂: Driver age — Age 50–69	1300	1400	900
IV₂: Driver age — Age 70+	1600	1500	1050

Braking onset time (ms) — Age 20–29 / Age 30–49 / Age 50–69 / Age 70+

FIGURE 12.23 A 3 × 4 factorial design. (Data are fabricated for illustration purposes.)

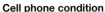

When independent variables have more than two levels, researchers can still investigate main effects and interactions by computing the marginal means and seeing whether they are different. The easiest way to detect interactions is to plot the results on a line graph and see whether the lines run parallel. As in a 2 × 2 factorial design, statistical tests would confirm whether any of the main effects or interactions are statistically significant.

Increasing the Number of Independent Variables

For some research questions, researchers find it necessary to have more than two independent variables in a crossed factorial design. For instance, suppose Strayer and Drews decided to study not only the cell-phone independent variable and the age independent variable, but also two kinds of traffic conditions: dense traffic and light traffic. Would this third independent variable make a difference?

Such a design is called a 2 × 2 × 2 factorial, or a three-way design. There are two levels of the first independent variable, two levels of the second, and two levels of the third. This design would create eight cells, or conditions, in the experiment (2 × 2 × 2 = 8). The best way to depict a three-way design is to construct the original 2 × 2 table twice, once for each level of the third independent variable, as shown in **Figure 12.24A**. To graph a three-way design, you create two side-by-side line graphs, as shown in **Figure 12.24B**.

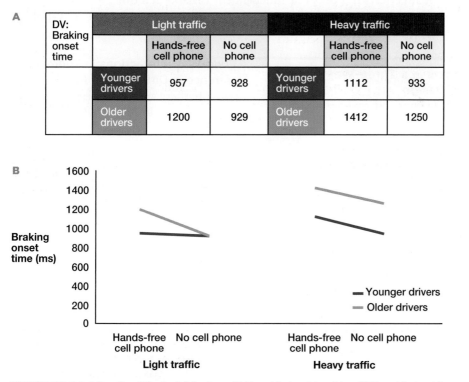

A

DV: Braking onset time		Light traffic			Heavy traffic	
		Hands-free cell phone	No cell phone		Hands-free cell phone	No cell phone
	Younger drivers	957	928	Younger drivers	1112	933
	Older drivers	1200	929	Older drivers	1412	1250

FIGURE 12.24 A 2 × 2 × 2 factorial design. (A) Two side-by-side tables. (B) Two side-by-side line graphs. (Data are fabricated for illustration purposes.)

To make this study a three-way design, Strayer and Drews might manipulate the new variable as independent-groups, having some participants drive in light traffic only and others drive in heavy traffic only. Or they might manipulate the new variable as within-groups, having all participants drive in light traffic and in heavy traffic. Either way, the design is considered a three-way factorial design.

Main Effects and Interactions from a Three-Way Design

When a factorial design has three independent variables, the number of differences to be investigated increases dramatically. In a three-way design, you are concerned with three main effects (one for each independent variable), plus three separate two-way interactions and a three-way interaction.

Main Effects: Is There a Difference? Because there are three independent variables in a $2 \times 2 \times 2$ design, there will be three main effects to test. Each main effect represents a simple, overall difference: the effect of one independent variable, averaged across the other two independent variables. In **Table 12.1**, you can see how the three main effects were computed. Table 12.1 indicates that, overall, drivers brake more slowly in the cell phone condition than in the control condition. Overall, older drivers brake more slowly than younger drivers. And overall, drivers are slower to brake in heavy traffic than in light traffic. Remember that main effects test only one independent variable at a time. When describing each main effect, you don't mention the other two independent variables, because you averaged across them.

TABLE 12.1 Main Effects in a Three-Way Factorial Design

Main effect for cell phone vs. control	
Cell phone (mean of 957, 1200, 1112, 1412)	1170.25
No cell phone (mean of 928, 929, 933, 1250)	1010.00
Main effect for driver age	
Younger drivers (mean of 957, 928, 1112, 933)	982.50
Older drivers (mean of 1200, 929, 1412, 1250)	1197.50
Main effect for traffic conditions	
Light traffic (mean of 957, 1200, 928, 929)	1003.50
Heavy traffic (mean of 1112, 1412, 933, 1250)	1176.75

Note: To estimate each main effect in a three-way factorial design, you average the means for braking onset time for each level of each independent variable, ignoring the levels of the other two independent variables. The means come from Figure 12.2. (These estimates assume that there are equal numbers of participants in each cell.)

Two-Way Interactions: Is There a Difference in Differences? In a three-way design, there are three possible two-way interactions. In the driving with cell phone example, these would be:

- Age × traffic condition (a two-way interaction averaging over the cell phone condition variable)
- Age × cell phone condition (a two-way interaction averaging over the traffic conditions variable)
- Cell phone condition × traffic condition (a two-way interaction averaging over the age variable).

To inspect each of these two-way interactions, you construct three 2×2

	Light traffic	Heavy traffic
Younger drivers	942.5 (average of 957 and 928)	1022.5 (average of 1112 and 933)
Older drivers	1064.5 (average of 1200 and 929)	1331 (average of 1412 and 1250)

	On cell phone	No cell phone
Younger drivers	1034.5 (average of 957 and 1112)	930.5 (average of 928 and 933)
Older drivers	1306 (average of 1200 and 1412)	1089.5 (average of 929 and 1250)

	Light traffic	Heavy traffic
On cell phone	1078.5 (average of 957 and 1200)	1262 (average of 1112 and 1412)
No cell phone	928.5 (average of 928 and 929)	1091.5 (average of 933 and 1250)

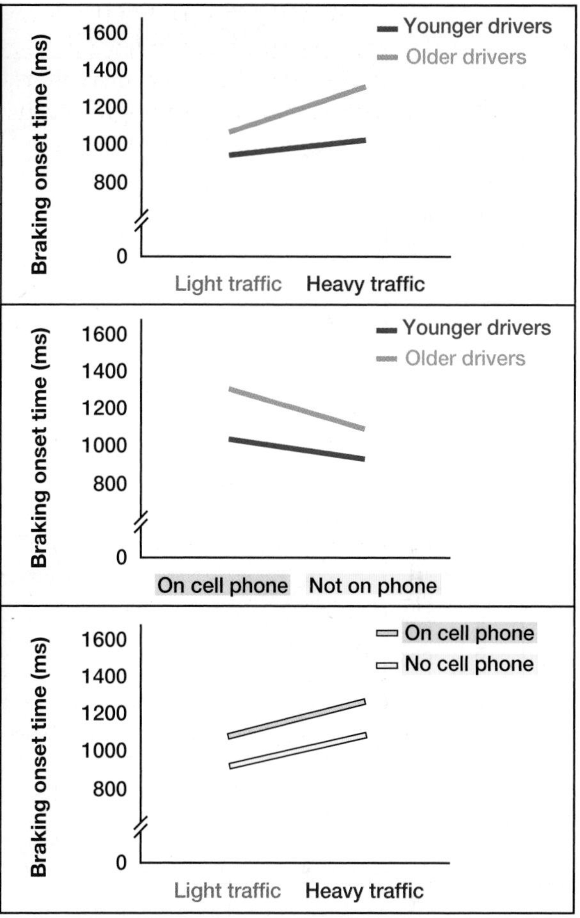

FIGURE 12.25 Two-way interactions in a 2 × 2 × 2 factorial design. Data are recombined to estimate the three two-way interactions in this study. The means come from Figure 12.24.

tables, as **Figure 12.25** shows. After computing the means, you can investigate the difference in differences using the table, just as you did for a two-way design. Alternatively, it might be easier to look for the interaction by graphing it and checking for nonparallel lines. (Statistical tests will show whether each two-way interaction is statistically significant or not.)

Three-Way Interactions: Are the Two-Way Interactions Different? In a three-way design, the final result is a single three-way interaction. In the cell phone example, this would be the three-way interaction among driver age, cell phone condition, and traffic condition. A three-way interaction, if it is significant, means that the two-way interaction between two of the independent variables *depends on* the level of the third independent variable. In mathematical

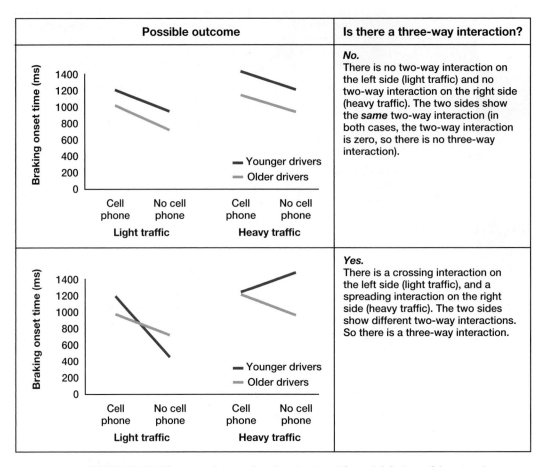

Possible outcome	Is there a three-way interaction?
	No. There is no two-way interaction on the left side (light traffic) and no two-way interaction on the right side (heavy traffic). The two sides show the *same* two-way interaction (in both cases, the two-way interaction is zero, so there is no three-way interaction).
	Yes. There is a crossing interaction on the left side (light traffic), and a spreading interaction on the right side (heavy traffic). The two sides show different two-way interactions. So there is a three-way interaction.

FIGURE 12.26 Three-way interactions in a 2 × 2 × 2 factorial design. If there is a three-way interaction, it means the two-way interactions are different, depending on the level of a third independent variable. This table shows different possible patterns of data in a 2 × 2 × 2 design. (Data are fabricated for illustration purposes.)

terms, a significant three-way interaction means that the "difference in differences . . . is different." (You are allowed to smile when you say this.)

A three-way interaction is easiest to detect by looking at line graphs of the data. Refer back to Figure 12.24B. Notice that in light traffic, there is a two-way interaction between driver age and cell phone condition, but in heavy traffic, there is no two-way interaction between these two independent variables. The two-way interaction of driver age × cell phone condition therefore depends on the level of traffic conditions. The interaction of driver age and cell phone is not the same on both sides of the graph. In other words, there is a difference in differences for the light traffic side of the graph, but there is no difference in differences for the heavy traffic side of the graph.

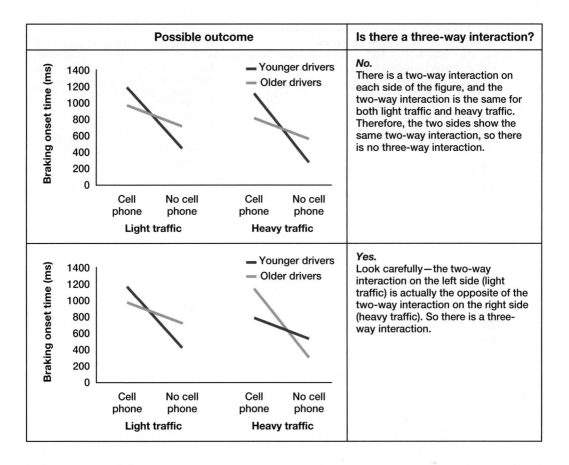

Possible outcome	Is there a three-way interaction?
	No. There is a two-way interaction on each side of the figure, and the two-way interaction is the same for both light traffic and heavy traffic. Therefore, the two sides show the same two-way interaction, so there is no three-way interaction.
	Yes. Look carefully—the two-way interaction on the left side (light traffic) is actually the opposite of the two-way interaction on the right side (heavy traffic). So there is a three-way interaction.

You would find a three-way interaction whenever there is a two-way interaction for one level of a third independent variable but not for the other (because the two-way interactions are different—there is a two-way interaction on one side but not on the other). You will also find a three-way interaction if a graph shows one pattern of two-way interaction on one side but a different pattern of two-way interaction on the other side—in other words, if there are different two-way interactions. However, if you found the same kind of two-way interaction for both levels of the third independent variable, there would not be a three-way interaction. **Figure 12.26** shows some of the possible outcomes of a three-way design.

Factorial designs are a useful way of testing theories and exploring outcomes that depend on multiple factors, and they provide researchers with a way of quantifying the interactions they want to study. Of course, a study can have more than three independent variables, and some may have four or five. With each additional independent variable (or factor), the researchers will be looking at more main effects and even more kinds of interactions.

Why Worry About All These Interactions?

Managing two-way and three-way interactions can be complicated, but in studying psychology and in thinking about daily life, you need to understand interaction effects. Why? Because we don't live in a main effect world. Most outcomes in psychological science studies—and, by extension, in life—are not main effects; they are interactions.

Consider, for instance, this main effect question: Is it good to be forgiving in a relationship? The answer would reflect an interaction: It depends on how severe the problems are in the relationship (McNulty, 2010). Here's another: Does daycare lead to social and emotional problems in children? This would probably have an interaction answer as well: It depends on the quality of the daycare. It might even have a three-way interaction answer: It depends on the quality of the care *and* the nature of the home environment.

CHECK YOUR UNDERSTANDING

1. Describe how the same 2 × 2 design might be conducted as an independent-groups factorial, a within-groups factorial, or a mixed factorial design. Explain how different designs change the number of participants required: Which design requires the most? Which requires the fewest?
2. What does the notation (e.g., 2 × 2, 3 × 4, 2 × 2 × 3) indicate about the number of independent variables in a study? How does it convey the number of cells?
3. In a 2 × 2 × 2 design, what is the number of main effects and interactions?
4. Describe how you can tell whether a study has a three-way interaction.

---

1. See pp. 362–363; an independent-groups factorial requires the most participants, and a within-groups factorial requires the fewest. 2. See pp. 363–365. 3. See pp. 366–369; three two-way interactions and one three-way interaction. 4. See pp. 367–369 and Table 12.1.

Identifying Factorial Designs in Your Reading

Whether you are reading original research published in a journal or secondhand reports of research published in the popular media, certain clues will alert you that the study had a factorial design.

Identifying Factorial Designs in Empirical Journal Articles

In an empirical journal article, researchers almost always describe the design they used in the Method section. You can tell the researchers used a factorial design if they refer to their study as a 2 × 2 design, a 3 × 2 design, a 2 × 2 × 2 design, or the like. Such descriptions also indicate the number of independent variables in the study, as well as how many levels there were for each independent variable.

In the study on using a cell phone while driving, for example, the researchers describe their experimental design as follows:

> The design was a 2 (Age: Younger vs. Older adults) × 2 (Task: Single- vs. Dual-task) factorial. Age was a between-subjects factor and the single- vs. dual-task condition was a within-subjects factor. (Strayer & Drews, 2004, p. 643)

In their article, they use "dual-task" for driving while using a cell phone and "single-task" for driving without a cell phone. Notice that Strayer and Drews use the notation 2 × 2, labeling each independent variable in parentheses. They also specify that the design was factorial. You can also infer they used a mixed factorial design, because they mentioned that one independent variable was independent-groups ("between-subjects") and one was within-groups ("within-subjects").

Whereas the Method section outlines the study's design, independent variables, and dependent variables, the Results section of an empirical journal article discusses whether the main effects and interactions are significant. Authors may use the term *significant*, the notation $p < 0.05$, or even an asterisk in a table to indicate that a main effect or interaction is statistically significant. Here is how Strayer and Drews described the main effects and interactions in their study:

> The MANOVA indicated significant main effects of age, $F(4, 35) = 8.74$, $p < 0.01$, and single- vs. dual-task, $F(4, 35) = 11.44$, $p < 0.01$. However, the Age × Single- vs. Dual-Task interaction was not significant, $F(4, 35) = 1.46$, $p = 0.23$. This latter finding suggests that older adults do not suffer a significantly greater penalty for talking on a cell phone while driving than do their younger counterparts. (Strayer & Drews, 2004, p. 644)

Although you might not know what MANOVA and F mean in the quoted text above, you should now be able to recognize the terms *main effect, interaction,* and *significant.*

Identifying Factorial Designs in Popular Press Articles

Whereas empirical journal articles must specify what kind of design was used in a study, popular press articles usually do not. These media outlets probably assume most of their readers would not know what a 2 × 2 factorial design means. Indeed, most journalists gloss over the details of an experimental design to make their articles simpler. However, you can detect a factorial design from a popular press report if you know what to look for.

Here's an example of how a journalist described the DeWall study on alcohol use, aggressive behavior, and body weight in the online news outlet, *Pacific Standard.* After explaining the study in some detail, the journalist described the interaction like this: "The researchers found that alcohol, compared to placebo, increased aggression among the heavier men but had little effect on the lighter men" (Best, 2010).

In other cases, you may need to read between the lines in order to know that a study had a factorial design. There are certain clues you can look for to identify factorial designs in the popular press.

Look for "It Depends"

Journalists might gloss over the details of a factorial design, but sometimes they will use the phrase "it depends" to highlight an interaction in a report of a factorial design. Here's an example from an article on gender differences and talking:

> In her own and others' work, La France noted, "the research is consistently showing either no sex differences in the amount that men and women talk, or if there *is* a difference, then it depends on the context. For example, in a professional context, men actually outspeak women by a long shot." (Mundell, 2007)

This passage is from an article on whether spending money makes people happy:

> Should I spend money on a vacation or a new computer? Will an experience or an object make me happier? A new study in the *Journal of Consumer Research* says it depends on different factors, including how materialistic you are. ("Do Experiences or Material Goods Make Us Happier?" 2009)

In these two examples, you can identify the dependent variable and then use the phrase "it depends" to find the independent variables. Notice that each article first mentions how a dependent variable is affected by only one factor; then it complicates that basic difference with a second factor. The first example starts with the dependent variable of how much people talk. It mentions one factor (gender) and then adds a second factor (the context: work, nonwork) to describe the interaction. The effect of gender on how much people talk *depends on* the context in which they are talking.

The second example starts with the dependent variable "happiness" and first asks whether happiness is affected by one factor—what a person spends money on (experiences or possessions). Then it adds the second factor, saying that the effect of experiences (versus possessions) on happiness *depends on* a person's level of materialism. Thus, materialism is a second factor that interacts with how people spend their money.

Look for Participant Variables

You can sometimes detect factorial designs when articles discuss a participant variable, such as age, gender, or ethnicity. In such stories, the participant variable often moderates another independent variable. And when there is a moderator, there is an interaction (as well as a factorial design to test it). For instance, the following article discusses how male and female monkeys respond to cocaine prenatally:

> Adult male monkeys exposed to cocaine while in the womb have poor impulse control and may be more vulnerable to drug abuse than female monkeys, even a decade or more after the exposure, according to a new study by researchers at Wake Forest University School of Medicine. The findings could lead to a better understanding of human drug abuse. . . .

For the study, researchers compared adult monkeys—both male and fe-male—prenatally exposed to cocaine more than 15 years ago, to monkeys who were raised under similar conditions, but not exposed to cocaine during gestation. To determine if the animals differed in impulse con-trol, they performed four tests. For one of the tests, the researchers gave the animals the choice between pushing a lever that delivered a single banana pellet reward immediately or a lever that delivered several ba-nana pellets, but required the animals to wait up to 5 minutes before the reward was delivered. ("Cocaine Exposure During Pregnancy," 2009)

You should be able to identify that the dependent variable was impulsivity, as tested with the banana pellet lever. The excerpt specifies that one independent variable, cocaine exposure, made a difference for males, but not for females—a sign of an interaction. Sex (a participant variable) interacted with cocaine expo-sure (an independent variable) to determine how the monkeys responded to a self-control task.

In the following example of a factorial design with a participant variable, the journalist again does not mention the study's factors or design. How can you tell that there is an interaction?

Joanne Wood of the University of Waterloo in Ontario and two col-leagues conducted experiments in which they asked students to repeat statements to themselves such as "I am a lovable person"—then mea-sured how it affected their mood. But in one of their studies involving 32 male and 36 female psychology students, the researchers found that repeating the phrase did not improve the mood of those who had low self-esteem, as measured by a standard test. They actually ended up feeling worse, and the gap between those with high and low self-esteem widened. (Stein, 2009)

The statement "the gap between those with high and low self-esteem widened" is a sign that there was a difference in differences—an interaction (probably a spreading interaction). Reading between the lines, you can infer that the depen-dent variable was mood. One factor in this design was self-esteem (high or low); the other was whether or not they repeated the sentence "I am a lovable person."

CHECK YOUR UNDERSTANDING

1. In an empirical journal article, in what section will you find the independent and dependent variables of the design? In what section will you find whether the main effects and interactions are statistically significant?

2. Describe at least two cues indicating that a popular press article is probably describ-ing a factorial design.

1. See pp. 370–371. 2. See pp. 371–373.

Summary

- Simple experiments involve one independent and one dependent variable. Many hypotheses in psychological science are more complex; they involve studying two or more independent variables.

Review: Experiments with One Independent Variable

- In a study with one independent variable, we look for a simple difference. For example, we might look for the difference between being drunk or sober, or the difference between being on a cell phone or not.

Experiments with Two Independent Variables Can Show Interactions

- When testing more than one variable, researchers are looking for interactions, asking whether the effect of one independent variable depends on the level of the other one. An interaction is a "difference in differences."
- Factorial designs cross two or more independent variables, creating conditions (cells) that represent every possible combination of the levels of each independent variable.
- Factorial designs can describe multiple influences on behavior; they enable researchers to test their theories and determine whether some manipulation affects one type of person more than another.

- Analyzing the data from a factorial design involves looking for main effects for each independent variable by estimating the marginal means, then looking for interaction effects by checking for a difference in differences (in a line graph, look for nonparallel lines).
- When there is an interaction effect, it is more important than any main effects found.

Factorial Variations

- The factors can be independent-groups or within-groups variables; the factors can be manipulated (independent) variables or measured, participant variables.
- When a factorial design has three or more independent variables, the number of interactions increases to include all possible combinations of the independent variables.
- In a design with three independent variables, the three-way interaction tests whether two-way interactions are the same at the levels of the third independent variable.

Identifying Factorial Designs in Your Reading

- In empirical journal articles, the type of design is given in the Method section.
- In popular press articles, factorial designs may be indicated by language such as "it depends" or descriptions of both participant variables and independent variables.

Key Terms

interaction effect, p. 345
factorial design, p. 347
cell, p. 348
participant variable, p. 348
main effect, p. 353
marginal means, p. 354

 To see samples of chapter concepts in the popular press, visit www.everydayresearchmethods.com and click the box for Chapter 12.

Review Questions

Psychologist Joanne Wood and her colleagues recruited people with high and low self-esteem to participate in a study of positive self-statements (Wood, Perunovic, & Lee, 2009). They asked participants to write their thoughts and feelings down for 4 minutes. They randomly assigned half the participants to repeat to themselves a positive self-statement, "I am a lovable person," at 15-second intervals (cued by a bell sound). The other half did not repeat this phrase. After the 4-minute session, all participants rated their mood on a subtle mood questionnaire. Here are the results:

DV: Positive mood	Low self-esteem participants	High self-esteem participants
"I am a lovable person"	11.18	30.47
No statement	16.94	24.59

1. Why might Wood and her team have conducted their study as a factorial design?
   a. To test how well positive self-statements work, compared to no statements.
   b. To compare the moods of high self-esteem and low self-esteem people.
   c. To test whether the effect of positive self-statements would depend on people's level of self-esteem.

2. What are the factors in this study?
   a. Self-esteem level: high versus low
   b. Self-statement instructions: positive versus none
   c. Self-esteem level: high versus low; and self-statement instructions: positive versus none
   d. Positive mood

3. There is an interaction in the results. How do you know?
   a. When the cell means are graphed, the lines are not parallel.

   b. The difference between low and high self-esteem is large for the positive self-statement condition, and smaller for the neutral statement condition.
   c. Positive self-statements made the mood of high self-esteem people go up, but they made the mood of low self-esteem people go down.
   d. All of the above.

4. Which of the following sentences describes the *main effect for self-esteem* in the Wood study?
   a. Overall, the moods of high self-esteem people are more positive than the moods of low self-esteem people.
   b. Mood depended on both the participants' level of self-esteem and what self-statement condition they were in.
   c. Overall, the moods of people in the "I am a lovable person" condition are about the same as the moods of people in the "No statement" condition.
   d. Positive self-statements made the moods of high self-esteem people go up, but they made the moods of low self-esteem people go down.

5. This study is an example of a(n):
   a. Independent-groups factorial design
   b. Within-groups factorial design
   c. Mixed factorial design

6. Suppose these researchers ran their study again, but this time they compared how high or low self-esteem people responded to three kinds of statements: Positive self-statements, negative self-statements, and no statements. What kind of design would this be?
   a. 2×2
   b. 2×3
   c. $2 \times 2 \times 2$
   d. 6×1

Learning Actively

1. Create a line graph of the data depicted in the review questions above (Wood et al., 2009). Create the graph both ways: *Self-statement type* on the x-axis; *Self-esteem level* on the x-axis. Describe in words the interaction that you see.

2. For practice, compute the marginal means in the two studies shown in the figures below. (Assume each cell has an equal number of participants.) You would need significance tests to be sure, but does it look as if there will be significant main effects for both the cell-phone condition and the driver age? Why or why not? Does it look as if there are main effects for the testing condition and the learning condition? Why or why not?

DV: Braking onset time (ms)	IV$_1$: Cell phone condition		Main effect for IV$_2$: Driver age
	Cell phone	Not on phone	
IV$_2$: Driver age — Younger drivers	912	780	
IV$_2$: Driver age — Older drivers	1086	912	
Main effect for IV$_1$: Cell phone condition			

DV: Number of words memorized	IV$_1$: Testing condition		Main effect for IV$_2$: Learning condition
	Water's edge	Underwater	
IV$_2$: Learning condition — Water's edge	13.5	8.6	
IV$_2$: Learning condition — Underwater	8.4	11.4	
Main effect for IV$_1$: Testing condition			

3. In one of their studies, Strayer and his students tested whether people would get better at driving while talking on a cell phone if they practiced doing so (Cooper & Strayer, 2008). They asked people to drive in a simulator, while talking on a hands-free cell phone and while not talking on a phone. In addition, the same people participated over several days, so that they had a chance to practice this multitasking. On the first day, they were considered to be least experienced. On the last day, they were considered to be most experienced. In addition, on the last day, they were tested in both a familiar environment and a slightly different driving environment, to see if the first days of practice would transfer to a new context. Cooper and Strayer collected data on how many collisions (accidents) the drivers got into on the simulator (trained in the "city" condition). Here are their data:

	Number of Collision		
	Day 1	Day 4 (driving in a familiar context)	Day 4 (driving in a new context)
Single-task (not using cell phone)	15	6	10
Dual-task (using cell phone)	20	7.5	24

a. What kind of design is this? (Put your answer in the form "___ × ___.")
b. What are the independent and dependent variables?
c. Indicate whether each independent variable was manipulated as independent-groups or within-groups.
d. Create a line graph depicting these results.

e. Estimate and describe any main effects and interactions in this study.

f. What might you conclude from the results of this study? Does experience affect cell phone use while driving?

4. Are participant variables independent-groups variables or within-groups variables? Why?

PART VI

Balancing
Research Priorities

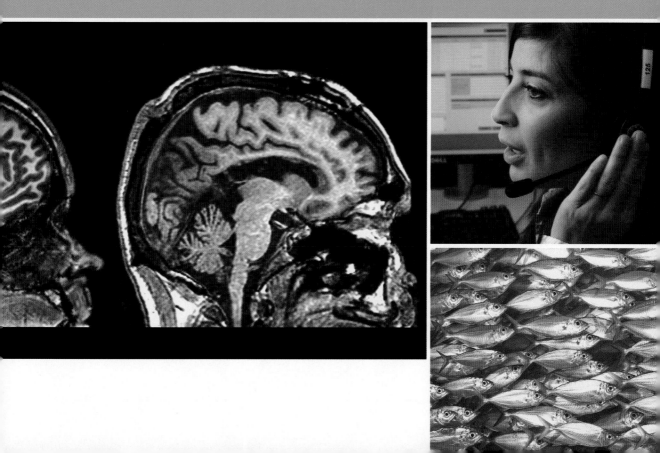

"What if you can't randomly assign participants to the independent variable levels?"

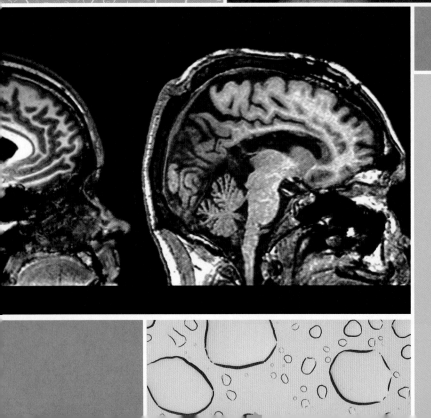

"What is the value of an experiment with just one participant?"

13

Quasi-Experiments and Small-*N* Designs

LEARNING OBJECTIVES

A year from now, you should still be able to:

1. Articulate how quasi-experiments differ from true experiments.

2. Analyze the design and results of quasi-experiments to evaluate the support they provide for causal claims.

3. Explain the major differences between small-*N* designs and large-*N* designs.

4. Analyze the design and results of small-*N* experiments to evaluate the support they provide for causal claims.

Previous chapters of this book have explained how to interrogate frequency claims (Chapters 6 and 7), association claims (Chapters 8 and 9), and causal claims (Chapters 10–12). The last two chapters focus on a more general issue: how researchers balance research priorities in conducting their studies. Of course, scientists always want to conduct the best studies possible, but they are constrained by practical issues, and they must conduct their work ethically. How do they balance scientific goals with practical realities?

This chapter discusses situations in which conducting a true experiment is not feasible. For example, a researcher might not be able to randomly assign participants to different groups or counterbalance conditions in a within-groups experiment. What are the trade-offs? How do scientists establish internal validity when full experimental control is impossible? In other instances, researchers may be able to collect data from only one case, such as a person with a rare disorder or unusual behavioral problem. How might practitioners and scientists balance priorities for internal and external validity when they study just a single case?

Quasi-Experiments

A **quasi-experiment** differs from a true experiment in that the researchers do not have full experimental control. They start by selecting an independent variable and a dependent variable. Then they study participants who are exposed to each level of the independent variable. However, in a quasi-experiment, they might not be able to randomly assign participants to one level or the other. Instead, participants are assigned to the independent variable conditions by teachers, political regulations, acts of nature—or even by their own choice.

Two Examples of Independent-Groups Quasi-Experiments

The following two examples of quasi-experiments use an independent-groups design. In these examples, there are different participants at each level of the independent variable. This type of quasi-experimental design is typically called a **nonequivalent control group design**: a quasi-experimental study that has at least one treatment group and one comparison group, but participants have not been randomly assigned to the two groups.

The Head Start Study

Head Start is a government-funded, early-childhood education program in the United States that gives a quality preschool experience to children from economically poor homes. Does the program really improve the academic performance of the children it serves? To find out, early in the program's history, educational researchers compared the academic performance of children in the Head Start program with that of children who were not in the program (Cicirelli & Associates, 1969). However, they soon ran into a real-world policy that could harm the internal validity of their studies: Any child who qualifies for Head Start has a right to enroll. Therefore, children are assigned to Head Start by social workers and administrators; they cannot be randomly assigned to Head Start versus some comparison program.

Nevertheless, one early study attempted to assess the efficacy of Head Start by finding a comparison group of children who had not been enrolled in Head Start programs but who seemed similar to Head Start children. Specifically, the comparison group's scores on an early childhood Stanford Achievement Test were about the same. (The researchers tried to match the children on their achievement test scores.) However, even though the Head Start children and the comparison children had similar achievement scores, they were probably different in other ways. One important difference was family income: The Head Start children were economically disadvantaged, while the comparison children were not (after all, economic disadvantage was the main eligibility requirement). Therefore, although this study had an independent variable (participating in Head Start or not) and a dependent variable (later academic achievement), the study was a quasi-experiment. The children were not randomly assigned to the two groups, so the groups were not perfectly equivalent (thus the name nonequivalent control group design).

Administrators of Head Start hoped to show that this intensive preschool program would help at-risk children perform better in school when they got to grade school. However, the results of the study showed that the achievement scores of the Head Start students were *worse* than the scores of the comparison group (**Figure 13.1**). As you read the rest of this chapter, consider what these results mean: Did the program simply fail to work? Did the Head Start program actually interfere with children's academic progress? Or was there something about the quasi-experiment that led to this result?

The Psychological Effects of Cosmetic Surgery

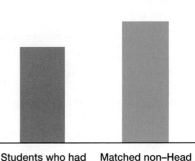

FIGURE 13.1 **Head Start and academic performance.** Students who had participated in Head Start programs scored lower than students who did not participate. According to this quasi-experiment, is the Head Start program a failure? (Source: Adapted from results reported by Cicirelli & Associates, 1969; Shadish & Luellen, 2006.)

Around the world, plastic surgeons perform about 8.5 million cosmetic surgeries each year (International Society of Aesthetic Plastic Surgery, 2011). Anecdotal evidence indicates that people who undergo such procedures think they will improve their self-esteem, well-being, and body image. But does cosmetic surgery really achieve these results? One way to answer this question would be to randomly assign people to have plastic surgery or not. In normal circumstances, though, this would not be ethically or practically feasible, because researchers cannot assign people to undergo an unnecessary and possibly risky surgery.

A team of psychological scientists found a way to study the effects of cosmetic surgery (Margraf, Meyer, & Lavallee, 2013). They recruited a sample of about 600 patients at a clinic in Germany who had already elected to undergo plastic surgery. The researchers administered a batch of psychological measures to this sample of patients. They measured their self-esteem, life satisfaction, self-rated general attractiveness, and other variables at four time periods: before surgery, and then 3 months, 6 months, and 1 year after surgery. As a comparison group, the researchers found a sample of about 250 people who had registered at the same plastic surgery clinic, having indicated their interest in receiving surgery, but who had not yet undergone any procedures. This comparison group filled out the self-esteem, life satisfaction, and attractiveness measures at the same times as the surgery group.

This study looks like an experiment. There is an independent variable (having cosmetic surgery or not), and there are dependent variables (measures of self-esteem, well-being, and attractiveness). However, the participants were not randomly assigned to the two conditions, and the lack of random assignment made this a quasi-experiment. People were self-assigned to the two independent variable groups according to whether they had actually had cosmetic surgery or not. The Margraf team's study is an example of a **nonequivalent control group pretest/posttest design**, because the participants were not randomly assigned to groups, and were tested both before and after some intervention.

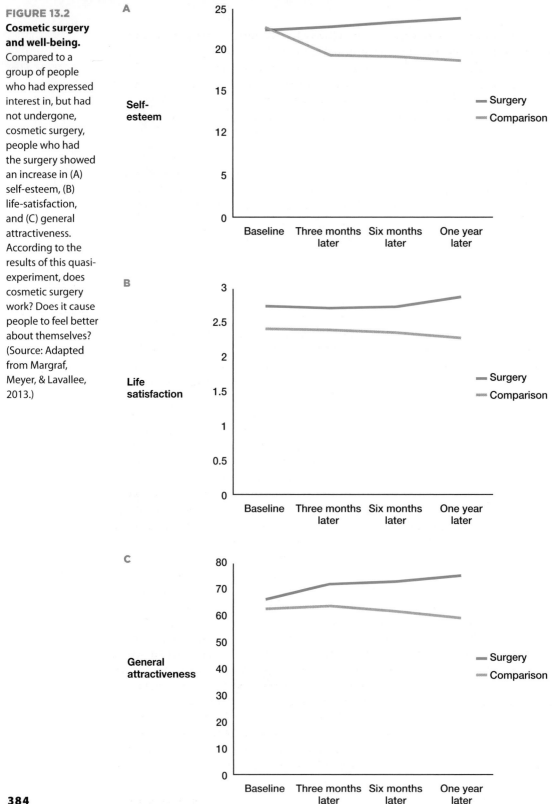

FIGURE 13.2

Cosmetic surgery and well-being. Compared to a group of people who had expressed interest in, but had not undergone, cosmetic surgery, people who had the surgery showed an increase in (A) self-esteem, (B) life-satisfaction, and (C) general attractiveness. According to the results of this quasi-experiment, does cosmetic surgery work? Does it cause people to feel better about themselves? (Source: Adapted from Margraf, Meyer, & Lavallee, 2013.)

The results of the study are shown in **Figure 13.2**. Although both groups started out the same on a standard measure of self-esteem, the two groups had diverged a year later. Similarly, the surgery group started out with slightly higher life satisfaction and general attractiveness than the comparison group, and the surgery group had increased on these measures 1 year later. Does this study allow us to say that the cosmetic surgery *caused* people's self-image and life satisfaction to improve?

Two Examples of Repeated-Measures Quasi-Experiments

Quasi-experiments can be repeated-measures designs, too, in which participants experience all levels of an independent variable. In a quasi-experimental version of this design, as opposed to a true repeated-measures experiment, the researcher takes advantage of an already-scheduled event, a new policy or regulation, or a chance occurrence to manipulate the independent variable. The following two studies are examples of repeated-measures quasi-experiments.

Food Breaks and Parole Decisions

Legal decisions, such as whether or not a prison inmate should be granted parole, are made by judges who presumably consider the facts of each case objectively. However, research on human biases in reasoning raises the possibility that even judicial decisions might be distorted by irrelevant, extraneous factors.

To review reasoning biases, see Chapter 2, pp. 30–35.

A team of researchers set out to investigate the effect of one particular extraneous factor on judicial decision making: a food break (Danziger, Levav, & Avnaim-Pesso, 2011). They collected data on more than 1,100 parole rulings that took place on 50 different days, for prisoners who were incarcerated in one of four major prisons in Israel. Judges had to decide whether each prisoner should be granted parole or not. The prisoners were both Israeli and Arab, male and female, and had committed crimes such as assault, theft, embezzlement, and murder. According to Danziger and his team, given the seriousness of most of the crimes, the easiest decision in each case would be to keep the prisoner in jail—to deny parole. Indeed, about 65% of the time, on average, judges decided to reject parole. In contrast, in order to justify approving parole, a judge would have had to pay close attention to the evidence, think carefully, and write a detailed justification.

The researchers recorded each prisoner's crime, the judge's decision (parole granted or denied), and crucially, the time of day each decision was made. The results of the study are depicted in **Figure 13.3**, which shows the proportion of cases that resulted in parole approval, listed by time of day (averaged over all 50 days in the study). The first few cases of the day were especially likely to be granted parole, and the probability declines quickly from there. However, judges had a mid-morning snack of a sandwich and fruit (marked with a circle and dotted line in the graph). After this food break the probability of parole approval jumped back up, and then declined again. After lunch break, judges were similarly more likely to approve parole, compared to cases heard at the very end of the day.

In the published study, the authors explain that this pattern of results is consistent with a theory of "decision fatigue" (Danziger et al., 2011). After making a series of complex choices, people become mentally tired and invest less effort in subsequent decision making. A short break can restore mental energy, because it

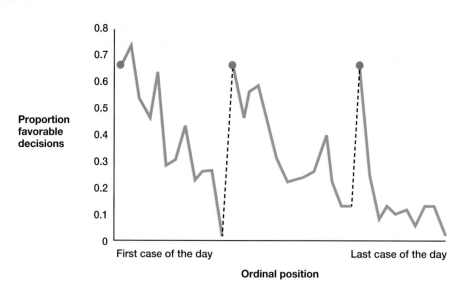

FIGURE 13.3 Judicial decision making. As the day went on, Israeli judges were increasingly less likely to approve parole, unless the case they heard came right after a snack or lunch break (dotted vertical lines). Does this quasi-experiment show that food breaks cause judges to consider a case more carefully? (Source: Danziger et al., 2011.)

provides rest and because the food restores glucose (blood sugar) that gets depleted in the decision-making process.

The judicial decision-making study is an example of an **interrupted time-series design**, a quasi-experimental study that measures participants repeatedly on a dependent variable (in this example, parole decision making) before, during, and after the "interruption" caused by some event (a food break).

Television Access and Crime Rates

Another quasi-experiment took advantage of a historical event. In the early days of television in the United States, individual cities had to apply for a license to transmit TV signals. After issuing licenses up to 1949, the Federal Communications Commission (FCC) stopped issuing broadcasting licenses for 3 years (1949–1952). During the early 1950s, therefore, some U.S. cities had access to television, and others did not. After 1952, the FCC resumed licensing cities bit by bit, and people in newly licensed cities began buying more TV sets.

Years later, some clever researchers took advantage of this situation to study crime rates in cities with and without widespread access to television (Hennigan et al., 1982). Specifically, they measured whether rates of larceny (nonviolent theft) rose in a city in the months after TV became available and after most citizens had purchased TVs. This quasi-experiment has an independent variable (TV exposure) and a dependent variable (larceny rate). The researchers measured larceny rates both before and after the introduction of television. This independent variable (the introduction of TV) was not controlled by the researchers but instead was a historical event. The lack of full experimenter control is what made the study a quasi-experiment.

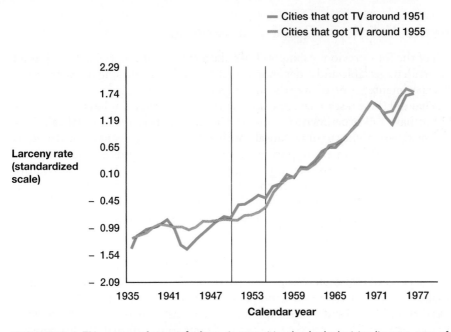

— Cities that got TV around 1951
— Cities that got TV around 1955

FIGURE 13.4 TV access and rates of crime. Among cities that had television licenses, rates of larceny (theft) were higher between 1951 and 1955. After 1955, an FCC freeze on broadcasting licenses had been lifted long enough for other cities to get access and the cities with newly introduced TV showed a rise in larceny rates. Does this quasi-experiment demonstrate that television caused larceny rates to increase? (Source: Adapted from Hennigan et al., 1982.)

The researchers also compared larceny rates in cities that had television with rates in cities that did not—an independent-groups comparison. This independent-groups manipulation of the independent variable was not controlled by the researchers, either: Cities were not randomly assigned to have TV access or not; instead, the FCC had inadvertently assigned cities to these two groups by imposing the freeze on new television licenses. Therefore, the comparison groups in the independent-groups part of the study were also quasi-experimental.

The results of this analysis are shown in **Figure 13.4**. Notice that larceny rates rose right after 1951, but only in cities that had earlier been granted access to television. After 1955, however, larceny rates similarly increased only in those cities in which citizens had recently acquired TV. Do these results show that television *caused* these increases in crime?

The design used in this study is sometimes called a **nonequivalent control group interrupted time-series design**. It combines two of the previous designs (the nonequivalent control group design and the interrupted time-series design). In this example, the independent variable was studied both as a repeated-measures variable (interrupted time-series) and as an independent-groups variable (non-equivalent control group). In both cases, however, the researchers did not have experimental control over the manipulation of the independent variable or the assignment of participants to conditions.

Internal Validity in Quasi-Experiments

Each of the four previous examples *looks* like a true experiment: Each one has an independent variable and a dependent variable. What is missing in every case is full experimenter control over the independent variable.

What did these researchers give up when they conducted studies in which they did not have full experimenter control? The main concern is internal validity—the researchers' ability to draw causal conclusions from the results. The degree to which a quasi-experiment supports a causal statement depends on two things: its design and its results. To interrogate internal validity, you ask about alternative explanations for an observed pattern of results. The internal validity threats for experiments discussed in Chapters 10 and 11 also apply to quasi-experiments. How well do the four examples of quasi-experiments hold up to an internal validity interrogation? Are they susceptible to the internal validity threats?

As you read this section, keep in mind that quasi-experiments can take a variety of designs, and the support that a quasi-experiment provides for a causal claim depends partly on its design and partly on the results a researcher obtains. Researchers do not have full control of the independent variable in a quasi-experiment (as they do in a true experiment), but they can choose better designs, and they can use the pattern of results to rule out some internal validity threats.

Selection Effects

Selection effects are relevant only for independent-groups designs, not for repeated-measures designs. A selection threat to internal validity applies when the groups at the various levels of an independent variable contain different types of participants. In such cases, it is not clear whether it was the independent variable or the different types of participants in each group that led to a difference in the dependent variable between the groups.

Consider the Head Start study in the first example. The results showed that the Head Start group performed more poorly than the non–Head Start group on achievement tests in grade school (Cicirelli & Associates, 1969; Shadish & Luellen, 2006). On the basis of these results, can you claim that the Head Start program *caused* the children to do worse? That's one explanation, but you can't rule out the alternative explanation of a selection effect. Even though the Head Start group's early childhood achievement scores were equivalent to those of the children in the comparison group (because the children were matched on this variable), the Head Start group was different in many other important ways. For example, the Head Start children were living in poverty, and the comparison children were not. The Head Start children were more likely to come from single-parent homes than the children in the comparison group. The internal validity threat is that you do not know whether the Head Start group's achievement scores in grade school were lower because of the Head Start program or because this group had different kinds of children in it (**Figure 13.5**). They might have performed more poorly over time because of their poverty or because they lived in single-parent homes, not because the Head Start program was detrimental.

Similarly, in the cosmetic surgery study, the people who actually had the surgery may have been different from those who simply expressed interest in it. Indeed, when the researchers asked, a full 61% of the comparison group reported they had not gone through with surgery because they couldn't afford it (Margraf et al., 2013). On the one hand, there may have been a selection effect in this study; people who had cosmetic surgery might have been more financially well-off than people who did not have the procedure. On the other hand, the pretest/posttest nature of the study helps rule out selection effects, too. Financial stability might explain why one group started out higher in life satisfaction, but it does not seem a reasonable explanation for why the surgery group increased in self-esteem and general attractiveness over time (see Figure 13.2).

FIGURE 13.5 Head Start studies and selection effects. In many studies, the children eligible for Head Start were different from children in comparison groups on several variables, including school achievement, family structure, family income, and cultural background.

The Margraf team took steps to help counteract selection effects in their study. For some of their analyses, they used information on age, gender, body mass index, income, and several other variables to create **matched groups**, matching 179 people from the surgery group with 179 people from the comparison group. They compared the results from the matched-groups data to the results from the full samples (about 500 people in the surgery group and 264 in the comparison group), and found similar results both times. The matched-groups version of the data gave these researchers confidence that selection effects were not responsible for the differences they observed.

Some researchers control for selection effects in a quasi-experiment by using a **wait-list design**, in which all the participants plan to receive treatment, but are assigned to do so at different times. The Margraf team could have studied a group of people, all of whom were scheduled for cosmetic surgery, instructing half to receive their surgery right away and placing others on a waiting list for surgery at a later time. They could then measure the patterns of self-esteem, life satisfaction, and general attractiveness in both groups over several months, when only one of the groups would have had surgery. When such a procedure is used, it can make the researchers more certain that the same kinds of people are in each group.

Design Confounds

In certain quasi-experiments, design confounds can be a problem. Recall that in a design confound, some outside variable accidentally and systematically varies with the levels of the targeted independent variable. In the Danziger study on food breaks and parole decision making, you might question whether the judicial cases that came up for ruling right after the food breaks were systematically different from those that occurred later (Danziger et al., 2011). For example, were the prisoners the judges saw right after they ate lunch guilty of less serious crimes? Had they been in prison less time? Did they have fewer previous incarcerations? If the early cases were less serious than the later ones, that would be an alternative explanation for why they were more likely to have been granted parole.

Danziger and his team, however, were able to use additional data from the study to rule out this design confound. When they tracked the seriousness of each case across its position during the day, they found absolutely no relationship. Compared to the later cases, earlier cases and those that occurred right after a food break involved prisoners who, on average, had the same number of previous incarcerations, had just as serious offenses, and had served the same amount of months. Therefore, by inspecting the data carefully, the researchers were able to rule out potential design confounds.

Maturation Threat

Maturation threats occur when, in an experimental or quasi-experimental design with a pretest and posttest, a treatment group shows an improvement over time, but it is not clear whether the improvement was caused by the treatment or whether the group would have improved spontaneously, even without a treatment.

The cosmetic surgery study had a pretest and posttest, so it was potentially susceptible to a maturation threat. Because the participants who had surgery did improve over time in self-esteem, life satisfaction, and general attractiveness (see Figure 13.2), you might ask whether the surgery was the reason, or whether it was maturation. Perhaps everybody simply improves in these qualities over time. Fortunately, the design of this quasi-experiment included a comparison group, and the results indicated that the comparison group did not improve over time; in fact, they got slightly worse on the same variables. Because of the design and the pattern of results, you can probably rule out maturation as an internal validity threat in this study.

In the fourth example, did access to television cause larceny rates to rise, or did larceny rates simply increase on their own? The overall trend in Figure 13.4, across all years, clearly shows that larceny rates went up over time. But this study's design lets you rule out maturation, or spontaneous change, as the sole explanation for the rise in larceny after the introduction of TV. Because this study used a comparison group, you can compare the increases in crime rates in the two types of cities (those with TV and those without). Larceny rates did rise between 1951 and 1955 in the cities without TV (a sign of possible maturation), but the rates rose even faster in cities with television. In addition, right after 1955, larceny rates continued to rise everywhere, but they rose even faster in cities that had more recently received TV licenses (**Figure 13.6**). In short, the design and results of the study let you conclude that larceny rates do go up everywhere over time, but television access accelerates this rise. You can rule out the maturation threat to internal validity.

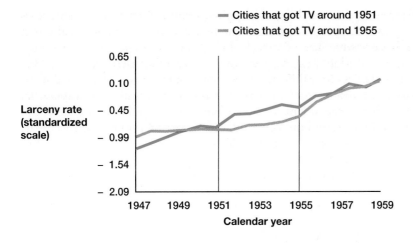

Legend:
— Cities that got TV around 1951
— Cities that got TV around 1955

Larceny rate (standardized scale)

y-axis: 0.65, 0.10, −0.45, −0.99, −1.54, −2.09

x-axis (Calendar year): 1947, 1949, 1951, 1953, 1955, 1957, 1959

History Threat

A history threat occurs when an external, historical event happens for everyone in a study at the same time as the treatment variable. With a history threat, it is unclear whether the outcome is caused by the treatment or by the common, external event or factor.

Crime rates between 1951 and 1955 may have risen, for instance, not because of television but because of a government policy introduced during that time period, because of economic recession, or even because of feelings of Cold War alienation. As you might imagine, history threats can be especially relevant when a quasi-experiment relies on external factors (such as the FCC's television policies) to manipulate its key variable. Fortunately, the design of this particular study (Hennigan et al., 1982) included a comparison group, which helped rule out most history threats. Public policies, a recession, or effects of the Cold War would have affected *all* cities, but according to the study results, only the cities with TV access showed the jump in larceny rates during this time period.

Of course, it is possible that the cities with earlier access to television also experienced some local historical event (perhaps a local economic downturn) that would explain the rise in larceny rates in only those cities. Such a threat would be a selection-history threat, because the history threat applies to only one group, not the other. In a selection-history threat, the historical event systematically affects participants only in the treatment group or only in the comparison group— not both. Although this kind of threat is a possibility in the Hennigan study, it seems unlikely that only the cities that happened to receive FCC TV licenses would also have some other historical event in common. In addition, it is unlikely that in 1952, when the remaining cities got their licenses, the same local historical event that had occurred in the cities licensed earlier just happened to occur again in the cities licensed later.

Similarly, perhaps the participants in the Margraf cosmetic surgery study experienced increased life satisfaction over time because the economy in Germany (where the study took place) was improving during the same time period.

Economic events like recessions can be potential history threats for any longitudinal study, but there are two reasons for ruling out this history threat in the cosmetic surgery study. First, the study design included a comparison group, and results showed that this group did not increase life satisfaction over the same time periods. Second, while good economic conditions provide an alternative explanation for increased life satisfaction, they are unlikely to explain an increase in the other dependent variables, such as self-esteem and general appearance. When quasi-experiments include a comparison group, history threats to internal validity can usually be ruled out.

Regression to the Mean

Regression to the mean occurs when an extreme finding is caused by a combination of random factors that are unlikely to happen in the same combination again, so the extreme finding gets less extreme over time. Chapter 11 gave the example of Portugal's 7–0 win in a World Cup soccer game. That extreme score was a lucky combination of random factors that did not repeat itself in the next game, so the next game's score regressed back toward the average, or mean.

Many educational researchers have suggested that regression to the mean was partly responsible for the surprising results of the Head Start study (Cicirelli & Associates, 1969; Shadish & Luellen, 2006). Recall that the researchers attempted to create equivalent groups of Head Start and non–Head Start children by matching them on their achievement scores at the beginning of the study. Because children who are eligible for Head Start typically have lower scores than those who are not eligible, the researchers had to select special subsets of these two types of children to create matched groups. Specifically, they may have selected a relatively *high-scoring* group of Head Start children and a relatively *low-scoring* group of non–Head Start children.

Although that process created groups that were matched at pretest, it may have also introduced the potential for regression. The high-scoring group of Head Start children had a high pretest average for a combination of reasons. They may have been smart, but they also benefited from a random combination of lucky factors. Some of the children may have happened to eat a great breakfast, others had an exceptionally good night's sleep, and a few others just happened to know some of the test questions perfectly. In short, this group's pretest average was partly a result of skill and partly a result of good luck. In turn, the comparison group of non–Head Start children may have had low scores, in part, because of an unlucky combination of random factors: Some had skipped breakfast, others had gone to bed late, and others had blanked on some of the easy questions. In short, this group's pretest average was partly a result of skill and partly a result of bad luck.

When the group of high-scoring Head Start students were tested again later, they would not all have experienced the same lucky combination of random factors, so their score regressed down, closer to the mean of other Head Starters. Similarly, when the low-scoring non–Head Start group of children were tested again later, they would not have experienced the same unlucky combination of random factors, so their score regressed up, closer to the mean of other non–Head

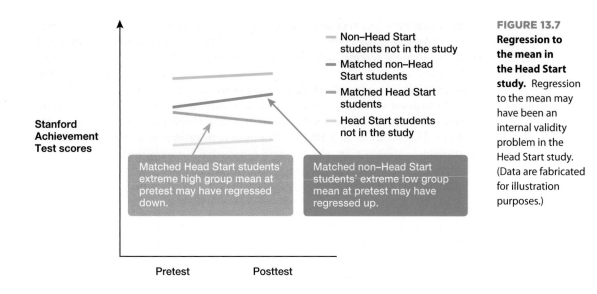

FIGURE 13.7

Regression to the mean in the Head Start study. Regression to the mean may have been an internal validity problem in the Head Start study. (Data are fabricated for illustration purposes.)

Start students (**Figure 13.7**). The outcome was a disappointing difference: The Head Start program appeared to have hurt the children's academic progress.

Many researchers have come to suspect that the posttest difference was at-tributable to regression. Indeed, this study is only one in a large body of research on the effectiveness of the Head Start program. In some other studies, Head Start students showed academic achievement gains; in addition, they showed more positive social outcomes, such as graduation from high school (Barnett, 1998; McKey et al., 1985).

Remember that regression effects are a threat to internal validity primarily when a group is selected because of its extremely high or low scores. Those scores may be extreme, in part, because of a combination of random factors that will not occur the same way twice. In the other quasi-experiments in this chapter, the groups were not selected on purpose for their high or low scores, so regression was less likely to be a problem. And true experiments use random assignment to place participants into groups, a practice that eliminates regression to the mean as an internal validity threat.

Attrition Threat

In designs with pretests and posttests, attrition occurs when people drop out of a study over time. Attrition becomes an internal validity threat when people drop out of a study for some systematic reason. In the cosmetic surgery study, for exam-ple, you might wonder whether people's self-image improved only because those who were disappointed with their surgery outcomes stopped responding to the study over time. If only the happiest, most satisfied participants complied with the study, that would explain the apparent increase in self-esteem, life satisfaction, and general appearance over time. In this case, it would not be the surgery, but the attrition of the most dissatisfied participants that caused the decrease.

Fortunately, attrition is easy to check for, and the researchers in the Margraf team made sure it was not an explanation for their results. Here is an excerpt from the Method section of the published study:

> *Missing Values Analysis.* Completers were defined as having available data at all four time points, as opposed to dropouts who did not. The comparison group contained more dropouts than the surgery group. . . . Completers did not differ from dropouts with respect to any analyzed outcome variable at baseline, 3- and 6-month follow-up, and neither with respect to the following eight features at baseline: clinic, occupation, treatment type, gender, age, body mass index, income. . . . (Margraf et al., 2013, pp. 7–8)

The statement above indicates that although some people—especially those in the comparison group—dropped out of the study, the dropouts were not systematically different from completers. Because the attrition was unsystematic, the researchers concluded that attrition was not a threat to internal validity.

Testing and Instrumentation Threats

Whenever researchers measure participants more than once, they need to be concerned about testing threats to internal validity. A testing threat is a kind of order effect in which participants tend to change as a result of having been tested before. Repeated testing might cause people to improve, regardless of the treatment they received. Repeated testing might also cause performance to decline because of fatigue or boredom.

Instrumentation, too, can be an internal validity threat when participants are tested or observed twice. A measuring instrument could change over repeated uses, and this change would threaten internal validity. If a study uses two versions of a test with different standards (e.g., one test is more difficult), or if a study uses coders who change their standards over time, then participants might appear to change, when in reality there is no change between one observation and the next.

You can use a study's results and design to interrogate testing and instrumentation threats to internal validity. Consider the design and results of the cosmetic surgery study. Participants in both the surgery group and the comparison group were tested multiple times on their self-esteem, life satisfaction, and body image. A simple testing effect or instrumentation effect would have caused both groups to improve or both to worsen, but the surgery group improved over time, while the comparison group declined. A comparison group like the one in this study almost always helps rule out a testing threat to internal validity.

The judicial decision making study provides a unique instance of an instrumentation effect. The measuring instrument in this case was the judge's assessment of a prisoner's readiness for parole. Danziger and his team's study illustrated how the judge's objectivity changed over time with fatigue. Although you might call this an instrumentation effect, rather than being a threat to internal validity, the effect is actually the study's central result!

Observer Bias, Demand Characteristics, and Placebo Effects

Three final threats to internal validity are related to human subjectivity. Observer bias, in addition to being a threat to construct validity, can also threaten internal validity when the experimenters' expectations influence their interpretation of the results. Other threats include demand characteristics, when participants guess what the study is about and change their behavior in the expected direction, and placebo effects, when participants improve, but only because they believe they are receiving an effective treatment. Fortunately, these three threats are easy to interrogate. For observer bias, you simply ask who measured the behaviors. Was the design blind (masked) or double-blind? For experimental demand, you can think about whether the participants were able to detect the study's goals and responded accordingly. For placebo effects, you can ask whether the design of a study included a comparison group that received an inert, or placebo, treatment.

Consider the study that evaluated the psychological effects of cosmetic surgery (Margraf et al., 2013). Even though this study was not double-blind (participants obviously knew whether or not they had had surgery), the chance of observer bias was low because the experimenters asked participants to self-report their own self-esteem and other variables. However, the study might have been susceptible to a placebo effect. People who have cosmetic surgery are usually aware that they chose to undergo such a procedure in order to feel better about themselves. Perhaps it's not surprising, then, that they increased their self-reported self-esteem and life satisfaction! A better way to study the question might be to disguise the fact that the longitudinal study was investigating cosmetic surgery; present it simply as a series of questionnaires. Although this approach might be difficult in terms of practicality, it might reduce the chance for participants in either group to consciously increase or decrease their scores. (**Figure 13.8**).

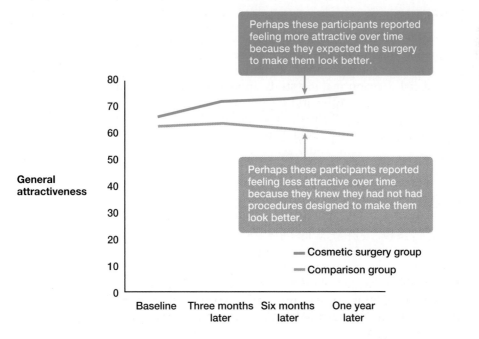

FIGURE 13.8
Interrogating placebo effects in the cosmetic surgery study.
(Source: Adapted from Margraf et al., 2013.)

Most of these threats can be ruled out in the other studies. Larceny rates are a matter of public record, so observer bias, demand characteristics, and/or placebo effects are unlikely to explain the increase in crime rates in cities without TV. In Danziger's study, judges probably value being objective, and would almost certainly not have intentionally changed their behavior in the observed direction. In fact, the judges' decisions in this study were simply analyzed through public records; the judges did not know they were part of a study, thereby eliminating demand characteristics as an internal validity threat.

Balancing Priorities in Quasi-Experiments

What does an experimenter gain by conducting a quasi-experiment? If quasi-experimental studies can be vulnerable to internal validity threats, why would a researcher use one?

Real-World Opportunities

One reason is that quasi-experimental designs, such as those in the TV access and crime rates study, the cosmetic surgery study, and the judicial decision making study, enable researchers to take advantage of real-world opportunities to study interesting phenomena and important events. Hennigan and his colleagues would never have been able to randomly assign towns to have television access (or not), but they took advantage of the research opportunity the FCC inadvertently provided. Similarly, Margraf and his colleagues did not manipulate cosmetic surgery and the Danziger team did not manipulate the timing of food breaks. However, both research teams took advantage of the next-best thing—events that occurred in real-world settings.

External Validity

The real-world settings of many quasi-experiments can enhance external validity: the likelihood that the patterns observed in the quasi-experiment will generalize to other settings and to other individuals. You don't have to ask whether the judicial decision making study applies to real-world settings, because the study occurred in a real-world setting. You don't have to wonder whether TV access increases rates of theft in the real world, because the events in the study did take place in the real world. You might still ask whether the judicial decision making study's results would generalize to other countries, or whether the TV and crime rate study's results would generalize to world regions other than the United States. In general, quasi-experiments capitalize on real-world situations, even as they give up some control over internal validity. (In contrast, as Chapter 14 will discuss, many laboratory experiments seek to maximize internal validity while giving up some external validity.)

Ethics

Ethical concerns are another reason researchers might choose a quasi-experimental design. Many questions of interest to researchers would be unethical to study in a true experiment. The Head Start study is a good example:

It would not be ethical to withhold free preschool education from a group of children by randomly assigning some children to be enrolled in the Head Start program and others not to be enrolled. Even a wait-list design would not be ethical here; by the time the wait-listed children started the program, they might be too old to benefit from it. Therefore, quasi-experiments are the only ethical way to study Head Start. Similarly, it would not be ethical to assign elective cosmetic surgery to people who don't want it, or to withhold television from residents of randomly assigned towns, but quasi-experiments can be an ethical option for studying these interesting questions.

Construct Validity and Statistical Validity in Quasi-Experiments

Thus far, this chapter has focused on internal validity, because researchers usually conduct quasi-experiments in order to make causal statements. External validity—the ability to generalize to real-world situations—was also mentioned as an advantage of many quasi-experimental designs. The other two validities should be interrogated as well.

For construct validity, you would interrogate how successfully the study manipulated or measured its variables. Usually, quasi-experiments show excellent construct validity for the independent variable, as illustrated by the examples in this chapter. In the cosmetic surgery study, people really did or did not undergo a procedure. In the judicial decision making study, judges really did get a food break or not. You also have to ask how successfully the dependent variables were measured in these studies: How well did the cosmetic surgery researchers measure self-esteem, life satisfaction, and general attractiveness? Were these measures internally reliable? And did they measure what they were intended to measure?

Finally, to assess a quasi-experimental study's statistical validity, you could ask how large the group differences were (the effect size), and whether the results were statistically significant.

Are Quasi-Experiments the Same as Correlational Studies?

Some quasi-experiments seem similar in design to correlational studies (see Chapters 8 and 9). When a quasi-experiment uses an independent-groups design—that is, when it compares two groups without using random assignment—the groups in the study can look similar to those in correlational studies.

Consider, for example, the Cacioppo et al. (2013) study about meeting one's spouse online and marital satisfaction (discussed in Chapter 8). The categorical variable in that study—whether people met online or in person—looks like a quasi-experimental independent variable. There are two categories (meeting online or not), and couples were not randomly assigned to one or the other category. It seems like a correlational study because there were two measured variables, but it also seems like a quasi-experiment, because it studied two groups of people who were not randomly assigned. Quasi-experiments and correlational designs also have similar internal validity concerns: Just as you might ask about third variables or unmeasured "lurking" variables in a correlational study, you might ask about selection effects in a quasi-experimental study.

Although the two are similar, in quasi-experiments the researchers tend to do a little more meddling than they do in most correlational designs. In correlational studies, researchers simply select a sample, measure two variables, and test the relationship between them. In quasi-experiments, however, the researchers might attempt to achieve internal validity by matching participants (as in the Head Start and cosmetic surgery studies), implementing a wait-list policy, or seeking out comparison groups provided by nature or by public policy (as in the judicial decision making and the TV and larceny studies). Therefore, whereas correlational researchers primarily measure variables in a sample and analyze their relationships, quasi-experimental researchers more actively select groups for an independent variable so they can achieve a greater degree of internal validity.

Ultimately, the distinction between quasi-experiments and correlational studies can be a blurry one, and some studies may be difficult to categorize. Rather than becoming too concerned about how to categorize a particular study as either quasi-experimental or correlational, focus instead on applying what you know about threats to internal validity and evaluating causal claims. These critical thinking tools apply regardless of how you classify the study's design.

CHECK YOUR UNDERSTANDING

1. How is a nonequivalent control group design different from a true independent-groups experiment?

2. How are interrupted time-series designs and nonequivalent control group interrupted time-series designs different from true within-groups experiments?

3. Describe why both the design and the results of a study are important for assessing a quasi-experiment's internal validity.

4. What are three reasons a researcher might conduct a quasi-experiment, rather than a true experiment, to study a research question?

1. See p. 382; only a true independent-groups experiment randomly assigns participants to the groups. 2. See pp. 385–387; only a true within-groups experiment can control the order of presentation of the levels of the independent variable. 3. See pp. 388–396. 4. See pp. 396–397.

Small-*N* Designs: Studying Only a Few Individuals

Sometimes researchers conduct experiments and studies with only a few participants. As discussed in earlier chapters, having a very large sample (a large *N*) is not always necessary. For the purpose of external validity, how a sample is selected is more important than the sample's size (see Chapter 7). Even a small sample can detect a large effect size (see Chapter 11), meaning that statistical

TABLE 13.1 Differences Between Large-*N* and Small-*N* Designs

Large-*N* designs	Small-*N* designs
1. *Participants are grouped.* The data from an individual participant are not of interest in themselves; data from all participants in each group are combined and studied together.	1. *Each participant is treated as a separate experiment.* Small-*N* designs are almost always repeated-measures designs, in which researchers observe how the person or animal responds to several systematically designed conditions.
2. Data are represented as *group averages.*	2. *Individuals' data* are presented.

validity is not necessarily undermined by a small sample. If small samples are often appropriate in research, how small can they be? Is it possible to draw conclusions from a study that uses only one or two participants? What priorities are researchers balancing when they study only a few people or animals at a time?

When researchers use a **small-*N* design**, instead of gathering a little information from a larger sample, they obtain a lot of information from just a few cases. They may even restrict their study to only one animal or one person, using a **single-*N* design**. Large-*N* designs and small-*N* designs differ in two key ways, summarized in **Table 13.1**.

Research on Split Brains

Along with his colleagues, neuroscientist Michael Gazzaniga (2005) performed research on only a few very unrepresentative people. This work has taught psychologists a great deal about how the human brain is organized—and even about the nature of human consciousness and the sense of self. Gazzaniga was a student of Nobel Laureate Roger Sperry, who pioneered techniques for studying the brain's two hemispheres (e.g., Sperry, 1961). The people Gazzaniga studied all had a history of severe epilepsy (Gazzaniga, Bogen, & Sperry, 1962). Their seizures were both strong and intractable; doctors could not control the electrical "storms" that would surge through their brains. All patients also underwent an effective last-resort treatment: surgery to cut apart the *corpus callosum*, a large band of nerve fibers at the center of the brain that allows neural messages to travel from the right hemisphere to the left hemisphere and back again. When neurosurgeons sever the corpus callosum of a patient with severe seizures, they essentially cut a main highway for the electrical storms, and the seizures become less debilitating.

People with so-called split brains appear to function normally, even though the two hemispheres do not communicate directly with each other. Gazzaniga and his colleagues wanted to create specially designed conditions in which they could study the two hemispheres separately—to try to send visual information to only one hemisphere of the brain at a time and observe what would happen.

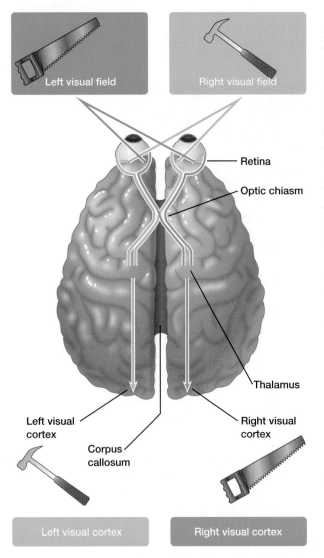

The researchers started with their existing understanding of how the visual system works. As **Figure 13.9** shows, an image from the left visual field goes to the right hemisphere, and an image from the right visual field goes to the left hemisphere. As a result, the normal human brain takes in a *full picture* of the visual field. Even with only one eye open, a person can process the whole scene, because the corpus callosum sends the images to both sides of the brain. A split-brain patient can take in a full picture of the visual field, too, by quickly shifting his or her eyes from right to left—that way, both hemispheres typically get the whole picture. But Gazzaniga and his colleagues wanted to send a different picture to each hemisphere. To do so, they used a device that presented the images to the split-brain patients so quickly that they did not have time to shift their eyes. The researchers thus ensured that the image from the left visual field went only to the right hemisphere of the brain, and the image from the right visual field went only to the left hemisphere of the brain.

As it turned out, if Gazzaniga presented a picture of a hammer to the left hemisphere (by showing on the right side of the visual field) and asked the split-brain patients what they saw, the patients could easily say they saw a hammer. But when a picture of a saw went only to the right hemisphere (it fell on the left side of the visual field), the patients reported that they did not see anything. This initial result supported what researchers had already learned—that, for most of us, speech is produced by the left hemisphere.

Even more interesting, when Gazzaniga placed a pen in the patients' left hand (the hand the right hemisphere controls) and asked them to draw what they had seen, the

FIGURE 13.9 The human brain, top view. The lenses of the eyes invert the right and left visual fields, so that the right visual field projects images onto the left half of each retina and vice versa. Meanwhile, the left half of each retina sends information to the left visual cortex, and the right half of each retina sends information to the right visual cortex. If the image of a hammer is presented to the right visual field, it will be processed by the left hemisphere of the brain.

split-brain patients could draw the tool that had been presented to the right hemisphere—the saw. The right brain knew what tool it had seen but could not articulate it. When the patients opened their eyes to look at the pictures they had drawn, the left hemisphere now got involved and could say verbally, "That's a saw." The patients could not say *why* they drew the saw, but they could recognize it just the same.

Based on research with people who have split brains, Gazzaniga and his colleagues (2005; Turk, Heatherton, Macrae, Kelley, & Gazzaniga, 2003) have also suggested that the left hemisphere may be responsible for making cause-and-effect judgments. For example, when shown an image with a chicken foot and a snow-covered farm, a person with a split brain chose two cards to represent what he saw. The left hand chose a picture of a chicken, to go with the chicken foot that the right brain had processed, while the right hand chose a picture of a shovel, to go with the snow that the left brain had processed. But when the experimenter asked why those two pictures had been chosen, the left hemisphere studied both selections (the shovel and the chicken foot) and concocted a plausible story: "Oh that's simple. The chicken claw goes with the chicken, and you need a shovel to clean out the chicken shed" (Turk et al., 2003, p. 71). The left hemisphere alone appears to be a "storyteller" that combines information into plausible cause-and-effect inferences—even if they are wrong.

Because the left hemisphere is apparently responsible for combining, interpreting, and telling a story about the many different inputs to the brain, Gazzaniga and colleagues have suggested that the left hemisphere may be a seat of the self-concept—responsible for the conscious "sense of self" that humans have (Turk et al., 2003). These are important conclusions from only a small sample of individuals.

Balancing Priorities in the Split-Brain Experiments

How convinced should you be by the results of split-brain research? These experiments, after all, were conducted with a very small number of participants. (Fortunately, only a small number of people require this kind of surgery.) Can you really conclude anything from research conducted on so few people?

Experimental Control, Manipulation, and Replication. Because of the empirical strengths of these studies, you can, in fact, make some conclusions on the basis of a small-N study. First, Gazzaniga and his colleagues used the power of experimental control: They controlled the eye movements of the participants, exposing images only briefly so the right and left hemispheres would view completely different information. Second, they used strong manipulations: Tasks that would be easy for someone with an intact brain (such as identifying a picture flashed to the left visual field) were simply impossible for a split-brain patient. By ensuring that some stimuli went only to one hemisphere or the other, the researchers could infer that the left hemisphere of the brain (but not the right) can produce language, construct stories, and make cause-and-effect explanations. Therefore, the research took advantage of the split-brain surgery to manipulate the independent variable—which part of the brain received the input. Finally, researchers were able to replicate the results across five split-brain patients.

Studying Special Cases. One feature of the split-brain experiments is that they took advantage of a unique population. Just as quasi-experiments can take advantage of natural accidents, laws, or historical events, small-N studies often take advantage of special medical cases. Using the split-brain patients gave researchers the opportunity to send information to only one brain hemisphere at a time under controlled conditions.

Disadvantages of Small-N Studies

One problem with small-N studies is that a few participants may not represent the human population very well. In the split-brain experiments, although it is important that the team obtained the same findings in all five patients, the history of epilepsy they shared means their brains may have had specific differences compared to the brains of nonepileptic people. This is a fair question about external validity: Can the results from these people, who all had severe epilepsy, generalize to other people?

You cannot be sure, of course, whether the Gazzaniga team results would apply to people without a history of epilepsy. Furthermore, it clearly would be unethical to sever the corpus callosum of a nonepileptic person's brain to create the necessary comparison. What could a researcher do to explore the generalizability of the findings from split-brain patients? One option would be to triangulate. For example, Gazzaniga's results were consistent with animal studies by Sperry (1961), as well as with contemporary research using functional brain imagery on nonepileptic adults. The results from these studies of animals and nonepileptic people often confirm what has been observed behaviorally in people with split brains. In sum, this is another example of how the weight of a variety of evidence supports a parsimonious theory about how the human brain is organized.

For more on pattern and parsimony, see Chapter 9, pp. 254–256.

Behavior-Change Studies in Clinical Settings: Three Small-N Designs

Split-brain research is only one example of the power of a small-N design. In clinical settings, practitioners can use small-N designs to learn whether their interventions work. For example, an occupational therapist might teach an elderly Alzheimer's patient a new memory strategy and then observe whether the patient's memory has improved. A special education teacher might try a behavioral correction technique to help a developmentally disabled student, and then observe to determine whether the student's behavior improves. In such clinical settings, practitioners, like researchers, need to think empirically: They develop theories about their clients' behaviors; make theory-based predictions about what treatments should help; and then implement changes, observe the results, and modify their treatments or understandings in response to these observations.

For a review of the theory-data cycle, see Chapter 1, pp. 9–13.

When practitioners notice an improvement after a treatment, they might wonder whether the improvement was caused by the intervention or by something else. Would the Alzheimer's patient's memory have improved anyway, or could the memory improvement have been caused by, say, a change in medication? Did the correction technique decrease the student's distracting behaviors in the classroom, or did the behaviors decrease simply because the teacher paid more attention to the student? Notice that all these questions are internal validity questions—questions about alternative explanations for the result. Carefully designed small-N or single-N studies can help practitioners decide whether changes are caused by their interventions or by some other influence.

Stable-Baseline Designs

A **stable-baseline design** is a study in which a researcher observes behavior for an extended baseline period before beginning a treatment or other intervention; if behavior during the baseline is stable, the researcher is more certain of the treatment's effectiveness. One example comes from a study of a memory strategy known as expanded rehearsal, which was used with a real Alzheimer's patient, Ms. S (Moffat, 1989). Before teaching her the new strategy, the researchers spent several weeks recording baseline information, such as how many words Ms. S could recall after hearing them only once. It was important that the baseline data were stable: Ms. S remembered very few words, and there was no upward trend. Then she was taught the new strategy, as researchers continued to monitor how many words she could remember. The researchers noticed a sudden improvement in her memory ability (**Figure 13.10**).

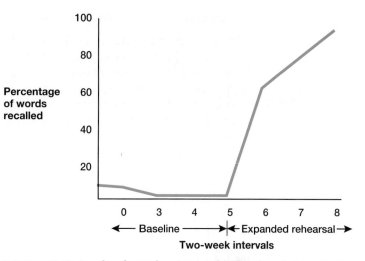

FIGURE 13.10 Results of a study using a stable-baseline design. Ms. S's memory was consistently low until the new expanded rehearsal technique was introduced. (Source: Adapted from Moffat, 1989.)

Why should these results convince you that the patient's improvement was caused by the new extended rehearsal strategy? One reason is that the baseline was stable. If the researchers had done a single pretest before the new training and a single test afterward (a before-and-after comparison), the improvement could be explained by any number of factors, such as maturation (spontaneous change) or a regression effect. (In fact, a single baseline record followed by a single post-treatment measure would have been a small-*N* version of the "really bad experiment"; see Chapter 11.) Instead, the researcher recorded an extended, stable baseline, which made it unlikely that some sudden, spontaneous change just happened to occur right at the time the new therapy began. Furthermore, the stable baseline meant that there was not a single, extreme low point from which improvement would almost definitely occur (a regression effect). Performance began low and stayed low until the experimental strategy was introduced.

The stable baseline gave this study internal validity, enabling the researcher to rule out some alternative explanations. In addition, the study was later repeated with a few other Alzheimer's patients (**Figure 13.11**). This replication provided further evidence that expanded rehearsal can help Alzheimer's patients.

FIGURE 13.11 A speech therapist testing a patient at home for Alzheimer's disease. Small-*N* designs can help therapists learn which therapies are effective for their clients.

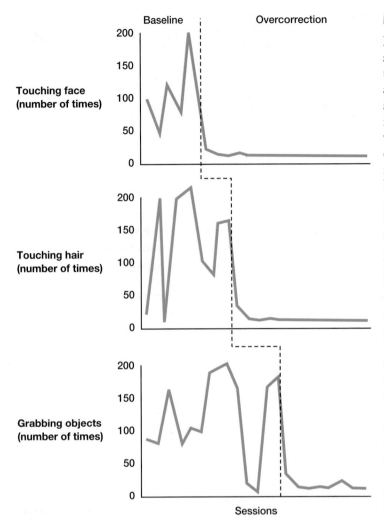

In a **multiple-baseline design**, researchers stagger their introduction of an intervention across a variety of contexts, times, or situations. For example, teachers in a special education classroom were trying to teach a 12-year-old developmentally disabled girl to refrain from several distracting behaviors, such as repeatedly touching her face, touching her hair, and grabbing objects in the classroom (described in Tawney & Gast, 1994). First they recorded baselines of each of the three behaviors for a few days. Then they started a treatment strategy, at first only targeting the face touching. If the girl touched her face, she was placed in a special "overcorrection" session for 3 minutes, when she was made to sit quietly with the palms of her hands on a table. At first, the overcorrection was applied only when face touching occurred. A few days later, the overcorrection was extended to include touching hair, and later still, to grabbing objects.

As each behavior was followed by an overcorrection consequence, the behavior was promptly and dramatically reduced. The results are shown in **Figure 13.12**. Notice how the three behaviors served as controls for one another to improve internal validity in this study, making it clear that it was the overcorrection that improved this girl's behavior and not something else. It is unlikely that each problem behavior just happened to have improved spontaneously, right at the time the teachers started using overcorrection. In addition, you can be sure that face touching did not improve just because the extra attention put the girl on her best behavior; if it had been the extra attention that caused the improvement, then all the behaviors would have decreased at the same time, and they did not. Therefore, by studying

FIGURE 13.12 Results of a study using a multiple-baseline design. In a special education classroom, an overcorrection consequence was first applied when a girl touched her face. Later, the teachers used overcorrection when the girl touched her hair and, still later, when she grabbed objects in the classroom. The graphs show how the rate of each behavior changed when the overcorrection consequence was introduced. (Source: Adapted from Tawney & Gast, 1994.)

multiple behaviors and collecting multiple baselines, these special education teachers could conclude that their overcorrection strategy improved the girl's behavior. This multiple-baseline design had enough internal validity to support a causal conclusion.

In this example, the multiple baselines were represented by a set of behaviors within a single person. In other studies, the baselines might be represented by different situations for one person (e.g., correcting a problem behavior at home, school, and work). The baselines might also be represented by three different people (e.g., correcting the problem behaviors of three children in the same classroom, but starting at different times). In any format, the multiple baselines provide comparison conditions to which a treatment or intervention can be compared.

Reversal Designs

In a **reversal design**, as in the other two small-*N* designs, a researcher observes a problem behavior both with and without treatment, but takes the treatment away for a while (the reversal period) to see whether the problem behavior returns (reverses). By discontinuing a treatment that seems to be working, the researcher can test for internal validity and make a causal statement: If the treatment was really working, the behavior should worsen again when the treatment is discontinued.

Here's an example. When a woman went into a severe depression following the death of her mother, her family participated in treating her at home, under the guidance of a behavioral therapist, by modifying the consequences of her actions (Liberman & Raskin, 1971). Her behavior was typical of depression—low energy, weakness, and expressions of helplessness. Her husband and children originally responded with sympathy and consolation to her actions. Their compassion was understandable, but also short-sighted: What if their sympathetic attention was actually reinforcing the woman's depressive behaviors?

On the advice of therapists, the family members forced themselves to change their reactions. They ignored her depressive behaviors and gave her attention and encouragement only when she coped in a positive way. **Figure 13.13** shows the results of this treatment. Baselines were initially stable (depressive behaviors were high, and coping behaviors were low), but when the family's reaction changed (during the treatment period), the patient's actions changed as well: She coped better and acted depressed less frequently. Then (still on advice from the therapist) the family went back

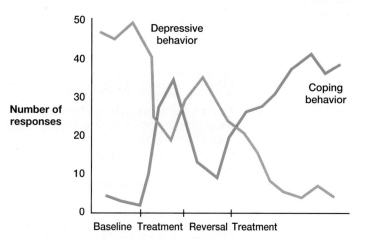

FIGURE 13.13 Results of a study using a reversal design. The patient's depressive behavior responded to nontreatment periods (baseline and reversal) compared to treatment periods. This pattern supports the idea that the treatment caused the patient's depressive behavior to decrease and her coping behavior to increase. (Source: Adapted from Liberman & Raskin, 1971.)

to its original ways of reacting; this was the reversal period. Sure enough, during reversal, the woman's depressive actions increased and her coping actions declined. Finally, the family resumed the treatment conditions once again. In response, the woman acted less depressed and coped more positively. It seemed clear that it was the family's actions, not a maturation or regression effect, that had influenced the woman's depressive versus coping behaviors in this situation.

Reversal designs are appropriate mainly for situations in which the treatment would not cause lasting change. For example, it would not make sense to use a reversal design to test an educational intervention. Once a student has learned a new skill (such as Ms. S's expanded rehearsal technique), it is unlikely that the skill will simply reverse, or go away. In addition, while the reversal design in the depression example enables the researcher to evaluate the efficacy of the treatment, some researchers would question the ethics of the choice to withdraw a treatment that appears to be working. In fact, two ethical priorities come into play here: On the one hand, it may be considered harmful to withdraw effective treatment from a patient; on the other hand, it also may be unethical to use a treatment that is not empirically supported as effective.

For a full discussion of ethics in psychological research, see Chapter 4.

Other Examples of Small-*N* Studies

Research in psychological science has boasted some influential and famous small-*N* and single-*N* studies. The Swiss scientist Jean Piaget (1923) developed a theory of child cognitive development through careful, systematic observations of his own three children. He found, for example, that as children get older, they learn that when a tall glass of liquid is poured into a shorter glass, the amount of liquid does not change (**Figure 13.14**). Younger children, in contrast, tend to respond that there is more liquid in the taller glass, because the level appears higher. Although Piaget observed only a few children, he designed systematic questions, made careful observations, and replicated his extensive interviews with each of them.

FIGURE 13.14
Studying how children think using a small-*N* design. Jean Piaget developed and tested his theories of child cognitive development by systematically testing his own children on carefully developed tasks, such as estimating which glass "has more."

Another early-20th-century researcher, Hermann Ebbinghaus (1913), made himself memorize long lists of nonsense words, such as *mip* and *pon*. In a series of studies conducted over many years, Ebbinghaus systematically varied the frequency and duration of studying each list, and carefully recorded how many syllables he remembered at different time intervals. Ebbinghaus was the first to document several fundamental memory phenomena, one of which is the "forgetting curve," shown in **Figure 13.15**. It depicts how memory for a newly learned list of nonsense syllables declines most dramatically over the first hour, but then declines more slowly after that. Although he studied only himself—a single-*N* design—Ebbinghaus created testing situations with experimental precision and, eventually, replicability.

Here's another example of a single-*N* study. Memory researchers recruited an average college student (known as S.F.) and asked him to come to their laboratory three to five times a week for 1.5 years (Ericsson, Chase, & Faloon, 1980). Each day, they read S.F. random digits—one digit per second. Later, S.F. would try to recall the digits in the correct order. Ordinarily, the average memory span is about 7 digits (Miller, 1956). After regularly practicing in the lab, S.F. developed the ability to recite back 79 random digits at a time (**Figure 13.16**).

S.F.'s remarkable performance was caused, in part, by his strategy of grouping clusters of numbers according to track and field times (e.g., a string of 3392 might become 3:39.2, "a great time for the mile"). In fact, the researchers tested whether the "running time" strategy *caused* his improved performance by generating some number strings that purposefully did not correspond well to running times. S.F.'s memory span for those special strings dropped down to his beginning performance level. S.F.'s remarkable performance demonstrates what can happen with extensive training and motivation. And the researchers' clever manipulation also demonstrated *why* S.F. got so good at learning strings of numbers—supporting a causal conclusion.

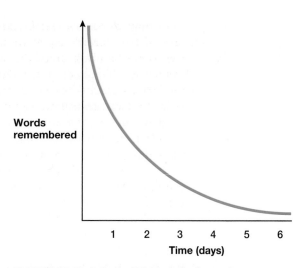

FIGURE 13.15 A single-*N* design: the forgetting curve. Hermann Ebbinghaus' carefully designed experiments on memory processes contributed to psychology, even though he used only one person—himself—as a subject.

2	7	1	2	5	8	2	3
7	0	8	7	5	0	9	9
9	2	5	4	1	6	1	8
7	9	6	1	0	0	5	6
7	8	0	0	1	1	5	6
6	2	6	2	5	3	4	8
2	1	1	9	1	8	4	3
1	1	3	9	5	4	9	2
3	9	9	9	5	6	5	8
7	8	0	5	6	8	5	5

FIGURE 13.16

Remembering random digits. Do you think you could recall up to 80 random digits like these, after hearing them only once? A college student known as S.F. learned to do so by practicing short-term memory skills for a year and a half.

Evaluating the Four Validities in Small-*N* Designs

The discussion of small-*N* designs has focused so far on how such designs can eliminate alternative explanations—how they can enhance internal validity. In all the examples described in this chapter, researchers designed careful, within-subject experiments that allowed them to draw causal conclusions. Even if there was only one participant, the researchers usually measured behaviors repeatedly, both before and after some intervention or manipulation. Therefore, the internal validity of these single-*N* designs is high.

It may seem easy to criticize the external validity of a small-*N* design. How can one person represent a population? Even when researchers can demonstrate that their manipulation, intervention, or procedure replicates in a second or third case, the question of generalizability remains. Remember, though, that researchers can take steps to maximize the external validity of their findings. First, they can triangulate by combining the results of single-*N* studies with other studies on animals or on larger groups, as Gazzaniga and his colleagues did when comparing split-brain study results with subsequent research results on animals and nonepileptic humans. Second, researchers can specify the population to which they want to generalize, and they rarely intend to generalize to everyone. They may not care, for example, if a memory strategy for Alzheimer's patients applies to everybody in the world, but they do care whether it generalizes to other Alzheimer's patients. Therefore, researchers sometimes limit a study's population of interest to a particular subset of possible participants. Third, sometimes researchers are not concerned about generalizing at all. It may be sufficient to a special education teacher to learn that the overcorrection technique works for one 12-year-old girl in the classroom. In such cases, even if the causal statement applies only to one person, it is still useful.

When interrogating a small-*N* design, you should also evaluate construct validity. Of course, researchers want to be sure that their measurements are reliable and valid. The researchers in the previous examples recorded what people drew, what objects they picked up, or what they said. They recorded how many words or numbers people remembered. They observed whether a girl grabbed objects or touched her face and hair. Construct validity is fairly straightforward when researchers are recording whether a split-brain patient reports seeing a hammer or a saw, and for objective measures such as memory for a string of numbers. But when researchers are recording the number of times a girl grabs objects in a special education classroom, they should use multiple observers and check for interrater reliability, in case one observer is biased or the behavior is difficult to identify.

Regarding statistical validity, in single-*N* designs, researchers do not typically use traditional statistics. However, they still draw conclusions from data, and they should treat data appropriately. In many cases graphs (such as those in Figures 13.10, 13.12, and 13.13) provide enough quantitative evidence. In addition, you might think about effect sizes more simply in small-*N* cases, by asking: By what margin did the client's behavior improve?

CHECK YOUR UNDERSTANDING

1. What are three small-*N* designs used in clinical settings?
2. Are small-*N* designs within-groups or between-groups designs?
3. How is a multiple-baseline design similar to a nonequivalent control group interrupted time-series design?
4. How do small-*N* researchers establish external validity?

3. See pp. 404–405; compare Figures 13.4 and 13.12. 4. See pp. 407–408.
1. See pp. 402–406. 2. Within-groups designs, see p. 399.

Summary

- Experiments do not always take place in ideal conditions, with clean manipulations, large samples of participants, and perfect random assignment. Quasi-experiments and small-*N* designs use strategies that optimize naturally occurring groups or single individuals.

Quasi-Experiments

- Quasi-experiments can use independent-groups designs, such as a nonequivalent control group design and a nonequivalent control group pretest/posttest design. They can also follow within-groups designs, as in an interrupted time-series design or a nonequivalent control group interrupted time-series design.
- When a quasi-experiment includes a comparison group and the right pattern of results, researchers can often support a causal claim, even when participants cannot be randomly assigned to conditions and the researchers do not have complete experimental control of the independent variable.
- Examining the results and design of a quasi-experiment reveals its vulnerablity to alternative explanations, such as selection, maturation, history, attrition, testing, and instrumentation effects; observer biases, demand characteristics, and placebo effects—the same kinds of internal validity threats that can occur in true experiments.

- In quasi-experiments, researchers balance confidence in internal validity with other priorities, such as opportunities to study in a real-world situation, to take advantage of a historical event, or to conduct an ethical investigation of a new program or other intervention.

Small-*N* Designs: Studying Only a Few Individuals

- Small-*N* studies balance an intense, systematic investigation of one or a few people against the usual approach of studying groups of people. The internal validity of small-*N* studies can be just as high as that of repeated-measures experiments conducted on larger samples.
- Three small-*N* designs used in clinical settings are the stable-baseline design, the multiple-baseline design, and the reversal design.
- Small-*N* designs can establish excellent construct and internal validity. They can achieve external validity by replicating the results in other settings, but in clinical settings, researchers might prioritize the ability to establish a treatment's effectiveness for a single individual over broad generalizability.
- Researchers must be aware of the trade-offs of each research decision, making conscious choices about which validities are most important—and most possible—to prioritize as they study a particular issue in psychological science.

Key Terms

quasi-experiment, p. 382
nonequivalent control group design, p. 382
nonequivalent control group pretest/posttest design, p. 383
interrupted time-series design, p. 386
nonequivalent control group interrupted time-series design, p. 387
matched groups, p. 389
wait-list design, p. 389
small-*N* design, p. 399
single-*N* design, p. 399
stable-baseline design, p. 403
multiple-baseline design, p. 404
reversal design, p. 405

 To see samples of chapter concepts in the popular press, visit www.everydayresearchmethods.com and click the box for Chapter 13.

Review Questions

1. What is the term for a quasi-experimental design with at least one treatment group and one comparison group, in which the participants have not been randomly assigned to the groups?
   a. Nonequivalent control group design
   b. Independent-groups design
   c. Factorial design
   d. Reversal design

2. Which of these is not a reason for a researcher to select a quasi-experimental design?
   a. To enhance external validity.
   b. To avoid the ethical issues a true experiment would cause.
   c. To ensure internal validity.
   d. To take advantage of real-world opportunities to study phenomena and events.

3. During a drought in California, some cities imposed fines for excess water consumption. This situation created the opportunity for a quasi-experiment to test the effectiveness of fines on water conservation behavior (Agras, Jacob, & Lebedeck, 1980). Three comparable cities were studied. Two had imposed fines at different times, and a third did not impose any fines. Using municipal water usage records, the researchers recorded each city's water consumption for an extended time period, from 3 years before the drought until the end of the drought. What type of design was this?
   a. Interrupted time-series design
   b. Nonequivalent control group interrupted time-series design
   c. Nonequivalent control group design
   d. Nonequivalent control group pretest/posttest design

4. In the drought and water fines study, you could ask: Are municipal water records a good measure of water usage? This would be asking about which kind of validity?

   a. Construct validity
   b. Statistical validity
   c. Internal validity
   d. External validity

5. The researchers found that in the two cities that imposed water usage fines, water use dropped dramatically in subsequent months. Which of the following would be a threat to internal validity in this study?
   a. If the cities that imposed fines also happened to use a public service ad campaign to reduce water usage.
   b. If the cities in the study were not representative of California's cities in general.
   c. If there was no significant difference in water usage between the fined cities and the comparison city.

6. A psychologist is working with the parents of four children, all of whom exhibit violent behavior toward one another. The parents were instructed to record the number of violent behaviors each child exhibits in the pre-dinner hour for 1 week. The parents then begin a using positive reinforcement technique to shape the behavior of the youngest child, while continuing to record the behavior of all children. The recording continues and the technique is used on one additional child each week. By the end of 6 weeks, there is a significant decrease in violent behaviors for each of the children. What type of design did the psychologist use?
   a. Stable-baseline design
   b. Multiple-baseline design
   c. Reversal design
   d. Interrupted time-series design

7. Which of these is not a method for maximizing the external validity of the conclusions of a small-N study?

a. Triangulate by comparing results with other research.
b. Specify a limited population to which to generalize.

c. Randomly assign people to the treatment and control conditions
d. Specify that the result applies only to the participant studied.

Learning Actively

1. Researchers Dutton and Aron (1974) wanted to test a theory of romantic attraction. They proposed that people can be fooled about their feelings of romantic attraction, and that feelings of anxiety can be similar to feelings of being in love. They suggested that if a man who happened to be feeling anxious met an attractive woman, he might feel especially attracted to her. In effect, the man might mistake his feelings of anxiety for feelings of romantic attraction.

   To test their theory, Dutton and Aron studied male tourists who were walking across one of two pedestrian bridges. One bridge was a solid, stable bridge, only 10 feet above a river. The other one (the Capilano Suspension Bridge) was 230 feet above the river and was made of wooden boards attached to wire cables, with a low wire handrail. Most people who cross this precarious bridge feel anxious. The researchers hired a female research assistant to approach male tourists, one by one, as they crossed one of the two bridges. After administering a short questionnaire, the woman handed each man her phone number, saying, "If you'd like to know the results, call me and I'll tell you about them." The researchers simply counted the number of calls the woman received—from men who had crossed the high bridge and from men who had crossed the low one. Of the men who crossed the high bridge, 50% phoned in for results, but of those on the safe bridge, only 12% did so.
   a. Is this study a nonequivalent control group design, an interrupted time-series design, or a nonequivalent control group interrupted time-series design?
   b. Graph the results of the study, according to the results in the description.
   c. What causal statement might the researcher be trying to make, if any? Is it appropriate? Use the results and design to interrogate the study's internal validity.
   d. If you notice any internal validity flaws, can you redesign the study to remove the flaw?
   e. Ask one question to address construct validity and one to address external validity.

2. Suppose you're a dog owner and are working with your 3-year-old Labrador retriever. When the dog goes for walks, he growls fiercely at other dogs. You want to reduce your dog's aggressive behavior, so you decide to try a technique you learned on television: pressing firmly on the dog's neck and saying a forceful, quick "Shhhhh!" sound when the dog begins to growl at other dogs. You decide to apply a small-N design to investigate the results of your training regimen.
   a. Which small-N design(s) would be appropriate for this situation?
   b. Choose one small-N design, and describe how you would conduct your study.
   c. Sketch a graph of the results you would predict from your design if your treatment worked.
   d. Explain whether you could conclude from your study that the treatment caused your dog's aggression to decrease.

"Would we find these same results in other cultural contexts?"

"Should this study use a random sample of participants?"

14

Replicability, Generalization, and the Real World

LEARNING OBJECTIVES

A year from now, you should still be able to:

1. Articulate, in a nuanced way, what makes a study important, including issues of scientific progress, replicability, external validity, and researchers' intent.

2. Determine whether a study has been conducted in theory-testing mode or generalization mode before deciding whether external validity is crucial for the study's importance.

What makes a study important? Judging a study's importance will be one of your goals as a consumer of research. As you read about studies, either in the popular press or in your classes, you will want to know not only whether the study was conducted well but also whether the study is important.

For a psychologist, an important study helps advance scientific progress by supporting or shaping psychological theories—that is, by contributing to the theory-data cycle (see Chapter 1). An important study, therefore, helps contribute a piece of knowledge to the body of scientific evidence.

This chapter outlines several dimensions to consider as you judge a study's importance. Some of the topics, such as replicability, have been discussed in previous chapters. Other topics, such as a study's applicability to real-world contexts, might challenge what you already think. To decide what makes a study important, you will keep in mind the researcher's priorities as well as the study's purpose.

To Be Important, a Study Must Be Replicable

Responsible researchers always consider whether the results of a study could be a fluke or whether they will get the same result if they do the study again—in other words, whether the study is **replicable** (or *reproducible*). In this context, notice that "replicable" does not mean a study has the potential to be replicated, but that the result has actually been replicated. When a finding is replicable, it means that the study has been conducted more than once and has yielded the same result.

It makes sense that a study must be replicable to be important. If a scientist claimed to have discovered evidence of life on Mars, but other scientists could not find similar evidence, nobody would believe there is life on Mars. If a study found that playing video games increased violent behavior but other studies did not yield the same result, the first result cannot be considered reliable. Replicability gives a study credibility, and it is a crucial part of the scientific process.

Replication Studies

When a researcher performs a study again, it is known as a replication study. In order to have their findings published, most researchers conduct replication studies, of which there are three major types: direct replication, conceptual replication, and replication-plus-extension. Even when the original study has a statistically significant result, researchers still need to conduct the study again to find out if the finding is replicable.

Direct Replication

In **direct replication** (or *exact replication*), researchers repeat an original study as closely as they can, to see whether the original effect shows up in the newly collected data. An example follows.

Researchers have theorized that because most people like themselves, they implicitly associate positive feelings with the letters in their own name and the numbers in their birthday. Because of these implicit associations, one team of researchers hypothesized that people might become more attracted to others who share their birthday, name, or initials (Jones, Pelham, Carvallo, & Mirenberg, 2004). In fact, a couple of correlational studies showed that people are slightly more likely to marry people who share similar first names (e.g., Frank is more likely to marry Francis, and Charles is more likely to marry Charlotte) than would be predicted just by chance. People seem to like those who share arbitrary features with them.

To test this theory experimentally, researcher John Jones and his team invited people to come to the laboratory to participate in a study that was ostensibly about "how much people can figure out about another person using only a limited amount of information" (Jones et al., 2004, p. 672). After completing a short survey about themselves, each person was handed the page of responses from a randomly selected partner. The page of responses had the selected partner's ID number printed in large type on the top, such as 12-27. In half the cases, the ID number had been matched to the participant's own birthday (i.e., if the participant's birthday was September 25, the number was 9-25). In the other half, it was not. Besides the ID number, all other information provided by the (invented) partner was exactly the same. A few minutes later, the experimenters asked each person to rate their anonymous partner on a variety of dimensions. They found that when the partner's ID number matched their own birthday, participants reported liking the partner more. Most importantly, they replicated the study almost exactly, and found virtually the same results (**Figure 14.1**).

Of course, a direct replication can never replicate the first study in every detail. In Jones and his team's studies, the two samples contained distinct sets of participants, and the authors noted that the chairs in the room were set up differently. In addition, the two studies may have been conducted at different times of the year. The experimenters themselves might not have been the same team of people. Some other minor circumstances might have changed. Despite these small variations, however, in a direct replication the researchers try to reproduce the original experiment as closely as possible.

Direct replication makes good sense. However, if there were any threats to internal validity or flaws in construct validity in the original study, such threats would be repeated in the direct replication, too. For this reason, researchers value other types of replication as a supplement to direct replication.

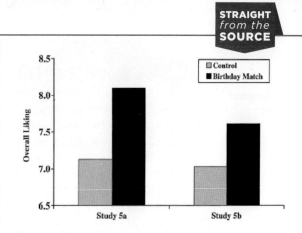

Figure 1. Liking of bogus partner as a function of experimental condition in Studies 5a and 5b. Liking scores are a composite of two liking measures: "How much do you look forward to getting to know this person during the upcoming conversation?" and "How much do you think you would like this person if you got to know her?"

FIGURE 14.1 Direct replication of the birthday similarity effect. This graph shows the results for the original study (Study 5a) and the direct replication study (Study 5b), as they appeared in the original journal article. (Source: Jones et al., 2004.)

Conceptual Replication

In a **conceptual replication**, researchers study the same research question but use different procedures. At the abstract level, the variables in the study are the same, but the procedures for operationalizing the variables are different.

Recall the van Kleef et al. pasta bowl study from Chapter 10. The basic finding has been studied in other ways by other researchers in the same lab, and each time the results demonstrated that serving container size affects how much people eat. In one replication, researchers manipulated the independent variable of serving container size by serving popcorn out of larger and smaller cardboard buckets, rather than larger and smaller bowls, as in the pasta study (Wansink &

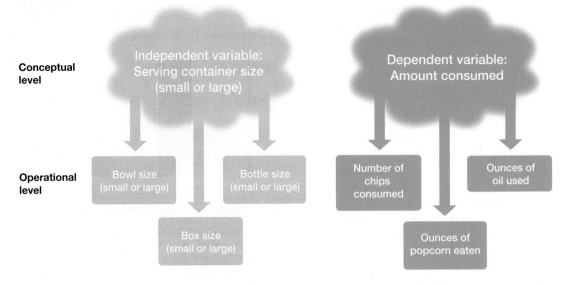

FIGURE 14.2 Conceptual replication: manipulating and measuring the same variables with different operationalizations. The abstract (conceptual) level of the variables is the same, but the operational level of the variables changes.

Kim, 2005). In another study, researchers continued to use serving bowls, but filled them with snack chips instead of pasta (Wansink & Cheney, 2005). In another study, people poured out more uncooked spaghetti from a large box than a small box, and used more cooking oil from a large bottle compared to a small bottle (Wansink, 1996). In all of these variations, researchers continued to find that larger serving containers cause people to serve themselves more food and to consume more calories (**Figure 14.2**).

Replication-Plus-Extension

In a direct replication study, researchers use the same methods to study the same variables as they did in an original study. In a conceptual replication, researchers use different methods to study the same variables as in the original study. In a **replication-plus-extension** study, researchers replicate their original study but add variables to test additional questions.

One example of a replication-plus-extension study comes from Strayer's research on the effect of cell phone use on driving performance, discussed in Chapter 12. As you might recall, Strayer and his colleagues first conducted experiments in which college students used a driving simulator. They found that talking on a hands-free cell phone caused the students to drive worse (Strayer, Drews, & Johnston, 2003). A later study extended this basic finding to a new population by using both college students and older adults (Strayer & Drews, 2004). The later study was a replication-plus-extension study, because it was an attempt to repeat the original study with college students (the replication) but also added a new population of elderly drivers (the extension).

Strayer's replication-plus-extension study was important for two reasons. First, it replicated a finding the researchers had noticed in their previous study: College students drove worse when they were talking on cell phones. Second, the study extended this original result into a new population: Older adults also drove worse when they talked on cell phones. Strayer's research is a good example of introducing a participant variable (in this case, participant age) to conduct a replication-plus-extension study—that is, extending an original finding to a new population. (Participants variables were introduced in Chapter 12.)

Another way to conduct a replication-plus-extension study is to introduce a new *situational variable*. For example, in one study, Strayer and his colleagues wanted to know whether the ability to drive and talk at the same time would improve with practice (Cooper & Strayer, 2008). Therefore, degree of practice became the new situational variable in this replication-plus-extension study. The researchers conducted a 4-day study in which people practiced driving in a simulator while talking on a hands-free cell phone. Cooper and Strayer compared the collision frequency on Day 1 (when participants had had no practice) with that on Day 4 (when they'd had 4 days of practice). On Days 1 and 4, people drove part of the course without a cell phone and drove part of the course while talking on a cell phone.

In this study, Cooper and Strayer therefore had two independent variables: being on a cell phone or not, and having had practice or not (Day 1 versus Day 4). (You might recognize this as a 2 × 2 factorial design.) The results showed that while people got into fewer accidents overall on Day 4, the effect of using a cell phone was the same: Talking on a cell phone made people get into more accidents on Day 4, by just as much as on Day 1; in other words, there was no interaction. This study was a replication-plus-extension because Cooper and Strayer extended the original finding—the effects of cell phone use on driving—to a new situation (performance after a few days of practice). The results are shown in **Figure 14.3**.

In yet another replication-plus-extension study, Strayer, Drews, and Crouch (2006) compared three driving conditions: driving alone, driving while talking on a cell phone, and driving drunk. They actually had people drink enough vodka to reach a 0.08 BAC (blood alcohol concentration); BAC 0.08 is legally drunk in many

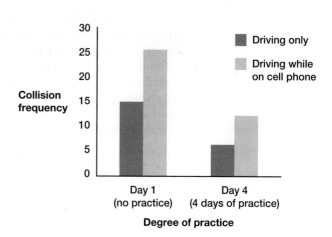

FIGURE 14.3 A replication-plus-extension study on cell phone use while driving. This graph shows the highway driving condition only. The study replicated Strayer's original study demonstrating that people get into more car accidents while talking on a cell phone, and extended their original finding to investigate the effect of practice. (Source: Adapted from Cooper & Strayer, 2008.)

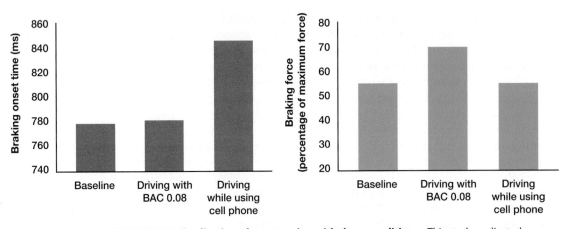

FIGURE 14.4 Replication-plus-extension with three conditions. This study replicated previous research showing that cell phone use while driving causes people to hit the brakes more slowly. Extending the study by adding the drunk-driving condition demonstrated that alcohol also impairs driving, but in different ways. (Source: Adapted from Strayer, Drews, & Crouch, 2006.)

U.S. states. In this replication, the extension involved adding a drunk driving condition to the independent variable. The results of the study showed that both talking on a cell phone and drinking affected people's driving, but in different ways. Drunk drivers braked just as quickly but with more force than nonimpaired drivers (those who were neither drunk nor on the phone). In contrast, drivers talking on cell phones were slower to hit the brakes, but they braked with the same amount of force as the unimpaired drivers (**Figure 14.4**).

This replication-plus-extension study first replicated the finding that driving while talking on a cell phone worsens people's driving performance. The study then directly compared the effect of driving drunk to the effect of driving while on a cell phone. By investigating all three conditions in the same study (talking on a cell phone, drinking, and baseline), the researchers learned more about the similarities and differences between various conditions that can affect driving ability.

Replications by Independent Researchers

Many psychological scientists give extra weight to replication studies that were conducted by independent researchers working outside the lab of the original experiment. As you may recall from Chapter 10, Elliot et al.'s original article showed several conceptual replications of the color effect on cognitive performance (Elliot et al., 2007). A couple of years later, another pair of researchers reported a similar effect of color on performance (Mehta & Zhu, 2009). However, when another independent researcher conducted an exact replication of Mehta and Zhu's study, he could not replicate the effect of red on performance (Steele, 2013).

Failure to replicate a finding in a completely different lab raises the possibility that the original effect can be obtained only in very specialized—and unidentified—conditions. In sum, although many effects in psychology have been replicated, others have not. When independent researchers are unable to replicate a result, you have to be more cautious about the importance of an effect (Ioannidis, 2012; Pashler & Wagenmakers, 2012). In psychology recently, the importance of replication has received much more critical attention (Kahneman, 2012), and psychologists are becoming more invested in replicating the key results in psychological science (Reproducibility Project: Psychology).

Replication, Importance, and the Weight of the Evidence

As the Chinese philosopher Lao Tzu is believed to have said, "The longest journey begins with a single step." Similarly, when researchers complete a single, well-conducted study, psychological science progresses a bit, but a single study is important only if it can be replicated. After all, if you can't be sure the same result occurs consistently under the same conditions, how can that result be important? Even statistically significant results must be tested through replication studies. Psychological science progresses only as researchers conduct systematic sets of direct replications, conceptual replications, and replication-plus-extension studies.

Meta-Analysis: What Does the Literature Say?

Because psychological science values replication, the most important conclusions in psychology are those based on a body of evidence—that is, a large scientific literature. A **scientific literature** (or simply *literature*) consists of a series of related studies, conducted by various researchers, that have tested similar variables. Thus, literatures are composed of several studies on a particular topic, often conducted by many different researchers. For example, you might hear your instructors or other students talk about the literature on the effects of cell phone use while driving, or the literature on the effects of color on behavior.

Sometimes, researchers collect all the studies on a topic and consider them together—generating what is known as a review article, or a literature review (see Chapter 2). One approach is simply to summarize the literature in a narrative way, verbally describing what the studies typically show, explaining how the body of evidence supports a theory.

Researchers can also use the quantitative technique of meta-analysis to create a mathematical summary of a scientific literature. A **meta-analysis**, as you learned in Chapter 2, is a way of mathematically averaging the results of all the studies that have tested the same variables, to see what conclusion that whole body of evidence supports. The following examples will help you understand the basic process involved in a meta-analysis.

Example: Religiosity and Depression

One group of researchers was interested in the relationship between degree of religious feeling (religiosity) and depressive symptoms (Smith, McCullough, & Poll, 2003). The researchers scoured the literature (using PsycINFO databases and other tools) to locate every study that had measured religiosity and depression. For example, one study found a correlation between religiosity and depression of $r = -.06$ in 146 college students (Blaine & Crocker, 1995). Another study,

TABLE 14.1 Cohen's Guidelines for Effect Sizes		
Effect size *d*	Strength of relationship	Effect size *r*
0.20	Small, or weak	.10
0.50	Medium, or moderate	.30
0.80	Large, or strong	.50

Source: Cohen, 1992.

using 44 adults, found a correlation of $r = -.13$ (Hertsgaard & Light, 1984). In total, Smith and his colleagues collected 147 studies. All of them used different samples, and many of them used slightly different operational measures of depression and religiosity (i.e., they were conceptual replications), but they all investigated the bivariate relationship between religiosity and depression, asking whether being religious is correlated with depression.

Using a meta-analytic formula, the Smith team found the average correlation across all 147 studies. (The formula is similar to that for a statistical mean, but it also weights studies with larger sample sizes more heavily.) The researchers found that the average correlation was $r = -.09$. Because this relationship is negative, it means that as religious belief increases, depressive symptoms decrease. Furthermore, the size of this relationship (.09) means that the strength of the association between depression and religiosity, while statistically significant, is small. Cohen's (1992) conventions for effect sizes can be applied to describe the average effect size as small, medium, or large (**Table 14.1**).

Meta-analysis, then, is the process of collecting all possible studies on a particular research question and combining them mathematically to study the overall trend in the data. Smith and his colleagues used their meta-analysis to conclude that there is a weak, negative relationship between depression and religiousness (**Figure 14.5**). Religious people are slightly less likely to be depressed. (Of course, because this is a correlation, you cannot conclude from it whether being religious causes a decrease in depression, whether being depressed causes a decrease in religiousness, or whether some outside factor causes both.)

FIGURE 14.5 Religiosity and depression. People who report being religious are also less depressed. How do meta-analysis data contribute to our understanding of this relationship?

Example: Violent Video Games and Behavior

Craig Anderson and seven colleagues (2010) collected all possible studies that investigated whether playing violent video games affects people's subsequent aggression, empathy, and prosocial behavior. The authors searched databases and contacted research colleagues to collect over 100 empirical articles that had studied exposure to violent video games and those three behavioral outcomes. The research they collected for this meta-analysis included a total of 92 experimental studies and 82 correlational studies.

For each study they collected, the researchers computed the effect size, comparing violent video game conditions to comparison conditions (either nonviolent video games or no video games). In these studies, the larger the effect size, the greater was the impact of violent video games on behavior. As in the previous example, the meta-analysis on religiosity and depression, this one computed the average of several effect sizes, as measured by r values. (However, meta-analyses might also compute the average of effect sizes as measured by d.)

These researchers separated out experiments that measured different dependent variables. Some had studied aggression, others had measured prosocial behavior, and others measured empathy. Some of their key findings are presented in **Table 14.2**. You can see that on average, playing violent video games causes increased aggressive behavior: the average effect size is .18, which is a small-to-medium effect size. In addition, playing violent video games also affects people's prosocial behavior and empathy. These average effect sizes are negative, indicating that violent games cause people to be less prosocial and to have less empathy for others' suffering.

Anderson and his team also conducted some follow-up analyses. They separated the studies into different categories. For example, some of the studies were conducted on North American samples, and others on Japanese samples. Because rates of violent crime are, on average, much lower in Japan than North

TABLE 14.2 Results for the Impact of Violent Video Games on Behavior, Experimental Studies Only

Type of outcome	Number of studies that measured this outcome	Total number of participants in these studies	Average effect size r (positive values mean violent video game groups scored higher)
Aggressive behavior	45	3,464	.181
Prosocial behavior	8	875	−.161
Empathy for others' suffering	11	537	−.148

Source: Adapted from Anderson et al., 2010, Tables 4, 7, and 8.

TABLE 14.3 Results for the Impact of Violent Video Games on Aggressive Behavior, Categorized into Methodologically Weak and Strong Studies

Category	Number of studies in category	Total number of participants in all studies	Average effect size *r* (positive values mean violent video game groups scored higher on aggression)
Methodologically weak	61	46,632	.163
Methodologically strong	79	21,681	.244

Source: Adapted from Anderson et al., 2010, Table 9.

To review moderators, see Chapter 8, pp. 227–230.

America, the researchers wondered if violent games caused aggression to the same extent in both nations. However, they reported that the average effect sizes were the same. In other words, the nationality of the sample did not moderate the relationship between violent video games and aggression.

In another follow-up analysis, Anderson's team separated the studies into those they considered to be of "weak" methodological quality and "strong" methodological quality. A "weak" study might have compared the violent video game group to a control group in which the game still contained some violence. Some "weak" studies might have measured the personality trait aggression as the outcome, not actual aggressive behavior. In **Table 14.3**, the results are broken down by these categories. You can see that study quality moderated the effects found when studying violent video games on behavior, such that methodologically strong studies actually show larger effect sizes than weak studies.

Strengths and Limitations of Meta-Analysis

The two examples just discussed illustrate several important features of meta-analysis. In a meta-analysis, researchers collect all possible examples of a particular kind of study. They then average all the effect sizes to find an overall effect size. Using meta-analyses, researchers can also sort a group of studies into categories (i.e., moderators), computing separate effect size averages for each category. From these follow-up analyses, researchers can detect new patterns in the literature as well as test new questions.

Because meta-analyses usually contain data that have been published in empirical journals, you can be more certain that the data have been peer-reviewed, providing one check on their quality. However, there is a publication bias in psychology: Significant relationships are more likely to be published than null effects. This phenomenon leads to the **file drawer problem**, the idea that a meta-analysis might be overestimating the true size of an effect because null effects, or even opposite effects, have not been included in the collection process. (The name comes from the notion that instead of being published, these studies sit forgotten in the researchers' filing cabinets.) To combat the problem, researchers who are conducting a meta-analysis should follow the practice of contacting their colleagues (via e-mail groups and subscription lists), requesting both published and unpublished data for their project.

Here's an illustration of the potential seriousness of the file drawer problem. A group of medical researchers analyzed data from a set of 74 studies on the effectiveness of antidepressant medications such as Paxil and Zoloft (Turner, Matthews, Linardatos, Tell, & Rosenthal, 2008). All the studies had been registered in advance, as required by law, with the U.S. Food and Drug Administration (FDA), which oversees pharmaceutical research. Of the 74 studies, only 38 had shown positive results for these drugs (i.e., they alleviated symptoms of depression). Of the rest, 24 studies showed negative and 12 showed "questionable" effects of antidepressants. However, Turner et al. reported that all but one of the positive studies had been published in medical journals, while the studies with null findings were much less likely to ever be published (**Figure 14.6**). In fact, only 3 of the 36 negative or questionable outcomes were ultimately published. This means that if you read only published studies, you'd conclude that 94% of them demonstrate antidepressants are effective, when in fact, only 51% of all registered studies have shown that they work!

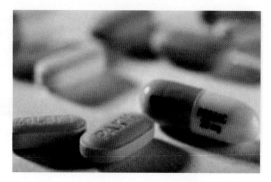

FIGURE 14.6 Selective publication rates.
About 51% of FDA-registered studies found that antidepressant medications are effective, yet the studies with positive effects are much more likely to have been ultimately published in medical journals.

Literature reviews and meta-analyses are considered valuable by many psychologists because they combine the findings of a variety of studies—direct replications and conceptual replications—into a single average. Therefore, a meta-analysis can be a valuable way to assess the weight of the evidence in a scientific literature. It tells you whether, across a number of studies, there is a relationship between two variables—and if so, how strong it is. However, a meta-analysis is only as powerful as the data that go into it. If researchers don't work hard to include even unpublished results, a meta-analysis would reach a biased conclusion.

Replicability in the Popular Press

Journalists do not always consider replicability when they report on science stories. Sometimes journalists will report on a single, hot-off-the-press study because it makes a splashy headline. Responsible journalists, however, not only report on the *latest* studies; they also give readers a sense of what the *entire literature* says on a particular topic. For example, rather than merely announcing the results of a recent study on chocolate and mood, a responsible journalist should talk about the context, too: How well does this latest study fit in with the entire literature on chocolate and mood? Does it contradict a study done last year on chocolate and mood? If journalists do not provide the context of the entire literature surrounding a study, then you would be right to reserve judgment about the study's importance.

CHECK YOUR UNDERSTANDING

1. Describe how the three types of replication studies are similar and different.
2. Compare the value of a single study to that of a body of research, or a scientific literature.
3. In your own words, describe the steps a researcher follows in a meta-analysis. What can a meta-analysis tell you?

---

1. See pp. 414–418. 2. See p. 419. 3. See pp. 419–423.

To Be Important, Must a Study Have External Validity?

Asking about replicability is one way to judge a study's importance. Reproducing a study's results is an essential step in the scientific process; it allows researchers to be far more confident in the accuracy of their results and more convinced of the importance of those results.

Replicability also helps you interrogate one of the four big validities: external validity—the degree to which a study's results are generalizable, to both other participants and other settings. Although direct replication studies do not support external validity, conceptual replications and replication-plus-extension studies can. When researchers test their questions using slightly different methods, different kinds of participants, or different situations, or when they extend their research to study new variables, they are demonstrating how their results generalize to other populations and settings. The more settings and populations in which a study is conducted, the better you can assess the generalizability of the findings.

Generalizing to Other Participants

Recall that to assess a study's generalizability to other people, you would ask *how* the participants were obtained. If a study is intended to generalize to some population, the researchers must draw a probability sample from that population. If a study uses a convenience sample (such as a haphazard sample of whoever is close by), you can't be sure of the study's generalizability to the population the researcher intends. So, for example, if a group of researchers wanted to generalize a study's results from a sample of U.S. soldiers to the population of all U.S. soldiers, they would have to draw the sample of soldiers using random sampling techniques.

It's *a* Population, not *the* Population

Bear in mind, too, that you learned how the population of interest—the one to which researchers want to generalize—usually is not the population of every living person. Instead, when researchers are generalizing from a sample to a population, they will specify what that target population is. It might be all U.S. soldiers. It might be all the college students in Toronto. It might be all the third graders in a London elementary school. It might be a group of lab-reared rhesus monkeys. Researchers are at liberty to specify what their population of interest is, based on the variables they are interested in and the theories they are testing.

External Validity Comes from *How*, not *How Many*

Recall that when you are assessing the generalizability of a sample to a population, "how" matters more than "how many." In other words, for the purposes of generalization, a randomly selected sample of 200 participants has external validity; a haphazardly selected sample of 2,000 participants does not.

For a review of sample size and generalizability, see Chapter 7, pp. 182–193.

Just Because a Sample Comes from a Population Doesn't Mean It Generalizes to That Population

Some students assume that if a convenience sample simply includes some members of a population (perhaps dog owners, or Asian men, or Methodist ministers) that the sample can therefore generalize to those populations (of all dog owners, Asian men, or Methodist ministers). Instead, the same rules apply. In order to generalize to any population, you would need a probability sample of dog owners, or a probability sample of Asian men or of Methodist ministers. If you had only a convenience sample, it might primarily contain the dog owners whom the researcher could contact and who were willing to participate in the study.

Generalizing to Other Settings

Recall that the other aspect of external validity is a study's generalizability to different settings. Conceptual replications illustrate this aspect of external validity very well. When researchers extended the studies of serving container size to chips, popcorn, and soup, as well as pasta, it showed that the results of a large serving container generalize from one setting (eating pasta in a laboratory kitchen) to another setting (eating popcorn during a movie).

Sometimes you want to know whether a laboratory situation created for a study generalizes to real-world settings. For example, you might ask whether the Elliot team's study on the color red and academic achievement (Elliot et al., 2007), which took place in a laboratory, would generalize to real-world settings, such as college examinations or achievement tests. A study's similarity to real-world contexts is sometimes called its **ecological validity**, or *mundane realism* (explained in detail later in this chapter). Many psychologists consider ecological validity to be one aspect of external validity (Brewer, 2000).

Does a Study Have to Be Generalizable to Many People?

How is external validity related to a study's importance? Read the following two statements, and decide whether each one is true or false:

1. The best research uses random samples from the population.
2. The best research studies people of both genders, of all ages and ethnicities, and from all socioeconomic classes, ages, regions, countries, and so on.

Of course, both of these statements address the external validity of a particular study. When the sample for a study has been selected from a population *at random* (using a probability sample), the results from that sample can be generalized to the population it was drawn from. It also makes sense that if a study's sample includes only men, you may not generalize its results to women; if a study's sample includes only college students from California, you may not generalize its results to elderly residents of Florida. Because most people have a strong intuitive understanding of external validity, they will agree with the two statements above.

However, the two statements are only *sometimes* right. The importance of external validity depends on a researcher's priorities. Whether a researcher strives for external validity in a study depends on what research mode he or she is operating in: theory-testing mode or generalization mode.

Theory-Testing Mode

When researchers work in **theory-testing mode**, they are usually testing association or causal claims to investigate support for a theory. As discussed in Chapter 1, the theory-data cycle is the process of designing studies to test a theory and using the data from the studies to reject, refine, or support the theory. In theory-testing mode, external validity matters much less than internal validity.

Example: The Contact Comfort Theory. Harlow's (1958) classic study of attachment in infant monkeys (described in Chapter 1) is a good example of theory-testing mode. Harlow created two artificial monkey "mothers" in order to test two competing theories of infant attachment: the cupboard theory (babies are attached to their mothers because their mothers feed them) and the contact comfort theory (babies are attached to their mothers because their mothers are soft and cozy). In a real monkey mother, of course, the features of food and coziness are confounded. So Harlow separated the two features by creating one "mother" that was soft and cozy but did not provide food and one "mother" that was cold and uncomfortable but did provide food. By separating the two confounded variables, Harlow was prioritizing internal validity.

Harlow was clearly in theory-testing mode here, wondering which theory, the cupboard theory or the contact comfort theory, was right. And the results from his study could not have been clearer: The baby monkeys in this study spent almost all of their time cuddling with the soft, cozy mother. The contact comfort theory was overwhelmingly supported.

The monkeys in Harlow's study were hardly representative of monkeys in the wild. Harlow did not even use a random sample of monkeys from his laboratory. But Harlow didn't care because he was in theory-testing mode: He created the artificial situation to test his *theory*—not to test the truth in some population of monkeys. In fact, according to the cupboard theory, *any* sample of monkeys—no matter how representative—should have been equally or more interested in the wire mother than they were in the cloth mother. The data, however, did not support the cupboard theory of attachment.

Example: The "Parent-as-Grammar-Coach" Theory. Another example of a study conducted in theory-testing mode comes from studies of how children learn grammar. Some psychologists used to believe that children learn correct grammar through reinforcement; they believed parents praise a child's grammatically correct sentences and correct the ungrammatical ones. They thought that children learned grammar through this constant correction process.

The reinforcement theory predicted that if a researcher were to observe a group of parents interacting with their children, the parents would praise their kids for grammatical sentences and correct the ungrammatical sentences. But read the following interaction, audiotaped by Brown and Hanlon (1970, cited in Mook, 1989, p. 27):

Child: Mama isn't boy, he girl.
Parent: That's right.

Child: There's the animal farmhouse.
Parent: No, that's a lighthouse.

What Brown and Hanlon noticed—and you probably did, too—is that the parent accepted the child's first sentence, which was ungrammatical but factually true. (That's right—he girl!) But the parent corrected the child's second sentence, which was grammatical but factually wrong. (Not a farmhouse—a lighthouse!) This one incident illustrates the overall trend in the data. After coding hours of conversations between parents and children, Brown and Hanlon found that most of the time, parents corrected their children's sentences for factual accuracy but not for grammar. Furthermore, the reinforcement theory predicted that the children in this study would not learn to speak correctly without corrections to their grammar. However, even though parents did not correct their children's grammar, the children did learn to speak grammatically. The reinforcement theory of speech development therefore appeared to be wrong.

This study included only upper-middle-class Boston families, so the children and parents were not representative of all children, or even of all U.S. children (Brown & Hanlon, 1970). Moreover, the parents in the study were willing to let a researcher record their interactions with their children on tape; they might have been especially eager to be involved in research and thus more educated

FIGURE 14.7 When is external validity crucial? Brown and Hanlon's sample included only upper-middle class Boston families. Why was it okay to study a nonrandom sample in this research?

than average (**Figure 14.7**). Yet the bias of this sample did not matter, because the researchers were testing a theory: If the reinforcement theory of grammar were true, *any* sample of parents should have corrected ungrammatical sentences, but the parents in this study did not.

Of course, the reinforcement theory of grammar might apply to some other population in the world, and if Brown and Hanlon had studied a wider sample of people, they might have found evidence that some parents, somewhere, do correct their children's grammar. Keep two things in mind: First, Brown and Hanlon chose a strong test of their theory. If the reinforcement theory of grammar should apply anywhere, it would be among precisely the kinds of parents who volunteered for the study: upper-middle class, well-educated, and interested in research. Such parents presumably use standard grammar themselves and are likely to be educated enough to explain grammar rules to their children. Second, if Brown and Hanlon had found some other cultural group of parents who did correct their children's grammar, the researchers would have to amend the reinforcement theory to fit these new data. They would need to change the theory to explain why reinforcement applies only in this population but not in others. In either case, the data from Brown and Hanlon's study mean that the grammar-coach theory must be rejected or at least modified.

Other Examples. In your psychology studies, you've probably encountered many other examples of research conducted in theory-testing mode. In fact, the overwhelming majority of studies in psychological science are of the theory-testing type (Mook, 1989). Most researchers design variables that enable them to test competing explanations, and confirm or disconfirm their hypotheses. For example, Wansink and his colleagues were testing the theory that portion size, rather than internal hunger cues, influences how much people eat. Research on the effect of violent video games on behavior tested the theory that people decide how to behave, in part, by modeling what they see in media representations. Strayer's research on cell phone use while driving tested the theory that cell phones are cognitively distracting to drivers. When researchers are in theory-testing mode, they are not very concerned (at least not yet) with the external validity of their samples or procedures (Berkowitz & Donnerstein, 1982).

Generalization Mode

Although much of the research in psychology is conducted in theory-testing mode, there are times when researchers work in **generalization mode**, when they want to generalize the findings from the sample in their study to a larger population. They are careful, therefore, to use probability samples with appropriate diversity of gender, age, ethnicity, and so on. In other words, researchers in generalization mode are concerned about external validity.

Applied research tends to be done in generalization mode, and basic research tends to be done in theory-testing mode. However, this distinction is not absolute: Applied researchers often test theories, too, and basic researchers may extend their findings to different populations.

For more on applied research versus basic research, see Chapter 1, pp. 13–14.

In addition, you'll probably notice that some research can have aspects of both modes, such as when researchers test an established theory to see if it applies in a new culture or for a different age group. For example, as covered in Chapter 12, Strayer and Drews (2004) were testing their theory about cognitive distractions of phone conversations, but they also were attempting to see if their original findings would generalize to an older group of drivers.

Frequency Claims: Always in Generalization Mode. Survey research that is intended to support frequency claims is done in generalization mode. A researcher must have a representative sample in order to answer such questions as: "How many U.S. teenagers text while driving?" "What percentage of voters support marriage equality?" "At what age do American children learn to read?" It would not be acceptable to estimate U.S. teenage texting-and-driving rates from a haphazard sample of teens in an upper-middle-class high school in New York City. It would not be acceptable to estimate the percentage of voters who support marriage equality by interviewing only people living in Dallas, Texas. And it would not be acceptable to estimate the age at which children learn to read by asking a self-selected sample on a web page dedicated to gifted children. All of these samples would be biased.

As you have learned, representative samples are essential for supporting frequency claims. (For a review, see Chapters 3 and 7.) Therefore, when researchers are testing frequency claims, they are always in generalization mode.

Association and Causal Claims: Sometimes in Generalization Mode. Most of the time, association and causal claims are conducted in theory-testing mode. But researchers sometimes conduct them in generalization mode, too.

Suppose a researcher tries out a new therapeutic technique on a limited sample of clients (e.g., a sample of American women of European descent) and finds that it works. If the therapy is effective in this sample, the researcher would then want to learn whether it will also be effective more generally, in other samples. Will it work on Latino women? Will it work on men? To learn whether the therapy's effectiveness generalizes to other populations, the researcher will need to determine how representative the first study's sample is. In this case, the researcher cares about generalizability from one cultural group to another.

Consider a marketing researcher who finds that a sample of local teenagers prefers an advertising campaign that features tattoo artists over an advertising campaign that features a professional skateboarder. The researcher would hope to generalize the pattern from this particular sample of teenagers to the teenagers around the country who will eventually view the advertising campaign. Therefore, the marketing researcher would care very much that the sample used in the study

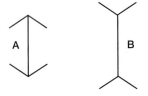

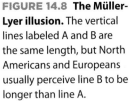

FIGURE 14.8 The Müller-Lyer illusion. The vertical lines labeled A and B are the same length, but North Americans and Europeans usually perceive line B to be longer than line A.

resembles teenagers nationwide. Are they the same age? Are they of the same social class? Do they show the same distribution of ethnicities? Is the focus group sample unusually interested in tattoos, compared with the rest of the U.S. teenage population? Only if the external validity were sound would the preferences of this sample be generalizable to the preferences of the nation's teens.

Cultural Psychology: A Special Case of Generalization Mode

Cultural psychology is a subdiscipline of psychology focusing on how cultural contexts shape the way a person thinks, feels, and behaves (Heine, 2012; Markus & Hamedani, 2007; Shweder, 1989). In conducting their studies, cultural psychologists primarily use generalization mode.

Cultural psychologists have challenged researchers who operate exclusively in theory-testing mode. While they understand why theory-testing mode focuses on internal validity, cultural psychologists point out that a theory that has been supported by a study in one human sample will not necessarily hold true for all people. Cultural psychologists have shown that many theories may be supported in some cultural contexts but not in others. Indeed, cultural psychologists have collected dozens of examples of theories that were supported by data in one cultural context but not in any other cultural context. Two of them follow.

The Müller-Lyer Illusion. You may already be familiar with the Müller-Lyer illusion, illustrated in **Figure 14.8**. Does the vertical line B appear longer than the vertical line A? If you take out a ruler and measure the two vertical lines, you'll find they are exactly the same length.

Almost all North Americans and Europeans fall for this illusion, but not all *people* do. Indeed, one team of researchers found that many people around the world, when tested, do not see line B as being longer than line A (Segall, Campbell, & Herskovits, 1966). **Figure 14.9** shows the cross-cultural results of this study.

FIGURE 14.9 Cross-cultural results for the Müller-Lyer illusion. Segall et al. tested the Müller-Lyer illusion on adults in 16 societies and found that North Americans are most likely to perceive the illusion. The y-axis shows how much longer line B appears to participants compared with line A. The higher the value, the greater the degree of the illusion. (Source: Adapted from Henrich, Heine, & Norenzayan, 2010.)

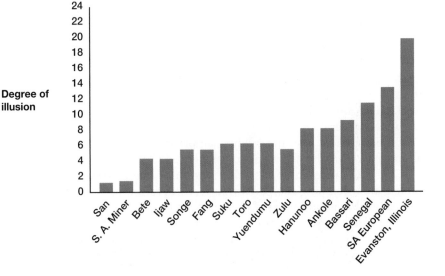

Suppose a group of North American researchers in theory-testing mode used the Müller-Lyer data from a single North American sample to formulate and test a theory about the human visual system and basic cognitive processes. Although they might briefly consider whether the results would generalize, they might discount the relevance of generalizability. After all, they might reason, culture would not affect such a basic cognitive process. But they would be wrong.

Indeed, the Segall team used their data from around the world to conclude that people who grow up in a "carpentered world" have more experience with right angles as cues for depth perception than people who grow up in other societies. (Look at the angles formed where two walls and the ceiling meet in the farthest corner of the room you are in right now. Do you see the patterns of line B in the Müller-Lyer illusion?) In cultures with few square buildings, a child's developing visual system never learns that end-lines angling in suggest that a corner is near, while end-lines angling out suggest that the corner is farther away. These culturally learned cues are the proposed explanation for the Müller-Lyer illusion.

Cultural psychologists such as Segall and his colleagues remind other researchers that they cannot take generalization for granted. Scientists cannot assume that psychological processes—even those that seem basic—are not influenced by culture.

Figure and Ground. Research conducted by Masuda and Nisbett (2001) provides another example of cultural psychology in action. When you look at the scene in **Figure 14.10**, what do you notice first? In the study, North Americans tended to comment on one of the three large fish swimming in the middle of the frame—the focal objects. As you study the image, you may also notice the objects in the background, such as the plants, water, and smaller fish. This makes sense, right? Of course we focus on what seems to be the most important—the big things in front.

When Masuda and Nisbett showed this image to a sample of Japanese college students, however, more students commented on the background first. Apparently, these Japanese participants attended to the background as much as, or even more

FIGURE 14.10 **Figure and ground.** This is the original image in Masuda and Nisbett's (2001) study.

FIGURE 14.11 Figure and ground: altering the background. To investigate how well people could remember the fish they saw, the researchers manipulated the background, presenting target fish against the original, a novel, or no background.

with original background   with no background   with novel background

than, the "focal" object. Later, Masuda and Nisbett quizzed participants from both groups on what they had seen. Sometimes the researchers showed people one of the original fish but changed the background (**Figure 14.11**). When the background was changed, North Americans could still recognize the fish, suggesting that they had processed the focal fish separately from the surrounding scene. In contrast, the Japanese students were less able to identify the fish when it was removed from the surrounding scene. (The graph in **Figure 14.12** shows the results.) Their errors suggested, in fact, that the Japanese participants had processed the fish in context, and when the context changed, their memories were less accurate.

If Masuda and Nisbett had been in theory-testing mode rather than generalization mode and had studied only the North American sample, they might have formed and tested theories about how *all people* perceive complex scenes. They might have theorized that human attention is drawn to "focal objects" first and foremost, whereas background objects receive much less visual attention. However, because the researchers were also in generalization mode, they found that visual attention worked differently in different cultures. Thus, this study is another good example of how cultural psychologists challenge other researchers to combine generalization mode with theory-testing mode—to test a theory in multiple cultures before assuming it applies to all people.

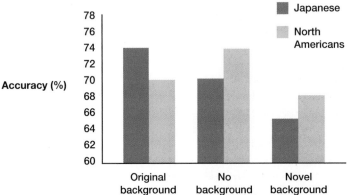

FIGURE 14.12 Figure and ground: context-sensitivity study results. North Americans were more accurate than Japanese at recognizing the target fish when it was presented without the original background. Japanese participants were more accurate than North Americans when the fish was presented in the original background. These results suggest that the way North Americans attend to "focal" and "ground" aspects of a scene does not generalize to a Japanese sample. (Source: Adapted from Masuda & Nisbett, 2001.)

Theory Testing Using WEIRD Participants

To understand the importance of cultural psychologists' work, consider that most research in psychological science has been conducted on North American college students. One researcher recorded the samples used in the top six journals in psychology for the year 2007. In these core journals, 68% of the participants were American, and 96% of the participants were from North America, Europe, Australia, or Israel (Arnett, 2008). Participants from these countries are from a unique subset of the world's population, which researchers refer to as WEIRD: Western, educated, industrialized, rich, and democratic (Henrich, Heine, & Norenzayan, 2010). Obviously, WEIRD samples are not very representative of all the world's people. The two examples above—the Müller-Lyer illusion and the figure and ground study—both demonstrate how seemingly basic human processes can work differently in different cultural contexts.

When psychological science researchers operate in theory-testing mode, they do not prioritize external validity, and they may even test their theories only on WEIRD participants. However, cultural psychologists raise the alarm, reminding researchers that their theories, when tested only on WEIRD people, may not apply to everyone (Arnett, 2008; Henrich et al., 2010; Sears, 1986).

Does a Study Have to Take Place in a Real-World Setting?

Another assumption people often make is that studies conducted in a real-world setting are more important to us than studies that take place in an artificial laboratory setting. Read the following descriptions of psychological science research, and ask yourself whether each study is important.

1. A researcher dressed a student model in black from head to toe and placed small lights on her wrists, elbows, shoulders, hips, knees, and ankles. The researcher then turned out the lights and made a movie of the model walking across the room. Later, the researcher showed either a photograph or the movie to a group of college students, asking them what they saw (**Figure 14.13**). Observers of the photograph saw a meaningless jumble of dots, and observers of the movie reported seeing a person walking (Johansson, 1973).

2. In split-brain studies (see Chapter 13), the neuroscientist Michael Gazzaniga (2005) placed patients in front of a computer, asked them to fixate on a dot in the center, and then flashed two images for a fraction of a second: one picture on the right and a different picture on the left. The people he studied could name any object presented on the right side of the computer screen but could not name objects presented on the left side.

3. A group of researchers studied helping behavior, by observing whether people in a library would intervene when a thief started rummaging through someone else's bookbag. In a staged event, a student (really an actor) sat down to study next to a library patron. After a few minutes, the student got up, leaving his or her bag at the table. Then another person—a "thief" (also an actor)—came along, rummaged through the abandoned bag, and removed either $20 or a wristwatch. The researchers were interested in whether the real student sitting at the table would say anything to stop the thief. When only the real student witnessed the theft, the real student intervened in the theft 32% of the time. However, when the real student was sitting at the table with one other "student," who was really a passive confederate of the researchers, the real student *never* intervened in the theft (Shaffer, Rogel, & Hendrick, 1975).

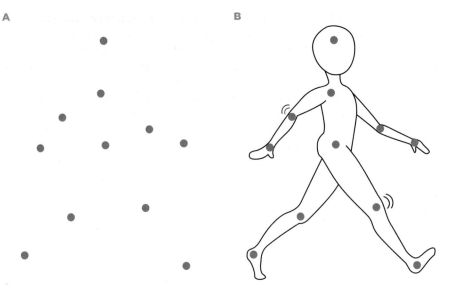

FIGURE 14.13 **Recognizing a human form.** The researcher placed small lights on the joints of a model and showed people either (A) a still photo of the model or (B) a movie of the model walking in a dark room. The results of this study demonstrated that people cannot recognize the human form from points of light alone; the model has to be moving. In the real world, you never observe people walking around in the dark with only small lights illuminating their joints. Is the Johansson (1973) study therefore unimportant?

Are these three studies important? You might argue, for instance, that the lights study does not tell you anything about the real world; after all, how often do you see someone walking around in a dark room with lights taped to his or her knees? For the split-brain study, you might argue that most people never have the corpus callosum in their brain severed, so the study does not apply to the majority. Finally, you might conclude that the library study is the most important, because it took place in a real-world setting. If so, you were probably guided by the assumption that a study should be similar to real-world contexts and daily life in order to be important. But is this always true?

External Validity and the Real World

When interrogating a study's external validity, you ask whether the results can generalize not only to other participants but also to other settings. When a study takes place in the real world, sometimes referred to as a **field setting**, it has a built-in advantage for external validity, because it clearly applies to real-world settings. As mentioned previously, ecological validity is a type of external validity that refers to how similar a study's manipulations and measures are to the kinds of situations participants might encounter in their everyday lives. The library study has excellent ecological validity because it did take place in a real-world setting. However, the ecological validity of a setting is only one aspect of the setting's generalizability; just because a setting seems realistic does not mean it represents all possible settings a person might encounter. Would the results of the library study also apply in a coffee shop, a doctor's office, or a movie theater?

Furthermore, the situation a scientist creates in a research laboratory is just as real as one that occurs in a restaurant or workplace. Although it may be easy to dismiss a study that does not seem realistic, remember that in daily life people find themselves in many different settings, all of which are "real." These settings can include not only libraries, theaters, and coffee shops but also classrooms and research labs.

Indeed, the emotions and behaviors generated by a laboratory manipulation (e.g., the anxiety about evaluation caused by seeing red ink, or the cell phone conversation a person conducts during a driving simulator task) can also be quite real, visible, and meaningful. Many laboratory experiments are high in what's known as **experimental realism**: They create settings in which people experience authentic emotions, motivations, and behaviors. People in lab settings have interacted with real other people, drunk real alcoholic beverages, and played real games with other participants. Many of these situations are truly engaging and emotionally evocative.

To what extent does the real-world similarity—the ecological validity—of a study affect your ideas about a study's importance? It depends on the mode it is conducted in: generalization mode or theory-testing mode.

Generalization Mode and the Real World

Because external validity is of primary importance when researchers are in generalization mode, they might strive for a representative sample of a population. But they might also try to enhance the ecological validity of their study in order to ensure its generalizability to nonlaboratory settings. By the time Shaffer and his team studied helping behavior in the library (Shaffer et al., 1975), several authors had already tested theories of helping in lab settings. When students, for instance, heard what sounded like a woman falling in a nearby lab (it was actually a realistic audio recording), they were more likely to investigate the accident if they were alone. When participants were with even one other person, however, the rates of helping went down dramatically. The results from these lab studies supported a theory of bystander intervention known as *diffusion of responsibility* (Darley & Latané, 1968; Latané & Nida, 1981). This theory predicts that as the number of witnesses to an emergency event increases, the likelihood that each individual will offer to help decreases.

After reading about lab research supporting the diffusion of responsibility theory, Shaffer et al. wanted to know whether the theory would hold up in the real world, so they conducted the library study. Indeed, the theory was also supported in that setting. People were more likely to report the theft when they were sole witnesses than when another person was there. By conducting the study outside the lab, in the real world, Shaffer and his colleagues were operating in generalization mode. Their results provided evidence for the theory's generalizability to other real-world settings. One recent review showed, in fact, that field studies often replicate lab research, especially when the laboratory effect sizes are large (Mitchell, 2012).

Theory-Testing Mode and the Real World

When a researcher is working in theory-testing mode, external validity and real-world applicability are lower priorities. Take, for instance, the Johansson (1973) study, in which the model had lights on her joints. Of course, no one is going to encounter these circumstances in the real world, but the ecological validity of the situation did not matter to the researcher. He was testing a research question: How much information do people need before they can conclude they are looking at a human being? By keeping the room dark and attaching lights only to the model's joints, Johansson was able to cut out all other visual information; only the location of the joints was visible. He was concerned with internal validity—eliminating alternative explanations for people's interpretations. It was not enough just to see the lights on the joints, however. Participants could not detect a human form from a still photo; the lights had to be moving in a coordinated way. To narrow down exactly what visual information people needed in order to detect a human form, Johansson had to create an extremely artificial situation.

Was Johansson's study important? In terms of the theory he was testing, it was invaluable, because he was able to show that both joint location and movement are necessary and sufficient to detect a human form. What about generalizability and real-world applicability? On the one hand, both the model and the study's participants were drawn haphazardly, not randomly, from a narrow group of North American college students. In addition, the situation created in the laboratory would never occur in a real-world setting. On the other hand, the ability to recognize human gestures and postures is undoubtedly essential for many aspects of human social life. The theoretical understanding gained from this seemingly artificial study contributes to our understanding of a perceptual process involved in basic social cognition.

TABLE 14.4 Responding Appropriately to the "Latest Scientific Breakthrough"

Say this:	Not that:
"Was that result replicated?" "That is a single study. How does the study fit in with the entire literature?"	"Look at this single, interesting result!"
"How well do the methods of this study get at the theory they were testing?"	"I don't think this study is important because the methods had nothing to do with the real world."
"Was the study conducted in generalization mode? If so, were the participants sampled randomly?"	"I reject this study because they didn't use a random sample." "This is a bad study because they used only North Americans as participants."
"The study had thousands of participants, but were they selected in such a way to allow generalization to the population of interest?"	"They used thousands of participants. It must have great external validity."
"Would the result hold up in another cultural context?" "Would that result apply in other settings?"	"That psychological principle seems so basic, I'm sure it's universal."

Gazzaniga and his colleagues' studies of split-brain patients (see Chapter 13) are another example of research done in theory-testing mode (Gazzaniga, 2005; Turk et al., 2003). Gazzaniga designed his two-sided, flashing pictures so he could better understand where language was localized in the brain. Do the situations he created in his laboratory occur in the real world? Absolutely not. They didn't even occur in the everyday lives of the split-brain patients in the study, who could usually move their eyes from right to left. If an image fell on the left side of the visual field, they could shift the input from the right side of the brain to the left with a quick movement of the eye.

The stimuli Gazzaniga presented to his participants were therefore about as unnatural as you can imagine. However, Gazzaniga specifically created these artificial conditions to test a theory. Despite the lack of real-world similarity in his methods, he was able to confirm an important theory about how the brain is organized—knowledge that has many real-world implications.

Finally, consider the study design that many people (quite correctly) respect as a pinnacle of behavioral research: the randomized, double-blind, placebo-controlled study, introduced in Chapter 11. In such a study, an experimenter goes to extreme artificial lengths to assign people at random to carefully constructed experimental conditions that control for placebo effects, experimenter bias, and experimental demand. Such studies have virtually no equivalent in everyday, real-world settings, yet their results can be among the most valuable in psychological science.

In short, theory-testing mode often demands that experimenters create artificial situations that allow them to minimize distractions, eliminate alternative explanations, and isolate individual features of some situation. Theory-testing mode prioritizes internal validity at the expense of all other considerations, including ecological validity. Nonetheless, such studies make valuable contributions to the field of psychology.

Table 14.4 summarizes the approach to external validity that has been emphasized in this chapter.

CHECK YOUR UNDERSTANDING

1. Describe the difference between generalization mode and theory-testing mode.
2. Which of the three types of claims (frequency, association, causal) is/are almost always conducted in generalization mode? Which of the three types of claims is/are usually conducted in theory-testing mode?
3. Explain why researchers who are operating in theory-testing mode might not try using a random sample in their study. What validity are they prioritizing? What aspects of their research are they emphasizing (for now)?
4. Summarize the goal of cultural psychology. What does this field suggest about working in theory-testing and generalization modes?
5. When an experiment tests hypotheses in an artificial laboratory setting, it does not necessarily mean the study does not apply to the real world. Explain why not.

---

1. See pp. 426–430. 2. See p. 429. 3. See pp. 426–428. 4. See p. 430. 5. See pp. 434–437.

Summary

- A nuanced approach can be used to evaluate a study's importance. Although a study should be replicated to be important, it might not need to be generalizable or have immediate, real-world applicability.

To Be Important, a Study Must Be Replicable

- Replication studies determine whether the findings are reproducible.
- A direct replication repeats the original study exactly. A conceptual replication has the same conceptual variables as the original study, but operationalizes the variables differently. A replication-plus-extension study repeats the original study and introduces new participant variables, situations, or independent variable levels. Replication studies are ideal when conducted by researchers independent of the original laboratory.
- A meta-analysis collects and mathematically averages the effect sizes from all studies that have tested the same variables. It helps quantify whether an effect exists in the literature and, if so, its size and what moderates it.

To Be Important, Must a Study Have External Validity?

- The importance of external validity depends on whether researchers are operating in generalization mode or theory-testing mode.
- In generalization mode, researchers focus on whether their samples are representative, whether the data from their sample apply to the population of interest, and even whether the data might apply to new population of interest.
- In theory-testing mode, researchers design studies that test a theory, leaving the generalization step for later studies, which will test whether the theory holds in a sample that is representative of another population.

- In contrast to what many casual observers assume, important research might not (1) use random samples from populations or (2) study people of both genders and all ethnicities, social classes, geographical location, and so on. Diverse, representative samples are primarily important when researchers are in generalization mode. In theory-testing mode, researchers do not (yet) consider whether their samples are representative of some population, so external validity is less important than internal validity.
- Researchers who make frequency claims are always in generalization mode, but they are also in generalization mode when asking whether an association or causal claim can be generalized to a different group of people.
- Cultural psychologists have documented how psychological discoveries are not always applicable cross-culturally, including basic cognitive or visual processes.
- When researchers collect data only from WEIRD (Western, educated, industrialized, rich, and democratic) samples, they cannot assume the theories they develop in theory-testing mode will apply to all people.
- To be important, research does not necessarily have to be conducted in the real world. A study has high ecological validity when it takes place in a setting similar to a common real-world setting. While studies (conducted in theory-testing mode) taking place in laboratories might be high in experimental realism, they may not resemble real-world settings outside the lab. Yet the data from such artificial settings help researchers test theories in the most internally valid way possible, and the results may still apply to other real-world situations.

Key Terms

replicable, p. 414
direct replication, p. 414
conceptual replication, p. 415
replication-plus-extension,
    p. 416

scientific literature, p. 419
meta-analysis, p. 419
file drawer problem, p. 422
ecological validity, p. 425
theory-testing mode, p. 426

generalization mode, p. 428
cultural psychology, p. 430
field setting, p. 434
experimental realism,
    p. 435

 To see samples of chapter concepts in the popular press, visit
www.everydayresearchmethods.com and click the box for Chapter 14.

Review Questions

1. If you repeat a study and find the same results as the first time, what can you say about the effect?
   a. It is replicable.
   b. It is statistically significant.
   c. It is valid.
   d. It is consistent.

2. When a researcher conducts a replication study in which she has the same variables at an abstract level, but uses different operationalizations of each variable, what type of study is it?
   a. Direct replication
   b. Meta-analysis
   c. Conceptual replication
   d. Replication-plus-extension

3. A _____ is a technique in which the researcher mathematically averages the results of all studies that have been completed with the same conceptual variables.
   a. meta-analysis
   b. correlation
   c. effect size measurement
   d. analysis of variance

4. Which of the following claims is most likely to have been tested in generalization mode?
   a. 8% of adults get news through Twitter.
   b. Reading stressful news makes adults anxious.
   c. People who walk faster live longer.

5. Which of these is a field setting?
   a. A psychology lab with a hidden camera
   b. A neuropsychology lab with an MRI machine
   c. A preschool playground with video cameras
   d. A biology lab with galvanic skin response detectors

6. Which of these statements is true of external validity?
   a. Psychologists usually strive to generalize to all people.
   b. The larger the sample the better.
   c. External validity comes from how the sample is obtained, rather than sample size.
   d. A sample that contains female college students can generalize to all female college students.

Learning Actively

1. Consider the study that recorded people's substantive conversations and their well-being, from Chapter 8 (Mehl et al., 2010). How would you conduct a direct replication of this study? A conceptual replication? A replication-plus-extension?

2. For each short study description below, indicate whether you think it would have been conducted in theory-testing mode or generalization mode, or whether it could be done in either mode. Explain your answer. For which of these studies would a random sample of participants be the most important? For which would external validity be the least important?

   a. A study found that most Holocaust survivors struggle with depression, sleep disorders, and emotional distress. The conclusion was based on a government data set that has tracked 220,000 Holocaust survivors ("Most Holocaust Survivors Battle Depression," 2010).

   b. A neuropsychologist exposed mice to radio waves from cell phones. In a pretest/posttest design, their cages were exposed to a typical cell phone's electromagnetic field for about 1 hour a day, for about 9 months. Later, the researchers tested each mouse's memory and found that the mice had better memory after their exposure to the electromagnetic fields than before, and better memory compared with the control group of mice that was not exposed (Hamzelou, 2010).

   c. A group of researchers studied three men in India who were born blind (Ostrovsky, Meyers, Ganesh, Mathur, & Sinha, 2009). At ages 7, 12, and 29, respectively, each man received surgery and treatment to correct his vision. (In all three cases, the families of the men had been too poor to afford treatment for the blindness.) After the patients regained their sight, the researchers studied how these three people developed their newly acquired abilities to decode the visual world. At first, each patient thought that a two-dimensional picture, such as the one labeled B in the figure, depicted three objects instead of two. With several months of experience, however, they all learned to interpret the images appropriately. By moving the objects apart from each other on some of the trials, the researchers discovered that the three men in their study could use motion cues to decode what lines belonged to which object (similar to how people in Johansson's study could identify that a lighted model was walking only when she was moving). The researchers concluded that as the brain learns about the visual world, it uses motion cues to decide which lines belong to which objects.

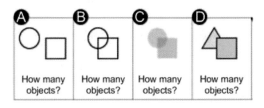

Statistics Review
Descriptive Statistics

In everyday language, the word *statistics* is used to describe quantitative records, such as a baseball player's batting average or the average life span of a country's citizens. In science, the word refers to the set of tools researchers use to make sense of data that they have collected in a study. This supplementary chapter provides a very brief overview of one set of such statistical tools: **descriptive statistics**, used for organizing and summarizing the properties of a set of data. The other set of statistical tools, inferential statistics, is covered in the supplementary chapter that follows this one.

Describing Data

Recall that when a researcher collects data from a group of people or animals, the group is often a sample from a larger population. If we tested 5 rhesus monkeys on their ability to discriminate blue from green, and the 5 came from a larger population of 25 monkeys in the lab, then the 5 monkeys would be the sample. If we tested 50 students on their anagram skills, the 50 students might be a sample from a larger population of students who could have signed up for the research. However, researchers don't always study a sample from a larger population.

If a midterm exam is given to 31 students, the 31 students are a complete set of cases; they are not a sample, because they are the whole population of interest. Or we might collect data on the average air temperature and teen pregnancy rates in all 50 states in the U.S. These 50 states are not a sample, either; they are a population. We might simply have a batch of scores—perhaps a set of prices from the local supermarket, or some data on reading speed from a group of third graders. Regardless of whether our data are best described as a sample, a population, or a simple set of scores, we can still apply the descriptive techniques explained here.

Variables are what researchers measure or manipulate in a study. If we study 31 students' grades on a midterm exam, then exam score is the variable. In other studies, variables might be the ability to discriminate blue from green, the average air temperature, or the pregnancy rate among teenagers. Variables vary: They take on different levels, or values, for the different members of a sample. Thus, the values for an exam score might range from 16 to 33 on a 35-point scale.

For a review of categorical and quantitative variables, see Chapter 5, p. 127.

Student name	Exam score
Henry	17
Emma	29
Caitlyn	19
Lonnie	27
Lalia	22
Alek	27
Rohan	22
Max	20
Shane	29
Yukiko	29
Alexi	18
Marianna	30
Mira	21
Cristina	27
Emmanuel	26
Raul	30
Ian	19
Sena	29
Jordan	27
Ayase	32
Luke	25
Miguel	32
Jon	30
Gabriel	31
Rhianna	32
Juniper	24
Malika	25
Shawn	30
Adhya	24
Harriet	33
Lucio	25

FIGURE S1.1

A data matrix of exam scores. A data matrix is the starting point for computing most statistics.

Ability to discriminate blue from green might have the categorical values of "yes" or "no." Average air temperature might have quantitative values ranging from 50 to 81 degrees Fahrenheit and anything in between.

Data Matrices

After we collect a set of data, we usually enter the data in a grid format, called a **data matrix**, using a computer program. Programs such as Excel, SPSS, SYSTAT, SAS, and STATA can not only calculate formulas, they can also facilitate making graphs and organizing data in various ways. **Figure S1.1** shows a data matrix with the scores of 31 students who took a short-answer exam consisting of 35 items. The first column identifies each person by name (this column might contain simple ID numbers instead). The second column shows the person's score on the exam. In a data matrix, each column represents a variable, and each row represents a case (such as a person, an animal, a state, a price, or any other case under study).

Frequency Distributions and Stemplots

Frequency distributions and stemplots are techniques for organizing a column of data in a data matrix. At first glance, the data matrix shows a disorganized list of scores. However, we can quickly bring some order to the scores by making a **frequency distribution**, a table that gives a visual picture of the observations on a particular variable. It clearly shows how many of the cases scored each possible value on the variable.

To make a frequency distribution, we list possible values for the variable from lowest to highest and tally how many people obtained each score, as in **Figure S1.2A**. Normally, we do not leave the tally marks there; we count them and enter the value in the table, as in **Figure S1.2B**. Based on the data from a frequency distribution, it is a fairly simple step to create a graph called a **frequency histogram** (often called simply a *histogram*), as in **Figure S1.3A**. Note that the possible exam scores are on the x-axis, while the frequency of each score is on the y-axis. We could also draw the histogram the other way, as in **Figure S1.3B**.

Instead of giving individual numerical scores, we could group the exam score values. For example, if we call any score between 30 and 33 an A, any score between 25 and 29 a B, and so on, the frequency histogram looks simpler, as in **Figure S1.4**.

Another option for organizing data visually is a graphical representation called a **stemplot**, also known as a *stem-and-leaf plot*. **Figure S1.5** shows the data from the midterm exam in stemplot form. The values on the left of the line are called *stems*, and the values on the right are called *leaves*. To make a stemplot, we would first decide the units for the stems—tens, hundreds, thousands—using the most appropriate level for the data. In this example, tens are used as the unit for the stems, because the possible scores on the exam could range from 0 to 35. After listing the stems (in this case, 10, 20, 30), we would enter the leaves, which represent each individual score. For example, there is one score of 17, so on the stem 10 there is one leaf marked with "7." There are two scores of 19, so on the stem 10 there are two leaves marked "9." The stemplot is useful because it is a table and a graph at the same time. It is simple to see all the scores in a stemplot.

A	Possible value	Number of cases
	17	I
	18	I
	19	II
	20	I
	21	I
	22	II
	23	
	24	II
	25	III
	26	I
	27	IIII
	28	
	29	IIII
	30	IIII
	31	I
	32	III
	33	I

B	Possible value	Number of cases
	17	1
	18	1
	19	2
	20	1
	21	1
	22	2
	23	0
	24	2
	25	3
	26	1
	27	4
	28	0
	29	4
	30	4
	31	1
	32	3
	33	1

FIGURE S1.2 A frequency distribution for exam scores. (A) List the possible values in one column and tally the number of times each value occurs in the data set in the next column. Then convert the tallies to numerals. (B) The final frequency distribution.

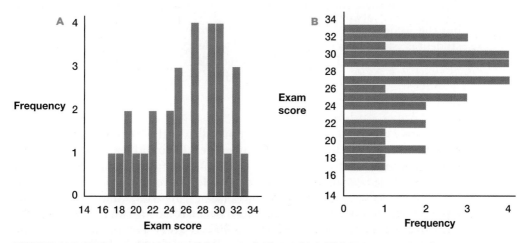

FIGURE S1.3 Frequency histogram of the scores in Figure S1.1. (A) Exam scores are on the x-axis. (B) Exam scores are on the y-axis.

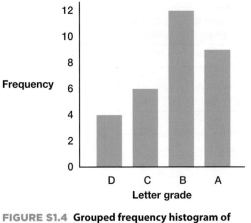

Frequency

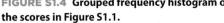

Letter grade

FIGURE S1.4 **Grouped frequency histogram of the scores in Figure S1.1.**

Stem	Leaves
10	7 8 9 9
20	0 1 2 2 4 4 5 5 5 6 7 7 7 7 9 9 9 9
30	0 0 0 0 1 2 2 2 3

FIGURE S1.5 **Stemplot of the 31 short-answer test scores.** A stemplot serves as both a table and a graph, making it easy to see all the scores in a batch and how they are distributed.

A grouped frequency distribution might tell us that nine students got an A in the class, but we would not know what the students' exact scores were. In contrast, a stemplot reveals this information.

Compared with a disorganized list of scores, a frequency distribution, frequency histogram, or stemplot makes it easier to visualize the scores collected.

Describing Central Tendencies (Mode, Median, and Mean)

Suppose I come into class carrying a bundle of exams in my hand, and a student asks me, "How did the class do?" I start to read off the individual exam scores, but the student says, "Too much information. What was a *typical* score?" The student is asking for a measure of **central tendency**—a measure of what value the individual scores tend to center on. Three values are commonly used to determine central tendency: the mode, the median, and the mean.

Mode

The **mode** is the value of the most common score—the score that was received by more members of the group than any other. To find the mode, we can look at the frequency histogram (as in Figure S1.3) and find the highest peak. The value below the peak on the x-axis is the mode. Or we can look at the stemplot and find the value with the most leaves (see Figure S1.5). Some distributions have more than one mode; they are called **bimodal**, having two modes or scores, or **multimodal**, having more than two modes or scores. For an example, see the distribution in Figure S1.3, which has three modes: 27, 29, and 30.

Median

The **median** is the value at the middlemost score of a distribution of scores—the score that divides a frequency distribution into halves. The median is a typical score in the sense that if we were to guess that every student in the class received the median score, we would not be consistently off in either direction. We would guess too high and too low equally often. To find the median of 31 scores, we would line up the scores in order (smallest to largest) and find the value of the 16th, or middlemost, score. A stemplot makes it easy to find the median. In the stemplot in Figure S1.5, the median is a score of 27, because if we count the leaves starting from the lowest score, the 16th leaf is the score of 27.

Mean

The **mean**, also called the *average*, is found by adding all the scores in the batch and then dividing by the number of scores. The mean is abbreviated with the symbol *M*. Here is the formula for determining the mean:

$$M = \frac{\Sigma X}{N}$$

The X in this formula stands for each student's score on the test. The sigma (Σ) means "the sum of." Therefore, ΣX means we must sum all the values of X—all the scores. The N stands for the number of scores. In our example, we would find the mean by adding up 33, 32, 32, 32, 31, 30, 30, 30, 30, 29, 27, 27, 27, 27, and so on (down to 17), and then we would divide by 31, the number of people who took the exam. We would find that the mean exam value in this class is 26.16.

Mode, Median, Mean: Which to Use?

The mean is by far the most common measure of central tendency. However, when a set of scores contains a few extreme scores on one end (outliers; see Chapter 8), the median or mode may be a more accurate measure of central tendency. Suppose we want to know the typical annual income in a community of only five families: four with modest incomes and a fifth that is very wealthy. Let's say the five incomes are as follows:

$20,000
$30,000
$40,000
$50,000
$1,000,000

The mean (average) would be $228,000—a very misleading idea of the community's income. In such a case, the median income—$40,000—would be a better estimate of what is typical for the community as a whole. In short, the mean is usually the most appropriate measure of central tendency, but when a set of data has outliers, the median (or sometimes the mode) may provide a better description.

When a distribution has a clear mode, the mode can be a good choice for describing central tendency. For example, a class's evaluations of a professor's teaching performance might be distributed as follows:

Overall, this professor's teaching was:	Number of respondents
1 = poor	0
2 = average	0
3 = good	1
4 = very good	4
5 = excellent	10

The professor's mean rating would be 4.60, but she might also wish to report the modal response—that the overwhelming majority of the students rated her "excellent," or 5.

Describing Variability (Variance and Standard Deviation)

Besides describing the central tendency of a set of scores, we can also describe how spread out the scores are. In **Figure S1.6**, compare the top set of scores to the bottom set. Notice that both sets have the same number of scores, and both have the same mean as well. However, the top set has less variability than the bottom one. In the top set, scores are, on average, closer to the mean. In the bottom set, scores are, on average, farther from the mean.

The two most common descriptive techniques that capture the relative spread of scores are the variance (sometimes abbreviated as SD^2) and the standard deviation

FIGURE S1.6 Two sets of scores with the same mean but different variability. (A) The top set has less variability than (B) the bottom set, but they both have the same mean and the same number of scores.

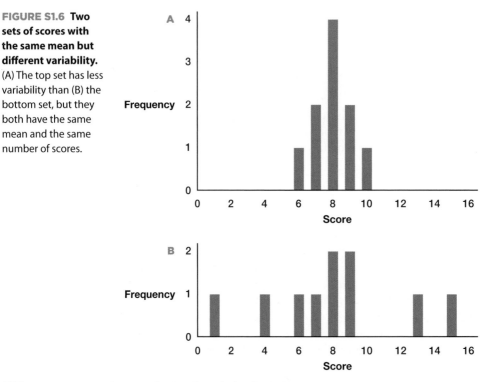

TABLE S1.1 Variance and Standard Deviation Computations for the Set of Scores in Figure S1.6A

Participant	Score	Deviation (score − mean)	Deviation squared
A	6	$6 - 8.0 = -2$	4
B	7	$7 - 8.0 = -1$	1
C	7	$7 - 8.0 = -1$	1
D	8	$8 - 8.0 = 0$	0
E	8	$8 - 8.0 = 0$	0
F	8	$8 - 8.0 = 0$	0
G	8	$8 - 8.0 = 0$	0
H	9	$9 - 8.0 = 1$	1
I	9	$9 - 8.0 = 1$	1
J	10	$10 - 8.0 = 2$	4
	Sum = 80		Sum = 12
	Mean = 80/10 = **8.0**		Variance = 12/10 = 1.20
			$SD = \sqrt{1.20} = 1.10$

(abbreviated *SD*). **Variance** is a computation that quantifies how spread out the scores of a sample are around their mean; it is the square of the standard deviation. **Standard deviation** is a computation that captures how far, on average, each score in a data set is from the mean. It's important to fully understand the logic behind these computations, because the logic applies to some other statistics, as well.

When computing the variance of a set of scores, we start by calculating how far each score is from the mean. The first two columns of **Table S1.1** present the set of scores that goes with Figure S1.6A.

The first step is to calculate the mean of this set of 10 scores. We add up all the scores in the second column, divide by 10, and get the mean: 8.0. Next, we create a deviation score for each participant. We subtract the mean, 8.0, from each score. The deviation scores are in the third column. One possible way to figure out the "average" deviation score would be simply to add up all the deviation scores in the third column and divide by 10. However, because some of the deviation scores are positive and some are negative, they would cancel each other out when added up. They would add up to zero for any distribution of scores, so merely summing them would not give us any sense of the variability in the scores.

To eliminate this problem, we square each deviation score, since the square of either a positive or a negative number is a positive number. The squared deviations are given in the fourth column of Table S1.1. We now compute the average of the squared deviations by summing them (to get 12) and dividing by the number of scores (10). The result is the variance. Finally, to reverse the step in which we squared the scores, we take the square root of the variance to find the standard deviation, or *SD* (1.10).

TABLE S1.2 Variance and Standard Deviation Computations for the Set of Scores in Figure S1.6B

Participant	Score	Deviation (score − mean)	Deviation squared
A	1	1 − 8.0 = −7	49
B	4	4 − 8.0 = −4	16
C	6	6 − 8.0 = −2	4
D	7	7 − 8.0 = −1	1
E	8	8 − 8.0 = 0	0
F	8	8 − 8.0 = 0	0
G	9	9 − 8.0 = 1	1
H	9	9 − 8.0 = 1	1
I	13	13 − 8.0 = 5	25
J	15	15 − 8.0 = 7	49
	Sum = 80		Sum = 146
	Mean = 80/10 = **8.0**		Variance = 146/10 = 14.6
			$SD = \sqrt{14.6} = 3.82$

Here is the mathematical formula for the variance when you are interested in describing only your current batch of scores:

$$SD^2 = \frac{\sum(X - M)^2}{N}$$

This formula can be explained as follows:

1. From each score X, we subtract the mean: $(X - M)$
2. We square each of the resulting deviation scores: $(X - M)^2$
3. We add up all the squared deviation scores: $\sum(X - M)^2$ (This quantity is called the "sum of squares" because we *sum* all of the *squared* deviation scores.)
4. We divide the sum of squares by the number of scores to get the mean squared deviation, called the variance:

$$SD^2 = \frac{\sum(X - M)^2}{N}$$

Finally, if we take the positive square root of the variance, we get the standard deviation:

$$SD = \sqrt{SD^2}$$

The standard deviation is more commonly reported than the variance because it better captures how far, on average, each score is from the mean. When the standard deviation is large, there is a great deal of variability in the set; the scores are spread out far from the mean, either above or below. When the standard deviation is small, there is less variability in the set; most of the scores are closer to the mean, above or below. Indeed, the standard deviation for Figure S1.6A is 1.10, but the *SD* for Figure S1.6B is 3.82. The standard deviation computations for the scores are shown in **Table S1.2**. The more spread out the scores are, the higher the standard deviation value will be.

When you are computing the standard deviation from a batch of scores and your goal is to estimate the population's standard deviation, you should know that the formula for *SD* changes a bit. Instead of using *N* in the denominator, you use $N - 1$. This small adjustment makes the *SD* from your sample a more accurate estimate of the true *SD* in the population from which your sample was drawn. Here are the formulas to use in that case:

$$SD^2 = \frac{\sum(X - M)^2}{N - 1}$$

$$SD = \sqrt{SD^2}$$

How Mean and Standard Deviation Are Represented in Journal Articles

In an empirical journal article, the mean and standard deviation information is usually presented either within the text of the Results section or as part of a table. Following are two examples of mean and standard deviation data that appeared in actual journal articles.

First is an example of how mean and standard deviation information can be presented in a text. Read the following excerpt from an article (discussed in Chapter 2) on using a punching bag to express anger (Bushman, 2002, p. 728):

> *How hard the punching bag was hit.* ...Overall, men hit the punching bag harder than did women, $M = 6.69$, $SD = 2.05$, and $M = 4.73$, $SD = 1.88$, $F(1, 396) = 99.14$, $p < .0001$, $d = 1.00$. No other effects were significant ($ps > .05$).
>
> *Number of times punching bag was hit.* Participants who thought about becoming physically fit hit the punching bag more times than did participants who thought about the person who insulted them, $M = 127.5$, $SD = 63.5$, and $M = 112.2$, $SD = 57.5$, $F(1, 396) = 6.31$, $p < .05$, $d = 0.25$. In other words, participants in the rumination group vented less than did participants in the distraction group. No other effects were significant ($ps > .05$).

Even if all of the statistical symbols are not familiar to you, look for the mean (*M*) and standard deviation (*SD*).

TEST YOURSELF 1

In the excerpt above, can you find the average force with which men hit the punching bag? Can you find the average force with which women hit the punching bag? Which group, males or females, has the higher variability? How can you tell?

The second example, involving amount of popcorn eaten and size of container (from Wansink & Kim, 2005) shows how mean and standard deviation information can be presented in table form. In **Figure S1.7**, focus on finding the mean and standard deviation, even if you do not recognize all of the statistical notation. Depending on the article and the journal, the tables will differ, but you can use the column labels or table captions to locate the means and standard deviations of particular cells.

Table 2. Larger Containers Influence Consumption Volume of Both Fresh and Stale Popcorn (Means ± Standard Deviations)

	Medium Container (120 g) n = 77		Large Container (240 g) n = 80		F Values (df = 154)	Statistical Significance of Container Size, Freshness, and Their Combined Impact	
	Fresh Popcorn	Stale Popcorn	Fresh Popcorn	Stale Popcorn		Container Size	Container Size × Freshness
Popcorn eaten, g	58.9 ± 16.7	38.0 ± 16.1	85.6 ± 19.8	50.8 ± 14.1	52.4**	101.8**	7.4**
'This popcorn tasted good'[1]	7.7 ± 1.4	3.9 ± 2.4	6.8 ± 1.5	2.2 ± 1.7	19.5**	201.1**	2.5**
'This popcorn was of high quality'[1]	7.3 ± 2.1	3.1 ± 1.5	6.8 ± 1.9	2.1 ± 2.1	5.6*	194.0**	0.4

[1]Means were measured on a 9-point scale (1 = strongly disagree; 9 = strongly agree).
*$P < .05$; **$P < .01$.

FIGURE S1.7 Mean and standard deviation information presented as a table in an empirical journal article. (Source: Wansink & Kim, 2005.)

TEST YOURSELF 2

In Figure S1.7, how much stale popcorn, on average, did people eat from a large container? What was the mean and standard deviation of how much fresh popcorn people ate from a medium container?

Describing Relative Standing (z Scores)

Thus far we have covered, among other tools, frequency distributions, means, and standard deviations. If we combine some of these techniques, we can also describe where an individual score stands in relation to the whole batch of scores. A **z score** describes whether an individual's score is above or below the mean and how far it is from the mean, in standard deviation units.

Describing Relative Standing in Standard Deviation Units

Let's start with the exam scores we used to illustrate frequency distributions, in Figure S1.1. Suppose Max, who has a score of 20, wants to know how good his exam score was in relation to the scores of the rest of the class. Because we already know that the mean score was 26.16, we can tell Max that his score, 20, was 6.16 points below the mean.

Perhaps Max also wants to know whether 6.16 points was far below mean or just a little below the mean. We might answer Max's question by using standard deviation units of distance.

The standard deviation for this group of test scores was 4.52—meaning that on average, scores were 4.52 points away from the mean. We can tell Max his score was 6.16 points below the mean, and that the standard deviation was 4.52. Therefore, Max's score was 1.36 standard deviation units below the mean. Now Max has learned that he did worse than average, by a fairly large margin. His score was more than one standard deviation below the mean.

Computing z Scores

To describe people's relative standing in standard deviation units, we compute z scores using the following formula:

$$z = \frac{(X - M)}{SD}$$

We start with the individual score, X, and subtract the mean from that score. Then we divide the difference by the standard deviation. When we follow the z score formula, any score below the mean (like Max's) will have a negative z score. Any score above the mean will have a positive z score. Any score that is directly at the mean will have a z score of zero.

TEST YOURSELF 3

Can you compute the z score for Emma, who got a 29 on the same exam Max took?

Using z Scores

One of the useful qualities of a z score is that it lets us compare the relative standing of individual cases on variables that might have been measured in different units. (For this reason, the z score is sometimes referred to as a *standardized score*.) Suppose, for example, the first exam was a midterm exam with only 35 questions on it, and Max's score was 20. Now imagine the final exam has 100 questions, and Max's score was 65. Was Max's score on the final, relative to those of his classmates, better than his relative score on the midterm? We could use z scores to find out.

If the mean score on the final was 80, with a standard deviation of 14 points, we can use this information to compute Max's z score on the final exam:

$$z = \frac{(65 - 80)}{14} = -1.07$$

Max's z score for the first exam was -1.34, and for the final it was -1.07. Both scores are below average, but his final exam score was closer to the mean than his midterm score. Therefore, Max's performance on the final was a little better, relatively, than his performance on the midterm.

TEST YOURSELF 4

Emma's score on the final exam was 94. Which test did she perform better on, relative to her classmates?

In this way, to describe the relative standing of the scores in a set, we can convert each score to a z score. The z score lets us describe how far any individual's score on a variable is from the mean, in standard deviation units. In addition, if we convert each person's scores on two or more variables to z scores, we can meaningfully compare the relative standings of each person on those variables, even when the variables are measured in different units.

One variable, for instance, might be height, measured in centimeters, and the other variable might be weight, measured in kilograms. If a person's z score for height is $z = 0.58$ and his z score for weight is $z = 0.00$, for example, we could conclude he is above average in height but at the mean in weight (and thus probably a rather thin person). Or perhaps one variable, such as a state's air temperature, is measured in degrees Fahrenheit, and the other variable, teen pregnancy rate, is measured as the number of pregnancies per 100,000 teens. The z scores can tell us whether a state is relatively warm or cool and whether its teen pregnancy rate is higher or lower than average.

Describing Associations Using Scatterplots or the Correlation Coefficient r

Three chapters in the main text introduced the logic of scatterplots and the correlation coefficient r (see Chapters 3, 5, and 8). We use scatterplots and r to describe the association between two variables that are measured in the same set of cases. For example, we might want to describe the association between 2-year-old height and adult height (see Figure 8.6). Or we might want to describe the association between how often people multitask and their ability to do so (see Figure 8.2).

Scatterplots

As discussed previously, one way to describe associations between two variables is to draw a scatterplot. With one variable on the x-axis and another variable on the y-axis, we plot each case as a dot on the graph so that it represents the person's score on both variables.

Figure S1.8 shows a hypothetical scatterplot for the association between 2-year-old height and adult height. The marked dot represents Eliana, one member of the group. The scatterplot shows that Eliana was fairly short at age 2 and is also fairly short as an adult. Other dots on the scatterplot represent other members of the group, showing their height at the two different ages.

Similarly, **Figure S1.9** shows a scatterplot of the association between frequency of media multitasking and ability to multitask, based on a study by David Sanbonmatsu and his colleagues (2013). The black dot represents Rhoslyn, a person who is not very good at media multitasking, and who engages in media multitasking a bit more than average. The other dots on that scatterplot represent other members of the batch, showing how much they engage in multitasking and how well they performed on the multitasking ability task (their OSPAN score).

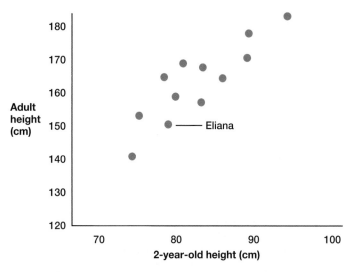

FIGURE S1.8 Scatterplot of adult height and 2-year-old height.

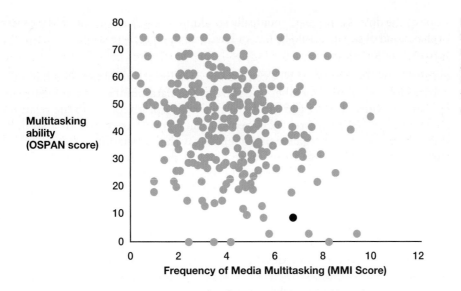

FIGURE S1.9
Scatterplot of multitasking ability and frequency.
(Source: Adapted from Sanbonmatsu et al., 2013.)

By inspecting a scatterplot, we can describe two important aspects of an association: the *direction* of the relationship between two variables (positive, negative, or zero) and the *strength* of the positive or negative relationship (strong or weak).

Direction of Association: Positive, Negative, or Zero. In Figure S1.8, notice that the cloud of points on the scatterplot slopes upward from left to right. The slope of the dots is positive; mathematically speaking, a line drawn through the center of that cloud of points would have a positive slope. Because the slope is positive, we call the association between the two variables positive. High scores on one variable go with high scores on the other variable, and low scores on one variable go with low scores on the other variable. In a positive association, "high goes with high and low goes with low."

In contrast, in Figure S1.9 notice that the cloud of points on the scatterplot slopes downward from left to right. Because the slope of the dots is negative—mathematically speaking, a line drawn through the center of that cloud of points would have a negative slope—the association between the two variables is referred to as negative (or an inverse association). High scores on one variable go with low scores on the other variable. In a negative association, "high goes with low and low goes with high."

Finally, we might draw a scatterplot like the one in **Figure S1.10.** Here, the cloud of points does not slope clearly upward or downward. The

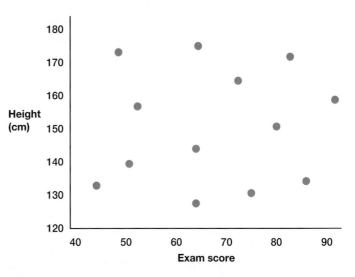

FIGURE S1.10 Hypothetical scatterplot of exam score and height.

slope of the dots is zero; mathematically speaking, a line drawn through the center of that cloud of points would be flat, or have a zero slope; there is no association, or zero association.

Strength of Association. Notice that the data points in Figure S1.8 hang together closer to a straight line; in contrast, the data points in Figure S1.9 are spread out wider. The spread of points in a scatterplot represents the relationship's strength (see Chapter 5). When the data points are closer to a straight line (either positive or negative in slope), we say the association is strong. When the data points are spread out more along a positively or negatively sloped line, we say the association is weak. Therefore, the data in Figure S1.8 depict a strong, positive association, while the data in Figure S1.9 depict a weak, negative association.

Correlation Coefficient *r*

Usually, researchers do not describe associations using scatterplots. Instead, they use the correlation coefficient *r*, a statistical computation that captures the direction and strength of a relationship (see Chapters 3, 5, and 8). The value of *r* can range from −1.0, which represents the strongest possible negative correlation, to 1.0, which represents the strongest possible positive correlation. For example, the relationship depicted in Figure S1.8 is $r = .64$; the relationship depicted in Figure S1.9 is $r = -.19$.

The sign of *r* indicates the direction of the relationship. If *r* is positive (such as $r = .64$), the relationship between the two variables is positive. If *r* is negative (such as $r = -.19$), the relationship between the two variables is negative. If *r* is zero, or very close to zero (such as $r = .02$), then the relationship between the two variables is essentially zero.

The magnitude of the absolute value of *r* indicates the strength of the relationship. If *r* is large (such as .64), the relationship between two variables is strong (the dots on the scatterplot would be closer together). If *r* is smaller (such as −.19), the relationship between two variables is weaker (the dots on the scatterplot would be more spread out). The strength of a correlation is independent of its sign, so an *r* of −.85 would represent a stronger correlation than an *r* of .35.

Computing *r*. The formula for computing the correlation coefficient *r* can be represented in many ways. Here is the simplest formula:

$$r = \frac{\sum z_x z_y}{N}$$

Let's break it down step by step. First, we have two variables per case (often that means two variables per person). **Table S1.3** shows how to carry out the steps in calculating *r* for a set of seven people. Notice that the first three columns of the table represent a data matrix for this data set, including one column for each variable (*X* and *Y*) and one row for each person. The three right-hand columns show the computations for *r*. In the formula, the variables are labeled *X* and *Y*. If we are computing the correlation between 2-year-old height and adult height,

TABLE S1.3 Computing the Correlation Coefficient r

(1) Person	(2) Score on X (2-year-old height, in cm)	(3) Score on Y (adult height, in cm)	(4) z_X (z score for 2-year-old height)	(5) z_Y (z score for adult height)	(6) $z_X z_Y$
Eliana	78	150	−1.00, or (78 − 83.3) / 5.3	−1.88, or (150 − 165.3) / 8.16	1.88, or (−1.00 × −1.88)
Ella	80	160	−0.62	−0.65	0.40
Eshaan	91	170	1.45	0.58	0.84
Ava	84	168	0.13	0.33	0.04
Annamaria	79	165	−0.81	−0.04	0.03
Oscar	90	175	1.26	1.19	1.50
Oliver	81	169	−0.43	0.45	−0.19
	$M = 83.3$	$M = 165.3$			$\Sigma z_X z_Y = 4.50$
	$SD = 5.3$	$SD = 8.16$			$\Sigma z_X z_Y / N = 0.64$
					$r = .64$

for example, 2-year-old height would be variable X (column 2), and adult height would be variable Y (column 3).

The second step is converting each person's scores on X and Y to z scores, z_X and z_Y, using the formula for computing z given earlier. If someone's 2-year-old height was above the mean, his or her z score (z_X) would be positive; if someone's 2-year-old height was below the mean, his or her z score (z_X) would be negative (columns 4 and 5 of Table S1.3). The third step is to multiply these two z scores, z_X and z_Y, for each person (column 6). Finally, we sum the products of the z scores and divide by the number of cases—in this example, seven people—to get r.

The Logic of the r Formula. It is worth reflecting on two aspects of the formula for r. First, notice that r can easily capture the association between adult height and 2-year-old height, even though the two variables have very different ranges of scores. The height for 2-year-olds ranges from 78 to 91 cm; adult height ranges from 150 to 175 cm. However, the formula for r converts each height value to its z score first. That way, it does not matter that the two heights fall within very different ranges.

Second, think about what it means that r multiplies the two z scores for each person. Take Eliana, for example. Her height is below average at age 2 and below average at adulthood, so both of her z scores are negative. When we multiply them together, we get a positive number. Now consider Oscar, whose height is above average at age 2 and above average at adulthood. Both of his z scores are positive, so when we multiply them, we also get a positive number. In Table S1.3, most of the products are positive, though some are negative. After summing all these products and dividing by N, we get an r value of .64—a positive r, meaning that "high goes with high and low goes with low." This makes sense; people with high 2-year-old height tend to have high adult height, and people with low 2-year-old height tend to have low adult height.

In contrast, if the relationship between two variables is negative, high goes with low and low goes with high. In this situation, when we compute the r, positive z scores for one variable will tend to be multiplied with negative z scores for the other variable, so the products will be mostly negative. When we sum these negative products and divide by N, the result will be a negative number, or a negative r, meaning that "high goes with low and low goes with high." Normally we use computers to calculate r values. However, knowing the mathematics behind the formula for r can help us understand what r values represent.

Describing Effect Size

Because the value of r indicates the strength of the relationship between two variables, many researchers use r as a measure of effect size, a computation that describes the magnitude of a study's result (see Chapters 8 and 14). There are several measures of effect size, and all of them are used for the same purpose: to describe the strength of the relationship between two variables. For example, when a study's outcome demonstrates a difference between two groups, the effect size describes how large or small that difference is.

Let's revisit the study that found that people ate more popcorn out of large containers than they did out of medium containers (Wansink & Kim, 2005; see Figure S1.7). If we were to ask about this study's effect size, we would ask how *much* more popcorn people ate from the large containers. Was it just a little more or a lot more? We are asking: Is the effect size large or small?

Describing Effect Size with Cohen's *d*

When a study involves group or condition means (such as the mean amount of popcorn eaten from a large container compared with the mean amount from a medium container), we can describe the effect size in terms of how far apart the two means are, in standard deviation units. This will also tell us how much overlap there is between the two sets of scores. This commonly used effect size measure is called d, also known as **Cohen's *d***.

For simplicity, let's focus on the results for the *fresh* popcorn condition in Wansink and Kim's study (see Figure S1.7):

- From the medium container, people ate a mean of 58.9 grams of popcorn, with a standard deviation of 16.7 grams.
- From the large container, people ate a mean of 85.6 grams of popcorn, with a standard deviation of 19.8 grams.

To determine how far apart these two means are in standard deviation units, we use the following formula for d:

$$d = \frac{M_1 - M_2}{SD_{(pooled)}}$$

TABLE S1.4 Cohen's Guidelines for Effect Size

d	Strength of relationship
0.20	Small, or weak
0.50	Medium, or moderate
0.80	Large, or strong

The numerator is the mean of one group minus the mean of the other group. The denominator is the *SD* of these two groups, "pooled." The pooled *SD* is an average of the two standard deviations for the two groups. If the two groups are the same size, we can take a simple mean of the two standard deviations, but when the two groups are different sizes, we need to compute a weighted mean of the two standard deviations; that is, we weight the *SD* of the larger group more.[1]

If we apply this formula to Wansink and Kim's data, the numerator is simply the mean difference between the two groups (the large container group and the medium container group), or 58.9 − 85.6. The denominator is the pooled *SD*, which is 18.3. So, for the fresh popcorn condition, we would compute the effect size for bucket size as follows:

$$d = \frac{58.9 - 85.6}{18.3} = \frac{-26.7}{18.3} = -1.46$$

In other words, the effect size of the container manipulation is $d = 1.46$. (We can omit the negative sign when it is clear which group is higher than the other.)

Effect Size Conventions for Cohen's d. What does a *d* of 1.46 mean? It means that the average of the large container group is 1.46 standard deviations higher than the average of the medium container group. But is that large or small? One way to tell is to consult Cohen's conventions for interpreting effect size (**Table S1.4**).

According to this table, the effect size in Wansink and Kim's study was very large, well above $d = 0.80$. Therefore, we can conclude that container size makes a large difference in the amount of popcorn people eat.

The effect size *d* could also be used to measure the difference between the red ink and green ink groups in the study of ink color and anagram performance (Elliot et al., 2007). As discussed in Chapter 10, the researchers manipulated the color in which an ID number was written on a test booklet, and then measured how many anagrams people could solve. The effect size was about $d = 0.63$; the mean of the red ink group and the mean of the green ink group were 0.63 of a

---

[1] The general formula for a pooled *SD* is as follows, where n_1 and n_2 are the number of observations in the two groups, and SD_1^2 and SD_2^2 are the variances of each group.

$$SD_{(pooled)} = \sqrt{\frac{(n_1 - 1)SD_1^2 + (n_2 - 1)SD_2^2}{n_1 + n_2 - 2}}$$

standard deviation apart. According to Cohen's conventions, this represents a medium to large effect of ink color on performance.

Effect Size *d* and Group Overlap. Another way of looking at group-difference effect sizes such as *d* is to know that *d* represents the amount of overlap between two groups. Parts A and B of **Figure S1.11** show how two groups might overlap at different effect sizes in our examples. The larger the effect size, the less overlap between the two experimental groups; the smaller the effect size, the more overlap. If the effect size is zero, there is full overlap between the two groups (Figure S1.11C).

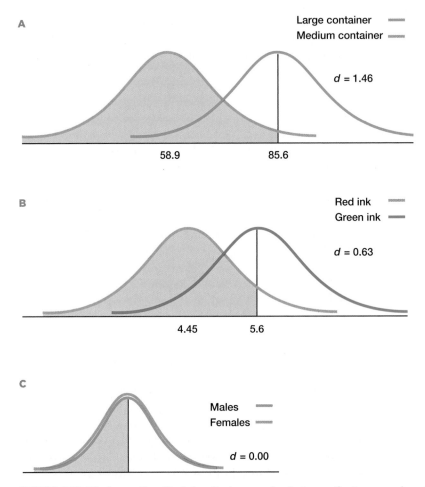

FIGURE S1.11 The larger the effect size, the less overlap between the two experimental groups. (A) At an effect size of 1.46, 92% of the medium container group members in the Wansink and Kim study (2005) ate less popcorn than the average member of the large container group. (B) At an effect size of 0.63, about 73% of the red ink group members in the Elliot et al. study (2007) solved fewer anagrams than the average member of the green ink group. (C) An effect size of *d* = 0.0 represents full overlap between the two groups, the greatest possible overlap, with 50% of Group 1 members (males) falling below the average member of Group 2 (females).

Which Effect Size Measure to Use?

Researchers generally use the effect size r to determine the strength of the relationship between two quantitative variables. The effect size d is more often used when one variable is categorical. These two measures of effect size are based on different scales: r can only range between 1 and -1, but d can be higher than 1 or lower than -1. Therefore, the size conventions for r are different from those for d (**Table S1.5**). In psychological science research, if a study finds an r of .50 or higher, that relationship (that effect size) is considered to be large, or strong. If the r is .10 or lower, that effect is considered small, or weak.

TABLE S1.5 Cohen's Guidelines for Two Measures of Effect Size: *d* and *r*

d	Strength of relationship	r
0.20	Small, or weak	.10
0.50	Medium, or moderate	.30
0.80	Large, or strong	.50

Other Effect Size Measures

As you read empirical journal articles, you may notice other indicators of effect size, such as Hedge's *g*. Hedge's *g* is very similar to *d*. Like *d*, it gives the distance between two means in standard deviation units, but it is computed with a different formula. The conventions for small, medium, and large for Hedge's *g* are the same as they are for Cohen's *d*.

Another effect size measure you might encounter is η^2, or eta squared. This effect size may be used when researchers describe differences among several groups (i.e., more than two means), or when they describe the effect sizes of interaction effects. Size conventions for η^2 have not been published in peer-reviewed sources; some Internet sources write that η^2 of .14 to .26 would be considered large, and .01 to .02 would be small.

Effect Size and Importance

Chapters 8 and 10 explored the relationship between effect size and importance. Generally speaking, the larger an effect size is, the more important a result seems to be. However, the converse is not always true: A small effect size is not always an unimportant one. Chapter 8 introduced the example of a very small effect size ($r = .03$) for the relationship between taking aspirin and risk of heart attack. This small effect size, however, translates into a very real decrease in deaths in the study's aspirin treatment group. Therefore, small effect sizes are generally less important than large ones—but sometimes even small effect sizes are important and valuable. It depends on the theoretical and real-world context of the research.

Effect Sizes and Practical Numbers

Effect sizes can certainly help indicate whether a study's result is strong, moderate, or weak. In some cases, however, we may not need to compute an effect size to assess the magnitude of some intervention. For example, the study on ink color found an effect size of $d = 0.63$ (Elliot et al., 2007). We could have noted simply that people whose ID numbers were written in red solved 1.2 fewer anagrams (out of a possible 15), on average, than people whose ID numbers were written in green. In addition, for Wansink and Kim's study (2005), instead of calculating the effect size, 1.46, we could have simply looked at the mean differences and found that people eating from large containers ate 26.7 more grams of popcorn (about 4 cups), on average.

In these two examples, it is relatively easy to evaluate the strength of the manipulation's impact. Red ink caused people to solve about 1.2 fewer anagrams. The large container caused people to eat 26.7 more grams of popcorn. (Depending on the fat content, that could contain as many as 140 calories.) These results may seem substantial and important enough—even without their effect size values.

Sometimes, however, we must rely on effect size values to put a result in perspective. Effect sizes are especially useful when we're not familiar with the scale on which a variable is measured. Suppose we conduct an experiment in which we praise the appearance of one group and say something neutral to members of another group. Then we ask each group to take a self-esteem test using a 5-point scoring scale. We compute the two group means and find a mean of 4.10 ($SD = 1.46$) for the people whose appearance was praised and a mean of 3.58 ($SD = 1.5$) for those who were not praised.

Because measures of self-esteem are abstract and subjective, it would be hard to put the difference between these two means into practical terms. Praising people's appearance seems to have made their scores on self-esteem increase about half of a point (0.52) on the 5-point scale, so we might say the two

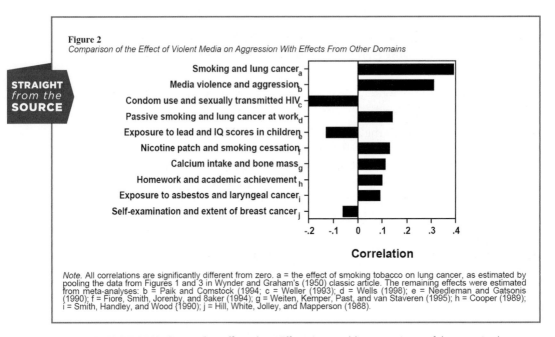

STRAIGHT *from the* **SOURCE**

Figure 2
Comparison of the Effect of Violent Media on Aggression With Effects From Other Domains

Note. All correlations are significantly different from zero. a = the effect of smoking tobacco on lung cancer, as estimated by pooling the data from Figures 1 and 3 in Wynder and Graham's (1950) classic article. The remaining effects were estimated from meta-analyses: b = Paik and Comstock (1994; c = Weller (1993); d = Wells (1998); e = Needleman and Gatsonis (1990); f = Fiore, Smith, Jorenby, and Baker (1994); g = Weiten, Kemper, Past, and van Staveren (1995); h = Cooper (1989); i = Smith, Handley, and Wood (1990); j = Hill, White, Jolley, and Mapperson (1988).

FIGURE S1.12 Comparing effect sizes. Effect sizes enable comparisons of the magnitudes of different studies, even ones that do not investigate the same interventions or risk factors. (Source: Bushman & Anderson, 2001.)

group means were about one-half of a "self-esteem unit" apart. Is half a point a large difference or a small one? Indeed, it is difficult to translate this self-report scale into a practical difference; it's not the same as counting correctly solved anagrams or grams of popcorn.

Now suppose we compute the effect size, d, for the two groups and come up with $d = 0.35$. We know this means that the groups are about 0.35 of a standard deviation unit apart, and we know this conventionally represents a medium effect size, so we have a somewhat better understanding of its magnitude. In isolation, of course, this might still not be very informative, so we might even compare the effect size to something else we know. For example, we might say the effect size of praising someone's appearance on self-esteem is $d = 0.35$, but the effect size of praising someone's personal qualities on self-esteem is even larger, say $d = 0.45$.

In addition, the effect size from one study can be compared to the effect size from another study—even a study using different variables. In one article, Brad Bushman and Craig Anderson (2001) were summarizing the evidence that violent media can cause aggressive behavior. They compared the average magnitude of the effect size for studies of the relationship between these two variables, which is about $r = .31$ (obtained from a meta-analysis), to studies of the impact of smoking on lung cancer, the effect of exposure to lead on IQ, and other effects whose scientific acceptance is more widely known among the general public (**Figure S1.12**). With the studies lined up in such a way, the authors were able to make a more convincing argument that violent media constitute a public health risk. (Meta-analysis is covered in Chapter 14.)

ANSWERS TO TEST YOURSELF

TEST YOURSELF 1 The average force for men was 6.69. The average force for women was 4.73. Men had a slightly higher SD on this variable (2.05) than women (1.88).

TEST YOURSELF 2 On average, people ate 50.8 grams from a large container. The mean was 58.9 grams, with a standard deviation of 16.7 grams.

TEST YOURSELF 3 Emma's z score on the midterm exam was 0.63. Her score is less than one standard deviation above the mean.

TEST YOURSELF 4 Emma's z score on the final was 1.0, so she did better on the final than she did on the midterm—relative to the rest of the class, at least.

Key Terms

descriptive statistics, p. 441
data matrix, p. 442
frequency distribution, p. 442
frequency histogram, p. 442
stemplot, p. 442
central tendency, p. 444
mode, p. 444
bimodal, p. 444

multimodal, p. 444
median, p. 445
mean, p. 445
variance, p. 447
standard deviation, p. 447
z score, p. 450
Cohen's d, p. 456

Statistics Review
Inferential Statistics

The preceding discussion reviewed descriptive statistics, a set of tools for organizing and summarizing certain characteristics of a sample. This supplementary chapter covers **inferential statistics**, a set of techniques that uses the laws of chance and probability to help researchers make decisions about what their data mean and what inferences they can make from that information.

The Logic of Statistical Inference

Inferential statistical techniques are not so much a process of mathematics (although some basic algebra is involved) as a process of *logic*—a way of thinking through a logical set of steps. Inferential statistical thinking involves theories about how chance operates: What kinds of results can happen just by chance? How often do such results occur just by chance? For example, suppose we conduct a study in which we test a new medication for schizophrenia. This randomized, controlled study finds that the group taking the drug experienced reduced symptoms. When we use inferential statistics, we follow a set of steps to decide whether the result from our study is statistically significant; that is, we estimate the probability that we would get a similar result just by chance, even if the drug does not work.

There are many different statistical tests, and four are covered here: the *t* test, the *F* test, and tests of the significance of a correlation and beta. All of them share the same underlying logical steps. Therefore, understanding the process of inferential statistics is the basis for understanding most other statistical tests, because they follow the same logic.

When researchers decide to investigate a phenomenon (such as whether the color red affects achievement, or whether religious belief, or religiosity, is related to depression), they do not test every possible individual to whom the phenomenon might apply. Instead, they conduct the study on a sample of people. Based on the results in that sample, they make an inference about what would happen if they tested the whole population.

Therefore, inferential statistics is (most commonly) the logical process of using data from a sample, whose characteristics are known, to make inferences about some population, whose characteristics are often unknown. Although we may never be able to study every person in a population, we can use the tools of inferential statistics to make decisions about what the population's values probably are and about what our data really mean.

An Example

Here's a fictional scenario to illustrate the process of inferential statistics. Imagine we encounter a woman named Sarah, who claims that in any crowd, she can pick out smart people—that is, she can identify people with high IQs. Her claim might seem a bit preposterous, so at first we're skeptical and assume she does not have this power. However, we're open to testing Sarah's claim. Across a large sample of people, IQ, as it is usually measured, has a mean of 100, with a standard deviation of 15, as shown in **Figure S2.1**. In addition, IQ is *normally distributed*, meaning that if we plot the IQ scores of a very large random sample on a frequency histogram, about 68% of people fall between one standard deviation above and one standard deviation below the mean. About 14% of people fall between one and two standard deviations above the mean, and 14% of people fall between one and two standard deviations below the mean. Furthermore, 2% fall higher or lower than two standard deviations. Armed with this basic knowledge, let's put Sarah to the test.

We take her to a local professional basketball stadium. It is full of people from all walks of life, both smart and dull, and their IQs span the usual range—with an average of 100 and an *SD* of 15. We ask Sarah to pick out a smart person. She looks around and chooses a woman in the 18th row. After obtaining the woman's permission, we take her to a private room and administer an IQ test with the help of a school psychologist. The woman's IQ is 115.

Are we convinced by this datum that Sarah has a special ability to detect smart people? Intuitively, we might think: 115 is a higher-than-average IQ, but it is not *that* much higher than average. So we might not be convinced that Sarah has special talents.

If we were to unpack this (correct) intuition, we would reason like this: Even if Sarah does not have special abilities, she could have selected a person with an

FIGURE S2.1 A normal distribution of IQ scores, where *M* = 100 and *SD* = 15.

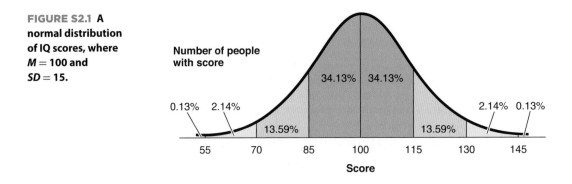

IQ of 115 or higher just by chance about 16% of the time. According to the normal distribution in Figure S2.1, 16% of the people in the stadium should have an IQ score of 115 or higher. Sarah could have selected a person at random with an IQ that high or higher 16% of the time, even if she does not have a special ability to pick out smart people. And 16% seems too high to rule out the possibility that she just happened to choose a smarter-than-average person by chance.

Now suppose the scenario has produced a different result. Suppose we take Sarah to the stadium and ask her to identify a smart person. This time, however, she identifies a person who, when tested, has an IQ of 130. Are we convinced now?

If we're thinking probabilistically, then we should find this second outcome much more convincing, because now there is a much smaller probability that Sarah could have guessed correctly just by chance. As Figure S2.1 shows, only 2% of the people in the stadium are likely to have an IQ of 130 or higher. We can interpret this 2% as follows: If Sarah does not have special powers, she would have to be extremely lucky to have picked a person with an IQ that high or higher—only 2% of the time would she be so lucky. Of course, it could happen. But because the chance of her getting lucky is very low, we feel confident that she does, in fact, have a special ability to detect smart people. In other words, the assumption you started with—the skeptical assumption that Sarah cannot identify smart people—is probably wrong. (This example is adapted from Aron, 2009.)

Incidentally, Sarah's ability to identify intelligent people is actually not uncommon. An entire line of research on this phenomenon finds that most people are fairly accurate at judging certain traits, such as extroversion, agreeableness, and intelligence, just by looking at other people for a few seconds. This phenomenon is known as *zero-acquaintance accuracy* (Borkenau & Liebler, 1993; Kenny & West, 2008).

The Steps of Inferential Statistics

The steps described in the example above illustrate those taken by researchers when they use inferential statistics. The steps are collectively referred to as **statistical hypothesis testing**. Although there are a few forms of statistical hypothesis testing, **null hypothesis testing** is the most common one used today. To apply the steps of null hypothesis testing to the scenario in which Sarah chose a person with an IQ of 130, we would proceed as follows.

Step 1: Assume There Is No Effect (the Null Hypothesis)

When we tested Sarah's abilities, we started with the skeptical assumption that she was not able to identify smart people. In statistical hypothesis testing, this kind of starting assumption is known as a **null hypothesis**. *Null* means "nothing," and colloquially, a null hypothesis means "assume that nothing is going on." Depending on the research question, the null hypothesis can mean that a person does not have special abilities, that an independent variable does not have an effect on the dependent variable, or that two variables are not correlated with each other.

Step 2: Collect Data

To test Sarah's ability to identify smart people, we asked her to demonstrate it by locating a smart person in the crowd. We then gave the person she chose an IQ test to see whether she was correct. That was the datum: She correctly identified a person with an IQ of 130.

Step 3: Calculate the Probability of Getting Such Data, or Even More Extreme Data, If the Null Hypothesis Is True

In this step, we calculated a probability: We used our knowledge of the normal distribution to compute the probability that Sarah could have chosen a person with an IQ of 130 or greater, just by chance, if the null hypothesis is true. What is the probability that Sarah could have chosen a person this smart or smarter by chance if she is not in fact able to identify smart people?

In making the calculations, we used what we know about IQ—that it is normally distributed with a mean of 100 and a standard deviation of 15—to estimate what percentage of people in the stadium would have each range of IQ scores. We also used our understanding of chance. Combined, these two pieces of knowledge directed us to predict that if Sarah had chosen a person at random, she would have chosen a person with an IQ of 130 or higher about 2% of the time.

Step 4: Decide Whether to Reject or Retain the Null Hypothesis

In the fourth step, we made a decision based on the probability we obtained in Step 3. Since the probability of choosing a person with an IQ of 130 or higher just by chance is so small, we rejected our original assumption. That is, we rejected the null hypothesis that Sarah is not able to identify smart people.

The Decision to Reject the Null Hypothesis. The probability we obtained in Step 3 was so small that we rejected the null hypothesis assumption. In other words, we concluded that our data on Sarah's abilities were statistically significant. When we reject the null hypothesis, we are essentially saying that:

Data like these could have come about by chance,

but

data like these happen very rarely by chance;

therefore

we are pretty sure the data were not the result of chance.

The Decision to Retain the Null Hypothesis. To clarify this decision, consider a situation in which we would retain the null hypothesis: the first scenario, in which Sarah identified a person with a score of 115. The probability that Sarah would identify a person who is at least that smart just by chance even if she is not special is 16%, or .16. That probability seemed high enough that we would not reject our initial assumption that she is not able to detect smart people (the null hypothesis).

TABLE S2.1 The Decision to Reject or Retain the Null Hypothesis

This term	Means the same as:	In other words:	You may see, in published work:	In a research context, may mean:
Rejecting the null hypothesis	The result is statistically significant.	The probability of getting a result this extreme, or more extreme, by chance, if the null hypothesis is true, is less than 5%.	$p < .05$ * (asterisk)	The difference is significantly larger than zero. The association is significantly stronger than zero.
Retaining the null hypothesis	The result is not statistically significant.	The probability of getting a result like this by chance, if the null hypothesis is true, is greater than or equal to 5%.	$p \geq .05$ n.s.	We cannot conclude that the difference is larger than zero. We cannot conclude that the relationship is stronger than zero.

When we retain the null hypothesis, we are saying that:

Data like these could have happened just by chance;

in fact

data like these are likely to happen by chance 16% of the time;

therefore

we conclude that we are not confident enough, based on these data,
to reject the null hypothesis.

Finally, at what probability level should we decide to reject the null hypothesis? Why did we reject the null hypothesis at $p = .02$ but not at $p = .16$? In psychological science, the level researchers typically use is 5% or less, or $p < .05$ (**Table S2.1**). This decision point is called the **alpha level**—the point at which researchers will decide whether the p is too high (and therefore will retain the null hypothesis) or very low (and therefore will reject the null hypothesis).

Samples, Populations, and Inference

The previous section outlined the four basic steps for drawing a conclusion based on statistical inference. The process involves using data from a sample (one of Sarah's guesses) to make an inference about the nature of a population (the population of all possible guesses Sarah could have made). In other words, we did not ask Sarah to demonstrate that she could classify every person in the

For details on sampling techniques, see Chapter 7, pp. 182–193.

basketball stadium as smart or not smart; we did not collect data on the entire *population* of possible guesses in the stadium. Instead, we measured a *sample* of the population of guesses.

Almost all research studies a sample of some population. For example, when researchers conduct a political poll, they do not attempt to telephone every member of the voting population; instead, they select a sample of the voting population and make inferences about the voting population based on what the sample tells them. In the average experiment, researchers draw samples from populations such as monkeys, college students, or children in third grade. Often, these samples are not selected randomly, but they are still drawn from a population.

Understanding Inference: Type I and Type II Errors

Recall that the process of statistical hypothesis testing requires us, in Step 4, to make a decision. We decide whether to reject or retain the null hypothesis. In the example of Sarah, if we reject the null hypothesis, we would conclude, based on this sample of data, that Sarah really is able to identify smart people. If we retain the null hypothesis, we would decide that we have insufficient evidence, based on this sample of data, to conclude that Sarah is able to identify smart people.

Because we are studying only a sample of Sarah's behavior, not the full population of her behavior, the decision we make about her abilities could be right, or it could be wrong. Therefore, when we follow the process of inferential statistics, there are two possible ways to be right and two possible ways to be wrong. These four possibilities come from the two decisions we might make, based on the sample, and the two possible states of affairs in the population.

Two Possible Correct Conclusions. There are two ways to make a correct decision. (1) We could conclude from the sample of behavior that Sarah has a special ability to identify smart people (reject the null hypothesis), and in truth, Sarah really does—so our conclusion is correct. (2) We could decide that we cannot confidently conclude that Sarah can identify smart people (retain the null hypothesis), and in truth, she really cannot. Again, our conclusion would be correct.

Two Possible Errors. There are also two ways to make an incorrect decision. (1) We could conclude that Sarah probably has special abilities, when she really does not. This kind of mistake is known as a **Type I error**, a "false positive." (2) We could conclude that Sarah probably does not have special abilities, when she really does. This kind of mistake is known as a **Type II error**, or a "miss." (These two types of errors were introduced in Chapter 3.)

Table S2.2 shows the four possibilities.

Which Error Is Worse? In the research context, the two types of errors can lead to different types of problems. On the one hand, if we make a Type I error, we may conclude that we have found something interesting in our study, which could encourage other researchers or practitioners to follow a false lead. For example, we might conclude from a study that a particular medication is effective for schizophrenia symptoms when it is not (a Type I error). This Type I error might be a

TABLE S2.2 Two Possible Correct Decisions and Two Possible Errors from the Process of Statistical Inference

Decision based on the sample:	True nature of the population	
	There is really no effect in the population	There is really an effect in the population
Reject the null hypothesis (conclude there is an effect).	Type I error	Correct conclusion
Retain the null hypothesis (conclude there is not enough evidence of an effect).	Correct conclusion	Type II error

Decision based on the sample:	True nature of Sarah's abilities	
	Sarah really cannot identify smart people	Sarah really can identify smart people
Reject the null hypothesis (conclude Sarah can identify smart people).	Type I error: We conclude Sarah can identify smart people, but she really cannot.	Correct conclusion: We conclude Sarah can identify smart people, and she really can.
Retain the null hypothesis (conclude there is not enough evidence that Sarah can identify smart people).	Correct conclusion: We have not shown that Sarah can identify smart people, and she really does not have this ability.	Type II error: Sarah really can identify smart people, but we have failed to show it.

Decision based on the sample:	True nature of the medication	
	Drug does not improve schizophrenia symptoms	Drug does improve schizophrenia symptoms
Reject the null hypothesis (conclude the drug does work).	Type I error: We conclude the drug works, but it really does not.	Correct conclusion: We conclude the drug works, and it really does.
Retain the null hypothesis (conclude there is not sufficient evidence that the drug works).	Correct conclusion: We have not shown the drug works, and it really does not work.	Type II error: The drug really does work, but we have failed to show it.

Note: The top section of this table shows the general case; the middle and bottom sections repeat the information in terms of two examples.

costly mistake in terms of false hopes, unnecessary side effects, or fruitless follow-up research.

On the other hand, we might conclude that a drug is not effective when it really is (a Type II error). This might be a costly mistake, too. Suppose the new schizophrenia drug is, in fact, effective, but an early study incorrectly finds that it is not effective. These results could delay the availability of the medication for people who could benefit from it—or even prevent it from ever becoming available.

Deciding which error is more costly depends on the context. We might decide it's important to be conservative, in which case avoiding Type I errors might be our priority. Especially if the schizophrenia drug is expensive or has troublesome side effects, we may not want to conclude that it works when it actually does not (i.e., we don't want to make a Type I error). We may not want to spend the money or make people endure side effects by prescribing a drug that is ineffective. To be conservative in this way, we would design our study to minimize the probability of making a Type I error.

In other situations, we might decide we don't want to overlook an effect that is really there, so our priority would be to avoid Type II errors (i.e., being sure to reject the null hypothesis if in fact it is false). We might decide that if the drug for schizophrenia really does work, we want to be able to detect that. Perhaps the disease being treated is particularly serious and there are no other cures. Or maybe we are running the first study on a research question, and we want to find the effect if it is really there; if there is an effect, we don't want to miss it, because we are thinking about investing time in a promising research direction. In such cases, we want to reduce the chances of missing something important, so we design our study to reduce the probability of making a Type II error.

Finally, no matter how we design our study, there is always the possibility that no matter what we conclude, we might make an error, because the true relationship, true difference, or true state of affairs in the population is often unknowable. The schizophrenia medication either has an effect or does not—but because we cannot evaluate the entire population of people who might use this drug, we will never know. However, we can choose the probability that we will make a Type I error, and we can estimate the probability of making a Type II error. We can design studies in order to minimize these probabilities.

Preventing Type I Errors

Only one aspect of a study affects the likelihood of making a Type I error: the level of probability (or p) at which we decide whether or not to reject the null hypothesis. As mentioned earlier, that decision point is called the alpha level. Researchers set the alpha level for a study in advance. They decide ahead of time that if the probability of their result happening just by chance (assuming the null hypothesis is true) is *less* than alpha, they will reject the null hypothesis. If the probability of their result happening just by chance (assuming the null hypothesis is true) is *greater* than alpha, they will retain the null hypothesis. In psychological science research, the convention is to set the alpha level at 5%, or alpha $= .05$.

To understand alpha level better, recall how we evaluated Sarah's abilities. In doing so, we used the conventional alpha level of alpha $= .05$. When Sarah identified a person with a 115 IQ, we knew the probability of her doing so by chance was $p = .16$ even if she didn't have any special ability to identify smart people. Because that probability was "high"—higher than .05—we thought it was possible that Sarah made a lucky guess this time. In other words, because the probability of the result turned out to be higher than .05, we retained the null hypothesis. In contrast, when Sarah identified someone with an IQ of 130, we knew the probability of her doing so by chance, even if she had no particular skill, was .02. Because that probability was "low"—less than .05—we assumed she probably didn't identify that person by chance, and therefore we rejected the null hypothesis.

Alpha Is the Type I Error Rate. The alpha we set in advance is also the probability of making a Type I error if the null hypothesis is true. Returning to our example, when we computed that the probability of Sarah choosing someone with a 130 IQ by chance was .02 (if the null hypothesis is really true), we rejected the null hypothesis. However, it's still possible that Sarah did not have special abilities and that she simply got lucky this time. In this case, we would have drawn the wrong conclusion.

When we set alpha in advance at alpha = .05, we are admitting that 5% of the time, when the null hypothesis is true, we will end up rejecting the null hypothesis anyway. Because we know how chance works, we know that if we asked someone who has no special abilities to select 100 people in the stadium at random, 5% of them will have an IQ of 125 or higher (the IQ score associated with the top 5% of people). However, we are admitting that we are comfortable with the possibility that we will make this particular mistake—a Type I error—5% of the time when the null hypothesis is true.

Alpha Conventions. Even though the alpha level is conventionally set at .05, researchers can set it at whatever they want it to be, depending on the priorities of their research. If they prioritize being conservative, they might set alpha lower than 5%—perhaps at 1%, or .01. By setting alpha lower, they are trying to minimize the chances of making a Type I error—of accidentally concluding there is a true effect or relationship when there actually is none.

In contrast, there may be situations in which researchers choose to set alpha higher—say, .10. In this case, they would be comfortable making false conclusions 10% of the time if, in truth, there is no effect. By setting alpha higher, they are also increasing the probability of making a Type I error. Researchers may wish to set alpha higher as one of the strategies to avoid missing an effect of a drug or intervention—that is, to avoid a Type II error.

Preventing Type II Errors (Power, Effect Size, and Alpha)

Whereas preventing a Type I error involves only one factor (alpha level), preventing a Type II error depends on a set of factors, collectively known as power. Formally defined, **power** is the likelihood of not making a Type II error when the null hypothesis is false. In positive terms, it is the probability that a researcher will be able to reject the null hypothesis if it should be rejected (i.e., if there is really some effect in the population). If we are testing a schizophrenia drug that, in truth, does reduce the symptoms of schizophrenia, then power refers to how likely a study is to detect that effect by finding a significant result (see Chapters 10 and 11).

The following analogy will further clarify Type II errors. Suppose the electricity goes out in your house, and all the rooms are dark. You think you left a book somewhere in the bedroom, so you go upstairs with a flashlight and shine the light around the room. Assuming the book is really there, can you find it?

If, in truth, the book is in the room, two things could happen. First, you might find it with your flashlight. Finding the book is analogous to making a correct research decision: You have rejected the null hypothesis (so in effect, you have decided, "The book is in this room"), and indeed, it is there. Second, you might *not* find the book with your flashlight. Failing to find the book is analogous to making a Type II error: You have retained the null hypothesis (you retained the assumption that the book is not in the room, implying "The book is not here"). Power is about the first case: being able to detect the book when it is really there.

In this example, one factor that will help you detect the missing book is to have a good, strong flashlight. If the flashlight puts out a lot of light, you will be able to find the book in the room much more easily. But if the flashlight's batteries are running low and its beam is weak, you might not see the book, and you might erroneously conclude it's not in the room when in fact it is there. That would be a Type II error.

Another factor that influences the Type II error rate is the size of what you are looking for. If you are looking for something large (your pet elephant, perhaps), you will probably find it, even if the flashlight is very weak. However, if you are looking for something very small (a lost earring), you may not detect it, even with a bright flashlight.

Similarly, when researchers predict the chance of making a Type II error, they consider several factors simultaneously. The alpha level, the sample size, the effect size, the degree of variability in the sample, and the choice of statistical test all have an impact on the power of a study, and thus they all influence the Type II error rate.

Alpha Level. The alpha level is the first factor that influences power. Usually set at .05, alpha is the point at which researchers decide whether or not to reject the null hypothesis. When researchers set alpha lower in a study (say, at .01), it will be more difficult for them to reject the null hypothesis. But if it is harder to reject the null hypothesis, it is also more likely that they will *retain* the null hypothesis even if it deserves to be rejected. Therefore, when researchers set the alpha level low (usually to avoid Type I errors), they increase the chances of making a Type II error. In this one sense, Type I and Type II errors compete: As the chance of Type I errors goes down, the chance of Type II errors goes up.

Because of this competition between Type I and Type II errors, alpha levels are conventionally set at .05. According to most researchers, this level is low enough to keep Type I error rates in control but high enough that they can still find a significant result (keeping Type II error rates down).

Sample Size. A second factor that influences power is the sample size used in a study. All else being equal, a study that has a larger sample will have more power to reject the null hypothesis if there really is an effect in the population. A large sample is analogous to carrying a big, bright flashlight, and a small sample is analogous to carrying a candle, or a weak flashlight. The bright, powerful flashlight will enable you to find what you are looking for more easily. If you carry a candle, you might mistakenly conclude that your missing object is not in the dark room when it really is (a Type II error). Similarly, if a drug really reduces the symptoms of schizophrenia in the population, we are more likely to detect that effect in a study with a larger sample than with a smaller sample. (How sample size works mathematically is discussed later.)

Effect Size. A third factor that influences power is the size of the effect in the population. All else being equal, when there is a large effect size in the population, there is a greater chance of conducting a study that rejects the null hypothesis. As an analogy, no matter what kind of light you use, you are much more likely to find an elephant than an earring. Elephants are just easier to see. Similarly, if, in the population, a drug has a large effect on schizophrenia symptoms, we would be likely to detect that effect easily, even if we used a small sample and a low alpha level. But if the drug has a small effect on schizophrenia symptoms in the population, we are less likely to find it easily, and we might miss it in our sample. When there is a small effect size in the population, Type II errors are more likely to occur.

Sample Size and Effect Size. It is a common misconception that a study should have the largest sample size possible. Suppose we come across a study that found a statistically significant result but had a very small sample size—only 10 participants. Should the researchers conducting this study have used twice as many participants? Or maybe 50 more?

In fact, sample size and effect size interact. Large samples are necessary *only* when researchers are trying to detect a small effect size. In contrast, if they are trying to detect a large effect size, a small sample may be all that is necessary. Think again about the lost object analogy. If, on the one hand, you are looking for a lost elephant, you can find it easily, even if you only have a small candle in the dark room. If the elephant is there (like a large effect size), your candle (like a small sample) is all you need to detect him. (Of course, you would also find him with a powerful flashlight, but all you need is the candle.) On the other hand, if you are looking for a lost earring, you may not be able to find it with the small candle, which is not powerful enough to illuminate the darkest corners. You need a big flashlight (like a large sample) to be sure to find the earring (like a small effect size) that is there.

Therefore, the smaller the effect size in the population, the larger the sample needed to reject the null hypothesis (and therefore to avoid a Type II error). But as the effect size in the population gets larger, researchers can get away with a smaller sample and still detect it.

Degree of Unsystematic Variability. A fourth factor that influences power is the amount of unsystematic variability in a sample's data. All else being equal, when a study's design introduces more unsystematic variability into the results, researchers have less power to detect effects that are really there. Unsystematic variability in the data prevents researchers from seeing a clear effect resulting from their experimental manipulation.

To review systematic and unsystematic variability, and how a study's design can reduce unsystematic variability, see Chapter 11, pp. 329–335.

Three sources of unsystematic variability are measurement error, individual differences, and situation noise. Measurement error occurs when the variables are measured with a less precise instrument or with less careful coding. Individual differences among study participants can also obscure the difference between two groups and thus weaken power. Using a repeated-measures design in an experiment reduces the impact of individual differences and strengthens the study's power. Situation noise can weaken power by adding extraneous sources of variability into the results. Researchers can conduct studies in controlled conditions to avoid such situation noise.

Statistical Choices. A fifth factor that influences power involves the statistical choices the researcher makes. A researcher selects a statistical test (e.g., a sign test, a chi-square test, a *t* test, an *F* test, analysis of covariance, or multiple regression) to compute the results from a sample of data. Some of these tests make it more difficult to find significant results and thus increase the chance of Type II errors. Researchers must carefully decide which statistical test is appropriate. (Some of the commonly used statistical tests are explained below.)

Another statistical choice that affects power is the decision to use a "one-tailed" or a "two-tailed" test. The choice is related to the researcher's hypothesis. For example, if we are only interested in finding out whether the schizophrenia drug significantly *reduces* symptoms, we use a one-tailed test. If we are interested in finding out whether the schizophrenia drug significantly reduces symptoms *or* significantly makes them worse, we use a two-tailed test. When we have a good idea about the direction in which the effect will occur, a one-tailed test is more powerful than a two-tailed test.

In summary, power is the probability of not making a Type II error. It is the probability that a researcher will be able to reject the null hypothesis if it deserves to be rejected. Researchers have more power to detect an effect in a population if:

1. They select a larger (less stringent) alpha level.
2. The effect size in the population is large rather than small.
3. The sample size is large rather than small.
4. The data have lower levels of unsystematic variability.
5. They use the most appropriate statistical test.

Common Inferential Statistical Tests

There are dozens of statistical tests used in psychological science. Researchers use different tests depending on whether they are testing frequency, association, or causal claims. They also use different tests depending on whether the variables are categorical (such as gender or political party affiliation), numeric (such as test grade or height), or a combination of the two.

This section describes four of the inferential tests commonly used in psychology research, all of which follow the same set of four logical steps outlined earlier. (A full-length statistics book will provide more detail on these and other statistical tests.)

Is That Difference Significant? The *t* Test

The **t test** (introduced in Chapter 8) allows researchers to test whether the difference between two group means in an independent-groups design is statistically significant. Let's recall the study from Chapter 14, in which 52 students were told they would be evaluating a person based on just a single information sheet about their partner (Jones, Pelham, Carvallo, & Mirenberg, 2004). The partner's ID number, printed on the information sheet, either matched the student's own birthday (the birthday match group), or it did not (the control group). The researchers were investigating whether participants would like the partner more if the person was similar to them in this superficial way. After the students read the person's description (and saw their ID number), the researchers had the students rate how much they liked the person on a scale of 1 to 9.

The researchers found the following results:

- Mean liking rating in the birthday match group: 8.10
- Mean liking rating in the control group: 7.15

To conduct inferential statistics for this study, we ask whether these two means, 8.10 and 7.15, are significantly different from each other. In other words, what is the probability that this difference, or an even larger one, could have been obtained by chance alone, even if there's no difference?

Step 1: Stating the Null Hypothesis

We begin by stating the null hypothesis for the Jones study. Here, the null hypothesis would be that there is no difference between the mean of the birthday match group and the mean of the control group.

Step 2: Computing the *t* Test for Independent Groups

The next step is to organize the data and decide which statistical test to use. The appropriate inferential test in this case is the *t* test for independent groups. The *t* test helps us estimate whether the difference in scores between two samples is significantly greater than zero.

As discussed in the section on effect size in Statistics Review: Descriptive Statistics, two features of the data influence the distance between two means. One is the difference *between* the two means themselves, and the other is how much variability there is *within* each group. The *t* test is a ratio of these two values. The numerator of the *t* test is the simple difference between the means of the two groups: Mean 1 minus Mean 2. The denominator of the *t* test contains information about the variance within each of the two means, as well as the number of cases (*n*) that make up each of the means. Here is the formula:

$$t = \frac{M_1 - M_2}{\sqrt{\left(\dfrac{SD^2_{pooled}}{n_1} + \dfrac{SD^2_{pooled}}{n_2}\right)}}$$

As you can see, t will be larger if the difference between M_1 and M_2 is larger. The value of t will also be larger if the SD^2 (variance) for each mean is smaller. (The SD^2_{pooled} in the formula means that we take a weighted average of the two samples' SD^2 estimates.) The less the two groups overlap—either because their means are farther apart or because there is less variability within each group—the larger the value of t will be. Sample size (n) also influences t. All else being equal, if n is larger, then the denominator of the t formula becomes smaller, making t larger.

The Jones team obtained a t value from their study of 2.57. Once we know this t value, we must decide whether it is statistically significant.

Step 3: Calculating the Probability of the Result, or One Even More Extreme, If the Null Hypothesis Is True

Next we calculate the probability of getting this result, or a result even more extreme, if the null hypothesis is true. To do so, we compare the t value from our sample of data to the types of t values we are likely to get if the null hypothesis is true.

By far the most common way to estimate this probability is to use a **sampling distribution** of t. This method estimates the probability of obtaining the t we got, just by chance, from a null hypothesis population.

Sampling Distribution of *t*. To start, it helps to know that we never actually create a sampling distribution; however, we can estimate what its properties will be. To do so, we theorize about what values of t we would get if the null hypothesis is true in the population. If we were to run the study many, many times, drawing different random samples from this same null hypothesis population, what values of t would we get? Most of the time, we should find only a small difference in the means, so t would be close to zero most of the time (i.e., the numerator of the t test would be close to zero, making t close to zero). Therefore, the average of the t values should be around 0.00. Half the time, just by chance, t might be a little higher than 0.00. And just by chance, half the time, t might be a little lower than 0.00. Sometimes, we might even get a t that is *much* higher or lower than 0.00. Thus, when the null hypothesis is true, we will still get a variety of values of t, but they will average around zero.

Sampling distributions of t are always centered at zero, because they are always created based on the assumption that the null hypothesis is true. But the width of the sampling distribution of t will depend on the sample size (i.e., the sample size of the study that we hypothetically run many times). As shown in **Figure S2.2**, when the sample size in our study is small, the sampling distribution will be wider and will result in more values at the extremes. This occurs in part because a small sample is more likely, just by chance, to obtain t values that are far from the mean because of sampling error. In contrast, in a large sample, the sampling distribution will be thinner.

Sampling distributions are created based on sample size, but they do not use sample sizes directly; instead, they use a slightly smaller number called *degrees of freedom*. A full-length statistics book will tell you more about this value. In the present example, the degrees of freedom are computed from the number of people in the first group, minus 1, plus the number of people in the second group, minus 1: $(26 - 1) + (26 - 1) = 50$. The sampling distribution of t for the example from Jones et al. (2004) would look like **Figure S2.3**.

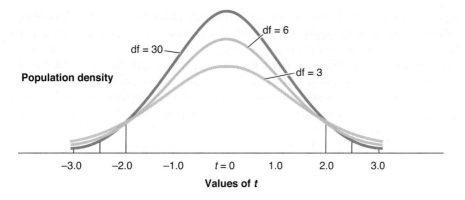

FIGURE S2.2 **Sampling distributions of *t* for small samples (degrees of freedom = 3 and 6) and large samples (degrees of freedom = 30 or larger).** As the sample size increases, the *t* distribution gets thinner and approximates a normal distribution.

This sampling distribution of *t* tells us what values of *t* we would be likely to get if the null hypothesis is true. In addition, this figure tells us that occasionally it is possible (but very rare) to get *t* values of 1.8, 2.0, or even larger, just by chance.

Using the Sampling Distribution to Evaluate Significance, or *p*. Why did we go to the trouble of estimating that sampling distribution anyway? Doing so helps us complete Step 3 of the null hypothesis testing process: Now that we have derived the sampling distribution, we can use it to evaluate the probability of getting the *t* obtained in the Jones study (2.57), or an even more extreme value of *t*, if the null hypothesis is true in the population.

One way to determine this probability is to find where our obtained *t* falls on the x-axis of the sampling distribution. Then we use calculus to determine the

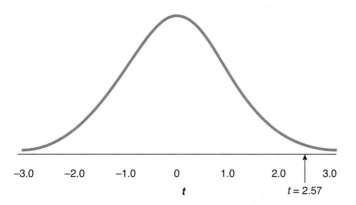

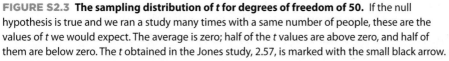

FIGURE S2.3 **The sampling distribution of *t* for degrees of freedom of 50.** If the null hypothesis is true and we ran a study many times with a same number of people, these are the values of *t* we would expect. The average is zero; half of the *t* values are above zero, and half of them are below zero. The *t* obtained in the Jones study, 2.57, is marked with the small black arrow.

area under the curve from that point outward, which gives us the probability of obtaining a t as large as, or larger than, 2.57 when the null hypothesis is true. Researchers typically compute this probability using a computer program, such as SPSS, STATA, or SYSTAT. The p that the computer reports is the exact probability of getting a t that extreme or more extreme if the null hypothesis is true. In the Jones et al. case, the computer reported that the probability of obtaining a t value of 2.57, with 50 degrees of freedom, is exactly .013.

Another way to determine the probability of a particular t value is to use the table in Appendix B, Critical Values of t. This table shows the probability of obtaining different values of t for different degrees of freedom. Such a table does not give the exact area under the curve, as the computer can do. However, using that table, we can look up the **critical value** of t—the t value that is associated with our alpha level. For example, we can look up the critical t value associated with a .05 alpha level and 50 degrees of freedom: 2.009. (As an analogy, this is like establishing that the IQ score associated with the .05 alpha level was 125.) The critical value of t means that in a sampling distribution of t based on 50 degrees of freedom, we would get a t of 2.009 or higher 5% of the time, just by chance. In Step 4, we will compare the critical value of t to the t we actually obtained, 2.57.

Using Randomization Tests to Evaluate Significance. To evaluate the probability of getting our results by chance if the null hypothesis is true, we could use a sampling distribution, as explained earlier, in which we evaluate the chances of randomly sampling the t we got from a null hypothesis population, using either a computer or a critical values table. However, a different way to estimate the power of chance is by conducting a randomization test (Edgington & Onghena, 2007).

In a randomization test, researchers use a computer to determine all of the possible ways the study could have come out (all possible permutations) if only chance were operating. For the Jones study, the computer would take the 52 scores actually obtained in the study and randomly assign them to the two groups in all possible ways, computing the t test after each permutation. This creates a distribution of all the possible t values the researchers could get in the study, just by chance. Using this distribution, they can see how often they would get the t value that they obtained or one more extreme, just by chance.

Randomization tests are much less commonly used, but they are in fact more appropriate than the method of using sampling distributions when samples in an experiment are not drawn randomly from a population (Bear, 1995). However, both methods—sampling distributions and randomization tests—allow researchers to estimate the probability of obtaining the t value they got, or a larger one, if only chance is operating (if the null hypothesis is true).

Step 4: Deciding Whether to Reject or Retain the Null Hypothesis

Now we are ready for Step 4 of the hypothesis-testing process. Again, according to the computer, the probability of the Jones team obtaining the t of 2.57 in a study with 52 people was $p = .013$. This p is smaller than the conventional alpha level of .05, so we reject the null hypothesis and conclude that the difference between the two groups is statistically significant.

In other words, we said:

It is possible to get a *t* of 2.57 just by chance,

but

the probability of getting a *t* of that size (or larger) is very small—only .013;

therefore

we assume the difference between the two means did not happen just by chance.

When we use a table of critical values of *t*, we compare the *t* we obtained to the critical value of *t* we looked up (see Appendix B). Because the *t* we obtained (2.57) is greater than the critical *t* associated with the alpha level of .05 (2.009), we conclude that the result is statistically significant. Because our *t* is even more extreme than the *t* associated with the .05 alpha level, we can reject the null hypothesis. This means the probability of getting the *t* we got is something less than .05 if the null hypothesis is true.

Notice that the two methods—the computer-derived probability and the critical value method—lead to the same conclusion from different directions. When using the computer's estimate of probability, we decide whether or not that estimate of *p* is *smaller* than our alpha level of .05. In contrast, when we use the critical values table, we are assessing whether our obtained *t* is *larger* than the critical value of *t*. *Larger* values of *t* are associated with *smaller* probabilities.

Is That Difference Significant? The *F* Test (ANOVA)

The *t* test is the appropriate test for evaluating whether two group means are significantly different. When a study compares two *or more* groups to each other, the appropriate test is the **F test**, obtained from an analysis of variance, also referred to as ANOVA.

A study conducted by Bushman (2002), introduced in Chapter 2, illustrates research for which the *F* test is appropriate. As you may recall, Bushman was testing the hypothesis that venting one's anger (by punching a punching bag) would reduce a person's subsequent anger and aggression. The study had three stages. In the first stage, a student wrote an essay, which was subsequently criticized by another student, who called it "one of the worst essays I have ever read!" In the second stage, Bushman divided the insulted (and angry) participants into groups. One group sat quietly in the lab room. Another group had the chance to punch a punching bag and was told to imagine the insulting student's face on it (this was the venting group). A third group had the chance to punch a punching bag, but they were told they were doing so for exercise. Finally, in the third stage, all three groups of participants rated their anger on a scale of mood, and they had a chance to punish the insulting student by playing a very loud noise blast.

The researchers obtained three group means. Here we present the means representing how angry each group reported feeling:

- Mean of group who sat quietly: 26.25
- Mean of venting group: 29.78
- Mean of exercise group: 27.32

To conduct inferential statistics for this study, we need to ask whether the three means—26.25, 29.78, and 27.32—are significantly different from one another. Could differences between means of this size plausibly have been obtained just by chance? The authors used an F test, or ANOVA, to find out.

The F test helps determine whether the differences among the three groups are statistically significant. Just as with the t test, two sources of variability will influence the distances between these three groups. One is the variability *between* the three means themselves. The other is how much variability there is *within* each of the groups. Like t, the F test is a ratio of these two values. The numerator contains the value representing the variability between the means, and the denominator contains the value representing the variability within the groups.

The computations of the F ratio are not that complicated, but they are also beyond the scope of this discussion. In brief, when the F ratio is large, it means there is more variability between the groups than there is within the groups; that is, the groups' scores are far apart and do not overlap much. When the F ratio is small, it means there is about the same (or even less) variability between the groups than there is within the groups; the groups overlap more.

Let's walk through how we would use an ANOVA in the example.

Step 1: Stating the Null Hypothesis

To go through the hypothesis-testing steps for the Bushman study, which compared groups who sat quietly, vented their anger, or exercised, we start by assuming the null hypothesis. In this case, we assume there is no difference among the three groups. In other words, the null hypothesis is that the difference between the means of the groups will be zero; all possible differences among the three means result in zero.

Step 2: Computing the F Ratio

Next, we calculate the F ratio for the study. In their article, the researchers reported that they obtained an F value of 5.23 for their results. We won't discuss the computations here, but this means the variability between the three means was 5.23 times larger than the variability within the three means. That sounds like a large ratio, but is it statistically significant?

Step 3: Calculating the Probability of the F Value We Obtained, or an Even Larger Value, If the Null Hypothesis Is True

Next, we compare the F we obtained in Step 2 to a sampling distribution of F values, similar to what we did for the t value. We derive the sampling distribution of F by assuming that the null hypothesis is true in the population, and then imagining that we run the study many more times, drawing different samples from that null hypothesis population. If we use the same design and run the study again and again, what values of F would we expect from such a population if the null hypothesis is true?

If there is no difference between means in the population, then most of the time the variance between the groups will be about the same as the variance within the groups. When these two variances are about the same, the F ratio will be close to 1 most of the time. Therefore, the sampling distribution of F is centered on 1.0—most of the F values we get from the null hypothesis population will be close to 1.0.

The sampling distribution of F is not symmetrical (**Figure S2.4**). While it is possible to get an F that is lower than 1 (e.g., when the between-groups variance is smaller than the within-groups variance), it is not possible to get an F that is less than zero. Zero is the lowest that F can be. However, F can be very large sometimes, such as when the between-groups variance is much larger than the within-groups variance.

Just like t, the sampling distribution of F will take on slightly different shapes, depending on the degrees of freedom for F. The degrees of freedom for the sampling distribution of F contain two values. For the numerator (the between-groups variance), it is the number of groups minus 1 (in this example, $3 - 1$, or 2). The degrees of freedom value for the denominator (the within-groups variance) is computed from the number of participants in the study, minus the number of groups. (There were 602 students in Bushman's study, about 200 in each group, so the degrees of freedom would be $602 - 3 = 599$.)

By deriving the sampling distribution, a computer program will calculate the probability of getting the F we got, or one more extreme, if the null hypothesis is true. The larger the F we obtained, the less likely it is to have happened just by chance if the null hypothesis is true. In the case of the Bushman study, the computer reported that value to be $p = .0056$. This means that if the null hypothesis is true, we could get an F value of 5.23 only 0.56% of the time, just by chance.

Usually we let the computer to tell us the exact probability of getting the F we got if the null hypothesis is true. If a computer is not available, we can use a table like the one in Appendix B, Critical Values of F. The critical value of F is the F value associated with our alpha level. According to that table, the critical value of F at 2 and 599 degrees of freedom is 3.10. This means that if we ran the study many times, we would get an F of 3.10 or higher 5% of the time when the null hypothesis is true.

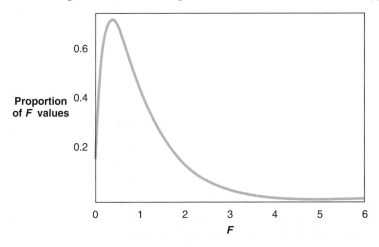

FIGURE S2.4 A sampling distribution of F. The sampling distribution of F is centered on 1.0 and is not symmetrical. If the null hypothesis is true, most of the F values would be close to 1.0. The F value cannot be lower than zero, but it can be infinitely large. The exact shape of the F distribution will differ slightly, depending on the degrees of freedom.

In Step 4, we will compare this critical value (3.10) to the one we obtained in our study (5.23).

Step 4: Deciding Whether to Reject or Retain the Null Hypothesis

When we use the computer, we simply compare the computer's estimated p value, $p = .0056$, to the conventional alpha level of .05. In this case, we will reject the null hypothesis and conclude that there is a significant difference among the means of the three groups in the Bushman study. In other words, we have concluded that there is a significant difference in anger among the control, venting, and exercise groups.

Using the critical values table, we can compare the value we obtained, 5.23, to the critical value we looked up, 3.10. Because the F we obtained is even *larger* than the critical value, we can also reject the null hypothesis and conclude that there is a significant difference among the means of the three groups in this study.

Just as with the t test, the two decision techniques lead to the same conclusion from different directions. When we use the computer's estimate of probability, we are assessing whether the computer's estimate of p is *smaller* than our alpha level of .05. But because larger F values are associated with smaller probabilities, when we use the critical values table, we are assessing whether our obtained F is *larger* than the critical value of F.

A statistically significant F means that there is some difference somewhere among the groups in your study. The next step is to conduct a set of post-hoc comparisons to identify which of the group means is significantly different from the others. A full length statistics text will explain the procedure for these post-hoc comparisons.

Is That Correlation Significant? Inferential Statistics with r

Two chapters (Chapter 8 and Statistics Review: Descriptive Statistics) discussed the correlation coefficient r in detail. The correlation coefficient is considered a descriptive test because it describes the direction and strength of a relationship between two numeric variables.

In addition to using r to describe an association, we can also evaluate the statistical significance of a correlation coefficient. As with t and F, we follow the four steps of null hypothesis testing. Step 1: We assume that there is no relationship in the population. Step 2: We collect some data and calculate r. Step 3: We estimate the probability of getting the r we got, or one more extreme, if the null hypothesis is true. Step 4: We decide whether to reject or retain the null hypothesis. When we reject the null hypothesis, we are concluding that the relationship (the r) we observed in our sample is statistically significant—in other words, that r we obtained is unlikely to occur just by chance in a null hypothesis population.

Sampling Distribution of r

Just as t and F had sampling distributions, so does the correlation coefficient. The sampling distribution of r is developed based on the probable values of r we would get if we ran the study many times on random samples from a population in which the null hypothesis is true. If the null hypothesis is true, most of the values of r

would be around .00. Some would be greater than .00, and some would be less than .00, but they would average at (or near) .00. If the null hypothesis is true and there is a large sample (greater than 30), then the sampling distribution of r is shaped very much like the t distribution. It is centered on zero, and it varies in width depending on degrees of freedom—that is, the number of cases in the sample.

The larger our study's r is (the closer it gets to 1.0 or -1.0), the less likely it becomes that we would get that value, just by chance, if the null hypothesis is true. (Therefore, the larger the r, the more likely that r is statistically significant.)

When we use a computer program to calculate r, the computer usually reports the value of r in the sample, along with an exact p value. That exact p tells us the probability of obtaining the r we got or a more extreme r if the null hypothesis is true. As in most statistical tests, when the p value is below alpha (usually, below a p of .05), we conclude that the result is statistically significant.

Sample Size and r

A larger r (a stronger r) is more likely to be statistically significant. However, the statistical significance of a value of r depends heavily on the sample size. When a study has a very small sample—fewer than 15 participants—it requires a large value of r to be statistically significant. In contrast, when a study has a very large sample—more than 1,000 participants—a small r (e.g., even an r of only .09 or $-.09$) will be statistically significant. Therefore, it is important to remember that r can also be used as a measure of effect size. In other words, an r of .09 may be statistically significant, but it still represents a very weak, or small, effect size (see Table S1.5).

For more on statistical significance, see Chapter 8, pp. 214–217.

As you evaluate the meaning of a correlation coefficient, recall what you have learned in this book about statistical significance, effect size, and practical importance. As you consider these three elements, you will be interrogating statistical validity.

Is That Regression Coefficient Significant? Inferential Statistics for Beta

Chapter 9 introduced beta, a value obtained from the multiple-regression process. Beta is similar to r in that both are used to estimate the association between two variables. However, beta goes further than r, because it usually represents the relationship between a predictor (independent) variable and a dependent variable, *controlling for* other ("third") variables. Chapter 9 presented a study that estimated the relationship between recess and school behavior problems, controlling for other variables such as family income, class size, and the percentage of boys in the classroom.

We can evaluate the statistical significance of beta by following a series of mathematical steps leading to a t value. After finding the t value associated with a beta, we use the sampling distribution of t to evaluate the statistical significance of that beta. The sampling distributions of the t that are used to evaluate beta are the same as those for evaluating the difference between two samples. (Recall that these sampling distributions vary in width depending on their degrees of freedom.)

Other than that, the steps are the same as for all other statistical tests. We assume there is no relationship in the population (Step 1). We collect some data and calculate beta (Step 2). We estimate the probability of getting the beta we got or one more extreme, if the null hypothesis is true (Step 3). We decide whether to reject or retain the null hypothesis (Step 4).

A multiple-regression table in an empirical journal article will usually have a column indicating whether each beta is statistically significant. As discussed in Chapter 9, sometimes the significance column will contain the actual t value associated with that beta, along with the p value associated with that t. Alternatively, it might contain only the p value associated with the beta and its t. Or this column may simply contain an asterisk (*), indicating the beta is statistically significant, or the letters n.s., indicating the beta is not significant.

Other Statistical Tests: Same Process, Different Letters

We have discussed four inferential statistical tests: the t test, the F test, and tests of the significance of r and beta. These four tests were developed for different research designs. The t test is for evaluating the difference between two group means. The F test is for evaluating the differences between two or more group means. The correlation coefficient r and its sampling distribution are used for evaluating whether an association between two variables is statistically significant. And beta, evaluated with a t test, indicates whether an association between two variables, controlling for some other variable(s), is statistically significant. **Table S2.3** presents a more comprehensive list of inferential statistical tests.

Although these tests are used for different research situations, they all follow the same general steps:

Step 1: We assume the null hypothesis.

Step 2: We collect data and calculate a statistical test (a t, F, r, or beta).

Step 3: We create a sampling distribution of that statistic: the distribution of the values of t, F, r, or beta we would get if we ran the study using many samples from a null hypothesis population. We then use the sampling distribution to evaluate the probability of getting the t, F, r, or beta that we got in our data, or one even more extreme, if the null hypothesis is true.

Step 4: We decide whether to reject or retain the null hypothesis based on this probability.

No matter what the test is, the inferential process is the same. In the future, you may see a statistical test you haven't seen before. If it is an inferential statistic, you can assume it will follow the same logic—the same null hypothesis testing process. For example, suppose a researcher reports a test that's unfamiliar, called Q. If the test is accompanied by a p value, you are safe to assume the researcher derived a sampling distribution of Q and then used the sampling distribution to evaluate the probability (p) of getting the Q she obtained in her sample, if the null hypothesis is true.

As you continue reading about psychological research in empirical journal articles, you will encounter new statistical tests, developed for different kinds of data and for different research designs. However, no matter what the test is, it will probably be accompanied by a p value, and in most cases, the p value will tell you whether or not the results are statistically significant.

	One variable is:	The other variable is:	Sample research questions	Use this test:
Testing the significance of a difference between two independent groups (comparing two group means)	Categorical/nominal e.g., gender e.g., experimental vs. control group	Quantitative e.g., exam score e.g., severity of symptoms	Did girls score significantly higher than boys? Did the experimental group show a significant reduction in symptom severity?	t test for independent groups (returns a t value)
Testing the significance of a difference between two groups (comparing group percentages)	Categorical e.g., gender	Categorical (2 levels) e.g., pass/fail rate	Are girls more likely to pass than boys?	Most common: chi-square test of goodness of fit (returns a χ^2 value)
Testing the significance of a difference between two or more groups (comparing group means)	Categorical e.g., major (chemistry, psychology, or biology)	Quantitative e.g., exam score	Is there a significant difference in exam score among the three groups?	One-way ANOVA (returns an F value)
Testing the significance of a difference between two or more groups (comparing group percentages)	Categorical e.g., grade level (grade 1, 3, or 5)	Categorical (2 levels) e.g., pass/fail rate	Is there a significant difference in the passing rate among the three groups?	Most common: chi-square test of goodness of fit (returns a χ^2 value)
Testing a difference between two means, measured in the same sample	Categorical e.g., kind of cola (regular or diet; people taste both kinds of cola)	Quantitative e.g., rating of cola flavor on a scale of 1 to 10	Which of the two colas do people rate the highest?	Paired-samples t test (also known as t test for dependent groups). Also used: sign test
Testing a difference between two or more means, all measured in the same sample	Categorical e.g., kind of cola (regular, diet, caffeine-free, or vitamin-fortified; people taste all kinds)	Quantitative e.g., rating of flavor on a scale of 1 to 10	Which of the four colas do people rate the highest?	Repeated-measures ANOVA (returns an F value)

(continued)

	One variable is:		The other variable is:	Sample research questions	Use this test:
Testing two or more independent variables at a time and their interaction (see Chapter 11)	First independent variable is categorical e.g., size of box (large or small)	Second independent variable is categorical e.g., price of product (cheap or expensive)	Dependent variable is quantitative e.g., grams of spaghetti poured from the box	Do people use more spaghetti from large or small boxes? Do people use more spaghetti when it is cheap, rather than expensive? Does the effect of box size depend on the price of the product?	Factorial analysis of variance (returns F values for each main effect and each interaction)
Testing an association between two variables	Quantitative e.g., hours of study for exam		Quantitative e.g., grade on exam	Do people who study longer get better grades?	Correlation coefficient (returns an r value)
Testing an association between two variables, controlling for a third variable	Quantitative e.g., hours of study for exam	Quantitative e.g., preference for material	Quantitative e.g., grade on exam	Do people who study longer get better grades, even when their preference for the material is controlled for?	Multiple regression (returns beta values or b values). Sampling distribution of beta and b is the t distribution.
Testing an association between two variables	Categorical e.g., class year: freshman, sophomore, junior, senior		Categorical e.g., form of transportation to campus: bike, bus, car	Do people in different class years differ systematically in what form of transportation they use?	Chi-square test of independence (returns a χ^2)

Note: Not all of the statistical tests in this table are included in this supplementary chapter.

Key Terms

inferential statistics, p. 463
statistical hypothesis testing, p. 465
null hypothesis testing, p. 465
null hypothesis, p. 465
alpha level, p. 467
Type I error, p. 468

Type II error, p. 468
power, p. 471
t test, p. 475
sampling distribution, p. 476
critical value, p. 478
F test, p. 479

Presenting Results
APA-Style Reports and Conference Posters

Scientists make the results of their research public in order to tell others about the advances they have made or the phenomena they have documented. The dissemination of research results can involve key aspects of scientific practice discussed in Chapter 1.

Publication contributes to the theory-data cycle because researchers write about the results in terms of how well they support a theory. Published data also become the basis for theory development and theory revision. Through the peer-review process, methods and results are scrutinized by peers who evaluate the quality of the research and the importance of the findings. Published data can contribute to either basic or applied research. Basic research findings can be adapted to applied settings, and when applied research is made public, basic researchers may be inspired to refine or develop new theories. Finally, data published in scientific journals or presented at a conference may also be transmitted to the public if a journalist decides the results would be interesting to a general audience. A well-written report can help ensure that journalists interpret and present scientific findings accurately.

This supplementary chapter covers two forms in which psychological scientists present their data: the written research report and the conference poster.

Writing Research Reports in APA Style

As part of your psychology courses, you will probably be required to prepare a research report. The most common format for report writing is APA style, outlined in the *Publication Manual of the American Psychological Association* (6th edition, 2009). In the classroom, your research reports will be read only by your professors and fellow students. However, psychological scientists use the same APA style to write research reports that may become empirical journal articles.

APA Style Overview

A scientific research report is different from other kinds of nonfiction writing you may have tried so far. All APA-style research reports contain the same sections, which present particular kinds of information (see Chapter 2). When you know what is contained in each section of an empirical journal article, it is simpler to locate the study's hypotheses, background, and methodological details. In turn, when you write an APA-style report, you will be expected to include certain information in each section for your readers to find easily. An APA-style report includes the following elements:

Title
Abstract
Introduction
Method
Results
Discussion
References

APA style prescribes not only the content that belongs in each section, but also the format, including margin specifications, heading styles, and the presentation of statistical tests.

Title

By reading the title alone, readers should understand the main idea of the article. The *APA Manual* recommends that the title be no more than 12 words long.

Table S3.1 presents examples of titles of research papers cited in this textbook. You can see that, overall, they are informative and concise. In some cases, they even communicate their message with style. Most of the titles in the table contain a colon and a subtitle. The main title, the words before the colon, are intended to attract readers' interest; the subtitle, the words after the colon, specify the article's content.

TABLE S3.1 Titles of Empirical Journal Articles

Article Title	Authors
Well-being from the knife? Psychological effects of aesthetic surgery	Margraf, Meyer, & Lavallee, 2013
Profiles in driver distraction: Effects of cell phone conversations on younger and older drivers	Strayer & Drews, 2004
Superbowls: Serving bowl size and food consumption	Wansink & Cheney, 2005
Eavesdropping on happiness: Well-being is related to having less small talk and more substantive conversations	Mehl et al., 2010
Extraneous factors in judicial decisions	Danziger, Levav, & Avnaim-Pesso, 2011

- A title should communicate the purpose of the research in about 12 words or less.
- A title does not typically contain abbreviations.
- A title does not use the words "method," "results," "a study of," or "an experimental investigation of."
- In an APA-style manuscript, the title is centered and presented in uppercase and lowercase letters; it is not boldfaced. It appears in two places in the typed manuscript: on the cover page, which is page 1, and on the first page of the introduction (see the sample paper, pp. 507 and 509).

Abstract

The abstract is a summary of the article's content. It does not present the nuances and details of the research—for that, readers will consult the full report. However, the abstract should clearly communicate the report's main research question, the methods used to test it, the major results, and an indication of why the results are important—for example, how the results support or shape a theory.

The abstract is the first section of your paper that most readers will encounter, but it is often the last thing you will write. After you complete the other sections of the paper, you can easily create an abstract by adapting one or two sentences each from the introduction and the Method, Results, and Discussion sections. Above all, the abstract should be concise, accurate, and clear. Readers should be able to get a good sense of your research question and the results you obtained by reading the abstract alone.

- An abstract clearly and accurately summarizes the research question, methods used, primary results, and interpretation of the results in terms of some theory or application.
- An abstract should be about 150 words long. (Different journals have different word limits for abstracts, and the APA Manual does not specify abstract length; ask your professor how long he or she would like your abstract to be.)
- In an APA-style manuscript, the abstract is presented on its own page, page 2. The page is labeled with the word Abstract in plain text at the top center. The abstract itself should be typed as a single paragraph with no indentation (see the sample paper, p. 508).

Introduction

The first major section of your paper is the introduction. This is where the main narrative of the research report begins.

Components of an Introduction. The main body of the introduction introduces the problem you studied and explains why it is important—usually because it tests some element of a theory. Your study may also be important because your particular approach or method has not been used in past research. Therefore, the bulk of your introduction is an explanation of the theory or theories your study is testing, as well as an explanation of any past research that is pertinent to the problem you studied. In the introduction, you describe what other researchers have found and explain why their research is relevant to yours.

In the last paragraph of the introduction, you briefly introduce the method you used. (Was it a correlational study? A single-*N* design? An experiment? Did you use a factorial design?) The introduction is not the place to explain all the methodological details, such as how many participants you used or what questionnaires or tasks they completed; that information belongs in the Method section. However, you do have to tell your readers whether your method was correlational or experimental, and what your primary variables were. Then, usually in the same paragraph, you state your hypothesis or research question. If you had a clear prediction about what would happen in the study, that's your hypothesis. If you conducted a study to see which of several interesting outcomes might happen (Will A happen? Or will B?), that's your research question. The hypothesis or research question is stated in terms of the variables you mentioned when you briefly described the method.

Here's an example of how you can combine a brief description of the method with a statement of hypothesis. These are the last two sentences of the introduction from an article by Barros, Silver, and Stein (2009), described in Chapter 9, on school recess and behavior:

> Therefore, this study examined the amount of recess that children 8 to 9 years of age receive in the United States and compared the group classroom behavior of children of the same age receiving daily recess or not receiving recess. We hypothesized that children who received recess would behave better in the classroom as a group, compared with those who did not receive recess. (p. 432)

Here's an example of how you might state an exploratory research question. This is the last paragraph of the introduction to an article by Wansink and Kim (2005). Earlier paragraphs had reviewed relevant literature:

> Past research in this area by Wansink and Park has not been conclusive because it did not objectively manipulate the palatability of food. The study described in this article directly manipulates the palatability of popcorn (fresh versus stale) and then presents it to moviegoers in either medium- or large-size containers. Although people tend to believe that how much they eat is largely based on the taste of food, this study investigated whether this was true or whether environmental factors could instead influence a food's intake independent of its palatability. (p. 243)

Writing the Introduction. For many students, the introduction is the hardest section to write. Although you'll probably have read review articles or empirical journal articles that inspired your study, writing about these sources to create a coherent introduction is a challenge.

If you are writing an introduction for the first time, try writing the last paragraph of it first. Write about the method you used and the variables you studied. State your research question or hypothesis.

Next, try writing the first paragraph. Introduce the main area of research (perhaps it is stereotyping, eating preferences, cultural differences, or brain activity during reading). You may introduce your topic in a creative way to describe why this area of research is potentially interesting. However, the balance can be tricky. It might be appropriate to link your topic to contemporary events, but it is not appropriate to explain why you personally became interested in the research topic. For the sake of your readers, you should avoid being too broad in this opening paragraph, lest you sound trite or say things you cannot back up (such as "From the dawn of time, stereotypes have plagued humankind" or "Cultural differences are a common source of tension in our society today"). You also want to avoid jumping into technical waters too early. A good balance is to link your topic to a concrete story—but to do so briefly. Here's how Brad Bushman (2002) introduced his report of an experimental study on venting anger, described in Chapter 2:

> The belief in the value of venting anger has become widespread in our culture. In movies, magazine articles, and even on billboards, people are encouraged to vent their anger and "blow off steam." For example, in the movie *Analyze This*, a psychiatrist (played by Billy Crystal) tells his New York gangster client (played by Robert De Niro), "You know what I do when I'm angry? I hit a pillow. Try that." The client promptly pulls out his gun, points it at the couch, and fires several bullets into the pillow. "Feel better?" asks the psychiatrist. "Yeah, I do," says the gunman. (p. 724)

It can be particularly challenging to organize the middle portion of the introduction—the paragraphs after the opening paragraph and before those containing the statement of your hypothesis or research question. In general, it's not effective simply to summarize each empirical journal article in isolation, one after another. Instead, try using past studies to build an argument that leads to your hypothesis. This requires planning. Reread the background articles you have. Write each article's results and arguments on separate index cards, summarizing the main point, and move the index cards around on your desk as you explore the most logical way to arrange them. What order of presentation will let you explain the past research so it leads to your hypothesis? Then you can turn your index card arrangement into an outline and start writing.

When summarizing past research, keep in mind that psychologists do not generally use direct quotes when describing work by other researchers. They almost always paraphrase it, putting it into their own words.

As you write your introduction, alternate between summaries of past research, including brief paraphrased descriptions (e.g., "In one study, Wansink and Cheney [2005] prepared bowls of chips in a party setting that were either large and small, and found that people ate more out of large bowls") and statements that reflect your own interpretations and arguments (e.g., "This study demonstrated that serving bowl size can affect how much people eat, but it was conducted with junk food; it does not indicate whether serving bowl size will affect how much people eat healthy food"). It might help to think of the past research descriptions as the "bricks" of your introduction, and the interpretations, arguments, and transitions you provide as the "mortar." As you build your introduction, you arrange the bricks in a logical order and then provide the mortar that connects them. By the end, it should be very clear to the reader why you conducted your study the way you did and why you formed your hypothesis.

INTRODUCTION CHECKLIST

- Follow the typical introduction format:
    - The first paragraph of the introduction describes the general area of research.
    - The middle paragraphs summarize past research studies (the "bricks") and give your interpretation of their meaning and importance (the "mortar"), arranged in a way that logically leads to your hypothesis.
    - The last paragraphs briefly describe the method used and the primary variables studied, and they state the hypothesis or research question.
- Document the sources you are summarizing by listing the authors' last names and year of publication, using parentheses or a signal phrase, as described below (in Citing Sources in APA Style, pp. 504–506). You should not type the full titles of the articles you describe.
- Describe past research by paraphrasing or summarizing, not quoting. Be careful to avoid plagiarizing (see p. 502), and be sure to cite each article you describe.
- Describe completed research in the past tense. In general, it is appropriate to write the entire introduction in the past tense.
- If needed for organizing a long introduction, use subheadings.
- In the opening paragraph, avoid phrases that are vague and undocumentable, such as "in our society today" and "since the beginning of time."
- In an APA-style manuscript, the introduction begins at the top of page 3. Retype the paper's title at the top of the introduction and begin the text on the next line. (The heading "Introduction" is not used.) Do not insert any extra line breaks or extra spacing throughout the introduction. If you use subheadings to organize a long introduction, they should be boldfaced, capitalized, and flush left.

Method

The Method section explains, in concise and accurate detail, the procedures you followed in conducting your study. When you write the Method section, your goal is to communicate the details of your study so completely that a reader who had only your report to go on could conduct an exact replication study.

A conventional Method section contains about four subsections. They will vary according to the study. Possible subsections include Design, Participants, Measures, Materials (or, alternatively, Apparatus), and Procedure.

Design. If you conducted a factorial experiment, it can be helpful to open the Method section with a statement of the study's design, naming its independent and dependent variables. You state whether the independent variables were manipulated as between-subjects or within-subjects. For example, you might write, "We conducted a 3 (serving bowl size: small, medium, or large) × 2 (type of food: healthy or unhealthy) between-subjects factorial experiment. The dependent variable was the amount of food participants consumed."

If your study is a simple experiment or if you conducted a correlational study, the Design subsection may not be necessary. But a complex correlational study may require a section headed Overview, in which you describe the variables you measured and the procedure you followed.

Participants (or for Animals: Subjects). Here you describe the number, type, and characteristics of the people or animals you studied. Human participants are referred to as "participants," and animals are usually called "subjects" in psychological science writing. For human participants, you say how many people participated, and give relevant demographic information, such as gender, ethnicity, socioeconomic status, age range, immigrant status, and native language. In addition, other characteristics may be relevant to report. Participants' intellectual abilities or disabilities may be relevant for a study on educational techniques; participants' sexual orientation may be relevant for a study on dating behaviors. In describing human participants, you also indicate how the participants were selected (randomly? by convenience?), recruited (by e-mail? in a shopping mall? in psychology classes?), and compensated (Were they paid? Did they get course credit? Did they volunteer?).

When describing animal subjects, it is conventional to give the species' common name and taxonomic name (e.g., "We observed 10 piping plovers [*Charadrius melodus*] in their natural environment") and indicate for laboratory animals the strain and provider used.

Materials (or Apparatus). Here you describe in detail the instruments you used to measure or manipulate the variables in your study. If you presented information on a computer screen, indicate how large the screen was and how far participants sat from it. If you used a commercially available computer program, specify the program you used. If animals were exposed to a particular piece of equipment, give its dimensions, manufacturer, and model.

If you used questionnaires or published scales to measure well-being or self-esteem, you'd devote one paragraph to each measurement scale. Indicate who wrote the items by citing the authors who first published the scale. Give one or two sample items from the questionnaire and indicate what the response scale was (e.g., "a 5-point scale ranging from 1 [*strongly disagree*] to 5 [*strongly agree*]"). Explain how you combined items for the scales, for example, if you computed a mean or a sum. Indicate what higher and lower scores signify (e.g., "high scores indicated higher self-esteem"). Also indicate the scale's reliability and validity. For example, you might give the Cronbach's alpha value you obtained in your own study, and the extent to which past researchers have validated the measure.

For types of reliability and validity that might be relevant, see Chapter 5, pp. 129–146.

Although the Materials section should be complete and detailed, you don't have to describe obvious features, such as what kind of paper a questionnaire was printed on (unless there was something special about it) or whether the participants used pens or pencils to record their answers.

Procedure. This is where you describe what happened in your study, in what order. Did participants come to a laboratory or classroom, or did they participate online? What did participants do first, next, and last? If there was a series of trials, what happened in each trial? If there were counterbalanced orders of presentation, what were they, and how were participants assigned to each order? How were participants assigned to independent variable groups (randomly or not)? Were participants or experimenters blind to conditions in the study? If so, how was this achieved? If there was a confederate in the study, what did the confederate say (exactly), and when?

In writing the Procedure subsection, be careful not to repeat information you already described in other sections. In the Method section, each element is presented only once, in the most appropriate place and the most appropriate order. Often it makes sense to put Procedure last, but in some cases it may need to go earlier in the Method section for more clarity.

METHOD CHECKLIST

- The reader should be able to use the Method section to conduct an exact replication study, without asking any further questions.
- In APA style, the heading should be "Method," not "Methods."
- Use subsections such as Design, Participants, Materials, and Procedure, presented in the order that is most appropriate and clear.
- Do not put the same information in more than one section. If you describe a measure in the Materials subsection, do not describe it again or give more detail about it in the Procedure subsection.
- If you used published questionnaires, describe each one in its own short paragraph, citing its source, sample items, relevant computations, and response options. Indicate relevant reliability and validity results for each questionnaire.
- In an APA-style manuscript, the Method section is labeled Method in boldface, centered. The Method section does not start on a new page; it begins directly after the introduction with no extra line spacing. Subheadings for Participants, Materials, or Procedure should be typed flush left, boldfaced, and capitalized. Do not insert extra line spacing between subsections.

Results

The Results section of a research report presents the study's numerical results, including any statistical tests and their significance, sometimes in the form of a table or figure. You don't report the values for individual participants; you present group means or overall associations. In the Results section, you type numerals for means, standard deviations, correlation coefficients, effect sizes, or other descriptive statistics. You also enter the results and symbols for any statistical tests you calculated. The *APA Manual* provides precise guidelines for presenting these values. Generally, the symbols for statistical computations and means (such as M for mean, SD for standard deviation, t for t test, and F for ANOVA) are presented in italics, but the numerals themselves are not (e.g., $M = 3.25$).

A well-organized Results section is systematic, and its sentence structure may even be a little repetitive. The priority is to be crystal clear. It is often best to begin with simple results and then move to more complicated ones. For example, if you included a manipulation check in an experiment, begin with its results. Then move to group means, followed by tests of significance. If your study was correlational, begin by presenting the simple bivariate correlations and then present multiple-regression results. If your study was a factorial design, present main effects first and then interactions. If your study included multiple dependent variables, present the results for each one in turn, but try to keep the sentence structure the same for each dependent variable, so the reader can follow a predictable pattern.

It might also be appropriate to refer to your study's hypothesis and expectations as you write your Results section. For example, you might write, "As predicted, people were less affected by bowl size when eating healthy food than when eating unhealthy food."

Tables and Figures. It is good practice to present certain results in a table or figure. While a sentence is appropriate for presenting one to three numerical values, a table can summarize a larger set of descriptive statistics, such as four or more means and standard deviations, much more clearly and easily than you could do in a sentence. Tables are also appropriate for presenting multiple-regression results.

Tables must follow APA style guidelines. They may be single- or double-spaced, but they must include only horizontal lines as spacers, not vertical lines. You should never simply copy and paste tables of output from a statistical program into your manuscript. Instead, you must reformat them in APA style, usually retyping the numbers and formatting them appropriately. Tables are not included within the main body of the text. They are placed near the end of the paper, after the References. If you have more than one table, number each one consecutively (Table 1, Table 2, and so on), and place each on its own page. A title for each table appears at the top of the page. The label (e.g., Table 1) is in plain text, and the title itself appears on the next line, italicized, in upper- and lowercase letters. In the text of the Results section, refer to each table you created (e.g., "Means and standard deviations for the main dependent variables are presented in Table 1"). An example of an APA-style table is provided in the sample paper (see p. 519).

A figure can often highlight your data's strongest result. For example, if your factorial design found a predicted interaction, you might want to present the result as a line graph or bar graph. Figures should be created using a computer program such as Excel. Each figure should have clearly labeled axes and should be presented in black and white rather than color, whenever feasible. Like tables, figures do not appear in the body of the Results section; they are placed at the end of the printed manuscript. If you have more than one figure, number each one consecutively (Figure 1, Figure 2, and so on), and place each on its own page. You must refer to each figure that you are including in the text of the Results section (e.g., "Figure 1 depicts the effect of food quality and bowl size on amount of food consumed"). Provide a descriptive caption for each figure, typed on the same page as the figure, appearing below it. The label (e.g., *Figure 1*) appears in italics followed by a period. The caption follows on the same line, in plain text.

If you present results in a table or figure, do not repeat the same numerical values (such as the same group means) in the text of the Results section. Mention the general pattern in the text, and refer readers to the table or figure for the full story (e.g., "As Figure 2 depicts, people ate more food from the largest bowl, especially when the food was unhealthy").

The key guideline for the Results section is to state the numerical findings clearly, concisely, and accurately, and then stop writing. The Results section is likely to be the shortest section of a student research report.

RESULTS CHECKLIST

- A good Results section is well organized and crystal clear. Present simple results first, and use repetitive sentence structures when presenting multiple, related results.
- Use a table to present multiple values such as means, correlations, or multiple inferential tests.
- Figures are always called figures, not graphs. Use figures to present the strongest results in your study. Don't overdo it; most papers contain only one to three figures.
- Call out all tables and figures in the text of the Results section, but place the tables and figures themselves at the end of the manuscript.
- Do not present the same results twice. If you present a result in the text, do not repeat it in a table or figure.
- In an APA-style manuscript, the Results section begins right after the Method section, with no page break or extra line spacing. It is labeled with the word Results in boldface. You may insert additional subheadings to organize a long Results section; such subheads should be boldfaced, capitalized, and flush left.
- Check the APA Manual or the sample paper on pp. 507–521 for examples of how to present statistical results.

Discussion

A well-written Discussion section achieves three goals. First, you summarize the results of your study and describe the extent to which the results support your hypothesis or answer your research question. You tell the reader how well the results fit with the theory or background literature that you described in the introduction. Second, you evaluate your study, advocating for its strengths and defending its weaknesses. Third, you suggest what the next step might be for the theory-data cycle.

Summarizing and Linking to the Theory-Data Cycle. The first paragraph or two of the Discussion section summarizes the hypotheses and major results of your study. Clearly indicate which results supported your hypothesis and which did not. Tie the results back to the literature and theories you mentioned in the introduction. In this sense, the Discussion section and introduction are like bookends to your paper—they both address the theory-data cycle. Describe how your results support the broader theory and why (or why not). If the results support the theory you were testing, you should explain how.

If the results do not support your theory, it will mean one of two things (as shown in Figure 1.5): Either the theory is incorrect (and therefore must be modified in some way), or your study was flawed (and therefore a better study should be conducted). The Discussion is the place to explore these options and explain what you think is going on. For example, if you conducted an experiment that found a null result, what factors might be responsible?

For some common reasons for a null result, see Table 11.2, p. 337.

Evaluating Your Study. In the next paragraphs of the Discussion section, you evaluate the choices you made in conducting your study. Generally speaking, authors advocate for the strengths of their own studies and anticipate criticisms others might make, so they can deflect them in advance. An excellent strategy is to write about the four big validities one by one.

Start by addressing the construct validity of your study, explaining whether your variables were manipulated or measured well, and how you know (review the evidence). Then, if you conducted an experiment, assess how well your study addressed potential internal validity threats. If your study was correlational, you might remind your readers that your data do not allow you to make a causal statement, and explain why. Address the statistical validity of your study by discussing the statistical choices you made. Finally, you might address the study's external validity. Because many student papers are not based on random samples of participants, however, you need to consider how much this matters in your case. Maybe it does not—if you were in theory-testing mode, for example. Reviewing your study in terms of the four big validities is an excellent way to make sure you have thoroughly evaluated and defended your study. The average student paper can probably include about one paragraph for each of the four big validities. (To review balancing research priorities, see Chapters 13 and 14.)

Specifying the Next Step. In the last paragraph or two, you write about some directions for further research. It's not sufficient to conclude with a vague statement, such as "Future research is needed." Suggest a specific, theory-driven direction for the next study to take. If your study was flawed in some way, could specific steps be taken to correct the flaws, and what results would you expect? If your study was conducted well, what part of the theory should be tested next? How could you test it, what results would you expect, and what would such results mean? If your study was correlational, could you conduct an experiment next? If so, how would you do so, what results would you expect, and what would those results mean? Could the next study be a conceptual replication? If so, what new contexts might you test, what results would you expect, and what would those results mean?

Push yourself to answer these questions, so you can write thoughtful suggestions about the next step. Who knows—you might even inspire yourself to conduct another study.

- The Discussion section has three components.
- The first one or two paragraphs summarize the results and interpret how the results fit with the theory and literature discussed in the introduction.
- The middle paragraphs evaluate your study. Work through each of the four big validities in turn, explaining the extent to which your study has fulfilled each one.
- The last one or two paragraphs give suggestions for future research. For each suggestion, explain four things: Why you would study that question, how you would study it, what your results might be, and what those results would mean.
- Do not report new statistical findings in the Discussion section; numerals and statistics belong in the Results section.
- The Discussion section and introduction are bookends; they both describe how your particular study fits in with the larger body of literature on a topic. If you opened your paper with a real-world example or story, you might consider closing it by reflecting on how your findings can help interpret that same example.
- In an APA-style manuscript, the Discussion section starts directly after the Results section with no page break or extra line spacing. Head the section with the word Discussion, boldfaced and centered. You may insert additional subheadings to organize a long Discussion section; such subheads should be boldfaced, capitalized, and flush left.

References

In the course of writing the introduction and the Discussion section, you consulted and summarized articles written by other authors. You cited these papers within the text using the authors' last names and the year of publication. Near the end of your paper, in a section titled References, you provide the full bibliographic information for each of the sources you cited, in an alphabetized list. The format is shown on p. 517.

Formatting an APA-Style Manuscript

When you prepare a research report in APA style, you'll follow a number of specific guidelines. It can be hard to assimilate all the rules the first time. A good strategy is to use the sample paper on pp. 507–521. Pay attention to every detail, such as line spacing, font size and style, and the use of boldface and italic terms. Here's an overview of APA format rules that apply to all sections of the research report:

- In an APA-style paper, everything is double-spaced, with the exception of tables and figures, which may contain single-spaced text.
- All text is in the same-sized font (usually 12-point) and printed in black. Section headings are the same font size and color as the main text.
- Margins on all sides should be 1 inch (2.54 centimeters). Do not right-justify the text. This means to leave the right side ragged; don't make the text line up in a straight line.
- The paper's title is not boldfaced but is centered and capitalized, both on the first page and at the top of page 3.

- Headings are boldfaced. The first-level heading—used for section headings such as Method, Results, and Discussion—is centered and capitalized. The second-level heading is boldfaced and flush left, and the first letters of major words are capitalized; the text following the heading begins on the next line. The third-level heading, if any, is boldfaced and indented and is followed by a period; only the first letter of the heading and any proper nouns are capitalized, and the text following the heading begins on the same line.

- The title page of the paper contains the title, the authors' names, the authors' institutional affiliations, an author note with contact information, and a running head, which is a shortened version of the title that appears at the top of each page.

- The following sections start on a new page: abstract, introduction, and References. (The Method, Results, and Discussion sections do not start on new pages.)

- The order of pages is as follows: title page, abstract, main body of paper (including introduction and Method, Results, and Discussion sections), References, footnotes (if any), appendices (if any), tables, figures. Tables and figures should be presented one per page.

- The top of each page includes the three- to four-word shortened title (running head), printed in all capitals and flush left, as well as the page number, which goes on the same line but flush right. In word processing programs, you might "insert header" or "view header" to add this information.

Writing Style: Five Suggestions

An APA-style research report should be written in clear, concise language. This is not the place to use long, complex sentences or show off a large vocabulary. In general, research writing is straightforward, not fancy.

Such writing is easier said than done: It takes practice, feedback, and attention. Here are five suggestions that can go a long way toward making your research report writing more sophisticated and clear. Your course instructor may have further suggestions to help you improve your writing.

Write in the First Person

In APA style, the first person ("I" or "we") is permitted because it can make a sentence more readable. First-person writing sounds especially natural and clear when there are two or more authors on a paper. Compare the following sentences:

The authors presented participants with three bowl sizes: large, medium, and small. It was expected that participants would consume more food from the larger bowls.

We presented participants with three bowl sizes: large, medium, and small. We expected that participants would consume more food from the larger bowls.

Whereas the first-person singular pronoun "I" is acceptable in report writing, it can sound awkward, so use it sparingly. In addition, the second person ("you") is considered too casual for report writing; in a research report, do not refer to the reader directly.

Choose the Most Appropriate Subject for Each Sentence

Sometimes, when you are comparing competing theories or briefly describing past research, it makes sense to use the author names as the subject of the sentence, as in the following example:

> Darley and Latané's (1968) laboratory studies supported a theory of bystander intervention known as diffusion of responsibility, but Shaffer and colleagues (1975) wanted to test the theory in a real-world context.

Often, however, when you are primarily describing the behavior of people, children, students, or animals, it is better to start a sentence with them, not with the researchers who studied them. Compare the following two sentences:

> Latané and Darley (1970) have found that in an emergency, people are less likely to help others when there are other people around who might also offer help.

> In an emergency, people are less likely to help others when there are other people around who might also offer help (Latané & Darley, 1970).

The first sentence emphasizes the *names* of the researchers, whereas the second sentence more appropriately emphasizes the *findings*: what people do in an emergency. Emphasizing the findings will make your descriptions of past research more vivid and interesting. Notice that in the second sentence above, the citation in parentheses makes it clear that the preceding statement is a research finding by Latané and Darley.

Prefer the Active Voice

The subject you use for a sentence can also determine whether the sentence is written in the active voice or the passive voice. Sentences in the active voice are more direct and usually easier to read, so you should strive to write in the active voice as much as possible. Compare the following examples:

> *Passive:* The target actions were never seen by the children.

> *Active:* The children never saw the target actions.

> *Passive:* Some of the action sequences were verbally commented upon by the adults.

> *Active:* The adults verbally commented on some of the action sequences.

In these examples, both options are grammatically correct, but the active sentences are clearer, shorter, and easier to read.

Sometimes, however, the passive voice makes the most sense. For example:

The rats were injected with ethanol 2 hours before each trial.

This sentence is written in the passive voice, but it appropriately places the focus of the sentence on the rats, not the people who injected them.

Use Strong Verbs

A precise verb can improve a sentence's clarity and style. Search your paragraphs for linking verbs such as *is, are,* and *be.* Try to replace them with stronger verbs, as in the following examples:

Our results are consistent with past research on eating behavior.

Our results replicate past research on eating behavior.

Portion size is an important influence on how much people eat.

Portion size influences how much people eat.

The manual was the guide for how to conduct the study.

The manual explained how to conduct the study.

Cut Clutter

Concise writing is more readable. You can often write clearer sentences simply by cutting needless words. For example, the following sentence originally appeared in an early draft of this material:

A precise verb can improve a sentence's clarity and make your writing easier to read. (15 words)

This shorter sentence conveys the same meaning without being repetitive:

A precise verb can improve a sentence's clarity. (8 words)

In the next example, the writer streamlined a long sentence by trimming unnecessary words:

When challenged to do so by their professors, most students find that they can cut out 20% of their manuscript's length simply by taking out a few extra words from each sentence. (32 words)

Most students can shorten their manuscript by 20% by removing unnecessary words from each sentence. (15 words)

Your writing becomes more readable when you cut redundant phrases and replace strings of short words with a single, effective one.

Avoiding Plagiarism[1]

When you use the words or ideas of others, you must acknowledge that by crediting the original published source. If you don't credit your sources, you are guilty of plagiarism. Plagiarism is often unintentional, such as when a writer paraphrases someone else's ideas in language that is close to the original. It is essential, therefore, to know what constitutes plagiarism: (1) using another writer's words or ideas without in-text citation and documentation, (2) using another writer's exact words without quotation marks, and (3) paraphrasing or summarizing someone else's ideas using language or sentence structures that are too close to the original, even if you cited the source in parentheses. The following practices will help you avoid plagiarizing:

- *Take careful notes*, clearly labeling quotations and using your own phrasing and sentence structure in paraphrases and summaries.
- *Know what sources you must document*, and credit them both in the text and in the reference list.
- *Be especially careful with online material*; copying material from a website directly into a document you are writing is all too easy. Like other sources, information from the web must be acknowledged.
- *Check all paraphrases and summaries* to be sure they are in your words and your style of sentence structure, and that you put quotation marks around any of the source's original phrasing.
- *Check to see that all quotations are documented*; it is not enough just to include quotation marks or indent a block quotation. (Remember, however, that in APA style it is not conventional to quote; you should paraphrase instead.)

Whether deliberate or accidental, plagiarism has consequences. Students who plagiarize may automatically fail a course or even be expelled from school. If you are having trouble completing an assignment, ask your instructor for help, or seek assistance at your school's writing center.

Using Appropriate Paraphrasing[2]

When you paraphrase, you restate information from a source in your own words, using your own sentence structures. (APA style requires paraphrasing and restricts direct quotes to very special circumstances.) Paraphrase when the source material is important but the original wording is not. Because it includes

---

[1] This section is adapted from "Avoiding Plagiarism" in *The Norton Field Guide to Writing, 3rd Edition* by Richard Bullock.

[2] This section is from "Using Appropriate Paraphrasing" in *The Norton Field Guide to Writing, 3rd Edition* by Richard Bullock. Copyright © 2013, 2009, 2006 by W. W. Norton & Company, Inc. Used by permission of W. W. Norton & Company, Inc. This selection may not be reproduced, stored in a retrieval system, or transmitted in any form or by any means without the prior written permission of the publisher.

all the main points of the source, a paraphrase is usually about the same length as the original.

Here is an excerpt from a source, followed by three paraphrased versions. The first two demonstrate some of the challenges of paraphrasing:

Original Source

In 1938, in a series of now-classic experiments, exposure to synthetic dyes derived from coal and belonging to a class of chemicals called aromatic amines was shown to cause bladder cancer in dogs. These results helped explain why bladder cancers had become so prevalent among dyestuffs workers. With the invention of mauve in 1854, synthetic dyes began replacing natural plant-based dyes in the coloring of cloth and leather. By the beginning of the twentieth century, bladder cancer rates among this group of workers had skyrocketed, and the dog experiments helped unravel this mystery.

—Sandra Steingraber, 2008, p. 976

Unacceptable Paraphrase: Wording Too Close to Original

<u>Now-classic experiments</u> in 1938 showed that when dogs were exposed to aromatic amines, chemicals used in <u>synthetic dyes derived from coal,</u> they developed bladder cancer. Similar cancers were <u>prevalent among dyestuffs workers,</u> and these experiments <u>helped</u> to <u>explain why.</u> Mauve, a synthetic dye, was invented in 1854, after which <u>cloth and leather</u> manufacturers replaced most of the natural plant-based dyes with synthetic dyes. <u>By the</u> early <u>twentieth century, this group of workers had skyrocketing</u> rates of bladder cancer, a <u>mystery the dog experiments helped to unravel</u> (Steingraber, 2008).

This paraphrase borrows too much of the language of the original or changes it only slightly, as the underlined words and phrases show.

Unacceptable Paraphrase: Sentence Structure Too Close to Original

In 1938, several path-breaking experiments showed that being exposed to synthetic dyes that are made from coal and belong to a type of chemicals called aromatic amines caused dogs to get bladder cancer. These results helped researchers identify why cancers of the bladder had become so common among textile workers who worked with dyes. With the development of mauve in 1854, synthetic dyes began to be used instead of dyes based on plants in the dyeing of leather and cloth. By the end of the nineteenth century, rates of bladder cancer among these workers had increased dramatically, and the experiments using dogs helped clear up this oddity (Steingraber, 2008).

This paraphrase uses different language but follows the sentence structure of Steingraber's text too closely.

Acceptable Paraphrase

Biologist Sandra Steingraber (2008) explains that path-breaking experiments in 1938 demonstrated that dogs exposed to aromatic amines (chemicals used in coal-derived synthetic dyes) developed cancers of the bladder that were similar to cancers common among dyers in the textile industry. After mauve, the first synthetic dye, was invented in 1854, leather and cloth manufacturers replaced most natural dyes made from plants with synthetic dyes, and by the early 1900s textile workers had very high rates of bladder cancer. The experiments with dogs proved the connection.

Use your own words and sentence structure. If you use a few words from the original, put them in quotation marks.

Citing Sources in APA Style

As you write, you must briefly document the sources you use within the text. You must also include the full documentation of every cited source in the References.

Brief Documentation in Text

When you are describing another researcher's ideas, words, methods, instruments, or research findings in your research report, you cite the source by indicating the author's last name and the year of publication. There are two ways to provide in-text documentation: by using a signal phrase or by placing the entire citation in parentheses.

When using a signal phrase, you present the last names as part of the sentence and place only the year of publication in parentheses:

Results by Wansink and Cheney (2005) indicate . . .

According to Elliot and his colleagues (2006), . . .

Alternatively, you can provide in-text documentation by putting both the author name(s) and the date in parentheses:

One study showed that people eat more junk food when it is presented in a large bowl (Wansink & Cheney, 2005).

With the second method, remember to use an ampersand (&) and to place the sentence's period outside the closing parenthesis.

As mentioned earlier, in APA-style papers, you will not usually quote directly; instead, you paraphrase the research descriptions in your own words. However, if you do quote directly from another author, use quotation marks and indicate the page number:

"Although a small bowl of raw carrots might make a good afternoon snack, a large bowl might be even better" (Wansink & Kim, 2005, p. 244).

When a source is written by either one or two authors, cite their names and the date every time you refer to that source, as in the previous example. When a source is written by three or more authors, cite all the names and the date the first time. The next time you cite the source, use the first author's name followed by "et al." and the date:

> The color red can affect our motivation (Elliot, Maier, Moller, Friedman, & Meinhardt, 2007). Even the color of paper on which a set of puzzles is printed can cause people to score worse if it is red (Elliot et al., 2007).

These are the rules for sources with obvious authors—the most common types of sources used by psychology students. You might need to cite other sources, such as websites with no author or government agency reports. In those cases, consult the *APA Manual* for the correct documentation style.

Full Documentation in the References

The References section contains an alphabetized list of all the sources you cited in your paper—and only those sources. If you did not cite an article, chapter, or book in the main body of your text, it does not belong in the References. Do not list the sources in the order in which you cited them in the text; alphabetize them by the first author's last name.

In the following examples, notice the capitalization patterns for the titles of different types of publications—articles, journals, books, and book chapters—and whether they are italicized or formatted as plain text. Notice that while the journal's name is capitalized, only the first word of the article title is capitalized. Also pay attention to the placement of periods and commas.

Journal Articles with One Author. Here and in the next set of examples, notice that only the volume number of a journal, not the issue, is included, and that the volume number is italicized along with the journal title.

> Gernsbacher, M. A. (2003). Is one style of autism early intervention "scientifically proven"? *Journal of Developmental and Learning Disorders, 7,* 19–25.

> McNulty, J. K. (2010). When positive processes hurt relationships. *Current Directions in Psychological Science, 19,* 167–171.

Journal Articles with Two or More Authors. These examples follow the same pattern as a single-authored article. Notice how a list of authors is separated with commas in APA style.

> Elliot, A. J., Maier, M. A., Moller, A. C., Friedman, R., & Meinhardt, J. (2007). Color and psychological functioning: The effect of red on performance in achievement contexts. *Journal of Experimental Psychology: General, 136,* 154–168.

> Mueller, C. M., & Dweck, C. S. (1998). Intelligence praise can undermine motivation and performance. *Journal of Personality and Social Psychology, 75,* 33–52.

Books. In the next two sets of examples, pay attention to how the publisher and its location are listed.

Tomasello, M. (1999). *The cultural origins of human cognition.* Cambridge, MA: Harvard University Press.

Wansink, B. (2005). *Marketing nutrition: Soy, functional foods, and obesity.* Champaign, IL: University of Illinois Press.

Chapters in Edited Books. Here, compare the way the chapter authors' names and those of the book editors are given, and notice how and where the page numbers appear.

Geen, R. G., & Bushman, B. J. (1989). The arousing effects of social presence. In H. Wagner & A. Manstead (Eds.), *Handbook of psychophysiology* (pp. 261–281). New York, NY: John Wiley.

Kitayama, S., & Bowman, N. A. (2010). Cultural consequences of voluntary settlement in the frontier: Evidence and implications. In M. Schaller, A. Norenzayan, S. J. Heine, T. Yamagishi, & T. Kameda (Eds.), *Evolution, culture, and the human mind* (pp. 205–227). New York, NY: Psychology Press.

CHECKLIST FOR DOCUMENTING SOURCES

- In the References, entries are listed in alphabetical order by the author's last name. They are not listed in the order in which you mentioned them in the paper.
- Within a source entry, the order of the authors matters; often the first author contributed the most to the paper, and the last author contributed the least. Therefore, if an article or book chapter has multiple authors, list them all in the same order that they appeared in the publication.
- The entry for each source starts on a new line, using a hanging indent format (see the examples and the sample paper). Do not insert extra line spacing between entries.
- The list is double-spaced and starts on a new page, after the Discussion section. The heading References appears at the top of the page, in plain text and centered. (Do not label this section Bibliography or Works Cited.)

The Effect of Negative "Child of Divorce" Stereotypes on

Thinking About Future Romantic Relationships

Kristina Ciarlo

Muhlenberg College

Author Note

Kristina Ciarlo, Psychology Department, Muhlenberg College.

This research was supported by an undergraduate research award

from Muhlenberg College.

Correspondence concerning this article should be addressed to:

123 Main Street, Bloomville, NY, 12000; E-mail: ciarlo@college.edu.

A short version of the title appears on the top of every page, in all caps. To edit this, view the "headers" area in your word processor. On the title page, the shortened title is preceded by "Running head" with a colon. On subsequent pages, only the shortened title appears.

Page numbers start with 1 on the title page and appear on the right corner of each page.

Provide a middle initial if you have one.

If there are multiple authors, list all their names, followed by their shared institution. If they are from different institutions, list name, institution, next name, next institution.

The word Abstract is centered and not bold. The abstract begins on page 2.

The abstract text is not indented.

It is appropriate to use the first person (I, we) in a research report. This student is presenting the results of a group project, so "we" is appropriate.

Avoid sexist language by using both "his" and "her" or by using plural rather than singular.

The abstract should be about 150 words long; some journals allow an abstract to be as long as 250 words.

Provide three to five keywords for your paper, centered under the abstract. Use the Thesaurus of Psychological Index Terms, available in psycINFO, for appropriate keywords.

Abstract

This study investigated whether negative stereotypes about children with divorced parents extend to beliefs about their romantic relationships. Specifically, we looked at whether people would use information about the level of conflict of a child's parents, as well as information about the marital status of the child's parents, in predicting a child's future relationship success. Undergraduates ($N = 38$) read a vignette about a child and his or her family and then predicted the child's future romantic relationships. We found that participants predicted the future relationships of children from divorced families to be more negative than those from married parents ($p = .02$), and predicted that the relationships of children from high-conflict families would be more negative than those from low-conflict families ($p < .001$). The results suggest that people use both the marital status of a child's parents and the conflict level of the child's parents to predict the child's future success in romantic relationships.

Keywords: conflict, parental divorce, stereotyping

The Effect of Negative "Child of Divorce" Stereotypes on

Thinking About Future Relationships

People use categories to simplify the task of processing the enormous amount of stimuli that confronts us (Gilovich, Keltner, & Nisbett, 2006). In social interactions, categorization may involve stereotypes, which are defined as "beliefs about attributes that are thought to be characteristic of particular groups" (Gilovich et al., 2006, p. 432). Even though stereotypes are not always accurate, we still knowingly or unknowingly use them as we interact with the social world. Stereotypes can apply to people from different ethnic populations, genders, or social classes, as well as other categories. The present study investigated the stereotype content and effects of one social category: children from divorced parents.

Past research has established that people hold stereotypes about children from divorced families, at least at the implicit level (Amato, 1991). In three studies, Amato (1991) assessed people's implicit beliefs about offspring of divorce. The first study demonstrated that people hold implicit negative stereotypes about individuals from divorced families, including the beliefs that they are distrustful, insecure, rebellious, prone to delinquency, shy, unpopular, have trouble relating to the opposite sex, and have nontraditional attitudes about marriage and family life. The results of the second study showed how these stereotypes work: Participants recalled fewer favorable facts about children from divorce than individuals from intact families. That is, participants implicitly ignored information that did not go along with the "child of divorce" stereotypes. However, when participants were explicitly asked if they thought that divorce caused negative effects for children, most responded that they thought divorce had few effects on children. Amato concluded that negative child of divorce stereotypes are widespread but implicit. They affect people's implicit beliefs even if they do not want them to.

One stereotype documented by Amato's study is that people perceive children of divorce as having trouble relating to the opposite sex. This particular stereotype is based upon some truth. Segrin, Taylor, and Altman (2005) found that children who come from divorced parents are more reluctant to enter into relationships because of the negative observations they made regarding their parents' committed relationship. The researchers also found that these children are less intimate even when they do enter into romantic relationships. The experimenters believe that this is the case because good communication skills were never modeled for them.

Although divorce may predict poor romantic relationships at an overall level, the context of the divorce seems to matter, too. The amount of parental conflict before the divorce moderates divorce's consequences for children (Kaslow & Schwartz, 1987). Some studies have shown that sometimes divorce has severe negative effects on children, and sometimes it has minimal effects or no consequences at all (Bartell, 2006). This discrepancy is partly due to the level of parental conflict that occurred prior to the divorce. Parental hostility and conflict have a stronger influence on children than the actual family structure does (Ensign, Scherman, & Clark, 1998). Furthermore, the cognitive-developmental model of the influence of parental divorce on romantic relationships explains that the level of parental conflict and proper modeling of relationships determines if children experience negative effects from the divorce or not (Bartell, 2006). Hence, the context surrounding the divorce matters more than the actual divorce does when considering the effects on future romantic relationships.

In the present study, we tested whether undergraduates' stereotypes about divorced children would be sensitive to the contextual factor of parental conflict. We predicted that although parental conflict matters in actual divorce cases, people's stereotypes would not be sensitive to this factor. Instead, we

Citation format for a two-author source

When possible, do not simply discuss past research articles one at a time; integrate them into an argument, as the student has done here.

The final paragraph of the introduction describes the method briefly and explains the hypotheses of the study in terms of this method.

hypothesized that people would ignore the context of the divorce and perceive overall negative effects of divorce across situations, because people fail
to notice or tend to discard information that does not confirm their previous
stereotypes (Amato, 1991). To test this prediction, we used a factorial design
that manipulated both parental conflict and parental marital status in a set of
vignettes. Participants read a high- or low-conflict vignette about parents who
were married or divorced, and then responded to statements about the future
romantic relationships of the couple's child.

Due to overall negative stereotypes about individuals whose parents are
divorced, we predicted that participants would perceive more harmful outcomes for such individuals' romantic relationships than for those who came
from intact families (a main effect for marital status). However, we predicted
that participants would fail to consider the effect of conflict, predicting that
participants would not make any distinction between the low- and high-paren-
tal conflict vignettes (no main effect for conflict). We hypothesized that these
predictions will hold true for all the participants regardless of their own family
situations because of how far-reaching negative child of divorce stereotypes are.

Method

Design

We conducted a 2 × 2 between-subjects factorial experiment. The independent variables were the level of parental conflict in the vignette, either low
conflict or high conflict, and the marital status of the parents in the passage,
either married or divorced. The dependent variable of the study was the participants' responses to the statements regarding the romantic relationships
of the children.

Participants

Participants were nine male students and 29 female students from
upper-level psychology classes at Muhlenberg College. Thirty-three

There is no extra
space between the
introduction and the
Method heading.

Format for a first-level
heading: centered and
boldfaced.

Format for a second-
level heading: flush
left, boldfaced, title
case. The text begins on
the next indented line.

Use numerals, not
words, to describe the
numbers in a factorial
design.

Numbers equal to or
greater than 10 are
presented as numerals.
Numbers less than 10
are presented as words.

At the start of a
sentence, any number
should be written as
a word.

participants came from parents who were married, three came from divorced parents, one came from parents who were separated, and one came from a single parent. In terms of class year, one was a first-year student, 20 were sophomores, 12 were juniors, and five were seniors. All the participants participated to fulfill a requirement in their psychology courses.

Materials

We randomly assigned each participant to read one of four vignettes and answer several dependent-variable questions.

Vignettes. We used four different vignettes representing each cell of the 2 × 2 design, specifically: high-conflict/divorced, high-conflict/married, low-conflict/divorced, and low-conflict/married (see Appendix). Each scenario described two parents, John and Elizabeth, who were involved in either a high-conflict or a low-conflict relationship. The last line of the passage stated either that the couple remain married or that they had gotten divorced.

We confirmed the effectiveness of the vignette manipulation by conducting a pilot test. Subjects answered questions pertaining to a passage thought to portray either high parental conflict or low parental conflict. Participants used a 5-point scale to rate the level of conflict that they felt the vignette represented ($1 = $ *very low conflict* to $5 = $ *very high conflict*). In addition, students were asked to rate how realistic they thought the scenario was, using a 5-point scale ($1 = $ *extremely unrealistic* to $5 = $ *extremely realistic*). We found a very large, significant effect for level of conflict, $t(9) = 6.43, p < .001, d = 4.29$. The students rated the high-conflict scenario as containing much more conflict than the low-conflict scenario (see Table 1 for the means). Hence, we determined that the parental conflict manipulation was effective. Furthermore, there was not a significant effect for realism, $t(9) = 0.98, p = .35, d = 0.65$. The participants did not rate the low-conflict scenario as being significantly more realistic than the high-conflict scenario. From these results, we concluded that the vignettes were equally realistic.

Dependent variables. The vignettes were followed by nine statements that addressed predictions about the future romantic relationships of John and Elizabeth's child. Each statement was assessed using a 5-point scale (1 = *strongly disagree* to 5 = *strongly agree*). We asked the students to circle the number that most appropriately corresponded with their feelings regarding the statements about the child from the previous passage. Examples of the statements include "This child will have difficulty sustaining a long term relationship" and "Their child will be able to effectively communicate with a significant other." After appropriate recoding, higher scores on the survey indicate a more negative view of the child's future romantic relationships. Possible scores could range from 9 to 45.

One survey question reassessed the construct validity of the vignettes, as we did in the pilot testing. Specifically, we asked, "What level of parental conflict does this vignette represent?" This statement was assessed using a different 5-point scale than the rest of the survey (1 = *very low conflict* to 5 = *very high conflict*).

The final four questions of the survey requested demographic information, including age, class year, sex, and parents' marital status.

Results

A factorial analysis of variance was calculated to determine if level of parental conflict or marital status had an effect on the students' perceptions of the children's future romantic relationships. Figure 1 presents the pattern of means. There was a significant main effect for level of conflict, $F(1, 34) = 55.88, p < .001$. The romantic relationships of children coming from high-conflict situations were rated more negatively than relationships of those

Indicate rating scales and anchors when describing self-report scales.

Use numerals for the point numbers and anchors of scales, and italicize scale anchors.

Give example items when describing self-report scales.

There is no extra space between the end of the Method section and the Results heading.

Call out all figures in the text. Do not repeat values in the text if they also appear in a figure.

Format for presenting an *F* statistic.

coming from low-conflict situations. There was also a significant main effect for parents' marital status, $F(1, 34) = 5.95, p = .02$. The romantic relationships of individuals coming from divorced parents were rated more negatively than children coming from married parents. Finally, there was not a significant interaction between level of conflict and marital status, $F(1, 34) = 0.09, p = .76$. Thus, the relationship ratings did not depend on the combined effects of parental conflict and marital status.

In addition, there was not a significant effect for the sex of the participant.[1] The female subjects rated the relationships ($M = 25.17, SD = 7.06$) slightly worse than the males ($M = 20.67, SD = 6.28$); however, this difference was not statistically significant, $t(36) = 1.71, p = .095, d = 0.67$.

To reassess construct validity, as was done in the pilot test, we computed another independent-samples t test to determine if the ratings of conflict level differed between the high- and low-conflict vignettes. The results replicated the findings from the pilot test: There was a very large, statistically significant difference between the two scenarios, $t(36) = 8.68, p < .001$, $d = 2.89$. Students rated the high-conflict vignette ($M = 4.53, SD = 0.61$) as containing much more conflict than the low-conflict vignette ($M = 2.37$, $SD = 0.90$).

Discussion

Due to globally negative child of divorce stereotypes, we hypothesized that people would ignore the context of divorce and perceive overall negative effects across situations. Our results supported this hypothesis; students rated the romantic relationships of the children from divorced parents more negatively than the relationships of those coming from married parents. This result replicates past research showing that negative child of divorce stereotypes include negative perceptions about their future romantic relationships (Amato, 1991). We had also hypothesized that participants' ratings would not be affected by the conflict level of the parents, but the results showed otherwise. Students rated the romantic relationships of children coming from high-conflict situations much more negatively than those coming from low-conflict circumstances. Hence, even though negative child of divorce stereotypes were activated, participants also took the context of the situation into account, contrary to predictions.

In our study, the contextual factor of conflict may have mattered because the vignettes were so extreme. The high-conflict passage contained an excessive amount of conflict, including verbal and physical violence, while the low-conflict vignette contained almost no conflict at all. The scenarios were made to represent opposite ends of a conflict spectrum in order to ensure that the manipulation was effective—it had good construct validity. However, this may also have increased demand characteristics. Participants may have realized what we were trying to study after reading such extreme situations. Thus, future studies should use vignettes that are more subtle in their differences and maybe even include a greater variety of conflict levels.

> **When the results do not support the hypothesis, offer an explanation.**

Our study was designed with good internal validity. We used a between-subjects design so that participants would not be easily aware of the comparisons we were making between divorced and married parents, or low- and high-conflict families. The vignette paradigm made it easy to keep extraneous variables controlled.

> **The middle paragraphs of the Discussion section evaluate the study's strengths and weaknesses.**

On the one hand, our external validity was not strong in this study; we recruited most of the participants from upper-level psychology classes, which means that they have all probably been taught a lot about stereotypes and biases. Additionally, all the subjects were college students and probably know someone whose parents are divorced. These individuals may realize that the effects of divorce depend on the context because of their personal experience. Such students may be better at controlling their implicit beliefs because they are aware of the automatic activation of certain stereotypes. Even so, they

> **In a student paper, address how well the study meets the four big validities.**

showed evidence of stereotypes that favor the children of married parents and low-conflict parents. Such stereotypes may, if anything, be even stronger among a non-student population.

We originally wanted to look at the difference between the relationship ratings of participants coming from married, divorced, separated, and single parents. However, the sample size was small and most of the students came from an intact family. Consequently, we could not run statistical tests to identify if there was a difference between the participants based on their family structure. However, we examined other sample characteristics, like participant sex, to look for discrepancies. Females rated the relationships more negatively than the males across all the conditions, but this difference was not statistically significant.

At the end of the Discussion, point to future research questions, explain what you would expect, and explain why they would be important.

A future study could examine the possible dissimilarities between the perceptions of people coming from married versus divorced parents. We predict that children of divorce would be even more sensitive to contextual factors because of their own personal experiences—that is, we would predict an interaction between the participant's own family status and the experimental factor of parental conflict.

References

Amato, P. R. (1991). The "child of divorce" as a person prototype: Bias in the
  recall of information about children in divorced families. *Journal of Marriage
  and the Family, 53,* 59–69. doi: 10.2307/353133

Bartell, D. (2006). Influence of parental divorce on romantic relationships in
  young adulthood: A cognitive-developmental perspective. In M. A. Fine &
  J. H. Harvey (Eds.), *Handbook of divorce and relationship dissolution*
  (pp. 339–360). London, England: Psychology Press.

Ensign, J., Scherman, A., & Clark, J. J. (1998). The relationship of family
  structure and conflict to levels of intimacy and parental attachment in
  college students. *Adolescence, 33,* 575–582.

Gilovich, T., Keltner, D., & Nisbett, R. E. (2006). *Social psychology.* New York,
  NY: W. W. Norton & Company.

Kaslow, F. W., & Schwartz, L. L. (1987). *The dynamics of divorce: A life cycle
  perspective.* Philadelphia, PA: Brunner/Mazel.

Segrin, C., Taylor, M. E., & Altman, J. (2005). Social cognitive mediators and
  relational outcomes associated with parental divorce. *Journal of Social and
  Personal Relationships, 22,* 361–377. doi: 10.1177/0265407505052441

The reference list begins on a new page. The heading is not boldfaced. Sources are listed in alphabetical order by first author.

Reference format for an empirical journal article with one author. Notice that the journal volume is italicized and the issue number is not included.

Reference format for a chapter in an edited book

Reference format for an empirical journal article with more than one author

Reference format for a book

Within a single source, preserve the order of authorship; do not list authors alphabetically unless they originally appeared that way.

When a DOI is available for a source, provide it at the end of the citation.

Footnotes

[1]We originally intended to test the effect of the participants' own family status, but we did not have enough participants in each category for this analysis.

Table 1

Pilot Testing Data: Conflict and Realism Perceived for the Two Vignettes

Rating	High-conflict vignette M (SD)	Low-conflict vignette M (SD)
Conflict	4.40 (0.55)	2.33 (0.52)
Realism	3.50 (0.55)	3.20 (0.45)

Note. n = 10 for all values. Conflict ratings ranged from 1 (*very low conflict*) to 5 (*very high conflict*). Realism ratings ranged from 1 (*extremely unrealistic*) to 5 (*extremely realistic*).

Tables are numbered consecutively and placed one per page.

Table titles are presented in italics and are printed in title case.

Do not simply copy output from a statistical program into a table. Retype the data and its labels in the APA format.

Tables may be double- or single-spaced.

Table format can include horizontal separation lines, but no vertical lines.

Use the table note to describe any abbreviations used in the table or explain the nature of measures used in the table. The table note should be double-spaced.

Prepare figures in a computer program, not by hand.

Do not use gridlines (horizontal lines across the figure).

Label both the x-axis and the y-axis clearly. Use shades of gray, not color, to represent levels of a variable.

Each figure goes on its own page and is numbered consecutively. Figure labels are italicized.

Figure captions are double-spaced and appear in plain text below each figure.

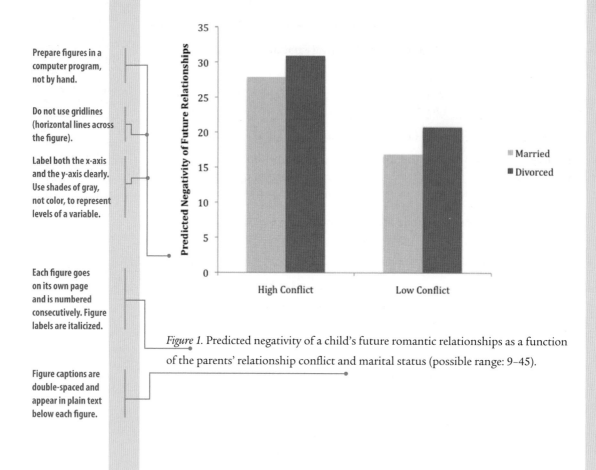

Figure 1. Predicted negativity of a child's future romantic relationships as a function of the parents' relationship conflict and marital status (possible range: 9–45).

Appendix

Vignettes Used in the Research

High Conflict:

John and Elizabeth have a child who just graduated from high school and is about to leave for college. Growing up, their child noticed that John and Elizabeth weren't always affectionate towards each other. They rarely hugged or held hands. The parents often fought over what was to be served for dinner, sometimes to the point that dinner was only served at 10:30 at night when they had finally settled on what to have. Their child had seen one parent or the other storm out of the house from time to time after a fight. Sometimes their verbal arguments turned violent, with either John hitting Elizabeth or Elizabeth hitting John. They would eventually apologize to each other only to get into another argument the next day. Their child often heard them yelling after going to bed, and it seemed that John and Elizabeth had more difficulties getting along than other parents.

Note. The vignette was followed by either of the following statements: "John and Elizabeth divorced about 1 year ago" or "John and Elizabeth remain married."

Low Conflict:

John and Elizabeth have a child who just graduated from high school and is about to leave for college. Growing up, their child noticed that John and Elizabeth were often affectionate toward each other. The parents sometimes had disagreements about what was to be served for dinner, but these problems were always resolved and dinner was served at 6:00 every evening. Their child had occasionally seen one parent or the other storm out of the room after a fight. However, they would apologize to each other soon after and the argument would be resolved. The child also noticed that John and Elizabeth could always make each other laugh and knew how to cheer each other up.

Note. The vignette was followed by either of the following statements: "John and Elizabeth divorced about 1 year ago" or "John and Elizabeth remain married."

An appendix is appropriate for presenting the full text of research materials, when such information is too long to present in the Method section.

If there is more than one appendix, they are called Appendix A, Appendix B, and so on.

Preparing Posters for Conferences

If you become involved in conducting original research—whether as part of a class project, for a student thesis, or as a research assistant for a professor—you may have the opportunity to present your research in a poster session. A poster is a brief summary of a research study, typed in a large, easy-to-read font and printed on a page as large as 4 to 5 feet wide. Poster sessions, in which several researchers present their posters simultaneously, are a common part of psychology conferences, both at undergraduate psychology conferences (where undergraduate research is the sole focus) and at regional and national psychology conferences (where faculty and graduate student research is the primary focus).

The Purpose of a Poster Session

A poster session is an informal way to share research results with the scientific community. At a typical poster session, dozens of researchers stand next to their posters in a large conference room (as in **Figure S3.1**). Other researchers mingle, stopping to read posters that attract their interest, and perhaps talking one-on-one with the poster authors about the research.

Besides sharing results with the scientific community, the other goal of a poster session is to enable researchers to talk informally. The one-on-one conversations and the nonthreatening context let people talk to potential collaborators, meet people they admire, or simply learn more about research conducted at other colleges and universities.

FIGURE S3.1 A poster session at a psychology conference.

Preparing the Poster

An APA-style research report will be the starting point for your poster, which should contain sections labeled Introduction, Method, Results, Discussion, and References. The poster format lends itself to less text and more images, as shown in the sample poster on pp. 524–525.

Keep the Text Short

A poster should give only a *brief* summary of the study you conducted. Many posters contain more text than most people are willing to read as they walk by, and it's best to keep the text short. Limit yourself to one or two paragraphs (perhaps even bulleted statements) for the introduction and the Discussion section. Keep the Method section focused on the bare minimum of information (such as the number of participants and the operationalizations of the primary variables). Let your tables and figures tell the story of your results.

Show, Don't Tell

Present as much information as you can in tables, images, and figures. Visual art attracts an audience: People are more likely to stop by a poster that contains a large, interesting photo or a colorful graph. Tables and figures can also help you talk about your results in an interactive way. (For example, while pointing to your poster, you could explain, "Here are the large and small bowls we used. And you can see in this figure that the large-bowl group ate about twice as much as the small-bowl group.")

Make the Poster Readable and Attractive

The typeface and formatting rules for a poster are flexible. Any text should be in a font that is large enough to read from a distance—at least 20-point. The title of your poster (printed across the top edge) should be even larger—at least 40-point. You can combine a variety of font sizes, colors, and backgrounds if you wish, as long as the poster is readable. (Be careful not to go overboard with too many visual effects.)

Attending a Poster Session

When you participate in a poster session, you will find your assigned space, hang up your poster with the pushpins provided, and stand next to it wearing your best outfit and a friendly expression. As people approach your poster, give them a moment to look it over, and then offer to explain your work. Some people prefer to read silently, but most of your audience will appreciate the chance to talk one-on-one.

It is a good idea to practice delivering a "poster talk," in which you describe your research in 1 minute or less. Using your poster's images as props, practice delivering the key points—the purpose of the study, the method, and the results—in this very short time period. After your brief description, a visitor can ask follow-up questions, and you can begin a conversation about the research. Congratulations—you are now participating in the scientific community!

In addition to preparing your poster, bring handouts to the session—regular-sized pages on which you have printed the text and images from the poster. You can offer handouts to interested people. Be sure to include your name and e-mail address, so people can contact you with questions.

Finally, during a poster session, it is perfectly appropriate to leave your poster for a few minutes to mingle and look at the other posters. This is especially important if your conference contains only one poster session. Don't miss this chance to learn about others' research as well as show off your own.

Effect of Negative "Child of Divorce" Stereotypes

Kristina Ciarlo, Muhlenberg College

Introduction

People hold negative stereotypes about children from divorced families; for example, they make negative predictions about such children's future relationships (Amato, 1991). For real families, studies show that divorce on its own is not the main factor in actual outcomes. Family conflict moderates the outcomes of divorce for children (Bartell, 2006).

The present study investigated whether people would stereotype children of divorced families as having less positive romantic relationships, and whether people would stereotype differently depending on whether the relationship had been high or low in conflict. We predicted that parental marital status alone, not marriage conflict, would affect people's predictions about a child's future relationships.

Method

Participants were 38 college students (29 female).

We used a 2 (marital status: divorced or married) × 2 (relationship conflict: high or low) between-subjects factorial design. Each student read one version of the story and predicted the child's future relationship success (see the vignettes to the right).

Statements about future relationships included "This child will have difficulty sustaining a long term relationship" and "Their child will be able to effectively communicate with a significant other."

Each statement was assessed using a 5-point scale (1 = *strongly disagree* to 5 = *strongly agree*).

Vignettes

HIGH CONFLICT:

John and Elizabeth have a child who just graduated from high school and is about to leave for college. Growing up, their child noticed that John and Elizabeth **weren't always affectionate towards** each other. **They rarely hugged or held hands.** The parents often fought over what was to be served for dinner, sometimes to the point that **dinner was only served at 10:30 at night** when they had finally settled on what to have. Their child had seen one parent or the other storm out of the house from time to time after a fight. Sometimes their **verbal arguments turned violent**, with either John hitting Elizabeth or Elizabeth hitting John. They would eventually apologize to each **other only to get into another argument the next day**.

Note. The vignette was followed by one of the following statements: "John and Elizabeth divorced about 1 year ago" or "John and Elizabeth remain married."

LOW CONFLICT:

John and Elizabeth have a child who just graduated from high school and is about to leave for college. Growing up, their child noticed that John and Elizabeth were **often affectionate toward each other**. The parents sometimes had disagreements about what was to be served for dinner, but these problems **were always resolved and dinner was served at 6:00 every evening**. Their child had occasionally seen one parent or the other storm out of the room after a fight. However, they **would apologize to each other soon after and the argument would be resolved**. The child also noticed that John and Elizabeth **could always make each other laugh and knew how to cheer each other up**.

Note. The vignette was followed by one of the following statements: "John and Elizabeth divorced about 1 year ago" or "John and Elizabeth remain married."

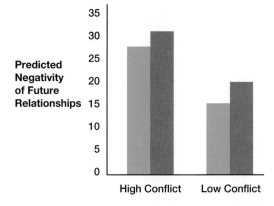

FIGURE 1. Predicted negativity of a child's future romantic relationships as a function of the parents' relationship conflict and marital status.

Table 1 *Pretesting data on the vignettes*

Rating	High-Conflict Vignette	Low-Conflict Vignette
Conflict	4.40 (0.55)	2.33 (0.52)
Realism	3.50 (0.55)	3.20 (0.45)

Note: Table presents Ms (SDs). The pretest was conducted on a sample of 10 undergraduates, using only the high- and low-conflict versions of the vignettes.

Results

There were main effects for conflict, $F(1,34) = 55.88, p < .001$, and marital status, $F(1,34) = 5.95, p = .02$, but no interaction.

Discussion

The results suggest that people used both marital status and marriage conflict when they predicted the future relationships of a child. As hypothesized, people predicted worse relationships for children of divorced parents than children of married parents. But counter to predictions, people also predicted worse relationships for children whose parents had high levels of conflict. These results suggest that people may, in fact, be sensitive to the level of conflict in a marriage, as well as marital status, when applying stereotypes to children of divorced parents.

References

Amato, P. R. (1991). The "child of divorce" as a person prototype: Bias in the recall of information about children in divorced families. *Journal of Marriage and the Family, 53*, 59–69.

Bartell, D. (2006). Influence of parental divorce on romantic relationships in young adulthood: A cognitive-developmental perspective. In M. A. Fine & J. H. Harvey (Eds.), *Handbook of divorce and relationship dissolution* (pp. 339–360). London, England: Psychology Press.

Appendix A
Random Numbers and How to Use Them

There are two uses of the term *randomization* in psychology, and it is important not to confuse them. Sometimes it refers to *probability sampling* (often called *random sampling*) from a population, and sometimes it refers to *random assignment* of participants to groups in a between-subjects experiment. Whereas random sampling (probability sampling) is a method for selecting participants from some population in an unbiased way, random assignment is a method for assigning participants to two or more experimental conditions in an unbiased way. Random sampling enhances a study's external validity, and random assignment enhances a study's internal validity. (For more on probability sampling, see Chapter 7; for more on random assignment, see Chapter 10.)

Table A.1 contains a random series of two-digit numbers, from 00 to 99. This kind of random number table is useful for both probability sampling and random assignment, but they are used differently in each case.

Random Sampling (Probability Sampling)

Suppose we have a classroom with no more than 100 people in it; that's our population. We want to sample 20 cases from this population using *simple random sampling*. The first step is to assign a number to each member of the population, from 00 to 99. Using the random numbers table, we select a starting value haphazardly—by dropping a pen onto the page, perhaps. Starting with this value, we then read across the rows. For example, if the pen drops on the third entry on the first row, 78, person number 78 will be sampled in our study. Then we continue moving along the row from there—persons 71, 21, 28, and so on—until we sample 20 cases. If a number is duplicated, we simply ignore the duplicate and go to the next number. If the population has fewer than 100 people in it—say, only 60 people—we ignore any random numbers that are greater than 60.

The example assumes we have a population of no more than 100 cases. If the population is larger than 100, we take the numbers in pairs, making the first entry on the table 7917. By using two columns at a time, we can handle populations up to 10,000 members.

We can also use the random number table for *systematic sampling*, another variation of random sampling. We drop a pen on Table A.1 and choose a value—say, 98. We split this into two digits, 9 and 8. Then we count off. Starting with the ninth person in a group, we select every eighth person after that until we have a full sample.

Random Assignment

Now let's assume we have already selected some sample of people who are going to be subjects in an experiment, and we're ready to assign participants to each experimental condition.

We plan to have 30 participants in our study, which includes three groups (say, red, green, and black). Thirty participants have agreed to be in our study, and we decide that red will be Group 1, green will be Group 2, and black will be Group 3. We can start anywhere on the random number table (perhaps by dropping a pen on it) and read along the row, considering only the digits 1, 2, and 3; we ignore any other numbers.

We assign our participants in sets of three. If we had a prearranged list of participant names, we would start with the first three on the list. If we did not have names in advance, we could set up a schedule based on the order in which participants show up for the experiment and start with the first three participants who arrive. Suppose we drop the pen on a part of the table that starts with the following row of random numbers:

93   94   17   15   28   07   16   87   22   06

Starting with the 9 in 93 and reading across, the first value of 1, 2, or 3 we encounter is a 3. That means the first person in the first set of three people will be in Group 3—black. The next value we encounter is 1, so the second person will be in Group 1—red. Therefore, by elimination, the final person in this group of three will be in Group 2—green.

Now we start again with the next set of three people. The next appropriate value we encounter is a 1, so the fourth person is in Group 1. Next is a 2, so the fifth person will be in Group 2, and, by elimination, the sixth person will be in Group 3, and so on.

Of course, if we had four experimental groups, we would consider the numbers 1, 2, 3, and 4. If we had two experimental groups, we might consider numbers 1 and 2. Or we could consider odd and even numbers—any odd number would mean an assignment to Group 1, and any even number would mean an assignment to Group 2. (In the case of two groups, we can also flip a coin to assign people to conditions.)

TABLE A.1 Random Numbers

79	17	78	71	21	28	49	08	47	79
17	33	72	97	86	45	44	65	97	29
27	65	06	82	98	28	36	03	72	93
33	57	70	34	39	91	78	99	64	53
76	81	31	42	31	04	00	10	82	13
27	72	54	77	94	97	92	56	20	98
97	95	39	36	02	43	10	08	19	00
87	84	51	57	65	03	46	70	94	69
40	80	05	81	12	90	02	90	44	38
21	90	78	37	47	61	92	69	35	30
40	61	04	23	42	76	72	13	08	83
59	02	28	10	82	77	75	89	13	34
91	37	80	64	61	39	19	38	91	28
24	42	44	77	45	44	03	46	25	94
66	49	81	89	88	40	81	60	25	26
57	55	52	54	53	31	49	38	14	72
83	26	59	05	42	05	89	74	68	10
16	97	26	84	41	14	94	94	94	03
53	16	08	29	29	28	19	28	01	83
87	73	84	55	94	57	52	68	56	90
56	55	60	96	53	21	18	59	55	86
83	59	56	38	86	84	07	40	77	20
37	39	88	49	43	00	49	13	02	51
14	20	68	04	90	94	70	05	83	10
11	16	82	54	39	36	56	00	52	07
46	97	32	82	63	13	42	30	20	64
25	04	76	44	88	19	61	20	56	97
05	54	35	78	93	94	17	15	28	07
16	87	66	77	22	06	50	76	95	09
67	78	65	43	99	96	82	04	48	30
50	70	46	81	33	52	89	59	09	49
57	90	31	77	96	04	97	17	87	54
51	85	26	99	70	46	88	58	00	99
45	07	47	13	64	79	44	06	15	07
46	72	46	81	14	12	17	48	07	33
04	62	90	98	01	48	00	54	91	65
75	83	67	58	01	28	14	42	41	00

(continued)

84	72	63	83	39	67	62	67	28	05
61	91	27	17	24	76	64	22	20	75
01	05	20	78	51	19	23	31	44	61
71	71	55	10	29	62	30	90	52	04
08	98	57	51	73	55	96	67	02	36
57	83	20	73	45	93	21	48	23	95
33	51	57	26	11	16	82	56	63	55
10	35	48	50	12	09	09	83	81	46
26	07	34	35	97	89	11	71	88	75
94	08	05	65	43	55	83	00	20	64
03	80	52	12	55	86	62	79	39	72
50	86	61	36	18	43	48	01	71	04
24	58	31	51	91	55	43	43	17	27
76	96	32	12	33	99	74	96	26	65
41	63	83	68	38	74	97	45	30	82
22	25	34	52	80	38	18	62	53	15
79	88	43	73	32	02	38	51	22	47
28	37	38	51	44	13	10	03	18	97
95	09	89	59	94	87	96	44	55	82
53	37	57	01	72	33	79	00	85	10
84	83	02	29	98	81	77	79	49	28
86	67	93	57	32	17	50	69	42	12
18	61	05	12	59	12	71	25	42	60
26	09	16	23	90	39	33	49	11	64
48	83	61	38	67	06	46	03	18	83
88	46	69	96	53	83	10	91	06	15
89	34	46	69	45	65	42	29	04	04
58	06	18	26	65	07	55	36	54	05
85	87	13	15	14	37	25	31	61	36
01	81	81	80	61	99	67	81	14	25
14	46	11	80	94	45	75	84	92	28
17	04	08	18	02	51	04	84	31	76
79	72	38	16	74	54	22	00	51	22
71	17	12	26	47	03	30	51	27	95
08	64	24	69	14	90	49	53	37	89
65	79	53	49	56	27	20	15	10	59
33	13	86	60	94	48	27	27	98	84

14	78	26	31	01	57	02	92	55	81
56	57	03	39	92	45	53	36	69	25
42	54	21	57	40	71	99	66	91	48
93	10	88	86	67	14	03	16	38	89
32	61	47	42	04	94	25	65	84	76
60	44	66	51	94	34	21	32	12	86
06	70	13	90	90	05	68	01	98	87
76	38	70	73	55	62	94	24	47	06
66	22	83	26	59	77	97	79	04	97
80	38	89	80	14	96	13	64	16	12
51	16	75	12	20	77	85	30	59	76
87	74	55	86	74	38	76	81	30	94
00	16	08	49	50	55	59	33	65	93
75	61	81	62	03	92	94	27	41	67
23	87	37	06	08	56	34	86	06	86
41	48	68	45	23	89	04	83	37	38
84	34	63	36	22	31	02	53	42	53
35	20	23	20	76	56	73	88	60	17
80	49	38	13	41	00	93	37	62	53
70	35	78	06	05	91	52	81	98	14
33	14	40	54	94	39	20	69	69	15
54	42	74	80	12	98	76	28	42	91
30	55	14	38	26	06	33	44	94	24
96	28	58	93	82	45	63	13	15	79
85	46	30	34	09	39	37	55	46	01
53	57	10	83	57	51	79	05	90	76
17	19	89	90	27	01	50	84	55	09
40	09	81	67	07	32	52	40	68	71
49	17	66	61	97	30	20	66	54	53
22	32	35	81	47	32	70	73	87	77
89	97	08	70	87	39	11	40	15	46
46	74	00	02	80	39	85	92	57	65
42	75	86	23	09	75	28	28	40	73
94	43	80	48	64	63	01	02	80	22
54	72	93	31	34	07	50	42	60	66
55	16	04	74	47	21	43	16	70	89
07	92	33	15	38	36	86	79	95	71

(continued)

54	11	73	86	13	49	10	10	89	36
05	52	32	81	69	27	76	65	87	73
93	65	64	46	20	42	68	34	85	95
09	38	86	01	19	06	94	71	04	16
71	01	97	48	42	07	38	90	53	56
37	65	03	46	22	79	31	84	70	20
04	81	54	72	34	51	85	03	07	83
13	57	23	30	11	58	68	32	83	96
67	61	33	63	86	59	14	58	99	17
60	35	99	45	88	44	76	17	69	96
22	03	82	01	22	27	58	50	89	24
87	30	73	72	02	93	22	09	27	89
99	94	97	86	75	02	95	33	44	88
45	52	41	35	79	56	51	82	60	26
41	94	12	01	61	24	15	62	89	77
52	14	05	73	11	94	46	70	97	64
60	00	84	59	49	21	31	13	02	92
39	68	23	26	03	47	31	65	19	44

Appendix B
Statistical Tables

Areas Under the Normal Curve (Distribution of z)

After computing a z score, we can use this table to look up the percentage of the scores between that z score and the mean in a normal distribution, or the percentage of scores that lie beyond that z score in a normal distribution.

The percentage of scores in the entire normal distribution is 100%, or an area of 1.00. A score that is directly at the mean would have a z score of 0.00, in the exact center of the distribution. Therefore, 0% of the scores fall between a z score of 0.00 and the mean, and 50% (i.e., half) of them fall beyond that z score.

For a z score of 1.11, using the table we can see that 36.65% of the scores fall between that z score and the mean, and 13.35% fall beyond that z score.

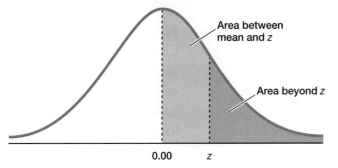

The normal distribution is symmetrical, so if our z score is negative, we use the absolute value of z to look up the relevant areas.

z Score	Area between mean and z	Area beyond z	z Score	Area between mean and z	Area beyond z
0.00	0.0000	0.5000	0.03	0.0120	0.4880
0.01	0.0040	0.4960	0.04	0.0160	0.4840
0.02	0.0080	0.4920	0.05	0.0199	0.4801

(continued)

z Score	Area between mean and z	Area beyond z	z Score	Area between mean and z	Area beyond z
0.06	0.0239	0.4761	0.40	0.1554	0.3446
0.07	0.0279	0.4721	0.41	0.1591	0.3409
0.08	0.0319	0.4681	0.42	0.1628	0.3372
0.09	0.0359	0.4641	0.43	0.1664	0.3336
0.10	0.0398	0.4602	0.44	0.1700	0.3300
0.11	0.0438	0.4562	0.45	0.1736	0.3264
0.12	0.0478	0.4522	0.46	0.1772	0.3228
0.13	0.0517	0.4483	0.47	0.1808	0.3192
0.14	0.0557	0.4443	0.48	0.1844	0.3156
0.15	0.0596	0.4404	0.49	0.1879	0.3121
0.16	0.0636	0.4364	0.50	0.1915	0.3085
0.17	0.0675	0.4325	0.51	0.1950	0.3050
0.18	0.0714	0.4286	0.52	0.1985	0.3015
0.19	0.0753	0.4247	0.53	0.2019	0.2981
0.20	0.0793	0.4207	0.54	0.2054	0.2946
0.21	0.0832	0.4168	0.55	0.2088	0.2912
0.22	0.0871	0.4129	0.56	0.2123	0.2877
0.23	0.0910	0.4090	0.57	0.2157	0.2843
0.24	0.0948	0.4052	0.58	0.2190	0.2810
0.25	0.0987	0.4013	0.59	0.2224	0.2776
0.26	0.1026	0.3974	0.60	0.2257	0.2743
0.27	0.1064	0.3936	0.61	0.2291	0.2709
0.28	0.1103	0.3897	0.62	0.2324	0.2676
0.29	0.1141	0.3859	0.63	0.2357	0.2643
0.30	0.1179	0.3821	0.64	0.2389	0.2611
0.31	0.1217	0.3783	0.65	0.2422	0.2578
0.32	0.1255	0.3745	0.66	0.2454	0.2546
0.33	0.1293	0.3707	0.67	0.2486	0.2514
0.34	0.1331	0.3669	0.68	0.2517	0.2483
0.35	0.1368	0.3632	0.69	0.2549	0.2451
0.36	0.1406	0.3594	0.70	0.2580	0.2420
0.37	0.1443	0.3557	0.71	0.2611	0.2389
0.38	0.1480	0.3520	0.72	0.2642	0.2358
0.39	0.1517	0.3483	0.73	0.2673	0.2327

z Score	Area between mean and z	Area beyond z	z Score	Area between mean and z	Area beyond z
0.74	0.2704	0.2296	1.08	0.3599	0.1401
0.75	0.2734	0.2266	1.09	0.3621	0.1379
0.76	0.2764	0.2236	1.10	0.3643	0.1357
0.77	0.2794	0.2206	1.11	0.3665	0.1335
0.78	0.2823	0.2177	1.12	0.3686	0.1314
0.79	0.2852	0.2148	1.13	0.3708	0.1292
0.80	0.2881	0.2119	1.14	0.3729	0.1271
0.81	0.2910	0.2090	1.15	0.3749	0.1251
0.82	0.2939	0.2061	1.16	0.3770	0.1230
0.83	0.2967	0.2033	1.17	0.3790	0.1210
0.84	0.2995	0.2005	1.18	0.3810	0.1190
0.85	0.3023	0.1977	1.19	0.3830	0.1170
0.86	0.3051	0.1949	1.20	0.3849	0.1151
0.87	0.3078	0.1922	1.21	0.3869	0.1131
0.88	0.3106	0.1894	1.22	0.3888	0.1112
0.89	0.3133	0.1867	1.23	0.3907	0.1093
0.90	0.3159	0.1841	1.24	0.3925	0.1075
0.91	0.3186	0.1814	1.25	0.3944	0.1056
0.92	0.3212	0.1788	1.26	0.3962	0.1038
0.93	0.3238	0.1762	1.27	0.3980	0.1020
0.94	0.3264	0.1736	1.28	0.3997	0.1003
0.95	0.3289	0.1711	1.29	0.4015	0.0985
0.96	0.3315	0.1685	1.30	0.4032	0.0968
0.97	0.3340	0.1660	1.31	0.4049	0.0951
0.98	0.3365	0.1635	1.32	0.4066	0.0934
0.99	0.3389	0.1611	1.33	0.4082	0.0918
1.00	0.3413	0.1587	1.34	0.4099	0.0901
1.01	0.3438	0.1562	1.35	0.4115	0.0885
1.02	0.3461	0.1539	1.36	0.4131	0.0869
1.03	0.3485	0.1515	1.37	0.4147	0.0853
1.04	0.3508	0.1492	1.38	0.4162	0.0838
1.05	0.3531	0.1469	1.39	0.4177	0.0823
1.06	0.3554	0.1446	1.40	0.4192	0.0808
1.07	0.3577	0.1423	1.41	0.4207	0.0793

(continued)

z Score	Area between mean and z	Area beyond z	z Score	Area between mean and z	Area beyond z
1.42	0.4222	0.0778	1.76	0.4608	0.0392
1.43	0.4236	0.0764	1.77	0.4616	0.0384
1.44	0.4251	0.0749	1.78	0.4625	0.0375
1.45	0.4265	0.0735	1.79	0.4633	0.0367
1.46	0.4279	0.0721	1.80	0.4641	0.0359
1.47	0.4292	0.0708	1.81	0.4649	0.0351
1.48	0.4306	0.0694	1.82	0.4656	0.0344
1.49	0.4319	0.0681	1.83	0.4664	0.0336
1.50	0.4332	0.0668	1.84	0.4671	0.0329
1.51	0.4345	0.0655	1.85	0.4678	0.0322
1.52	0.4357	0.0643	1.86	0.4686	0.0314
1.53	0.4370	0.0630	1.87	0.4693	0.0307
1.54	0.4382	0.0618	1.88	0.4699	0.0301
1.55	0.4394	0.0606	1.89	0.4706	0.0294
1.56	0.4406	0.0594	1.90	0.4713	0.0287
1.57	0.4418	0.0582	1.91	0.4719	0.0281
1.58	0.4429	0.0571	1.92	0.4726	0.0274
1.59	0.4441	0.0559	1.93	0.4732	0.0268
1.60	0.4452	0.0548	1.94	0.4738	0.0262
1.61	0.4463	0.0537	1.95	0.4744	0.0256
1.62	0.4474	0.0526	1.96	0.4750	0.0250
1.63	0.4484	0.0516	1.97	0.4756	0.0244
1.64	0.4495	0.0505	1.98	0.4761	0.0239
1.65	0.4505	0.0495	1.99	0.4767	0.0233
1.66	0.4515	0.0485	2.00	0.4772	0.0228
1.67	0.4525	0.0475	2.01	0.4778	0.0222
1.68	0.4535	0.0465	2.02	0.4783	0.0217
1.69	0.4545	0.0455	2.03	0.4788	0.0212
1.70	0.4554	0.0446	2.04	0.4793	0.0207
1.71	0.4564	0.0436	2.05	0.4798	0.0202
1.72	0.4573	0.0427	2.06	0.4803	0.0197
1.73	0.4582	0.0418	2.07	0.4808	0.0192
1.74	0.4591	0.0409	2.08	0.4812	0.0188
1.75	0.4599	0.0401	2.09	0.4817	0.0183

z Score	Area between mean and z	Area beyond z	z Score	Area between mean and z	Area beyond z
2.10	0.4821	0.0179	2.44	0.4927	0.0073
2.11	0.4826	0.0174	2.45	0.4929	0.0071
2.12	0.4830	0.0170	2.46	0.4931	0.0069
2.13	0.4834	0.0166	2.47	0.4932	0.0068
2.14	0.4838	0.0162	2.48	0.4934	0.0066
2.15	0.4842	0.0158	2.49	0.4936	0.0064
2.16	0.4846	0.0154	2.50	0.4938	0.0062
2.17	0.4850	0.0150	2.51	0.4940	0.0060
2.18	0.4854	0.0146	2.52	0.4941	0.0059
2.19	0.4857	0.0143	2.53	0.4943	0.0057
2.20	0.4861	0.0139	2.54	0.4945	0.0055
2.21	0.4864	0.0136	2.55	0.4946	0.0054
2.22	0.4868	0.0132	2.56	0.4948	0.0052
2.23	0.4871	0.0129	2.57	0.4949	0.0051
2.24	0.4875	0.0125	2.58	0.4950	0.0050
2.25	0.4878	0.0122	2.59	0.4952	0.0048
2.26	0.4881	0.0119	2.60	0.4953	0.0047
2.27	0.4884	0.0116	2.61	0.4955	0.0045
2.28	0.4887	0.0113	2.62	0.4956	0.0044
2.29	0.4890	0.0110	2.63	0.4957	0.0043
2.30	0.4893	0.0107	2.64	0.4959	0.0041
2.31	0.4896	0.0104	2.65	0.4960	0.0040
2.32	0.4898	0.0102	2.66	0.4961	0.0039
2.33	0.4901	0.0099	2.67	0.4962	0.0038
2.34	0.4904	0.0096	2.68	0.4963	0.0037
2.35	0.4906	0.0094	2.69	0.4964	0.0036
2.36	0.4909	0.0091	2.70	0.4965	0.0035
2.37	0.4911	0.0089	2.71	0.4966	0.0034
2.38	0.4913	0.0087	2.72	0.4967	0.0033
2.39	0.4916	0.0084	2.73	0.4968	0.0032
2.40	0.4918	0.0082	2.74	0.4969	0.0031
2.41	0.4920	0.0080	2.75	0.4970	0.0030
2.42	0.4922	0.0078	2.76	0.4971	0.0029
2.43	0.4925	0.0075	2.77	0.4972	0.0028

(continued)

z Score	Area between mean and z	Area beyond z	z Score	Area between mean and z	Area beyond z
2.78	0.4973	0.0027	3.13	0.4991	0.0009
2.79	0.4974	0.0026	3.14	0.4992	0.0008
2.80	0.4974	0.0026	3.15	0.4992	0.0008
2.81	0.4975	0.0025	3.16	0.4992	0.0008
2.82	0.4976	0.0024	3.17	0.4992	0.0008
2.83	0.4977	0.0023	3.18	0.4993	0.0007
2.84	0.4977	0.0023	3.19	0.4993	0.0007
2.85	0.4978	0.0022	3.20	0.4993	0.0007
2.86	0.4979	0.0021	3.21	0.4993	0.0007
2.87	0.4979	0.0021	3.22	0.4994	0.0006
2.88	0.4980	0.0020	3.23	0.4994	0.0006
2.89	0.4981	0.0019	3.24	0.4994	0.0006
2.90	0.4981	0.0019	3.25	0.4994	0.0006
2.91	0.4982	0.0018	3.26	0.4994	0.0006
2.92	0.4982	0.0018	3.27	0.4995	0.0005
2.93	0.4983	0.0017	3.28	0.4995	0.0005
2.94	0.4984	0.0016	3.29	0.4995	0.0005
2.95	0.4984	0.0016	3.30	0.4995	0.0005
2.96	0.4985	0.0015	3.31	0.4995	0.0005
2.97	0.4985	0.0015	3.32	0.4995	0.0005
2.98	0.4986	0.0014	3.33	0.4996	0.0004
2.99	0.4986	0.0014	3.34	0.4996	0.0004
3.00	0.4987	0.0013	3.35	0.4996	0.0004
3.01	0.4987	0.0013	3.36	0.4996	0.0004
3.02	0.4987	0.0013	3.37	0.4996	0.0004
3.03	0.4988	0.0012	3.38	0.4996	0.0004
3.04	0.4988	0.0012	3.39	0.4997	0.0003
3.05	0.4989	0.0011	3.40	0.4997	0.0003
3.06	0.4989	0.0011	3.41	0.4997	0.0003
3.07	0.4989	0.0011	3.42	0.4997	0.0003
3.08	0.4990	0.0010	3.43	0.4997	0.0003
3.09	0.4990	0.0010	3.44	0.4997	0.0003
3.10	0.4990	0.0010	3.45	0.4997	0.0003
3.11	0.4991	0.0009	3.46	0.4997	0.0003
3.12	0.4991	0.0009	3.47	0.4997	0.0003

z Score	Area between mean and z	Area beyond z	z Score	Area between mean and z	Area beyond z
3.48	0.4997	0.0003	3.57	0.4998	0.0002
3.49	0.4998	0.0002	3.58	0.4998	0.0002
3.50	0.4998	0.0002	3.59	0.4998	0.0002
3.51	0.4998	0.0002	3.60	0.4998	0.0002
3.52	0.4998	0.0002	3.70	0.4999	0.0001
3.53	0.4998	0.0002	3.80	0.4999	0.0001
3.54	0.4998	0.0002	3.90	0.49995	0.00005
3.55	0.4998	0.0002	4.00	0.49997	0.00003
3.56	0.4998	0.0002			

Note: This table is included for basic statistical reference. It is not discussed in detail in this book.

Critical Values of t

To use this table, we first decide whether a one- or a two-tailed test is appropriate. We decide the level of significance. Then we read down the corresponding column to the number of degrees of freedom. The tabled entry gives the value of t that must be *exceeded* in order to be significant. For example, if we do a two-tailed test with 20 degrees of freedom, our t must be greater than 2.086 to be significant at the 0.05 level.

df	One-tailed tests			Two-tailed tests		
	.10	.05	.01	.10	.05	.01
1	3.078	6.314	31.821	6.314	12.706	63.657
2	1.886	2.920	6.965	2.920	4.303	9.925
3	1.638	2.353	4.541	2.353	3.182	5.841
4	1.533	2.132	3.747	2.132	2.776	4.604
5	1.476	2.015	3.365	2.015	2.571	4.032
6	1.440	1.943	3.143	1.943	2.447	3.708
7	1.415	1.895	2.998	1.895	2.365	3.500
8	1.397	1.860	2.897	1.860	2.306	3.356
9	1.383	1.833	2.822	1.833	2.262	3.250
10	1.372	1.813	2.764	1.813	2.228	3.170
11	1.364	1.796	2.718	1.796	2.201	3.106
12	1.356	1.783	2.681	1.783	2.179	3.055

(continued)

	One-tailed tests			Two-tailed tests		
df	.10	.05	.01	.10	.05	.01
13	1.350	1.771	2.651	1.771	2.161	3.013
14	1.345	1.762	2.625	1.762	2.145	2.977
15	1.341	1.753	2.603	1.753	2.132	2.947
16	1.337	1.746	2.584	1.746	2.120	2.921
17	1.334	1.740	2.567	1.740	2.110	2.898
18	1.331	1.734	2.553	1.734	2.101	2.897
19	1.328	1.729	2.540	1.729	2.093	2.861
20	1.326	1.725	2.528	1.725	2.086	2.846
21	1.323	1.721	2.518	1.721	2.080	2.832
22	1.321	1.717	2.509	1.717	2.074	2.819
23	1.320	1.714	2.500	1.714	2.069	2.808
24	1.318	1.711	2.492	1.711	2.064	2.797
25	1.317	1.708	2.485	1.708	2.060	2.788
26	1.315	1.706	2.479	1.706	2.056	2.779
27	1.314	1.704	2.473	1.704	2.052	2.771
28	1.313	1.701	2.467	1.701	2.049	2.764
29	1.312	1.699	2.462	1.699	2.045	2.757
30	1.311	1.697	2.458	1.698	2.042	2.750
35	1.306	1.690	2.438	1.690	2.030	2.724
40	1.303	1.684	2.424	1.684	2.021	2.705
45	1.301	1.680	2.412	1.680	2.014	2.690
50	1.299	1.676	2.404	1.676	2.009	2.678
55	1.297	1.673	2.396	1.673	2.004	2.668
60	1.296	1.671	2.390	1.671	2.001	2.661
65	1.295	1.669	2.385	1.669	1.997	2.654
70	1.294	1.667	2.381	1.667	1.995	2.648
75	1.293	1.666	2.377	1.666	1.992	2.643
80	1.292	1.664	2.374	1.664	1.990	2.639
85	1.292	1.663	2.371	1.663	1.989	2.635
90	1.291	1.662	2.369	1.662	1.987	2.632
95	1.291	1.661	2.366	1.661	1.986	2.629
100	1.290	1.660	2.364	1.660	1.984	2.626
∞	1.282	1.645	2.327	1.645	1.960	2.576

Critical Values of F

This table can handle up to seven independent treatment groups. To use it, we decide our level of significance (.01, .05, or .10). We determine degrees of freedom for the numerator (number of conditions minus 1) and degrees of freedom for the denominator (sum of the number of subjects, minus 1 in each group). The table then gives the value of F that must be *exceeded* to be significant at the specified level.

Thus, if we have three treatment groups with 10 subjects each, we have 2 df for the numerator and $9 + 9 + 9 = 27$ df for the denominator. If we set our significance criterion at .05, we need an F larger than 3.36 to reject the null hypothesis.

Denominator df	Significance level	Numerator degrees of freedom 1	2	3	4	5	6
1	.01	4,052	5,000	5,404	5,625	5,764	5,859
	.05	162	200	216	225	230	234
	.10	39.9	49.5	53.6	55.8	57.2	58.2
2	.01	98.50	99.00	99.17	99.25	99.30	99.33
	.05	18.51	19.00	19.17	19.25	19.30	19.33
	.10	8.53	9.00	9.16	9.24	9.29	9.33
3	.01	34.12	30.82	29.46	28.71	28.24	27.91
	.05	10.13	9.55	9.28	9.12	9.01	8.94
	.10	5.54	5.46	5.39	5.34	5.31	5.28
4	.01	21.20	18.00	16.70	15.98	15.52	15.21
	.05	7.71	6.95	6.59	6.39	6.26	6.16
	.10	4.55	4.33	4.19	4.11	4.05	4.01
5	.01	16.26	13.27	12.06	11.39	10.97	10.67
	.05	6.61	5.79	5.41	5.19	5.05	4.95
	.10	4.06	3.78	3.62	3.52	3.45	3.41
6	.01	13.75	10.93	9.78	9.15	8.75	8.47
	.05	5.99	5.14	4.76	4.53	4.39	4.28
	.10	3.78	3.46	3.29	3.18	3.11	3.06
7	.01	12.25	9.55	8.45	7.85	7.46	7.19
	.05	5.59	4.74	4.35	4.12	3.97	3.87
	.10	3.59	3.26	3.08	2.96	2.88	2.83

(continued)

Denominator df	Significance level	Numerator degrees of freedom					
		1	2	3	4	5	6
8	.01	11.26	8.65	7.59	7.01	6.63	6.37
	.05	5.32	4.46	4.07	3.84	3.69	3.58
	.10	3.46	3.11	2.92	2.81	2.73	2.67
9	.01	10.56	8.02	6.99	6.42	6.06	5.80
	.05	5.12	4.26	3.86	3.63	3.48	3.37
	.10	3.36	3.01	2.81	2.69	2.61	2.55
10	.01	10.05	7.56	6.55	6.00	5.64	5.39
	.05	4.97	4.10	3.71	3.48	3.33	3.22
	.10	3.29	2.93	2.73	2.61	2.52	2.46
11	.01	9.65	7.21	6.22	5.67	5.32	5.07
	.05	4.85	3.98	3.59	3.36	3.20	3.10
	.10	3.23	2.86	2.66	2.55	2.45	2.39
12	.01	9.33	6.93	5.95	5.41	5.07	4.82
	.05	4.75	3.89	3.49	3.26	3.11	3.00
	.10	3.18	2.81	2.61	2.48	2.40	2.33
13	.01	9.07	6.70	5.74	5.21	4.86	4.62
	.05	4.67	3.81	3.41	3.18	3.03	2.92
	.10	3.14	2.76	2.56	2.43	2.35	2.28
14	.01	8.86	6.52	5.56	5.04	4.70	4.46
	.05	4.60	3.74	3.34	3.11	2.96	2.85
	.10	3.10	2.73	2.52	2.40	2.31	2.24
15	.01	8.68	6.36	5.42	4.89	4.56	4.32
	.05	4.54	3.68	3.29	3.06	2.90	2.79
	.10	3.07	2.70	2.49	2.36	2.27	2.21
16	.01	8.53	6.23	5.29	4.77	4.44	4.30
	.05	4.49	3.63	3.24	3.01	2.85	2.74
	.10	3.05	2.67	2.46	2.33	2.24	2.18
17	.01	8.40	6.11	5.19	4.67	4.34	4.10
	.05	4.45	3.59	3.20	2.97	2.81	2.70
	.10	3.03	2.65	2.44	2.31	2.22	2.15
18	.01	8.29	6.01	5.09	4.58	4.25	4.02
	.05	4.41	3.56	3.16	2.93	2.77	2.66
	.10	3.01	2.62	2.42	2.29	2.20	2.13

Denominator df	Significance level	Numerator degrees of freedom					
		1	2	3	4	5	6
19	.01	8.19	5.93	5.01	4.50	4.17	3.94
	.05	4.38	3.52	3.13	2.90	2.74	2.63
	.10	2.91	2.61	2.40	2.27	2.18	2.11
20	.01	8.10	5.85	4.94	4.43	4.10	3.87
	.05	4.35	3.49	3.10	2.87	2.71	2.60
	.10	2.98	2.59	2.38	2.25	2.16	2.09
21	.01	8.02	5.78	4.88	4.37	4.04	3.81
	.05	4.33	3.47	3.07	2.84	2.69	2.57
	.10	2.96	2.58	2.37	2.23	2.14	2.08
22	.01	7.95	5.72	4.82	4.31	3.99	3.76
	.05	4.30	3.44	3.05	2.82	2.66	2.55
	.10	2.95	2.56	2.35	2.22	2.13	2.06
23	.01	7.88	5.66	4.77	4.26	3.94	3.71
	.05	4.28	3.42	3.03	2.80	2.64	2.53
	.10	2.94	2.55	2.34	2.21	2.12	2.05
24	.01	7.82	5.61	4.72	4.22	3.90	3.67
	.05	4.26	3.40	3.01	2.78	2.62	2.51
	.10	2.93	2.54	2.33	2.20	2.10	2.04
25	.01	7.77	5.57	4.68	4.18	3.86	3.63
	.05	4.24	3.39	2.99	2.76	2.60	2.49
	.10	2.92	2.53	2.32	2.19	2.09	2.03
26	.01	7.72	5.53	4.64	4.14	3.82	3.59
	.05	4.23	3.37	2.98	2.74	2.59	2.48
	.10	2.91	2.52	2.31	2.18	2.08	2.01
27	.01	7.68	5.49	4.60	4.11	3.79	3.56
	.05	4.21	3.36	2.96	2.73	2.57	2.46
	.10	2.90	2.51	2.30	2.17	2.07	2.01
28	.01	7.64	5.45	4.57	4.08	3.75	3.53
	.05	4.20	3.34	2.95	2.72	2.56	2.45
	.10	2.89	2.50	2.29	2.16	2.07	2.00
29	.01	7.60	5.42	4.54	4.05	3.73	3.50
	.05	4.18	3.33	2.94	2.70	2.55	2.43
	.10	2.89	2.50	2.28	2.15	2.06	1.99

(continued)

Denominator df	Significance level	Numerator degrees of freedom					
		1	2	3	4	5	6
30	.01	7.56	5.39	4.51	4.02	3.70	3.47
	.05	4.17	3.32	2.92	2.69	2.53	2.42
	.10	2.88	2.49	2.28	2.14	2.05	1.98
35	.01	7.42	5.27	4.40	3.91	3.59	3.37
	.05	4.12	3.27	2.88	2.64	2.49	2.37
	.10	2.86	2.46	2.25	2.11	2.02	1.95
40	.01	7.32	5.18	4.31	3.83	3.51	3.29
	.05	4.09	3.23	2.84	2.61	2.45	2.34
	.10	2.84	2.44	2.23	2.09	2.00	1.93
45	.01	7.23	5.11	4.25	3.77	3.46	3.23
	.05	4.06	3.21	2.81	2.58	2.42	2.31
	.10	2.82	2.43	2.21	2.08	1.98	1.91
50	.01	7.17	5.06	4.20	3.72	3.41	3.19
	.05	4.04	3.18	2.79	2.56	2.40	2.29
	.10	2.81	2.41	2.20	2.06	1.97	1.90
55	.01	7.12	5.01	4.16	3.68	3.37	3.15
	.05	4.02	3.17	2.77	2.54	2.38	2.27
	.10	2.80	2.40	2.19	2.05	1.96	1.89
60	.01	7.08	4.98	4.13	3.65	3.34	3.12
	.05	4.00	3.15	2.76	2.53	2.37	2.26
	.10	2.79	2.39	2.18	2.04	1.95	1.88
65	.01	7.04	4.95	4.10	3.62	3.31	3.09
	.05	3.99	3.14	2.75	2.51	2.36	2.24
	.10	2.79	2.39	2.17	2.03	1.94	1.87
70	.01	7.01	4.92	4.08	3.60	3.29	3.07
	.05	3.98	3.13	2.74	2.50	2.35	2.23
	.10	2.78	2.38	2.16	2.03	1.93	1.86
75	.01	6.99	4.90	4.06	3.58	3.27	3.05
	.05	3.97	3.12	2.73	2.49	2.34	2.22
	.10	2.77	2.38	2.16	2.02	1.93	1.86
80	.01	6.96	4.88	4.04	3.56	3.26	3.04
	.05	3.96	3.11	2.72	2.49	2.33	2.22
	.10	2.77	2.37	2.15	2.02	1.92	1.85

Denominator df	Significance level	Numerator degrees of freedom					
		1	2	3	4	5	6
85	.01	6.94	4.86	4.02	3.55	3.24	3.02
	.05	3.95	3.10	2.71	2.48	2.32	2.21
	.10	2.77	2.37	2.15	2.01	1.92	1.85
90	.01	6.93	4.85	4.01	3.54	3.23	3.01
	.05	3.95	3.10	2.71	2.47	2.32	2.20
	.10	2.76	2.36	2.15	2.01	1.91	1.84

r to z' Conversion

r	z'	r	z'	r	z'
0.00	0.0000	0.18	0.1820	0.36	0.3769
0.01	0.0100	0.19	0.1923	0.37	0.3884
0.02	0.0200	0.20	0.2027	0.38	0.4001
0.03	0.0300	0.21	0.2132	0.39	0.4118
0.04	0.0400	0.22	0.2237	0.40	0.4236
0.05	0.0500	0.23	0.2342	0.41	0.4356
0.06	0.0601	0.24	0.2448	0.42	0.4477
0.07	0.0701	0.25	0.2554	0.43	0.4599
0.08	0.0802	0.26	0.2661	0.44	0.4722
0.09	0.0902	0.27	0.2769	0.45	0.4847
0.10	0.1003	0.28	0.2877	0.46	0.4973
0.11	0.1104	0.29	0.2986	0.47	0.5101
0.12	0.1206	0.30	0.3095	0.48	0.5230
0.13	0.1307	0.31	0.3205	0.49	0.5361
0.14	0.1409	0.32	0.3316	0.50	0.5493
0.15	0.1511	0.33	0.3428	0.51	0.5627
0.16	0.1614	0.34	0.3541	0.52	0.5763
0.17	0.1717	0.35	0.3654	0.53	0.5901

(continued)

r	z'	r	z'	r	z'
0.54	0.6042	0.70	0.8673	0.86	1.2933
0.55	0.6184	0.71	0.8872	0.87	1.3331
0.56	0.6328	0.72	0.9076	0.88	1.3758
0.57	0.6475	0.73	0.9287	0.89	1.4219
0.58	0.6625	0.74	0.9505	0.90	1.4722
0.59	0.6777	0.75	0.9730	0.91	1.5275
0.60	0.6931	0.76	0.9962	0.92	1.5890
0.61	0.7089	0.77	1.0203	0.93	1.6584
0.62	0.7250	0.78	1.0454	0.94	1.7380
0.63	0.7414	0.79	1.0714	0.95	1.8318
0.64	0.7582	0.80	1.0986	0.96	1.9459
0.65	0.7753	0.81	1.1270	0.97	2.0923
0.66	0.7928	0.82	1.1568	0.98	2.2976
0.67	0.8107	0.83	1.1881	0.99	2.6467
0.68	0.8291	0.84	1.2212		
0.69	0.8480	0.85	1.2562		

Note: This table is included for basic statistical reference. Its use is not discussed in detail in this book.

Glossary

A

acquiescence Answering "yes" or "strongly agree" to every item in a survey or interview. Also called *yea-saying*.

alpha level The value, determined in advance, at which researchers decide whether the *p* value obtained from a sample statistic is low enough to reject the null hypothesis or too high, and thus retain the null hypothesis.

applied research Research whose goal is to find a solution to a particular real-world problem. *See also* basic research, translational research.

association claim A claim about two variables, in which the value (level) of one variable is said to vary systematically with the value of another variable.

attrition threat In a repeated-measures design or quasi-experiment, a threat to internal validity that occurs when a systematic type of participant drops out of a study before it ends.

autocorrelation In a longitudinal design, the correlation of one variable with itself, measured at two different times.

availability heuristic The tendency to rely predominantly on evidence that easily comes to mind rather than use all possible evidence in evaluating a conclusion.

B

basic research Research whose goal is to enhance the general body of knowledge, without regard for direct application to practical problems. *See also* applied research, translational research.

beneficence *See* principle of beneficence.

bias blind spot The tendency for people to think that compared to others, they are less likely to engage in biased reasoning.

biased sample A sample in which some members of the population of interest are systematically left out, and as a consequence, the results from the sample cannot generalize to the population of interest. Also called *unrepresentative sample*.

bimodal Having two modes, or most common scores.

bivariate correlation An association that involves exactly two variables. Also called *bivariate association*.

C

carryover effect A type of order effect, in which some form of contamination carries over from one condition to the next.

categorical variable A variable whose levels are categories (e.g., male/female). Also called *nominal variable*.

causal claim A claim arguing that a specific change in one variable is responsible for influencing the value of another variable.

ceiling effect An experimental design problem in which independent variable groups score almost the same on a dependent variable, such that all scores fall at the high end of their possible distribution. *See also* floor effect.

cell A condition in an experiment; in a simple experiment, it can represent the level of one independent variable; in a factorial design it represents one of the possible combinations of two independent variables.

census A set of observations that contains all members of the population of interest.

central tendency A value that the individual scores in a data set tend to center on. *See also* mean, median, mode.

claim The argument a journalist, researcher, or scientist is trying to make.

cluster sampling A probability sampling technique in which clusters of participants within the population of interest are selected at random, followed by data collection from all individuals in each cluster.

Cohen's *d* A measure of effect size indicating how far apart two group means are, in standard deviation units.

comparison group A group in an experiment whose level on the independent variable differs from those of the treatment group in some intended and meaningful way. Also called *comparison condition*.

conceptual definition A researcher's definition of a variable at the theoretical level. Also called *construct*. *See also* conceptual variable.

conceptual replication A replication study in which researchers examine the same research question (the same conceptual variables) but use different procedures for operationalizing the variables. *See also* direct replication, replication-plus-extension.

conceptual variable A variable of interest, stated at an abstract, or conversational, level. Also called *construct*. *See also* conceptual definition.

concurrent-measures design An experiment using a within-groups design in which participants are exposed to all the levels of an independent variable at roughly the same time, and a single attitudinal or behavioral preference is the dependent variable.

condition One of the levels of the independent variable in an experiment.

confederate An actor who is directed by the researcher to play a specific role in a research study.

confirmatory hypothesis testing The tendency to ask only the questions that will lead to the expected answer.

confound A general term for a potential alternative explanation for a research finding (a threat to internal validity).

constant An attribute that could potentially vary but that has only one level in the study in question.

construct A variable of interest, stated at an abstract level, usually defined as part of a formal statement of a psychological theory. *See also* conceptual variable.

construct validity An indication of how well a variable was measured or manipulated in a study.

content validity The extent to which a measure captures all parts of a defined construct.

control for Holding a potential third variable at a constant level while investigating the association between two other variables.

control group A level of an independent variable that is intended to represent "no treatment" or a neutral condition.

control variable A potential variable that an experimenter holds constant on purpose.

convenience sampling Choosing a sample based on those who are easiest to access and readily available; a biased sampling technique.

convergent validity An empirical test of the extent to which a measure is associated with other measures of a theoretically similar construct. *See also* discriminant validity.

correlate To occur or vary together (covary) systematically, as in the case of two variables. *See also* correlational study, covariance.

correlational study A study that includes two or more variables, in which all of the variables are measured; can support an association claim.

correlation coefficient *r* A single number, ranging from −1.0 to 1.0, that indicates the strength and direction of an association between two variables.

counterbalancing In an repeated-measures experiment, presenting the levels of the independent variable to participants in different sequences to control for order effects. *See also* full counterbalancing, partial counterbalancing.

covariance One of three criteria for establishing a causal claim, which states that the proposed causal variable must vary systematically with changes in the proposed outcome variable. *See also* internal validity, temporal precedence.

criterion validity An empirical form of measurement validity that establishes the extent to which a measure is correlated with a behavior or concrete outcome that it should be related to.

criterion variable The variable in a multiple-regression analysis that the researchers are most interested in understanding or predicting. Also called *dependent variable*.

critical value A value of a statistic that is associated with a desired alpha level.

Cronbach's alpha A correlation-based statistic that measures a scale's internal reliability. Also called *coefficient alpha*.

cross-lag correlation In a longitudinal design, a correlation between an earlier measure of one variable and a later measure of another variable.

cross-sectional correlation In a longitudinal design, a correlation between two variables that are measured at the same time.

cultural psychology A subdiscipline of psychology concerned with how cultural settings shape a person's thoughts, feelings, and behavior, and how these in turn shape cultural settings.

curvilinear association An association between two variables which is not a straight line; instead, as one variable increases, the level of the other variable increases and then decreases (or vice versa). Also called *curvilinear correlation. See also* positive association, negative association, zero association.

D

data (plural; singular **datum**) A set of observations representing the values of some variable, collected from one or more research studies.

data fabrication A form of research misconduct in which a researcher invents data that fit the hypothesis.

data falsification A form of research misconduct in which a researcher influences a study's results, perhaps by deleting observations from a data set or by influencing participants to act in the hypothesized way.

data matrix A grid presenting collected data.

debrief To inform participants afterward about a study's true nature, details, and hypotheses.

deception The withholding of some details of a study from participants (deception through omission) or the act of actively lying to them (deception through commission).

demand characteristic A threat to internal validity that occurs when some cue leads participants to guess a study's hypotheses or goals. Also called *experimental demand.*

dependent variable In an experiment, the variable that is measured. In a multiple-regression analysis, the single outcome, or criterion variable, the researchers are most interested in understanding or predicting. Also called *outcome variable. See also* independent variable.

descriptive statistics A set of statistics used to organize and summarize the properties of a set of data.

design confound A threat to internal validity in an experiment in which a second variable happens to vary systematically along with the independent variable and therefore is an alternative explanation for the results.

directionality problem A situation in which it is unclear which variable in an association came first.

direct replication A replication study in which researchers repeat the original study as closely as possible to see whether the original effect shows up in the newly collected data. Also called *exact replication. See also* conceptual replication, replication-plus-extension.

discriminant validity An empirical test of the extent to which a measure does not associate strongly with measures of other, theoretically different constructs. Also called *divergent validity. See also* convergent validity.

double-barreled question A type of question in a survey or poll that is problematic because it asks two questions in one, thereby weakening its construct validity.

double-blind placebo control study A study that uses a treatment group and a placebo group and in which neither the research staff nor the participants know who is in which group.

double-blind study A study in which neither the participants nor the researchers who evaluate them know who is in the treatment group and who is in the comparison group.

E

ecological validity The extent to which the tasks and manipulations of a study are similar to real-world contexts. Also called *mundane realism.*

effect size The magnitude of a relationship between two or more variables.

empirical journal article A scholarly article that reports for the first time the results of a research study.

empiricism The use of verifiable evidence as the basis for conclusions; collecting data systematically and using it to develop, support, or challenge a theory. Also called *empirical method* or *empirical research.*

evidence-based treatment A psychotherapy technique whose effectiveness has been supported by empirical research.

experiment A study in which one variable is manipulated and the other is measured.

experimental realism The extent to which a laboratory experiment is designed so that participants experience authentic emotions, motivations, and behaviors.

external validity An indication of how well the results of a study generalize to, or represent, individuals or contexts besides those in the study itself. *See also* generalization.

F

face validity The extent to which a measure is subjectively considered a plausible operationalization of the conceptual variable in question.

factorial design A study in which there are two or more independent variables, or factors.

faking bad Giving answers on a survey (or other self-report measure) that make one look worse than one really is.

faking good *See* socially desirable responding.

falsifiability A feature of a scientific theory, in which it is possible to collect data that will prove the theory wrong.

fence sitting Playing it safe by answering in the middle of the scale for every question in a survey or interview.

field setting A real-world setting for a research study.

file drawer problem The idea that reviews and meta-analyses of published literature might overestimate the support for a theory, because studies finding null effects are less likely to be published than studies finding significant results, and are thus less likely to be included in such reviews.

floor effect An experimental design problem in which independent variable groups score almost the same on a dependent variable, such that all scores fall at the low end of their possible distribution. *See also* ceiling effect.

forced-choice format A survey question format in which respondents give their opinion by picking the best of two or more options.

frequency claim A claim that describes a particular rate or degree of a single variable.

frequency distribution A table showing how many of the cases in a batch of data scored each possible value, or range of values, on the variable.

frequency histogram A graph showing how many of the cases in a batch of data scored each possible value or range of values on the variable.

F test A statistical test based on analysis of variance that determines degree of difference among two or more group means.

full counterbalancing A method of counterbalancing in which all possible condition orders are represented. *See also* counterbalancing, partial counterbalancing.

G

generalizability The extent to which the subjects in a study represent the populations they are intended to represent; how well the settings in a study represent other settings or contexts.

generalization mode The intent of researchers to generalize the findings from the samples and procedures in their study to other populations or contexts. *See also* theory-testing mode.

H

history threat A threat to internal validity that occurs when it is unclear whether a change in the treatment group is caused by the treatment or by a historical factor or event that affects everyone or almost everyone in the group.

hypothesis A statement of the specific relationship between a study's variables that the researcher expects to observe if a theory is accurate. Also called *prediction*.

I

independent-groups design An experimental design in which different groups of participants are exposed to different levels of the independent variable, such that each participant experiences only one level of the independent variable. Also called *between-subjects design* or *between-groups design*.

independent variable A variable that is manipulated in an experiment. In a multiple-regression analysis, a predictor variable used to explain variance in the criterion variable. *See also* dependent variable.

inferential statistics A set of techniques that uses the laws of chance and probability to help researchers make decisions about what their data mean and what inferences they can make from them.

informed consent The right of research participants to learn about a research project, know its risks and benefits, and decide whether to participate.

institutional review board (IRB) A committee responsible for ensuring that research using human participants is conducted ethically.

instrumentation threat A threat to internal validity that occurs when a measuring instrument changes over time from having been used before. Also called *instrument decay*.

interaction effect A result from a factorial design, in which the difference in the levels of one independent variable changes, depending on the level of the other independent variable; a difference in differences. Also called *interaction*.

internal reliability In a measure that contains several items, the consistency in a pattern of answers, no matter how a question is phrased. Also called *internal consistency*.

internal validity One of three criteria for establishing a causal claim; the ability to rule out alternative explanations for a causal relationship between two variables. *See also* covariance, temporal precedence.

interrater reliability The degree to which two or more coders or observers give consistent ratings of a set of targets.

interrupted time-series design A quasi-experiment in which participants are measured repeatedly on a dependent variable before, during, and after the "interruption" caused by some event.

interval scale A quantitative measurement scale that has no "true zero," and in which the numerals represent equal intervals (distances) between levels (e.g., temperature in degrees). *See also* ordinal scale, ratio scale.

J

journal A monthly or quarterly periodical containing peer-reviewed articles on a specific academic discipline or subdiscipline, written for a scholarly audience.

journalism News and commentary published or broadcast in the popular media and produced for a general audience.

justice *See* principle of justice.

K

known-groups paradigm A method for establishing criterion validity, in which a researcher tests two or more groups, who are known to differ on the variable of interest, to ensure that they score differently on a measure of that variable.

L

Latin square A formal system of partial counterbalancing that ensures that each condition in a within-groups design appears in each position at least once.

leading question A type of question in a survey or poll that is problematic because its wording encourages only one response, thereby weakening its construct validity.

level One of the possible variations, or values, of a variable.

Likert scale A survey question format; a rating scale containing multiple response options that are anchored by the terms *strongly agree, agree, neither agree nor disagree, disagree*, and *strongly disagree*. A scale that does not follow this format exactly is called a *Likert-type scale*.

longitudinal design A study in which the same variables are measured in the same people at different points in time.

M

main effect In a factorial design, the overall effect of one independent variable on the dependent variable, averaging over the levels of the other independent variable.

manipulated variable A variable in an experiment that a researcher controls, such as by assigning participants to its different levels (values). *See also* measured variable.

manipulation check In an experiment, an extra dependent variable researchers can include to determine how well an experimental manipulation worked.

marginal means In a factorial design, the arithmetic means for each level of an independent variable, averaging over the levels of another independent variable.

margin of error estimate A statistic, based in part on sample size for a poll, indicating the probable true value in the population.

masked design A study design in which the observers are unaware of the experimental conditions to which participants have been assigned. Also called *blind design*.

matched groups An experimental design technique in which participants who are similar on some measured variable are grouped into sets; the members of each matched set are then randomly assigned to different experimental conditions. Also called *matching*.

maturation threat A threat to internal validity that occurs when an observed change in an experimental group could have emerged more or less spontaneously over time.

mean An arithmethic average; a measure of central tendency computed from the sum of all the scores in a set of data, divided by the total number of scores.

measured variable A variable in an experiment whose levels (values) are observed and recorded. *See also* manipulated variable.

measurement error The degree to which the recorded measure for a participant on some variable differs from the true value of the variable for that participant. Measurement errors may be random, if over a sample they both inflate or deflate true scores, or they may be systematic, in which case they may result in biased measurement.

median A measure of central tendency that is the value at the middlemost score of a distribution of scores, dividing the frequency distribution into halves.

mediator A variable that helps explain the relationship between two other variables. Also called *mediating variable*.

meta-analysis A way of mathematically averaging the effect sizes of all the studies that have tested the same variables to see what conclusion that whole body of evidence supports.

mode A measure of central tendency that is the most common score in a set of data.

moderator A variable that, depending on its level, changes the relationship between two other variables.

multimodal Having two or more modes, or most common scores.

multiple-baseline design A small-*N* design in which researchers stagger their introduction of an intervention across a variety of contexts, times, or situations.

multiple regression A statistical technique that computes the relationship between a predictor variable and a criterion variable, controlling for other predictor variables. Also called *multivariate regression*.

multistage sampling A probability sampling technique involving at least two stages: a random sample of clusters followed by a random sample of people within the selected clusters.

multivariate design A study designed to test an association involving more than two measured variables.

N

negative association An association in which high levels of one variable go with low levels of the other variable, and vice versa. Also called *inverse association*, *negative correlation*. *See also* curvilinear association, positive association, zero association.

negatively worded question A question in a survey or poll that contains negatively phrased statements, making its wording complicated or confusing and potentially weakening its construct validity.

noise The unsystematic variability among the members of a group in an experiment. Also called *error variance, unsystematic variance*.

nonequivalent control group design An independent-groups quasi-experiment that has at least one treatment group and one comparison group, but participants have not been randomly assigned to the two groups.

nonequivalent control group interrupted time-series design A quasi-experiment with two or more groups in which participants have not been randomly assigned to groups; and participants are measured repeatedly on a dependent variable before, during, and after the "interruption" caused by some event, and the presence or timing of the interrupting event differs among the groups.

nonequivalent control group pretest/posttest design An independent-groups quasi-experiment that has at least one treatment group and one comparison group, in which participants have not been randomly assigned to the two groups, and

in which at least one pretest and one posttest are administered.

null effect A finding that an independent variable did not make a difference in the dependent variable; there is no significant covariance between the two. Also called *null result*.

null hypothesis In a common form of statistical hypothesis testing, the assumption that there is no difference, no relationship, or no effect in a population.

null hypothesis testing A common form of statistical hypothesis testing in which researchers calculate the probability of obtaining their result if the null hypothesis is true; they then decide whether to reject or retain the null hypothesis based on their calculations.

O

observational measure A method of measuring a variable by recording observable behaviors or physical traces of behaviors. Also called *behavioral measure*.

observational research The process of watching people or animals and systematically recording how they behave or what they are doing.

observer bias A bias that occurs when observers' expectations influence their interpretation of the participants' behaviors or the outcome of the study.

observer effect A change in behavior of study participants in the direction of an observer's expectation. Also called *expectancy effect*.

one-group, pretest/posttest design An experiment in which a researcher recruits one group of participants; measures them on a pretest; exposes them to a treatment, intervention, or change; and then measures them on a posttest.

open-ended question A survey question format that allows respondents to answer any way they like.

operational definition The specific way in which a concept of interest is measured or manipulated as a variable in a study. Also called *operationalization* or *operational variable*.

operational variable *See* operational definition.

operationalize To turn a conceptual definition of a variable into a specific measured variable or manipulated variable in order to conduct a research study.

order effect In a within-groups design, a threat to internal validity in which exposure to one condition changes participants' responses to a later condition. *See also* carryover effect, practice effect, fatigue effect, testing threat.

ordinal scale A quantitative measurement scale whose levels represent a ranked order, in which it is unclear whether the distances between levels are equal (e.g., a 5-star rating scale). *See also* interval scale, ratio scale.

outlier A score that stands out as either much higher or much lower than most of the other scores in a sample.

oversampling A form of probability sampling; a variation of stratified random sampling in which the researcher intentionally overrepresents one or more groups.

P

parsimony The degree to which a theory provides the simplest explanation of some phenomenon. In the context of investigating a claim, the simplest explanation of a pattern of data; the best explanation that requires making the fewest exceptions or qualifications.

partial counterbalancing A method of counterbalancing in which some, but not all, of the possible condition orders are represented. *See also* counterbalancing, full counterbalancing.

participant variable A variable such as age, gender, or ethnicity whose levels are selected (i.e., measured), not manipulated.

physiological measure A method of measuring a variable by recording biological data.

pilot study A study completed before (or sometimes after) the study of primary interest, usually to test the effectiveness or characteristics of the manipulations.

placebo effect A response or effect that occurs when people receiving an experimental treatment experience a change only because they believe they are receiving a valid treatment.

placebo group A control group that is exposed to an inert treatment (e.g., a sugar pill). Also called *placebo control group*.

plagiarism Representing the ideas or words of others as one's own; a form of research misconduct.

poll A method of posing questions to people on the telephone, in personal interviews, on written questionnaires, or via the Internet. Also called *survey*.

population A larger group from which a sample is drawn; the group to which a study's conclusions are intended to be applied. Also called *population of interest*.

positive association An association in which high levels of one variable go with high levels of the other variable, and low levels of one variable go with low levels of the other variable. Also called *positive correlation. See also* curvilinear association, negative association, zero association.

posttest-only design An experiment using an independent-groups design in which participants are tested on the dependent variable only once. Also called *equivalent groups, posttest-only design*.

power The likelihood that a study will show a statistically significant result when some effect is truly present in the population; the probability of not making a Type II error.

practice effect A type of order effect in which people's performance improves over time because they become practiced at the dependent measure (not because of the manipulation or treatment). *See also* fatigue effect, order effect, testing threat.

predictor variable A variable in multiple-regression analysis that is used to explain variance in the criterion variable. Also called *independent variable*.

present/present bias The tendency to rely only on evidence that is present (e.g., instances in which both a treatment and a desired outcome are present) and ignore evidence that is absent (e.g., instances in which a treatment is absent or the desired outcome is absent) when evaluating the support for a conclusion.

pretest/posttest design An experiment using an independent-groups design in which participants are tested on the key dependent variable twice: once before and once after exposure to the independent variable.

principle of beneficence An ethical principle from the Belmont Report stating that researchers must take precautions to protect participants from harm and to promote their well-being. *See also* principle of justice, principle of respect for persons.

principle of justice An ethical principle from the Belmont Report calling for a fair balance between the kinds of people who participate in research and the kinds of people who benefit from it. *See also* principle of beneficence, principle of respect for persons.

principle of respect for persons An ethical principle from the Belmont Report stating that research participants should be treated as autonomous agents and that certain groups deserve special protection. *See also* principle of beneficence, principle of justice.

probabilistic Describing the empirical method, stating that science is intended to explain a certain proportion (but not necessarily all) of the possible cases.

probability sampling The process of drawing a sample from a population of interest in such a way that each member of the population has an equal chance of being included in the sample, usually via random selection. Also called *random sampling*.

purposive sampling A biased sampling technique in which only certain kinds of people are included in a sample.

Q

quantitative variable A variable whose values can be recorded as meaningful numbers.

quasi-experiment A study that is similar to an experiment except that the researchers do not have full experimental control (e.g., they may not be able to randomly assign participants to the independent variable conditions).

quota sampling A biased sampling technique in which a researcher identifies subsets of the population of interest, sets a target number for each category in the sample, and nonrandomly selects individuals within each category until the quotas are filled.

R

r *See* correlation coefficient.

random assignment The use of a random method (e.g., flipping a coin) to assign participants into different experimental groups.

ratio scale A quantitative scale of measurement in which the numerals have equal intervals and the value of zero truly means "nothing." *See also* interval scale, ordinal scale.

reactivity A change in behavior of study participants (such as acting less spontaneously) because they are aware they are being watched.

regression threat A threat to internal validity related to regression to the mean, a phenomenon in which any extreme finding is likely to be closer to its own typical, or mean, level the next time it is measured (with or without the experimental treatment or intervention).

reliability The consistency of the results of a measure.

repeated-measures design An experiment using a within-groups design in which participants respond to a dependent variable more than once, after exposure to each level of the independent variable.

replicable Pertaining to a study whose results have been obtained again when the study was repeated.

replication-plus-extension A replication study in which researchers replicate their original study but add variables or conditions that test additional questions. *See also* conceptual replication, direct replication.

representative sample A sample in which all members of the population of interest are equally likely to be included (usually through some random method), and therefore the results can generalize to the population of interest. Also called *unbiased sample*.

respect for persons *See* principle of respect for persons.

response set A shortcut respondents may use to answer items in a long survey, rather than responding to the content of each item. Also called *nondifferentiation*.

restriction of range A situation involving a bivariate correlation, in which there is not a full range of possible scores on one of the variables in the association, so the relationship from the sample underestimates the true correlation.

reversal design A small-*N* design in which a researcher observes a problem behavior both before and during treatment, and then discontinues the treatment for a while to see if the problem behavior returns.

review journal article An article summarizing all the studies that have been published in one research area.

S

sample The group of people, animals, or cases used in a study; a subset of the population of interest.

sampling distribution A theoretical prediction about the kinds of statistical outcomes likely to be obtained if a study is run many times and the null hypothesis is true.

scatterplot A graphical representation of an association, in which each dot represents one participant in the study measured on two variables.

scientific literature A series of related studies, conducted by various researchers, that have tested similar variables. Also called *literature*.

selection effect A threat to internal validity that occurs in an independent-groups design when the kinds of participants at one level of the independent variable are systematically different from those at the other level.

selection-attrition threat A threat to internal validity in which members are likely to drop out of either the treatment group or the comparison group, not both.

selection-history threat A threat to internal validity in which a historical or seasonal event systematically affects only the subjects in the treatment group or only those in the comparison group, not both.

self-report measure A method of measuring a variable in which people answer questions about themselves in a questionnaire or interview.

self-selection A form of sampling bias that occurs when a sample contains only people who volunteer to participate.

semantic differential format A response scale whose numbers are anchored with contrasting adjectives.

simple random sampling The most basic form of probability sampling, in which the sample is chosen completely at random from the population of interest (e.g., drawing names out of a hat).

single-N design A study in which researchers gather information from only one animal or one person.

situation noise Unrelated events or distractions in the external environment that create unsystematic variability within groups in an experiment.

slope direction The upward, downward, or neutral slope of the cluster of data points in a scatterplot.

small-N design A study in which researchers gather information from just a few cases.

snowball sampling A variation on purposive sampling, a biased sampling technique in which participants are asked to recommend acquaintances for the study.

socially desirable responding Giving answers on a survey (or other self-report measure) that make one look better than one really is. Also called *faking good*.

spurious association A bivariate association that is attributable only to systematic mean differences on subgroups within the sample; the original association is not present within the subgroups.

stable-baseline design A small-N design in which a researcher observes behavior for an extended baseline period before beginning a treatment or other intervention; if behavior during the baseline is stable, the researcher is more certain of the treatment's effectiveness.

standard deviation A computation that captures how far, on average, each score in a data set is from the mean.

statistical hypothesis testing The steps taken by researchers when they use inferential statistics.

statistical significance A conclusion that a result from a sample (such as an association or a difference between groups) is so extreme that the sample is unlikely to have come from a population in which there is no association or no difference.

statistical validity The extent to which statistical conclusions derived from a study are accurate and reasonable. Also called *statistical conclusion validity*.

stemplot A graphical representation of the values obtained on some variable in a sample of data. Also called *stem-and-leaf plot*.

stratified random sampling A form of probability sampling; a random sampling technique in which the researcher identifies particular demographic categories of interest and then randomly selects individuals within each category.

strength A description of an association indicating how closely the data points in a scatterplot cluster along a line of best fit drawn through them.

survey A method of posing questions to people on the telephone, in personal interviews, on written questionnaires, or via the Internet. Also called *poll*.

systematic sampling A probability sampling technique in which the researcher counts off members of a population to achieve a sample, using a randomly chosen interval (e.g., every nth person, where n is a randomly selected number).

systematic variability In an experiment, the levels of a variable coinciding in some predictable way with experimental group membership, creating a potential confound. *See also* unsystematic variability.

T

temporal precedence One of three criteria for establishing a causal claim, stating that the proposed causal variable comes first in time, before the proposed outcome variable. *See also* covariance, internal validity.

testing threat In a repeated-measures experiment or quasi-experiment, a kind of order effect in which scores change over time just because participants have taken the test more than once; includes practice effects and fatigue effects.

test-retest reliability The consistency in results every time a measure is used.

theory A statement or set of statements that describes general principles about how variables relate to one another.

theory-testing mode A researcher's intent for a study, testing association claims or causal claims to investigate support for a theory. *See also* generalization mode.

third-variable problem A situation in which a plausible alternative explanation exists for the association between two variables. *See also* internal validity.

translational research Research that uses knowledge derived from basic research to develop and test solutions to real-world problems. *See also* applied research, basic research.

treatment group The participants in an experiment who are exposed to the level of the independent variable that involves a medication, therapy, or intervention.

t test A statistical test used to evaluate the size and significance of the difference between two means.

Type I error A "false positive" result from a statistical inference process, in which researchers conclude that there is an effect in a population when there really is none.

Type II error A "miss" in the statistical inference process, in which researchers conclude that there is no effect in a population when there really is one.

U

unobtrusive observation An observation in a study made indirectly, through physical traces of behavior, or made by someone who is hidden or is posing as a bystander.

unsystematic variability In an experiment, when levels of a variable fluctuate independently of experimental group membership, contributing to variability within groups. *See also* systematic variability.

V

validity The appropriateness of a conclusion or decision. *See also* construct validity, external validity, internal validity, statistical validity.

variable An attribute that varies, having at least two levels, or values. *See also* dependent variable, independent variable, manipulated variable, measured variable.

variance A computation that quantifies how spread out the scores of a sample are around their mean; it is the square of the standard deviation.

W

weight of the evidence A conclusion drawn from reviewing scientific literature and considering the proportion of studies that is consistent with a theory.

within-groups design An experimental design in which each participant is presented with all levels of the independent variable. Also called *within-subjects design*.

Z

zero association A lack of systematic association between two variables. Also called *zero correlation*. *See also* curvilinear association, positive association, negative association.

z score A computation that describes how far an individual score is above or below the mean, in standard deviation units. Also called *standardized score*.

Answers to End-of-Chapter Questions

Review Questions

Chapter 1
1. b
2. a
3. d
4. b
5. d

Chapter 2
1. a
2. c
3. b
4. b
5. b
6. a

Chapter 3
1. c
2. c
3. b
4. a
5. a
6. c
7. a

Chapter 4
1. d
2. c
3. d
4. a
5. b
6. a
7. c

Chapter 5
1. a. Quantitative, ratio
   b. Quantitative, ratio
   c. Quantitative, ordinal
   d. Categorical
   e. Categorical
   f. Quantitative, interval
2. b
3. a. Test-retest
   b. Interrater reliability
   c. Internal reliability
4. a. Criterion validity
   b. Convergent and discriminant validity
   c. Face validity
   d. Content validity

Chapter 6
1. c
2. d
3. d
4. b
5. c
6. a

Chapter 7
1. d
2. c
3. c
4. a

Chapter 8
1. b
2. c
3. d
4. d
5. a

Chapter 9
1. a
2. a
3. b
4. c
5. c
6. b
7. b
8. a

Chapter 10
1. b
2. d
3. a
4. b
5. b

Chapter 11
1. a
2. d
3. b

4. a
5. a
6. d

Chapter 12
1. c
2. c
3. d
4. a
5. a
6. b

Chapter 13
1. a
2. c
3. b
4. a
5. a
6. b
7. c

Chapter 14
1. a
2. c
3. a
4. a
5. c
6. c

Guidelines for Selected Learning Actively Exercises

Chapter 1
Answers will vary.

Chapter 2
1. Example A.

   a. How hard is it to read books in regular print, compared to e-books? (Regular books are the comparison group.)

   b.

	Read e-books (treatment)	Read regular books (no treatment)
Feel pain in eyes (outcome present)		
No pain in eyes (outcome absent)		

c. Is it possible that the books I read in e-book format are more difficult than those I read as regular printed books? Could it be that the font I use for reading e-books is smaller than the standard font used in printed books? Is it possible that the lighting in the room when I read e-books is different from the lighting when I read regular books?

Example C.
a. Are older teachers just as good with students? (Older teachers are the comparison group.)
b.

	Younger teachers ("treatment" group)	Older teachers (comparison group)
Good rapport with students (outcome present)		
Poor rapport with students (outcome absent)		

c. What else might be confounded with young teacher age that would account for rapport with kids? Perhaps younger teachers are more common in a school, and it's familiarity, not their age. Perhaps younger teachers are more likely to teach early grades, and early-grade children are better behaved, anyway.

2. a. This statement reflects intuitive reasoning, specifically the availability heuristic. The speaker bases the conclusion on evidence that comes easily to mind (what he or she sees the cousin eating). The speaker also shows some overconfidence ("I'm positive...").

b. The conclusion your friend is talking about seems to be supported by empirical evidence, so this is a good source of evidence. You might also want to ask whether the newspaper source reported the research findings accurately.

c. This statement reflects intuitive reasoning, specifically focusing on only some of the evidence: While watching the debate, the speaker was more motivated to notice the preferred candidate's successes and to ignore the candidate's lapses.

d. This speaker is relying on authority; in this case, information from marketing and advertising. She should ask: How good is the science on which this advertisement's conclusions are based, and is the ad reporting the science accurately?

e. This statement reflects intuitive reasoning, namely the availability heuristic—dogs need to be outdoors, so they are more visible than cats, many of which are only indoors. Just because something is visible doesn't mean it is necessarily more prevalent.

f. This statement reflects intuitive reasoning, specifically the present-present bias. (It's much easier to notice the students who are drinking, and much more difficult to factor in the many students on campus who are not drinking.)

g. This statement reflects faulty intuition and the availability heuristic. Because airplane crashes get so much attention in the media, the speaker erroneously concludes that they are frequent. (Statistically, driving a car is much more dangerous than flying.)

h. This speaker is basing her conclusions on her own experience. Experience lacks a comparison group. (What would have happened if the speaker didn't declutter the closet?) Experience may have confounds. (Maybe decluttering the closet coincided with other positive changes, such as eating better or getting more sleep.)

i. The Match.com advertisement is exploiting people's intuitive reasoning. By failing to show people who met on Match.com but who are not happily married, they may portray a distorted image of how successful the dating site is.

3. Answers will vary.
4. Answers will vary.

Chapter 3

1.

Variable in context	Conceptual level (boldfaced in the description)	Levels of this variable	Measured or manipulated	Operational definition
A questionnaire study asks for various demographic information, including participant's **gender**.	Participant's gender	Male, female	Measured	Asking participants to circle "male" or "female" on a form
A questionnaire study asks about **self-esteem**, measured on a 10-item Rosenberg self-esteem scale.	Self-esteem	Self-esteem from low to high, represented by a numerical score	Measured	Score on 10-item Rosenberg self-esteem scale
A study of readability gives people a passage of text. The passage to be read is printed in one of three **colors** (black, red, or blue).	Color of text	Black, red, blue text	Manipulated	Printed color of the text of a passage
A study of **school achievement** requests each participant to report his or her SAT score, as a measure of college readiness.	School achievement	SAT score, from 600 to 2400	Measured	SAT score
A researcher studying self-control and **blood glucose levels** asks participants to come to an experiment at 1:00 pm. Some of them are told not to eat anything before the experiment; others are told to eat lunch before arriving.	Blood glucose levels	High glucose (after lunch), low glucose (fasting)	Manipulated	Coming to the experiment after lunch versus fasting
A professor who wants to know more about **study habits** among his students asks students to report the number of minutes they studied for the midterm exam.	Amount of studying	Time in minutes	Measured	Students' reports of number of minutes they studied for the midterm
In a study on **self-esteem**'s association with self-control, the researchers give a group of students a self-esteem inventory. Then they invite participants who score in the top 10% and the bottom 10% of the self-esteem scale to participate in the next step.	Self-esteem	High and low	Measured	Students whose scores are at the top 10% and bottom 10% of a self-esteem inventory

2. a. Causal.
   Variables: chewing gum (or not), level of focus.
   - You might ask: How well did they measure level of focus? (Construct validity)
   - How well did they manipulate chewing gum or not? (Construct validity)
   - Did they conduct an experiment, randomly assigning people to chew gum or not? (Internal validity)
   - How did they get their sample? (External validity)
   - How strong is the relationship between chewing gum and focus? Is it statistically significant? (Statistical validity)

   b. Association.
   Variables: body weight (obese or not), sensitivity to stress.
   - How accurately did they measure body weight? How accurately did they measure sensitivity to stress? (Construct validity)
   - How strong is the relationship between obesity and sensitivity to stress? (Statistical validity)
   - How did they get their sample? Is the sample representative? (External validity)

   c. Frequency.
   Variable: report of doing Zumba.
   - How well did they measure people's exercise behaviors? (Construct validity)
   - How did they get their sample? Is the sample representative of the readers of this magazine? (External validity)

3. You would randomly assign a sample of people to either chew gum or not, then have everyone participate in a task that requires careful focus. The two variables would be gum chewing (or not) and degree of focus.

The results may be graphed as follows:

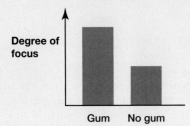

The experiment would fulfill covariance if the results turned out as depicted in the graph, because the causal variable (gum chewing) is covarying with the outcome (degree of focus). There is temporal precedence because gum chewing began before task focus was measured. There would be internal validity as long as participants were randomly assigned and all other aspects were kept the same (the two groups performed the same task under the same conditions).

Chapter 4

1. The IRB members might consider that publicly observable behavior is usually exempt from informed consent requirements, but children are considered a "vulnerable population." Children may not be able to give informed consent, and they may not monitor their public behavior to the same extent as adults do. Depending on the case, the IRB may require the researcher to request informed consent from parents in the play area before proceeding. In addition, the researcher has not yet explained what the purpose of the study will be. The IRB, in its evaluation of the research proposal, should consider the benefits of the knowledge to be gained from the study.
2. Normally, researchers using anonymous, low-risk questionnaires may be exempted from informed consent procedures, but a review board might be concerned about the risk of coercion in this situation. The IRB might wonder if students in the professor's class will feel coerced into completing the questionnaire, even if they do not wish to. (However, if there is truly no way to link responses back to the participants, then a student who does not wish to participate

might be instructed to turn in a blank questionnaire.) In a small class, the students' handwriting might be recognized by the professor, so the surveys may not be truly anonymous. The IRB would probably evaluate this proposal more negatively if the questions on the survey were about personal values or private behaviors, rather than study habits.
3. You might have listed some of the following costs and benefits: Deception might harm participants by making them feel tricked or embarrassed. Such negative feelings may make participants less likely to participate in future research and may make them less willing to accept or read research findings in the future. On the one hand, people might become aware of negative information about themselves, such as what kinds of actions they will perform—knowledge that may not be welcome or comfortable (e.g., in the Milgram studies, delivering shocks to the "learner"). On the other hand, deceived research participants may gain some valuable self-knowledge from their participation, thereby feeling they are contributing to the enterprise of science.

    Deception studies can be valuable to society because, as noted in the chapter, the results of such studies may provide important lessons about obedience, helping behavior, subliminal persuasion, or other research topics. In addition, human welfare might be improved when scientists or practitioners apply the knowledge from a deception study. However, when members of society read or hear about deceptive research studies, they may begin to mistrust scientists. They may also become more suspicious of others around them. (Text from this question and answer is based on an analysis by Dunn, 2009.)
4. Answers will vary.
5. Answers will vary.

Chapter 5

1. a. Coders will need to be tested on their inter-rater reliability. A scatterplot should have "Coder 1" on the x-axis and "Coder 2" on the y-axis; there would be a tight, upward-sloping cloud of points to show strong interrater reliability.

Test-retest reliability may also be relevant. If you assume children's video game playing is stable over time, you should observe a positive relationship on a scatterplot, or a strong, positive correlation coefficient. The labels on the scatterplot should be "Gaming level at first recording" on one axis and "Gaming level at second recording" on the other axis.

b. Since this scale has seven items that are likely to be averaged together, it will be important to establish internal reliability, to make sure all seven items are answered consistently by most people. In addition, since risk for panic disorder is something that should be fairly stable over time, you should assess test-retest reliability. A scatterplot should have "Time 1 test" on the x-axis and "Time 2 test" on the y-axis. There would be a tight, upward-sloping cloud of points to show strong interrater reliability.

c. Since observers are coding the eyeblink response, coders will need to be tested on their interrater reliability. A scatterplot should have "Coder 1" on the x-axis and "Coder 2" on the y-axis; there would be a tight, upward-sloping cloud of points to show strong interrater reliability.

d. If the restaurant owner wants to use the card to rate the overall quality of his restaurant, he might be interested in combining these items into a single scale. If he does this, then internal reliability is the most relevant. However, if he plans to treat the four items as separate aspects of quality, then he will not combine them, and internal reliability will not be relevant.

e. Interrater (interteacher) reliability is relevant here. So is test-retest reliability, assuming that shyness is stable over time.

2. To measure criterion validity, you would see whether the teacher ratings correlated with some behavioral measure of classroom shyness. For example, you might see if the shyness ratings correlated (negatively) with the number of times the student was seen to raise his hand in a classroom setting during the day.

   For convergent validity, you would want to show that the classroom shyness rating is correlated with other ratings of shyness, perhaps parent ratings of shyness in the children, or therapist ratings of shyness. To show convergent and discriminant validity, the ratings of shyness should be more strongly correlated with a measure of

shyness than they are with a measure of autism or basic anxiety, for example.

Chapter 6

1. Answers will vary.
2. Answers will vary.
3. Your decisions will depend on where you are planning to code, but the one thing to attend carefully to is interrater reliability. To establish interrater reliability, you will need to have two coders each rate each person, yielding two ratings per observation. The association between the two coders' ratings is the interrater reliability.

Chapter 7

1. Many people are frustrated that opinion pollsters never call them, and they may even volunteer to contribute polling data for opinion polls during an election. Of course, the polling organizations cannot accept volunteer respondents. If they did, their polls would have poor external validity—or at least, they would be able to generalize only to other people who voluntarily call pollsters to share their opinions.

   One reason this woman has not been called by pollsters is that each poll needs to sample only about 1,000 to 2,000 voters. With millions of voters in the population, the chance of being selected by a poll is extremely small.

2. a. The sample is the 200 titles you select, and the population is the entire set of 13,000 titles.

   b. To collect a random sample, use the database of all 13,000 titles. In that list, assign each book a random number, use the computer to sort the books into a list with the smallest numbers on top, and select the first 200 books on the sorted list. For each of the 200 books in the sample, you would record the price and take the average. That sample average would be a good estimate of the average price of the full book population in the store.

   c. To collect a stratified random sample, you would first choose some categories, or strata, that might be important to you. For example, you might stratify the sample into textbooks and trade books. If the population includes 60% textbooks and 40% trade books, you could select a random sample of 120 textbooks and 80 trade books (so your sample is proportional to the true strata). Alternatively, you could categorize according to whether the books are paperback or hardback, fiction or nonfiction, or you might even stratify by topic (literature, foreign language, self-help, etc.). After identifying the categories, you would select at random the number of books you need in each stratum, according to the proportion they represent in the full list of titles.

d. A convenience sample would involve recording the price of the first 200 books you can pick up in the store, simply walking around and choosing books. (This would bias your sample toward books on the most reachable shelves.) Or you could stand by the cash register and record the price of the next 200 books sold at that store. (This convenience sample might bias your sample to include mainly the cheaper books, or mainly the sale books, or mainly the popular books.)

e. To conduct a systematic random sample, you would select two random numbers (say, 15 and 33). You would list the 13,000 books in the store, start with the 15th book, and then count off, selecting every 33rd book in the list until you get 200 books. Record the prices and take the average of the 200 books in the sample.

f. To conduct a cluster sample, you could make a list of all the display shelves in the store (say there are 20 bookshelves). You could select four of the 20 bookshelves at random and then record the price of all the books on each of the four selected shelves. Alternatively, you could randomly sample 50 books from each of the four selected shelves.

g. To conduct a quota sample, you would first choose some categories that might be important to you. For example, you might decide to study textbooks and trade books. If the population includes 60% textbooks and 40% trade books, you would decide to study 120 textbooks and 80 trade books. However, you would choose these books nonrandomly—perhaps by choosing the first 120 textbooks and the first 80 trade books you encounter.

Chapter 8

1. a. Measured variables: degree of stomach pain in childhood (present or absent) and level of anxiety disorders as adults. This should be plotted with a bar graph, since stomach pain was a categorical, yes or no variable. The x-axis should have "Stomach pain in childhood" or "No stomach pain" and the y-axis should have "Level of anxiety disorders in adulthood." The bar for "Stomach pain in childhood" should be higher.

Construct validity: How accurately can they measure the degree of stomach pain in childhood? (The measures are probably good because they were medically diagnosed.) How well did they measure anxiety disorders as adults? Are self-reports appropriate here?

Statistical validity: As for effect size, the rates of 51% and 20% are rather far apart, so the effect size seems large. You would want to know if this difference is statistically significant, however.

External validity: This was probably a purposive sample; they started by identifying kids who had stomach pain. Because purposive sampling is not a representative sampling technique, you do not know if the results will generalize to a population.

Internal validity: Can you make the claim that "Stomach pain in childhood causes anxiety disorders later on?" Clearly there is covariance: Stomach pain goes with anxiety. There is also temporal precedence: The stomach pain is measured before the anxiety disorder. However, there may be third variables that provide alternative explanations. For example, perhaps family stress is associated with both stomach pain and anxiety disorders.

b. Measured variables: diagnosis of ADHD and likelihood of bullying. If ADHD is considered categorical (ADHD diagnosis or not), it could be plotted as a bar graph, but if it is considered quantitative (level of ADHD), then a scatterplot is appropriate.

To interrogate construct validity, you could ask how well the researchers measured each of the two variables in this association: level of ADHD and level of bullying. You could first ask how the ADHD diagnosis was made. If a professional psychologist diagnosed each child, you could feel more confident in the construct validity of this measure. You would then ask about the measure of bullying. How well was this variable measured? The article mentions only that the researchers asked the children about bullying. You might wonder how valid a child's report of his or her own bullying behavior would be. Would a child's self-ratings correlate with teachers' ratings?

For statistical validity, you could ask about effect size first. The article reports that children with ADHD are "four times more likely to bully" than non-ADHD children, which seems like a strong effect size. You might ask, as well, about subgroups—perhaps children from one socioeconomic group are more likely both to bully and to have an ADHD diagnosis. Finally, when the variables are categorical, as they seem to be in this study (children either have ADHD or they don't, and they are either bullies or not), outliers are typically not a problem, because a person cannot have an extreme score on a categorical variable.

For external validity, the article reports that all the children in one grade level were studied. This study used a census, not a sample, so the findings clearly generalize to children in this Swedish town.

2. a. This strong correlation means that scientists who drank more beer published fewer articles.

b. This means that the correlation is statistically significant—it is unlikely to have occurred by chance if there is really no relationship.

c. The correlation would become stronger with this outlier.

d. No, the result establishes covariance, but it does not establish temporal precedence. (It could also be the case that the scientists drank beer to cope with a lower publication rate.) It does not establish internal validity, either: A third variable might be institution type; scientists working at universities might publish more and socialize less with beer, while scientists at working companies might publish less and socialize more with beer.

e. One possible table:

	Correlation between beer consumption and publication rate
Ecologists	−.63
Physicists	−.04

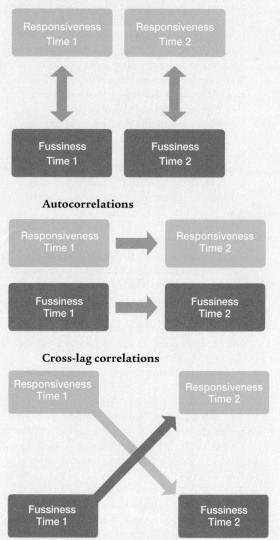

Chapter 9

1. a. **Cross-sectional correlations**

Autocorrelations

Cross-lag correlations

b. A significant correlation between responsiveness at Time 1 and fussiness at Time 2 would suggest that responsiveness causes less fussiness. A significant correlation between responsiveness at Time 2 and fussiness at Time 1 would suggest that infant fussiness causes less responsiveness. A mutually reinforcing relationship would be indicated if both cross-lag correlations were significant.

2. a. Education is a third variable problem.

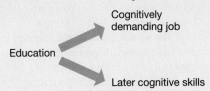

Education
→ Cognitively demanding job
→ Later cognitive skills

b. Gender is a moderator.

Gender	Relationship between having a cognitively demanding job and later cognitive skills
Male	Significant r
Female	Nonsignificant r

c. "Building lasting connections in the brain" is the mediator.

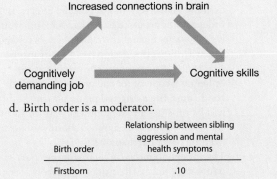

Increased connections in brain

Cognitively demanding job → Cognitive skills

d. Birth order is a moderator.

Birth order	Relationship between sibling aggression and mental health symptoms
Firstborn	.10
Later-born	.18

e. Loneliness is a mediator.

Loneliness

Sibling aggression → Mental health symptoms

f. Parental conflict is a third variable problem.

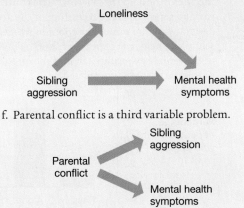

Parental conflict
→ Sibling aggression
→ Mental health symptoms

3. a. The criterion variable is mental health, measured by the Trauma Symptom Checklist. It is at the top of the table, in the table title.

b. There are 17 predictors in this table (you don't count R^2 as a predictor).

c. Kids who experience more total types of sibling victimization experience more mental health symptoms, controlling for parent education, ethnicity, language, age, gender, child maltreatment, sexual victimization, school victimization, Internet victimization, witnessing family or community violence, total types of peer victimization, and the interaction of peer and sibling victimization.

d. Kids who experience more total types of peer victimization experience more mental health symptoms, controlling for parent education, ethnicity, language, age, gender, child maltreatment, sexual victimization, school victimization, Internet victimization, witnessing family or community violence, total types of sibling victimization, and the interaction of peer and sibling victimization.

e. Kids who experience childhood maltreatment experience more mental health symptoms, controlling for parent education, ethnicity, language, age, gender, sexual victimization, school victimization, Internet victimization, witnessing family or community violence, total peer victimization, total types of sibling victimization, and the interaction of peer and sibling victimization.

f. Kids who experience Internet victimization do not experience more mental health symptoms, at least when controlling for parent education, ethnicity, language, age, gender, sexual victimization, school victimization, witnessing family or community violence, total peer victimization, total types of sibling victimization, and the interaction of peer and sibling victimization.

g. Since the beta for peer victimization is larger than the beta for sibling aggression, you can conclude that peer victimization is more strongly related to mental health. The strongest beta on the table is peer victimization.

Chapter 10

1. (*Sample answer*)

   a. You could randomly assign students to two groups. Both groups will be taught the same material, using the same teaching methods, homework, and examples. However, you would train a teacher to act either friendly or stern as he or she teaches the two groups of students. After the teaching unit, students would take the same school achievement test.

   The bar graph should look something like this:

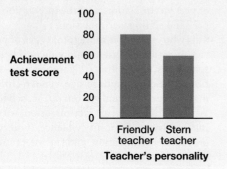

   The independent (manipulated) variable is teacher's personality, with two levels (friendly and stern). The dependent (measured) variable is the achievement test score. The control variables might include the teacher's appearance, the content of the material taught, the teaching method, the examples used, and the homework used.

   Your assessment of covariance will depend on how your graph is prepared; however, this study would show covariance if the results came out as depicted in the graph shown above, in which the achievement test scores covary with the teacher's personality. This study also shows temporal precedence: The teacher's personality was manipulated, so it came first in time, followed by the achievement test. This study would also have internal validity if the researchers controlled for potential alternative explanations—for example, by keeping the teaching methods and homework the same. If the study has met all three causal rules, you can make a causal statement that a friendlier teacher causes students to score higher on school achievement tests.

2. (*Sample answer*)

   c. If you manipulated the piano practice independent variable as independent-groups, you would have some participants practice the piano for 10 minutes per day and other participants practice for 30 minutes per day. You would randomly assign people to the two groups.

   If you manipulated the piano practice variable as within-groups, you could have participants alternate blocks of practice months—some months practicing 10 minutes per day, and other months practicing 30 minutes per day. You would measure piano performance at the end of each monthly block. To control for carryover effects, you would counterbalance the months, so that some participants practice 10 minutes a day first, and others practice 30 minutes a day first.

   For this independent variable, the advantage to using the independent-groups design is that most participants probably believe that 30 minutes of practice will work better than 10, so this design may be more susceptible to demand characteristics or placebo effects. In an independent groups design, participants would be less aware of what the experiment is testing. The within-groups design has the advantage that each participant will be serving as his or her own control for the two experimental conditions; their original piano playing ability will be constant for all conditions. In addition, the within-groups design has the advantage of needing fewer participants.

3. a. The independent variable is whether participants were doing their questionnaires alone or with a passive confederate. The dependent variable was whether people stopped filling out their questionnaires to investigate the "accident" or help the "victim." The control variables were the tape recording of the accident (always the same), the room in which the study was held, the appearance and behavior of the female experimenter, and the questionnaires participants completed.

   b.

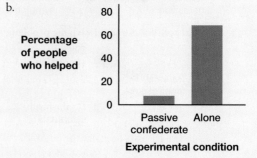

c. This was an independent-groups manipulation. People were in either the alone group or the passive confederate group.

d. For construct validity, you would ask whether getting up to help is a good measure of helping behavior (it seems to be). You would also ask whether participating alone or with a passive confederate is a reasonable manipulation of the presence of bystanders. For internal validity, you would make sure that the experimenters used random assignment (they did) and appropriate control variables to avoid confounds. Are any other control variables unaccounted for? For external validity, you would ask how the experimenters gathered their sample: Was it a random sample of some population? You can also ask if this situation—helping a woman falling from a chair in another room—would generalize to other emergencies, such as helping a man bleeding on the street, helping somebody who fainted, or helping in other kinds of situations.

For statistical validity, you could ask how large the effect size was. Indeed, the difference was 7% versus 70%, and this is an extremely large effect size. You would make sure it was statistically significant, too. (An effect size that large probably is.)

Chapter 11

1. a. IV: Exposure to alcohol advertising. DV: Reported level of drinking.
   b. Design: One-group, pretest/posttest design (a within-groups design).
   c.

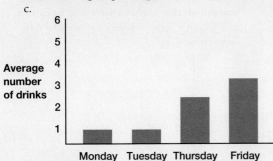

   d. IV threats: Because this is a one-group, pretest/posttest design, it is subject to multiple internal validity threats. Perhaps the most obvious is history: It is plausible that students drank

more after exposure to the advertising simply because the posttest was on a weekend.

   e. To redesign the study, Jack could add a comparison group that is also tested on the same days but does not see the alcohol advertising.

2. a. IV: The use of the categorization strategy. DV: the memory rate.
   b. Design: one-group, pretest/posttest (a within-groups design).
   c.

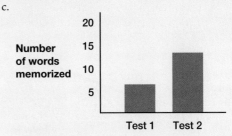

   d. Because this is a one-group, pretest/posttest design, it is subject to multiple internal validity threats. Perhaps the most obvious here is testing: The students probably recalled more words the second time because they had a second chance to learn the same list of words.

   e. To fix this problem, the student presenters should use a new word list the second time—when categorization is used as a mnemonic. To control for the possibility that one word list might be more difficult than the other (which would be a design confound), the presenters should also counterbalance the use of the two word lists.

3. *Increasing between-groups variability:* Was 3 ounces of chocolate enough to cause a difference in well-being? Was the well-being questionnaire sensitive enough to detect differences in this variable?

   Reducing within-group differences: With such a small sample, Dr. Dove might need to use a within-groups design, because there are likely to be individual differences in well-being. Otherwise, she might try using a larger number of participants (30 in each group might be better), thus reducing the impact of measurement errors or individual differences. The participants in this study also seemed to be going about their normal routines in real-world settings. There may have been innumerable sources of situation noise in their lives over this 4-week period. In a future study, Dr. Dove might consider quarantining participants for some period of time.

Chapter 12

1. Below are two possible line graphs that represent the Wood et al. (2009) data. You can describe this interaction in words as follows: People with low self-esteem feel worse after telling themselves "I am a lovable person," but people with high self-esteem feel better after telling themselves "I am a lovable person."

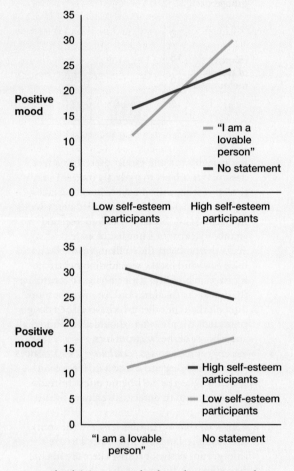

2. In the driving example, there does appear to be a main effect for driver age, such that older drivers are slower to brake. And there does appear to be a main effect for the cell phone condition, such that drivers using cell phones are slower to brake. Although you would need statistics to confirm that these differences are significant, you know that in the actual study, both main effects were statistically significant (see p. 371).

DV: Brake onset time (ms)		IV₁: Cell phone condition		
		On cell phone	Not on phone	Main effect for IV₂: Driver age
IV₂: Driver age	Younger drivers	912	780	846
	Older drivers	1066	912	989
Main effect for IV₁: Cell phone condition		989	846	

In the memory test example, there does not appear to be a main effect for the testing condition, since the two marginal means are almost the same. There also does not appear to be a very large main effect for the learning condition, since the two marginal means are almost the same here, too. You would need inferential statistics to determine whether the difference between 11.05 and 9.90 is statistically significant.

DV: Number of words memorized		IV₁: Testing condition		
		Water's edge	Underwater	Main effect for IV₂: Learning condition
IV₂: Learning condition	Water's edge	13.5	8.6	11.05
	Underwater	8.4	11.4	9.90
Main effect for IV₁: Testing conditions		10.95	10.00	

3. a. This is a 3 × 2 within-groups factorial design.
   b. The independent variables are cell phone condition (two levels) and testing condition (three levels). The dependent variable is the number of collisions.
   c. Both independent variables are within-groups variables.
   d. Notice that you could put either independent variable on the x-axis; either would be correct, and you can detect interactions equally well from either graph.

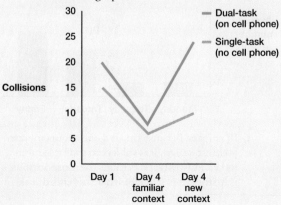

e. There is a main effect for cell phone condition, such that talking on a cell phone causes more collisions. (You can say "cause" here because this was an experimental design with no confounds.) There is also a main effect for testing day: People had the fewest collisions on Day 4, familiar context, and the most collisions on Day 4, new context. There appears to be an interaction: The difference between single and dual task is about the same on Day 1 and Day 4, familiar context, but the difference is greater on Day 4, new context.

f. The results of this study seem to show that regardless of experience level, using cell phones impairs people's driving skill.

4. Participant variables are usually independent-groups variables. In the case of gender, participants usually are not both male and female; they are usually one or the other. Ethnicity, too, is an independent-groups variable. Sometimes personality traits (such as high self-esteem versus low self-esteem or introversion versus extroversion) are used as participant variables; these, too, are independent-groups variables. Age, however, could go either way. Strayer and his colleagues recruited some people in their 20s and other people in their 70s, so age was an independent-groups variable in this design. However, if a researcher recruits one sample of people and tests them in their 20s, 30s, 40s, and 50s, age becomes a participant variable that is studied as a repeated-measures variable. (This kind of study is called a longitudinal design; see Chapter 9.)

Chapter 13

1. a. This is a nonequivalent control group design.
   b.

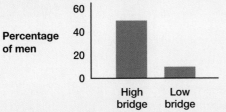

Percentage of men (y-axis: 0, 20, 40, 60; x-axis: High bridge, Low bridge)

   c. The causal claim would be that being on the high bridge caused men to call the female experimenter (presumably because they thought they were attracted to her). This design has covariance (the participants from the high bridge called more

than those from the low bridge) and temporal precedence (the participants crossed the bridge before they called the woman). However, in this quasi-experimental design, it is possible that a selection effect is threatening internal validity. Different kinds of men might choose to cross a precarious high bridge versus a safer low bridge. Furthermore, a man who would cross the exciting bridge might also be more likely to take the risk of calling an attractive woman. Therefore, the internal validity is questionable in this study.

   d. There is a selection effect in this study, as noted above. You could redesign this study by somehow studying only the men who chose to cross the bridge but studying them either before they were about to cross it or after they had already crossed it. In fact, Dutton and Aron (1974) ran a second study to rule out the selection effect problem. The female experimenter approached only men who had crossed the tall bridge. However, half the men she approached had just crossed the bridge, and the other half were approached after they had taken a long rest; their heart rates had returned to normal. The results showed that the men approached right after crossing were more likely to call than the men who had rested; this finding helped the researchers rule out the selection effect explanation for the first study.

   e. Construct validity of the dependent variable: How well does a phone call operationalize a man's attraction to a woman? (Probably very well.) External validity: How well does the situation of crossing a bridge represent other situations in which a person might be aroused? (The researchers could also study other arousing activities, such as exercising or watching a scary movie.)

2. a. Either the stable-baseline design or the reversal design is appropriate here. Since there is only one context for the growling behavior, the multiple-baseline design would not be appropriate.

   b. Using a stable-baseline design, you would observe and record your dog's growling behavior daily in the presence of other dogs for a long period of time (2–3 weeks). Then you would continue to observe and record your dog's growling behavior daily as you began to implement the behavioral technique.

   c. The graph would look similar to Figure 13.10, except the growling behavior would be consistently high (rather than low) during the baseline period and would then decrease after the intervention starts.

d. If the results were as depicted in the graph you drew, you could rule out maturation and regression explanations for the dog's behavior, because the stable-baseline period shows that the dog's behavior has not changed on its own. A history threat might still apply to your data if some other change (such as a change in diet) happened to occur in the dog's life at the same time you started using the behavioral technique. However, in the absence of some other explanation, you could infer the causal success of the therapy if the dog's growling behavior began to decrease at the time you started the therapy.

Chapter 14

1. Answers will vary.
2. a. This study could be conducted in theory-testing mode, because it may test a theory that exposure to a very stressful event is a potential cause of mental suffering and emotional problems. However, this study is also being conducted in generalization mode, since it appears to be testing a frequency claim about the population of Holocaust survivors: What percentage of survivors experience mood or sleep disorders? Frequency claims are always in generalization mode.

b. This study appears at first to be conducted in theory-testing mode. It is testing a link between electromagnetic radiation and brain activity. (Does this kind of radiation affect the brain?) However, because the type of radiation is tied to cell phones, the researchers may be interested, eventually, in generalizing the results to humans who use cell phones and may be worried about the technology's long-term benefits and risks.

c. Because this study used a restricted sample of a special kind of person—being born blind and later regaining sight is rare—it probably was not conducted in generalization mode. It is a good example of theory-testing mode because the results from this special sample allowed the researchers to learn that the brain uses motion (more than color or lines) to decode the visual world.

References

Abelson, R. P. (1995). *Statistics as principled argument.* Hillsdale, NJ: Erlbaum.

Agras, W. S., Jacob, R. G., & Lebedeck, M. (1980). The California drought: A quasi-experimental analysis of social policy. *Journal of Applied Behavior Analysis, 13,* 561–570.

American Psychological Association. (1994). Resolution on Facilitated Communication by the American Psychological Association Adopted in Council, August 14, 1994, Los Angeles, CA.

American Psychological Association. (2002, with 2010 amendments). *Ethical principles of psychologists and code of conduct.* Retrieved from http://www.apa.org/ethics/code/index.aspx

American Psychological Association. (2010). *Publication manual of the American Psychological Association* (6th ed). Washington, DC: American Psychological Association.

Anderson, C. A., Berkowitz, L., Donnerstein, E., Huesmann, L. R., Johnson, J., Linz, D., . . . Wartella, E. (2003). The influence of media violence on youth. *Psychological Science in the Public Interest, 4,* 81–110.

Anderson, C. A., Shibuya, A., Ihori, N., Swing, E. L., Bushman, B. J., Sakamoto, A., . . . Barlett, C. P. (2010). Violent video game effects on aggression, empathy, and prosocial behavior in Eastern and Western countries: A meta-analytic review. *Psychological Bulletin, 136,* 151–173.

Animal Welfare Act. (1966). Title 9 Code of Federal Regulations (CF), Chapter 1, Subchapter A: Animal Welfare. Retrieved from http://www.gpo.gov/fdsys/pkg/CFR-2009-title9-vol1/xml/CFR-2009-title9-vol1-chapI-subchapA.xml

Arnett, J. (2008). The neglected 95%: Why American psychology needs to become less American. *American Psychologist, 63,* 602–614.

Aron, A. (2009). *Instructor's manual with tests for statistics for psychology* (5th ed.). New York: Pearson.

Back, M. D., Schmuckle, S. C., & Egloff, B. (2008). Becoming friends by chance. *Psychological Science, 19,* 439–440.

Bakalar, N. (2005, May 3). Ugly children may get parental short shrift. *New York Times.* Retrieved from www.nytimes.com

Barnett, W. S. (1998). Long-term effects on cognitive development and school success. In W. S. Barnett & S. S. Boocock (Eds.), *Early care and education for children in poverty: Promises, programs, and long-term outcomes* (pp. 11–44). Buffalo, NY: SUNY Press.

Baron, R. (1997). The sweet smell of . . . helping: Effects of pleasant ambient fragrance on prosocial behavior in shopping malls. *Personality and Social Psychology Bulletin, 23,* 498–503.

Baron, R. M., & Kenny, D. A. (1986). The moderator-mediator variable distinction in social psychological research: Conceptual, strategic and statistical considerations. *Journal of Personality and Social Psychology, 51,* 1173–1182.

Barros, R. M., Silver, E. J., & Stein, R. E. K. (2009). School recess and group classroom behavior. *Pediatrics, 123,* 431–436.

Bartholow, B. D., & Heinz, A. (2006). Alcohol and aggression without consumption: Alcohol cues, aggressive thoughts, and hostile perception bias. *Psychological Science, 17,* 30–37.

Baumrind, D. (1964). Some thoughts on the ethics of research: After reading Milgram's "Behavioral Study of Obedience." *American Psychologist, 19,* 421–423.

Bear, G. (1995). Computationally intensive methods warrant reconsideration of pedagogy in statistics. *Behavior Research Methods, Instruments, and Computers, 27,* 144–147.

Beck, A. T., Ward, C., & Mendelson, M. (1961). Beck Depression Inventory (BDI). *Archives of General Psychiatry, 4,* 561–571.

Beck, A. T., Ward, C. H., Mendelson, M., Mock, J., & Erbaugh, J. (1961). An inventory for measuring depression. *Archives of General Psychiatry, 4,* 53–63.

Beecher, H. K. (1955). The powerful placebo. *Journal of the American Medical Association, 159,* 1601–1606.

Benedetti, F., Amanzio, M., Vighetti, S., & Asteggiano, G. (2006). The biochemical and neuroendocrine bases of the hyperalgesic nocebo effect. *Journal of Neuroscience, 26,* 12014–12022.

Berkowitz, L. (1973, July). The case for bottling up rage. *Psychology Today, 7,* 24–31.

Berkowitz, L., & Donnerstein, E. (1982). External validity is more than skin deep: Some answers to criticisms of laboratory experiments. *American Psychologist, 37,* 245–257.

Best, E. (2010). Alcohol makes bigger guys more aggressive. *Pacific Standard.* http://www.psmag.com/culture-society/alcohol-makes-bigger-guys-more-aggressive-15485/

Bick, J., & Dozier, M. (2010, May). Mothers' and children's concentrations of oxytocin following close, physical interactions with biological and non-biological children. *Developmental Psychobiology, 52,* 101–107.

Blaine, B., & Crocker, J. (1995). Religiousness, race and psychological well-being: Exploring social psychological mediators. *Personality and Social Psychology Bulletin, 21,* 1031–1041.

Blass, T. (2002). The man who shocked the world. *Psychology Today, 35,* 68–74.

Bogg, T., & Roberts, B. W. (2004). Conscientiousness and health-related behaviors: A meta-analysis of the leading behavioral contributors to mortality. *Psychological Bulletin, 130,* 887–919.

Borkenau, P., & Liebler, A. (1993). Convergence of stranger ratings of personality and intelligence with self-ratings, partner ratings, and measured intelligence. *Journal of Personality and Social Psychology, 65,* 546–553.

Borsboom, D., & Wagenmakers, E. J. (2013). Derailed: The rise and fall of Diederik Stapel [Book review]. *APS Observer.* Retrieved from http://www.psychologicalscience.org/index.php/publications/observer/2013/january-13/derailed-the-rise-and-fall-of-diederik-stapel.html

Bothwell, R. K., Deffenbacher, K. A., & Brigham, J. C. (1987). Correlations of eyewitness accuracy and confidence: Optimality hypothesis revisited. *Journal of Applied Psychology, 72,* 691–695.

Boucher, J., Mayes, A., & Bigham, S. (2012). Memory in autistic spectrum disorder. *Psychological Bulletin, 138,* 458–496.

Bowker, A., Boekhoven, B., Nolan, A., Bauhaus, S., Glover, P., Powell, T., & Taylor, S. (2009). Naturalistic observations of spectator behavior at youth hockey games. *Sport Psychologist, 23,* 301–316.

Bratskeir, K. (2012, April 3). Color me creative: Study says green sparks inventiveness. *Huffington Post.* Retrieved from http://www.huffingtonpost.com/2012/04/03/green-colors-creative_n_1386190.html

Brewer, M. (2000). Research design and issues of validity. In H. Reis & C. Judd (Eds.), *Handbook of research methods in social and personality psychology.* Cambridge, England: Cambridge University Press.

Brewer, N., & Wells, G. L. (2006). The confidence-accuracy relationship in eyewitness identification: Effects of lineup instructions, foil similarity, and target-absent base rates. *Journal of Experimental Psychology: Applied, 12,* 11–30.

Brice, G. C., Gorey, K. M., Hall, R. M., & Angelino, S. (1996). The STAYWELL program: Maximizing elders' capacity for independent living through health promotion and disease prevention activities. *Research on Aging, 18,* 202–218.

Bröder, A. (1998). Deception can be acceptable. *American Psychologist, 53,* 805–806. doi:10.1037/0003-066X.53.7.805.b

Brown, R., & Hanlon, C. (1970). Derivational complexity and order of acquisition in child speech. In J. R. Hayes (Ed.), *Cognition and the development of language* (pp. 11–54). New York: Wiley.

Bushman, B. J. (2002). Does venting anger feed or extinguish the flame? Catharsis, rumination, distraction, anger and aggressive responding. *Personality and Social Psychology Bulletin, 28,* 724–731.

Bushman, B. J., & Anderson, C. A. (2001). Media violence and the American public: Scientific facts versus media misinformation. *American Psychologist, 56,* 477–489.

Bushman, B. J., Baumeister, R. F., & Phillips, C. M. (2001). Do people aggress to improve their mood? Catharsis beliefs, affect regulation opportunity, and aggressive responding. *Journal of Personality and Social Psychology, 81,* 17–32.

Cacioppo, J., Cacioppo, S., Gonzaga, G. C., Ogburn, E. L., & VanderWeele, T. J. (2013). Marital satisfaction and break-ups differ across on-line and off-line meeting venues. *Proceedings of the National Academy of Sciences,* doi: 10.1073/pnas.1222447110

Camara, W. J., & Echternacht, G. (2000). The SAT I and high school grades: Utility in predicting success in college. Research Notes, College Entrance

Examination Board, New York, NY. http://files.eric.ed.gov/fulltext/ED446592.pdf

Campos, B., Wang, S., Plaksina, T., Repetti, R. L., Schoebi, D., Ochs, E., & Beck, M. E. (2013). Positive and negative emotion in the daily life of dual-earner couples with children. *Journal of Family Psychology*, *27*, 76–85.

Cantril, H. (1965). *The pattern of human concerns*. New Brunswick, NJ: Rutgers University Press.

Carey, B. (2007, June 22). Research finds firstborns gain the higher IQ. *New York Times*. Retrieved from www.nytimes.com.

Carlson, N. (2009). *Physiology of behavior* (10th ed.). New York: Allyn & Bacon.

Carroll, L. (2008, January 29). Kids with ADHD may be more likely to bully. NBC News [Online edition]. Retrieved from http://www.nbcnews.com/id/22813400/ns/health-childrens_health/t/kids-adhd-may-be-more-likely-bully/#.U1bKavldV8E

Carroll, L. (2013, August 12). Chronic stomach pain in kids linked to later anxiety. NBC News (Health). Retrieved from http://www.nbcnews.com/health/chronic-stomach-pain-kids-linked-later-anxiety-6C10887554

CDC: Nearly 60% of Teens Text While Driving (MSNBC.com, 2012): *Chapter 3 opening headline*. Stobbe, M. (2012, June 8). CDC: Nearly 60 percent of teens text while driving. MSNBC.com. Retrieved from http://www.nbcnews.com/id/47723985/ns/ health-health_care/t/cdc-nearly-percent-teens-text-while-driving/#.Uu_gxfZ6NxN

Centers for Disease Control and Prevention. (2000). Clinical growth charts. Retrieved from http://www.cdc.gov/growthcharts/clinical_charts.htm

Centers for Disease Control and Prevention. (2008). Youth risk behavior surveillance—United States 2007. Retrieved from http://www.cdc.gov/mmwr/preview/mmwrhtml/ss5704a1.htm

Childress, J. F., Meslin, E. M., & Shapiro, H. T. (2005). *Belmont revisited: Ethical principles for research with human subjects*. Washington, DC: Georgetown University Press.

Christian, L., Keeter, S., Purcell, K., & Smith, A. (2010). Assessing the cell phone challenge. Pew Research Center. Retrieved from http://pewresearch.org/pubs/1601/assessing-cell-phone-challenge-in-public-opinion-surveys

Cicirelli, V. G., & Associates. (1969). *The impact of Head Start: An evaluation of the effects of Head Start on children's cognitive and affective development* (Vols. 1–2) (Report to the Office of Economic Opportunity). Athens, OH: Ohio University and Westinghouse Learning Corporation.

Cimpian, A., Arce, H. C., Markman, E. M., & Dweck, C. S. (2007). Subtle linguistic cues affect children's motivation. *Psychological Science*, *18*, 314–316.

Cocaine exposure during pregnancy leads to impulsivity in male, not female, monkeys (2009, October 24). Retrieved from http://www.sciencedaily.com/releases/2009/10/091022114309.htm

Cohen, J. (1992). A power primer. *Psychological Bulletin*, *112*, 155–159.

Cohen, S., Kamarck, T., & Mermelstein, R. (1983). A global measure of perceived stress. *Journal of Health and Social Behavior*, *24*, 385–396.

Coile, D. C., & Miller, N. E. (1984). How radical animal activists try to mislead humane people. *American Psychologist*, *45*, 1304–1312.

Coleman, N. (2008, September 13). Hockey moms? Hockey dads set the example. *Star Tribune*. Retrieved from http://www.startribune.com

Conner Snibbe, A., & Markus, H. R. (2005). You can't always get what you want: Educational attainment, agency, and choice. *Journal of Personality and Social Psychology*, *88*, 703–720.

Cooper, J., & Strayer, D. L. (2008). Effects of simulator practice and real world experience on cell-phone-related driver distraction. *Human Factors*, *50*, 893–902.

Copeland, J., & Snyder, M. (1995). When counselors confirm: A functional analysis. *Personality and Social Psychology Bulletin*, *21*, 1210–1220.

Cozby, P. C. (2007). *Methods in Behavioral Research* (9th ed.). New York: McGraw-Hill.

Crane, M. (2013, February 18). Kids' aggressive behavior tied to TV violence in studies. *Columbus Dispatch* [Online edition]. Retrieved from http://www.dispatch.com/content/stories/local/2013/02/18/kids-aggressive-behavior-tied-to-tv-violence-in-studies.html

Cronbach, L. J., & Meehl, P. E. (1955). Construct validity in psychological tests. *Psychological Bulletin*, *52*, 281–302.

Crowne, D. P., & Marlowe, D. (1960). A new scale of social desirability independent of psychopathology. *Journal of Consulting Psychology*, *24*, 349–354.

Dachis, A. (2010, August 18). Venting frustration will only make your anger worse. *Lifehacker.com* [Online magazine]. Retrieved from http://www.lifehacker.com.au/2010/08/venting-frustration-will-only-make-your-anger-worse

Danziger, S., Levav, J., & Avnaim-Pesso, L. (2011). Extraneous factors in judicial decisions. *Proceedings of the National Academy of Sciences*, *108*, 6889–6892.

Darley, J. M., & Latané, B. (1968). Bystander intervention in emergencies: Diffusion of responsibility. *Journal of Personality and Social Psychology*, *8*, 377–383.

Deary, I. J., Penke, J., & Johnson, W. (2010). The neuroscience of human intelligence differences. *Nature Reviews: Neuroscience, 11*, 201–212.

DeNoon, D. J. (2008, May 7). Perk of a good job: Aging mind is sharp. Retrieved from http://www.webmd.com/brain/news/20080507/perk-of-good-job-aging-mind-is-sharp

DeWall, C. N., Bushman, B. J., Giancola, P. R., & Webster, G. D. (2010). The big, the bad, and the boozed-up: Weight moderates the effect of alcohol on aggression. *Journal of Experimental Social Psychology, 46*, 619–623.

Diener, E., & Diener, C. (1996). Most people are happy. *Psychological Science, 7*, 181–185.

Diener, E., Emmons, R. A., Larsen, R. J., & Griffin, S. (1985). The satisfaction with life scale. *Journal of Personality Assessment, 49*, 71–75.

Diener, E., Horwitz, J., & Emmons, R. A. (1985). Happiness of the very wealthy. *Social Indicators, 16*, 263–274.

Do Experiences or Material Goods Make Us Happier? (2009, February 23). Esciencenews.com. Retrieved from http://esciencenews.com/articles/ 2009/02/23/do.experiences.or.material.goods.make.us.happier

Does Venting Anger Feed or Extinguish the Flame? (*Personality and Social Psychology Bulletin*, 2002): *Chapter 2 opening headline.* Bushman, B. J. (2002). Does venting anger feed or extinguish the flame? Catharsis, rumination, distraction, anger and aggressive responding. *Personality and Social Psychology Bulletin, 28*, 724–731.

Doyle, A. C. (1892/2002). Silver blaze. In *The complete Sherlock Holmes.* New York: Gramercy.

Duke, A. A., Giancola, P. R., Morris, D. H., Holt, J. C. D., & Gunn, R. L. (2011). Alcohol dose and aggression: Another reason why drinking more is a bad idea. *Journal of Studies on Alcohol and Drugs, 72*, 34–43.

Dunn, D. (2009). *Research methods for social psychology.* New York: Wiley-Blackwell.

Dunn, L. M., & Dunn, L. M. (1981). *PPVT: Revised manual.* Circle Pines, MN: American Guidance Service.

Dutton, D. G., & Aron, A. P. (1974). Some evidence for heightened sexual attraction under conditions of high anxiety. *Journal of Personality and Social Psychology, 30*, 510–517.

Ebbinghaus, H. (1913). *Memory: A contribution to experimental psychology.* New York: Columbia University Press. (Originally published 1885.)

Edgington, E. S., & Onghena, P. (2007). *Randomization tests* (4th ed). London: Chapman and Hall/CRC.

Eisenberg, L. (1977). The social imperatives of medical research. *Science, 198*, 1105–1110.

Elliot, A. J., & Aarts, H. (2011). Perception of the color red enhances the force and velocity of motor output. *Emotion, 11*, 445–449.

Elliot, A. J., & Maier, M. A. (2012). Color-in-context theory. *Advances in Experimental Social Psychology, 45*, 61–126.

Elliot, A. J., Maier, M. A., Moller, A. C., Friedman, R., & Meinhardt, J. (2007). Color and psychological functioning: The effect of red on performance in achievement contexts. *Journal of Experimental Psychology: General, 136*, 154–168.

Ericsson, K. A., Chase, W. G., & Faloon, S. (1980). Acquisition of a memory skill. *Science, 208*, 1181–1182.

Eron, L. D., Huesmann, L. R., Lefkowitz, M. M., & Walder, L. O. (1972). Does television violence cause aggression? *American Psychologist, 27*, 253–263.

Estes, A. C. (2011, June 2). The color red makes you stronger, but more distractable. *The Wire* [Online magazine]. Retrieved from http://www.thewire.com/technology/2011/06/color-red-makes-you-stronger-faster/38435/

Family Dinner Benefits: Do Meals Together Really Make a Difference for Children? (POLL) (2012, September 26). *Huffington Post.* Retrieved from http://www.huffingtonpost.com/2012/09/26/family-dinner-benefits-make-a-difference-poll_n_1916602.html

Federal Register. (2000, December 6). FR Doc 06de00-72. Federal Research Misconduct Policy. Washington, DC: Department of Health and Human Services.

Federal Register. (2001). FR Doc 01-30627. Washington, DC: Department of Health and Human Services.

Feshbach, S. (1956). The catharsis hypothesis and some consequences of interaction with aggression and neutral play objects. *Journal of Personality, 24*, 449–462.

Final Report of the Tuskegee Syphilis Study Ad Hoc Advisory Panel. Washington, DC: U.S. Department of Health, Education, and Welfare; Public Health Service, 1–3, 6–15, 23–24, 47.

Frey, D., & Stahlberg, D. (1986). Selection of information after receiving more or less reliable self-threatening information. *Personality and Social Psychology Bulletin, 12*, 434–441.

Gabriel, T. (2010, May 1). Despite push, success at charter schools is mixed. *New York Times.* Retrieved from www.nytimes.com.

Gallup Healthways (n.d.). *Gallup Healthways Well-Being Index: Methodology report for indexes.* Retrieved from http://wbi.meyouhealth.com/files/GallupHealthways WBI-Methodology.pdf

Gallup Worldview Interactive Database (2014). Feel well-rested item. Retrieved February 3, 2014, from https://worldview.gallup.com

Gay, P. (Ed.). (1989). *A Freud reader.* New York: Norton.

Gazzaniga, M. (2005). Forty-five years of split-brain research and still going strong. *Nature Reviews Neuroscience, 6*, 653–649.

Gazzaniga, M. S., Bogen, J. E., & Sperry, R. W. (1962). Some functional effects of sectioning the cerebral commissures in man. *Proceedings of the National Academy of Science, 48*, part 2, 1765–1769.

Geen, R. G., & Quanty, M. B. (1977). The catharsis of aggression: An evaluation of a hypothesis. *Advances in Experimental Social Psychology, 10*, 2–39.

Gernsbacher, M. A. (2003). Is one style of autism early intervention "scientifically proven"? *Journal of Developmental and Learning Disorders, 7*, 19–25.

Giancola, P. R. (2000). Executive functioning: A conceptual framework for alcohol-related aggression. *Experimental and Clinical Psychopharmacology, 8*, 576–597.

Gidus, T. (2008, June 19). Mindless eating [Blog post]. Retrieved from http://www.healthline.com/blogs/diet_nutrition/2008/06/mindless-eating.html

Gilbert, D. (2005). *Stumbling on happiness*. New York: Vintage.

Godden, D. R., & Baddeley, D. (1975). Context-dependent memory in two natural environments: On land and underwater. *British Journal of Psychology, 66*, 325–331.

Goldacre, B. (2008, September 6). Cheer up, it's all down to random variation [Web log post]. Retrieved from http://www.guardian.co.uk/commentisfree/2008/sep/06/medicalresearch

Goldacre, B. (2011, August 19). Unemployment is rising—or is that statistical noise? *Guardian* [Online]. Retrieved from http://www.guardian.co.uk/commentisfree/2011/aug/19/bad-science-unemployment-statistical-noise

Gottfredson, L. S. (Ed.). (1997). Intelligence and social policy. *Intelligence, 24* (Special Issue).

Gould, S. J. (1996). *The mismeasure of man* (revised and expanded). New York: Norton.

Gray, F. D. (1998). *The Tuskegee syphilis study: The real story and beyond*. Montgomery, AL: River City Publishers.

Greenwald, A. G., Nosek, B. A., & Banaji, M. R. (2003). Understanding and using the Implicit Association Test: I. An improved scoring algorithm. *Journal of Personality and Social Psychology, 85*, 197–216.

Grim, T. (2008). A possible role of social activity to explain differences in publication output among ecologists. *Oikos, 117*, 484–487.

Gross, J. J., & John, O. P. (2002). Wise emotion regulation. In L. F. Barrett & P. Salovey (Eds.), *The wisdom in feeling: Psychological processes in emotional intelligence* (pp. 297–319). New York: Guilford Press.

Halavis, A. (2004, August 29). The Isuzu experiment. Retrieved from http://alex.halavais.net/the-isuzu-experiment

Haller, M. (2012, January). The reason why you're an angry drunk. *Men's Health* [Online edition]. Retrieved from http://news.menshealth.com/the-reason-why-you%E2%80%99re-an-angry-drunk/2012/01/06/

Hamzelou, J. (2010, January). Cell phone radiation is good for Alzheimer's mice. *New Scientist Health*. Retrieved from http://www.newscientist.com/article/dn18351-cellphone-radiation-is-good-for-alzheimers-mice.html

Happiness Facts and Fiction (webmd.com): *Chapter 5 opening headline*. Stuart, A. (n.d.) Don't fall for these happiness myths: Learn how to overcome them. Webmd.com. Retrieved from http://www.webmd.com/balance/guide/happiness-6-myths-and-truths

Harlow, H. (1958). The nature of love. *American Psychologist, 13*, 673–685.

Hastorf, A., & Cantril, H. (1954). They saw a game: A case study. *Journal of Abnormal and Social Psychology, 49*, 129–134.

Heine, S. J. (2008). *Cultural psychology*. New York: Norton.

Heller, J. (1972, July 26). Syphilis victims went untreated for 40 years. *New York Times*. Retrieved from www.nytimes.com.

Hennigan, K. M., Del Rosario, M. L., Heath, L., Cook, T. D., Wharton, J. D., & Calder, B. J. (1982). Impact of the introduction of television on crime in the United States: Empirical findings and theoretical implications. *Journal of Personality and Social Psychology, 42*, 461–477.

Henrich, J., Heine, S. J., & Norenzayan, A. (2010). The weirdest people in the world? [Target article, commentaries, and response]. *Behavioral and Brain Sciences, 33*, 61–83.

Hertsgaard, D., & Light, H. (1984). Anxiety, depression, and hostility in rural women. *Psychological Reports, 55*, 673–674.

Herzog, H. A., Jr. (1993). "The movement is my life": The psychology of animal rights activism. *Journal of Social Issues, 49*, 103–119.

Hill, P. L., & Roberts, B. W. (2011). The role of adherence in the relationship between conscientiousness and perceived health. *Health Psychology, 30*, 797–804.

Hirst, W., Phelps, E. A., Buckner, R. L., Budson, A. E., Cuc, A., Gabrieli, J. D. E., . . . Chandan J. (2009). Long-term memory for the terrorist attack of September 11: Flashbulb memories, event memories, and the factors that influence their retention. *Journal of Experimental Psychology: General, 138*, 161–176.

Holmes, T. H., & Rahe, R. H. (1967). The social readjustment rating scale. *Journal of Psychosomatic Research, 11*, 213–218.

Hsu, J. (2009, April 12). Facebook users get worse grades in college. Retrieved from http://www.livescience.com/culture/090413-facebook-grades.html

Hubbard, F. O. A., & van Ijzendoorn, M. H. (1991). Maternal unresponsiveness and infant crying across the first 9 months: A naturalistic longitudinal study. *Infant Behavior and Development, 14*, 299–312.

International Society of Aesthetic Plastic Surgery. (2011). *ISAPS International Survey on Aesthetic/Cosmetic Procedures Performed in 2010*. Retrieved from http://www.isaps.org/isaps-global-statistics-2011.html

Ioannidis, J. P. A. (2012). Why science is not necessarily self-correcting. *Perspectives on Psychological Science, 7*, 645–654.

Jacobson, J. W., Mulick, J. A., & Schwartz, A. A. (1995). A history of facilitated communication: Science, pseudoscience, and antiscience. (Science Working Group on facilitated communication). *American Psychologist, 50*, 750–765.

Janzen-Wilde, M. L., Duchan, J. F., & Higginbotham, D. J. (1995). Successful use of facilitated communication with an oral child. *Journal of Speech and Hearing Research, 38*, 658–676.

Johansson, G. (1973). Visual perception of biological motion and a model for its analysis. *Perception and Psychophysics, 14*, 201–211.

Johnson, J. G., Cohen, P., Smailes, E. M., Kasen, S., & Brook, J. S. (2002). Television viewing and aggressive behavior during adolescence and adulthood. *Science, 295*, 2468–2471.

Jones, J. H. (1993). *Bad blood: The Tuskegee syphilis experiment* (Rev. ed.). New York: Free Press.

Jones, J. T., Pelham, B. W., Carvallo, M., & Mirenberg, M. C. (2004). How do I love thee? Let me count the J's: Implicit egotism and interpersonal attraction. *Journal of Personality and Social Psychology, 87*, 665–683.

Jonsen, A. R. (2005). On the origins and future of the Belmont Report. In J. F. Childress, E. M. Meslin, & H. T. Shapiro (Eds.), *Belmont revisited: Ethical principles for research with human subjects* (pp. 3–11). Washington, DC: Georgetown University Press.

Kagay, M. (1994, July 8). Poll on doubt of Holocaust is corrected. *New York Times*. Retrieved from www.nytimes.com.

Kahneman, D. (2012, September 26). A proposal to deal with questions about priming effects. Retrieved from http://www.nature.com/polopoly_fs/7.6716.1349271308!/suppinfoFile/Kahneman%20Letter.pdf

Kamenetz, A. (2013). Eharmony-funded study shows meeting online leads to better marriages. *Fast Company*. Retrieved from http://www.fastcompany.com/3012421/updated-eharmony-funded-study-shows-meeting-online-leads-to-better-marriages

Keeter, S., Christian, L., & Dimock, M. (2010). The growing gap between landline and dual-frame election polls. Retrieved from http://www.pewresearch.org/2010/11/22/the-growing-gap-between-landline-and-dual-frame-election-polls

Kenny, D. A. (2008). Mediation. Retrieved from http://davidakenny.net/cm/mediate.htm

Kenny, D. A. (2009). Moderator variables. Retrieved from http://davidakenny.net/cm/moderation.htm

Kenny, D. A., & West, T. V. (2008). Zero acquaintance: Definitions, statistical model, findings, and process. In J. Skowronski & N. Ambady (Eds.), *First impressions* (pp. 129–146). New York: Guilford Press.

Kids' Aggressive Behavior Tied to TV Violence in Studies (*Columbus Dispatch*, 2013): *Chapter 9 opening headline*. Crane, M. (2013, February 18). Kids' aggressive behavior tied to TV violence in studies. *Columbus Dispatch* [Online edition]. Retrieved from http://www.dispatch.com/content/stories/local/2013/02/18/kids-aggressive-behavior-tied-to-tv-violence-in-studies.html

Kienle, G. S., & Kiene, H. (1997). The powerful placebo effect: Fact or fiction? *Journal of Clinical Epidemiology, 50*, 1311–1318.

Kimmel, A. J. (1998). In defense of deception. *American Psychologist, 53*, 803–805.

Kimmel, A. J. (2007). *Ethical issues in behavioral research* (2nd ed.). Malden, MA: Blackwell.

Kirsch, I., & Sapirstein, G. (1998). Listening to Prozac and hearing placebo: A meta-analysis of antidepressant medication. *Prevention & Treatment, 1*(2).

Klayman, J., & Ha, Y. W. (1987). Confirmation, disconfirmation, and information in hypothesis testing. *Psychological Review, 94*, 211–228.

Klewe, L. (1993). An empirical evaluation of spelling boards as a means of communication for the multihandicapped. *Journal of Autism and Developmental Disorders, 23*, 559–566.

Kringelbach, M. L., & Berridge, K. C. (2009). Towards a functional neuroanatomy of pleasure and happiness. *Trends in Cognitive Sciences, 13*, 479–487.

Krosnick, J. (1999). Survey research. *Annual Review of Psychology, 50*, 537–567.

Kubicek, L. F., & Emde, R. N. (2012). Emotional expression and language: A longitudinal study of typically developing earlier and later talkers from 15 to 30 months. *Infant Mental Health Journal, 33*, 553–584.

Langer, E. J., & Abelson, R. P. (1974). A patient by any other name . . . clinician group differences in labeling bias. *Journal of Consulting and Clinical Psychology, 42*, 4–9.

Latané, B., & Darley, J. M. (1968). Bystander "apathy." *American Scientist, 57*, 244–268.

Latané, B., & Nida, S. (1981). Ten years of research on group size and helping. *Psychological Bulletin, 89,* 308–324.

Lee, J. (1993). *Facing the fire: Experiencing and expressing anger appropriately.* New York: Bantam.

Lelkes, Y., Krosnick, J. A., Marx, D. M., Judd, C. M., & Park, B. (2012). Complete anonymity compromises the accuracy of self-reports. *Journal of Experimental Social Psychology, 48,* 1291–1299.

Leonhardt, D. (2007, May 2). Your plate is bigger than your stomach. *New York Times.* Retrieved from http://www.nytimes.com/2007/05/02/business/02leonhardt.html?pagewanted=all

Leppik, P. (2005, December 1). How authoritative is Wikipedia? Retrieved from http://66.49.144.193/C2011481421/E652809545/index.html

Liberman, R. P., & Raskin, D. E. (1971). Depression: A behavioral formulation. *Archives of General Psychiatry, 24,* 515–523.

Likert, R. (1932). A technique for the measurement of attitudes. *Archives of Psychology, 22,* 1–55.

Lohr, J. M., Olatunji, B. O., Baumeister, R. F., & Bushman, B. J. (2007). The psychology of anger venting and empirically supported alternatives that do no harm. *Scientific Review of Mental Health Practice, 5,* 54–65.

Lovaas, O. I. (1987). Behavioral treatment and normal educational and intellectual functioning in young autistic children. *Journal of Consulting and Clinical Psychology, 55,* 3–9.

Lutsky, N. (2008). Arguing with numbers: A rationale and suggestions for teaching quantitative reasoning through argument and writing. In B. L. Madison & L. A. Steen (Eds.), *Calculation vs. context: Quantitative literacy and its implications for teacher education* (pp. 59–74). Washington, DC: Mathematical Association of America.

Lyubomirsky, S., King, L. A., & Diener, E. (2005). The benefits of frequent positive affect. *Psychological Bulletin, 131,* 803–855.

Margraf, J., Meyer, A. H., & Lavallee, K. L. (2013). Well-being from the knife? Psychological effects of aesthetic surgery. *Clinical Psychological Science, 3,* 1–14.

Markus, H. R., & Hamedani, M. G. (2007). Sociocultural psychology: The dynamic interdependence among self systems and social systems. In S. Kitayama & D. Cohen (Eds.), *Handbook of cultural psychology* (pp. 3–39). New York: Guilford Press.

Markus, H. R., & Kitayama, S. (1991). Culture and the self: Implications for cognition, emotion, and motivation. *Psychological Review, 98,* 224–253.

Marshall, B. J., & Warren, J. R. (1983). Unidentified curved bacillus on gastric epithelium in active chronic gastritis. *Lancet, 1*(8336), 1273–1275.

Marshall, B. J., & Warren. J. R. (1984). Unidentified curved bacilli in the stomach patients with gastritis and peptic ulceration. *Lancet, 1*(8390), 1311–1315.

Masuda, T., & Nisbett, R. E. (2001). Attending holistically vs. analytically: Comparing the context sensitivity of Japanese and Americans. *Journal of Personality and Social Psychology, 81,* 922–934.

McCallum, J. M., Arekere, D. M., Green, B. L., Katz, R. V., & Rivers, B. M. (2007). Awareness and knowledge of the U.S. Public Health Service syphilis study at Tuskegee: Implications for biomedical research. *Journal of Health Care for the Poor and Underserved, 17,* 716–733.

McCartney, K., & Rosenthal, R. (2000). Effect size, practical importance, and social policy for children. *Child Development, 71,* 173–180.

McKey, R., Condelli, L., Ganson, H., Barrett, B., McConkey, C., & Plantz, M. (1985). *The impact of Head Start on children, families, and communities.* (Final report of the Head Start Evaluation, Synthesis, and Utilization Project). Washington, DC: U.S. Department of Health and Human Services.

McNulty, J. K. (2010). When positive processes hurt relationships. *Current Directions in Psychological Science, 19,* 167–171.

Meeting Spouse Online Linked to a Better Marriage (PsychCentral, 2013): *Chapter 8 opening headline.* Nauert, R. (2013, June 4). Meeting spouse online linked to better marriage. Retrieved from http://psychcentral.com/news/2013/06/04/meeting-spouse-online-linked-to-better-marriage/55590.html

Mehl, M. R., Gosling, S. D., & Pennebaker, J. W. (2006). Personality in its natural habitat: Manifestations and implicit folk theories of personality in daily life. *Journal of Personality and Social Psychology, 90,* 862–877.

Mehl, M. R., & Pennebaker, J. W. (2003). The sounds of social life: A psychometric analysis of students' daily social environments and natural conversations. *Journal of Personality and Social Psychology, 84*(4), 857–870.

Mehl, M. R., Vazire, S., Holleran, S. E., & Clark, C. S. (2010). Eavesdropping on happiness: Well-being is related to having less small talk and more substantive conversations. *Psychological Science, 21,* 539–541.

Mehl, M. R., Vazire, S., Ramirez-Esparza, N., Slatcher, R. B., & Pennebaker, J. W. (2007). Are women really more talkative than men? *Science, 317,* 82.

Mehta, R., & Zhu, R. J. (2009). Blue or red? Exploring the effect of color on cognitive performances. *Science, 323,* 1226–1229.

Meier, B. P., D'Agostino, P. R., Elliot, A. J., Maier, M. A., & Wilkowski, B. M. (2012). Color in context: Psychological context moderates the influence of red on approach- and avoidance-motivated behavior. *PLoS ONE, 7*, e40333.

Milgram, S. (1963). Behavioral study of obedience. *Journal of Abnormal and Social Psychology, 67*, 371–378.

Milgram, S. (1974). *Obedience to authority.* New York: Harper & Row.

Miller, D. P., Waldfogel, J., & Han, W. J. (2012). Family meals and child academic and behavioral outcomes. *Child Development, 83*, 2104–2120.

Miller, G. E. (1956). The magic number seven plus or minus two: Some limits on our capacity for processing information. *Psychological Review, 63*, 81–97.

Mitchell, G. (2012). Revisiting truth or triviality: The external validity of research in the psychological laboratory. *Perspectives on Psychological Science, 7*, 109–117.

Moffat, N. J. (1989). Home-based cognitive rehabilitation with the elderly. In L. W. Poon, D. C. Rubin, & B. A. Wilson (Eds.), *Everyday cognition in adulthood and late life* (pp. 659–680). Cambridge, England: Cambridge University Press.

Mook, D. (1989). The myth of external validity. In L. W. Poon, D. C. Rubin, & B. A. Wilson (Eds.), *Everyday cognition in adulthood and late life* (pp. 25–43). Cambridge, England: Cambridge University Press.

Mook, D. (2001). *Psychological research.* New York: Norton.

Most Holocaust survivors battle depression. (2010, January 26). NBC News [Online edition]. Retrieved from http://www.nbcnews.com/id/35082451/ns/health-mental_health/t/most-holocaust-survivors-battle-depression/#.U1bHs_ldV8E

Mozart Effect—Shmozart Effect (*Intelligence,* 2010): *Chapter 1 opening headline.* Pietschnig, J., Voracek, M., & Formann, A. K. (2010). Mozart effect—Shmozart effect: A meta-analysis. *Intelligence, 38*, 314–323.

Mueller, C. M., & Dweck, C. S. (1998). Intelligence praise can undermine motivation and performance. *Journal of Personality and Social Psychology, 75*, 33–52.

Mundell, E. J. (2007, July 5). Science quiets myth of "chatterbox" females. Sexualhealth.com. Retrieved from http://sexualhealth.e-healtsource.com/index.php?p=news1&id=606134

Myers, D. (2000). The funds, friends, and faith of happy people. *American Psychologist, 55*, 56–67.

Nasaw, D. (2012, July 24). Meet the "bots" that edit Wikipedia. BBC News Magazine [Online edition]. Retrieved from http://www.bbc.co.uk/news/magazine-18892510

National Institutes of Health, Office of Human Subjects Research. (1979). *Belmont Report.* Retrieved from http://ohsr.od.nih.gov/guidelines/belmont.html

National Research Council. (2011). *Guide for the care and use of laboratory animals* (8th ed.). Washington, DC: National Academies Press.

Nauert, R. (2013, June 4). Meeting spouse online linked to better marriage. Retrieved from http://psychcentral.com/news/2013/06/04/meeting-spouse-online-linked-to-better-marriage/55590.html

Neisser, U., & Harsch, N. (1992). Phantom flashbulbs: False recollections of hearing the news about Challenger. In E. Winograd and U. Neisser (Eds.) *Affect and accuracy in recall.* New York: Cambridge University Press.

Newport, F., Witters, D., & Agrawal, S. (2012, February 16). Religious Americans enjoy higher well-being. *Gallup Well-Being* [Online magazine]. Retrieved from http://www.gallup.com/poll/152723/religious-americans-enjoy-higher-wellbeing.aspx

New York Times (2009, July 18). Should cell phone use by drivers be illegal? *New York Times* [Online edition]. Retrieved from http://roomfordebate.blogs.nytimes.com/2009/07/18/should-cellphone-use-by-drivers-be-illegal/

Nisbett, R. E., & Wilson, T. (1977). Telling more than we can know: Verbal reports on mental processes. *Psychological Review, 84*, 231–259.

O'Connor, A. (2012). The chocolate diet? *New York Times Well Blog.* Retrieved from http://well.blogs.nytimes.com/2012/03/26/the-chocolate-diet/?src=me&ref=general

Ortmann, A., & Hertwig, R. (1997). Is deception acceptable? *American Psychologist, 52*, 746–747.

Ostrovsky, Y., Meyers, E., Ganesh, S., Mathur, U., & Sinha, P. (2009). Parsing images via dynamic cues. *Psychological Science, 20*, 1484–1491.

Paik, H., & Comstock, G. (1994). The effects of television violence on antisocial behavior: A meta-analysis. *Communication Research, 21*, 516–546.

Pashler, H., & Wagenmakers, E. J. (2012). Editors' introduction to the special section on replicability in psychological science: A crisis of confidence? *Perspectives on Psychological Science, 7*, 528–529.

Pavot, W., & Diener, E. (1993). Review of the Satisfaction with Life Scale. *Psychological Assessment, 5*, 164–172.

Perry, G. (2013). *Behind the shock machine: The untold story of the notorious Milgram psychology experiments.* New York: New Press.

Pew Research Center. (n.d.). Cell phone surveys. Retrieved from http://www.people-press.org/methodology/collecting-survey-data/cell-phone-surveys/

Pew Research Center. (n.d.). Random digit dialing—Our standard method. Retrieved from http://people-press.org/methodology/sampling/#1

Pezdek, K. (2004). Event memory and autobiographical memory for the events of September 11, 2001. *Applied Cognitive Psychology, 17*, 1033–1045.

Pfungst, O. (1911). *Clever Hans (The horse of Mr. Von Osten): A contribution to experimental animal and human psychology*. New York: Henry Holt.

Piaget, J. (1923). *The language and thought of the child* (M. Worden, trans.). New York: Harcourt, Brace, & World.

Pietschnig, J., Voracek, M., & Formann, A. K. (2010). Mozart effect—Shmozart effect: A meta-analysis. *Intelligence, 38*, 314–323.

Piff, P. K., Stancato, D. M., Côté, S., Mendoza-Denton, R., & Keltner, D. (2012). Higher social class predicts increased unethical behavior. *Proceedings of the National Academy of Sciences, 109*, 4086–4091.

Pittenger, D. J. (2002). Deception in research: Distinctions and solutions from the perspective of utilitarianism. *Ethics & Behavior, 12*, 117–142.

Plous, S. (1996a). Attitudes toward the use of animals in psychological research and education: Results from a national survey of psychologists. *American Psychologist, 51*, 1167–1180.

Plous, S. (1996b). Attitudes toward the use of animals in psychological research and education: Results from a national survey of psychology majors. *Psychological Science, 7*, 352–358.

Plous, S. (1998). Signs of change within the animal rights movement: Results from a follow-up survey of activists. *Journal of Comparative Psychology, 112*, 48–54.

Plous, S., & Herzog, H. A., Jr. (2000). Poll shows researchers favor lab animal protection. *Science, 290*, 711.

Pope, T. (2009, February 24). The three R's? A fourth is crucial, too: Recess. *New York Times*, p. D4.

Pronin, E., Gilovich, T., & Ross, L. (2004). Objectivity in the eye of the beholder: Divergent perceptions of bias in self versus others. *Psychological Review, 111*, 781–799.

Pronin, E., Lin, D. Y., & Ross, L. (2002). The bias blind spot: Perceptions of bias in self versus others. *Personality and Social Psychology Bulletin, 28*, 369–381.

Quinn, P. C., Yahr, J., Kuhn, A., Slater, A. M., & Pascalis, O. (2002). Representation of the gender of human faces by infants: A preference for female. *Perception, 31*, 1109–1121.

Rabin, R. C. (2010, March 17). Talk deeply, be happy? *New York Times* [Online]. Retrieved from http://well.blogs.nytimes.com/2010/03/17/talk-deeply-be-happy/?src=me

Rampell, C. (2010, April 19). Want a higher GPA? Go to a private college [Blog post]. Retrieved from http://economix.blogs.nytimes.com/2010/04/19/want-a-higher-g-p-a-go-to-a-private-college/

Raskin, R., & Terry, H. (1988). A principle components analysis of the Narcissistic Personality Inventory and further evidence of its construct validity. *Journal of Personality and Social Psychology, 54*, 890–902.

Rauscher, F. H., Shaw, G. L., & Ky, K. N. (1993). Music and spatial task performance. *Nature, 365*, 611.

Raven, J. C. (1976). *Standard progressive matrices*. Oxford: Oxford Psychologists Press.

Reiss, J. E., & Hoffman, J. E. (2006). Object substitution masking interferes with semantic processing: Evidence from event-related potentials. *Psychological Science, 17*, 1015–1020.

Religion can spur goodness (2008, April 28). World-science.net. Retrieved from http://www.world-science.net/othernews/081002_religion

Religious Americans Enjoy Higher Well-Being (Gallup, 2012): *Chapter 5 opening headline*. Newport, F., Witters, D., & Agrawal, S. (2012, February 16). Religious Americans enjoy higher well-being. *Gallup Well-Being* [Online magazine]. Retrieved from http://www.gallup.com/poll/152723/religious-americans-enjoy-higher-wellbeing.aspx

Rentfrow, P. J., & Gosling, S. D. (2003). The do-re-mi's of everyday life: The structure and personality correlates of music preferences. *Journal of Personality and Social Psychology, 84*, 1236–1256.

Reproducibility Project: Psychology [Website]. Retrieved from https://osf.io/project/EZcUj/wiki/home/

Rettner, R. (2012, August 17). Shy people are better at reading facial expressions. *LiveScience* [Online magazine]. Retrieved from http://www.livescience.com/22468-shy-people-faces.html

Reverby, S. (2009). *Examining Tuskegee: The infamous syphilis study and its legacy*. Chapel Hill: University of North Carolina Press.

Roberts, B. W., & Robins, R. W. (2000). Broad dispositions, broad aspirations: The intersection of personality traits and major life goals. *Personality and Social Psychology Bulletin, 26*, 1284–1296.

Ropeik, D., & Gray, G. (2002). *Risk: A practical guide for deciding what's really safe and what's really dangerous in the world around you*. New York: Houghton Mifflin.

Rosenberg, M. (1965). *Society and the adolescent self-image*. Princeton, NJ: Princeton University Press.

Rosenthal, R., & Fode, K. (1963). The effect of experimenter bias on the performance of the albino rat. *Behavioral Science, 8*, 183–189.

Russell, D. (2011, December 12). Three things you might not know about the relationship between income and happiness. *PsychologyToday.com* [Online magazine]. Retrieved from http://www.psychologytoday.com/blog/distress-in-context/201112/three-things-you-might-not-know-about-the-relationship-between-incom

Sanbonmatsu, D. M., Strayer, D. L., Medeiros-Ward, N., & Watson, J. M. (2013). Who multitasks and why? Multitasking ability, perceived multi-tasking ability, impulsivity, and sensation-seeking. PLOS ONE, *8*(1) e54402.

Sasaki, J., & Kim, H. (2011). At the intersection of culture and religion: A cultural analysis of religion's implications for secondary control and social affiliation. *Journal of Personality and Social Psychology, 101,* 401–414.

Saxe, L. (1991). Lying: Thoughts of an applied social psychologist. *American Psychologist, 46,* 409–415.

Schellenberg, G. (2004). Music lessons enhance IQ. *Psychological Science, 15,* 511–514.

Sears, D. O. (1986). College freshmen in the laboratory: Influences of a narrow data base on social psychology's view of human nature. *Journal of Personality and Social Psychology, 51,* 515–539.

Seeing Red Affects Achievement. (*World Science,* 2007): *Chapter 10 opening headline. World Science* (2007, March 2) [Online]. Retrieved from http://www.world-science.net/othernews/ 070301_red.htm

Segal, D. L., Coolidge, F. L., Cahill, B. S., & O'Riley, A. A. (2008). Psychometric properties of the Beck Depression Inventory-II (BDI-II) among community-dwelling older adults. *Behavior Modification, 32,* 3–20.

Segall, M. H., Campbell, D. T., & Herskovits, M. J. (1966). *The influence of culture on visual perception.* Indianapolis, IN: Bobbs-Merrill.

70% of Canadians "Felt Well-Rested Yesterday" (Gallup Worldview, 2014): *Chapter 7 opening headline.* Gallup Worldview Interactive Database (2014). Feel well-rested item. Retrieved February 3, 2014, from https://worldview.gallup.com/

Shadish, W. R., & Luellen, J. K. (2006). Quasi-experimental design. In J. L. Green, G. Camilli, & P. B. Elmore (Eds.), *Handbook of complementary methods in education research* (pp. 539–550). Mahwah, NJ: Erlbaum.

Shaffer, D. R., Rogel, M., & Hendrick, C. (1975). Intervention in the library: The effect of increased responsibility on bystanders' willingness to prevent a theft. *Journal of Applied Social Psychology, 5,* 303–319.

Sharpe, D., Adair, J. G., & Roese, N. J. (1992). Twenty years of deception research: A decline in subjects' trust? *Personality and Social Psychology Bulletin, 18,* 585–590.

Should Cell Phone Use by Drivers Be Illegal? (*New York Times,* 2009): *Chapter 12 opening headline. New York Times* (2009, July 18). Should cell phone use by drivers be illegal? *New York Times* [Online edition]. Retrieved from http://roomfordebate.blogs.nytimes.com/2009/07/18/should-cellphone-use-by-drivers-be-illegal/

Shuster, E. (1997). Fifty years later: The significance of the Nuremberg Code. *New England Journal of Medicine, 337,* 1436–1440.

Shy People Are Better at Reading Facial Expressions (*LiveScience,* 2012): *Chapter 3 opening headline.* Rettner, R. (2012, August 17). Shy people are better at reading facial expressions. *LiveScience* [Online magazine]. Retrieved from http://www.livescience.com/ 22468-shy-people-faces.html

Shweder, R. (1989). Cultural psychology: What is it? In J. Stigler, R. Shweder, & G. Herdt (Eds.), *Cultural psychology: The Chicago symposia on culture and development* (pp. 1–46). New York: Cambridge University Press.

Silver, N. (2012). Fivethirtyeight: Nate Silver's political calculus. Retrieved from http://fivethirtyeight.blogs. nytimes.com

61% Said This Shoe "Felt True to Size" (Zappos.com): *Chapter 7 opening headline.* Zappos.com, online review data.

Smith, G. T. (2005a). On construct validity: Issues of method and measurement. *Psychological Assessment, 17,* 396–408.

Smith, G. T. (2005b). On the complexity of quantifying construct validity. *Psychological Assessment, 17,* 413–414.

Smith, S. S., & Richardson, D. (1983). Amelioriation of deception and harm in psychological research: The important role of debriefing. *Journal of Personality and Social Psychology, 44,* 1075–1082.

Smith, T. B., McCullough, M. E., & Poll, J. (2003). Religiousness and depression: Evidence for a main effect and the moderating influence of stressful life events. *Psychological Bulletin, 129,* 614–636.

Snyder, M., & Campbell, B. (1980). Testing hypotheses about other people: The role of the hypothesis. *Personality and Social Psychology Bulletin, 6,* 421–426.

Snyder, M., & Swann, W. B. (1978). Hypothesis-testing processes in social interaction. *Journal of Personality and Social Psychology, 36,* 1202–1212.

Snyder, M., & White, M. (1981). Testing hypotheses about other people: Strategies of verification and falsification. *Personality and Social Psychology Bulletin, 7,* 39–43.

Sowislo, J. F., & Orth, U. (2013). Does low self-esteem predict depression and anxiety? A meta-analysis of longitudinal studies. *Psychological Bulletin, 139,* 213–240.

Sperry, R. W. (1961). Cerebral organization and behavior. *Science, 133,* 1749–1757.

Spiegel, A. (2010, June 28). "Mozart effect" was just what we wanted to hear. National Public Radio transcript. Retrieved from http://www.npr.org/templates/story/story.php?storyId=128104580

Stanovich, K. E. (2010). *How to think straight about psychology* (9th ed.). Boston, MA: Allyn & Bacon.

Stapel Investigation (2012). Flawed science: The fraudulent research practices of social psychologist Diederik Stapel. Retrieved from https://www.commissielevelt.nl

Steele, K. M. (2013). Failure to replicate the Mehta and Zhu (2009) color-priming effect on anagram solution times. *Psychonomic Bulletin and Review*. Advance online publication.

Steenhuysen, J. (2010, April 26). Depressed? You must like chocolate. MSNBC mental health. Retrieved from http://www.msnbc.msn.com/id/36786824/ns/health-mental_health

Stein, R. (2009, June 22). Positive is negative. *Washington Post*. Retrieved from www.washingtonpost.com.

Steingraber, S. (2008). Pesticides, animals, and humans. In L. H. Peterson & J. C. Brereton (Eds.), *The Norton Reader* (11th ed., pp. 971–982). New York: Norton. (Reprinted from *Living downstream: An ecologist looks at cancer and the environment*, by S. Steingraber, 1997, New York: Perseus Books.)

Stobbe, M. (2012, June 8). CDC: Nearly 60 percent of teens text while driving. MSNBC.com. Retrieved from http://www.nbcnews.com/id/47723985/ns/health-health_care/t/cdc-nearly-percent-teens-text-while-driving/#.Uu_gxfZ6NxN

Strauman, T. J., Vieth, A. Z., Merrill, K. A., Woods, T. E., Kolden, G. G., Klein, M. H., . . . Kwapil, L. (2006). Self-system therapy as an intervention for self-regulatory dysfunction in depression: A randomized comparison with cognitive therapy. *Journal of Consulting and Clinical Psychology, 74*, 367–376.

Strayer, D. L., & Drews, F. A. (2004). Profiles in distraction: Effects of cell phone conversations on younger and older drivers. *Human Factors, 46*, 640–650.

Strayer, D. L., Drews, F. A., & Crouch, D. J. (2006). A comparison of the cell phone driver and the drunk driver. *Human Factors, 48*, 381–391.

Strayer, D. L., Drews, F. A., & Johnston, W. A. (2003). Cell phone induced failures in visual attention during simulated driving. *Journal of Experimental Psychology: Applied, 9*, 23–52.

Stuart, A. (n.d.) Don't fall for these happiness myths: Learn how to overcome them. Webmd.com. Retrieved from http://www.webmd.com/balance/guide/happiness-6-myths-and-truths

Suds seem to skew scientific success. (2008, March 18). UT San Diego. Retrieved from http://www.utsandiego.com/uniontrib/20080318/news_1n18science.html

Talk Deeply, Be Happy? (*New York Times*, 2010): *Chapter 8 opening headline*. Rabin, R. C. (2010, March 17). Talk deeply, be happy? *New York Times* [Online edition]. Retrieved from http://well.blogs.nytimes.com/2010/03/17/talk-deeply-be-happy/?src=me

Tavris, C. (1989). *Anger: The misunderstood emotion*. New York: Simon & Schuster.

Tawney, J. W., & Gast, D. L. (1994). *Single subject research in special education*. Columbus, OH: Merrill.

The Color Red Makes You Stronger, but More Distractable (*The Wire*, 2011): *Chapter 1 opening headline*. Estes, A. C. (2011, June 2). The color red makes you stronger, but more distractable. *The Wire* [Online magazine]. Retrieved from http://www.thewire.com/technology/2011/06/color-red-makes-you-stronger-faster/38435/

The Reason Why You're an Angry Drunk (*Men's Health,* 2012): *Chapter 12 opening headline*. Haller, M. (2012, January). The reason why you're an angry drunk. *Men's Health* [Online edition]. Retrieved from http://news.menshealth.com/the-reason-why-you%E2%80%99re-an-angry-drunk/2012/01/06

The Three R's? A Fourth Is Crucial, Too: Recess (*New York Times*, 2009): *Chapter 9 opening headline*. Pope, T. (2009, February 24). The three r's? a fourth is crucial, too: Recess. *New York Times*, p. D4.

Three Things You Might Not Know About the Relationship Between Income and Happiness (*PsychologyToday.com*, 2011): *Chapter 5 opening headline*. Russell, D. (2011, December 12). Three things you might not know about the relationship between income and happiness. *PsychologyToday.com* [Online magazine]. Retrieved from http://www.psychologytoday.com/blog/distress-in-context/201112/three-things-you-might-not-know-about-the-relationship-between-incom

Tucker, C. J., Finkelhor, D., Turner, H., & Shattuck, A. (2013). Association of sibling aggression with child and adolescent mental health. *Pediatrics, 132*, 79–84.

Turk, D. J., Heatherton, T. F., Macrae, C. N., Kelley, W. M., & Gazzaniga, M. S. (2003). Out of contact, out of mind: The distributed nature of the self. *Annals of the New York Academy of Sciences, 1001*, 65–78.

Turner, E. H., Matthews, A .M., Linardatos, E., Tell, R. A., & Rosenthal, R. (2008). Selective publication of antidepressant trials and its influence on apparent efficacy. *New England Journal of Medicine, 358*, 252–260.

Tversky, A., & Kahneman, D. (1974). Judgments under uncertainty: Heuristics and biases. *Science, 185*, 1124–1131.

Twachtman-Cullen, D. (1997). *A passion to believe: Autism and the facilitated communication phenomenon*. Boulder, CO: Westview Press.

U.S. Department of Health and Human Services. Data from the National Health Interview Survey. December, 2012. Retrieved from http://www.cdc.gov/nchs/data/series/sr_10/sr10_256.pdf

U.S. Department of Health and Human Services, National Institutes of Health. (2009). Public welfare, protection of human subjects. Code of Federal Regulations: HHS Regulation 45 CFR, Part 46. Retrieved from http://www.hhs.gov/ohrp/humansubjects/guidance/45cfr46.html

Vandell, D., Henderson, L. V., & Wilson, K. S. (1988). A longitudinal study of children with day-care experiences of varying quality. *Child Development, 59*, 1286–1292.

Van Kleef, E., Shimizu, M., & Wansink, B. (2012). Serving bowl selection biases the amount of food served. *Journal of Nutrition Education and Behavior, 44*, 66–70.

Van Orden, K. A., Witte, T. K., Cukrowicz, K. C., Braithwaite, S. R., Selby, E. A., & Joiner, T. E. (2010). The interpersonal theory of suicide. *Psychological Review, 117*, 575–600.

Vazire., S., & Carlson, E. N. (2011). Others sometimes know us better than we know ourselves. *Current Directions in Psychological Science, 20*, 104–108.

Venting Frustration Will Only Make Your Anger Worse (*Lifehacker.com*, 2010): *Chapter 2 opener*. Dachis, A. (2010, August 18). Venting frustration will only make your anger worse. *Lifehacker.com* [Online magazine]. Retrieved from http://www.lifehacker.com.au/2010/08/venting-frustration-will-only-make-your-anger-worse

Vickery, T. J., Chun, M. M., & Lee, D. (2011). Ubiquity and specificity of reinforcement signals throughout the human brain. *Neuron, 72*, 166–177.

Wansink, B. (1996). Can package size accelerate usage volume? *Journal of Marketing, 60*, 1–14.

Wansink, B. (2006). *Mindless eating: Why we eat more than we think*. New York: Bantam Books.

Wansink, B., & Cheney, M. M. (2005). Superbowls: Serving bowl size and food consumption. *Journal of the American Medical Association, 293*, 1727–1728.

Wansink, B., & Kim, J. (2005). Bad popcorn in big buckets: Portion size can influence intake as much as taste. *Journal of Nutrition Education and Behavior, 37*, 242–245.

Webb, E., Campbell, D., Schwartz, R., & Sechrest, L. (1966). *Unobtrusive measures: Nonreactive research in the social sciences*. Chicago, IL: Rand McNally.

Wechsler, D. (2004). *The Wechsler Intelligence Scale for Children* (4th ed.). London: Pearson Assessment.

Westman, M., & Eden, D. (1997). Effects of a respite from work on burnout: Vacation relief and fade-out. *Journal of Applied Psychology, 82*, 516–527.

What's the Difference Between a Pit Bull and a Hockey Dad? There Is No Difference (*Star Tribune*, 2008): *Chapter 6 opening headline*. Coleman, N. (2008, September 13). Hockey moms? Hockey dads set the example. *Star Tribune*. Retrieved from http://www.startribune.com

Whiff of Rosemary Gives Your Brain a Boost (*Body Odd*, nbcnews.com, 2012): *Chapter 3 opening headline*. Winner, A. (2012, February 25). A whiff of rosemary gives your brain a boost. *Body Odd* [Online magazine]. Retrieved from http://bodyodd.nbcnews.com/_news/2012/02/25/10498152-a-whiff-of-rosemary-gives-your-brain-a-boost?d=1

Wilson, D. C. (2006, December). Framing the future of race relations. *Public Opinion Pros*. Retrieved from http://www.publicopinionpros.norc.org

Wilson, D. C., Moore, D. W., McKay, P. F., & Avery, D. R. (2008). Affirmative action programs for women and minorities: Support affected by question order. *Public Opinion Quarterly, 73*, 514–522.

Winner, A. (2012, February 25). A whiff of rosemary gives your brain a boost. *Body Odd* [Online magazine]. Retrieved from http://bodyodd.nbcnews.com/_news/2012/02/25/10498152-a-whiff-of-rosemary-gives-your-brain-a-boost?d=1

Wood, J. V., Perunovic, E. W. Q., & Lee, J. W. (2009). Positive self-statements: Power for some, peril for others. *Psychological Science, 20*, 860–866.

Worthington, E. L., Wade, N. G., Height, T. L., Ripley, J., McCullough, M. E., Berry, J. W., Schmitt, M. M., Berry, J. T., Bursley, K. H., & O'Connor, L. (2003). The religious commitment inventory-10: Development, refinement, and validation of a brief scale for research and counseling. *Journal of Counseling Psychology, 50*, 84–96.

Your Plate Is Bigger Than Your Stomach (*New York Times*, 2007): *Chapter 10 opening headline*. Leonhardt, D. (2007, May 2). Your plate is bigger than your stomach. *New York Times*. Retrieved from http://www.nytimes.com/2007/05/02/business/02leonhardt.html?pagewanted=all

Zajonc, R. B., Heingartner, A., & Herman, E. M. (1969). Social enhancement and impairment of performance in the cockroach. *Journal of Personality and Social Psychology, 13*, 83–92.

Credits

conduct (2002, amended June 1, 2010). Retrieved from http://www.apa.org/ethics/code/index.aspx. No further reproduction or distribution is permitted without written permission from the American Psychological Association; **p. 102:** Beth Morling; **p. 103:** Diego Cervo/Fotolia; **p. 106:** From Stapel & Lindenberg, *Science* 332:251 (2011) Reprinted with permission from AAAS; **p. 107:** Morling, Beth. *Research Methods in Psychology* 2e, WW Norton; **p. 110:** Courtesy PETA; **p. 111:** Courtesy Foundation for Biomedical Research; **pp. 116–119:** Copyright © 2010 by the American Psychological Association. Reproduced with permission. The official citation that should be used in referencing this material is: American Psychological Association. (2010a). Ethical principles of psychologists and code of conduct (2002, amended June 1, 2010). Retrieved from http://www.apa.org/ethics/code/index.aspx. No further reproduction or distribution is permitted without written permission from the American Psychological Association.

Chapter 5

Page 120 (top): Dreamstime; **(center):** AP Photo; **(bottom):** Anne Marie Weber/Getty Images; **p. 126:** Vickery et al. (2011). Ubiquity and specificity of reinforcement signals throughout the human brain. *Neuron*, 72(1): 166–177, supplemental Figure S1, panel B. © 2011 Elsevier; **p. 135:** Table 2, p.167, from Pavot, W., & Diener, E. (1993). Review of the Satisfaction With Life Scale. Psychological Assessment, 5(2), 164–172. doi:10.1037/1040-3590.5.2.164; **p. 136:** Topham/The Image Works; **p. 143:** Copyright © 2013 Gallup, Inc. All rights reserved. The content is used with permission; however, Gallup retains all rights of republication; **p. 148:** Ocean/Corbis; **p. 149:** Copyright © 2013 by the American Psychological Association. Reproduced with permission. Worthington et al. (2003). The religious commitment inventory-10: Development, refinement, and validation of a brief scale for research and counseling. *Journal of Counseling Psychology*, 50, 84–96. No further reproduction or distribution is permitted without written permission from the American Psychological Association.

Part Opener III

Page 155 (clockwise): Dreamstime; Shutterstock (2).

Chapter 6

Page 156 (from top down): Dreamstime; Shutterstock; WW Norton; Shutterstock; **p. 159:** Courtesy Zappos.com; **p. 164:** Diener, E., Emmons, R. A., Larsen, R. J., & Griffin, S. (1985). The Satisfaction with Life Scale. *Journal of Personality Assessment*, 49, 71–75; **p. 167:**

NovaStock/Superstock; **p. 170:** Courtesy Matthias Mehl, University of Arizona; **p. 171 (both):** Copyright 2013 by the American Psychological Association. Reproduced with permission. Campos et al. (2013). Positive and negative emotion in the daily life of dual-earner couples with children. *Journal of Family Psychology*, 27(1), 76–85. doi:10.1037/a0031413. No further reproduction or distribution is permitted without written permission from the American Psychological Association; **p. 173:** Mary Evans Picture Library/Alamy; **p. 174:** Reprinted with permission from Bowker et al. 2009, Naturalistic observations of spectator behavior at youth hockey games. *The Sport Psychologist*, 23(3) 301–316. © 2009 Human Kinetics, Inc; **p. 176:** Spencer Grant/Science Source.

Chapter 7

Page 180 (from top down): Phil Rees/Alamy; Blend Images/Superstock; Courtesy Zappos.com; **p. 185:** Bonnie Jo Mount/The Washington Post via Getty Images; **p. 187 (left):** RayArt Graphics/Alamy; **(right):** © 2013 Carol Bainbridge (http://giftedkids.about.com/). Used with permission of About Inc., which can be found online at www.about.com. All rights reserved; **p. 188:** AP Photo/PRNewsFoto/PowerSchool, a division of Apple Computer, Inc.; **p. 189:** Urbaniak, G. C., & Plous, S. (2013). Research Randomizer (Version 4.0) [Computer software]. Retrieved on June 22, 2013, from http://www.randomizer.org.

Part Opener IV

Page 201 (clockwise): H. Mark Weidman Photography Alamy; Matthew Staver/The New York Times/Redux; Dreamstime.

Chapter 8

Page 202 (from top down): ZenShui/Sigrid Olson/Getty Images; Matthew Staver/The New York Times/Redux (2); **p. 214:** i love images/Alamy; **p. 216:** Mehl et al. Eavesdropping on Happiness: Well-Being Is Related to Having Less Small Talk and More Substantive Conversations. Psychological Science April 2010 21: 539–541, first published 2/18/10. Copyright © 2010, APS.

Chapter 9

Page 234 (from top down): Megapress/Alamy; Diego Vito Cervo/Dreamstime; Dreamstime; **p. 241:** Andia/Alamy; **p. 252:** Dimitrios Pappas/Dreamstime.com; **p. 253:** Megapress/Alamy; **p. 255:** David J. Green-Lifestyle/Alamy; **p. 262:** Barros et al. (2009). School recess and group classroom behavior. *Pediatrics*, 123, 431–436. © 2009, American Academy of Pediatrics.

Part Opener V

Page 269 (clockwise): Geoff Manasse/Getty Images; Andrew Scrivani /The New York Times /Redux; iStockphoto.

Chapter 10

Page 270 (from top down): iStockphoto; Andrew Scrivani/The New York Times/Redux; iStockphoto; **p. 272 (clockwise):** Elopaint/Dreamstime.com; devon/FeaturePics; Batman2000/FeaturePics; **p. 299:** Andrei Cimpian.

Chapter 11

Page 306 (from top): Dorling Kindersley/UI/agefotostock; Geoff Manasse/Getty Images; **p. 320:** The Photo Works/Alamy.

Chapter 12

Page 342 (top): Edward Frazer/Corbis; **(center):** Fred Prouser/Reuters; **(bottom):** Novastock Stock Connection Worldwide/Newscom; **p. 349:** Strayer, D. L., & Drews, F. A. (2004). Profiles in driver distraction: Effects of cell phone conversations on younger and older drivers. *Human Factors*, 46, 640-649. Photo courtesy David Strayer.

Part Opener VI

Page 379 (top right): Benoit Decout/REA/Redux; **(bottom right):** iStockphoto.

Chapter 13

Page 380 (top): Elleringmann/laif/Redux; **(bottom):** Shutterstock; **p. 389:** Antonio Perez/MCT/Newscom; **p. 403:** Mendil/Science Source; **p. 406 (left):** Farrell Grehan/Corbis; **(right):** Maya Barnes Johansen/The Image Works.

Chapter 14

Page 412 (top): Barbara Davidson/Los Angeles Times; **(bottom):** Benoit Decout/REA/Redux; **p. 415:** Jones et al. (2004). How do I love thee? Let me count the J's: Implicit egotism and interpersonal attraction. *Journal of Personality and Social Psychology*, 87, 665-683. © APA; **p. 420:** Robert Harding Picture Library/Alamy; **p. 423:** Tom Grill/age footstock; **p. 428:** Gallery Stock; **pp. 431-432:** Masuda & Nisbett (2001), JPSP, 81, 922-934. © Takahiko Masuda, All rights Reserved.

Statistics Review: Descriptive Statistics

Page 450: Wansink & Kim (2005) Bad Popcorn in Big Buckets: Portion Size Can Influence Intake as Much as Taste. *Journal of Nutrition Education and Behavior*, Volume 37, Issue 5, Pages 242-245. Table 2. Copyright © 2005. Elsevier; **p. 460:** Bushman, B. J., & Anderson, C. A. (2001). Media violence and the American Public. *American Psychologist*, 56, 477-489. © Copyright 2001 by Brad J. Bushman & Craig A. Anderson.

Presenting Results: APA-Style Reports and Conference Posters

pp. 502-504: From *The Norton Field Guide to Writing, Third Edition* by Richard Bullock. Copyright © 2013, 2009, 2006 by W. W. Norton & Company, Inc. Used by permission of W. W. Norton & Company, Inc.

Name Index

A

Aarts, H., 15
Abelson, R. P., 172, 175, 255
Adair, J. G., 104
Agras, W. S., 410
Amanzio, M., 320
Anderson, C. A., 39, 46, 241, 256, 421, 422, 460, 461
Arce, H. C., 299
Arekere, D. M., 91
Arnett, J., 433
Aron, A., 465
Aron, A. P., 411
Asteggiano, G., 320
Avery, D. R., 163
Avnaim-Pesso, L., 385

B

Baddeley, D., 352, 353
Banaji, M. R., 166
Barnett, W. S., 393
Baron, R. M., 259
Barros, R. M., 242, 249, 262, 490
Bartholow, B. D., 351, 352, 354–56
Baumeister, R. F., 28
Baumrind, D., 93, 94
Bear, G., 478
Beck, A. T., 141
Beck, M. E., 170
Beecher, H. K., 320
Benedetti, F., 320
Berkowitz, L., 28, 29, 428
Bick, J., 289, 291
Bigham, S., 46
Blaine, B., 419
Blass, T., 94

Bogen, J. E., 399
Borkenau, P., 465
Boucher, J., 46
Bowker, A., 169, 174, 189, 192
Brewer, M., 425
Bröder, A., 104
Brook, J. S., 239
Brown, R., 427
Bushman, B. J., 28, 29, 39, 41, 241, 350, 449, 460, 461, 479, 491

C

Cacioppo, J., 204, 205, 208, 209, 397
Cacioppo, S., 204
Cahill, B. S., 144
Camara, W. J., 218
Campbell, B., 35
Campbell, D., 176
Campbell, D. T., 430
Campos, B., 170, 171, 174, 195
Cantril, H., 123
Carey, B., 252
Carlson, E. N., 164, 166
Carlson, N., 126
Carroll, L., 233
Carvallo, M., 414, 475
Chase, W. G., 407
Cheney, M. M., 416, 491
Childress, J. F., 91
Christian, L., 186
Chun, M. M., 126
Cicirelli, V. G., & Associates, 382, 383, 388, 392
Cimpian, A., 299
Cohen, J., 207, 420

Cohen, P., 239
Coile, D. C., 111
Comstock, G., 236, 238
Connor Snibbe, A., 185
Coolidge, F. L., 144
Cooper, J., 376, 417
Copeland J., 35
Côté, S., 125
Crocker, J., 419
Cronbach, L. J., 137
Crouch, D. J., 417, 418

D

D'Agostino, P. R., 15
Danziger, S., 386, 390
Darley, J. M., 305, 435
Deary, I. J., 126
DeNoon, D. J., 251
DeWall, C. N., 355, 358
Diener, C., 123
Diener, E., 122, 123, 135, 142, 204, 336
Dimock, M., 186
Donnerstein, E., 428
Doyle, A. C., 32
Dozier, M., 289, 291
Drews, F. A., 344, 345, 349, 357, 358, 371, 416–18, 429
Duchan, J. F., 7
Duke, A. A., 350
Dutton, D. G., 411
Dweck, C. S., 286, 287, 295, 298, 299, 301

E

Ebbinghaus, H., 407
Echternacht, G., 218

Edgington, E. S., 478
Eisenberg, L., 25
Elliot, A. J., 7, 15, 17, 104, 273, 280, 285, 297, 301, 319, 418, 425, 457, 459
Emmons, R. A., 336
Erbaugh, J., 141
Ericsson, K. A., 407
Eron, L. D., 237–39, 241

F

Faloon, S., 407
Feshbach, S., 28, 29
Finkelhor, D., 266
Fode, K., 173, 175
Formann, A. K., 19
Frey, D., 33

G

Ganesh, S., 440
Gast, D. L., 404
Gay, P., 31
Gazzaniga, M., 399, 401, 433, 437
Gazzaniga, M. S., 399, 401
Geen, R. G., 29
Gernsbacher, M. A., 281
Giancola, P. R., 344, 350
Gilbert, D., 32
Gilovich, T., 35
Godden, D. R., 352, 353
Goldacre, B., 19
Gonzaga, G. C., 204
Gosling, S. D., 227
Gottfredson, L. S., 138
Gould, S. J., 126, 136
Gray, F. D., 91, 92
Gray, G., 31
Green, B. L., 91
Greenwald, A. G., 166
Gunn, R. L., 344

H

Ha, Y. W., 35
Hamediani, M. G., 430
Hamzelou, J., 440
Han, W. J., 248, 251
Hanlon, C., 427
Harlow, H., 10, 288, 426
Harsch, N., 168
Heatherton, T. F., 401
Heine, S. J., 430, 433

Heingartner, A., 175
Heinz, A., 351, 352, 354–56
Heller, J., 91
Henderson, L. V., 347
Hendrick, C., 103, 433
Hennigan, K. M., 386, 387, 391
Henrich, J., 430, 433
Herman, E. M., 175
Herskovits, M. J., 430
Hertsgaard, D., 420
Hertwig, R., 104
Herzog, H. A., Jr., 109, 110
Higginbotham, D. J., 7
Hill, P. L., 257
Hoffman, J. E., 44
Holmes, T. H., 124
Holt, J. C. D., 344
Horwitz, J., 336
Hsu, J., 264
Hubbard, F. O. A., 265
Huesmann, L. R., 237

I

Ioannidis, J. P. A., 419

J

Jacob, R. G., 410
Jacobson, J. W., 7
Janzen-Wilde, M. L., 7
Johansson, G., 433–35
Johnson, J. G., 239
Johnson, W., 125
Johnston, W. A., 416
Jones, J. H., 90–92
Jones, J. T., 414, 415, 475
Jonsen, A. R., 95, 98
Judd, C. M., 164

K

Kagay, M., 161, 162
Kahneman, D., 31, 106, 419
Kasen, S., 239
Katz, R. V., 91
Keeter, S., 186
Kelley, W. M., 401
Keltner, D., 125
Kenny, D. A., 257, 259, 350, 465
Kiene, H., 321
Kienle, G. S., 321
Kim, H., 147, 150
Kim, J., 416, 449, 450, 455, 460, 490

Kimmel, A. J., 97, 98, 104, 110, 111
King, L. A., 336
Kirsch, I., 320
Klayman, J., 35
Klewe, L., 7
Krosnick, J. A., 164
Kuhn, A., 288
Ky, K. N., 7

L

Langer, E. J., 172, 175
Latané, B., 305, 435
Lavallee, K. L., 383, 384
Lebedeck, M., 410
Lee, D., 126
Lee, J., 37
Lee, J. W., 375
Lefkowitz, M. M., 237
Lelkes, Y., 164, 166
Levav, J., 385
Liberman, R. P., 405
Liebler, A., 465
Light, H., 420
Likert, R., 159
Lin, D. Y., 35
Linardatos, E., 423
Lohr, J. M., 28, 29
Lovaas, O. I., 281
Luellen, J. K., 383, 392
Lyubomirsky, S., 336

M

Macrae, C. N., 401
Maier, M. A., 15, 17
Margraf, J., 383, 384, 389, 394, 395
Markman, E. M., 299
Markus, H. R., 185, 430
Marshall, B. J., 31
Marx, D. M., 164
Masuda, T., 431, 432
Mathur, U., 440
Matthews, A. M., 423
Mayes, A., 46
McCallum, J. M., 91
McCartney, K., 214
McCullough, M. E., 419
McKay, P. F., 163
McKey, R., 393
McNulty, J. K., 347, 370
Medeiros-Ward, N., 205
Meehl, P. E., 137

Mehl, M. R., 169, 170, 176, 190, 196, 204–6, 216, 217, 220, 227–29, 336, 440
Mehta, R., 418
Meier, B. P., 15
Mendelson, M., 141
Mendoza-Denton, R., 125
Meslin, E. M., 91
Meyer, A. H., 383, 384
Meyers, E., 440
Milgram, S., 92–94, 107
Miller, D. P., 248, 251
Miller, G. E., 407
Miller, N. E., 111
Mirenberg, M. C., 414, 475
Mitchell, G., 435
Mock, J., 141
Moffat, N. J., 403
Mook, D., 334, 427, 428
Moore, D. W., 163
Morris, D. H., 344
Mueller, C. M., 286, 287, 295, 298, 301
Mulick, J. A., 7
Mundell, E. J., 372
Myers, D., 336

N

Nasaw, D., 48
Neisser, U., 168
Nida, S., 435
Nisbett, R. E., 167, 431, 432
Norenzayan, A., 430, 433
Nosek, B. A., 166

O

Ochs, E., 170
O'Connor, A., 252
Ogburn, E. L., 204
Olatunji, B. O., 28
Onghena, P., 478
O'Riley, A. A., 144
Orth, U., 46
Ortmann, A., 104
Ostrovsky, Y., 440

P

Paik, H., 236, 238
Park, B., 164
Pascalis, O., 288
Pashler, H., 419

Pavot, W., 122, 135, 142, 204
Pelham, B. W., 414, 475
Penke, J., 125
Pennebaker, J. W., 169, 176, 227, 336
Perry, G., 94
Perunovic, E. W. Q., 375
Pezdek, K., 168
Pfungst, O., 173
Phillips, C. M., 28
Piaget, J., 406
Pietschnig, J., 19
Piff, P. K., 125
Pittenger, D. J., 104
Plaksina, T., 170
Plous, S., 109, 110
Poll, J., 419
Pope, T., 242, 250
Pronin, E., 35

Q

Quanty, M. B., 29
Quinn, P. C., 288

R

Rabin, R. C., 221
Rahe, R. H., 124
Ramirez-Esparza, N., 169, 336
Raskin, D. E., 405
Raskin, R., 158
Rauscher, F. H., 7
Raven, J. C., 296
Reiss, J. E., 44
Repetti, R. L., 170
Reverby, S., 90, 91
Richardson, D., 104
Rivers, B. M., 91
Roberts, B. W., 257
Roese, N. J., 104
Rogel, M., 103, 433
Ropeik, D., 31
Rosenberg, M., 159
Rosenthal, R., 173, 175, 214, 423
Ross, L., 35

S

Sanbonmatsu, D. M., 205–7, 220, 226, 452, 453
Sapirstein, G., 320
Sasaki, J., 147, 150
Saxe, L., 141
Schellenberg, G., 73, 77

Schoebi, D., 170
Schwartz, A. A., 7
Schwartz, R., 176
Sears, D. O., 433
Sechrest, L., 176
Segal, D. L., 144, 145
Segall, M. H., 430
Shadish, W. R., 383, 388, 392
Shaffer, D. R., 103, 433, 435
Shapiro, H. T., 91
Sharpe, D., 104
Shattuck, A., 266
Shaw, G. L., 7
Shimizu, M., 274
Shuster, E., 95
Shweder, R., 430
Silver, E. J., 242, 490
Silver, N., 194
Sinha, P., 440
Slatcher, R. B., 169, 336
Slater, A. M., 288
Smailes, E. M., 239
Smith, G. T., 137, 144
Smith, S. S., 104
Smith, T. B., 419
Snyder, M., 34, 35
Sowislo, J. F., 46
Sperry, R. W., 399, 402
Spiegel, A., 17, 18
Stahlberg, D., 33
Stancato, D. M., 125
Stanovich, K. E., 12
Steele, K. M., 418
Stein, R., 373
Stein, R. E. K., 242, 490
Strauman, T. J., 14
Strayer, D. L., 205, 344, 345, 349, 357, 358, 371, 376, 416–18, 429
Swann, W. G., 34

T

Tawney, J. W., 404
Tell, R. A., 423
Terry, H., 158
Tucker, C. J., 266, 267
Turk, D. J., 401, 437
Turner, E. H., 423
Turner, H., 266
Tversky, A., 31
Twachtman-Cullen, D., 7, 12

V

Vandell, D., 347
VanderWeele, T. J., 204
van Ijzendoorn, M. H., 265
van Kleef, E., 274
Vazire, S., 164, 166
Vickery, T. J., 126
Vighetti, S., 320
Voracek, M., 19

W

Wagenmakers, E. J., 419

Walder, L. O., 237
Waldfogel, J., 248, 251
Wang, S., 170
Wansink, B., 274, 298, 415, 416, 449, 450, 455, 460, 490, 491
Ward, C. H., 141
Warren, J. R., 31
Watson, J. M., 205
Webb, E., 176
Webster, G. D., 350
West, T. V., 465
White, M., 35

Wilkowski, B. M., 15
Wilson, D. C., 160, 163
Wilson, K. S., 347
Wilson, T., 167
Wood, J. V., 375, 376
Worthington, E. L., 147–49

Y

Yahr, J., 288

Z

Zajonc, R. B., 175
Zhu, R. J., 418

Subject Index

A

Abelson, R. P., 175
Abelson, Robert, 254–55
abstract
  in empirical journal articles, 44–45
  in research reports, 489
abstract constructs, measurement validity of, 136–37
academic achievement
  color and, 272–78, 280–82, 284, 285, 297–98, 301, 319, 418, 447–68
  of Head Start students, 382–83, 388, 392–93
acquiescence (yea-saying), 164, 165
"adjusting for," 251–52
advice, 65
aggression
  alcohol use and, 343–44, 350–52, 355, 358–59, 362–63, 371
  venting of anger and, 23, 24, 28–29, 36–37, 41, 479
  violent media and, 237–41, 256, 261, 421–22, 461
alpha level, 467, 470–72
Alzheimer's patients, expanded rehearsal by, 403
Amen, Daniel, 47
American Psychological Association (APA)
  conference posters in APA style, 522–25
  Ethical Principles of Psychologists and Code of Conduct, 98–111

Ethical Standard 8, 99–111, 116–19
  research reports in APA style, 487–521
analysis of variance (ANOVA), 479–82
Anderson, Craig, 421–22, 461
Anger (Tavris), 47
anger, venting, 23, 24, 28–29, 36–37, 41, 479
animal research, Ethical Standard 8 on, 108–11
animal rights groups, 109–10
Animal Welfare Act (AWA), 108
ANOVA (analysis of variance), 479–82
antidepressant medications, 423
APA, *see* American Psychological Association
APA Ethics Office, 100
applied research, 13–14
approach orientation, 272
Arce, H. C., 299
areas under the normal curve (distribution of z), 533–39
association claims, 61–64
  and causal relationships, 235–36; *see also* causation
  construct validity of, 210
  defined, 61
  distinguishing features of, 61
  external validity of, 226–30
  internal validity of, 221–26
  interrogating, 68–71, 203–4, 210, 235–36

phrases distinguishing causal claims from, 65
  reliability as special example of, 130
  research mode for, 429
  statistical validity of, 210–21; *see also* multivariate correlational research (multivariate designs)
associations
  bivariate, 204–9, 217
  in causal claims, 64
  curvilinear, 220–23
  described with categorical data, 208–9
  descriptive statistics for, 452–56
  generalization of, 227
  making predictions based on, 64
  negative, 62–64, 453
  outliers affecting, 217–18
  positive, 62–64, 453
  spurious, 225
  statistical significance of, 70
  zero, 62–64, 215, 453
attachment
  in infant monkeys, 10–11, 278, 288, 426–27
  theories of, 9–11
attrition threats
  in experiments, 315–16, 322
  in quasi-experiments, 393–94
authorities, trust in, 36–39
autism
  childhood vaccines and, 37
  discriminant validity of scales, 145, 146

autism *(cont.)*
  intensive therapy for, 281–82
autocorrelations, 238, 239
availability heuristic, 31–32
average, *see* mean
Avnaim-Pesso, L., 385–86, 389–90, 395
avoidance orientation, 272, 297–98
AWA (Animal Welfare Act), 108

B
b (unstandardized coefficient), 246–47
Baddeley, D., 352–53
bar graphs
  associations on, 208–9
  detecting interactions from, 357–58
Barros, R. M., 242–43, 249, 261
Bartholow, Bruce, 351–54, 362
basic research, 14
BDI, *see* Beck Depression Inventory
Beck, Aaron, 141
Beck, M. E., 170–71, 195–96
Beck Depression Inventory (BDI)
  convergent validity of, 144
  discriminant validity of, 145–46
  known-groups criterion validity of, 141–42
behavioral measures (observational measures), 125
behavior-change studies in clinical settings (small-*N*), 402–6
  multiple-baseline designs, 404–5
  reversal designs, 405–6
  stable-baseline designs, 403
beliefs, sources of evidence for, *see* sources of information
Belmont Report, 95–98
beneficence, principle of, 96–97, 99, 100
beta
  inferential statistics for, 483–84
  and number of predictor variables, 250
  in testing for third variables, 246–49
between-groups design, *see* independent-groups designs
between-groups difference, null effects and, 326–29

between-subjects design, *see* independent-groups designs
bias blind spot, 35
biased samples (unrepresentative samples), 182–88, 192–93
  from convenience sampling, 185–86
  from self-selection, 187–88
  techniques resulting in, 192–93
bias(es)
  cognitive, 30–33
  countering, 36
  motivational, 33–35
  observer, 172–75, 318, 319, 323, 395–96
  present/present, 32–33
  publication, 422–23
  in sampling, 184–88, 192–93
Bick, J., 289, 291, 292
bimodal distributions, 444
bivariate correlational research, 203–31
  bivariate correlations, 204–9
  construct validity of, 210
  external validity of, 226–30
  internal validity of, 221–26
  for interrogating association claims, 210
  statistical validity of, 210–21
bivariate correlations (bivariate associations), 204–9
  with categorical data, 208–9
  defined, 204
  outliers with, 217
  with quantitative variables, 206–7
books
  edited, chapters in, 42, 46
  scientific, 42, 44
  trade, 47–48
Bowker, A., 169, 170, 176
brain
  fMRI scanning of, 125–26
  scent of rosemary and, 78–81
  split brain research, 399–402, 408, 437
Brook, J. S., 239
Brown, R., 427–28
Bushman, B. J., 28–29, 350, 355, 358–59, 362, 371, 461, 479
Buxtun, Peter, 91

C
Cacioppo, John, 204–5, 208–9, 211, 214, 216, 397
Campbell, D. T., 430–31
Campos, B., 170–71, 195–96
Carey, B., 251, 252
carryover effects, 291
Carvallo, M., 414–15, 475
categorical variables
  describing associations with, 208–9
  quantitative variables versus, 127, 128
catharsis hypothesis, 28–29, 31–33
causal claims, 64–65, 271
  construct validity of, 295–98
  defined, 64
  experiments supporting, 277–84
  external validity of, 298–300
  internal validity of, 302, 308–23
  interrogating, 71–77, 295–302
  interventions and treatments resulting from, 271
  phrases distinguishing association claims from, 65
  research mode for, 429
  statistical validity of, 300–301; *see also* experiments
causal temptation, 221
causation
  associations and, 235–36
  criteria for, 72–73, 236–37
  mediation and, 257–60
  pattern and parsimony and, 254–56
  temporal precedence and, 237–41
  third variable problem and, 242–54; *see also* multivariate correlational research (multivariate designs)
CDC (U.S. Centers for Disease Control and Prevention), 61
ceiling effect, 326–28
cell phone use, while driving, 344–45, 347–49, 363, 371, 416–18, 433
cells (in factorial designs), 348
census, 183
Center for Epidemiologic Studies Depression scale (CES-D), 144, 145

central tendency, 444–46
Cham, Jorge, 18
chapters in edited books, 42, 46
Chase, W. G., 407
"cherry-picking" information, 33
child cognitive development, 406
Cicirelli, V. G., & Associates, 382–83, 388, 392–93
Cimpian, A., 299
citations, 107
citing sources, 504–6
claims, 60–66
    association, 61–64, 68–71
    causal, 64–65
    defined, 60
    frequency, 60–61, 67–68
    validity of, 66–78; *see also* association claims; causal claims; frequency claims
Clever Hans, 173–75
Clinton, Bill, 91
cluster sampling, 189
codebooks, 174
coefficient alpha (Cronbach's alpha), 135
cognitive biases, 30–33
Cohen, Jacob, 207
Cohen, P., 239
Cohen's *d,* 456–59
color(s)
    academic achievement and, 272–78, 280–82, 284, 285, 297–98, 301, 319, 418, 447–68
    associations with, 7–8
    behavior and, 15
combined threats, 317–18
comparison groups
    in anger-venting research, 28–29
    covariance and, 277
    defined, 25, 277
    personal experience and, 25–27
conceptual definitions, *see* conceptual variables
conceptual replication, 415–16
conceptual variables (conceptual definitions, constructs), 57–59
    defined, 57
    operationalization of, 58–59, 122–24
concurrent-measures design, 288
conditions (of variables), 274–75

confederate, 28
conference posters (APA style), 522–25
confirmatory hypothesis testing, 34–35
confounds
    controlling for, 28
    defined, 27, 279
    with experience, 27
    in research, *see* design confounds
constant, 56
construct, 57; *see also* conceptual variables
construct validity
    of abstract constructs, 136–37
    of association claims, 68–69, 210
    of causal claims, 76, 295–98
    defined, 67, 69
    evidence of, 147–50
    of frequency claims, 67
    of measured variables, *see* measurement
    of multivariate designs, 261
    of observational research, 168–77
    in quasi-experiments, 397
    of small-*N* designs, 408
    of surveys and polls, 158–68
consumers of research information, 4–8
    interrogation tools for, *see* interrogating information
    judging of studies' importance by, 413
contact comfort theory, 10–11, 426–27
content validity, 137–38
control for (term)
    popular press' use of, 250–51
    in regression analysis, 243–45
control group
    defined, 278
    in experiments, 278
control variables, in experiments, 276
convenience sampling, 185–86, 192
convergent validity, 143, 144, 146
Cooper, J., 417
Cornell University Food and Brand Lab, 274–75
"correcting for," 251–52

correction for restriction of range, 220
correlate (covary)
    defined, 61; *see also* association; covariance
correlational studies
    bivariate, 203–31
    defined, 68
    multivariate, 235–63
    quasi-experiments versus, 397–98
    supporting association claims, 209
correlation coefficient (*r*), 454–56
    computing, 454–55
    defined, 132
    inferential statistics for, 482–83
    reliability evaluation with, 132–35
    r to *z'* conversion, 545–46
    sampling distribution of, 482–83
correlations
    autocorrelations, 238, 239
    bivariate, 204–9, 217
    for criterion validity, 139–40
    cross-lag, 238, 239
    cross-sectional, 238
    curvilinear, 220–23
    in establishing reliability, 130
    in longitudinal designs, 238–39
    negative, 62–64, 453
    positive, 62–64, 453
    zero, 62–64, 215, 453
cosmetic surgery, psychological effects of, 383–85, 389–91, 395
counterbalancing
    defined, 292
    in within-groups designs, 292–93
Couples Satisfaction Index (CSI), 205
covariance
    as criterion for causation, 72, 222
    defined, 72
    in experiments, 277–78
    in longitudinal studies, 240
    in multivariate designs, 236
crime rates, access to television and, 386–87, 390, 391, 395
criterion validity, 139–43
criterion variables, 246; *see also* dependent variable

critical value (of *t*), 478
Cronbach's alpha (coefficient alpha), 135
cross-lag correlations, 238, 239
cross-sectional correlations, 238
Crouch, D. J., 417–18
CSI (Couples Satisfaction Index), 205
cultural psychology, 430–33
cupboard theory, 10, 11
curvilinear association (curvilinear correlation), 220–23

D

Danziger, S., 385–86, 389–90, 395
data
  defined, 11
  theories supported by, 12
  in theory-data cycle, 9–13
  unobtrusive, 176
database searches, 42–44
data fabrication, 105–6
data falsification, 105–6
data matrices, 442
debriefing
  Ethical Standard 8 on, 104–5
  in Milgram obedience study, 94
deception
  defined, 104
  Ethical Standard 8 on, 103–4
decision making
  ethical, 112
  judicial, food breaks and, 385–86, 389–90, 395
Declaration of Helsinki, 95
deep talk, 204–7, 210, 211, 222, 224–26, 229
degrees of freedom, 476
demand characteristics (experimental demand)
  controlling for, 319
  defined, 294
  in experiments, 294, 318–19, 323
  in quasi-experiments, 395–96
DeNoon, D. J., 251
dependent variable (outcome variable, criterion variable)
  ceilings, floors, and, 327
  construct validity of, 295–96
  defined, 73, 276
  in experiments, 276

on graphs, 276
  measurement error with, 330–31
depression
  BDI measurement of, 144, 145
  and discriminant validity of measures, 146
  religiosity and, 419–20
  reversal study of, 405–6
descriptive statistics, 441–61
  for associations, 452–56
  for central tendencies, 444–46
  data matrices, 442
  for effect size, 456–61
  frequency distributions, 442–44
  for relative standing, 450–52
  stemplots, 442, 444
  for variability, 446–50
design confounds
  in experiments, 280–81, 308, 322, 329
  in quasi-experiments, 389–90
DeWall, C. N., 350, 355, 358–59, 362, 371
DeWall, Nathan, 42
Diener, Ed, 122–24, 130, 134, 142, 164
directionality problem, 222; *see also* temporal precedence
direct replication (exact replication), 414–15
discriminant validity (divergent validity), 143, 145–46
Discussion section
  in empirical journal articles, 45
  in research reports, 496–98
distracting behaviors, in special education student, 404–5, 408
divergent validity (discriminant validity), 143, 145–46
double-barreled questions, 161
double-blind placebo control study, 320–22, 437
double-blind studies, 319
Dozier, M., 289, 291, 292
Drews, F. A., 344–45, 347–49, 363, 371, 416–18
Duke, Aaron, 344
Dweck, C. S., 286–87, 295–302

E

eating disorders, 74–75

Ebbinghaus, Hermann, 407
ecological validity (mundane realism), 425, 434–36
edited books, 42, 46
effect size, 39, 42
  descriptive statistics for, 456–61
  power and, 473
  of small samples, 398, 399
  statistical significance and, 215–16
  statistical validity and, 210–14, 300–301
election polls, 185–86, 194, 196
Elliot, Andrew, 272–78, 280–82, 284, 285, 297–98, 301, 319, 447–68
empirical journal articles, 39, 42, 44
  components of, 44–45
  identifying factorial designs in, 370–71
  reading, 45–46
empiricism (empirical method/empirical research), 3, 8–9
epilepsy, split brain research and, 399–402
equivalent groups, posttest-only design, 285
equivalent groups, pretest/posttest design, 286–87, 294–95
Ericsson, K. A., 407
Eron, L. D., 237–41, 261
error variance (noise), 329
η^2 (eta squared), 459
Ethical Principles of Psychologists and Code of Conduct (APA), 98–111
  Ethical Standard 8, 99–111
  general principles, 98–99
  specific ethical standards, 99
Ethical Standard 8 (APA), 99–111
  animal research, 108–11
  debriefing, 104–5
  deception, 103–4
  informed consent, 101–3
  institutional review boards, 100–101
  research misconduct, 105–8
  text of, 116–19
ethical standards (APA), 99–100
ethics, 89–113
  APA Ethical Principles, 98–111
  APA Ethical Standard 8, 116–19

core ethical principles, 95–98

in decision making, 112

Milgram obedience studies, 92–95

in observational research, 176–77

in quasi-experiments, 396–97

Tuskegee Syphilis Study, 90–93

ethics violations

and Milgram study, 93–94

in Tuskegee Syphilis Study, 91–92

Everything Guide to Narcissistic Personality Disorder (Lechan and Leff), 47

evidence-based treatments, 6

exact replication (direct replication), 414–15

exit polls (elections), 185–86

expanded rehearsal (memory), 403

expectancy effects, *see* observer effects

experience, 24–30

confounded, 27

lack of comparison group for, 25–27

research versus, 28–30

experimental demand, *see* demand characteristics

experimental realism, 435

experiments

causal claims supported by, 73–74

defined, 73

interaction effect in, 345–47

interrogating null effects in, 323–38

intuitive interactions in, 346–47

with one independent variable, 343–45

simple, *see* simple experiments

threats to internal validity in, 308–23

with two independent variables, 345–61; *see also specific experimental designs, e.g.:* factorial designs

external validity

of association claims, 69, 70, 226–30

of bivariate correlational research, 226–30

of causal claims, 76, 298–300

defined, 67, 69

of frequency claims, 67–68, 194–97

of important studies, 424–37

of multivariate designs, 261

of quasi-experiments, 396

of small-*N* designs, 408; *see also* generalizability of results

F

face validity, 137

facial electromyography (EMG), 125

facial preferences, of infants, 288–90

facilitated communication (FC), 6–7, 12–13

factorial designs, 347–73

identifying, 370–73

increasing levels of independent variables in, 363–65

increasing number of independent variables in, 365–70

independent-group, 362

interactions in, 355–61

interpreting results of, 353–61

main effects in, 353–61

mixed, 363

to test limits, 348–50

to test theories, 351–53

within-groups, 362–63

faking bad, 166

faking good, 166

falling, death by, 31–32

Faloon, S., 407

false positives, *see* Type I errors

falsifiability (theories), 12–13, 25

families

evening observations of, 170–71, 195–96

meals together and academic success, 248

fatigue effects (practice effects), 291

faulty thinking, bias by, 30–33

FC (facilitated communication), 6–7, 12–13

Federal Communications Commission (FCC), 386, 387

fence sitting, 165

fidelity and responsibility, principle of, 99, 100

field settings, 433–37

figure and ground, 431–32

file drawer problem, 422–23

fire, death by, 31–32

"flashbulb memories," 167

floor effect, 326–28

fMRI (functional magnetic resonance imaging), 125–26

Fode, K., 173, 175

food breaks, judicial decision-making and, 385–86, 389–90

forced-choice format (survey questions), 158

forgetting curve, 407

formatting manuscript (research reports), 498–99

Fredrickson, Barbara, 47

frequency claims, 60–61

defined, 61

distinguishing features of, 61

external validity of, 194–97

generalizability of, 182–93

interrogating, 67–68, 71, 194–97

observational research of, 168–77

surveys and polls supporting, 158–68

frequency distributions, 442–44

frequency histograms, 442–44

Freud, Sigmund, 31

Friedman, R., 272–78, 280–82, 284, 285, 297–98, 301, 319

F test, 479–82

critical values of *F*, 541–45

steps in, 480–82

full counterbalancing, 292–93

full-length books, 42

functional magnetic resonance imaging (fMRI), 125–26

G

Gallup, 150, 160

Gallup Healthways Well-Being Index, 123, 140, 142, 143

Gast, D. L., 404–5

Gazzaniga, Michael, 399–402, 408, 433, 437

gender

amount of talking and, 169, 170, 176, 196, 227–29

infants' preference for female faces, 288–90

gender *(cont.)*
   operational definitions of, 124
   preference for violent TV and, 240–41
generalizability of results, 182–93
   and biased sampling techniques, 192–93
   defined, 67
   from important studies, 424–37
   to other participants, 424–25
   to other people, 298
   to other settings, 425
   to other situations, 298–99
   and population sampled, 182–84
   and probability sampling techniques, 188–92
   research mode and, 426–33
   and sample bias, 184–87; *see also* external validity
generalization mode, 428–30, 432, 435
Giancola, P. R., 350, 355, 358–59, 362, 371
Godden, D. R., 352–53
Goldacre, Ben, 19
Goodall, Jane, 176
"good stories," 31
Google Scholar, 44
Gosling, S. D., 227–29
grammar, learning, 427–28
graphs
   bar graphs, 208–9, 357–58
   dependent and independent variables on, 276
   detecting interactions from, 356–58
Gray, John, 47–48
Guide for the Care and Use of Laboratory Animals, 108–9, 111

H
Han, W. J., 248
Handbook of Social Exclusion, The (DeWall), 42
Hanlon, C., 427–28
happiness
   measuring, 121, 137
   Mehl's study of, 204
   misrepresentation of study results, 19
   operational definitions of, 124

operationalizing, 122–23
physiological measures of, 125; *see also* subjective well-being (SWB)
Harlow, Harry, 10–11, 278, 288, 426–27
Head Start study, 382–83, 388, 392–93, 396–97
Healing ADD (Amen), 47
health care use, 220–21
heart attacks, aspirin and, 214
Heatherton, T. F., 401, 437
Hedge's *g,* 459
Heinz, Adrienne, 351–54, 362
helping behavior study, 433, 435
Hendrick, C., 433, 435
Hennigan, K. M., 386–87, 390, 391
Herskovits, M. J., 430–31
Herzog, H. A., Jr., 110
histograms, 442–44
history threats
   in experiments, 311–12, 322
   in quasi-experiments, 391–92
Hoarder in You, The (Zasio), 47
hockey games, parent behavior at, 169, 170, 176
Holocaust denial, 161–62
Huesmann, L. R., 237–41, 261
human form, recognizing, 433–36
hypothesis, 11
hypothesis testing, statistical, 465–67

I
IACUC (Institutional Animal Care and Use Committee), 108–9, 111
Implicit Association Test, 166
important studies, 413–38
   external validity of, 424–37
   real-world settings and, 433–37
   replicability of, 414–24
independent-group factorial designs, 362
independent-groups designs (between-subjects design, between-groups design), 284–88
   defined, 284
   posttest-only, 285
   pretest/posttest, 286–87
   within-groups designs versus, 284

independent-groups quasi-experiments, 382–85
independent researchers, replication by, 418–19
independent variables (predictor variables)
   ceilings, floors, and, 326–27
   construct validity of, 296–97
   covariance and, 277
   defined, 73, 246
   in experiments, 275–76
   in factorial designs, 347, 363–70
   on graphs, 276
   levels of, in factorial designs, 363–65
   number of, in factorial designs, 365–70
   in regressions, 249–50
individual differences, 331–33
inferential statistics, 463–86
   F test (ANOVA), 479–82
   logic of, 463–64
   population inferences from samples, 467–74
   process of, 464–65
   for significance of beta, 483–84
   for significance of correlation coefficient *r,* 482–83
   steps of, 465–67
   t test, 475–79
   Type I errors, 468–71
   Type II errors, 468–74
information sources, *see* sources of information
informed consent
   as core principle, 95–96
   Ethical Standard 8 on, 101–3
   form for, 102
insensitive measures, 326
Institutional Animal Care and Use Committee (IACUC), 108–9, 111
institutional review boards (IRBs), 100–101
instrumentation threats (instrument decay)
   in experiments, 317, 323
   in quasi-experiments, 394
integrity, principle of, 99, 100
intelligence
   conceptual definitions of, 137, 138

and Mozart effect, 17–19
music lessons and IQ, 73
physiological measures of, 125, 126
intelligence tests (IQ tests)
analyzing information about, 33
criterion validity of, 139
as interval scale, 127
as observational measures, 125
test-retest reliability of, 133
validity and reliability of, 146
interaction effect (interaction), 345
in experiments with two variables, 345–47
in factorial designs, 355–61
intuitive, 346–47
three-way, 365–70
internal reliability (internal consistency), 130
assessing, 134
defined, 129
internal validity (third-variable criterion)
of association claims, 221–26
attrition threats to, 315–16, 322, 393–94
of causal claims, 302, 308–23
combined threats to, 317–18
as criterion for causation, 72, 222
defined, 69, 72
demand characteristics and, 318–19, 323, 395–96
design confounds and, 308, 322, 389–90
in experiments, 277, 279–84
history threats to, 311–12, 322, 391–92
instrumentation threats to, 317, 323, 394
in longitudinal studies, 240
maturation threats to, 310–11, 322, 390–91
in multivariate designs, 237
observer bias and, 318, 323, 395–96
in one-group, pretest/posttest designs, 310–18
order effect and, 308, 322
placebo effects and, 319–21, 323, 395–96

in quasi-experiments, 388–96
regression threats to, 312–15, 322, 392–93
ruling out third variables with multiple regression, 242–54
selection effects and, 308, 322, 388–89
of small-*N* designs, 402, 407
temporal precedence and, 73
testing threats to, 316–17, 323, 394
Internet polls, 187–88
Internet ratings, 159
interrater reliability, 129–30
assessing, 134
defined, 129
scatterplots showing, 131–32
interrogating information, 66–81
association claims, 68–71
causal claims, 71–77
external validity, 194–97
frequency claims, 67–68, 71, 194–97
and journals versus journalism, 16
prioritizing validities in, 77–78, 308; *see also individual types of claims*
interrupted time-series design, 386
interval scale, 127, 128
introduction
in empirical journal articles, 45
in research reports, 489–92
intuition, 30–36
cognitive bias with, 30–33
motivational bias with, 33–35
scientific reasoning versus, 36
IQ, music lessons and, 73, 74; *see also* intelligence
IQ tests, *see* intelligence tests
IRBs (institutional review boards), 100–101

J
Johansson, G., 433–36
Johnson, J. G., 239
Johnston, W. A., 416
Jones, J. T., 414–15, 475
journal articles, 39–42
empirical, 39, 42, 44–46, 370–71

mean and standard deviation represented in, 449–50
reliability information in, 135
review, 39, 42, 46
statistical significance information in, 216–17
journalism, 16–19
accuracy of, 17–19
choice of research covered in, 16–17
defined, 16
psychological science coverage, 48–49
journals, 15–16, 40
articles in, *see* journal articles
journalism and, 16
judicial decision-making study, 385–86, 389–90, 395
justice, principle of, 97–100

K
Kasen, S., 239
Kelley, W. M., 401, 437
Kim, H., 147
Kim, J., 456–58
Kirsch, I., 320
known-groups paradigm
for criterion validity, 140–43
defined, 140
Kuhn, A., 288–90

L
laboratory animals
ethical guidelines for research using, 108–11
legal protection for, 108–9
Ladder of Life, 123, 124, 140, 142, 143, 150
Langer, E. J., 175
language skills, preschool tantrums and, 75–76
Lao Tzu, 419
large-*N* designs, 399
Latin square, 293
Lavallee, K. L., 383–85, 389, 390, 391, 395
leading questions, 160–61
learning disabilities, 146
Lechan, Cynthia, 47
Lee, John, 36–37
Leff, Barbara, 47

Lefkowitz, M. M., 237–41, 261
Levav, J., 385–86, 389–90, 395
levels (of variables), 56, 363–65
Liberman, R. P., 405–6
lie detectors, 141
life satisfaction, 122–23; *see also* happiness
light study (human form), 433–36
Likert scale, 159
limits testing, factorial designs for, 348–50
Linardatos, E., 423
literature (scientific literature), 419
longitudinal research, 237–41
Lovaas, O. I., 281
Love 2.0 (Fredrickson), 47
lying, 104; *see also* deception

M

Macrae, C. N., 401, 437
Maier, M. A., 272–78, 280–82, 284, 285, 297–98, 301, 319
main effects
  defined, 353
  in factorial designs, 353–61
  in three-way factorial design, 366
manipulated variables, 57
  construct validity and, 296–97
  defined, 275
  factorial design studies of, 348
manipulation checks, 296, 297, 328
marginal means, 354
margin of error
  estimates of, 68
  sample size and, 197
Margraf, J., 383–85, 389–91, 395
marital satisfaction, of couples who met online, 204–5, 208–9, 211, 214, 216, 223–24, 397
Markman, E. M., 299
masked design (blind design), 175, 319
Masuda, T., 431–32
matched groups (matching)
  avoiding selection effects with, 283–84
  in cosmetic surgery study, 389
Matthews, A. M., 423
maturation threat
  in experiments, 310–11, 322

in quasi-experiments, 390–91
McCarthy, Jenny, 37
McCartney, K., 214
McCullough, M. E., 419–20
McRaney, David, 47
mean (average), 445, 446, 449–50
measured variables, 56–57, 122
  construct validity and, 295–96
  defined, 275
measurement, 121–51
  identifying good measurement, 147–50
  process of, 122–28
  reliability of, 129–36, 146
  scales of, 126–28
  types of measures, 124–26
  validity of, 136–46
measurement error, 330–31
media multitasking, 205–7, 220, 226, 452, 453
Media Multitasking Inventory (MMI), 205–6
median, 445
mediation, in multivariate correlational research, 257–60
Mehl, Matthias, 169, 176, 196, 204–6, 210, 211, 220, 227–29
Meinhardt, J., 272–78, 280–82, 284, 285, 297–98, 301, 319
memory
  accuracy of, 167–68
  context-dependent, 352–54
  expanded rehearsal study, 403
  forgetting curve, 407
  of nonsense words, 407
  random digits recall, 407
meta-analysis, 419–23
  defined, 419
  effect size in, 39, 42
  religiosity and depression example, 419–20
  strengths and limitations of, 422–23
  violent video games and behavior example, 421–22
Method section
  in empirical journal articles, 45
  in research reports, 492–94
Meyer, A. H., 383–85, 389–91, 395
Milgram, Stanley, 92–94, 97
Milgram obedience studies, 92–95

Miller, D. P., 248
Mirenberg, M. C., 414–15, 475
misses, *see* Type II errors
mixed factorial designs, 363
MMI (Media Multitasking Inventory), 205–6
mode, 444–46
moderators (moderating variables), 227–30
  interactions showing, 350
  mediators versus, 259–60
Moffat, N. J., 403
Moller, A. C., 272–78, 280–82, 284, 285, 297–98, 301, 319
monkeys, infant attachment in, 10–11, 278, 288, 426–27
motivational biases, 33–35
Mozart effect, 17–19
Mueller, C. M., 286–87, 295–302
Müller-Lyer illusion, 430–31
multimodal distributions, 444
multiple-baseline designs (small-*N*), 404–5
multiple regression (multivariate regression), 242
multiple-regression analyses, 242–54
  adding more predictors, 249–50
  causation not established by, 252–53
  controlling for third variables, 243–45
  indicating effect of third variables, 245–49
  measuring more than two variables, 242–45
  in popular press articles, 250–52
multistage sampling, 189–90
multivariate correlational research (multivariate designs), 235–63
  causal criteria and, 236–37
  interrogating validities of, 261–62
  longitudinal designs, 237–41
  mediation in, 257–60
  multiple-regression analyses, 242–54
  pattern and parsimony in, 254–56
  ruling out third variables in, 242–54

multivariate regression (multiple regression), 242
mundane realism (ecological validity), 425, 434–36
Mundell, E. J., 372
music lessons, IQ and, 73, 74

N

Narcissistic Personality Inventory (NPI), 158–59
National Rifle Association, 161
NBCNEWS.com, 78
negative association (negative correlation), 62–64, 453
negatively worded questions, 161–62
Nisbett, R. E., 167, 431–32
NIST (U.S. National Institute of Standards and Technology), 136
noise (error variance, unsystematic variance)
  situation, 333–34
  within-groups variability obscured by, 329
nonequivalent control group design, 382
nonequivalent control group interrupted time-series design, 387
nonequivalent control group pretest/posttest design, 383–85
nonrandom samples
  in the real world, 195
  in research studies, 195–96
nonrepresentative samples, 194–97
NPI (Narcissistic Personality Inventory), 158–59
null effects (null results), 323–38
  between-groups difference and, 326–29
  finding, 336, 338
  lack of significant difference and, 336
  reasons for, 337
  within-groups variability obscuring group differences and, 329–35
null hypothesis
  defined, 465
  rejecting or retaining, 466–67, 478–79

null hypothesis testing, 465–67
Nuremberg Code, 95
Nuremberg Trials, 95

O

Obama, Barack, 194
obedience studies (Milgram), 92–95, 97
observational measures (behavioral measures), 125
observational research
  construct validity of, 168–77
  ethics in, 176–77
  examples of claims based on, 169–71
  observer bias/observer effects in, 172–75
  reactivity in, 175–76
  self-reports versus, 172–77
observer bias
  controlling for, 319
  defined, 172
  in experiments, 318, 323
  in observational research, 172–75
  preventing, 174–75
  in quasi-experiments, 395–96
observer effects (expectancy effects)
  in observational research, 172–75
  preventing, 174–75
Occam's razor, 13
Ochs, E., 170–71, 195–96
O'Connor, A., 252
Office of Research Integrity, Department of Health and Human Services, 106
Offit, Paul, 37
one-group, pretest/posttest designs, 309–18
  attrition threats in, 315–16
  combined threats in, 317–18
  history threats in, 311–12
  instrumentation threats in, 217
  maturation threats in, 310–11
  regression threats in, 312–15
  testing threats in, 316–17
online-originated marriages, 204–5, 208–9, 211, 214, 216, 223–24, 397
online polls, 187–88
open-ended questions, 158

operational definitions (operational variables, operationalizations), 57–59, 122
  categorical, 127, 128
  of conceptual variables, 58–59, 122–24
  defined, 57
  of happiness, 122–23
  quantitative, 127–28
operationalize (term), 57
order effects
  defined, 291
  internal validity and, 308, 322
  in within-groups designs, 291–92
ordinal scale, 127, 128
outcome variable, see dependent variable
outliers
  affecting association, 217–18
  defined, 217
oversampling, 190
oxytocin, social bonding and, 289, 291, 292

P

paraphrasing, 107, 502–4
parole decisions study, 385–86, 389–90, 395
parsimony, 13
  defined, 254
  in multivariate correlational research, 254–56
partial counterbalancing, 293
participant variables, 348, 372–73
Pascalis, O., 288–90
pasta servings study, 274–80, 284, 415
pattern and parsimony approach, 254–56
peer-review process, 16
Pelham, B. W., 414–15, 475
Pennebaker, J. W., 227–29
Pennebaker, James, 47
People for the Ethical Treatment of Animals (PETA), 110
Personality and Social Psychology Bulletin, 39
Pew Research Center, 187, 191
Pfungst, Oskar, 173
PHS (U.S. Public Health Service), 90, 91

physiological measures, 125–26
Piaget, Jean, 406
pilot studies, 296–97
placebo effects
    in experiments, 319–21, 323
    in quasi-experiments, 395–96
placebo groups (placebo control
        groups)
    defined, 278
    in experiments, 278
plagiarism, 107–8, 502
Plaksina, T., 170–71, 195–96
Plous, S., 110
political opinion polls, 196–97
Poll, J., 419–20
polls, *see* surveys and polls
popcorn serving sizes, 456–58
Pope, T., 242
popular press
    articles about psychology
        research in, 55
    identifying factorial designs in
        articles, 371–73
    multiple-regression analyses and,
        250–52
    pattern and parsimony not
        represented in, 256
    replication in, 423–24
    as source of information, 48–49
population of interest, 183, 425
populations, 182–84
    defined, 182
    target, 425
positive association (positive
        correlation), 62–64, 453
poster sessions, 522–25
posttest-only designs (equivalent
        groups, posttest-only design),
        285
power, 334–35
    defined, 290, 471
    factors influencing, 471–74
practice effects (fatigue effects), 291
praise, process versus person,
        286–87, 295–302
predictions
    based on associations, 64, 212–13
    hypotheses as, 11
predictor variables, 246; *see also*
    independent variables

preschool tantrums, language skills
        and, 75–76
present/present bias, 32–33
pretest/posttest designs (equivalent
        groups, pretest/posttest
        design), 286–87, 294–95
principle of beneficence, 96–97, 99,
        100
principle of fidelity and
        responsibility, 99, 100
principle of integrity, 99, 100
principle of justice, 97–100
principle of respect for persons,
        95–96, 99, 100
probabilistic (term)
    defined, 30
    research as, 29–30
probability sampling (random
        sampling), 188–92
    cluster sampling, 189
    combined techniques, 191
    defined, 188
    multistage sampling, 189–90
    oversampling, 190
    random assignment versus, 192
    random numbers for, 527–28
    simple random sampling, 188–89
    stratified random sampling, 190
    systematic sampling, 190
producers of research information,
        4–5
proof of theories, 13
psychological science, 3
    applied and basic research in,
        13–14
    empirical nature of, 8–9
    journalism's coverage of, 16–19
    publication process in, 15–16
    research producers and
        consumers in, 4–8
    theory-data cycle in, 9–13
Psychology of Twilight, The (Klonsky
        et al.), 47
Psychology Today, 49
PsycINFO, 42–43, 44
publication bias (in psychology),
        422–23
*Publication Manual of the American
        Psychological Association* (APA),
        44, 107

publication process, 15–16
purposive sampling, 192–93

Q

quantitative variables
    categorical variables versus,
        127–28
    describing associations with,
        206–7
quasi-experiments, 382–98
    balancing priorities in, 396–97
    correlational studies versus,
        397–98
    defined, 382
    independent-groups, 382–85
    internal validity in, 388–96
    repeated-measures, 385–87
questions
    biased, 34–35
    double-barreled, 161
    forced-choice, 158
    leading, 160–61
    negatively worded, 161–62
    open-ended, 158
    for surveys and polls, 158–63
Quinn, P. C., 288–90
quota sampling, 193

R

random assignment, 192
    avoiding selection effects with,
        282–83
    in counterbalancing, 292
    random numbers for, 528
random digits recall, 407
randomization tests, 478
randomized double-blind placebo
        control study, 437
random numbers, 527–632
    for probability sampling, 527–28
    for random assignment, 528
    table of, 529–32
random sampling, *see* probability
    sampling
range, restriction of, 218–20
Raskin, D. E., 405–6
ratemyprofessors.com, 159
ratio scale, 128
rats, "maze-bright" versus "maze-
        dull," 173, 175

Rauscher, Frances, 16
RCI (Religious Commitment Inventory), 147–50
reactivity
    defined, 175
    in observational research, 175–76
reading research, 44–46
real-world settings (field settings), 433–37
recess, behavior and, 242, 257–58, 261–62
References section
    in empirical journal articles, 45
    in research reports, 498
regression threats
    in experiments, 312–15, 322
    in quasi-experiments, 392–93
regression to the mean, 312–13
reinforcement theory of grammar, 427–28
relative standing, descriptive statistics for, 450–52
reliability, 129–36
    correlation coefficient evaluation of, 132–35
    defined, 129
    internal, 129, 130, 134
    interrater, 129–32, 134
    journal article information on, 135
    scatterplot evaluation of, 130–32
    test-retest, 129, 131–33
    validity versus, 146
religiosity
    depression and, 419–20
    interrogating measures of, 147–50
    operational definitions of, 124
Religious Commitment Inventory (RCI), 147–50
repeated-measures designs, 289
repeated-measures quasi-experiments, 385–87
Repetti, R. L., 170–71, 195–96
replicable (reproducible), 414
replication, 414–24
    conceptual, 415–16
    direct, 414–15
    by independent researchers, 418–19
    meta-analysis and, 419–23

in popular press, 423–24
    replication-plus-extension, 416–18
    weight of evidence and, 419
replication-plus-extension, 416–18
representative samples (unbiased samples), 182–83, 188–92
research, 3–4
    applied, 13–14
    basic, 14
    experience versus, 24–30
    intuition versus, 30–36
    judging importance of, see important studies
    less-scholarly, 46–49
    reading, 44–46
    translational, 14; see also specific topics; specific types of research
research consumers, 4–8
research misconduct, 105–8
    data fabrication and data falsification, 105–6
    plagiarism, 107–8
research producers, 4–5
research reports (APA style), 487–521
    abstract, 489
    avoiding plagiarism, 502
    citing sources, 504–6
    Discussion section, 496–98
    example of, 507–21
    formatting manuscript, 498–99
    introduction, 489–92
    Method section, 492–94
    overview of, 488
    paraphrasing in, 502–4
    References section, 498
    Results section, 494–96
    title, 488–89
    writing style for, 499–501
respect for persons, principle of, 95–96, 99, 100
response sets (nondifferentiation), 164–65
restriction of range, 218–20
Results section
    in empirical journal articles, 45
    in research reports, 494–96
reversal designs (small-N), 405–6
review journal articles, 39, 42, 46
Rogel, M., 433, 435

Roper poll, 161–62
rosemary, brain and, 78–81
Rosenberg self-esteem inventory, 159
Rosenthal, R., 173, 175, 214, 423
Rush, Benjamin, 25–27, 32

S
samples
    biased (unrepresentative), 182–88, 192–93
    defined, 182
    nonrepresentative, 194–97
    population inferences from, 467–74
    representative (unbiased), 182–83, 188–92
    WEIRD, 432–33
sample size, 196–97
    external validity and, 425
    outliers and, 218
    power and, 473
    statistical significance and, 215–16
sampling, 181–98
    biased techniques for, 192–93
    bias in, 184–88
    cluster, 189
    convenience, 185–86, 192
    external validity of, 194–97
    generalizability of results and, 182–93
    multistage, 189–90
    oversampling, 190
    populations and, 182–84
    probability sampling techniques, 188–92
    purposive, 192–93
    quota, 193
    random, 527–28
    simple random, 188–89
    snowball, 193
    stratified random, 190
    systematic, 190
sampling distribution
    of r, 482–83
    of t, 476–77
Sanbonmatsu, David, 205–7, 220, 226, 452, 453
Sapirstein, G., 320

Sasaki, J., 147
SAT tests
  criterion validity of, 139, 140
  statistical validity of, 218–20
scales of measurement, 126–28
scatterplots, 452–54
  outliers on, 217
  plotting data on, 208
  reliability evaluation with,
    130–32
Schellenberg, Glen, 74, 77
Schoebi, D., 170–71, 195–96
Scientific American Mind, 49
scientific literature (literature), 419
scientific research, 39–44
scientific sources of information,
  39–44
Scott, Kristin, 42
Secret Life of Pronouns, The
    (Pennebaker), 47
Segal, D. L., 145
Segall, M. H., 430–31
selection-attrition threat, 318
selection effects
  defined, 281
  in experiments, 281–84, 308, 322
  in quasi-experiments, 388–89
selection-history threat, 317–18
self-esteem, 460–61
self-report measures (self-reports),
  124–25
  accuracy of, 166–67
  of event memories, 167–68
  known-groups criterion validity
    for, 141
  meaningful information from,
    163–64
  observational research versus,
    172–77; *see also* surveys and
    polls
self-selection, 187–88, 195
semantic differential format, 159
Shaffer, D. R., 433, 435
Shellenberg, Glen, 73
Sherlock Holmes, 32
Shimizu, Mitsuru, 274–80, 284
Silver, E. J., 242–43, 249, 261
Silver, Nate, 194
"Silver Blaze" (Doyle), 32
similarity effect, 414–15, 475
simple experiments, 343–45

causal claims supported by,
    277–84
covariance established in,
    277–78
examples of, 272–75
independent-groups designs,
    284–88
internal validity established in,
    279–84
temporal precedence established
    in, 278–79
variables in, 275–76
within-groups designs, 288–95
simple random sampling, 188–89
single-*N* designs, 399, 407
situational variables, 417
situation noise, 333–34
Slater, A. M., 288–90
slope direction, 132
Smailes, E. M., 239
small-*N* designs, 398–408
  behavior-change studies in
    clinical settings, 402–6
  disadvantages of, 402
  evaluating validities in, 407–8
  multiple-baseline designs, 404–5
  reversal designs, 405–6
  split brain research, 399–402
  stable-baseline designs, 403
Smith, T. B., 419–20
smoking, lung cancer and, 254–55
snowball sampling, 193
Snyder, M., 45
socially desirable responding, 166
social psychology, 106
sources of information, 23–50
  experience, 24–30
  intuition, 30–36
  journalism, 16–19
  less-scholarly research, 46–49
  and reading research, 44–46
  scientific research, 39–44
  and trust in subject authorities,
    36–39
Sperry, Roger, 399
split brain research, 399–402, 408,
  437
spontaneous remission, 310; *see also*
  maturation threat
spreading interaction, 346
spurious association, 225

stable-baseline designs (small-*N*),
  403
standard deviation (*SD*), 446–50
standardized tests, criterion validity
  of, 139, 140
Standard Progressive Matrices,
  295–96
Stanovich, K. E., 12
Stapel, Diederik, 105, 106
statistical choices, power and, 474
statistical conclusion validity, *see*
  statistical validity
statistical hypothesis testing,
  465–67
statistical inference, 214–15; *see also*
  inferential statistics
statistical significance, 214–17
  of associations, 70
  of beta, 247
  defined, 214
  of difference between means, 300
  lack of, 336
  of main effects, 354–55
statistical tables
  critical values of *F,* 541–45
  critical values of *t,* 539–40
  distribution of *z,* 533–39
  r to *z'* conversion, 545–46
statistical validity (statistical
  conclusion validity)
  of association claims, 70–71,
    210–21
  of causal claims, 76–77, 300–301
  defined, 68, 69
  of frequency claims, 68
  of multivariate designs, 261–62
  in quasi-experiments, 397
  of small-*N* designs, 408
statistics, *see* descriptive statistics;
  inferential statistics
Stein, R., 373
Stein, R. E. K., 242–43, 249, 261
stemplots (stem-and-leaf plots),
  442, 444
stories, bias from, 31
stratified random sampling, 190
Strayer, D. L., 344–45, 347–49, 363,
  371, 416–18
strength
  of associations, 207, 212, 213,
    454

of relationships on scatterplots, 132

statistical, 70

stress
    observational measures of, 125
    physiological measures of, 126
subjective well-being (SWB)
    deep talk and, 204–7, 211, 222, 224–26, 229
    internal reliability of measures, 134
    interrater reliability of measures, 129–30
    known-groups criterion validity for, 142–43
    operational definition of, 123, 124
    reliability of scales of, 135; *see also* happiness
surveys and polls
    choosing question formats for, 158–60
    confirming external validity of, 194
    construct validity of, 158–68
    defined, 158
    encouraging accurate responses to, 163–68
    sample size for, 196–97
    telephone, 77–78, 189–91
    writing questions for, 160–63
Swann, W. B., 45
SWB, *see* subjective well-being
syphilis study (Tuskegee Institute), 90–93, 96–97
systematic sampling, 190
systematic variability
    defined, 280
    design confounds and, 280–81

T
tables
    detecting interactions from, 355–56
    statistical, *see* statistical tables
"taking into account," 251
talking
    deep talk, 204–7, 210, 211, 222, 224–26, 229
    gender and amount of, 169, 170, 176, 196, 227–29
target population, 425

Tawney, J. W., 404–5
telephone surveys, 77–78, 189–91
television
    aggression and TV violence, 237–41, 256, 261
    crime rates and access to, 386–87, 390, 391, 395
Tell, R. A., 423
temporal precedence
    as criterion for causation, 72, 222
    defined, 72
    in experiments, 277–79
    internal validity and, 73
    in longitudinal studies, 237–41
    in multivariate designs, 236–37
testing threats
    in experiments, 316–17, 323
    in quasi-experiments, 394
test-retest reliability, 129
    assessing, 133
    defined, 129
    scatterplots showing, 131–32
Thau, Stefan, 42
theory-data cycle, 9–13
theory(-ies)
    defined, 11
    features of, 12–13
theory testing
    construct validity and, 297–98
    factorial designs for, 351–53
theory-testing mode, 426–30, 432, 435–37
Therapeutic Advances in Psychopharmacology, 78
third-variable problem, *see* internal validity; multiple-regression analyses
"three R's" for animal research, 109
three-way designs, 365–70
title (research reports), 488–89
trade books, 47–48
translational research, 14
treatment groups
    defined, 278
    in experiments, 278
trust
    deception and, 104
    in subject authorities, 36–39
t test, 475
    critical values of *t*, 539–40

steps in, 475–79
Turk, D. J., 401, 437
Turner, E. H., 423
Tuskegee Institute, 90, 91
Tuskegee Syphilis Study, 90–93, 96–97
TV, *see* television
Type I errors (false positives), 70, 468–71
    preventing, 470–71
    Type II errors versus, 468–70
Type II errors (misses), 70, 468–74
    preventing, 471–74
    Type I errors versus, 468–70

U
ulcers, 31
unbiased samples (representative samples), 182–83, 188–92
unobtrusive data, 176
unobtrusive observations, 176
unrepresentative samples, *see* biased samples
unstandardized coefficient (*b*), 246–47
unsystematic variability
    defined, 280
    in experiments, 281
    group differences and, 329
    power and, 473–74
unsystematic variance (noise), 329
U.S. Centers for Disease Control and Prevention (CDC), 61
U.S. National Institute of Standards and Technology (NIST), 136
U.S. Public Health Service (PHS), 90, 91
uSamp, 204–5

V
vaccines, autism and, 37
validity(-ies), 66–81, 136–46
    of abstract constructs, 136–37
    applying, 80–81
    of association claims, 68–71
    of causal claims, 72–77
    construct, 67–69, 76
    content, 137–38
    convergent, 143, 144, 146
    criterion, 139–43

validity(-ies) *(cont.)*
  defined, 66, 129
  discriminant, 143, 145–46
  ecological, 425
  external, 67–70, 76
  face, 137
  of frequency claims, 67–68
  prioritizing, 77–78, 308
  reliability versus, 146
  statistical, 68, 70–71, 76–77; *see also each type of validity*
van Kleef, Ellen, 274–80, 284, 415
variability, descriptive statistics for, 446–50
variables, 56–59
  conceptual, 57–59
  defined, 56
  dependent, 73
  in experiments, 275–76
  independent, 73
  manipulated, 57, 275
  measured, 56–57, 275
  measuring, 122–28
  operational, 57
  ruling out third variables, 242–54; *see also* internal validity [third-variable criterion]
variance *(SD2)*, 446–49
video games, violence and, 421–22

violence, aggression and, 237–41, 256, 261, 421–22, 461
von Osten, William, 173

W
wait-list design, 389
Walder, L. O., 237–41, 261
Waldfogel, J., 248
Wang, S., 170–71, 195–96
Wansink, Brian, 274–80, 284, 456–58
weak manipulations, 326, 328
wealth
  happiness and, 123
  operational definitions of, 124
Webster, G. D., 350, 355, 358–59, 362, 371
weight of the evidence, 13, 419
WEIRD samples, 432–33
Why Mars and Venus Collide (Gray), 47–48
Wikipedia, 48
wikis, 48
Wilson, David, 163
Wilson, Timothy, 167
within-groups designs (within-subjects design), 288–95
  advantages of, 289–91
  causal criteria in, 291–93
  concurrent-measures design, 288

defined, 284
  disadvantages of, 293–94
  independent-groups designs versus, 284
  pretest/posttest designs and, 294–95
  repeated-measures design, 289
within-groups factorial designs, 362–63
within-groups variability, group differences obscured by, 329–35
working memory span, operational definitions of, 124
Worthington, E. L., 147–50
writing style, for research reports, 499–501

Y
Yahr, J., 288–90
You Are Not So Smart (McRaney), 47

Z
Zajonc, Robert, 175
Zasio, Robin, 47
zero-acquaintance accuracy, 465
zero association (zero correlation), 62–64, 215, 453
z scores, 450–52
  distribution of z, 533–39
  r to z' conversion, 545–46